W9-BPK-792

Edited and designed by
Time Out Paris
15-17 rue des Martyrs
75009 Paris
Tel: +33(0)1.44.87.00.45
Fax:+33(0)1.44.73.90.60
Email editors@timeout.fr
www.timeout.com/paris

For
Time Out Guides Ltd
Universal House
251 Tottenham Court Road
London W1T 7AB
Tel: +44(0)20 7813 3000
Fax:+44(0)20 7813 6001
Email guides@timeout.com
www.timeout.com

Editorial

Editor Paul Hines
Consultant Editor Natasha Edwards
Production Editor Alison Culliford
Assistant Editors Ella Green, Emily Rueb, Dora Whitaker
Sightseeing Consultant Maryanne Blacker

Managing Director Paris Karen Albrecht

Guides Editorial/Managing Director Peter Fiennes
Series Editor Ruth Jarvis
Deputy Series Editor Lesley McCave
Guides Co-ordinator Anna Norman

Design

Art Director Paris Richard Joy
Ad Design Richard Randall, Philippe Thareaut

Art Director Mandy Martin
Acting Art Director Scott Moore
Picture Editor Jael Marschner

Advertising

Sales & Administration Manager Philippe Thareaut
Advertising Executives Ellen Green, Keri Stone, Deborah Vidal

Sales Director Mark Phillips
International Sales Manager Ross Canadé

Time Out Group

Chairman Tony Elliott
Managing Director Mike Hardwick
Group Financial Director Richard Waterlow
Group Commercial Director Lesley Gill
Group Marketing Director Christine Cort
Marketing Manager Mandy Martinez
Group General Manager Nichola Coulthard
Group Art Director John Oakey
Production Manager Mark Lamond
Production Controller Samantha Furniss
Accountants Sarah Bostock, Abdus Sadique

Contributors

History Michael Fitzpatrick, Paul Hines (*Historical (s)hit parade, Give peace a chance, A dead heat* Paul Hines; *The path to purgatory – a walk through Revolutionary Paris* Alison Culliford). **Paris Today** Stéphanie Janicot (translated by Emily Rueb and Paul Hines) (*Tainted love, 2003's thrusters & busters* Paul Hines). **Minority Report** Jon Henley, Paul Hines, Emily Rueb. **Capital Creatives** Claire Thomson. **French Film: Fini?** Elizabeth Bard and Paul Hines. **Architecture** Natasha Edwards (*Field works* Natalie Whittle). **Where to Stay** Ella Green (*The climax of canine comfort* Natalie Whittle). **Sightseeing Introduction** Paul Hines (*Paris on a need-to-know basis* Emily Rueb, Dora Whitaker). **The Islands**, **Right Bank**, **Left Bank**, **Beyond the Périphérique** Maryanne Blacker, Emily Rueb, Dora Whitaker (*Le Fab Four, The beach is back!, Bones, thugs 'n' harmony* Paul Hines; *Canal go to? Beyond the fringe theatre, Peripheral vision* Emily Rueb; *Bridge it, Jones!* Dora Whitaker). **Museums** Natasha Edwards (*Hidden treasures, Musée de l'Erotisme* Dora Whitaker, Emily Rueb). **Restaurants** Adapted from *Time Out Paris Eating & Drinking* (*What a corking good vin plan* Maryanne Blacker; *Couldn't stand the heat* Paul Hines). **Bars, Cafés & Tearooms** Adapted from *Time Out Paris Eating & Drinking* (*Froth & Mania* Natalie Whittle; *Tearooms for the Noëls & Gerties* Rosa Jackson). **Shops & Services** Anna Brooke, Rosa Jackson, Anna Sansom, Lucy Cohen, Alison Culliford (*Tati-bye? High street chic* Anna Brooke; *Vinyl fantasy* Lucia Scazzocchio; *Only in Paris, Posh spice & vanilla paradis* Rosa Jackson). **Festivals & Events** Natalie Whittle, Kate van den Boogert. **Cabaret, Circus & Comedy** Anna Brooke. **Children** Louise Rogers. **Clubs** Lucia Scazzocchio, Emily Rueb, Alison Culliford (*Ain't no doubt, we are here to party* Anna Sansom; *Titz & glitz: the British are coming!* Paul Hines, Richard Joy). **Dance** Natalie Whittle. **Film** Dora Whitaker. **Galleries** Natasha Edwards. **Gay & Lesbian** Paul Clements. **Music: Classical & Opera** Stephen Mudge. **Music: Popular Music** Emily Rueb. **Sport & Fitness** Paul Hines (*One- (or two-) session gyms* Liz Krieger; *The crawl of nature* Natalie Whittle, Paul Hines. **Theatre** Emily Rueb. **Trips Out of Town** Anna Brooke, Natasha Edwards. **Directory** Dora Whitaker, Emily Rueb. **Index** Emily Rueb, Dora Whitaker.

Maps pp398-409 by Mapworld, pp410-412 courtesy RATP.

Photography by Karl Blackwell, Tom Craig, Adam Eastland, Oliver Knight, Jon Perugia.
Additional photography Daniel Agneli, Jean-Louis Faverole, Nathalie Jacqualt, Crescenzo Mazza, PMVP: Habouzit, Joffre, Pierrain, Ladet **Additional photos courtesy** Collections Photographiques du Musée Carnavalet, Opéra National de Paris, Théâtre de la Ville, Photothèque des Musées de la Ville de Paris, Mairie de Paris, Parc Astérix.

The editor would like to thank Ted Hines and all contributors to previous editions of *Time Out Paris*.

Paris

timeout.com/paris

Penguin Books

PENGUIN BOOKS

Published by the Penguin Group
Penguin Books Ltd, 80 Strand, London WC2R ORL, England
Penguin Books USA Inc., 375 Hudson Street, New York, New York 10014, USA
Penguin Books Australia Ltd, 250 Camberwell Road, Camberwell, Victoria 3124, Australia
Penguin Books Canada Ltd, 10 Alcorn Avenue, Toronto, Ontario, Canada M4V 3B2
Penguin Books (NZ) Ltd, cnr Rosedale and Airborne Rds, Albany, Auckland, New Zealand

Penguin Books Ltd, Registered Offices: Harmondsworth, Middlesex, England

First published 1989
Second edition 1990
Third edition 1992
Fourth edition 1995
Fifth edition 1997
Sixth edition 1998
Seventh edition 1999
Eighth edition 2000
Ninth edition 2001
Tenth Edition 2002
Eleventh Edition 2003
Twelfth Edition 2004

10 9 8 7 6 5 4 3 2 1

Reprographics by Quebecor Numeric, 56 bd Davout, 75020 Paris
Cover reprographics by Precise Litho, 34-35 Great Sutton Street, London EC1
Printed and bound by Cayfosa-Quebecor, Ctra. de Caldes, Km 3 08 130 Sta Perpètua de Mogoda, Barcelona, Spain

Contents

Introduction

Voltaire, for all his genius, was known for missing the punchline. When he said, 'If God didn't exist, it would be necessary to invent him' the Enlightenment hero was only half-way there. What he should have said was, 'If God didn't exist, it would be necessary to invent him *so he could invent Paris*'.

Whoever did design Paris, it's impossible not to be moved by delights like Notre-Dame, the Sainte-Chapelle, the Louvre – not to mention more ancient glimpses at the Crypte Archéologique and modern visions such as Beaubourg, the Pyramid or the Grande Arche. (We could go on – and we do, not only about this but about cinema, shopping and, of course, gastronomy).

The city's power to impress is legendary. Sixty years ago, in May 1944, the dedicated Nazi Dietrich von Choltitz was named commander of Paris precisely because he had a reputation for being prepared to flatten cities that were about to break free from Nazi domination. The Allies invaded Normandy in June, and were under pressure to secure Paris. Dietrich was the demolition man. Yet, when he arrived here, the beauty of the city astonished him into a state of uncharacteristic indecision. According to his personal testimony, he spent 48 sleepless hours deciding whether he should disobey the man he was convinced would still win the war (thus signing his own death warrant) or destroy the magnificence of Paris. In the end, the city won. Von Choltitz chose to save Paris.

Paris still has the power to move romantics and cynics alike. Even the clichés stay great: you can still find showbiz sleaze around Pigalle, and the real down and dirty stuff on rue St-Denis. And people with no discernible musical talent will still wreck your Métro journey with the wailing of their accordions.

But to put an end to the granddaddy of all clichés, you wanna wake up in a city that doesn't sleep? You wanna wake up in Paris.

ABOUT THE TIME OUT CITY GUIDES

Time Out Paris is one of an expanding series of *Time Out* City Guides produced by the people behind London's and New York's successful listings magazines. This 12th edition has been thoroughly revised and updated by writers resident in Paris who have striven to provide you with all the most up-to-date information you'll need to explore the city.

For events each week, see the *Time Out Paris* section (in English) inside French listings magazine *Pariscope*, available at all Paris-area newsstands. The quarterly *Time Out Paris Free Guide* is available in selected hotels, bars and visitor centres. For detailed reviews of 850 Paris restaurants, cafés and bars, buy the new book *Time Out Paris Eating & Drinking*. Penguin's *Time Out Book of Paris Walks* features 23 themed itineraries by eminent writers and journalists.

THE LOWDOWN ON THE LISTINGS

We've tried to make this book as useful as possible. Addresses, telephone numbers, transport details, opening times, admission prices, credit card details and, where possible, websites, are all included. As far as possible, we've given details of facilities, services and events, all checked and correct at the time we went to press. However, arrangements, exhibitions and entire venue entities can change at any time. Before you go out of your way, we'd advise you to telephone and check opening times, dates of exhibitions and other particulars. While every effort has been made to ensure the accuracy of the information contained in this guide, the publishers cannot accept responsiblity for any errors it may contain.

There is an online version of this guide, and guides to over 40 international cities, at www.timeout.com.

PRICES AND PAYMENT

The prices we've supplied should be treated as guidelines, not gospel. Our editorial team checks and checks again, but of course inflation, fluctuations in exchange rates and sometimes even a mood-swing on the part of a retailer can cause prices to change. If you encounter prices that vary wildly from those we've quoted, ask whether there's a good reason. If not, go elsewhere. We have noted whether venues such as shops, hotels, restaurants, bars and clubs accept credit cards or not but have listed only the major cards – American Express (**AmEx**), Diners Club (**DC**), MasterCard (**MC**) and Visa (**V**). Note that shops, restaurants, cafés and museums often will not accept credit cards for sums of less than €15.

CROSS-REFERENCING
Where we mention important places or events that are also listed elsewhere in the guide, they are in **bold,** or cross-referenced to relevant chapters.

THE LIE OF THE LAND
Paris is divided into 20 arrondissements, in a spiral beginning at Notre-Dame and finishing at the Porte de Montreuil. Paris postcodes include the arrondissement, following the prefix 750. We have referred to the arrondissements as 1st, 2nd, 3rd, 4th etc. Chapters on **Where to Stay, Sightseeing** and **Eating & Drinking** are divided into areas that follow arrondissement guidelines. In the other listings categories, entries are listed in order of arrondissement. Addresses within the area covered on the **colour street maps** also have map references. An **arrondissement map** is on page 398.

TELEPHONE NUMBERS
All French phone numbers, including mobile numbers, have ten digits. The area code for Paris is 01. From outside France, dial the country code (33) and leave off the zero at the beginning .

ESSENTIAL INFORMATION
All the practical information you might need – including visa and customs information, disabled access, health and emergency telephone numbers, information on the euro and the lowdown on local customs – can be found in the **Directory** chapter (*see p366*).

MAPS
We've included fully indexed colour maps to the city, along with a map of Paris areas and arrondissements and complete public transport maps, at the back of the guide. We have printed a page reference and map grid for all venues that appear on these maps.

LET US KNOW WHAT YOU THINK
We hope you enjoy *Time Out Paris* and we'd like to know what you think of it. We welcome tips for places we should include in future editions and we value and take notice of your criticism of our choices. There's a reader's reply card at the back of this book – or you can email us on editors@timeout.fr.

Advertisers
We would like to stress that no establishment has been included in this guide because it has advertised in any of our publications and no payment of any kind has influenced any review. The opinions in this book are those of *Time Out* writers and are entirely independent.

In Context

Features

History

Blood-baths, bunk-ups and right royal punch-ups. Any British pub on a Friday night? No: Paris, throughout its history.

INTRODUCTION

The purpose of this chapter is to cover the main events, trends and personalities that have added up to create the Paris you'll find in 2004. It is by no means a conventional history of France: you'll find, for example, no mention of the Battle of Hastings and no account of the Normandy beach landings in 1944. You will, by contrast, find that, towards the end of the chapter, the subject matter broadens out to consider France's current role on the international stage: that's because that subject currently provides material for debate and discussion all over the capital, from its national media headquarters to the cafés and bars that you might well visit.

Places in **bold** appear in other sections of the book (most often in the **Sightseeing** section). Please refer to the **Index** if you want to find out on which pages they can be found.

THE FIRST VISITORS

The earliest settlers seem to have arrived in Paris around 120,000 years ago. One of them lost a flint spear-tip on the hill we now call Montmartre, and the still dangerous-looking weapon is to be seen today in the Stone Age Collection at the **Musée des Antiquités Nationales**. There was a Stone Age weapons factory under present-day Châtelet, and the redevelopment of Bercy in the 1980s unearthed five Neolithic canoes, now high and dry in the **Musée Carnavalet**. The fluctuating level of the river, however, probably forced people to dwell on one of the area's many hills.

By 250BC, some Celts (known as the Parisii) had put the place on the map, and given the modern capital its name. Some of them kept going northwards and settled in the English city of York. The ones who stayed behind became river traders, wealthy enough to mint their own gold coins. The **Musée de la Monnaie** has a collection of their small change. Their most important *oppidum*, a primitive fortified town, was located on an island in the Seine, which is generally thought to have been the present **Ile de la Cité**.

ROMAN PARIS

Superb strategic location and the capacity to generate hard cash were guaranteed to attract the attention of the Romans. Julius Caesar arrived in southern Gaul as proconsul in 58BC and soon used the pretext of dealing with invading Germans to stick his Roman nose into the affairs of northern Gaul. The Gauls didn't appreciate the attention, and in 54BC the Eburones from the Meuse valley rebelled against the Romans. Soon other tribes joined in: in 51BC the Parisii rose up with the rest of Gaul.

'Superb strategic location and the capacity to generate hard cash were guaranteed to attract Roman attention.'

Caesar had his hands full trying to deal with the great Gaul marauder Vercingetorix, so he sent his general Labienus with four legions and part of the cavalry to secure the passage of the Seine at Lutetia, as they called Paris. The Gauls were decimated, although a contingent of Parisii escaped the slaughter only to be defeated with Vercingetorix at the battle of Alesia. The surrender of Vercingetorix in 52BC left the Parisian region along with the rest of Gaul in Roman hands. Roman Lutetia was a prosperous town of around 8,000 inhabitants. Apart from centrally-heated villas and a temple to Jupiter on the main island (remains of both are visible in the **Crypte Archéologique**), there were the sumptuous baths (now the **Musée de Cluny**), and the 15,000-seater **Arènes de Lutèce**.

Christianity arrived in around 250 in the shape of Denis of Athens, who went on to become first bishop of Paris. Legend has it that he was decapitated by Valerian on Mons Martis, the mount of the martyrs, thus giving Montmartre its name.

Gaul kept its allure. Waves of barbarian invaders – Alamans, Francs and others – began crossing the Rhine from 275 onwards. They sacked more than 60 cities in Gaul, including Lutetia, where the population was decimated and the buildings on the Montagne Ste-Geneviève were pillaged and burned. The bedraggled survivors used the rubble to build a rampart around the Ile de la Cité and to fortify the forum, although few citizens remained in the shadow of its walls.

It was at this time that the city was renamed Paris. Protected by the Seine and the new fortifications, its main role now was as a rear base for the Roman armies defending Gaul, and it was here in 360 that Julian was proclaimed emperor by his troops. In the same year, the first Catholic council of Paris was held, condemning the Arian branch of Christianity as heresy. The city's inhabitants, however, had concerns more pressing than theology.

THE IMPACT OF CHRISTIANITY

Around 450, with the arrival of the Huns in the region, the people of Paris prepared once again to flee. They were dissuaded by a feisty woman named Geneviève, who was famed in the Christian community for her fervent piety. Seeing the walls of the city defended against him, no less a pillager than Attila the Hun turned back and was defeated soon afterwards.

In 464, Paris managed to resist another siege, this time by the Francs under Childeric. However by 486, after a further blockade lasting ten years, Geneviève had no option but to surrender the city to Childeric's successor, Clovis, who went on to conquer most of Gaul and founded the Merovingian dynasty. He chose Paris as capital of his new kingdom, and it stayed that way until the 7th century, in spite of various conflicts among his successors.

Under the influence of his wife, Clotilde, Clovis converted to Christianity. He founded and was buried in the basilica of the Saints Apôtres, later re-dedicated to Sainte Geneviève when the saviour and future patron saint of Paris was interred there in 512. All that remains of the basilica today is a single pillar in the grounds of the modern Lycée Henri IV; but there's a shrine dedicated to Sainte Geneviève and some relics in the fine Gothic church of **St-Etienne-du-Mont**, just next door.

Geneviève and Clovis had set a trend. The Ile de la Cité was still the heart of the city, but, under the Merovingians, the Left Bank was the up-and-coming area for fashion-conscious

Christians, with 11 churches built here in the period (against only four on the Right Bank and one on the Ile de la Cité).

Not everyone was sold on the joys of city living, though. From 614 onwards, the Merovingian kings preferred to hang out in the *banlieue* at Clichy, or wandered the kingdom trying to keep rebellious nobles in check. When one of their number, Pippin 'the Short', decided to do away with the last Merovingian in 751, Paris was starting to look decidedly *passé*.

Pippin's son, Charlemagne, built his capital at Aix-la-Chapelle, while his successors, known as the Carolingian dynasty, moved from palace to palace, consuming the local production.

Paris, meanwhile, was doing quite nicely for itself as a centre for Christian learning, and the city had grown to house a population of 20,000 by the beginning of the 9th century. This was the high point in the popularity and political power of the great abbeys like St-Germain-des-Prés, where transcription of the Latin classics was helping to preserve much of Europe's Roman cultural heritage. Power in the Paris region was exercised by the Counts of Paris.

THE VIKINGS

In 845 the Vikings appeared before the walls. Unopposed, the Norsemen sacked the city, and king Charles II, 'the Bald', had to cough up 7,000 pounds of silver to get them to leave. Recognising a soft touch when they saw one, the Vikings returned to sack the city repeatedly between 856 and 869, burning churches with heathen abandon. Deciding that matters were getting out of hand, Charles 'the Bald' at last organised the defence of the city. Fortified bridges were constructed – the Grand Pont over the northern and the Petit Pont over the southern branch of the Seine, blocking the passage of the Viking ships further upstream.

In 885, Gozlin, bishop of Paris, had just finished repairing the Roman walls when the Vikings showed up once again; this time they found the city defended against them. After a siege lasting a year, king Charles III 'the Fat' arrived at the head of an army but, deciding that discretion is indeed the better part of valour, handed over 700 pounds of silver and politely invited the Norsemen to pillage some other part of his kingdom. The Count of Paris, Eudes, having performed valiantly in the siege of 885-886, was offered the royal crown when Fat Chas was deposed in 888. Although the Carolingians recovered the throne after his death in 898, Eudes' great-nephew, Hugues Capet, was finally elected king of France in 987, adding what remained of the Carolingian dominions to his territories around Paris.

15th-century illuminations: **Ste-Chapelle...**

PARIS FINDS ITS IDENTITY

Under the Capetian dynasty, although Paris was now at the heart of the royal domains, the city did not yet dominate the kingdom. Hugues was elected at Senlis and crowned at Noyon, while his successors divided their time between Senlis, Paris, Étampes and Orléans.

Robert 'the Pious', king from 996 to 1031, stayed more often in Paris than his father, restoring the royal palace on the Ile de la Cité, while Henri I (1031-1060) issued more of his charters in Paris than in Orléans. In 1112, the abbey of **St-Denis** replaced St-Benoît-sur-Loire as principal monastery, so confirming the pre-eminence of Paris over Orléans.

Paris itself still consisted of little more than the Ile de la Cité and small settlements under the protection of the abbeys on each bank. On the Left Bank, royal largesse helped to rebuild the abbeys of St-Germain-des-Prés, St-Marcel, and Ste-Geneviève, although it took more than 150 years for the destruction wrought there by the Vikings to be fully repaired. The Right Bank, where mooring was easier, prospered from river commerce, and three boroughs grew up around the abbeys of St-Germain-l'Auxerrois,

and **The Louvre**, from the *Très Riches Heures*.

St-Martin-des-Champs and St-Gervais. Bishop Sully of Paris began building the cathedral of **Notre-Dame** in 1163.

The growing complexity of government during the 12th century, and the departure of kings on crusade, meant that the administration tended to stay in the **Palais de la Cité** and the royal treasure in the fortress of the Temple (built by the newly founded order of the Templars). The wisdom of this approach was confirmed by the disaster of Fréteval in 1194, where King Philippe-Auguste was defeated by Richard the Lionheart, losing much of his treasure and his archives in the process.

This minor hiccup aside, the reign of Philippe-Auguste (1180-1223) was a turning point in the history of Paris. Before, the city was a confused patchwork of royal, ecclesiastical and feudal authorities, exercising various powers, rights and privileges. Keen to raise revenues, Philippe favoured the growth of the guilds, especially the butchers, drapers, furriers, haberdashers and merchants: so began the rise of the bourgeoisie.

When Philippe went on crusade in 1190, he nominated representatives of this new bourgeoisie to govern the city in preference to the feudal lords, even leaving them the keys to the royal treasure kept at the Temple. He also ordered the building of the first permanent market buildings at **Les Halles**.

At the same time he ordered the construction of a new city wall, first on the Right Bank to protect the commercial heart of Paris, and later on the Left Bank. At the western end of the wall, Philippe built a new castle, the **Louvre**, to defend the road from the ever-menacing Normandy, only 100 km away (and whose duke was also King of England). The Louvre was where he imprisoned his conquered enemies after the battle of Bouvines (1214), which set the seal on a remarkable reign.

THE GOLDEN AGE

Paris was now the principal residence of the king and the uncontested capital of France. No longer threatened by foreign invasion, the city found itself overrun by a new and altogether deadlier menace that exists to this day: lawyers. And barristers, bailiffs, prosecutors, sergeants, accountants, judges, clerks and all the bureaucratic paraphernalia of royal government.

> **'The English were clearly impressed: they soon came back for a long stay.'**

To accommodate the growing royal administration, the Palace of the Cité, site and symbol of power for the previous thousand years, was remodelled and enlarged. The work was begun by Louis IX (later Saint Louis) in the 1240s, and continued under Philippe IV ('le Bel'). This vast architectural complex, of which the **Ste-Chapelle** and the **Conciergerie** can still be seen today, was inaugurated with great pomp at Pentecost 1313. Philippe invited Edward II of England and his Queen, Isabelle of France. The English were clearly impressed: they soon came back for a long stay.

The palace was quickly filled with functionaries, so the king spent as much of his time as he could outside Paris at the royal castles of **Fontainebleau** and, especially, **Vincennes**. The needs of the plenipotentiaries left behind to run the kingdom were met by a rapidly growing city population, piled into rather less chic buildings.

Paris was also reinforcing its identity as a major religious centre: as well as the local clergy and dozens of religious orders, the city was home to the masters and students of the university of the **Sorbonne** (established in 1253), who were already gaining a reputation for chemically-induced rowdiness. An influx of scholars and pilgrims from all over Europe gave the capital an intellectual and cultural cachet it was never to lose.

By 1328, Paris housed around 200,000 inhabitants, making it the most populous city in Europe. However, that year was to be the last of the golden age: the line of Capetian kings spluttered to an inglorious halt as Charles IV died heirless, leaving the kingdom up for grabs.

The English claimed the throne for the young Edward III, son of Philippe IV's daughter. Refusing to recognise his descent through the female line the late king's cousin, Philippe de Valois, claimed the crown as Philippe VI. So began the Hundred Years' War, which, as a lot of people know, went on for a bit longer than that.

TROUBLE AND STRIFE

It went on for 116 years. To make matters worse, the Black Death (bubonic plague) ravaged Europe from the 1340s. Those not done for by the plague had to contend with food shortages, ever-increasing taxes, riots, repression, currency devaluations and marauding mercenaries.

'The people of the city were increasingly exasperated by the futility of the sacrifices they were making.'

Meanwhile, back in Paris, the honeymoon period for the king and the bourgeoisie was coming to an end. Rich and populous, Paris was expected to bear the brunt of the war burden; and as defeat followed defeat (notably the disaster at Crécy in August 1346) the bourgeoisie and people of the city were increasingly exasperated by the futility of the sacrifices they were making.

When King Jean II 'le Bon' called the Estates General (a sort of parliament) in November 1355 to beg for yet more money for the war effort, one Etienne Marcel, provost of the merchants of Paris, started making a name for himself as spokesman for the cities of the realm in favour of reform. By 1356 Jean II and the Estates General had failed to agree on a new tax system and the king devalued the currency again, something always guaranteed to rile a bourgeoisie accustomed to growing rich on fixed incomes from rents. As a result, the contingents of Paris, Rouen and Amiens were withdrawn from the royal army: which at least saved them from a whipping at the battle of Poitiers in October 1356, where Jean II was captured by the English and held for ransom, leaving the kingdom in a fix.

Taking advantage of the situation, Etienne Marcel seized control of Paris, hoping to force the Dauphin Charles to grant the city increased autonomy. By 1358, however, Marcel was well and truly hoisted on his own petard, dying at the hands of an angry mob. Charles went on to improve the defences of the Louvre and begin building the fort at **La Bastille**, not only to protect the city, but also to protect himself against its inflamed citizens. One day, the inflamed citizens would make their feelings abundantly clear on the site of this building.

By 1420, following the French defeat at Agincourt, Paris was in English hands. In 1431, Henry VI of England was crowned King of France in Notre-Dame. He didn't last. Five years later, Henry and his army had been driven back to Calais by the Valois king, Charles VII. Charles owed his grasp on power to Jeanne d'Arc, who led the victorious French in the battle of Orléans, only to be betrayed by her compatriots who decided she was getting too big for her boots. She was captured and sold to the English, who had her burnt as a witch.

By 1436, Paris was once again the capital of France. But the nation was nearly ruined by war, still sharply divided politically, with powerful regional rulers continuing to threaten the monarchy. The ambitions of the Austrian Hapsburg dynasty represented a serious external worry. In a general atmosphere of instability, disputes over trade, religion and taxation were all simmering dangerously.

RENAISSANCE AND REFORMATION

In the closing decades of the 15th century, the restored Valois monarchs sought to reassert their position. A wave of building projects was the public sign of this effort, giving us such masterpieces as St-Etienne-du-Mont, St-Eustache and private homes like Hôtel de Cluny (which now houses the **Musée National du Moyen-Age**) and Hôtel de Sens. The renaissance in France climaxed under François 1er. As well as being involved in the construction of magnificent châteaux at **Fontainebleau**, Blois and **Chambord**, François was responsible for transforming the Louvre from a fortress into a royal palace. He held open house for such luminaries as Leonardo da Vinci and Benvenuto Cellini. He also established the Collège de France to encourage humanist learning outside the control of the clergy-dominated universities.

Despite publicly burning heretics by the dozen, François was unable to stop the spread of Protestantism, launched in Germany by Martin Luther in 1517. Resolutely Catholic, Paris was the scene of some horrific violence against Huguenots, as supporters of the new

Historical (s)hit parade

Gilles de Rais, 1404-40

By day a nobleman and Joan of Arc's Chief of Staff at the siege of Orléans. By night, a party animal who had trouble reining in his passions. He kidnapped and killed at least 150 children in sexual orgies. Not only that, but he seems to have been a shopaholic, too. De Rais tried to solve his debt problem by the novel method of turning to Satanism to raise funds. He was eventually hanged and then – just in case – burned. Not the sort of chap you could take home to meet mother.

Gilles de Rais, the tonsure-fringed torturer.

Catherine Monvoisin Deshayes, 1629-1682

So what would you do if *your* husband's jewellery business failed? The supportive and resourceful Catherine became a freelance witch, specialising in black masses, potions, contract poisoning and those aphrodisiac sprays that all too often result in your being hunted down, cornered and mounted by every stray dog within a five-male radius. Tragically, most of her recipes had children's blood as a base ingredient, so it was a quick trial and straight on the fire for Cath.

Jean Baptiste Carrier, 1756-94

Hey, Members of the Revolutionary Tribunal, tired of those Nantes dudes getting up your grill? Why not build a fleet of ships with trap-door bottoms and sail those muthas into the middle of the Loire; then you just pull the lever, the poop deck disappears and – bingo – they all drown. If you put your mind to it, you can kill 16,000 people that way. Jean Baptiste Carrier did.

Henri-Désiré Landru: would you buy a used oven from this hunk?

Henri-Désiré Landru, 1869-1922

Henri-Désiré Landru was a bit of a lad with the ladies, especially those who were recently widowed, rich and gullible. Once he'd got his hands on their assets, he somehow seemed to tire of them, so, perhaps too sensitive to do the 'something seems to have died between us' routine, he strangled at least ten of them, chopped them up and shoved them in his incinerator. Rather mysteriously, canine remains were also found in his deadly oven. Hey, Mr Landru, a dog's not just for Christmas, you know.

Dr Marcel Petiot, 1897-1946

When, in March 1944, police broke into the Paris house of Dr Marcel Petiot because the neighbours were complaining of strange smells, Petiot told them that he was head of a resistance cell (he wasn't) and that the arm that was hanging out of his incinerator was that of a collaborator (it wasn't). They believed him and he slipped away for seven months. When the penny finally dropped, the police went after him and he admitted 107 random murders. Petiot, who had invented a suction machine for the relief of constipation, was condemned to the guillotine tonsillectomy.

faith were called. The picture was complicated by the political conflict opposing the Huguenot Prince de Condé and the Catholic Duc de Guise.

By the 1560s, the situation had degenerated into open warfare. Catherine de Médicis, the scheming Italian widow of Henri II, was the real force in court politics. It was she who connived to murder prominent Protestants gathered in Paris for the marriage of the king's sister on St Bartholomew's Day (23 August 1572). Catherine's main aim was to dispose of her powerful rival, Gaspard de Coligny, but the situation got out of hand, and as many as 3,000 people were butchered. Henri III attempted to reconcile the religious factions and eradicate the powerful families directing the conflict, but the people of Paris turned against him and he was forced to flee. His assassination in 1589 brought the Valois line to an end.

THE BOURBONS

The throne of France being up for grabs, Henri of Navarre declared himself King Henri IV, getting the Bourbon dynasty off the mark. Paris was not impressed. The city closed its gates against the Huguenot king and the inhabitants endured a four-year siege by supporters of the new ruler. Henri broke the impasse by becoming a Catholic. It was he who quipped 'Paris vaut bien une messe' (Paris is well worth a Mass).

The new king set about rebuilding his ravaged capital. He completed the **Pont-Neuf**, the first bridge to span the whole of the Seine. He commissioned place Dauphine and the city's first enclosed residential square – the place Royale – now **place des Vosges**. The square was the scene of jousting competitions and countless duels.

Henri also tried to reconcile his Catholic and Protestant subjects, issuing the Edict of Nantes in 1598, effectively giving each religion equal status. The Catholics hated the deal, and the Huguenots were suspicious. Henri was the victim of at least 23 attempted assassinations by fanatics of both persuasions. Finally, in 1610, one François Ravaillac – a Catholic – fatally stabbed the king while he was stuck in traffic on rue de la Ferronnerie.

TWO CARDINALS

Since Henry's son, Louis XIII, was only eight at the time of his father's death, the widow, Marie de Médicis, took up the reins of power. We can thank her for the **Palais du Luxembourg** and the 24 paintings she commissioned from Rubens, now part of the Louvre collection.

Louis took up his royal duties in 1617, but Cardinal Richelieu, chief minister from 1624, was the man who ran France. Something of a schemer, he outwitted the king's mother, his wife, Anne of Austria, and a host of princes and

The cessation of wars frees funds for the 1660s refurbishment of the Louvre.

Palais de la Cité, centre of the legal system from the 12th century until today. *See p9.*

place-seekers. Richelieu helped to strengthen the power of the monarch, and he did much to limit the independence of the aristocracy. The cardinal was also a great architectural patron. He commissioned Jacques Lemercier to build what is now the **Palais-Royal**, and ordered the rebuilding of the **Sorbonne**.

The Counter-Reformation was at its height, and lavish churches such as the Baroque **Val-de-Grâce** were an important reassertion of Catholic supremacy. The 16th century was also *Le Grand Siècle*, a time of patronage of art and artists, even if censorship forced the brilliant mathematician and philosopher, René Descartes, into exile.

The first national newspaper, *La Gazette*, hit the streets in 1631, with Richelieu using it as a propaganda tool. The cardinal founded the **Académie Française**, a sort of literary think-tank which is still working, slowly, on the dictionary of the French language which Richelieu commissioned from them in 1634. Richelieu died in 1642; Louis XIII followed him a few months later. The new king, Louis XIV, was barely five years old. Anne of Austria became regent, with the Italian Cardinal Mazarin, a Richelieu protégé, as chief minister. Mazarin's nifty townhouse is now the home of the **Bibliothèque Nationale Richelieu**.

Endless wars against Austria and Spain had depleted the royal coffers, and left the nation drained by exorbitant taxation. In 1648, the royal family was chased out of Paris by a popular uprising, 'la fronde', named after the catapults used by some of the rioters. Parisians soon tired of the resulting anarchy. When Mazarin's army retook the city in 1653, the boy-king was warmly welcomed. Mazarin died in 1661 and Louis XIV, now 24 years old, decided he would rule France without the intervention of a chief minister.

THE SUN ALSO RISES

The Sun King was an absolute monarch. 'L'état, c'est moi,' (I am the State) was his vision of power. To emphasise his grandeur, the king embarked on wars against England, Holland and Austria. He also refurbished and extended the **Louvre**, commissioned **place Vendôme** and **place des Victoires**, constructed the Observatory and laid out the *grands boulevards* along the lines of the old city walls. The triumphal arches at **Porte St-Denis** and **Porte St-Martin** date from this time, too. His major project was the palace at **Versailles**, a massive complex which drew on the age's finest architectural, artistic and landscape-design talent. Louis moved his court there in 1682.

Louis XIV owed much of his brilliant success to the work of Jean-Baptiste Colbert, nominally in charge of state finances, but eventually taking control of all the important levers of the state machine. Colbert was the force behind the Sun King's redevelopment of Paris.

The **Hôtel des Invalides** was built to accommodate the crippled survivors of Louis' wars, the **Salpêtrière** to shelter fallen women. In 1702, Paris was divided into 20 'quartiers'

The path to purgatory – a walk

If you can keep your head while all those around you are losing theirs, get on the blocks for our Revolutionary Walk, a unique promenade through the goriest spots of regicidal fever. You'll need: stout shoes, water and a fervent imagination.
Start: Place de la Concorde, Mº Concorde. The key date here is 21 January 1793. Since 8am the gates of Paris have been locked, the shutters barred. A crowd of 20,000 has assembled in the place Louis XV, renamed place de la Révolution. At 10am there is a drum roll, the king is strapped to a plank and pushed towards the 'iron razor', the guillotine. The device slices through his neck, executioner Samson holds up the head, the crowd roars and clamours to soak their hankies in the monarch's blood. But to see how the nation reached this bloodthirsty state, we have to step back in time.

So walk through the gates from Concorde and into the sedate **Tuileries gardens**. The Tuileries Palace that used to stand here was the scene of repeated Revolutionary fracas. On 13 July 1789, the eve of Bastille Day, a crowd ransacked the royal *garde-meubles* for weapons, raining stones on the guards from the balustraded terrace. This was only a taster for what was to come. Inadvisedly, perhaps, the Royal family moved here from Versailles in October 1789. On the night of the King's arrest in 1792, 600 of his Swiss guards were murdered, their genitals hacked off and fed to dogs. It was, said Robespierre, 'the most beautiful Revolution that has ever honoured humanity'.

Turn left at the first path, which takes you to the side gates of the Tuileries. On the railings opposite 230 rue the Rivoli there's a plaque commemorating the site of the old **Salle du Manège**. This was the seat of Revolutionary government through November 1789 until a Republic was declared on 21 September 1792. At 202 rue de Rivoli is the **Hôtel Saint James et d'Albany**, the home of Général Lafayette, whose celebrated meeting with Marie-Antoinette in 1779 is commemorated by a plaque in the courtyard.

Turn up rue St-Roch to the rue St-Honoré, where Danton, Robespierre and friends met at the Couvent des Jacobins, and follow the road to the **Palais-Royal**. The dandy Duc d'Orléans' pleasure palace was a hotbed of revolutionary thought as nobles and plebs mingled in the coffee shops and sideshows. This was the scene, on 12 July 1789, for Camille Desmoulins' pistol-waving speech, while revolutionaries stormed into salon No 7, Monsieur Curtius' wax museum, to grab the wax heads of their heroes.

Walk through the arch in the Louvre's north wing to the Place du Carrousel, where the guillotine briefly stood. Cross the Seine at Pont des Arts and head down rue Bonaparte. On your left you'll see the **Ecole des Beaux-Arts**, where Alexandre Lenoir tried to save France's heritage from the mob – he threw himself on the grave of Richelieu and took a stab in the back for his pains.

The fourth left, rue de l'Abbaye, was the site of one of the Revolution's worst atrocities, in September 1792, when 115 priests were trapped in the garden and butchered. The red brick Abbot's Palace is now the **Institut Catholique**. Take rue de l'Echaudé right, cross the road and take rue Mabillon and rue Garancière past St-Sulpice to the **Palais du Luxembourg**. Now the Senate, the palace was commandeered as a prison and housed, among others, Danton and Thomas Paine. Take rue Rotrou through **place de l'Odéon**, where Camille Desmoulins lived at No 2, and follow rue de l'Odéon, where Paine, having escaped the guillotine, lived at No 10. Cross boulevard St-Germain to find the **Café Procope** at 13 rue de l'Ancienne Comédie. A favourite slugging ground of Voltaire, Rousseau, Danton and Marat, it contains a host of portraits, Voltaire's desk and even a postcard from Marie-Antoinette.

Backtrack to the other side of boulevard St-Germain and the rue de l'Ecole de Médecine, where at No 15 the Cordeliers' Club met in the former **Couvent des Cordeliers**. No 18 was the scene of pamphleteer **Marat**'s infamous demise, when Charlotte Corday stabbed him in the bath with a kitchen knife. The martyred Marat's rotting corpse was exhibited for public display in the chapel of the Cordeliers, with a false arm that had been sewn on from another dead man.

Follow the road east and cut up rue St-Jacques and rue Dante until you meet rue Galande. By the time the Terror started, every available space was being used as a prison. At No 52 the Caveau des Oubliettes jazz club gets its name from a gory death sentence whereby prisoners were thrown into cells and 'forgotten'. At No 56 the Trois Mailletz pub found torture instruments in its cellar during

through Revolutionary Paris

renovation, while the Caveau de la Huchette jazz club (5 rue de La Huchette), was a tribunal, prison and place of execution where a well washed away the traces of 'justice'.

At Pont St-Michel, cross onto the Ile de la Cité where you can call in at the **Conciergerie**. This 'vast antechamber of death' was one of the most appalling prisons of the Revolution, where prisoners slept in their own excrement. Not so Marie-Antoinette, who had an 11-by-six-foot room with a bed and wallpaper. Didn't stop her getting dispatched for the big sleep on 12 October 1793.

Cross the Seine at Pont d'Arcole and you'll find yourself in front of the **Hôtel de Ville** from whence, in October 1789, a mob of 3,000 fishwives and others commandeered guns and cannon before marching to Versailles to lynch the King. They returned with the severed heads of two guards. This was also the seat of the military tribunal set up in August 1792 to dispense instant 'justice'. The original building was destroyed in the 1871 Commune.

Take rue du Temple, the road of no return for Louis XVI, turn right into rue St-Croix-de-la-Bretonnerie and left into **rue Vielle-du-Temple**. At No 47 (with the medusa heads on the door) is the townhouse where Beaumarchais ran a fictitious trading company that secretly channelled arms to America. Now take rue des Francs-Bourgeois on the right, which will bring you to the **Musée Carnavalet** (*see p169*) with its fine collection of Revolutionary history. Follow rue de Sévigné south to the church of **St-Paul-St-Louis** on rue St-Antoine, from which the hearts of Louis XIII and XIV were seized and sold to a painter. Now you're on the road to the Bastille. Take boulevard Henri IV and notice the brown bricks in the road as you approach **place de la Bastille**. These mark the spot where the Bastille prison stood; similar marks can be seen on rue St-Antoine, where No 5 is the site of the main gate and the famous 'storming' on 14 July 1789. On place de la Bastille, in June 1794, the guillotine claimed 73 victims in three days.

From here on in, things get grim, in terms of both the tale and the trudging. Lightweights can hop on the 86 bus to place de la Nation, leaving hardier souls to ponder Mirabeau's remark that 'There is nothing more lamentable or revolting in its details than a revolution but nothing finer in its consequences for the regeneration of empires'.

Nation, formerly place du Trône, was the guillotine's last stand before the murderous device moved back to Concorde to give Robespierre the chop. But this is where French collective denial steps in. In 1794 the machine claimed more than 1,000 lives at place de la Réunion, just to the north-east of the twin pillars of the Fermiers-Généraux wall. But is there anything to commemorate the slaughter? Nothing. The proof is found at the **Cimetière de Picpus** (*see p101*), down rue Fabre d'Eglantine and left. Here two mass graves contain the bodies of 1,306 people killed by the guillotine in the last, brutal period of the Terror in June and July 1794. Also buried here is Général Lafayette, who, languishing in an Austrian prison all this time, escaped the guillotine and lived on to the ripe old age of 74. Which just goes to show you: there are far worse places to be than the big house.

Statement of intent: the King's Guard is massacred in the **Tuileries** in 1792. *See p14.*

(not until the Revolution was it re-mapped as arrondissements). **Le Procope**, the city's first café, opened for business in 1686. Even if the original proprietor, Francesco Procopio dei Coltelli, wouldn't recognise it following a 1989 facelift, the place is still doing business. Colbert died in 1683, and Louis' luck on the battlefield ran out. Hopelessly embroiled in the War of the Spanish Succession, the country was devastated by famine in 1692.

The Sun King died in 1715, leaving no direct heir. His five-year-old great-grandson, Louis XV, was named king, with Philippe d'Orléans as regent. The court moved back to Paris. Installed in the **Palais-Royal**, the regent set about enjoying his few years of power, hosting lavish dinners which regularly degenerated into orgies. The state, meanwhile, remained chronically in debt.

PARIS GETS ENLIGHTENED

Some of the city's more sober residents were making Paris the intellectual capital of Europe. Enlightenment thinkers like Diderot, Montesquieu, Voltaire and Rousseau were all active during the reign of Louis XV. Literacy rates were increasing – 50% of French men could read, 25% of women – and the publishing industry was booming.

The king's mistress, Madame de Pompadour, encouraged him to finance the building of the **Ecole Militaire** and the laying out of place Louis XV, known to us as **place de la Concorde**. The massive church of **St-Sulpice** was completed in 1776. Many of the great houses in the area bounded by rue de Lille, rue de Varenne and rue de Grenelle date from the first half of the 18th century. The private homes of aristocrats and wealthy bourgeois, these were the venues for numerous *salons*, informal discussion sessions devoted to topics raised by Enlightenment questioning.

The Enlightenment spirit of rational humanism finally took the venom out of the Catholic-Protestant power struggle, and the increase in public debate helped to change views about the nature of the State and the place and authority of the monarchy. As Jacques Necker, Louis XVI's finance minister on the eve of the Revolution, put it, popular opinion was 'an invisible power that, without treasury, guard or army, gives its laws to the city, the court and even the palaces of kings.' Thanks to the Enlightenment, that power was about to change the history of Europe.

BASTILLE DAY

Enlightened debate had made the inequalities of society impossible to ignore. The majority of the population, the so-called Third Estate (the commoners), generated most of France's economic output and yet was systematically exploited by the First and Second Estates (respectively, the clergy and the nobility).

Added to this, Louis XVI was a poor advert for a monarchy that had fallen into disrepute by engaging France in a succession of ruinous wars; living in ostenatious luxury at Versailles was not the most sensitive course of action. A disastrous harvest meant that, by July 1789, starving farm labourers joined the angry crowds who were already roaming Paris; and then the weather turned oppressively hot.

'The possibility of a negotiated settlement was no longer an option.'

On 14 July 1789, the storm broke. Early in the day, a crowd stormed the **Tuileries** and carried off tons of weapons. They then marched across town to the royal prison at the **Bastille**. A pitched battle ensued, in which 83 people died. When the mob finally took control of the jail, they decapitated its governor and freed its seven bemused prisoners. It was a modest start, but the Revolution at least had its symbolic act of violence against the *ancien régime*.

The Bastille was eventually razed to the ground. A plaque on the westbound side of the tunnel of Line 1 of the Métro, 50 metres from Bastille station, marks the foundations of one of the prison's eight towers.

Life almost returned to 'normal' after the initial revolutionary success. The king visited the Hôtel de Ville on 16 July and delighted the crowd by accepting a tricolour badge. A new era of constitutional monarchy was hailed as the future. The city council voted to erect a statue to the king on the site of the hated prison. As the summer wore on, there were isolated acts of violence and riot, as reformers pushed for further insurrection. Sensing that the worst was to come, many noble families tried to move out of France, thus adding thousands of domestic servants to the ranks of the angry unemployed.

Louis made his move on 21 June 1791, attempting to escape with his family in disguise to Germany. He was stopped at the town of Varennes and brought back in disgrace to the Tuileries. Financed by worried European monarchs, a Prussian army invaded France and advanced on Paris. The possibility of a negotiated settlement was no longer an option.

THE TERROR

The revolutionaries were anything but united. They fought among themselves for everything from immediate gain to increased political power. Those in the provinces deeply distrusted those in the capital. In September 1792, as the Prussians approached Paris, a wave of paranoia led to the massacre of at least 2,000 suspected traitors. Later in the same month, the monarchy was formally abolished and the French Republic proclaimed. A citizens' army defeated the Prussians at Valmy.

The year 1793 saw the execution of Louis and his queen, Marie-Antoinette, as well as the brutal murder of those revolutionaries believed to be too moderate. In the *Grande Terreur* of 1794, the guillotine stationed in place du Trône Renversé (now place de la Nation) dispatched 1,300 souls in six blood-sodden weeks.

The remaining years of the century saw more violence, famine and war, as the new republic fought off the armies of neighbouring monarchs, defeated royalist factions within France, and endured its own internal power struggles. When the dust settled, a young Corsican general emerged as the unlikely winner. The citizens' revolution had paved the way for dictatorship.

NAPOLEON

Napoléon I gave France muscle and leadership. After a decade of murderous chaos, it was a winning combination. Boney had himself declared emperor in 1804, and waged wars of massive scope against Britain, Russia and Austria. On his way to the decisive disasters of Moscow and Waterloo, Napoléon gave France

Napoléon: portraiture as spin, even then.

the *lycée* educational system, the Napoléonic Code of civil law, the Legion of Honour, the Banque de France, the **Pont des Arts**, the **Arc de Triomphe**, the **Madeleine** church (he cunningly re-established Catholicism as the State religion), the **Bourse**, and the **rue de Rivoli**. He also started the centralised bureaucracy which is still driving people mad. And so the Little Corsican died on the south Atlantic prison island of Ste Helena in 1821.

ANOTHER ROUND OF BOURBONS

Having sampled revolution and military dictatorship, the French were now ready to give monarchy a second chance.

The Bourbons got back in business, briefly, in 1815 in the person of Louis XVIII, Louis XVI's elderly brother. Several efforts were made to adapt the monarchy to the new political realities, but the forces unleashed during the Revolution, and the divisions which had opened in French society as a result, were not to be ignored. When another brother of Louis XVI, Charles X, became king in 1824, he decided that enough royal energy had been wasted trying to reconcile the nation's myriad factions. It was time for a spot of old-fashioned absolutism. The people responded with old-fashioned rebellion.

'The poor were as badly off as ever, only there were more of them.'

In July 1830, the king abolished press freedom and dissolved the Chamber of Deputies. Print workers took to the streets, and three newspapers defiantly published. Police attempts to seize copies led to full-scale rioting and the defection of Paris regiments. After three days of fighting in the streets (*Les Trois Glorieuses*), Charles X was forced to abdicate. Another leftover from the *ancien régime* was now winched onto the throne – Louis-Philippe, Duc d'Orléans, who had some Bourbon blood in his veins. A father of eight who never went out without his umbrella, he was eminently acceptable to the newly powerful bourgeoisie. But the poor who had risked their lives in two attempts to change French society were unimpressed by the new king's promise to embrace a moderate and liberal version of the Revolutionary heritage.

The population of Paris doubled to one million over the first half of the 19th century. Most of the new arrivals were rural labourers who came to work on the ever-expanding city's building sites. The middle classes were doing well, thanks to the late arrival of the industrial revolution in France, and the solid administrative structures inherited from Napoléon. The poor were as badly off as ever, only there were more of them.

ONCE MORE, WITH FEELING

When troops fired on a crowd of the unemployed on boulevard des Capucines on 23 February 1848, they triggered another revolution. The monarchy was no longer the target: this time the antagonists divided on class lines, rich against poor. The city was soon embroiled in barricade fighting. When the National Guard sided with the revolutionaries, Louis-Philippe stood down.

This workers' revolution ushered in the Second Republic. But in the elections of May 1848, provincial conservatives won the day against Paris progressives. When disappointed workers in the capital again took to the streets, they were massacred by government troops. As the pamphleteer Adolphe Karr said of the aftermath of the 1848 revolution, 'plus ça change, plus c'est la meme chose' (the more things change, the more they stay the same).

In December 1848, Louis Bonaparte – nephew of Napoléon – was elected president. By 1852, he had moved into the **Tuileries Palace** and declared himself Emperor Napoléon III.

THE SECOND EMPIRE

The emperor appointed a lawyer as Préfet to oversee the reconstruction of Paris. Yet Little Napoléon, as Hugo called him, held on to power for 22 years, and the lawyer, Georges-Eugène Haussmann, went on to create the most magnificent city in Europe. Haussmann's wide avenues were not only better ventilated and more hygienic than the squalid lanes they replaced; they were also more difficult to barricade. The tree-lined streets radiating from place de l'Etoile are the classic expression of Haussmann's vision, while the rich mix of styles in Charles Garnier's **Opéra** is often seen as typical of Second Empire self-indulgence.

The emperor's attempt to remain neutral in the Austro-Prussian war ended in disaster. At Sedan, in September 1870, 100,000 French troops were forced to surrender to Bismarck's Prussians, and Napoléon III was imprisoned in Germany. He never came back. In the humiliating deal which put a temporary end to hostilities, France lost the industrial heartlands of Alsace and Lorraine to Germany.

Out of the ruins of the Second Empire rose the Third Republic, a hastily flung together compromise given little chance of survival even by those who supported it. In fact, this makeshift constitution was to survive until 1940, thus becoming the most enduring – so far – in modern French history.

Occupational hazard: Hitler dreamed of Paris as a showcase of the Third Reich. *See p20.*

THE PARIS COMMUNE

Things started badly. Paris was surrounded by German forces, who had to be paid off to leave. The place was seething with revolt. The new president, Adolphe Thiers, had moved the seat of government to Versailles, further inflaming opinion in the city. On 26 March 1871, the Commune of Paris was proclaimed by an ill-organised group of radicals. The city was immediately surrounded by government troops, and systematic slaughter became the order of the day. In a celebrated shoot-out in the cemetery of **Père Lachaise**, 147 communards were cornered and executed against the Mur des Fédérés, now a memorial to the insurrection. In less than a week 30,000 Parisians were summarily executed by Thiers' troops, with 40,000 more being taken prisoner. A third of the city was destroyed by fire. The tragic story of the Paris Commune is memorably documented in the collection of the **Musée d'Art et d'Histoire de St-Denis**.

Thanks mainly to the huge economic boost provided by colonial expansion in Africa and Indo-China, the horrors of the Commune were soon forgotten in the self-indulgent materialism of the turn of the century. The **Eiffel Tower** was built as the centrepiece of the 1889 Universal Exhibition. In 1891 the first line of the Métro opened, linking Porte Maillot and Vincennes in 25 minutes. For the World Exhibition of 1900, the Grand and Petit Palais, the Pont Alexandre III and the Gare d'Orsay (now **Musée d'Orsay**) were built to affirm France's position as a dominant world power. The first cinema had opened (1895), and clubs like the **Moulin Rouge** (1890) were buzzing.

AN AFFAIR TO REMEMBER

In 1894, a Jewish army officer, Captain Alfred Dreyfus, had been dismissed in disgrace from the army and deported to Devil's Island, convicted of selling state secrets to the Prussians. The affair rocked the French establishment to its self-satisfied roots.

Emile Zola famously championed the Jewish officer's cause, as did statesmen such as Georges Clemenceau and Jean Jaurès. The Catholic right wing sided with the army, and lost heavily when Dreyfus was proven innocent.

THE GREAT WAR

The Germans never made it to Paris in the course of the First World War. They were stopped 20 kilometres short by French victory in the Battle of the Marne. But the city, and French society generally, suffered terribly as a result of this war, despite ultimate victory.

The interwar years were a whirl of activity in both artistic and political circles. Paris became the avant-garde capital of the world, spiritual home to Surrealism and Cubism. Hemingway, F. Scott Fitzgerald and Gertrude Stein made the city their home and source of inspiration. The Depression unleashed a wave of political violence, Fascists fighting Socialists and Communists for control. The election in 1936 of Léon Blum's Front Populaire saw the introduction of such social benefits as paid holidays for workers.

THE SECOND WORLD WAR

Paris was in German hands within weeks of the start of hostilities. The city fell without a fight. A pro-German government in Vichy was headed by Maréchal Pétain, while a young army officer, Charles de Gaulle, went to London to organise the Free French opposition. For those happy to get along with the German army, the period of the Occupation presented few real hardships. Food was rationed and tobacco and coffee went out of circulation.

> **'For those happy to get along with the German army the Occupation presented few real hardships.'**

Each month during the winter of 1939-40, 800,000 Parisians still managed to go to the cinema. For those few who chose to resist, there were the Gestapo torture chambers at avenue Foch or rue Lauriston. The Vichy government was eager to please the Germans. From the spring of 1941, the French authorities deported Jews to the death camps, frequently via the internment camp at **Drancy**, in what prime minister Pierre Laval claimed was a necessary concession to his Third Reich masters.

In July 1942, 12,000 Jewish French citizens were rounded up in the Vélodrome d'Hiver, a sports complex on quai de Grenelle, and then dispatched to Auschwitz. In July 1994, a memorial to the victims was finally erected near the site of the long-demolished sports arena.

Paris survived the war practically unscathed, ultimately due to the bravery of one of its captors. On 23 August 1944, as the Allied armies of liberation approached the city, Hitler ordered his commander, Dietrich Von Choltitz, to detonate the explosives which had been set all over town in anticipation of a retreat. Von Choltitz refused. On 25 August 1944, French troops, discreetly placed at the head of the US forces, entered the city, and General de Gaulle, sporting his London tan, vogued his way triumphantly in the butch-but-distinguished way he had, down the Champs-Elysées. Thank God, he'd won the war.

Give peace a(nother) chance?

In February 2003 Jacques 'Le Bulldozer' Chirac announced that, as he believed that UN weapons inspectors in Iraq needed more time to do their job, he would deploy France's veto against any US-led attempt to construct a UN resolution authorising military action against Iraq.

This was no coquettish hissy fit of the type that's occasionally thrown by always-the-bridesmaid French presidents when the cloying nature of Anglo-American relationships goes beyond the pale; this was a serious case of Jacques hurling his toys out of the pram at a time when he seemed to have settled grumpily into the role of the Pauline Fowler of international politics. Perhaps understandably, people wondered what on earth had come over the old rascal.

Some cynics saw Chirac's stance as an attempt to raise France's flagging international profile, and, if it was, he certainly had a most distinguished precedent to guide him: as far back as the 1950s, Charles de Gaulle was advocating the long-term benefits of France's counter-balancing Anglo-American influence by forging special ties with Arab states. The Ba'ath Party certainly appreciated the gesture: *Babel*, the newspaper controlled by Sadam's son Uday, awarded Chirac the title 'Great Combatant' in recognition of his position. Meanwhile, at home, a poll in *Le Figaro* newspaper showed that 62% of French people felt that their nation had risen in international standing as a result of Chirac's relative pacificism.

Other cynics interpreted Chirac's stance as a devious method of pepping up his profile in France. Certainly, his pre-2003 image had degenerated into that of, at best, an amiable spiv: while he was running for his second term of presidential office in 2002, he was under investigation for no fewer than three sets of alleged criminal offences.

If image regeneration was Chirac's aim, it worked like a charm. In March 2003, a poll suggested that 92% of the French electorate thoroughly approved of him, an impressive transformation from ten months earlier when the same people were bewailing the fact that they would have to re-elect a man many considered a crook in order to keep the National Front's Jean-Marie Le Pen out of power. Monsieur Sleazeball Hyde was now Jackie Jekyll, the Presidential peacenik, a Greenham Common woman for the newish millennium and new best friend of France's five million Muslims (and their votes).

Still more cynics – the sneering sort – claimed that Le Bulldozer's stand had its origin in the fact that, for once, France had a Foreign Minister, Dominique de Villepin, who spent as much time away with the fairies as his boss and thus was unable to perform a vital part of his role, namely, preventing Chirac's crackpot attempts at being butch on the international level from becoming public.

So why the cynicism? Why did so few commentators (especially abroad, and most especially – surprise, surprise – in the US and UK) conclude that Chirac was simply trying to avoid, or at least postpone, a war and its inevitable cost in terms of human life and the French government's business deals with the Iraqi regime? *Bon dieu de bois*, what a bitterly rum business it is when a chap's well-meaning attempt at keeping the peace is subjected to all manner of perverse speculation, merely because so many indications – to those unable or unwilling to see the messianic degree of philanthropic virtue that motivates this Gallic Gandhi's every action – seemed to point to less-than-lily-white motives. When all he was saying was give peace a chance.

THE ALGERIAN WAR AND MAY 1968

The postwar years were marked by the rapid disintegration of France's overseas interests. When revolt broke out in Algeria in 1956, almost 500,000 troops were sent in to protect national interests. A protest by Algerians in Paris on 17 October 1961 led to the deaths of hundreds of people at the hands of the city's police. The extent of the violence was officially concealed for decades, as was the use of torture against Algerians by French troops. Algeria became independent in 1962.

Charles de Gaulle's Fifth Republic was felt by many to be grimly authoritarian. There are certainly those who believe that he designed it to be an elected monarchy, which is interesting when you consider that it's the constitution that is still in use today. In the spring of 1968, students unhappy with overcrowded university conditions took to the streets of Paris at the same time as striking Renault workers. The protest turned violent, and six million people went on strike. The real significance of May 68 is still debated, but President de Gaulle certainly took it seriously, fleeing to Germany on 29 May as the street violence reached its peak. He came back, of course, and won the June elections, but his career was over.

MITTERRAND

Following the largely anonymous presidencies of Georges Pompidou and Valéry Giscard d'Estaing, the Socialist François Mitterrand took up the task in 1981. The verdict on Mitterrand is still not in: the early part of his Presidency saw him introducing some radical political and economic reforms, but the necessities of pragmatism and compromise led to their reversal, and he left the Socialist party in some disarray. At any rate, Mitterrand made a big difference to Paris and visitors to the city can thank him for his *Grands Projets* without worrying about suggestions that they represent a most unrepublican form of self-aggrandissement. Mitterrand gave us: I M Pei's **Louvre Pyramid**, the **Grande Arche de la Défense**, the **Opéra Bastille**, and the **Bibliothèque Nationale de France François Mitterrand**.

CHIRAC, BUSH AND IRAQ

France may still boast the world's fourth-largest economy, the nuclear deterrent and a permanent seat on the UN Security Council, but her influence on the world stage had been waning for years until President Chirac, flushed from re-election and well aware he was onto a PR no-brainer, stood up in early 2003 to shout

May 1968: yesterday's rebels, today's establishment.

(metaphorically speaking, of course), 'Hey guys, look out, old Jacques is back'.

The jury is still out on whether France's remarkable and determined opposition to the US-led invasion of Iraq, culminating in the threat to use its Security Council veto against any resolution authorising the use of force without UN approval, was inspired by Chirac's deep-seated need to throw his weight around a bit, his fear of the consequences of an attack on Iraq on France's five million Muslims, traditional Gallic anti-Americanism, or (strange as it may seem) a genuine belief that this particular war at this particular time in this particular place was wrong.

Whatever the reason, it did our Jacques no harm at all. His personal approval ratings soared at home, at one stage breaking the 80% barrier, and abroad he became the darling of the Islamic world, Africa, Asia and large swathes of continental Europe. He also acquired a most-hated-man status in America rivalled only by bin Laden, O. and Hussein, S., but that was a small price to pay.

Chirac's domestic popularity at least did not last. His prime minister, Jean-Pierre Raffarin, and the centre-right government began attacking some of France's more prized national institutions with a programme of long-overdue reforms, starting with the state pension system. The blindingly obvious fact that a steadily greying population plus fewer people in work equals serious pension shortfall did not prevent some of the largest nationwide protests France has seen since 1995, with striking Métro, hospital workers, postmen, teachers and binmen bringing the city to a virtual standstill.

Planned restrictions on the uniquely Gallic, exceptionally generous (and heavily indebted) system of unemployment benefit for out-of-work performing arts professionals like actors, musicians and backstage staff led to a further round of major protests, as well as the cancellation of France's equivalents of Edinburgh and Glyndebourne, the Avignon and Aix summer festivals.

Then came the official mismanagement and aloofness that characterised, for all of France, the murderous two-week heatwave of August 2003, during which as many as 15,000 elderly people died, Government ministers endlessly intoned 'Crisis, what crisis?', and Chirac himself did not deign to open his mouth, still less cut short his lumber-jack shirt, one-of-the-guys holiday in Canada.

Result: by the time this guide went to press, the popularity of both president and prime minister had plummeted to all-time lows, and the future of Raffarin at least was looking increasingly shaky beyond spring 2004.

A dead heat

August 2003. One minute, the Parisians who hadn't escaped the city for the month were enjoying the breathing spaces of its empty streets, cafés and public transport. The next minute, they were forced to spend nights trying to sleep in baths full of cold water, they were avoiding leaving their flats and, in a lot of cases, they were dying.

Things turned nasty on the weekend of 2/3 August, when the weather changed from hot to unbearable. By 13 August, day-time temperatures in Paris had been over 35 degrees Celsius for over a week and hundreds of casualties of the heat – mainly the elderly and the homeless – were arriving in the city's hospitals. As these casualties began dying (a total of 14,802 people died that month in Paris), the mortuaries were filling up. They couldn't cope, either, and bodies had to be stored in refrigerated lorries. Priests were told to stop conducting marriages and devote all their time to funerals. At the end of August there were still 400 unidentified bodies awaiting burial, 400 Parisians who presumably hadn't yet been missed by friends or family. The emergency workers who had found the corpses, sometimes after days of decomposition in boiling conditions, were offered counselling.

Predictably the tragedy of how many vulnerable people died because of a change in the weather became a political point-scoring match. François Hollande, the Socialist Party leader, accused Prime Minister Jean-Pierre Raffarin's government of being too slow to react. A great deal of popular fury was directed at President Chirac, who refused to cut short his summer holiday in Canada; when he did return to Paris, at the very end of August, he promised extra funding for the health service in case there are similar weather conditions in 2004. The newspaper Le Monde said that it was the state's responsibility to care for the weak, while Le Figaro declared that it was up to individuals to look out for people at risk. And what of the hidden victims? What of the psychological effects upon the bronzed and bitchin' bodies beautiful as, splayed seductively on the imported sand of Paris-Plage, the catastrophe unfolded around their factor-38-smeared loins?

Key events

EARLY HISTORY

250 BC Lutétia founded on the Ile de la Cité by a Celtic tribe, the Parisii.
52 BC Paris conquered by the Romans.
260 AD St Denis executed on Mount Mercury.
360 Julian, Governor of Lutétia, is proclaimed Roman Emperor by his troops.
451 Attila the Hun nearly attacks Paris.
496 Frankish king Clovis baptised at Reims.
508 Clovis makes Paris his capital.
543 Monastery of St-Germain-des-Prés founded.
635 King Dagobert establishes Fair of St-Denis.
800 Charlemagne becomes first Holy Roman Emperor. Moves capital from Paris to Aix-la-Chapelle (Aachen).
845-880 Paris sacked by the Vikings.
987 Hugues Capet, Count of Paris becomes king of France.

THE CITY TAKES SHAPE

1136 Abbot Suger begins Basilica of St-Denis.
1163 Building of Notre-Dame begins.
1181 Philippe-Auguste establishes market at Les Halles.
1190-1202 Philippe-Auguste constructs new city wall.
1215 University of Paris recognised with Papal Charter.
1246-48 Louis IX (St-Louis) builds the Sainte-Chapelle.
1253 Sorbonne founded.
1340 Hundred Years War with England begins.
1357 Revolt by Etienne Marcel.
1364 Charles V moves royal court to the Louvre and builds Bastille and Vincennes fortresses.
1420-36 Paris under English rule.
1422 Henry V of England dies at Château de Vincennes.
1463 First printing press in Paris.

THE WARS OF RELIGION AND AFTER

1528 François 1er begins rebuilding the Louvre.
1572 23 Aug: St Bartholemew's Day massacre of Protestants.
1589 Henri III assassinated.
1593 Henri IV converts to Catholicism, ending Wars of Religion.
1605 Building of place des Vosges and Pont Neuf.
1610 Henri IV assassinated.
1635 Académie Française founded.
1643 Cardinal Mazarin becomes regent.
1648-53 Paris occupied by the *Fronde* rebellion.
1661 Louis XIV begins personal rule – and transformation of Versailles; fall of Fouquet.
1667 Paris given its first street lighting.
1671 Building of Les Invalides.
1672 Creation of the Grands Boulevards on line of Charles V's city wall. Portes St-Denis and St-Martin built.
1680 Comédie Française founded.
1682 Louis XIV transfers court to Versailles.

ROYALTY TO REPUBLICANISM

1700 Beginning of War of the Spanish Succession.
1715 Death of Louis XIV; Philippe d'Orléans becomes regent.
1753 Place Louis XV (later place de la Concorde) begun.
1785 Fermiers Généraux Tax Wall built.
1789 First meeting of Etats-Généraux since 1614.
1789 14 July: Paris mob takes the Bastille. Oct: Louis XVI forced to leave Versailles for Paris.
1791 21 June: Louis XVI attempts to escape Paris.
1792 September Massacres. 22 Sept: Republic declared. Royal statues removed.
1793 Execution of Louis XVI and Marie-Antoinette. Louvre museum opens to the public.
1794 The Terror – 1,300 heads fall in six weeks. July: Jacobins overthrown; Directoire takes over.
1799 Napoléon stages coup, becomes First Consul.
1804 Napoléon crowns himself emperor in Notre-Dame.
1806 Napoléon commissions the Arc de Triomphe.
1814 Napoléon defeated; Russian army occupies Paris; Louis XVIII grants Charter of Liberties.
1815 Napoléon regains power (the 'Hundred Days'), before defeat at Waterloo. Bourbon monarchy restored, with Louis XVII.

1830 July: Charles X overthrown; Louis-Philippe of Orléans becomes king.
1836 Completion of Arc de Triomphe.
1838 Daguerre creates first daguerreotype photos.
1848 Louis-Philippe overthrown, replaced by Second Republic. Most men get the vote. Louis-Napoléon Bonaparte elected President.

CULTURAL EVOLUTION

1852 Louis-Napoléon declares himself Emperor Napoléon III: Second Empire. Bon Marché, first department store, opens.
1853 Haussmann made Préfet de Paris.
1862 Construction of Palais Garnier begins. Hugo's *Les Misérables* published.
1866 *Le Figaro* daily newspaper founded.
1870 Prussian victory at Sedan; siege of Paris. Napoléon III abdicates.
1871 Commune takes over Paris; May: *semaine sanglante.*
1874 First Impressionist exhibition in Nadar's *atelier* on bd des Capucines.
1875 Bizet's *Carmen* at Opéra Comique.
1889 Paris Exhibition on centenary of Revolution: Eiffel Tower built. Moulin Rouge opens.
1894-1900 Dreyfus case polarises opinion.
1895 Dec: world's first public film screening by the Lumière brothers at the Jockey Club (Hôtel Scribe).
1900 Paris' *Exposition Universelle*: Grand Palais, Petit Palais, Pont Alexandre III built. First Métro line.

THE WORLD WAR YEARS

1914 As World War I begins, Germans beaten back from Paris at the Marne.
1918 11 Nov: Armistice signed in the forest of Compiègne.
1919 Peace conference held at Versailles.
1927 La Coupole opens in Montparnasse.
1934 Fascist demonstrations.
1936-37 France elects Popular Front under Léon Blum; first paid holidays.
1940 Germans occupy Paris. 18 May: De Gaulle's call to arms from London.
1941-42 Mass deportations of Paris Jews.
1943 Nativity of Jean-Philippe Smet (aka Johnny Hallyday).
1944 25 Aug: Paris liberated.
1946 Fourth Republic established. Women given the vote.
1947 Christian Dior launches the New Look. Marshall Plan gives post-war aid to France.
1949 Simone de Beauvoir's *The Second Sex* published.
1955-56 Revolt begins in Algeria; demonstrations on the streets in Paris.
1957 Opening of CNIT in new La Défense business district.
1958 De Gaulle President: Fifth Republic.

EUROPEAN UNION AND NEW WORLD ORDER

1959 France founder member of the EEC.
1962 Algerian War ends.
1968 May: student riots and workers' strikes in Paris and across France.
1969 De Gaulle resigns, Pompidou becomes President.
1973 Boulevard Périphérique inaugurated.
1977 Centre Pompidou opens. Jacques Chirac wins first mayoral elections. Marie Myriam wins the Eurovision Song Contest with *L'Oiseau et l'enfant.*
1981 François Mitterrand elected President; abolition of the death penalty.
1989 Bicentenary of the Revolution: Louvre Pyramid and Opéra Bastille completed.
1995 Jacques Chirac elected President.
1997 General election: Socialist government elected under Lionel Jospin.
2001 Socialist Bertrand Delanoë elected Mayor of Paris. *Le Monde* declares 'We Are All Americans' following the destruction of the World Trade Center.
2002 The success of National Front leader Jean-Marie Le Pen in the first round of the presidential elections paves the way for Jacques Chirac's landslide re-election. Jean-Pierre Raffarin becomes Prime Minister as France choses to be governed by the centre-right.
2003 Jacques Chirac threatens to veto any US-led attempt to construct a UN resolution authorising military action against Iraq. Parliament approves legislation to devolve wide-ranging powers to France's regions and departments, perhaps signalling a move away from highly centralised government. Jean-Pierre Raffarin's government's proposals to reform the state retirement pension and unemployment benefit allowance causes wide-spread strikes. An estimated 15,000 French people die in the August heat wave. Compensation awarded to orphaned victims of the Nazi occupation.

Paris Today

A fuming Stéphanie Janicot relates a striking year in Paris: teachers held a strike. So did doctors. Then disaster struck.

If ever there was an activity, my dear Anglo-Saxon chums, that requires the application of the old bulldog spirit, the blood, the sweat, the toil and – yes – the tears, it's giving up smoking in Paris. Location, you see, is all. Last year, my own habit was curtailed (albeit temporarily) while I was on holiday in California. Now, there's a land that's devoid of temptation, a land where restaurants, hotels, and city-centre sidewalks can be braved without fear of a soul lighting up. At cocktail parties, luminaries chat charismatically while drinking tall lemonades. For this particular Parisienne, the novelty value of it all was dazzling enough to fill me with hope for a better, cleaner and, mayhap (as I know you Anglophones never say), less wheezy future.

One week back in Paris put paid to that, and my hopes for a better life dissolved into whimsy. But, after re-girding my loins, I have decided that this year, even without California, I'm going for it. I'm plunging head-first into terra incognita: I'm quitting smoking in Paris. In the middle of the *rentrée littéraire*, no less. 'The literary what?' you cry, but fear not: I'll introduce this strange and unfamiliar concept to your virginal Anglo minds. Dig this: in France, two-thirds of all the year's novels are released in one fell-swoop at the end of August. The crazy thing about this is that the time of the year we French literary types get our knickers most in a twist is September, the time when fewest books are sold in France. Call it charmingly French, or, more accurately, charmingly Parisian, because in the rest of France normal people spend September rushing down to their local supermarket to buy their children's schoolbooks. But I digress.

So, for two weeks in the autumn of 2003, despite the *rentrée littéraire* (for which I am one of a mere 691 competitors in the 2003 literary market), I had the brilliant idea to quit smoking in Paris. In September the weather's still summery and the Paris streets are a fire walk of temptation. I shouldn't really go out, I told myself. Terraces heaved with chic caffeine-quaffers, taking long drags from their Marlboros. I walked on by. I couldn't even look. At every bus stop, some hedonist who was fed up with waiting for his number 63 lit up and emitted an orgasmic sigh. Pervert. Sicko. As for setting foot inside a restaurant, forget about it.

Once upon a time there was a law in France, and it was called the 'Loi Evin' after the genius who invented it. The theory – and stop me if I'm going too fast here – was to create smoking and non-smoking areas in public places. The result, in all Parisian restaurants, was this: smokers on the right, non-smokers on the left, and a 70cm gap (max) separating them. The only thing that could save non-smokers from an orgy of passive inhalation was major nasal congestion. File 'Evin' under 'which planet, exactly?'

As I say, I should really put myself under house arrest. In the streets here, people light up insouciantly, take one puff, toss the cigarette onto the pavement, then light up again. You can follow some people by their trail of cigarette ends. As unsavoury as that might be, it still makes me crave a drag. Each passing moment is a struggle against the urge to dabble. My sufferings have brought forth this observation (that never once crossed my mind in 15 years of heavy-duty smoking): Paris is but an enormous ashtray.

It is also a faecal battleground… I remember my childhood neighbourhood (the 6th arrondissement), where the streets were infested with dog excrement. They were even dirtier than they are today: it was before Jacques Chirac had, as Mayor of Paris, brought us the *motocrotte*, the scooterised shitmobile, astride which butch chaps sucked dog droppings through enlarged vacuum nozzles. The poops were stored in a container for disposal God-knows-where. The suburbs, I'd say. (Bear in mind that, for the Parisian, the mere word '*banlieue*' evokes images of a mysterious, far-away land: think Central Asian Steppe or downtown Nuneaton.) The result today is that sanitary workers, buffed up and bitchin' thanks to new laws imposing fines on owners of unruly, unlawful or incontinent canines, have relieved us pedestrians, to an extent, of this particular abomination. But the behavioural cycle has continued: dog droppings were replaced by fag ends. It's as if Parisians are genetically programmed to leave trash behind. In 2003, this attitude assumed an exponential seriousness that has plunged insanitary Parisian cliché into unpalatable Parisian disgrace.

OK, dog crap can be avoided via the dainty and judicious step; fag ends pose little risk once extinguished. But our elderly population… the entire world watched in horror. Witness an e-mail from an American friend: 'We heard about

Tainted love

If you want a handle on how Franco-US relations broke down so dramatically over Iraq in 2003, think *A Streetcar Named Desire*. America is the virile, brutish Stanley Kowalski; France is deluded, fading beauty, Blanche. The wrath Stanley turns against her at the end of the play is, in real-world terms, George W. Bush's threat not to invite Chirac to his ranch.

Things did get bitchy. Renaming French fries 'freedom fries' and blaming axes of weasels was the least of it: France's ambassador to Washington complained to the White House about an alleged smear campaign. French spectators were booing American cyclists in the Tour de France. And then there was Miami's now-famous Ken Wagner, who was televised pouring bottles of French wine into the gutter.

Something was certainly keeping US visitors away from Paris. Ready for some stats? Over the past decade, Americans have made up 20% of the city's foreign visitors; in 2003, their numbers fell by 30%, which is very bad news for a country where tourism makes up 12% of the GDP.

Needing, as ever, to appeal to the kindness of *étrangers* and their dollars, Mademoiselle DuBois is offering Stanley the same olive branch she was flapping around so wantonly when things got steamy over Iraq. The French Tourist Office has launched the 'Let's Fall In Love Again' initiative, the flower of which is the video of the same name, featuring Woody Allen, Wynton Marsalis, the late George Plimpton and others rhapsodising over the charms of America's oldest ally. The angle of this video seems to be one of 'let's forgive France'. Will Blanche's videogram be enough to rekindle Kowalski's fervour, especially with Tony 'Stella' Blair fussing about in the background drawing up guest lists for ranch barbecues?

Only the tourist profile for 2004 will tell us, but let's hope that, in the intervening months, the French Tourist Office is steeped in a profound enough depth of culture to be able to seek comfort in the poetry of Tammy Wynette, poetry that explains how to survive bad times when your man's having good times, doing things that you just don't understand. Like invading Iraq.

the catastrophe. We sincerely hope your mother's OK.' (I assure you, dear readers, that my mother is in good health, she's not old and she doesn't live in Paris.) The knowledge that my friends in Sacramento were aware via TV and Internet that Parisians had plumbed a new low of civic irresponsibility, a nadir rarely seen in a first-world nation, struck me as inglorious.

As I write, the Mayor of Paris has three hundred unclaimed corpses in his possession, and doesn't know quite what to do with them. The Parisians, used to having others clean up after them, don't see why he doesn't go and bury them himself. It appears (or, at least, it's been reported in certain mayoral departments) that the few people who bothered to call to report a heat wave-related death were immediately slamming down receivers after being asked by public servants if they wouldn't like to 'take care' of the corpse themselves. Thanks so much for calling and goodbye! God, the shame.

'How did we ever come to this level of indifference and I'm-alright-Jacques collective inactivity?'

We should have seen it coming in spring; the Ides of March, and all that. For it was a harsh spring indeed for us here in the capital. Strikes struck. Many a public transport worker and school teacher hoisted the middle finger, and, of course, we all felt the knock-on. Consider, for example, the scenario of a working mother (the same sort of working mother who's now trying to give up smoking, despite the rigours of the literary *rentrée*): on days when the RATP was not on strike, this particular babe was able to arrive fresh, fragrant and relaxed at work while, outside, teachers picketed against retirement reforms. On these days, she arrived at 8.45am, happy just to have got there in one piece. But then came the call from her jubilant 11-year-old. 'No school today, mum! I'm out with the posse.'

Cue maternal breakdown, brought on by the pressure of having to: leave work to try and save the child from the road to perdition, at the risk of ending up on the dole (these strike-related trials and tribulations continued for two months without interruption); stay put, but with every tick of the clock worry about the unsupervised child in question running rampantly on the streets of the city, cohorting with God-knows-whom in the cafés of Paris (the very same cafés, I may remind you, that are infested with the temptations of noxious fumes).

During these harrowing days, Parisian woman was obliged to put her nerves on ice, to remain preternaturally calm and in tip-top health. Actually, the latter was especially important because doctors gave striking a whirl, too. First of all, the quacks who ply their trade in town were fighting for the right to hike up their consultation fee. Then the hospital guys laid down their specula. The only possible option for the Parisian chick was to avoid being ill. Thus, in order to keep her stress levels down and maintain her svelte and athletic physique, she upped her nicotine intake.

You can understand then how Parisian woman, this miracle of modern motherhood, this literary genius, this paragon of iron self-control, needed badly to escape teachers, doctors and a public transport system that wasn't transporting the public anywhere because its operatives were on strike in support of the teachers and doctors. She had but one desire: a well-deserved holiday – provided, of course, that the holiday plans did not include the Avignon theatre festival, or indeed any other arts festival: this year, going on a cultural break was no guarantee of avoiding the strikes as *intermittents*, the people who work in the arts, also took industrial action. But let us not go into that; you'd think I was gilding the lily or using you as guinea pigs for the plot for my upcoming sci-fi blockbuster – *The Land That Modern Industrial Relations Forgot* or something.

So, once we were actually on holiday, do you really imagine that Parisians were going to rush back to the furnace that the city became in early August, lugging bottles of water up to the flats of aged, distant cousins? We didn't bother. This is how we found ourselves slap bang in the middle of an unparalleled health crisis. Of course, we all blamed the government, because that's what we do; it's how we deal with our embarrassment and shame. How did we ever come to this level of indifference and I'm-alright-Jacques collective inactivity?

However, it wasn't over. No, there was one group who hadn't yet exercised its right to strike – tobacconists. Incredibly, on 20 October the government put the price of cigarettes up by 20% to €4.60, and the *buralistes* shut up shop to show their grievance at the loss of income that would result when people decided to quit smoking. It worked. The government has agreed to subsidise their profits in order to uphold its commitment to public health. I'm not sure if our gorgeous Prime Minister, Monsieur Raffarin, is a smoker, but if I were in his shoes, I certainly wouldn't choose this as a good time to try to kick the habit. French kisses from Paris, Stéphanie.

Stéphanie Janicot is a journalist and author whose eighth novel, La Constante de Hubble, *was published in September 2003.*

2003's thrusters and busters

The vicissitudes, near-missitudes and hissy-fittitudes of life in the public eye.

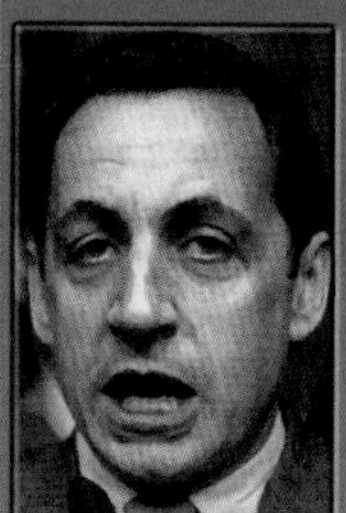

Now established as Chirac's pet, Interior Minister Nicolas Sarkozy has been closing nightclubs, patronising Muslims and wooing the left. What next for Mr Serious Knickers? Representing France in the Eurovision Song Contest?

France may be a republic, but 60-years-young Johnny Hallyday is King. King of rrheuk, of course (his new CD is France's fastest-selling ever), but also of lucrative ad contracts – reading specs and personal insurance, anyone?

Paris: stylesville, right? And what was 2003's hair rage? The lock mess monster that is the mullet. No kidding: these days, the business-at-the-front, party-at-the-back look is chic city central's all-conquering coiffure.

Former PM Alain Juppé was accused of inventing jobs to get his mates bungs from the Mairie (he denies it). Enemies have accused Chirac of similar charges, so the trial's outcome will be followed avidly. How could people be so cynical?

French TV. Oft-derided as 'crap', the ugly duckling that is French TV was given the chance to shine by the *intermittents'* strike (*see p321*). Deprived of live entertainment, we tuned in. You know what? It's crap.

Prime Minister Jean-Pierre Raffarin's policies have pissed off a lot of people, especially when it comes to pension reforms. Give, as they say, that man a handbag (and a new job, if the economy doesn't pull out of its nosedive).

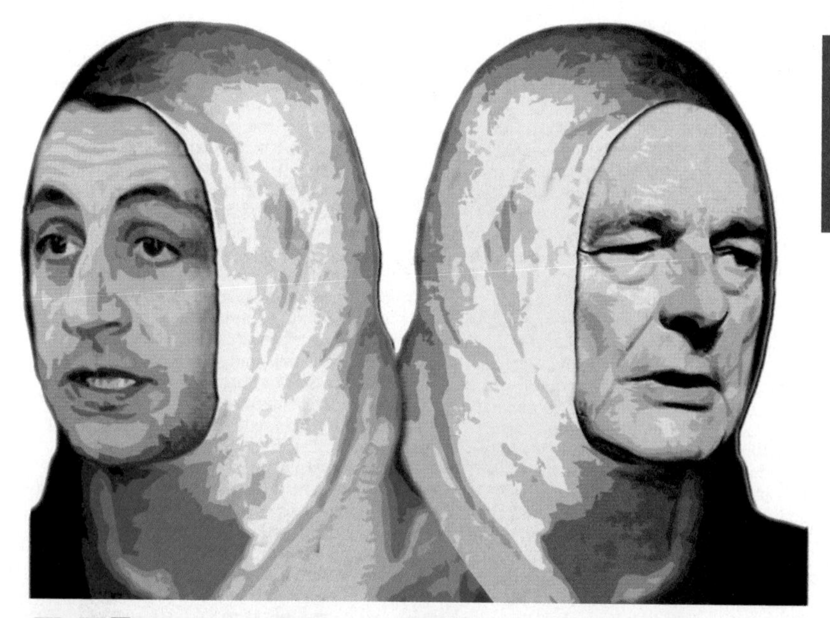

Minority Report

Liberté, égalité, fraternité was such a Utopian recipe for society. Then colonialism led to multiculturalism. And now?

Amid much fanfare and an unmissable post-World-Cup-triumph embrace between Jacques Chirac and then-Prime Minister Lionel Jospin, footballer Zinedine Zidane became the first Frenchman of North African origin to be declared the country's favourite figure – an annual popularity contest usually dominated by the likes of Jacques Cousteau, Johnny Hallyday, Jean-Paul Belmondo, Gérard Depardieu and a legendary charity worker called Abbé Pierre.

Zidane's triumph in and of itself wasn't so surprising. But that was back in 1998, days that seem distinctly halcyon when we look at French society today.

That the status of nation's favourite son should have fallen to the footballing offspring of Algerian immigrants was, of course, a reason for not-so-quiet pride in the French ideal of *égalité* of opportunity. Here, the commentators said, was proof that France was changing, that the land that spawned Jean-Marie Le Pen and his far-right Front National had at last embraced multiculturalism. But, five years on, can we really affirm that this is the case?

True, France's mixed football team did show the way, at least for a while. True, Le Pen and his party, despite knocking France for six in the first round of the 2002 presidential elections, are still far from being a real force on the national political scene. And true, overtly racist incidents in France are, on the whole, rare.

But appearances, of course, can be deceptive. Racism, especially in France – except during the Vichy era – has rarely been about grand public gestures. Discrimination on grounds of race is seldom of the violent, jackbooted variety. Instead, it emerges in everyday incidents, in coy double-thinks. It is in its way genteel, but it is very real, very hurtful and exceedingly potent.

Discrimination in employment is widespread. Many Frenchmen close their eyes to it, but the effects of institutionalised racism are apparent everywhere: have you seen a black waiter in a central Paris bistro? A black or North African newsreader on French television (there is one, but you'll be lucky to catch him), or – despite the country's 2.5 million voters of North African origin – an Arab MP in the National Assembly?

In the social arena, too, French men and women of immigrant origin get a hard deal: the anti-racist group *SOS Racisme* organises around 40 'testings' in bars and clubs per year, which have shown that discriminatory door policies are widespread.

And if any proof were needed of what newspaper *Le Monde* has called the 'hidden realities of everyday racism in France', it came with the launch of the government's racism hotline. Its counsellors reckon they deal with 500 genuine cases of unlawful discrimination a day: some 38% relating to employment problems, 15% to housing, and 11% to the way immigrants are treated by the police.

Val-Fourré, 80 km outside Paris, is western Europe's largest council estate; over 28,000 people living in high-rise blocks built in the 1960s and 70s. What you'll see, half-an-hour's drive from the Louvre, is muggings, thefts, drug deals, battles with rival gangs, sky-high unemployment and soaring school drop-out rates. To most intents and purposes, the French Republic does not exist there; residents say they live 'next door to France'. Because France, sadly for them, is founded on the sacred principle that all its people are equal in the eyes of the unitary state; that no matter where they come from, French citizens are identical in their Frenchness. That's why France does not keep many statistics relating to immigrants beyond the number of foreigners legally resident in France. Only non-official reports are available to show that unemployment among 20-29 year-olds of North African origin is running at 40% against 10% for youths of French origin.

Sociologists say Arab youths whose parents emigrated from the former North African colonies and who often live in places like Val-Fourré feel they are the victims of institutionalised racism. The Republic likes to deal with citizens, not individuals. The problem in places like Val-Fourré, of which every large city in France has at least one equivalent, is that their inhabitants do not know what they are, or at least where their roots lie. They are not Algerian, Moroccan or West African, but they are not entirely French either. What they are is unrecognised and unrepresented, so it's not surprising they lash out.

The so-called rebellion of France's immigrant-filled suburbs has fomented what is almost a national psychosis in France, fanning the fears that led some six million people to vote for Le Pen in 2002. The current, right-wing government's uncompromising response has been to launch an unprecedented zero-tolerance crime crackdown, spearheaded by the hardline interior minister and super-cop (and, some would say, Superman), Nicolas Sarkozy. Since taking office, Sarkozy has budgeted an extra €9.2 billion to fight crime and announced plans to hire 13,500 more police officers. Youths who gather in stairwells are now liable to two months in jail, and young offenders can be banged up in youth detention centres from the age of 13. Swearing at a policeman could bring a two-year jail sentence; wearing a short skirt and hanging around on street corners is now 'passive soliciting' and subject to fines and jail.

Sarkozy is also steering a tough bill on immigration, and said recently he would be setting targets he expects police to meet on the number of illegal foreigners they capture and succeed in expelling. Opponents say he is 'repression-crazy'; he says human rights should be 'first and foremost for the victims'. Tellingly, the majority of the French think he's wonderful; one recent poll saw him as by far the best future candidate for the Presidency.

'The French Republic likes to deal with citizens, not individuals.'

Unlike in the US or Britain, under France's much-vaunted 'republican model of integration', the idea that different ethnic, linguistic and religious groups might enjoy rights and recognition that stem from their particular minority status is unthinkable. Places like Val-Fourré are the living demonstration that this republican model has broken down. And, on the whole, French politicians do not grasp it. What they do grasp, particularly since the US-led invasion of Iraq, is a potential religious – rather than citizenship – problem. France has between five and six million Muslims, one of the factors often cited as explaining President Jacques Chirac's determined anti-war stance. If he didn't oppose this war, the argument went, he could have had bloodshed on French streets.

Chirac's opposition was equally as much to do with avoiding trouble at home as increasing his international status. Genuine concern that the war against Iraq could trigger violence in France was in part behind the state's backing of a new national Islamic council aimed at giving the faith's diverse factions a unified voice, and representing their views to government.

The creation of the CFCM (the Conseil français du culte musulman – the French Islamic Council), in which Sarkozy (again) was

heavily involved, is seen as critical to France's efforts to satisfy the needs and expectations of its Muslims, and also as a potentially vital bulwark against the rise of Islamic fundamentalism. Its respected, moderate president, the rector of the Paris Mosque, Dalil Boubakeur, has warned that the war in Iraq risked creating 'a new and far tougher breed of Islam' in France – it is no surprise that youngsters left homes and families in France to fight in Afghanistan and Iraq.

At some 650,000 strong, France's Jewish population is also the biggest in Europe. The community has come under considerable strain in the past two years following the surge in Middle East violence in the second Palestinian uprising. Although physical violence is rare, scores of anti-Jewish attacks have been recorded, including several firebombings of synagogues and assaults on Jews.

Members of the government and almost all Jewish leaders say that the sporadic violence and rising inter-community tensions are mainly due to political, rather than religious, differences. But some foreign Jewish groups seemed to provide more ammunition to France's critics early in 2003 when they said that 2,556 French Jews had emigrated to Israel the year before. In fact, most of the evidence suggests serious racist incidents against Muslims and Jews are in decline, particularly since some particularly tough laws on racial and religious discrimination were pushed by (who else?) Nicolas Sarkozy. But if there has been little real threat to public order, France faces some testing challenges to the secular state guaranteed by the Republic.

Both left and right are divided over whether the government should forbid Muslim girls wearing headscarves to school. The question may sound trivial, but it cuts to the heart of the separation of church and state (and also affects whether Catholic children should be allowed to display crucifixes). In the 21st century, how far can France realistically hope to 'integrate' immigrant families when it insists that they abandon their national and cultural roots, then effectively ignores and ghettoises them? How far can it continue to insist on secularism in the state apparatus (including schools) when some Muslims see the headscarf debate as an attempt to force them into an outmoded mould of what French citizens should be?

But there is hope. In a sign of what could be to come, France's first Muslim secondary school opened in Lille earlier this year. Girls there can study without fear of being suspended or kicked out by their headteacher on the legal grounds that their headgear constitutes 'an act of intimidation, provocation, proselytism or propaganda'. Sometime fairly soon, there seems little doubt that the ground rules of the French Republic are going to have to change. What this country needs is a Tom Paine for the 21st century. What it's got is Nicolas Sarkozy.

Capital Creatives

When it comes to new artists, Paris is a fount of fecundity. Get out on the streets and look, says Claire Thomson.

Don't you dare! Just don't you dare pay heed to those hideous wretches who claim that Paris is a city that uses the glories of its artistic past as a fig leaf behind which to hide the nakedness of its impotence in current avenues of expression. You tell 'em: happenings, openings, deviations, limited editions, mixed media… Paris 2004-style is a kaleidoscope of creative dynamism.

For the young Parisian, attending a contemporary art exhibition is commonplace, and the proliferation of galleries on rue Louise-Weiss has created a Parisian equivalent of New York's Chelsea. The strong *vernissage* (private exhibition openings) circuit, where art/fash pack liggers socialise, confirms exhibition-hopping as a sport in which Parisians excel; and while there is often a mirage of consensus in the London art world, the Paris scene remains complex, layered and critical. Boundaries between corporate design, art direction, fashion styling, graffiti and visual arts are blurred and there is a great deal of room for experimentation and crossover. Bonjour to the French generation of 'creators without categories', for whom influences are everything and nothing in particular.

Fashion's favourite Paris-based design group, M/M (Mathias Augustyniak and Michael Amzalag) are redefining the role of graphic design and ensuring that a 'French touch' is firmly stamped on the contemporary creative consciousness. Their highly contemporary work with fashion designers including Yohji Yamamoto, Martine Sitbon and Balenciaga led to a meeting of minds at Paris *Vogue*, where they've totally rocked the art direction. Their artisan-inspired approach is apparent in quirky typefaces, hand-drawn motifs and collage and has injected the 'Frenchness' lost under the previous American editor's reign. Minimalist style photographs of animal heads on shelves and lank-haired

In Context

cover-girls are in stark contrast with the magazine's traditional aesthetic glossiness.

M/M, and fellow Frenchman Michel Gondry, the man behind Levi's $2.5m mice advertising campaign, Kylie's videos and recent Smirnoff ads, are in demand by musicians looking for some edgy *je ne sais quoi*. A collaboration between M/M and Björk (Matthew Barney's missus) on her *Hidden Place* video, and design for Madonna's *American Life* album, show that experimental can be commercially successful. Marrying mainstream and cool is no mean feat. M/M are now as heavily involved in art as they are in fashion and music, and their graphic work is as much acclaimed by the art world as by those who value its functionality.

FLIP FLOP FLYIN' FASHION

'Tu connais Colette?' Disciples of the cult of Colette are not championing the early-20th century author, but the fashion store on the rue du Faubourg-St-Honoré. Like Milan's Corso Como, Colette is one store leading the way in crossover culture, the young affluent Parisian jetsetera (identifiable these days by their mullets) listen to Colette albums mixed by 2ManyDJs at Colette fashion week parties, featuring art exhibited at the in-store gallery. The store borrows from art and flirts with it – the presentation and design of the place give more than a nod and a wink to Dominique Gonzalez-Foerster (winner of the 2002 Prix Duchamp art prize and designer of the new Balenciaga store in Paris, a minimalist's wet dream). Retail tourists get their claws into Jeremy Scott and Raf Simons and clamour for an Anya Hindmarsh 'be a bag' featuring their own photograph, or a Gwen Stefani Sport Sac. Of course, the clothes won't fit you unless you're shaped like a chopstick, but the gallery, which shows the bright (and often subversive) young things of the art world is a reassuring distraction. Stylists, models and media-whores flick vacantly through street-style magazine *Fruits*, hit on each other and laugh knowingly at books like *How to be Fashionable* or *Consume like Me*. A recent live graffiti demo in the shop window proves that fashion's love affair with all things urban rools OK. With more people shooting from the hip than the NRA, Colette is the swoosh of designer shopping.

Art collective Surface2air have a following to rival Colette – but they're not going to shout about it. The guys are 'big in Japan' – their customised Reebok trainers, Masspop T-shirts emblazoned with models, *Heavy Change* book (comprised of T-shirts designed by artists), and photography tome *Pour la Victoire* (co-produced with *Spoon* magazine) have our techno types in a frenzy. The seven-strong collective is based between Paris and New York, with the Parisian boutique on rue de l'Arbre-Sec combining a studio, shop and exhibition space. Artists such as Kenneth

Cappello and Faile are exhibited alongside Tatty Devine accessories, and labels such as Folk, Griffin and Vexed Generation. The space has played host to ad hoc private concerts for New York rockers ARE weapons, parties for guest artists such as graffiti artist Banksy, and acts as a private meeting place for artistic types responsible for all that is innovative and interesting (but resolutely not faddy or trendy). The collective members have so many strings to their bow they could start their own orchestra. Member Gordon Hull is collaborating with artist Philippe Parreno to produce the music for a short film, while member Jeremie and artist Payam Sharifi (www.bruise.ws) consult for Nike, Egg and other brands. Along with producing films, books and winning the Tokion road race this year, the crew is responsible for artistic direction at more fashionable publications than you can shake a stick at.

Agnès b – now there's a new-art-nuturing babe. She's exhibited the artwork of graffiti artists such as Ease, O'Clock and Futura, collaborating with them on a number of projects to bring their artwork to a wider, less streetwise audience. A partnership with Alanna Heiss on the popular PS1 summer event in New York where music, fashion and art are brought together has established Agnès as a magpie for all things shiny and new. Each new edition of her *Point d'ironie* publication showcases a new artist. Her Paris gallery exhibits cult artists such as Harmony Korine, Ryan McGinley and photographer Martin Parr.

GEEZERS NEED EXCITEMENT

Street art is big business. No longer the black, slightly moth eaten sheep of the art family, graffiti has evolved and mutated to innovative new levels. The streets are the galleries of today. Of course, not all of it is worth the wall it is daubed on. Obey's silkscreen posters of Mao and Nixon, Andre's Mr A and Zeuss' shadow paintings may be some of the most visible pieces on the streets, but Sam Bern, HNT, and Trane are also providing something new and vibrant. An ongoing trial in Paris involving 65 of France's biggest train-taggers is an attempt to emulate New York's clampdown on unofficial street art. Spoilsports!

French artist Sam Bern is producing some of the street's most arresting work. Though he is a classically trained artist, his tubular, calligraphy-esque symbols painted around Paris seem to speak in an illegible language. Despite the public nature of their work, street artists are remarkably antisocial creatures and Bern's desire to work alone has led him to locations as diverse as Boston and Beirut. Bucking a trend by refusing to exhibit with Agnès b ('graffiti doesn't work on canvas'), he accepts individual commissions and has shown at alt-gallery Galerie 64 on rue Jean-Pierre-Timbaud. On his website www.crust.fr.st photographs of the homeless juxtaposed with images of abandoned mattresses reveal a social conscience with humour, and artful squiggles daubed on the ground are only obvious to those looking for them. One of several reasons to mind your step next time you cross the road…

With eclectic influences that are more art nouveau than Americana, HNT's gothic/romantic pieces can be found in surprising locations across Paris – from underground passages to motorway sidings. First prize-winner at Deauville contemporary art show, this young French artist enjoys the challenge of eccentric exhibition spaces. The esoteric website www.hnt.europa.fr.st offers an insight into his very personal universe with huge paintings of gypsy-esque characters, Communist-inspired designs and photographs of Eastern Europe mixed with art nouveau and moody artisan touches. Another artist spurning the traditional gallery route, HNT prefers to seek out isolated spots in which to display his work.

'Street art is big business. But not all of it is worth the wall it's daubed on.'

Regardless of one's opinion of graffiti, the handiwork of Trane, France's number one *graffeur*, has certainly made its mark. With a geek-like dedication to his craft, this young member of the notorious UV crew has consistently decorated Paris, showing *puissance* is the quality he cultivates. He has quickly made a name for himself and established a form of brand recognition to rival Monoprix in its scope. Initially graffiti insiders criticised Trane's lack of artistic aesthetic – no apparent graphic quality, detail or real variation in his pieces – but the sheer scale of his work has diminished any doubt as to who holds France's 'most wanted' title. Rumours about the kid – not least his real identity – circulate, but all is mystery. Oh how the effect would be cheapened if he were seen at a *vernissage* at Yvon Lambert. From the sides of trains and vans, to shutters, phoneboxes and walls, it is apparent that Trane has got marketing skills and a lot of time on his hands. Even if he stopped tomorrow his tag would leave a lasting impression on the urban art scene – his aggressiveness has certainly jump-started his fellow French *graffeurs*, and anyway it would take years to wash all that paint off.

French Film: Fini?

The Parisian cinema scene is buzzing, but French film was fading until a documentary resuscitated the 'seventh art'.

Occupying consciousness space somewhere between sex and eating, film – cinema-going and doing the pseudo-critic routine while waving a Gauloise and your copy of *Le Film Français* – is a top-rating French pastime. Going to the flicks may not be exactly what you travelled all this way to do but if you don't indulge in some film in this city, you'll be missing part of the cultural itinerary.

Paris is a city of international cinema. In a single week you might have the release of a feature-length Japanese animation, a French tale of domestic entanglements or a restored copy of an American classic. Cinema's place here among the more elevated forms of culture ensures that history is not lost, and a programme of 1920s silent films is just as likely to draw a crowd as the newest vehicle for Gérard 'I'm in every French film' Depardieu.

Now, if you are ever brave, drunk or bored enough to sally an opinion on film at a French dinner party, there's some cultural information you'll need to know. Please – please – be aware that the legacy of *la nouvelle vague* dictates that discussion of the art often revolves around the cult of the director rather than the actor. Translation: you've seen the latest David Lynch, not the latest Keanu Reeves.

Sometimes it seems that part of the French national curriculum is the daily recitation that French films are the best in the world; but the dirty little secret of going to the movies in Paris in 2004 is that the best films aren't French. Like food before nouvelle and fusion, France's films have become fusty and formulaic: hubby's having a torturous affair, grandpapa did something fishy during the war ('it was collaborate or starve, plus I'd lose the Volkswagen'), sis must get laid (and get hurt) to gain that wounded aloofness, that thinness and subtle rash that makes French women so damn sexy.

Nope: French film is due for a shake-up, but don't worry, it'll get it. Like the revolution in cuisine, it's the international element that will get things jumping. Last year's winners' circle at Cannes included Afghanistan, Denmark, Turkey, Serbia, Mexico and Quebec, and France is one of the few countries in the world that will regularly distribute films from such countries. The hope for a triumphant renaissance in French film is that a thriving festival scene and a public prepared to pay good money to see an obscure Cuban propaganda film from the 1950s or a digitally remastered copy of Chaplin's *The Dictator* ensures that Paris has become the keeper, if not currently the maker, of much that is worthy in the world of cinema.

The problems confronting the French film industry are simple: lack of funds, and competition from the Hollywood machine. The native scene is kept afloat by forced subsidies, many in the form of funds redirected back to cinema from Canal + TV, an agreement now in some turmoil ever since Jean-Marie Messier flushed Vivendi Universal down *les toilettes*.

'Documentaries capture something the French love about film – the truth, only better edited.'

Sometimes, the solution has to imitate the problem. Director Luc Besson (*Fifth Element*, *The Big Blue*) wants to shift French cinema production towards the Hollywood system. His privately owned Europa Corp is the first major movie studio to open in France since before World War I. Located west of Paris, Europa Corp was meant to jumpstart movie making in France by centralising pre-production, filming and post-production. But while Besson's plans to make Frenchified Hollywood blockbusters will certainly be good for business, he risks losing that European *je ne sais quoi* that New York and London luvvies don their black polo necks especially to luxuriate in.

French stars, too, are increasingly interested in following the Juliette Binoche model of trans-Atlantic success. Audrey Tautou has been working overtime (and in English) to shed her saccharine Amélie Poulain image. Stephen Frears' *Dirty Pretty Things* is a step in the right direction – illegal traffic in bodily organs ought to add some grime. Perhaps it was an overdose of Amélie that fuelled the recent success of documentary films in France. This form of storytelling – a carefully distilled version of life through the camera lens – captures something the French love about film – the truth, only better edited.

Documentary filmmaking here is as old as the medium itself. When the Frères Lumière made the first moving pictures, they set their cameras up in the middle of crowded streets – filming men picking their noses along the Champs-Elysées was special effects enough for 1895. At the 1900 Exposition Universelle, where an entire village was imported from Colonial Africa, they didn't hesitate to film 'bathing time', ie, Africans jumping in and out of the water at a furious pace to the delight of parasol-toting tourists.

Two documentaries have made a big impression on the French public in the past two years – one from either side of the Atlantic. 2003 saw the biggest chill in French/American relations since McDonalds invaded the Champs-Elysées. The only thing the French love more than criticising Americans is Americans who criticise themselves. Enter Michael Moore and *Bowling for Columbine*. Moore is the kind of pet American that French intellectuals love. A defiantly crappy dresser, and a sincere political activist at a time when political activism is, well… quaint. It gives those ageing 1968 'revolutionaries' a thrill to know that someone is still throwing a wet Wal-Mart bag in the face of the powers-that-be. Moore's take on America's self-perpetuating fear factor had the French sanctimoniously nodding their heads in agreement, all the while ignoring the fact that their very own Minister of the Interior, Nicolas Sarkozy, is using just such a campaign against vague public menaces to position himself as the next President of France.

While Moore was busy confronting 21st-century America, Nicolas Philibert was quietly creating the most successful French film since *Amélie*. *Etre et Avoir* (pictured) was an unlikely hit. A simple documentary about a schoolhouse in rural Auvergne, it featured Georges Lopez, the kind of old-style schoolmaster, wise and tender, that is normally reserved for reruns of *Little House on the Prairie*. The film follows a group of children as they learn to read, write and play together. A slow and awkward student makes the transition to upper school, toddlers make photocopies, and Jojo, the impish teacher's pet, declares he wants to become a teacher when he grows up. Certainly the film recalled simpler times, an innocence that forms a chillingly stark contrast to the Columbine shootings. Yet what could have been a heavy-handed dose of nostalgia was actually something timeless – suddenly the French filmic talent for catching small looks and pensive silences seemed worthwhile once again. And of course, Mr Lopez has since sued Philibert for a slice of the film's profits. How's that for cultural exchange? French film is on its way back.

Architecture

Be ready to gawp in the city that gave the world Gothic grace and Modern Movement masterpieces.

ROMANESQUE & GOTHIC

Medieval Paris was centred on the Ile de la Cité and the Latin Quarter. The main thoroughfares, rue St-Jacques and rue Mouffetard, followed those of Roman Paris. Paris had several powerful Romanesque abbeys outside the city walls, but remains of this simple style are few. The tower of **St-Germain-des-Prés**, topped by a later spire, still has its rounded arches, and some decorated capitals survive in the nave.

It was in the **Basilique St-Denis** that the Gothic trademarks of pointed arches, ogival vaulting and flying buttresses were first combined. Vaulting allowed buildings to span large spaces and let light in, hence an aesthetic of brightness and verticality. A spate of building followed with cathedrals at Chartres, Sens and Laon, as well as **Notre-Dame**, which incorporated all the features of the style: twin-towered west front, soaring nave, intricate rose windows and buttressed east end.

In the 1190s, Philippe-Auguste began the first **Louvre**, part of whose keep can still be seen within the museum complex. In the following century, ribbed vaulting became more refined and columns more slender, in the Rayonnant or High Gothic style. Mason and architect Pierre de Montreuil continued work on St-Denis, and his masterpiece, the 1246-48 **Sainte-Chapelle**, took Gothic to its height.

The later Flamboyant-Gothic style saw a wealth of decoration, in **Eglise St-Séverin**, with its twisting spiral column, the pinnacles and gargoyles of the early-16th-century **Tour St-Jacques**, the porch of **St-Germain-l'Auxerrois** and the Hôtel de Cluny (now **Musée National du Moyen-Age**).

THE RENAISSANCE

The Italian Renaissance came late to Paris, and was largely due to François 1er. He installed Leonardo da Vinci at **Amboise** and called in Primaticcio and Rosso at **Fontainebleau**. Pretty **Eglise St-Etienne-du-Mont** shows that Renaissance style remained largely superficial, its ornate roodscreen tacked on to a Flamboyant

Gothic structure. **Hôtel Carnavalet** (altered by Mansart) and **Hôtel Lamoignon**, both in the Marais, are Paris' best examples of Renaissance mansions.

THE ANCIEN REGIME

Henri IV built the **Pont Neuf** and **place Dauphine** on the Ile de la Cité and **place des Vosges** in the Marais. The latter were both symmetrical, with red brick vaulted galleries and steeply pitched roofs. The 17th century was a high point in French power; the monarchy desired buildings to reflect its grandeur: *bonjour*, Baroque. The **Palais du Luxembourg** combined classic French château with elements of the Pitti Palace in Marie de Médici's native Florence. Counter-Reformation churches, such as the **Chapelle de la Sorbonne** and the grandiose **Eglise du Val-de-Grâce**, designed by Mansart and Lemercier, followed the Gésu in Rome. But even at **Versailles**, Baroque style never reached the excesses of Italy or Austria, as French architects followed Cartesian principles of harmony and balance.

Nouveaux-riches flocked to build mansions in the Marais and the Ile-St-Louis. Those in the Marais follow a symmetrical U-shaped plan, with a secluded courtyard: look through the archways to the *cour d'honneur* of the **Hôtel de Sully** or Hôtel Salé (now **Musée Picasso**), where facades are richly decorated.

Under Colbert, Louis XIV's chief minister, the creation of stage sets to magnify the Sun King's power proceeded apace. The Louvre grew as Claude Perrault created the sweeping west facade, while Hardouin-Mansart's **place des Victoires** and **place Vendôme** were designed to show off equestrian statues of the king.

ROCOCO & NEO-CLASSICISM

In the early 18th century, the Faubourg-St-Germain overtook the Marais in fashion. Under Louis XV, the severe lines of the previous century were softened by rounded corners and decorative detailing, such as satyr masks over doorways, at the Hôtel Chenizot (51 rue St-Louis-en-l'Ile) and **Hôtel d'Albret** (31 rue des Francs-Bourgeois). The main developments came in interior decoration, as frivolous rococo style reached a peak in the **Hôtel de Soubise**, decorated by Boucher, Restout and Van Loo.

From the 1750s, geometry was back as Ancient Rome inspired another monument to royal majesty, Jacques Ange Gabriel's neo-classical **place de la Concorde**; and Soufflot's domed **Panthéon**, inspired by the one in Rome. Utopian Claude-Nicolas Ledoux's **toll gates** played games with pure geometrical forms; circular at parc Monceau and La Rotonde de la Villette, and rectangular pairs at place Denfert-Rochereau and place de la Nation.

THE NINETEENTH CENTURY

The Revolution largely confined itself to pulling buildings down. Royal statues bit the dust, and churches became 'temples of reason' or grain stores. Napoléon brought Paris back to a proper sense of its grand self. Land confiscated from aristocracy and church was built up. A stern classicism was preferred for the **Arc de Triomphe**, Greek temples inspired the **Madeleine** and the **Bourse**. By the 1840s, classical style was under challenge from a Gothic revival led by Eugène Viollet-le-Duc. Eclecticism ruled, though, with the neo-renaissance **Hôtel de Ville** and **Eglise de la Trinité**, while Byzantium and the Romanesque made a comeback from the 1870s.

The greatest change to the face of Paris came from Baron Haussmann. Appointed Napoléon III's *Préfet de la Seine* in 1853, Haussmann was not an architect but an administrator. Aided by architects and engineers including Baltard, Hittorff, Alphand and Belgrand, he set about shooshing up the rapidly growing capital. Broad boulevards were cut through the old city, answering communication and health problems but also ensuring that the city could be more easily governed. Haussmann constructed asylums, prisons, schools, churches (**Eglise St-Vincent de Paul**), hospitals, and the water and sewage systems. He landscaped the **Bois de Boulogne** and gave Paris its new cast-iron market pavilions at Les Halles. Charles Garnier's sumptuous **Palais Garnier** of 1862-75 epitomised Second Empire style. The city also acquired the Haussmannian apartment block, setting a model until well into the 20th century.

Breakthroughs in engineering made the use of iron frames increasingly popular. Henri Labrouste's reading room at the **Bibliothèque Ste-Geneviève** (1844-50), Hittorff's **Gare du Nord** (1861-65), the Grande Galerie de l'Evolution (**Muséum d'Histoire Naturelle**) and **Musée d'Orsay** are but shells around an iron frame. The most daring iron structure of them all was of course the **Eiffel Tower**, built in 1889, then the tallest structure in the world.

THE TWENTIETH CENTURY

The past century began with an outburst of extravagance for the 1900 Exposition Universelle. Laloux's Gare d'Orsay (now **Musée d'Orsay**) and the **Train Bleu** brasserie were ornate examples of the heavy beaux arts floral style and eclectic classical motifs of the period.

Art nouveau looked to nature and fluid forms for inspiration. It is seen at its most flamboyant in Guimard's Métro entrances and **Castel Béranger**, as well as restaurant interiors, notably Julien and Maxim's.

After World War I, two dudes rule – Auguste Perret and Le Corbusier. Perret stayed within a classical aesthetic, but his use of reinforced concrete gave new liberty to floor plans and facades, as in his flats/office (rue Raynouard, 16th) and the Conseil Economique et Social (place d'Iéna). Le Corbusier tried out his ideas in luxury houses, such as Villa La Roche (**Fondation Le Corbusier**). His Pavillon Suisse at the **Cité Universitaire** can be seen as an intermediary between these villas and the mass housing of his Villes Radieuses, which became so influential and so debased across Europe after 1945. Robert Mallet-Stevens is unrivalled for his elegance, most clearly on **rue Mallet-Stevens**. Modern Movement influence spread beyond avant-garde studios to town halls, public housing and schools built in the socially conscious 1930s, while art deco love of chrome, steel and glass found its way into **La Coupole** brasserie and **Grand Rex** cinema.

POST-WAR PARIS

The aerodynamic aesthetic of the 1950s saw the **UNESCO** building and the beginnings of La Défense. The shanty-towns that had emerged to house immigrant workers cried out for a solution. In the 1960s and 70s tower blocks sprouted in the suburbs. Redevelopment inside Paris was limited, but regulations allowed taller buildings, noticeably **Tour Montparnasse** and in the 13th arrondissement. Piano and Rogers' high-tech **Centre Pompidou**, opened in 1977, was the first of the prestige projects that have become a trademark of modern Paris.

INTO THE NEW MILLENNIUM

Mitterrand's *Grands Projets* dominated the 1980s and early 90s as he sought to leave his stamp on the city with Nouvel's **Institut du Monde Arabe**, Sprecklesen's **Grande Arche de la Défense**, as well as Ott's controversial **Opéra Bastille**, Perrault's **Bibliothèque Nationale** and Chemetov's Bercy finance ministry. Urban renewal has transformed previously industrial areas to return the balance of Paris eastwards. Stylistically, the word is 'transparency' – from I M Pei's **Louvre Pyramid** and Nouvel's **Fondation Cartier**, to Wilmotte's recent **MK2 Bibliothèque**.

Although the age of *Grands Projets* is over, Chirac's Musée du Quai Branly (Nouvel again) is currently under construction by the Seine. Paris has gained two footbridges: **passerelle de Solférino** by architect-engineer Mimram and future passerelle de Bercy by the Austrian Feichtinger. Building continues apace in the **ZAC Rive Gauche** around the Bibliothèque Nationale, bringing in countless architects under masterplanner Christian de Portzamparc.

Field works

'Oooh Champs-Elysées' crooned Joe Dassin. Oooh really? The Champs don't do it for everyone. As a vista of national egoism, it steamrolls through a huge strip of Paris: close-up it's all rip-off cafés and commercial giants like Virgin Megastore. But, this being the Champs, even Virgin's CD collection is stored in a grandiloquent 1930s building, complete with sweeping staircase. To most it looks easily 'historic', but relative to most of the architecture along the Champs, it is modern. All that is changing.

Two projects have been given the green light for construction. The first is Citroën's new showroom, due to open in summer 2005. The second is the renovation of the advertising agency Publicis' Drugstore, billed to be completed by early 2004.

Citroën invited six architects, including Daniel Libeskind, to submit blueprints. The winning design was by France's up-and-coming Manuelle Gautrand. She has envisaged a helix glass-twist showcase housing seven turning platforms stacked above one another, each bearing the latest car models like TV dinners on microwave platters. A tad tricksy perhaps but, next to its neighbours, an impressive architectural anomaly. Citroën will undoubtedly want to eclipse the success of Renault's mutely modern showroom-cum-restaurant, the Franck Hammoutène-designed Atelier Renault up the road. The project has been approved by architectural watchdog Bâtiments de France, which admitted in *Le Parisien* that there is 'not much opportunity for modern architecture in Paris.' The Champs is seen as a suitable space for innovation, as long as projects avoid what Bâtiments de France calls 'extravagances'.

Whatever Citroën's and Publicis' designs actually look like once completed, they will certainly be noticeable. Publicis, wanting to makeover its rather drab 1970s Drugstore (a night pharmacy and mini-mart), chose Italo-American architect Michele Saee to do something lively, and above all, something modern. His answer is a glass-and-steel structure, fronted with a 20-metre barbed spiral. Extravagant, *moi*? The design is bound to draw critics, but as Publicis well knows, there's no such thing as bad publicity. And it'll give the guidebooks something to talk about, too.

Where to Stay

Features

Where to Stay

You don't want to blow your budget on your billet but you don't want to hang your hat in a hovel. Stay cool: Paris offers choice and this chapter offers expertise.

The place you choose to establish as base camp as you explore Paris is, of course, one of the most vital decisions you'll make as you plan your trip. Skipping around such a beautiful city only to return to a dump resembling a bus shelter can take the edge off one's *joie*. One thing you can be sure of is that you'll be spoilt for choice in Paris, where the accommodation possibilities span the palatial to the, er, functional in that bus-shelter style.

There is an official star rating system that operates here. It's meant to sort out the châteaux from the shit-holes, but we haven't used it in this guide. The star ratings usually reflect room size and mere presence of a lift, rather than decor, staff or atmosphere, so we do not think that this system is of any great practical value when making your choice. Instead we have divided the hotels into four categories, roughly representing the following price ranges for one night in a double room with shower/bath facilities: Deluxe €300+; Expensive €200-€300; Moderate €100-€200; Budget up to €100. All hotels are assumed to have amenities such as TV in the rooms and lifts and safes within the hotel, though there are some exceptions.

All our deluxe hotels offer air conditioning, double glazed windows, bar(s), and restaurant(s) and can arrange baby-sitting; in-room services include modem link, room service plus other extras depending on the hotel. Expensive hotels offer a similar standard of amenities and services. The moderate hotels should have in-room phone and modem link and at the budget hotels you can normally be assured of a TV and in-room phone. Any additional services are listed below each review.

Please note that all hotels in France charge an additional room tax (*taxe de séjour*) of around €1 per person. Hotels are often booked solid during the major trade fairs and it's difficult to find a quality place to lay your head during fashion weeks (January and early July for couture, March and October for *prêt-a-porter*). However, in quieter times, including July and August, hotels often offer reasonable special price deals at short notice; phone ahead to find out. Same-day reservations can be made in person (for a small fee) at the Office de Tourisme de Paris (*see chapter* **Directory**).

The Islands

Expensive

Hôtel du Jeu de Paume

54 rue St-Louis-en-l'Ile, 4th (01.43.26.14.18/ fax 01.40.46.02.76/www.hoteldujeudepaume.com). M° Pont Marie. **Rates** single €157-€215; double €215-€285; suite €465; breakfast €14. **Credit** AmEx, DC, MC, V. **Map** p406 K7.

Set back through a tiny courtyard, this charming hotel boasts original 17th-century beams. It is now filled with a tastefully slung-together array of modern and classical art. The unique timbered breakfast room was once a real tennis court, built under the orders of Louis XIII. Rooms are simple and tasteful with Pierre Frey fabric walls.

Hotel services *Baby-sitting. Bar. Billiards. Conference services. Fitness room. Internet. Laundry. Sauna.*

Moderate

Hôtel des Deux-Iles

59 rue St-Louis-en-l'Ile, 4th (01.43.26.13.35/fax 01.43.29.60.25). M° Pont Marie. **Rates** single €133; double €150; breakfast €10. **Credit** AmEx, MC, V. **Map** p406 K7.

This peaceful 17th-century townhouse offers 17 rooms done out in a faintly colonial style. Accessible through the lobby, the tiny courtyard at the centre is more of a quaint feature than any kind of facility with a practical usage (but what are you going to do? Practise your juggling?) The very pleasant Hôtel Lutèce up the road at No 65 (01.43.26.23.52) is under the same management.

Hotel services *Air con. Baby-sitting. Laundry.*
Room services *Double glazing. Modem link. Radio.*

Hôtel St Louis

75 rue St-Louis-en-l'Ile, 4th (01.46.34.04.80/fax 01.46.34.02.13/www.hotelsainlouis.com). M° Pont Marie. **Rates** single €130; double €145-€210; breakfast €9. **Credit** MC, V. **Map** p406 K7.

The 1970s tiled floor and mish-mash of furniture in the lobby of this hotel contrast with the exposed stone walls and wooden beams, and make a drunken return after a night's fun quite a sensory/balance challenge. Rooms are simple and bathrooms clean. But the only really special features here are the two suites on the top floor, which offer great views, and some nice-sized rooms.

Hotel services *Air con.* **Room services** *Double glazing. Modem link..*

Hôtel Costes. *See p47.*

Budget

Hospitel Hôtel Dieu

1 pl du Parvis Notre Dame, 4th (01.44.32.01.00/ fax 01.44.32.01.16). M° Cité or Hôtel de Ville.
Rates double €95.50; Breakfast €11. **Credit** MC, V. **Map** p406 J7.
Hospitel offers 14 rooms with a limited vista of the spires of Notre-Dame. The hotel is used by families of the hospital's in-patients and medical staff who have priority and usually take up about half the hotel's capacity. That distinctive hospital smell is not overpowering, the rooms are spotless and you couldn't ask for a better sightseeing base.
Hotel services *Air con.* **Room services** *Double glazing.*

The Louvre, Palais-Royal & Les Halles

Deluxe

Hôtel Costes

239 rue St-Honoré, 1st (01.42.44.50.00/ fax 01.42.44.50.01/www.hotelcostes.com). M° Tuileries. **Rates** double €460-€540; suite €620-€1,150; breakfast €30. **Credit** AmEx, DC, MC, V. **Map** p401 G5.
We're talking posh, we're talking attitude and we're talking of the distinct possibility of bumping into A-listers at the hotel and/or its restaurant, so don't forget your autograph book. This hotel boasts possibly the best pool in Paris, a sybaritic Eastern-inspired affair with an under-water CD system. We dare you to go down for a dip wearing your water-wings and flappers.
Hotel services *Bureau de change. Laundry. Fitness centre. Pool. Sauna. Nightclub.* **Room services** *CD-player. Fax. Radio. Wheelchair access.*

Hôtel de Crillon

10 pl de la Concorde, 8th (01.44.71.15.00/fax 01.44.71.15.03/www.crillon.com). M° Concorde. **Rates** single €480-€575; double €575-€855; suite €775-€5,100. **Credit** AmEx, DC, MC, V. **Map** p401 F4.
This magnificent neo-classical palace, favoured by no less a goddess than Madonna, groans with marble, mirrors and gilt. The Ambassadeurs restaurant is sublime and the Winter Garden tearoom has a gorgeous terrace; the Institut Guerlain has its own beauty salon here.
Hotel services *Fitness centre. Garden.* **Room services** *CD player. Fax.*

Hôtel Ritz

15 pl Vendôme, 1st (01.43.16.30.30/fax 01.43.16.31.78/www.ritz.com). M° Concorde or Opéra. **Rates** single €580-€730; double €680-€690; suite €800-€7,700; breakfast €32.50-€56.50. **Credit** AmEx, DC, MC, V. **Map** p401 G4.
Coco Chanel, the Duke of Windsor and Proust stayed here; Hemingway hoped heaven would be as good. Now owned by Mohamed Al Fayed, the Ritz was the setting for Dodi and Di's last supper. The Oriental-carpeted corridors go on forever and the windows on place Vendôme are bullet-proof. There are 142 bedrooms and 45 suites, from the romantic 'Frédéric Chopin' to the glitzy 'Impérial'.
Hotel services *Baby-sitting. Fitness centre. Pool.* **Room services** *CD-player. Fax. Modem link. Radio. Room service (24hr). Wheelchair access.*

Hôtel Sofitel le Faubourg

15 rue Boissy d'Anglas, 8th (01.44.94.14.00/ fax 01.44.94.14.28/www.accor-hotels.com). M° Concorde. **Rates** single €320-€354; double €380-€480; suites €502-€870; apartment €2,000; breakfast €27. **Credit** AmEx, DC, MC, V. **Map** p401 G4.
With a strong fashion pedigree (it used to be the offices of *Marie Claire*) and within schlepping distance of all the major labels, it's not surprising that this Sofitel's wardrobes are big enough for any fashion editor's spree. The rooms have Louis XVI armchairs, large balconies and Roger & Gallet smellies in the bathrooms. For male shopping widows, there's a small gym and a hammam. And it's quiet. Since 9/11, the street has been closed to traffic (the American Embassy is on the corner).
Hotel services *Air con. Bar. Restaurant. Fitness centre. Steam rooms. Business centre.* **Room services** *Double glazing. Room service (24hr). Hairdryer. Dataport. Safe. TV.*

Moderate

Le Relais Saint-Honoré

308 rue St-Honoré, 1st (01.42.96.06.06/fax 01.42.96.17.50). M° Tuileries. **Rates** double €190; suite €280-€320; breakfast €12 **Credit** AmEx, DC, MC, V. **Map** p401 G5.
This entirely renovated 17th-century hotel offers a delightfully warm welcome. With elegant, traditional decor at a modern standard, attention to detail in the 13 rooms and two suites is immaculate.
Hotel services *Parking (€17). Free Internet access.* **Room services** *Double glazing. Minibar. Flat screen TV. Safety deposit box.*

Hôtel Brighton

218 rue de Rivoli, 1st (01.47.03.61.61/fax 01.42.60.41.78/www.esprit-de-france.com). M° Tuileries. **Rates** double €109-€226; triple €164-€252; suite €226; breakfast €8 **Credit** AmEx, DC, MC, V. **Map** p401 G5.
Excellent value for its location, the faux-marble and mosaic Hôtel Brighton dates back to the end of the 19th century when, for once in their history, France and England shared a friendship. Book early and reserve one of the beautifully refurbished rooms overlooking the Tuileries gardens. The rest of the rooms are reasonably priced and spacious.
Hotel services *Bureau de change. Tea salon.* **Room services** *Double glazing. Hairdryer (some rooms). Room service (breakfast only).*

Hôtel des Tuileries

10 rue St-Hyacinthe, 1st (01.42.61.04.17/ fax 01.49.27.91.56/www.hotel-des-tuileries.com). M° Tuileries. **Rates** single €125-€190; double €140-€220; triple €205-€235; breakfast €12. **Credit** AmEx, DC, MC, V. **Map** p401 G5

This 18th-century building was the former property of Marie-Antoinette's lady-in-waiting. It's current style is a kind of comfy ab-fab, with ethnic rugs, the odd splattering of animal print and bright art, combine with traditional antique furniture, exposed beams and a listed staircase. The fashion world has singled it out as a cool address, so book ahead.

Hotel services *Air con. Baby-sitting. Bureau de change.* **Room services** *Double glazing. Radio. Room service (24hr). Safe.*

Hôtel Mansart

5 rue des Capucines, 1st (01.42.61.50.28/fax 01.49.27.97.44/www.esprit-de-france.com). M° Opera. **Rates** double €106-€290; extra bed €17; breakfast €10. **Credit** AmEx, DC, MC, V. **Map** p401 G4.

Just steps away from place Vendôme, this friendly 57-room hotel offers genuine style at a fraction of the price of nearby palaces. The light, spacious lobby has geometric murals inspired by formal gardens. Bedrooms in assorted colour schemes boast pleasant fabrics, period furniture and paintings, and the lovely Vendôme duplex has an excellent view of the square (ideal if anyone's planning a jewel heist).

Hotel services *Bar. Internet.*
Room services *Double glazing. Minibar.*

Budget

Hôtel du Cygne

3 rue du Cygne, 1st (01.42.60.14.16/ fax 01.42.21.37.02). M° Etienne Marcel or Châtelet. **Rates** single €85; double €99-€110; suite €121; breakfast €7. **Credit** AmEx, MC, V. **Map** p402 J5.

Situated in pedestrianised Les Halles, this traditional hotel in a 17th-century building offers compact, cosy and simple rooms with thoughtful, distinctive touches such as homemade furnishings. The collection of antique furniture adds interest and 'La Grande' under the eaves is delightful.

Hotel services *Bar.*

Hôtel Tiquetonne

6 rue Tiquetonne, 2nd (01.42.36.94.58/fax 01.42.36.02.94). M° Etienne Marcel. Closed Aug and Christmas. **Rates** single €28-€38;double €46; shower €5; breakfast €5. **Credit** MC, V. **Map** p403 J5.

Situated down a charming pedestrianised cobbled street, this superb-value hotel has basic but clean rooms and some are surprisingly large considering the price. Madame described her baby as 'kitsch', and it would seem that salmon pink is a favourite colour. It ain't no crime.

Opéra & the Grands Boulevards

Deluxe

Le Grand InterContinental

2 rue Scribe, 2nd (01.40.07.32.32/fax 01.42.66.12.51/ www.intercontinental.com). M° Opéra. **Rates** double €740-€850; suite €1,650-€3,270; breakfast €31. **Credit** AmEx, MC, V. **Map** p401 G4.

Not your average cookie-cutter InterContinental, this is the chain's European flagship – but given its sheer size, perhaps 'mothership' would be more appropriate. An enormous palace with almost 500 rooms spread over three wings, the Le Grand lives up to its name, swallowing up the entire block next to the Opéra Garnier. Following an 18-month, multi-million-euro refit, this *grande dame* of the *deuxième* reopened in 2003. And, as Flash Harry used to say, 'What a dame, what a dame', her splendid innards retouched by renowned French decorator Pierre-Yves Rochon (who also did up the George V).

Hotel services *Air con. Bar. Restaurant. Fitness centre and spa. Business centre.*
Room services *Double glazing. Room service (24hr). Hairdryer. Safe.*

Expensive

Hôtel Edouard VII

39 av de l'Opéra, 2nd (01.42.61.56.90)/fax 01.42.61.47.73/www.edouard7hotel.com). M° Opéra. **Rates** single €225-€275; double €297-€420; suite €320-€540; breakfast €20. **Credit** AmEx, MC, V, DC, JCB. **Map** 406 H7.

Coloured Murano-glass-suspended lights, smooth wooden sculptures and potted orchids add a touch of refined funk to this family-run gem. The stylish bar and restaurant, Angl'Opéra (with resident star chef Gilles Choukroun) are decked in dark mahogany and comfortable stripes while the individually decorated bedrooms offer wonderful views up to the Palais Garnier from the balconies.

Hotel services *Air-con. Bar. Lift. Restaurant.*
Room services *Hairdryer. Minibar. Safe.*

Hôtel Victoires Opéra

56 rue Montorgueil, 2nd (01.42.36.41.08/ fax 01.45.08.08.79/ www.hotelvictoiresopera.com). M° Sentier. **Rates** double €214-€275; suite €335; breakfast €12. **Credit** AmEx, DC, MC, V. **Map** p402 J5.

Sexily (in terms of being in the centre of the action) situated on the colourful and authentic rue Montorgueil, this hotel is decorated in a modern style with browns and creams. Smooth lighting, unobtrusive artworks, and fresh flowers give a calming atmosphere and staff are genuinely friendly. Though rooms are a little small, the overall package is a good one.

Room services *Radio. Wheelchair access.*

Hôtel Sofitel le Faubourg. *See p47.*

Moderate

Résidence Hôtel des Trois Poussins

15 rue Clauzel, 9th (01.53.32.81.81/ fax 01.53.32.81.82/www.les3poussins.com). M° St-Georges. **Rates** single €125; double €140-€175; triple or quad €210; breakfast €10. **Credit** AmEx, DC, MC, V. **Map** p401 H2.

First and foremost, mention *Time Out Paris* upon reservation, and receive a 15% discount. The Residence also offers the rare opportunity of self-catering facilities in half of its rooms. Decor is traditional, and very yellow.

Hotel services. *Air con. Garden.*
Room services *Double glazing. Modem link. Room service. Wheelchair access (two rooms).*

Budget

Hôtel L'Anglois (Hôtel des Croisés)

63 rue St-Lazare, 9th (01.48.74.78.24/fax 01.49.95.04.43/www.hotel-langlois.com). M° Trinité. **Rates** single €79-€89; double €89-€99; suite €132; breakfast €7.80. **Credit** AmEx, DC, MC, V. **Map** p405 G3.

Built in 1870 and a bank until 1896, the 27 rooms of this great-value Art Nouveau hotel are individually decorated; watch out for the delightful hidden bathrooms in some of the larger rooms (if you can't find yours after an hour max, phone for help). In 2001 the hotel changed its name after featuring in the Jonathan Demme film *Charade*.

Room services *Double glazing. Minibar.*

Hôtel Madeleine Opéra

12 rue Greffuhle, 8th (01.47.42.26.26/ fax 01.47.42.89.76/www.hotel-madeleine-opera.com). M° Madeleine. **Rates** double €78-84; triple €98; breakfast €6. **Credit** AmEx, DC, MC, V. **Map** p402 J4.

The sunny lobby of this hotel sits behind a two-century-old façade that was once a shop front. Situated behind the Madeleine church and the *grands magasins*, an ideal bargain location for a shopping weekend. The 24 rooms are maybe a touch basic but plenty good enough for non-royalty.

Room services *Double glazing. Minibar.*

Hôtel Vivienne

40 rue Vivienne, 2nd (01.42.33.13.26/ fax 01.40.41.98.19). M° Bourse or Grands Boulevards. **Rates** single €48; double €75-€84; triple €109; breakfast €6. **Credit** MC, V. **Map** p405 H7.

The lobby has recently been subject to a vast refurbishment – whereas before it was homely and traditional it is now something much more modern and formal. Staff are trying to get used to the change (evolution, guys?), but still put huge emphasis on making guests feel welcome – just as one should in a hotel, one might venture.

Room services *Double glazing.*

Beaubourg & the Marais

Deluxe

Pavillon de la Reine

28 pl des Vosges, 3rd (01.40.29.19.19/ fax 01.40.29.19.20/www.pavillon-de-la-reine.com). M° Bastille or St-Paul. **Rates** double €350-€570; duplex €445-€570; suite €570-€700; breakfast €20-€25. **Credit** AmEx, DC, MC, V. **Map** p406 L6.

Sheer class emanates from this place, and there's a real effort to help guests feel at home. Set back from place des Vosges, the style appropriately oozes traditional Parisian, with smatterings of the modern – reflected in some of the newer duplex suites, which are decked out in plush purple velvets and taffeta.

Hotel services *Bureau de change. Garden. Laundry. Meeting room. Parking.* **Room services** *Room service (24-hr). TV/VCR.*

Moderate

Hôtel Axial Beaubourg

11 rue du Temple, 4th (01.42.72.72.22/fax 01.42.72.03.53/www.axialbeaubourg.com). M° Hôtel de Ville. **Rates** single €105-€120; double €140-€175; breakfast €10. **Credit** AmEx, DC, MC, V. **Map** p406 K6.

The modern interior of this hotel may well be unusual for its 17th-century surroundings, but those who have dared poke their hooters through its doors have been amazed by its white marble floors, mud coloured walls, crushed velvet sofas and exposed beams. Rooms are not large, but are every bit as tasteful as the lobby. Great value.

Hotel services *Air con.* **Room services** *Double glazing. Modem point.*

Hôtel de la Bretonnerie

22 rue Ste-Croix-de-la-Bretonnerie, 4th (01.48.87.77.63/fax 01.42.77.26.78/ www.bretonnerie.com). M° Hôtel de Ville. **Rates** double €110-€145; suite €180; breakfast €9.50. **Credit** MC, V. **Map** p406 K6.

A labyrinth of corridors and passages; this 17th century *hôtel particulier* has plenty of historic atmosphere with its beams, exposed stone and wrought ironwork. Lavish fabrics, rich colours and the odd four-poster bed give a sense of individuality to the 29 suites and bedrooms.

Room services *Double glazing. Minibar*

Hôtel de la Place des Vosges

12 rue de Birague, 4th (01.42.72.60.46/ fax 01.42.72.02.64). M° Hôtel de Ville. **Rates** double €120-€140; breakfast €6. **Credit** AmEx, MC, V. **Map** p406 K6.

The best feature this hotel has to offer is its location. With exposed stone walls and wooden beams the 'Louis XIII-style decor' is now unfortunately looking a little shabby. However, room No 10 has been updated (let's hope a few more follow), and for the extra €20 is worth asking for.

Hôtel St-Louis Marais

1 rue Charles V, 4th (01.48.87.87.04/ fax 01.48.87.33.26/www.saintlouismarais.com). M° Sully-Morland or Bastille. **Rates** single €91; double €107-€125; breakfast €7.50. **Credit** MC, V. **Map** p406 L7.

Built as part of a 17th-century Célestin convent, this peacefully located hotel was undergoing refurbishment in 2003 to match the new rooms in the recently purchased, second location just along the road. It is compact and cosy with characteristic wooden beams and traditional decor. Room 105 resembles a mini apartment; it stretches over two floors and there are plans for a small kitchenette.

Hotel services *Internet* **Room services** *Double glazing. Modem link.*

Hôtel St-Merry

78 rue de la Verrerie, 4th (01.42.78.14.15/ fax 01.40.29.06.82www/hotelmarais.com). M° Hôtel de Ville. **Rates** double €160-€230; triple €250; suite €335; breakfast €11. **Credit** MC, V. **Map** p406 K6.

Once part of the neighbouring church, this Gothic-styled hotel could indeed be the setting of an eerie vampire tale. Wooden beams, stone walls and plenty of iron only add to its charm. Behind the door of room No 9 a flying buttress straddles the bed. This hotel is filled with such religious oddities. Because it's a historic building, there is no lift. The Hôtel Saintonge Marais, 16 rue de Saintonge, (01.42.77.91.13) is under the same management.

Hotel services *Baby-sitting.* **Room services** *Double glazing. TV in suite only.*

Hôtel Caron de Beaumarchais

12 rue Vieille du Temple, 4th (01.42.72.34.12/fax 01.42.72.34.63/ www.carondebeaumarchais.com). M° Hôtel de Ville. **Rates** double €137-€162; breakfast €9.80. **Credit** AmEx, MC, V. **Map** p402 L6.

Named after the 18th-century playwright who wrote the *Marriage of Figaro* and was known for his radical views, this elegant hotel appropriately offers traditional French style of the period. The lobby contains, among other things, a harp, piano-forte and chandeliers. Rooms are equally tasteful.

Hotel services *Air con.*
Room services *Double glazing. Minibar.*

Grand Hôtel Malher

5 rue Malher, 4th (01.48.87.77.63/ fax 01.42.72.60.92/ www.grandhotelmalher.com). M° St-Paul. **Rates** single €86-111; double €103-€128; suite €170; breakfast €8. **Credit** AmEx, DC. MC, V. **Map** p406 K6.

The hallways of this hotel have recently been refurbished in a serene blue, chilling you out in readiness for the contrast with the vibrant- coloured guest rooms. The lobby is airy, with marble floors, black leather seating and a narrow stairway leading down to the 17th-century vaulted breakfast room.

Hotel services *Lift. Conference room. Cooking facilities. Safe.* **Room services** *Double glazing. Hairdryer. Minibar. TV.*

Hôtel Axial Beaubourg. *See p51.*

Budget

Grand Hôtel Jeanne d'Arc

3 rue de Jarente, 4th (01.48.87.62.11/ fax 01.48.87.37.31). M° St-Paul. **Rates** single €55-€78; double €78-€125; breakfast €5.80. **Credit** MC, V. **Map** p406 L6.

Though this bold, burnt-orange-coloured hotel may not suit all tastes, to others it may be a real gem. Recent refurbishment has made the reception area striking, and the huge mirror on the wall gives a real wow factor (plus, of course, that clever old more-space optical illusion). Rooms are equally colourful, and for this price range are well sized, comfortable and clean. But when we say it's orange, we're not taking the pith.

Hôtel du Septième Art

20 rue St-Paul, 4th (01.44.54.85.00/ fax 01.42.77.69.10). M° St-Paul. **Rates** single €59-€75; double €75-€130; breakfast €7. **Credit** AmEx, DC, MC, V. **Map** p406 L7.

This black-and-white styled hotel is a homage to the 'seventh art' of cinema no less. Delightfully different, this hotel will have you peering at the walls for the duration of your stay. Before dining in the breakfast room with the likes of Clark Gable, Vivienne Leigh and Donald Duck, you can work out in the fitness room in the cellar.

Hotel services *Bar. Fitness room. Laundry.* **Room services** *Double glazing.*

The Bastille, eastern & north-eastern Paris

Moderate

Hôtel Beaumarchais

3 rue Oberkampf, 11th (01.53.36.86.86/ fax 01.43.38.32.86/www.hotelbeaumarchais.com). M° Filles du Calvaire or Oberkampf. **Rates** single €69-€85; double €99-€140; breakfast €7. **Credit** AmEx, MC, V. **Map** p402 L5.

This stylish hotel in the Oberkampf area has been modernised with brightly coloured walls, mosaics in the bathrooms, wavy headboards and Milan glass bedlamps. Rooms range from singles to suites.

Hotel services *Air con.* **Room services** *Double glazing. Room service (24hr).*

Libertel Terminus Est

5 rue du 8 mai 1945, 10th (01.55.26.05.05/fax 01.55.26.05.00/www.libertel-hotels.com). M° Gare de l'Est. **Rates** single €143-168; double €151-€213; suite €227-€382; breakfast €13. **Credit** AmEx, DC, MC, V. **Map** p402 K3.

A great railway hotel, the Terminus Est combines modern interior design with elements that evoke the age of steam: leather luggage handles on wardrobes, old-style bathroom fittings and a library in the lobby.

Hotel services *Air con. Baby-sitting. Bar. Health club.* **Room services**. *Room service.*

Le Pavillon Bastille

65 rue de Lyon, 12th (01.43.43.65.65/fax 01.43.43.96.52/www.pavillon-bastille.com). M° Bastille. **Rates** double €130; suite €213; breakfast €12. **Credit** AmEx, DC, MC, V. **Map** p407 M7.

Though offering an ideal location for the Bastille Opera, this hotel is a contemporary-wannabe, run-of-the-mill affair. Rooms follow a strict yellow and blue dress code, but are clean and fresh. If you're feeling particularly classy, try out the €24 Forfait VIP, for a bathrobe, bowl of fruit, slippers, and more flexible checking out times.

Hotel services *Air con. Bar. Patio.* **Room services** *Room service (24-hr). Wheelchair access. Non-smoking rooms.*

Budget

Hôtel Apollo

11 rue Dunkerque, 11th (01.48.78.04.98/fax 01.42.85.08.78). M° Gare du Nord. **Rates** single €53; double €70; breakfast €6. **Credit** AmEx, DC MC,V. **Map** p407 M7.

Opposite the Gare du Nord, the Apollo is a great find. The 45 rooms have the rustic charm of a traditional railway hotel; rooms are decorated with large wardrobes and florid wallpaper and are thankfully not invaded by the roar of the TGV.

Top ten Modern

Hôtel Victoires Opéra
Oh, the creams! The browns! (*See p48.*)

Hôtel Vivienne
So mod they can hardly stand it. (*See p49.*)

Hôtel Axial Beaubourg
Old without, glistening within. (*See p51.*)

Hôtel Costes K
Jagger-lipped and ultra-hip. (*See p56.*)

Hôtel Square
Big-name artists exhibit here. (*See p56.*)

Pershing Hall
DJ bar and design by Putman. (*See p56.*)

Pavillon de Paris
All yer business mod cons. (*See p59.*)

Hôtel la Demeure
Exciting shower heads? (*See p60.*)

ArtusHotel
Custom-graffitied staircase. (*See p64.*)

Le Montalembert
100 per cent WiFi-compatible. (*See p69.*)

Hôtel Gilden Magenta

35 rue Yves Toudic, 10th (01.42.40.17.72/ fax 01.42.02.59.66). M° République or Jacques Bonsergent. **Rates** single €59; double €69-€72; triple €80; quad €90; breakfast €7. **Credit** AmEx, DC, MC, V. **Map** p402 L4.

Though it's not in a sightseer's paradise, you could certainly do a lot worse for the price. The reception is a little brassy and the rooms may tend towards an over-abundance of wood panelling and terracotta-coloured paint, but it is clean, the staff are friendly and there is a very attractive garden terrace.

Hotel services *Parking.* **Room services** *Double glazing. Room service.*

Hôtel de Nevers

53 rue de Malte, 11th (01.47.00.56.18/ fax 01.43.57.77.39/www.hoteldenevers.com). M° République. **Rates** double €32-€45; triple €60-€74; breakfast €4.20. **Credit** MC, V. **Map** p402 L4.

Alain and Sophie are the charming couple behind this hotel. Though rooms are floral and chintzy, they are clean and well looked after. If you're a lover of the feline, what will make your stay here special are the two resident cats, which, judging by the very complimentary comments inscribed in the guest-book, are loved by everyone.

Hotel services *Internet access.*

Hôtel Moderne du Temple

3 rue d'Aix, 10th (01.42.08.09.04/ www.hotelmodernedutemple.com). M° Goncourt or Republique. **Rates** single €24-€40; double €32-€44; breakfast €4. **Credit** MC, V. **Map** .

The owners have made a big effort to make very basic comfort as pleasant and enjoyable as possible at this hotel, just off the bazaar-like Faubourg-du-Temple. Many of the rooms have big mirrors and all have TV, and there's a little patio that's so quaint it makes you feel like painting your fingernails puce. If that were not enough, the top floor has a small lounge complete with cane furniture.

The Champs-Elysées & west

Deluxe

Four Seasons George V

31 av George V, 8th (01.49.52.70.00/ fax 01.49.52.70.10/www.fourseasons.com). M° George V. **Rates** double €670-€890; triple €880; suite €1,250-€2,200; breakfast €35-€46. **Credit** AmEx, DC, MC, V. **Map** p400 D4.

While hardcore George V fans may lament the alleged Disneyfication of the hotel, there is no denying that the new version churns out serious *luxe:* almost over-attentive staff, glorious flower arrangements, divine bathrooms and ludicrously, lavishly comfy beds. The sybaritic spa boasts whirlpools, saunas, murals and a relaxation room where you can recover from the haute cuisine food and hip bar.

Hotel services *Fitness centre. Pool.* **Room services** *CD player. PlayStation.*

Pavillon de Paris. See p59.

Hôtel Costes K

81 av Kléber, 16th (01.44.05.75.75/ fax 01.44.05.74.74.). M° Trocadéro. **Rates** single €300; double €380; suite €460-€540; breakfast €19. **Credit** AmEx, MC, V. **Map** p400 B5.

A Jagger-lips sofa greets you in the foyer of this ultra-hip modern hotel. The rooms are beautifully designed in a sleek, unconventional manner, with individual artworks. The reception room and restaurant are spread out, rather bizarrely, around the inner courtyard, adding to the sense of alienation on entering the hotel, as your voice bounces unforgivingly off marble walls. Some of the staff act a bit cooler-than-thou, but then they probably are.

Hotel services *Bureau de change. Health club. Laundry. Pool.* **Room services** *CD player. Fax. Radio. Room service (24hr). Wheelchair access.*

Pershing Hall

49 rue Pierre-Charron, 8th (01.58.36.58.00/ fax 01.58.36.58.01/www.pershinghall.com). M° George V. **Rates** double €380-€500; suite €720-€1,000; breakfast €26. **Credit** AmEx, DC, MC, V. **Map** p400 D4.

A recent addition to Paris' arsenal of luxury hotels, Pershing Hall offers a clever mix of 19th-century splendour and contemporary comfort, combined with the intimacy of only 26 rooms. An eagle over the entrance is a reminder that this was once the American Legion's World War I HQ, but inside the emphasis is on warm colours and natural materials. You even get a blast of nature in the form of a dramatic vertical garden. Bedrooms, designed by Andrée Putman, offer stained grey oak floors, and bathrooms are particularly fine with geometric styling and copious towels.

Hotel services *DJ bar. Health spa.* **Room services** *CD-DVD player. Fax. Internet.*

Hôtel de Vigny

9 rue Balzac, 8th (01. 42. 99. 80. 80/ fax 01. 40. 75. 05.81) M° George V. **Rates**: single €335; double €390; breakfast €20. **Credit**: AmEx, MC, V. **Map** p401 H5.

The only Relais & Château hotel in Paris, the Vigny offers total discretion and country-house style to a discerning, low-key clientele. Just off the Champs-Elysées but worlds away from the tourist tat, the individually decorated rooms are beautiful, the staff both discreet and charming and the overall experience pretty sublime.

Hotel services *Air-con. Baby-sitting. Bar. Lift. Safe.* **Room services** *Hairdryer. Minibar. TV.*

Hôtel Royal Monceau

37 av Hoche, 8th (01.42.99.88.00/ fax 01.42.99.89.90/www.royalmonceau.com). M° Charles de Gaulle-Etoile. **Rates** single €410-€550;

double €456-€596; suite €610-€5,336; breakfast €27-€40. **Credit** AmEx, DC, MC, V. **Map** p401 H5.
Trompe l'oeil clouds on the ceilings, acres of marble and four florists arranging a gargantuan display in the lobby shout *'luxe'* at the Royal Monceau. The hotel recently amalgamated some rooms into 45 new suites. One belongs to Omar Sharif, who often enjoys an *apéro* in the English bar (but, please, no shouts of 'Oi, it's Doctor Zhivago!'). The Royal Monceau's other main boast is its fabulous health club *Les Thermes*, and there's a romantic garden restaurant.
Hotel services *Fitness club. Pool.* **Room services** *CD player. Fax. Internet. Radio. Wheelchair access.*

Expensive

Hôtel Pergolèse

3 rue Pergolèse, 16th (01.53.64.04.04/ fax 01.64.04.40/www.hotelpergolese.com). M° Charles de Gaulle-Etoile. **Rates** single €175-€310; double €195-€350; breakfast €12/€18 **Credit** AmEx, DC, MC, V. **Map** p400 B3.
With all the modern/contempory boutique hotels popping up around town, this hotel that was decorated in 1991 by Rena Dumas-Hermès (yes, as in the scarf), may be having a run for its money. Ha! That's the kind of challenge it loves! The interior is filled with Philippe Starck furniture and Hilton McConnico rugs, and though it hasn't been done up for a while, it's looking pretty sprightly.
Hotel Services *Babysitting. Limousine. Internet. Laundry.*

Hôtel Square

3 rue de Boulainvilliers, 16th (01.44.14.91.90/ fax 01.44.14.91.99/www.hotelsquare.com). M° Passy/RER Kennedy-Radio France. **Rates** single or double €245-€390; suite €480; breakfast €20. **Credit** AmEx, DC, MC, V. **Map** p404 A7.
Though the polished granite curtain wall may look forbidding, the dramatic interior of this courageously modern hotel is welcoming, aided by the personalised service that comes with that extra gleam of sincerity that having to look after only 22 rooms brings. The exotic woods, quality fabrics and paint finishes are striking, with temporary exhibitions in the atrium by well-known artists, such as Ben and Viallat.
Hotel services *Baby-sitting. Laundry. Parking €20.* **Room services** *CD player. Fax. Radio. TV/VCR. Wheelchair access.*

Moderate

Hôtel Elysées Ceramic

34 av de Wagram, 8th (01.42.27.20.30/ fax 01.46.22.95.83/www.elysees-ceramic.com). M° Charles de Gaulle-Etoile. **Rates** single €180; double €200; triple €223; breakfast €9.50. **Credit** AmEx, DC, MC, V. **Map** p400 C3.
Standing out from the crowd with its ceramic facade, this celebrated art nouveau hotel was built in 1904 by Jules Lavirotte. The theme continues inside with

Value hotels

Littered – nay, sprinkled – throughout this chapter – are some truly great budget hotels. However, we felt it only meet to throw a spotlight on the creme de la cheap, as it were. Here follows a selection of some real value-for-money Versailles where, at the time of going to press, you'll find a decent room for less than €85.

Hôtel de Lille *8 rue du Pélican, 1st (01.42.33.33.42). Mº Palais Royal or Louvre.* **Rates** *single* €35 (basin), €40 (shower & WC); *double* €40 (basin)-€50 (shower & WC); *no breakfast.* **No credit cards.**
The spotless bedrooms have all just been renovated in *belle époque* style and there are even plans to create a breakfast room.

Hôtel de la Herse d'Or *20 rue St-Antoine, 4th (01.48.87.84.09/fax 01.48.87.94.01). Mº Bastille.* **Rates** *single* €32 (basin); *double* €42 (basin), €52-€54 (shower & WC); *breakfast* €4. **Credit** MC, V.
Enter this 17th-century Marais building down a stone-walled corridor, and you'll find a cheap hotel with good-sized rooms.

Hôtel de Nesle *7 rue de Nesle, 6th (01.43.54.62.41/www.hoteldenesle.com). Mº Odéon.* **Rates** *single* €50 (basin)-€60 (shower & WC); *double* €75 (basin), €75-€100 (shower & WC); *no breakfast.* **Credit** MC, V.
The eccentric Nesle draws an international backpacker clientele.

Hôtel des Arts *7 cité Bergère, 9th (01.42.46.73.30/fax 01.48.00.94.42). Mº Grands Boulevards.* **Rates** *single* €64-€66; *double* €68-€70; *breakfast* €6. **Credit** AmEx, DC, MC, V.
This is the best and most unconventional of a tiny alley of hotels. A parrot, fish tank, and gaudy grandfather clock watch over reception. The stairwells are covered with theatre and museum posters.

Hôtel Chopin *46 passage Jouffroy or 10 bd Montmartre, 9th (01.47.70.58.10/fax 01.42.47.00.70). Mº Grands Boulevards.* **Rates** *single* €63-€71; *double* €71-€82; *breakfast* €7. **Credit** AmEx, MC, V.
The old-fashioned Chopin was built with the glass-roofed passage in 1846 and forms part of its magical appeal. Behind the entrance hall, with its Chesterfield and piano, a warren of salmon-coloured corridors leads to 36 rooms.

a ceramic cornice around the reception. The 57 rooms are clean and modern, with stencilled patterns, and there's an airy, cactus-filled breakfast room in the basement.
Hotel services *Air con. Babystting. Laundry*
Room services *Double glaing. Safe. Minibar.*

Hôtel Regent's Garden

6 rue Pierre-Demours, 17th (01.45.74.07.30/ fax 01.40.55.01.42/ www.bw-paris-hotels.com). M° Charles de Gaulle-Etoile or Ternes. **Rates** single €134; double €145-€249; breakfast €11. **Credit** AmEx, DC, MC, V. **Map** p400 C3.
High ceilings and plush upholstery hark back to the Second Empire, when this house was built for Napoléon III's physician. There are 39 large bedrooms, some with gilt mirrors and fireplaces. With its lovely walled garden, this is an oasis of – you guessed it – calm just ten minutes from the hubbub of the Arc de Triomphe.
Hotel services *Air con. Baby-sitting. Bureau de change. Garden. Parking.* **Room services** *Double glazing. Modem link. Room service.*

Budget

Hôtel Keppler

12 rue Keppler, 16th (01.47.20.65.05/ fax 01.47.23.02.29/www.hotelkeppler.com). M° Kléber or George V. **Rates** double €86-€90; triple €100; breakfast €6. **Credit** AmEx, MC, V. **Map** p400 C4.
Situated just steps away from the Champs-Elysées, this budget hotel is a real haven of down-to-earth value in this high-flying neighbourhood. It has the high ceilings and spacious rooms typical of the area, with a pleasingly old-fashioned style.
Hotel services *Bar.* **Room services** *Room service (24hr).*

Montmartre & Pigalle

Expensive

Terrass Hôtel

12-14 rue Joseph-de-Maistre, 18th (01.46.06.72.85/ fax 01.42.52.29.11/www.terrass-hotel.com). M° Place de Clichy. **Rates** single €188-€214; double €225-€248; suite €302; breakfast included. **Credit** AmEx, DC, MC, V. **Map** p401 H1.
Entering the rather dated lobby of the Terrass you may wonder what draws such stars as Pierce Brosnan and MC Solaar (the latter's a rap star, in France at least) to the hotel. Go up to the seventh floor and there's your answer – possibly the best view in the whole of Paris from the rooftop restaurant. Those in the know ask for room 704, from which you can lie in the bath and look out at the Eiffel Tower (of course, people on the Eiffel Tower could train their binoculars on you in the bath).
Hotel services *Baby-sitting. Bureau de change. Laundry.* **Room services** *Some non-smoking rooms. Wheelchair access.*

Pavillon de Paris

7 rue de Parme, 9th (01.55.31.60.00/fax 01.55.31.60.01/www.pavillondeparis.com) M° Liège or Place de Clichy. **Rates** single €195-€230; double €245-€285; breakfast €15. **Credit** AmEx, DC, MC, V. **Map** p401 G2.
Compact yet stylish are most assuredly the apposite epithets for this bijou hotel that borrows much from the Japanese aesthetic. Downstairs is inviting, with sleek geometrical lines, dark wood and modern art exhibitions – there's a funky bar and welcoming smiles from what reports describe as Paris' only Buddhist cocktail barman. The 30 bedrooms all have fax, voicemail and Web TV, perfect for the young, hip, business-person – and human beings, too.
Hotel services *Air con. Bar. Disabled room.*

Moderate

Timhotel Montmartre

11 rue Ravignan (pl Emile-Goudeau), 18th (01.42.55.74.79/fax 01.42.55.71.01/ www.timhotel.fr) M° Abbesses. **Rates** double €110-€125; breakfast €8.50. **Credit** AmEx, DC, MC, V. **Map** p402 H1.
Situated in the picturesque place Emile-Goudeau, this chain hotel has romantic-weekend-in-Paris written all over it. And, if you do come over all ooh-la-la and decide that you don't want to set foot outside the front door, the hotel is lovely enough for you not to have to. The rooms are comfortable without being spectacularly plush; what you need to do is get yourself into one of the fourth- or fifth-floor numbers, and you'll get the benefit of stunning views.
Hotel services *Internet access.*

Villa Royale Pigalle

2 rue Duperre, 9th (01.55.31.78.78/ fax 01.55.31.78.70/www.leshotelsdeparis.com). M° Pigalle. **Rates** single €120-160; double €150-€210; suite €180-€300. **Credit** AmEx, DC, MC, V. **Map** p402 H2.
This hotel really is something quite different, and we're not just saying that to be euphemistic. The flamboyant mock-baroque style means you can be sure of plenty of golds, reds, purples and plush furnishings. Rooms are individually named and quite decadent, with a nifty device for refreshing one's clothes after a long spell schlepping around. Guests raved about this hotel in the guestbook, highlighting the fabulous rooms and wonderful service.
Hotel services *Air con. Laundry.* **Room services** *Plasma TV. Jacuzzi baths.*

Budget

Hôtel des Batignolles

26-28 rue des Batignolles, 17th (01.43.87.70.40/ fax 01.44.70.01.04/www.batignolles.com). M° Rome or Place de Clichy. **Rates** double €58-€63; triple €73; breakfast €6. **Credit** AmEx, DC, MC, V. **Map** p401 F2.

This 1920s building still feels a bit like the girls' boardinghouse it once was, but once you've done your homework and mastered the optative, it provides a good base within easy reach of Montmartre. The Batignolles is simple, quiet and clean, with 33 spacious rooms and a tranquil courtyard.
Room services *Double glazing.*

Hôtel Ermitage

24 rue Lamarck, 18th (01.42.64.79.22/ fax 01.42.64.10.33). M° Lamarck-Caulaincourt. **Rates** single €74; double €84; triple €107; quad €124; breakfast included. **No credit cards.** **Map** p401 H1.
This 12-room hotel is only five minutes from the Sacré-Coeur, but it's on a nice quiet street that's just over the hill from the tourist madness of the place du Tertre. Rooms are large and endearingly over-decorated; some on upper floors have great views.
Room services *Double glazing.*

Royal Fromentin

11 rue Fromentin, 9th (01.48.74.85.93/fax 01.42.81.02.33/www.hotelroyalfromentin.com). M° Pigalle. **Rates** single €79-€109; double €89-€129; triple €109-€139; quad €129-€159; breakfast included. **Credit** AmEx, DC, MC, V. **Map** p401 H2.
The lobby of this hotel was once a 1930s cabaret hall, and previous sleepers have included such rock legends as the Spice Girls, Blondie and Nirvana. Maybe only aspiring superstars will appreciate the bargain basement rock-star chic, but it's got to be good on all that riffing atmosphere, and the possibility that you're leaning against the same bar where Kurt Cobain enjoyed his first pink gin of the evening.
Hotel services *Baby-sitting. Bar. Laundry.* **Room services** *Double glazing. Room service.*

Blanche Hôtel

69 rue Blanche, 9th (01.48.74.16.94/fax 01.49.95.95.98). M° Blanche. **Rates** single €26-€58; double €31-€89; triple €50-€95; quad €61-€100; breakfast €5.34. **Credit** MC, V. **Map** p401 G2.
If you're prepared to go without frills (go on: pretend you're in the SAS or something), a good-value stay is yours for the taking here. Be warned, the interior is not noticeably palatial and contains not-noticeably-luxurious seventies furniture, but rooms are a good size and the bar in the lobby serves the same kind of booze that'll get you as not-noticeably-sober as the very swishest of the capital's establishments.
Hotel services *Bar.* **Room services** *Double glazing.*

The Latin Quarter & the 13th

Moderate

Les Degrés de Notre-Dame

10 rue des Grands-Degrés, 5th (01.55.42.88.88/ fax 01.40.46.95.34). M° St-Michel. **Rates** single €70; double €100-€140; studio €100; breakfast included. **Credit** MC,V. **Map** p406 J7.
Masses of dark wood and lovingly tended rooms make this hotel set back from the Seine a real find. If the ten hotel rooms are taken, ask about their two studios a few streets away from the hotel, where you can pretend to be a real Parisian. The studios come complete with washing machine, power shower and, in one flat, a conservatory filled with fresh flowers.
Hotel services *Bar. Restaurant.* **Room services** *Double glazing. Modem link. Room service (24hr).*

Hôtel des Grandes Ecoles

75 rue du Cardinal-Lemoine, 5th (01.43.26.79.23/ fax 01.43.25.28.15/www.hotel-grandes-ecoles.com). M° Cardinal Lemoine. **Rates** double €100-€120; extra bed €20; breakfast €8. **Credit** MC, V. **Map** p406 K8.
A taste of the country in central Paris, this wonderful hotel, with 51 old-fashioned rooms, is built around a leafy garden where breakfast is served in the summer. The largest of the three buildings houses the reception area and an old-fashioned breakfast room with gilt mirror and piano.
Hotel services *Garden. Lift. Parking.* **Room services** *Double glazing. Wheelchair access.*

Hôtel la Demeure

51 bd St-Marcel, 13th (01.43.37.81.25/ fax 01.45.87.05.03). M° Les Gobelins. **Rates** double €105-€125; suite €179; breakfast €10. **Credit** AmEx, DC, MC, V. **Map** p406 K10.
This 43-room establishment was recently bought and totally revamped by a charming father-son team. Suites have sliding doors to separate sleeping and living space, with direct Internet access from both. The wrap-around balustrades of the corner rooms offer lovely views of the city, and bathrooms feature either luxurious tubs, or elaborate shower heads with endless massaging possibilities.
Hotel services *Air con. Baby-sitting. Parking.* **Room services** *ADSL Internet.*

Hôtel du Panthéon

19 pl du Panthéon, 5th (01.43.54.32.95/ fax 01.43.26.64.65/www.hoteldupantheon.com). RER Luxembourg/M° Cardinal Lemoine. **Rates** double €168-€213; triple €198-€229; breakfast €10. **Credit** AmEx, DC, MC, V. **Map** p406 J8.
An elegant, classy hotel with 34 individually decorated rooms which take their scheme from the *toile de Jouy* fabric on the walls. Some rooms have impressive views of the Panthéon; others squint out on to a charming courtyard, complete with its own chestnut tree. The Hôtel des Grands Hommes (01.46.34.19.60) next door is run by the same people.
Hotel services *Air con. Baby-sitting. Bar. Bureau de change.* **Room services** *Double glazing. Modem link. Wheelchair access.*

Hôtel Résidence Henri IV

50 rue des Bernardins, 5th. (01.44.41.31.81/ 01.46.33.93.22/www.residencehenri4.com). M° Maubert-Mutualité. **Rates** double €123-€145; apartments (one-or two-person) €153-€190, (three-person) €183-€220, (four-person) €213-€250; breakfast €9. **Credit** AmEx, DC. **Map** p406 K7.

Hôtel Duc de St-Simon. *See p69.*

Hidden in a tiny cul-de-sac next to the leafy square Paul Langevin, this 16-room hotel is decorated in the standard *belle époque* fashion, but with more genuine style than many similarly priced hotels. The apartment rooms are equipped with a handy mini-kitchen, although you may be reduced to eating on the beds in the smaller apartments.

Hôtel Les Rives de Notre-Dame

15 quai St-Michel, 5th (01.43.54.81.16/ www.rivesdenotredame.com). M° St-Michel.
Rates double €183-€243; suite €237-€550; breakfast €10.70-€13.70. **Credit** AmEx, DC, MC, V. **Map** p406 J7.
Saturated in everything Provençal, the colourful ten-room Les Rives seems miles away from the busy Paris quais. Tile floors, beams and a glass roof set the scene in the salon. It's worth spending a little extra for the 2nd, 3rd or 4th floors which are not only comfortably spacious, but also have a good view of the Seine.

Select Hôtel

1 pl de la Sorbonne, 5th (01.46.34.14.80/ fax 01.46.34.51.79/www.selecthotel.fr). M° Cluny-La Sorbonne. **Rates** double; €139-€165; triple €169-€179; duplex; €202; breakfast included. **Credit** AmEx, DC, MC, V. **Map** p406 J7.
Twenty years ago this was a cheap hotel used by students arriving at the Sorbonne. The owners really went to town on the refurb, introducing a brave art deco scheme that incorporates a waterfall atrium and a very 1920s basement bar. The deco rooms are smart with Starck-ish bathrooms, but for the less adventurous one wing remains more trad.
Hotel services *Air con. Baby-sitting. Bar. Laundry. Safe.* **Room services** *Double glazing. Hairdryer. Modem link. Room service. TV.*

Budget

Hôtel Esmeralda

4 rue St-Julien-le-Pauvre, 5th (01.43.54.19.20/ fax 01.40.51.00.68). M° St-Michel or Maubert-Mutalité. **Rates** single €30; double €60-€80; triple €95; quad €105; breakfast €6. **No credit cards.** **Map** p406 J7.
This 1640 building (recently renovated) looks on to a tree-lined square and over the Seine to Notre-Dame. In the plant-filled entrance, the resident cat may be curled up in a velvet chair. Upstairs are 19 floral rooms with antique furnishings and uneven floors. Do book ahead.
Hotel services *Room service.*

Familia Hôtel

11 rue des Ecoles, 5th (01.43.54.55.27/ fax 01.43.29.61.77/www.hotel-paris-familia.com). M° Maubert-Mutualité or Jussieu. **Rates** single €73.50; double €90-€120; triple €143.50; quad €180; breakfast included. **Credit** AmEx, DC, MC, V. **Map** p406 J7.
An enthusiastic welcome awaits at this old-fashioned hotel whose balconies are hung with tumbling plants. Chatty owner Eric Gaucheron is immensely proud of the sepia murals and cherry wood furniture that feature in some of the 30 rooms. The Gaucheron family also owns the Minerve (01.43.26.26.04), just next door, offering the same fantastic package.
Hotel services *Parking €18.* **Room services** *Double glazing. Minibar.*

Hôtel de la Sorbonne

6 rue Victor-Cousin, 5th (01.43.54.58.08). M° Cluny-La Sorbonne. **Rates** double €80-€90; breakfast €5. **Credit** AmEx, MC, V. **Map** .
This Latin Quarter hotel has cosy charm with wood floors, beams and a fire in the salon. Rooms are pink and cheery with geranium-filled windowboxes. Bathrooms are tiny but new, though you're probably better off with choosing one with a shower than one with the gnome-sized tubs.

St-Germain-des-Prés, Odéon & Montparnasse

Deluxe

Hôtel Bel-Ami

7-11 rue St-Benoît, 6th (01.42.61.53.53/ fax 01.49.27.09.33/www.hotel-bel-ami.com) M° St-Germain-des-Prés. **Rates** double €260-€380; suite €490; breakfast €20. **Credit** AmEx, MC, V **Map** p405 H6.
The transformation of Grace-Leo Andrieu's design-standard St-Germain bolthole is now complete, following a lively new paint job last summer. Serene greenery rules – there are beautiful bowls of green apples or mini-ferns everywhere and a hangover-soothing breakfast room. The cute ground floor espresso bar, set in the corner of the Orientalish lobby, now also houses a couple of whizzy PCs for web-surfing. The smiley, cosmopolitan staff are young, smart and unbuttoned. As the rooms tend to be small, it's worth asking for one of the the larger, lighter corner rooms.
Hotel services *Air con. Bar. Internet PCs. Lift (except to basement breakfast bar)*
Room services *Double glazing. Room service. CD players (suites: TV and DVD also). Hairdryer. Safe.*

Hôtel Lutétia

45 bd Raspail, 6th (01.49.54.46.46/fax 01.49.54.46.00/www.lutetia-paris.com). M° Sèvres Babylone. **Rates** double €400-€530; suite €650-€2,300; breakfast €15-¤ 19. **Credit** AmEx, DC, MC, V. **Map** p405 G7.
A masterpiece of art nouveau and early art deco architecture, the Lutétia opened in 1910 to accommodate shoppers coming to the Bon Marché. Today its plush bar and lively brasserie are still fine places for resting weary feet. Its 250 rooms, revamped in purple, gold and pearl grey, maintain a 1930s feel so slip out of those wet clothes into a dry martini.
Hotel services *Fitness centre. Laundry. Parking.*
Room services *Fax. Radio.*

Expensive

Hôtel de l'Abbaye

10 rue Cassette, 6th (01.45.44.38.11/ fax 01.45.48.07.86/www.hotel-abbaye.com). M° St-Sulpice. **Rates** double €206-€305; suite €383-€438; breakfast included. **Credit** AmEx, MC, V. **Map** p405 G7.

This tranquil hotel was originally part of a convent. Wood panelling, well-stuffed sofas and an open fireplace in the drawing room make for a relaxed atmosphere but, best of all, there's a surprisingly large garden where breakfast is served in the warmer months. The 42 rooms are tasteful and luxurious and the suites have roof-top terraces.

Hotel services *Bureau de change. Garden. Laundry.* **Room services** *Radio. Room service.*

L'Hôtel

13 rue des Beaux-Arts, 6th (01.44.41.99.00/ fax 01.43.25.64.81/www.l-hotel.com). M° St-Germain-des-Prés. **Rates** double €259-€344; suite €595-€687; breakfast €17. **Credit** AmEx, DC, MC, V. **Map** p405 H6.

Longtime favourite with the fashion pack – poor old Oscar Wilde died here, by his own admission a loser in a duel with the wallpaper – L'Hôtel has been taken well in hand by new owner Jean-Paul Besnard (a biologist, strangely). Jacques Garcia's revamp has restored the central stairwell to its former glory; Mistinguett's *chambre* retains its art deco mirror bed and Oscar's deathbed room has, appropriately, been decorated with green peacock murals. Don't miss the cellar swimming pool and *fumoir*.

Hotel services *Laundry. Pool. Steam room.* **Room services** *CD player. Fax..*

La Villa

29 rue Jacob, 6th (01.43.26.60.00/fax 01.46.34.63.63). M° St-Germain-des-Prés. **Rates** double €240-€335; suite €440; extra bed €40; breakfast €14. **Credit** AmEx, DC, MC, V. **Map** p405 H6.

What a find. There's something winkingly, maybe even naughtily, stylish about this hotel. It's like a long cool drink of something refreshing and sparkly, and it's freshly renovated. Maybe it's the cool-to-the-nth faux crocodile skin on the bedheads or the crinkly taffeta on the taupe-coloured walls. This place is charismatic and likeable. Wonderfully, the room numbers are projected on to the floor in front of your door (in case it's a challenge to see straight when you make it back of an evening).

Hotel services *Laundry.* **Room services** *Modem link. Room service (24hr). Wheelchair access.*

ArtusHotel

34 rue de Buci, 6th (01.43.29.07.20/ fax 01.43.29.67.44/www.artushotel.com). M° St-Germain-des-Prés. **Rates** double €190-€300; suite €320; breakfast included. **Credit** AmEx, DC, MC, V. **Map** p405 H7.

Zebra-print chairs and crushed-velvet sofas in the lobby; graffiti-style stairway – painted by American Artist Jonone; young artists commissioned to paint the doors to each room: these are all sure signs telling you something hip is afoot. Back in the lobby, the self-service bar introduces you to the hell that is real alcoholic temptation.

Hotel services *Baby-sitting. Bar. Café. Laundry. Safe.* **Room services** *Hairdryer. Modem link. Radio. Room service (24-hr). Wheelchair access.*

Moderate

Hôtel Aviatic

105 rue de Vaugirard, 6th (01.53.63.25.50./ fax 01.53.63.25.50/www.aviatic.fr). M° Montparnasse-Bienvenüe or St-Placide. **Rates** double €121-€191; breakfast €11. **Credit** AmEx, DC, MC, V. **Map** p405 H7.

This vintage hotel has been totally overhauled in the inimitable style of the Corbel sisters, resulting in a smart joint with bags of character. The polished floor in the lobby (ideal for that unrehearsed moment of precision skating when the place is crowded) and the hints of marble and brass do lend an impressive touch of glamour. The slightly more expensive '*supérieure*' rooms are worth it for the extra space and solid, old-fashioned furniture. This hotel is very handy for access to the busy Montparnasse area.

Hotel services *Air Con. Baby-sitting.* **Room services** *Double glazing.*

Le Clos Médicis

56 rue Monsieur-le-Prince, 6th (01.43.29.10.80/ fax 01.43.54.26.90/www.closmedicis.com). M° Odéon/RER Luxembourg. **Rates** single €125; double €150-€180; triple €220; breakfast €10. **Credit** AmEx, DC, MC, V.**Map** p406 H7.

In a 1773 building built for the Médicis family is this extremely stylish hotel designed by Jean-Philippe Nuël. The brand-new decor is refreshingly modern and very chic, with taffeta curtains (remember when they were the last word in naff?), chenille bedcoverings and antique floor tiles in the bathrooms.

Hotel services *Air con. Baby-sitting. Bar. Internet access.* **Room services** *Double glazing. Modem link.*

Grand Hôtel de l'Univers

6 rue Grégoire-de-Tours, 6th (01.43.29.37.00/ fax 01.40.51.06.45/www.hotel-paris-univers.com). M° Odéon. **Rates** single €170; double €185-€215; breakfast included. **Credit** AmEx, DC, MC, V. **Map** p406 H7.

15th-century beams, high ceilings and *toile*-covered walls are the trademarks of this hotel. Fans of the posh French decorating magazine *Côté Sud* will love the Manuel Canovas fabrics, but there are also nice little touches such as as a laptop for rent. The same helpful team also runs the nearby Hôtel St-Germain-des-Près (36 rue Bonaparte, 6th/01.43.26.00.19/ www.hotel-st.ger.com), which boasts a medieval-themed room and what has to be the sweetest attic in Paris.

Hotel services *Air con.* **Room services** *Double glazing. Modem point.*

The climax of canine comfort

A new pedigree of VIP hotel guest is off the leash. Make way for the Very Important Pet. Rabies? Schmabies. That's in the past, all that froth and biting. Now in Paris your cute little bundle of I-swear-to-God-he-understands-every-word-I-say can get his paws on room service, groom service and top dog's dinners. Goodbye doghouse, hello Gucci basket.

Venturing the first sniff around the possibilities of this new luxury canine travel sector is the über-grand **Trianon Palace** hotel (*pictured*), situated just outside Paris, appropriately in Versailles. The hotel clearly knows how to satisfy its market – today's Yappies (young, affluent pooches) expect to be very well-treated indeed.

Since September 2003, the Trianon, which has always been dog-friendly, has answered this demand with its 'Heavenly Pets' package. The mutt gets Oh My Dog! perfume and shampoo, upmarket bedding from dog boutique Les Cadors, 24-hour room service with a slobber-worthy selection of beef burgers and the like, plus an al fresco obstacle course so he can stay in executive shape and still fit into his little tartan doggie coat next season.

And for the pet owner? A night in a deluxe double bed, all the usual luxury benefits, plus dog-sitters on call if you should fancy a spell in the hotel's beauty spa (oh, and, the dog can get beauty treatments,too). Other services, such as canine style consultations and even poochie psychotherapy (working through the trauma of years of tinned dog food and cold tree trunks, no doubt) are available upon request. Just whistle, and the staff will come running.

The Trianon's owners, Westin Hotels & Resorts, are currently honing the concept for the American market. Can you imagine? Ruff trade is about to get a whole lot ruffer.

Trianon Palace

1 bd de la Reine, 78000 Versailles (01.30.84.50.00/www.westin.com). SNCF Versailles Rive-Droite (from Gare St-Lazare). 'Heavenly Pets' Deluxe double: €365 per night, including breakfast.

Other hotels that welcome dogs

Hôtel Aviatic (*see p64.*)
Hôtel Edouard VII (*see p48.*)
Le Montalembert (*see p69.*)

Hôtel des Marronniers

21 rue Jacob, 6th (01.43.25.30.60/ fax 01.40.46.83.56). M° St-Germain-des-Prés. **Rates** single €110; double €150-€165; triple €205; breakfast €10-€12. **Credit** MC, V. **Map** p405 H6.

A most welcome bit of peace and quiet in lively St-Germain, this hotel has a courtyard in front and a lovely conservatory and garden at the back, where you'll find the chestnut trees (you could say they're all-conkering) that give the hotel its name. The 37 rooms are mostly reasonably sized, with pretty canopies and fabrics.

Hotel services *Air con. Baby-sitting. Bar. Garden. Tea salon.* **Room services** *Double glazing.*

Hôtel des Saints-Pères

65 rue des Sts-Pères, 6th. (01.45.44.50.00/fax 01.45.44.90.83). M° St-Germain-des-Prés. **Rates** double €105-€195; suite €280; breakfast €11. **Credit** AmEx, MC, V. **Map** p405 G7.

Right in the middle of designer shopping heaven, this *hôtel particulier* built in 1658 by Gittard, one of Louis XIV's architects, is wonderfully calm. Discreet and low-key, the hotel has a charming garden, and a sophisticated, though small, bar. The most coveted room is No. 100, with its impressive 17th-century ceiling by painters from the Versailles school. The room also features an open bathroom so you can gaze at the myth of Leda and the Swan while loofahing those areas where the sun doesn't shine.

Hotel services *Air con. Bar.* **Room services** *Double glazing.*

Budget

Hôtel Delambre

35 rue Delambre, 14th (01.43.20.66.31/fax 01.45.38.91.76/www.hoteldelambre.com). M° Edgar Quinet or Vavin. **Rates** double €80-€95; suite €140; breakfast €8. **Credit** AmEx, MC, V. **Map** p406 H7.

Elegant cast-iron touches in the 30 rooms give this friendly hotel an individual style, much updated from the 1920s when the 'Pope of Surrealism' – and certainly its main man – André Breton lived here. The mini-suite in the attic is particularly pleasing, if not really suitable for the more generously framed.

Hotel services *Laundry.* **Room services** *Double glazing.*

Hôtel du Globe

15 rue des Quatre-Vents, 6th (01.43.26.35.50/ fax 01.46.33.62.69). M° Odéon. Closed Aug. **Rates** single or double €66-€100; breakfast €9. **Credit** MC, V. **Map** p406 H7.

The Globe is an hotel with an appealing mix of styles. Gothic wrought-iron doors lead into florid corridors, and an unexplained suit of armour supervises guests from the tiny salon. Fancy a chuckle? Rush at it with a tin opener and see what happens. Take heed: a small, winding staircase may lead to suitcase trouble.

Room services *Double glazing. Radio. Room service.*

Auberge Jules Ferry. *See p71.*

Hôtel Istria-Montparnasse

29 rue Campagne-Première, 14th (01.43.20.91.82/fax 01.43.22.48.45). M° Raspail. **Rates** double €92-€106; breakfast €8. **Credit** AmEx, DC, MC, V. **Map** p405 G9.

If you're in Montparnasse in order to relive its artistic heyday, you can't do better than stay here – Man Ray, Kiki, Marcel Duchamp, Francis Picabia, Erik Satie and Louis Aragon all did. The Istria has been modernised since the days when the windswept-and-interesting mob graced its halls, but it still has great vats of charm with 26 simply furnished, compact rooms, a cosy cellar breakfast room and a comfortable living area. Film fans take note, the tiled artists' studios next door featured in Godard's *A Bout de Souffle*.

Hotel services *Garden. Laundry. Photocopier.* **Room services** *Double glazing. Room service (24hr).*

Regents Hôtel

44 rue Madame, 6th (01.45.48.02.81/fax 01.45.44.85.73). M° St-Sulpice. **Rates** single €75-€80; double €85-€100; triple €110; quad €125; breakfast €7. **Credit** AmEx,MC, V. **Map** p405 G7.

This discreet hotel has a surprising degree of style for its price and a location ideal for St-Germain, yet on a quiet street. Its courtyard garden is used for breakfast in summer. Reception rooms are a sunny Provençal blue and yellow, bedrooms are comfortable with new bathrooms, and some have balconies.

Room services *Double glazing.*

The 7th & the 15th

Deluxe

Hôtel Duc de St-Simon

14 rue de St-Simon, 7th (01.44.39.20.20/ fax 01.45.48.68.25). M° Rue du Bac. **Rates** double €220-€240; suite €320-€340; breakfast €14. **Credit** AmEx, MC, V. **Map** p405 F6.

Step off the quiet side street into a pretty courtyard – you'll be following in the footsteps of Lauren Bacall and Toni Morisson. The 34 romantically decorated bedrooms include four with terraces above a leafy garden (sadly not accessible to visitors). A perfect pitch for the amorous, though if you can do without a four-poster bed there are cheaper and more spacious rooms than the 'Honeymoon Suite'.

Hotel services *Laundry.* **Room services** *Room service. TV (on request).*

Le Montalembert

3 rue de Montalembert, 7th (01.45.49.68.68/ fax 01.45.49.69.49/www.montalembert.com). M° Rue du Bac. **Rates** double €320-€440; suite €490-€760; breakfast €20. **Credit** AmEx, DC, MC, V. **Map** p405 G6.

A benchmark of quality and impeccable service. There's everything the fasherati (who decamp here for fashion week) could want – bathrooms stuffed with Contemporel toiletries, a set of digital scales, and 360° mirrors to check that silhouette. The Montalembert, designed by superstar Christian Liaigre, is WiFi-compatible, and the clattery two-person staircase lifts are a nice nod to old-fashionability in a hotel that is otherwise *tout moderne*. If there's one oversight, however, it's the lack of wardrobe. If the owners can add a super-low-fat 'allégé' option to the breakfast menu, surely a few more hanging rails wouldn't be too much trouble?

Hotel services *Air con. Bar. Restaurant. Lift (except top floor). CD/DVD library* **Room services** *Double glazing. Room service (24hr). Hairdryer. Modem link. Safe. CD. DVD.*

Moderate

Hôtel Lenox

9 rue de l'Université, 7th (01.42.96.10.95/ fax 01.42.61.52.83/www.lenoxsaintgermain.com). M° St-Germain-des-Prés. **Rates** double €115-€200; duplex €255-€270; breakfast €10-€12.50. **Credit** AmEx, DC, MC, V. **Map** p405 G6.

This venerable literary and artistic haunt (TS Eliot booked Joyce in on the recommendation of Ezra Pound) has been reborn with a wink to art deco and the jazz age. The Lenox Club Bar, open to the public, is a bravura creation with marquetry scenes of jazz musicians. Bedrooms, reached by a ride in an astonishing glass lift, have more traditional decor and ever-so-Parisian views.

Hotel services *Air con. Baby-sitting. Bar. Internet connection.* **Room services** *Double glazing. Radio.*

Budget

Hôtel Eiffel Rive Gauche

6 rue du Gros-Caillou, 7th (01.45.51.24.56/fax 01.45.51.11.77/www.123france.com). M° Ecole Militaire. **Rates** double €85-€92; triple €110; quad €145; breakfast €7. **Credit** MC, V. **Map** p404 D6.

For the quintessential Paris view at a bargain price, ask for one of the upper floors of this well-situated hotel; you can see the Eiffel Tower from nine of the 30 rooms. They feature Empire-style bedheads and modern bathrooms. There is also a tiny, tiled courtyard with a bridge.

Room services *Double glazing. Radio.*

Grand Hôtel Lévêque

29 rue Cler, 7th (01.47.05.49.15/ fax 01.45.50.49.36/www.hotel-leveque.com). M° Ecole Militaire. **Rates** single €53; double €84-€91; triple €114; breakfast €7. **Credit** AmEx, MC, V. **Map** p404 D6.

Located on a market street near the Eiffel Tower, the Lévêque is good value for such a chic area. The tiled entrance is charming, while the 50 rooms are well-equipped: there are sparkling bathrooms in all the doubles; singles just have a basin.

Room services *Double glazing. Modem link.*

Hôtel de Nevers

83 rue du Bac, 7th (01.45.44.61.30/ fax 01.42.22.29.47). M° Rue du Bac. **Rates** double €83-€93; breakfast €6. **No credit cards**. **Map** p405 G6.

This characterful 11-room hotel was once part of a convent. Everything is dinky, divine and dainty, with mini-wardrobes and neat bathrooms. Rooms are smart, but the paintwork on the staircase has suffered regular torment as guests have to carry up their own luggage. Call it charmingly battered. There are two rooms on the fourth floor with tiny, charming terraces.

Room services *Double glazing. Minibar.*

Youth accommodation

MIJE

Fourcy *6 rue de Fourcy, 4th (01.42.74.23.45/ fax 01.40.27.81.64/www.mije.com). M° St-Paul.* **Fauconnier** *11 rue du Fauconnier, 4th (01.42.74.23.45). M° St-Paul.* **Maubisson** *12 rue des Barres, 4th (01.42.74.23.45). M° Hôtel de Ville.* **Open** 7am-1am daily. **Rates** dorm €22 per person (18-30s sharing rooms); single €38; double €30; triple €25; membership €2.50; breakfast included. **No credit cards**. **Map** p406 L6, L7, K6.

Two 17th-century aristocratic Marais residences and a former convent are the most attractive hostel sleeps to be found in Paris. Plain but clean rooms have well-made beds, snow-white sheets (at least, they are when you get in them) and sleep up to eight; all have a shower and basin. Fourcy even has its own restaurant. Do make sure you don't miss the 1am curfew.

BVJ Paris/Quartier Latin

44 rue des Bernardins, 5th (01.43.29.34.80/ fax 01.53.00.90.91). M° Maubert-Mutualité.
Open 24-hr. **Rates** dormitory €25 per person; single €30; double €27; breakfast included. **No credit cards**. **Map** p406 K7.
BVJ hostel has clean rooms, with 138 beds and homely tartan quilts in bare modern dorms (for up to ten) and singles. There is also a TV lounge and a work room for writing up your journal in.
Hostel services *Kitchen. Internet access. Safe.*
Branch: BVJ Paris/Louvre, 20 rue Jean-Jacques-Rousseau, 1st (01.53.00.90.90). 200 beds.

Auberge Internationale des Jeunes

10 rue Trousseau, 11th (01.47.00.62.00/ fax 01.47.00.33.16/www.aijparis.com). M° Ledru-Rollin. **Open** 24hrs daily; rooms closed 10am-3pm. **Rates** *Nov-Feb* €13; *Mar-Oct* €14; breakfast included. **Credit** MC, V. **Map** p407 N7.
Cleanliness is a high priority at this large (120 beds) hostel close to the lively Bastille and within walking distance of the Marais. There are rooms for two to six people. Larger rooms have their own bathroom.
Hostel services *Vending machine. Internet access. Safe.*

Auberge Jules Ferry

8 bd Jules-Ferry, 11th (01.43.57.55.60/ fax 01.43.14.82.09/www.fuaj.fr). M° République or Goncourt. **Open** office and hostel 24hrs daily, rooms closed 10am-2pm. **Rates** €18.50 per person; breakfast included. **Credit** AmEx, MC, V. **Map** p403 M4.
Friendly IYHF hostel has 100 beds in rooms for two to six. There is no need to – indeed no way to – make advance reservations.
Hostel services *Kitchen. Safe. Lockers. Internet access.*

The best Gardens

Hôtel Brighton

Overlooks the Tuileries gardens, filled with trees, flowers, sculpture and sometimes even a funfair. (*See p47.*)

Pavillon de la Reine

Florals and hardies. (*See p51.*)

Pershing Hall

250 species of plant! Count them, you saddo! (*See p56.*)

Regents Hôtel

Breakfast al fresco: heaven. (*See p56.*)

Le Clos Médicis

Indoor garden equals no damp Pringles at picnics. (*See p64.*)

Hôtel de Marronniers

All-conkering chestnut garden. (*See p64.*)

Bed & breakfast

Alcove & Agapes

Le Bed & Breakfast à Paris, 8bis rue Coysevox, 18th (01.44.85.06.05/fax 01.44.85.06.14).
This B&B service offers more than 100 homes (€50-€110 for a double) with hosts ranging from artists to grandmothers.

Good Morning Paris

43 rue Lacépède, 5th (01.47.07.28.29/ fax 01.47.07.44.45). **Open** 9am-5.30pm Mon-Fri.
This company has 40 rooms in the city. Prices range from €38 for one person to €75 for three.

Apart-hotels & short-stay rental

A deposit is usually payable on arrival. Small ads for private short-term rentals can be found in the Anglophone magazine *Fusac* or on its website www.fusac.fr.

Apparthotel Citadines

Central reservations 01.41.05.79.79/ fax 01.41.05.78.87/www.citadines.com **Rates** studio from €87; apartment for four from €141. **Credit** AmEx, DC, MC, V.
Seventeen modern complexes attract a mainly business clientele. Rooms are on the cramped side, but a kitchenette and table make them practical for those with children. Discounts can be had for longer stays.
Room services *CD player. Dishwasher. Double glazing. Kitchen. Microwave.*

Home Plazza Bastille

74 rue Amelot, 11th (01.40.21.20.00/ fax 01.47.00.82.40/ www.homeplazza.com). M° St-Sébastien-Froissart. **Rates** double €155-€198; single €137; suite €295-€443; breakfast €18. **Credit** AmEx, DC, MC, V. **Map** p402 L5.
Aimed at both business people and tourists, this carefully constructed 'village' of 290 apartments built around a street is reminiscent of a stage set. Rooms are clean and modern with well-equipped kitchenette and spacious bathrooms.
Hotel services *Air con. Bar. Business services. Garden. Parking. Restaurant.*
Branch: Home Plazza St-Antoine, 289bis rue du Fbg-St-Antoine, 11th (01.40.09.40.00/fax 01.40.09.11.55).

Paris Appartements Services

69 rue d'Argout, 2nd (01.40.28.01.28/ fax 01.40.28.92.01/www.paris.appartements-services.fr). **Open** 9am-7pm Mon-Fri; 10am-noon Sat. **Rates** studio from €61 per week; apartment from €135 per week. **Credit** MC, V.
This organisation provides furnished studios and one-bedroom flats in the 1st to 4th *arrondissements*, with weekly maid service, and a 24-hour helpline. The staff are bilingual.

Sightseeing

Features

Introduction

Paris has it all: grandeur and gaudiness, history and hearsay, culture and charisma, even a sandy summer beach draped with tanned hides.

Left. Right. Left. Right. No, not the sound of marching in the street but Parisians debating which side of the river they favour. Paris is divided physically, and some say psychologically, by the Seine, with the **Ile de la Cité** and the **Ile St-Louis** in the middle. The majestic **Palais du Louvre** exemplifies the Right Bank – elegant and affluent, while the Left Bank is more romantic and literary. Well, not quite. The old adage 'Sur la Rive Gauche on pense, sur la Rive Droite on dépénse' (on the Left Bank one thinks, on the Right Bank one spends) has all but lost its relevance. In reality, just as much large scale retail therapy happens in St-Germain-des-Près as in the Faubourg St-Honoré, and intellectuals and jazz mavericks no longer blow instinctively to the Left. It's more about *quartiers* and arrondissements.

The arrondissements, which begin at the Louvre and spiral out clockwise from one through to 20, are all important in Parisian life. It's a magic circle contained by the Périphérique. Your postcode says a lot about you, good or bad. The 16th: smug and embassy heavy; the 6th: chic and civilised; the 13th: Chinatown and towering apartment blocks; the 19th & 20th: young, artistic, multicultural. Stereotyping and snobbery have a lot to answer for in terms of an arrondissement's rep.

These days it's more about East and West. Western Paris on both sides of the river is home to the *haute bourgeoisie* while eastern Paris attracts genuine artists and whatever passes for a bohemian these days, with its cheap rents and fashionable pockets in working-class areas.

We have divided the **Sightseeing** chapter into four sections: The Islands, Right Bank, Left Bank and Beyond the Périphérique. The Right and Left Banks are arranged into areas which roughly follow arrondissement guidelines: start from the centre and work out. If you want to cut to the chase, follow our 48, 24 and 72-hour itineraries (*see p76*, **Paris on a need-to-know basis**), or simply visit the four unmissable sights, **Notre-Dame**, **Sacré-Coeur**, the **Arc de Triomphe** and the **Eiffel Tower** (*see p81, 104, 110 and 132,* **Le Fab Four**). Clichéd? *Nous*? Read on and you'll see there is life in the old monuments yet.

Getting around is usually pleasurable and easy by Métro and bus (barring heatwaves and strikes) or on foot (*see chapter* **Directory** for details of public transport). Paris is a compact city, perfect for walking; plentiful bridges make it easy to cross back and forth as moods or monuments dictate. Or if you crave something more laid-back, lazy even, see the sights via a riverboat cruise.

Guided tours

Boat trips

Bateaux-Mouches *pont de l'Alma, Rive Droite, 8th (01.42.25.96.10/recorded info 01.40.76.99.99/www.bateaux-mouches.fr). Mº Alma-Marceau.* **Departs** *summer* every 30 min 10am-8pm; every 20 min 8-11pm daily; *winter* 11am, 2.30pm, 4pm, 6pm and 9pm. **Tickets** €7; €4 4-12s; free under-4s; lunch €50, €25 under-12s; dinner €125. **Credit** MC, V. *Wheelchair access.*

Bateaux Parisiens *Tour Eiffel, port de la Bourdonnais, 7th (01.44.11.33.55/ www.bateauxparisiens.com). RER Pont de l'Alma.* **Departs** *Easter-Oct* every 30 min (except 12.30pm and 5.30pm) 10am-11pm daily; *Nov-Easter* every hr (every half hr at peak times) 10am-10pm daily. **Tickets** €9; €4.10 under-12s; €90-125, dinner 8.30pm daily. **Credit** AmEx, DC, MC, V. *Wheelchair access.*

Bateaux Vedettes de Paris *port de Suffren, 7th (01.47.05.71.29/www.vedettesdeparis.com). Mº Bir-Hakeim.* **Departs** *Apr-Oct* every 30 min 10am-10pm Mon-Fri; 10am-11pm Sat, Sun; *Nov-Mar* 11am-7pm Mon-Fri; 11am-9pm Sat, Sun. **Tickets** €8; €3 under-12s. **Credit** AmEx, DC, MC, V. Also offers a Bacchus cruise and a chocolate cruise.

Bateaux Vedettes du Pont-Neuf *square du Vert Galant, 1st (01.46.33.98.38/ www.pontneuf.net). Mº Pont-Neuf.* **Departs** *Mar-Oct* approx every 30 min 10.30am-10.30pm daily; *Nov-Feb* approx every 45 min 10.30am-10pm daily. **Tickets** €9; €4.50 under-12s. **No credit cards**.

Coach tours

Cityrama *4 pl des Pyramides, 1st (01.44.55.61.00/www.cityrama.com). Mº Palais Royal.* **Departs** times vary depending on season. **Tickets** €24; free under-12s. **Credit** AmEx, DC, MC, V. *Wheelchair access.*

Les Cars Rouges *(01.53.95.39.53/ www.lescarsrouges.com).* **Departs** from Trocadéro 9.30am-7pm every 10-15 min daily. **Tickets** 2-day pass €22; €11 4-12s. **Credit** AmEx, DC, MC, V. Recorded commentary in English. Hop-on, hop-off at any of nine stops (including Eiffel Tower, Notre-Dame, Louvre, Opéra). *Wheelchair access.*

Paris Vision *214 rue de Rivoli, 1st (01.42.60.30.01/www.parisvision.fr). Mº Tuileries.* **Departs** (2hr) *winter* 10.30am, 3.30pm, 7pm daily; *summer* 10.30am, 3.30pm, 9pm daily. Full-day tours also available. **Tickets** €24; free 4-11s. **Credit** AmEx, MC, DC, V.

Cycle tours

Mike's Bike Tours *(01.56.68.10.54/ www.mikesbiketoursparis.com). Meet Eiffel Tower, Pilier Sud, Champ de Mars, 7th. Mº Bir-Hakeim.* **Departs** *Mar, Apr, mid-Aug to Oct* 11am daily; 7pm Tue, Thur, Sun; *May to mid-Aug* 11am, 3.30pm, 7pm daily (no night tour Sat); *Nov-Feb* by appointment. **Tickets** day €22/$19; night €26/$23. **No credit cards** but US dollars accepted. Day and night tours in English hit the major sights. Wet-weather gear is provided in rain. Call for Segway tours.

Paris à vélo, c'est sympa! *28 rue Baudin, 11th (01.48.87.60.01/www.parisvelosympa.com). Mº Richard Lenoir.* **Departs** *Apr-Oct* Mon, Fri, Sat 10am, 3pm, 8.30pm; Sun 6am *(May-Sept only)* 10am, 3pm, 8.30pm. *Nov-Mar* on demand. **Tickets** (incl bike hire) €30; €16 under-26s, under-12s. Group rates available. **Credit** MC, V. Multilingual guided tours follow a variety of routes and themes, including Paris at dawn. Reservation required.

Walking tours

Guided walks in French are listed weekly in *Pariscope* under 'Promenades'. Walks in English are usually listed in the *Time Out Paris* section in *Pariscope* and the guides below can organise group walks on request. Prices exclude entrance fees for sights.

Paris Contact Jill Daneels (01.42.51.08.40/ www.realfrance.com). **Tickets** €12; €10 students, over-60s; €8 children. 2-hr tours by appointment daily, minimum four people (or €48 solo).

Paris Walking Tours Oriel and Peter Caine (01.48.09.21.40/www.paris-walks.com). Choice of 2-hr tours daily. Tickets €10; €7 students; €5 children.

Edible Paris (www.edible-paris.com). Parisian food writer Rosa Jackson tailors a journey of taste discovery in Paris to fit your likes, dislikes and budget.

Paris on a need-to-know basis

You could spend years discovering Paris: but what if you only have a few days?

Familiarising yourself with with highlights of Paris, especially our **Fab Four** unmissables *(see p81, 104, 110 & 132)*, on a brief stay may seem challenging. *Mais non*! You got us, babe. Here's what to do and where to go if days you have but few (*see* **Index** for where to find our recommendations).

If you only have one day

- **A river trip** (*see p75* **Guided tours**)! This minimises time spent not doing too much on the Métro and, of course, you get to see all the major sights (the **Eiffel Tower** springs to mind, as do **Notre-Dame** and the **Louvre**). Wave gaily at Parisians as you glide beneath their stunning bridges.
- Link arms (unless you're on your own, and you don't want to pose as a Cossack) and stroll through the **Islands**. Stand and gaze on Pont Neuf and join other tourists in the queue for a Berthillon ice cream.
- Take in the **Musée d'Orsay**. Shun the Louvre in favour of the demon brush-strokes of Renoir, Manet, Monet and Vince Van Gogh.
- Get ye down to the **Champs-Elysées**, the oft-called most beautiful avenue in the world, and focalise on the **Arc de Triomphe**.
- Walk down to **Place de la Concorde**, wonder at the Luxor obelisk, the wedding-cake fountains and drink in the view – especially at night – from the terrace by the Jeu de Paume in the **Tuileries** gardens.
- For one-stop Parisian shopping, **La Samaritaine** is a great place to secure that 'This? Dahling, I snapped it up in Paris' number. Then nip up to the top-floor restaurant and get a great view of the city.

If you have two days

- Go on, be a devil – go to the **Marais**. What a lot it's got: fantastic, one-off boutiques, kooky bars and some great art galleries. The vibe created by its being at once Paris' Jewish and gay centres is unique, and you'll notice a distinct beat back in tempo from the rest of the city. Do treat yourself to a falafel lunch on rue des Rosiers.
- One of the most raisiny *raisons d'etre* of your visit will be to brush up on your culture. And God created the **Musée du Louvre**, where the whole lot, from the first plip to the last plop, is explained in paintings and artefacts more stunning than you'll see anywhere else.
- Squares are cool, and never more so than when they're arcaded, symmetrical and the birthplace of Madame de Sévigné. The square of which we treat is the **Place des Vosges**, which transcends cliché and superlatives and can be simply stunning. If it weren't for the cars, this could be the 17th century.
- From the Place des Vosges, 'tis but a hop, skip and a Madison to the **place de la Bastille**, where the peasants had a major hissy fit and the Revolution really got started. There's not much left in terms of memorials, so don't bother with your Che Guevara hat. And please, while you're marvelling at the Colonne de Juillet (which commemorates the 1830 July Revolution) and the **Opéra Bastille** just across the square, don't get yourself mown down by the traffic.
- Now that you may be ready to brave the Métro (it's actually very good, of course), buzz along on line one – the yellow one – and have a look at **Hôtel de Ville**, the official (not actual) digs of the city's Mayor since 2001, Bertrand Delanoë.

Or maybe even three

- Shall we have a day on the Left Bank (the bit to the south of the Seine)?
- If you're the sensitive type, the artistic type, or if you've come over to Paris to recuperate from a massive nervous breakdown or something of that ilk, the place for you is the **Musée National Rodin**. Not only will you be able to swoon at such masterpieces as *The Kiss* and the *Walking Man*, but you can enjoy a nibble in the profound peace of the gardens. It is calmness itself.
- Mon Dieu, we haven't done any shopping today! Fear not: we have at our disposal **Le Bon Marché**, Paris' oldest, prettiest and swishest department store. Just next door (well, sort of joined on, actually) is the Grande Epicerie, where you can find fab foodstuffs from all over the world.
- Now, you can say what you like about old Napoléon, but he's almost certainly dead, and his little corpse is almost certainly entombed in Les Invalides' Eglise du Dome, which is astonishingly visually impressive. **Les Invalides**, which was built to house old and wounded soldiers, has a fabulous domed roof. And a great War Museum.
- The emotional import of the above (little guy, big ideas, huge embarrassment) may leave you in need of another stroll in the park. Luckily, the Left Bank provides us with the **Jardins du Luxembourg**, a must for saunterers, musers and general park-life lovers. Ladies: watch out for the guys with those tell-tale eyeholes in their newspapers.

You got four? That's a sabbatical!

- As you'll know by now, Paris has got the balance between culture, bohemia and sleaze absolutely right. Today's the day we're going to weigh it all up. Shall we digest our croissant over some culture?
- You read our mind, didn't you? An excursion to the **Musée Jacquemart-André** to see its magnificent illustration of the life of the 19th-century bourgeoisie. This is the lifestyle that revolutions lead to. For some.
- Fancy a bit of filth? We know you don't, but one must acquaint oneself with the underbelly, must one not? Head north for **Montmartre**, the place whose former plethora of windmills now focuses on one, the **Moulin Rouge**, which is first-rate for showbiz but far from ooh-la-la. You'll find some real porn and some pros on boulevard de Clichy. If that's too grimy, skip along to **Amélie Poulain's** neighbourhood, up rue Lepic to rue des Abbesses. It's less sleazy but might well give you a sweet tooth ache instead.
- So, it's up the steps to **Sacré-Coeur**. What a great way to find out if you've got cardiac problems; but if you do make it to the top, you'll get the most wonderful view of the most wonderful city in the world.

The Islands

Quasimodo was île suited; so too, Baudelaire. Even Marie-Antoinette made a pre-chop pitstop. So why not join them in the medieval heart of Paris?

Ile de la Cité

In the 1st and 4th arrondissements.

Paris began life on the Ile de la Cité around 250 BC when the Parisii, a tribe of Celtic Gauls, moved into the neighbourhood (see chapter History). It went on to be a centre of political and religious power right into the Middle Ages.

When Victor Hugo wrote Notre-Dame de Paris in 1831, the Ile de la Cité was still a bustling quarter of narrow medieval streets and tall houses: 'the head, heart and very marrow of Paris'. In that case, then, Baron Haussmann performed a marrow transplant when he supervised the expulsion of 25,000 people from the island, razing tenements and some 20 churches. The lines of the old streets are traced into the parvis in front of Notre-Dame. The people resettled to the east, leaving behind a few large, official buildings – the law courts, Conciergerie, Hôtel-Dieu hospital, the police headquarters the cathedral of Notre-Dame. The capital's oldest love story unfolded at 9 quai aux Fleurs, where Héloïse lived with her ball-breaking uncle Canon Fulbert, who had her lover Abélard castrated. A medieval feel persists in the few streets untouched by Haussmann northeast of the cathedral, such as rue Chanoinesse and the rue des Chantres.

The most charming spot, though, is the western tip, where the Pont-Neuf spans the Seine. Despite its name, it is in fact the oldest remaining bridge in Paris, begun under the reign of Catherine de Médicis and Henri III in 1578 and taking 30 years in all to complete.

Down the steps is a leafy triangular garden, the square du Vert-Galant, a perfect spot for summer picnics. Alternatively, take to the water on the Vedettes du Pont-Neuf moored just on the quai (see p75). In the centre of the bridge is an equestrian statue of Henri IV, erected in 1635, destroyed in the Revolution and replaced in 1818 (indecisive, nous?). On the island side of the bridge, the secluded place Dauphine, home to restaurants, wine bars and the ramshackle Hôtel Henri IV, was built in 1607. It was commissioned by Henri IV, who named it in honour of his son, the dauphin Louis, the future King Louis XIII. The red brick and stone houses look out on both quais and square, whose third, eastern side was demolished in the 1870s. André Malraux, borrowing from Freud no doubt, summed up its appeal – 'the sight of its triangular formation with slightly curved lines, and of the slit which bisects its two wooded spaces. It is, without doubt, the vagina of Paris'. One wonders if he should have got out a little more, perhaps.

The towers of the Conciergerie dominate the island's north bank. Along with the Palais de Justice, it was originally part of the Palais de la Cité, residential and administration complex of the Capetian kings. It occupies the site of an earlier Merovingian fortress and, before that, the Roman governor's house. Etienne Marcel's uprising prompted Charles V to move the royal retinue to the Louvre in 1358, and the Conciergerie was assigned a more sinister role as a prison where hapless souls awaited execution. The interior is worth a visit with its prison cells and Gothic vaulted halls.

Sainte-Chapelle, Pierre de Montreuil's masterpiece of stained glass and slender Gothic columns, is nestled amid the nearby law courts.

The Seine from Ile de la Cité.

Surrounding the chapel, the Palais de Justice evolved alongside the Conciergerie. After passing through security, visit the Salle des Pas Perdus, busy with plaintiffs and barristers, and sit in on cases in the civil and criminal courts. The Palais is still the centre of the French legal system, although it has long been rumoured that the law courts will be moved out to the 13th or 15th arrondissement.

Caged birds are on sale on Sundays at the **Marché aux Fleurs** behind the tribunal du Commerce at place Louis Lepine. During the rest of the week it's a flower market. The legal theme continues to the south with the Préfecture de Police, known by its address, quai des Orfèvres, and immortalised in Simenon's Maigret novels.

The Hôtel-Dieu, east of the market place, was founded as a hospital in the seventh century. During the Middle Ages your chances of survival here were, at best, slim; today the odds are much improved (providing it's not August and there's no heatwave). The hospital was rebuilt in the 1860s on the site of a nearby foundling hospital.

Notre-Dame cathedral dominates the eastern half of the island. In front of the cathedral, the bronze marker known as Kilomètre Zéro is the point from which all distances are measured. The Crypte Archéologique under the parvis gives a sense of the island's multi-layered past, when it was a tangle of alleys, houses, churches and cabarets. Behind the cathedral is the **Mémorial de la Déportation**, a sobering reminder of the French citizens (and people who fled the Nazis in the hope of finding refuge in France) deported to concentration camps.

Cathédrale Notre-Dame de Paris

pl du Parvis-Notre-Dame, 4th (01.42.34.56.10). M° Cité/RER St-Michel. **Open** 8am-6.45pm Mon-Fri; 8am-7.45pm Sat-Sun; towers (01.53.10.07.02) 9.30am-5pm daily. **Admission** free; towers €6.10; €4.10 18-25s; free under-18s. **Credit** MC, V. **Map** p406 J7. (*See p81* **Le Fab Four: Notre-Dame.**)

La Conciergerie

1 quai de l'Horloge, 1st (01.53.40.60.97). M° Cité/RER Châtelet-Les Halles. **Open** *Apr-Sept* 9.30am-6.30pm daily; *Oct-Mar* 9am-5pm daily. **Admission** €6.10; €4.10 12-25s, students; free under-12s; €9 with Sainte-Chapelle. **No credit cards. Map** p406 J6.

Marie-Antoinette was held here during the Revolution and Danton and Robespierre also did a pre-guillotine pitstop. The Conciergerie looks every inch the forbidding medieval fortress, yet the pseudo-medieval facade was added in the 1850s. The 13th-century Bonbec tower survives from the Capetian palace, and the Tour de l'Horloge built in 1370, on the corner of boulevard du Palais, was the first public clock in Paris. The fortress became a prison under the watch of the Concierge. The wealthy had private cells with their own furniture, which they paid for; others were crowded together on beds of straw. A list of Revolutionary prisoners,

including a hairdresser, shows that far from all victims were nobles. Marie-Antoinette's cell, the Chapelle des Girondins, contains her crucifix, some portraits and a guillotine blade.

La Crypte Archéologique

pl du Parvis-Notre-Dame, 4th (01.55.42.50.10). M° Cité/RER St-Michel. **Open** 10am-6pm; closed Mon. **Admission** €3.30; €2.20 over 60s; €1.60 under-26s; free under-14s. **No credit cards. Map** p406 J7.

The excavations under the parvis span 16 centuries, from the remains of Gallo-Roman ramparts to a 19th-century drain.

Marché aux Fleurs

pl Louis-Lépine, quai de la Corse, quai des Fleurs. M° Cité. **Open** Mon-Sat 8am-7.30pm; Sun 8am-7pm.

This ancient market sells not only flowers but potted plants and trees; specialist stallholders offer cacti and orchids. On Sundays it is all a-sqwark with the sounds of birds and small animals.

Paris Mémorial de la Déportation

Square de l'Ile de France, 4th M° Cité/RER St-Michel. **Open** 10am-6pm Tue-Sun; last ticket 5.30pm. **Admission** free. **Map** p406 J7.

This tribute to the 200,000 people deported to death camps during World War II lies on the eastern tip of the island. A blind staircase descends to river level, where simple chambers are lined with tiny lights and the walls are inscribed with poetry. A barred window looks out onto the Seine.

Sainte-Chapelle

4 bd du Palais, 1st (01.53.40.60.97). M° Cité/RER Châtelet-Les Halles. **Open** *Apr-Sept* 9.30am-6.30pm daily; *Oct-Mar* 10am-5pm daily. **Admission** €6.10; €4.10 12-25s, students; free under-12s; €9 with Conciergerie. **Credit** (shop) MC, V. **Map** p406 J6.

Seriously devout King Louis IX (1226-70) had a hobby of collecting holy relics (and children; he fathered 11). In the 1240s he bought what was advertised as the Crown of Thorns, and ordered Pierre de Montreuil to design a suitable shrine. The result was the exquisite High Gothic Sainte-Chapelle. The upper level, intended for the royal family and the canons, appears to consist almost entirely of stained glass. The windows depict Biblical scenes, and on sunny days coloured reflections dapple the stone. The lower chapel was for the use of palace servants.

Ile St-Louis

In the 4th arrondissement.

Ever wondered how the other half lives? The Ile St-Louis is one of the most exclusive residential addresses in the city. Delightfully unspoiled, it offers fine architecture, narrow streets and pretty views from the tree-lined quais.

For hundreds of years the island was a swampy pasture belonging to Notre-Dame and a retreat for fishermen, swimmers and courting couples; then it was known as the Ile Notre-Dame. In the 14th century Charles V built a fortified canal through the middle, thus creating the Ile aux Vaches ('Island of Cows'). Its real-estate potential wasn't realised until 1614, when speculator Christophe Marie persuaded Louis XIII to fill in the canal (now rue Poulletier) and plan streets, bridges and houses. The island was renamed in honour of the King's pious predecessor and the venture proved a huge success, thanks to society architect Louis Le Vau, who from the 1630s on built fashionable new residences on quai d'Anjou, quai de Bourbon and quai de Béthune, as well as the **Eglise St-Louis-en-l'Ile**. By the 1660s the island was filled and, unlike the Marais, where the smart reception rooms were at the rear of the courtyard, here they were often at the front to allow their residents riverside views.

The rue St-Louis-en-l'Ile, lined with quirky gift shops, quaint tearooms, lively stone-walled bars and restaurants and fine historic buildings, runs the length of the island. The grandiose Hôtel Lambert (2 rue St-Louis-en-l'Ile/1 quai d'Anjou) was built by Le Vau in 1641 for Louis XIII's secretary with interiors by Le Sueur, Perrier and Le Brun. At No 51, Hôtel Chenizot, look out for the bearded faun adorning the rocaille doorway and the stern dragons supporting the balcony. The **Hôtel du Jeu de Paume**, at No 54 was once a real tennis court, while legendary ice cream shop **Berthillon** (No 31) still draws a lip-licking queue. There are great views of the flying buttresses of Notre-Dame at the western end, where a footbridge crosses to the Ile de la Cité.

Baudelaire wrote part of *Les Fleurs du Mal* while living at the Hôtel de Lauzun. He and fellow poet Théophile Gautier also held meetings of their dope smokers' club here. Earlier, Racine, Molière and La Fontaine resided as guests of La Grande Mademoiselle, cousin of Louis XIV. The *hôtel* stands out for its scaly sea-serpent drainpipes and trompe l'oeil interiors. There are further literary associations to be found at 6 quai d'Orléans, where the Adam Mickiewicz library-museum (01.43.54.35.61/open 2-6pm Thur) is dedicated to the Romantic poet, journalist and zealous campaigner for Polish freedom from Russia, who lived in Paris 1832-40.

Eglise St-Louis-en-l'ile

19bis rue St-Louis-en-l'Ile, 4th (01.46.34.11.60). M° Pont Marie. **Open** 9am-noon, 3-7pm Tue-Sun. **Map** p406 L7.

The church was built between 1664 and 1765, following plans by Louis Le Vau and completed by Gabriel Le Duc. The interior follows the classic Baroque model with Corinthian columns and a sunburst over the altar, and is a popular classical concert venue.

Le Fab Four: Notre-Dame

As we float past Notre-Dame on our river trip and the full meaning of the English-language commentary dawns upon us, some of us have had to hit the hot, sweet tea and the smelling salts when we realised that the cathedral wasn't actually designed by Walt Disney. The better educated have gone into shock when someone managed to convince them that its architect wasn't Victor Hugo and that it isn't maintained exclusively by souls stricken with scoliosis. In fact, we don't know who this Gothic masterpiece's architect was.

Here's what we do know: it was commissioned in 1160 by Bishop Maurice de Sully and replaced an earlier basilica begun in the 4th century. It was constructed between 1163 and 1334 on the site of a Gallo-Roman temple to Jupiter, and the amount of time and money spent on it reflected Paris' growing prestige. Pope Alexander III laid the foundation stone, the choir was completed in 1182, the nave in 1208, the west front and twin towers went up between 1225 and 1250, chapels were added to the nave between 1235 and 1250 and to the apse between 1296 and 1330. The Cathedral was plundered wildly during the French Revolution, and then, ironically, re-dedicated to the cult of Reason. The original statues of the Kings of Judah from the west front were torn down by the mob and rediscovered in 1977 (they are now on view in the Musée National du Moyen-Age). Viollet-le-Duc restored Notre-Dame to her former glory in the mid-19th century.

Notre-Dame, like any old dame worth her salt, has seen a few things: in 1239 the supposed Crown of Thorns was placed here; in 1430, Henry IV of England was crowned here; Napoléon made himself Emperor in 1804, and in 1909 the beatification of Joan of Arc occurred here; in August 1944, Charles de Gaulle was present for the Te Deum mass that was supposed to celebrate the liberation of Paris, and he managed to resist the urge to flee to a safer country when the ceremony was disturbed by German snipers.

So there's your Cathédrale Notre-Dame. Better go and see it, and you've got to hand it to us: did we mention rose windows, flying buttresses or Quasimodo?

The Right Bank

From right royal residences to funky couscous corners, cheap frills and frou-frou to pristine pearls and poodles, the Right Bank has a healthy balance.

The Louvre to Concorde

In the 1st arrondissement.

In the 14th century the monarchs and their minions upped stumps from the Ile de la Cité and took a turn to the Right (bank); the Louvre and the secondary palaces of the Tuileries and Palais-Royal became the centre of royal power. The area is, even today, genetically genteel.

Now one of the world's great art museums, the **Palais du Louvre** has grandiose state rooms, fine courtyards and galleries stretching to the **Jardin des Tuileries**. Begun as a fortress and turned into a sumptuous Renaissance palace, the Louvre was designated a museum in 1793. Two hundred years later, Mitterrand's Grand Louvre scheme added I. M. Pei's pyramid in the Cour Napoléon, doubled the exhibition space, uncovered medieval remains and resulted in the subterranean Carrousel du Louvre shopping mall, auditorium and food halls. When floodlit at night, the pyramid's steel and glass structure creates mesmerising optical effects with the fountains.

On place du Louvre, opposite the palace, is **St-Germain-l'Auxerrois**, once the French kings' parish church and home to the only original Flamboyant Gothic porch in Paris, built in 1435. Mirroring it to the left is the 19th-century neo-Gothic 1st arrondissement town hall, alongside chic bar **Le Fumoir** (which has its very own Mona Lisa – Amaretto, orange juice and Champagne).

Thanks to the Grand Louvre scheme, the **Musée des Arts Décoratifs**, the **Musée de la Mode et du Textile** and the **Musée de la Publicité** (*see chapter* **Museums**) have all been refreshed, and the Arc du Carrousel, a mini-Arc de Triomphe built by Napoléon in 1806-09, has been restored. From the arch the extraordinary symmetry of the Jardin des Tuileries, the **Champs-Elysées** up to the **Arc de Triomphe** and beyond to the **Grande Arche de la Défense** is evident. Originally stretching to the Tuileries palace, the Tuileries gardens were laid out in the 17th century by André Le Nôtre and remain a living space with cafés, ice-cream stalls and summer fun fair; they also act as an open-air gallery for modern art sculptures. Flanking the Tuileries overlooking **place de la Concorde** stand the **Musée de l'Orangerie**, and the **Jeu de Paume**, the latter built for playing real tennis, now used for contemporary art exhibitions (*see chapter* **Museums**).

Along the north side of the Louvre, the rue de Rivoli is remarkable for its arcaded facades rather than its jaded souvenir shops. It runs in a perfect line to place de la Concorde in one direction, and to the Marais in the other, where it becomes rue St-Antoine. Elegant, old-fashioned hotels remain, along with gentlemen's tailors, bookshops **WH Smith** and **Galignani** and tearoom **Angelina**. The area germinated into a little England in the 1830s-40s as aristocracy, writers and artists flooded across the Channel after the Napoleonic Wars, staying at the Hôtel Meurice and dining in the restaurants of the **Palais-Royal**.

Place des Pyramides, at the western end of the Louvre where rue de Rivoli meets rue des Pyramides, contains a shiny gilt equestrian statue of Joan of Arc. One of four statues of her in the city, it is appropriated every year on May Day by supporters of Jean-Marie Le Pen as a symbol of French Nationalism. Ancient rue St-Honoré, running parallel to rue de Rivoli, is one of those streets that changes style in different districts – all smart shops towards place Vendôme, local cafés and inexpensive bistros towards Les Halles. No 296, the Baroque church of **St-Roch**, is pitted with bullet holes left by Napoléon's troops when they crushed a royalist revolt in 1795. With its old houses, rue St-Roch still feels like *vieux Paris*; a couple of shops are even built into the side of the church. Across the road, at 263bis, the 1670-76 Chapelle de l'Assomption has a dome so disproportionately large that contemporaries dubbed it 'dumb dome' (*sot dôme*), a pun on Sodom. Just west of here, much talked-about boutique **Colette** at No 213 has added some oomph to what was a

► For detailed museum information and opening times, turn to **Sightseeing: Museums**, starting on page 147.
► For information on arts events turn to **Arts & Entertainment**, starting on page 275.
► For shopping information turn to **Shops & Services**, starting on page 235.

Place de la Concorde

staid shopping area, drawing a swarm of high-concept fashion boutiques such as Joseph, Mandarina Duck and Marcel Marongiu. For older Parisians, though, it's the original Colette, novelist and naughty revue performer, who remains the area's icon.

Opposite is rue du Marché St-Honoré, where Le Rubis wine bar hosts Beaujolais Nouveau quaffers every November. The street formerly led to the covered Marché St-Honoré, but that has been replaced by the shiny glass-and-steel offices of the BNP-Paribas bank. Further west along rue St-Honoré lies wonderful, eight-sided **place Vendôme** (thank you Louis XIV), with a perspective stretching from rue de Rivoli up to Opéra. At the west end of the Tuileries, **place de la Concorde**, laid out to the glorification of Louis XV, is a masterclass in the use of open space. André Malraux may have been OTT when he called it 'the most beautiful architectural complex on this planet', but it's hard not to be impressed by its grandeur. The winged Marly horses (actually copies of the originals, which are now in the **Louvre**) frame the entrance to the Champs-Elysées. The smart rue Royale, leading to the Madeleine, boasts superior tearoom Ladurée and the mythic Maxim's restaurant (featured in Lehár's opera *The Merry Widow*), which has a fabulous art nouveau interior. The rue Boissy d'Anglas proffers stylish shops and the perennially popular **Buddha Bar**; while the ultimate sporting luxuries can be found at Hermès on rue du Fbg-St-Honoré (westward extension of rue St-Honoré), as well as designer divas Yves Saint Laurent, Gucci, Guy Laroche, Karl Lagerfeld, Chloé and more. More tearooms and fine porcelain lurk in the Galerie Royale and Passage Royale.

Eglise St-Germain-l'Auxerrois

2 pl du Louvre, 1st (01.42.60.13.96). M° Pont Neuf or Louvre. **Open** 8am-8pm daily. **Map** p406 H6.

The architecture of this former royal church spans several eras: most striking though is the elaborate Flamboyant Gothic porch. Inside, there is the 13th-century Lady Chapel and splendid canopied, carved bench designed by Le Brun in 1682 for the royal family. The church achieved notoriety on 24 August 1572, when its bell, Marie, rang to signal the St-Bartholomew's Day massacre.

Eglise St-Roch

296 rue St-Honoré, 1st (01.42.44.13.20). M° Pyramides or Tuileries. **Open** 8am-7.30pm daily. **Map** p405 G5.

Begun in the 1650s in what was then the heart of Paris, this long church was designed chiefly by

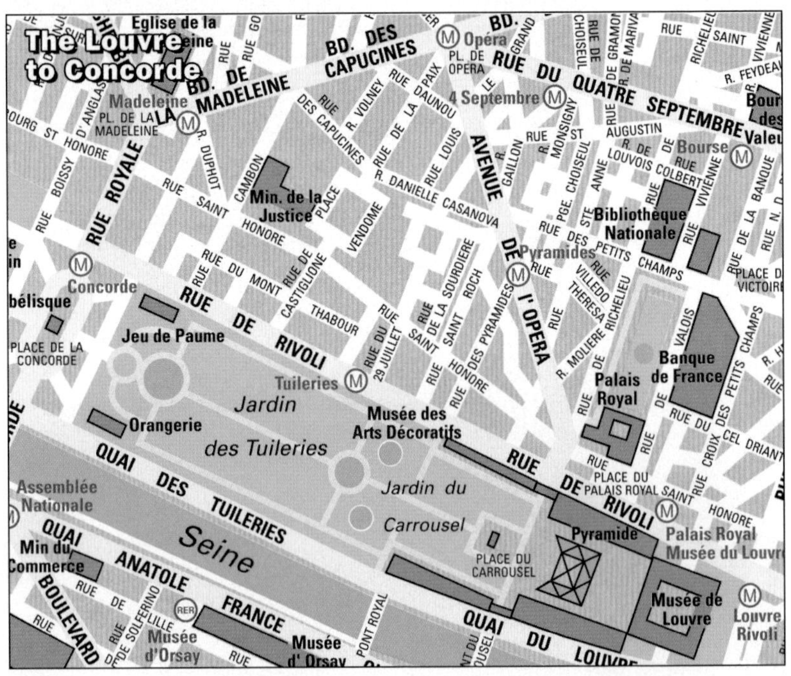

Jacques Lemercier. Illustrious, and pious, parishioners and patrons left funerary monuments: Le Nôtre, Mignard, Corneille and Diderot are all here, so too busts by Coysevox and Coustou as well as Falconet's statue *Christ on the Mount of Olives* and Anguier's superb *Nativité*. Plus, a Baroque pulpit and a cherub-adorned retable behind the rear altar. Out front, bullet holes from a 1795 shoot-out between royalists and conventionists still pit the church's facade.

Jardin des Tuileries

rue de Rivoli, 1st. M° Tuileries or Concorde. **Open** *Apr-Sept* 7am-9pm; *Oct-Mar* 7.30am-7.30pm.
Map p405 G5.

Stretching between the Louvre and place de la Concorde, the gravelled alleyways of the gardens have been a fashionable promenade ever since they opened to the public in the 16th century. André Le Nôtre, who began his illustrious career as royal gardener here in 1664 before going on to such exalted commissions as Versailles and Vaux-le-Vicomte, created the prototypical jardin à la française with its terraces and central vista running through ponds, and continuing along what would become the Champs-Elysées. When the Tuileries palace was burnt down by the Paris Commune in 1871, the park was expanded. As part of the Grand Louvre project, the most fragile sculptures, including Coysevox's winged horses, were transferred to the Louvre and replaced by copies and the Maillol sculptures returned to the Jardins du Carrousel, while replanting has restored parts of Le Nôtre's design and renewed damaged trees. Several modern sculptures have been added to develop a 'living museum', including bronzes by Laurens, Moore, Ernst, Martin and Giacommetti and Dubuffet's *Le Bel Costumé*. For gardeners, there's a specialist bookshop by place de la Concorde.

Palais du Louvre

entrance through Pyramid, Cour Napoléon, 1st (01.40.20.50.50/recorded information 01.40.20.51.51/www.louvre.fr). M° Palais-Royal.
Open 9am-6pm Thur-Sun; 9am-9.45pm Mon, Wed.
Closed 1 Jan, 1 May, 11 Nov, 25 Dec. Temporary exhibitions, Medieval Louvre 10am-9.45pm Mon, Wed-Sun. **Admission** Permanent collection and temporary exhibitions €7.50 (until 3pm); €5 after 3pm, Sun; Hall Napoléon €7; all-access €11.50; €9.50 after 3pm, Sun; free under-18s, first Sun of month.
Credit MC, V. **Map** p401 G5.

Arguably the world's greatest art collection, the Louvre's vast galleries boast antiquities and such icons as the *Mona Lisa* and Delacroix's *Liberty Leading the People*. Home to generations of French monarchs from the 14th century, a section of the massive keep, built in the 1190s by Philippe-Auguste and turned into a royal residence in the mid-14th century by Charles V, is now on view in the new underground complex. In the 1540s, François 1er asked Pierre Lescot to begin a Renaissance palace (now the western wing of

Canal go to?

Sure those clichéd old *bateaux mouches* let you kick back your heels and take in the sights along the Seine, but the quadrilingual quartet of announcers on the horn are so *tired*. Those partial to the Right Bank will tell you that a much more dynamic view of Paris can be seen from Canals de l'Ourcq, St-Denis and St Martin (81 miles long in all). Originally constructed by Napoléon Bonaparte in the 1800s, they served as alternate sources of barge traffic to maintain the Seine as the pristine centrepiece of the city. Today these service arteries, less industrial and more picturesque, are bumping with pre-requisite waterside activity: punters, joggers and the occasional topless sunbather. True, tours are more Centrum Silver than Quiksilver; but if grandma's hip is acting up, this might be just the thing. Pretend you're in Panama as onlookers flock to watch your boat free itself from the locks (nine on St-Martin) or sway a swing-bridge to make way. Or better yet, imagine yourself in a scene from the 1934 Marcel Carné classic *Hotel du Nord* ('Atmosphère!'). Depending on which tour you take, you might even get subterranean though Bastille. Plans are currently underway to feed €75,000 to make needed repairs and further develop the canal's cobblestone promenades.

Canauxrama *(01.42.39.15.00/ www.canauxrama.com). Tours from Bassin de La Villette, 13 quai de la Loire, 19th, Mº Jaurès or opposite 50 bd de la Bastille, 12th, Mº Bastille.* **Departs** 9.45am, 2.30pm daily. Bords de Marne trip: from Port de l'Arsenal 9am daily (Thur, Sat, Sun in July & Aug). **Tickets** Canal St-Martin (2½hrs) €13; €11 over-60s and students; €8 6-12s Bords de Marne (day cruise) €33 (children discouraged). **No credit cards.**

Paris Canal *(01.42.40.96.97/ www.pariscanal.com). Musée d'Orsay (Mº Solférino) to Parc de La Villette (Mº Porte de Pantin) or reverse.* **Departs** mid-Mar to mid-Nov Musée d'Orsay 9.30am daily; Parc de La Villette 2.30pm daily. **Tickets** €16; €12 12-25s, over-60s; €9 4-11s; no reductions Sun, bank holidays. **No credit cards.** Three-hour trip with commentary in French and English. Reservation required.

enclosed Cour Carrée). Continued by his successors, the different facades are etched with royal monograms – H interlaced with C and D for Henri II, his queen Catherine de Médicis and favourite Diane de Poitiers. Henri IV and Louis XIII completed the Cour Carrée and built the wing along the Seine. The pedimented facade along rue du Louvre was added by Perrault under Louis XIV, who also brought in Le Vau and Le Brun to refurbish the interior. After Louis XIV's court left for Versailles, the royals abandoned the palace and the apartments were often occupied by artists and state servants. After the Revolution, Napoléon had architects Percier and Fontaine add the grand stairway and also built the galleries along rue de Rivoli. His nephew Napoléon III added the Cour Napoléon.

The art collection was first opened to the public in 1793, but the Ministry of Finance remained in the palace until the 1980s, when the Louvre's latest great transformation, the Grand Louvre project, began. In 1989, the glass pyramid in the Cour Napoléon, designed by Sino-American architect I. M. Pei, became the museum's main entrance, and in 1993 the opening of the Richelieu Wing doubled the exhibition space. (*See also chapters* **Museums** and **Music: Classical & Opera**.)

Place de la Concorde

1st/8th. M° Concorde. **Map** p405 F5.

Place de la Concorde is Paris' largest square, with grand perspectives stretching east-west from the Louvre to the Arc de Triomphe, and north-south from the Madeleine to the Assemblée Nationale across the Seine. Famously in 1792, the centre statue of Louis XV was replaced with the revolutionaries' guillotine for the execution of Louis XVI, Marie-Antoinette and many more. The royal architect Gabriel designed the square and the two colonnaded mansions on either side of rue Royale; the west one houses the exclusive **Crillon** hotel and the Automobile Club de France, the other is the Navy Ministry. The place was embellished in the 19th century with sturdy lampposts, the Luxor obelisk, a present from the Viceroy of Egypt, and the tiered fountains. The best view is by night, from the terrace by the **Jeu de Paume** in the Tuileries gardens.

Place Vendôme

1st. M° Tuileries or Opéra. **Map** p405 G4.

Elegant place Vendôme got its name from the *hôtel particulier* built by the Duc de Vendôme previously on this site. Inaugurated in 1699, the eight-sided place was conceived by Hardouin-Mansart to show off an equestrian statue of the Sun King, which was torn down in 1792 and eventually replaced in 1806 by the Colonne de la Grande Armée. Modelled on Trajan's column in Rome and decorated with a spiral comic strip illustrating Napoléon's military exploits, it was made out of 1,250 Russian and Austrian cannons captured at the battle of Austerlitz. During the 1871 Commune this symbol of 'brute force and false glory' was pulled down; the present column is a replica. Hardouin-Mansart only designed the facades; the buildings behind were put up by nobles and speculators. Today the square is home to sparkling names like Cartier, Boucheron, Van Cleef & Arpels, Trussardi and other prestigious jewellers and fashion names, as well as banks, the Justice Ministry and the **Ritz** hotel, from where Di and Dodi set off on their fateful last journey that summer night in 1997. Incidentally, Chopin died at No 12, in 1849.

Palais-Royal & Bourse

In the 1st and 2nd arrondissements.

Across the rue de Rivoli from the Louvre, past the **Louvre des Antiquaires** antiques emporium (*see chapter* **Shops & Services**), stands the understatedly elegant **Palais-Royal**, once Cardinal Richelieu's private mansion and now the Conseil d'Etat and Ministry of Culture. The **Comédie-Française** theatre ('La Maison de Molière') stands on the southwest corner. The company, created by Louis XIV in 1680, moved here in 1799. Brass-fronted Café Nemours on place Colette is also thespian territory.

In the 1780s the **Palais-Royal** was a rumbustious centre of Parisian life, where aristocrats and the financially challenged inhabitants of the faubourgs rubbed shoulders and the coffee houses in its arcades attracted radical debate. Here Camille Desmoulins called the city to arms on the eve of Bastille Day. After the Napoleonic Wars, Wellington and Field Marshal von Blücher supposedly lost so much money at the gambling dens that Parisians claimed they had won back their entire dues for war reparations. Only haute cuisine restaurant Le Grand Véfour (founded as Café de Chartres in the 1780s) survives from this era, albeit with decoration from a little later. A more contemporary attraction at Palais-Royal is its Métro entrance: artist Jean-Michel Othoniel put a kitsch slant on Guimard's classic art nouveau design by decorating the aluminium struts with glass baubles.

Browse an eccentric world of antique dealers, philatelists and specialists in tin soldiers and musical boxes nestled under the arcades. Check out profoundly fashionable vintage clothes specialist **Didier Ludot**. Go through the arcades to rue de Montpensier to the west, and the neo-Rococo Théâtre du Palais-Royal. Opposite, next to busy bar **L'Entracte**, is one of several narrow, stepped passages that run between this road and rue de Richelieu, which, with parallel rue Ste-Anne, is a focus of Paris' Japanese community.

Paris' traditional business district is squeezed between the elegant calm of the Palais-Royal and the shopping-rabid Grands

Palais-Royal

Boulevards. The Banque de France, France's central bank, has occupied the 17th-century Hôtel de Toulouse since 1811, and its long gallery is still hung with old masters. Nearby, the pretty place des Victoires was designed, like place Vendôme, by Hardouin-Mansart, forming an intimate circle of buildings that are today dedicated to fashion. West of the place, poke your nose in shop-lined, beautifully decorated **galerie Vivienne** and **galerie Colbert** (*see p88* **The mall's first call**) and temporary exhibitions at the **Bibliothèque Nationale Richelieu**. Linger at luxury épicerie and wine merchant **Legrand** on the corner of galerie Vivienne and rue de la Banque, or take a detour along the passage des Petits Pères to see Eglise Notre-Dame-des-Victoires, the remains of an Augustine convent with paintings by Van Loo.

Rue de la Banque now leads to the **Bourse** (stock exchange), behind a commanding neo-classical colonnade. Generally, the area has a relaxed feel, positively sleepy on weekends, but animated pockets exist at places like Le Vaudeville brasserie where stockbrokers and journalists converge for lunch and after-work drinks. Rue des Colonnes is a quiet street lined with graceful porticos and acanthus motifs dating from the 1790s, while its design nemesis, the 1970s concrete and glass HQ of Agence France-Presse, France's biggest news agency, lies just across the busy rue du Quatre-Septembre. This street and rue Réaumur house some striking art nouveau buildings contrived by the press barons of the time. Although most newspapers have left, *Le Figaro* remains in rue du Louvre.

On the other side of the palace, off rue Jean-Jacques Rousseau, **galerie Véro-Dodat**, built by prosperous charcutiers in the Restoration, has neo-classical shopfronts in excellent condition (*see p88* **The mall's first call**).

Bibliothèque Nationale Richelieu

58 rue de Richelieu, 2nd (01.53.79.53.79/ www.bnf.fr). Mº Bourse. **Open** Galeries Mansart/Mazarine during exhibitions only 10am-7pm Tue-Sat; noon-7pm Sun. **Cabinet des Médailles** 1-5.45pm Mon-Fri; 1-4.45pm Sat; noon-6pm Sun. **Admission** Galerie Mansart/Mazarine €5; €4 under-26s. Cabinet des Médailles free.
Map p405 H4.

The genesis of the French National Library dates from the 1660s, when Louis XIV moved manuscripts that could not be housed in the Louvre to this lavish Louis XIII townhouse. The library was first opened to the public in 1692, and by 1724 the institution had received so many new acquisitions that the neighbouring Hôtel de Nevers was added. Some of the original painted decoration can still be seen in Galeries Mansart and Mazarine, now used for exhibitions of manuscripts and prints. Antique coins (originally known as 'médailles') and curious royal memorabilia collected by kings from Philippe-Auguste onwards are in the **Musée du Cabinet des Médailles** (*see chapter* **Museums**). Transformed in the 1860s by the innovative circular vaulted reading room designed by Henri Labrouste, the library is now curiously empty as the books have been relo-

The mall's first call

In early 19th-century Paris, the covered galleries and passages that seem so dinky and quaint today were the very latest in comfort, effluent-free shopping. You could skip from shop to shop without fear of getting the contents of last night's bedpan on your *perruque* and – adding to the carefree nature of your skipping motion – you had no worries about the nature of what your gaskins might land in. These days, of course, when it comes to choice, we've been spoilt by more modern purchasing paradises such as Mall of America and Lakeside Thurrock; but when it comes to charm and tantric browsing, Paris' covered passages still whack those suckers. Around 20 galleries and passages remain; here's a selection of the primae inter pares.

Galerie Véro-Dodat

2 rue du Bouloi/19 rue Jean-Jacques-Rousseau, 1st. Mº Louvre or Palais-Royal. **Map** p402 J5.

Probably the premium passage (thanks to its beautiful shop fronts), this is the place to cruise if you're into dolls (as in dollies) and teddy bears, at Robert Capia. By Terry has a veritable cosmos of cosmetics.

Passage Verdeau

9 rue de la Grange-Bateliere, 9th. Mº Richelieu Drouot. **Map** p402 J4.

If you like intriguing old relics – or even if you're one yourself – you'll love the antique shops in this passage that's very close to antique city central, rue Drouot. You'll find old everything in the shops here – cameras, stamps, jewels, furniture, etc.

Passage Jouffroy

10-12 bd Montmartre, 9th. Mº Richelieu-Drouot. **Map** p402 J4.

Tacked onto Passage Verdeau, Jouffroy is very much a story of the roof, the whole roof and nothing but the roof – it's a killer-diller, grand barrel-vaulted glass and iron spectacular, 'neath which lurk such delights as Mr Segas, walking stick specialist. Film buffs should beat a path to Ciné Doc for prints, stills and posters.

Passage Choiseul

40 rue des Petits-Champs/23 rue St-Augustin, 2nd. Mº Pyramides or Quatre-Septembre. **Map** p402 H4.

It's not big and it's not clever, but Choiseul proves that you can have a lot of fun in a small passage. It's great for bargain clothes, sarnies that a hod-carrier would struggle with and fantastic discount stores for those insulting gifts for the in-laws.

Passage des Panoramas

10 rue St-Marc/11 bd Montmartre, 2nd. Mº Richelieu-Drouot. **Map** p402 J4.

Tired of those same old, same old fonts on your headed notepaper? Look no further than 'Graveur', which has been knocking out personalised notelets since 1840. Fancy some lingerie that twangs sexier than Bill Black's bass? Hit César's, purveyor of pulse-raising panty-matter since the days when a glimpse of stocking was looked on as something shocking (it still is, on cops).

Passage Brady

46 rue du Fbg-St Denis, 10th. Mº Strasbourg-St-Denis. **Map** p402 K4.

This passage is wicked if you're after a curry, cheap haircut or fancy dress. Go for the hat-trick by having a short-back-and-sides at one of the barbers, hiring a sultan's costume and ordering a phaal and three pints. The closest thing Paris has to Southall.

cated to the **Bibliothèque Nationale François Mitterrand** (*see chapter* **Left Bank**), though medieval manuscripts, maps, engravings, musical scores and performing arts material remain here.

La Bourse

Palais Brongniart, pl de la Bourse, 2nd (01.49.27.55.55/www.bourse-de-paris.fr). Mº Bourse. Guided tours call a week in advance. **Admission** €8; €5 students. **No credit cards. Map** p406 H4.
After a century at the Louvre, the Palais-Royal and rue Vivienne, the stock exchange was transferred in 1826 to this building, a dignified testament to First Empire classicism designed under Napoléon by Alexandre Brongniart. It was enlarged in 1906 to create a cruciform interior, where brokers buzzed around a central enclosure, the *corbeille* (or crow's nest). Computers have rendered that design obsolete, but the daily dash for dosh ensures that the atmosphere remains frenetic.

Palais-Royal

main entrance pl du Palais-Royal, 1st (www.palais-royal.org). Mº Palais Royal. **Open** gardens only dawn-dusk daily. **Admission** free. **Map** p406 H5
Built for Cardinal Richelieu by Jacques Lemercier, the building was originally known as the Palais Cardinal. Richelieu left it to Louis XIII, whose widow, Anne d'Autriche, preferred it to the chilly Louvre and rechristened it when she moved in with her son, the young Louis XIV. In the 1780s, the Duc d'Orléans, Louis XVI's fun-loving brother, enclosed the gardens in a three-storey peristyle and filled it with cafés, theatres, sideshows, shops and apartment to raise money to reconstruct the burnt-down opera. In complete contrast to Versailles, the Palais-Royal encouraged people of all social classes to mingle and its arcades came into their own as a society trysting place. Daniel Buren's once-controversial modern installation of black and white striped columns of different heights graces the main courtyard, while the stately buildings house the Conseil d'Etat and the Ministry of Culture.

Place des Victoires

1st, 2nd. Mº Bourse. **Map** p406 H5.
The place was designed by Hardouin-Mansart in 1685 to show off a statue of Louis XIV which commemorated victories against Holland. The original disappeared in the Revolution and was replaced in 1822 with an equestrian statue by Bosio. Today, the sweeping facades shelter fashion brands Kenzo and Thierry Mugler.

Opéra & the Grands Boulevards

Mainly in the 2nd, 8th and 9th arrondissements.
Charles Garnier's wedding cake **Palais Garnier** opera (supposed birthplace of the Phantom of the Opera legend) is all gilt and grandeur as an opera house should be. Garnier was also responsible for the ritzy Café de la Paix, overlooking place de l'Opéra. In the Jockey Club (now **Hôtel Scribe**) just behind, the Lumière brothers held the world's first public cinema screening in 1895. Old England, just opposite on the boulevard des Capucines, with its antiquated wooden counters, Jacobean-style plaster ceilings and equally dated goods and service, could easily have served as their costume consultants. The **Olympia** concert hall, at 28 boulevard des Capucines, the legendary venue of Piaf and Jimi Hendrix, was knocked down but rose again just a few metres away. Across the road at No 35, pioneering portrait photographer Nadar opened a studio in the 1860s, soon frequented by writers, actors and artists including Dumas père, Doré and Offenbach. In 1874 it was the setting for the first Impressionists' exhibition. Pretty sidestreet rue Boudreau contains the 1880s **Théâtre de l'Athénée-Louis Jouvet**.

The **Madeleine**, a monument to Napoléon, guards the end of the boulevard. Its huge Corinthian columns mirror the Assemblée Nationale over the Seine, while the interior is a riot of marble and altars. Also worth contemplation is **Fauchon**, Paris' most extravagant delicatessen, **Maison de la Truffe**'s tubers and the other luxury foodstores, plus haute cuisine restaurant **Lucas Carton**, with art nouveau interior by Majorelle.

The *grands magasins* (department stores) **Printemps** and **Galeries Lafayette**, which opened behind the Palais Garnier in the late 19th century, also deserve investigation. Behind the latter, on rue Caumartin, stands the Lycée Caumartin, designed as a convent in the 1780s by Bourse architect Brongniart to become one of Paris' most prestigious lycées under Napoléon. West along Haussmann's boulevard is the small square containing the **Chapelle Expiatoire** dedicated to Louis XVI and Marie-Antoinette.

Chapelle Expiatoire

29 rue Pasquier, 8th (01.42.65.35.80). Mº St-Augustin. **Open** 1-5pm Thur-Sat. **Admission** €2.50; free under 18. **Map** p405 F3.
The chapel was commissioned by Louis XVIII in memory of his executed predecessors, his brother Louis XVI and Marie-Antoinette. Their remains, along with those of almost 3,000 revolutionary victims, including Philippe-Egalité, Charlotte Corday, Mme du Barry, Camille Desmoulins, Danton, Malesherbes and Lavoisier, were found in 1814 on the exact spot where the altar stands. The year after that, the bodies of Louis XVI and Marie-Antoinette were transferred to the **Basilique St-Denis** (*see chapter* **Beyond the Périphérique**). The chapel draws ardent (if currently unfulfilled) royalists for a memorial service in January.

Eglise St-Augustin

46 bd Malesherbes, 8th (01.45.22.23.12). M° St-Augustin. **Open** 10am-12.45pm, 3pm-6pm Mon-Fri; 10am-noon, 4-7.30pm Sat; 10am-noon, 4-7.30pm Sun. **Map** p405 F3.

St-Augustin, designed in 1860-71 by Victor Baltard, architect of the Les Halles pavilions, is not what it seems. The domed, neo-Renaissance stone exterior is merely a shell, inside is an iron vault structure; even the decorative angels are cast in metal. Bouguereau paintings hang in the transept.

Eglise de la Madeleine

pl de la Madeleine, 8th (01.44.51.69.00). M° Madeleine. **Open** 8am-6pm daily. **Map** p405 G4.

The building of a church on this site began in 1764 and in 1806, Napoléon sent instructions from Poland for Barthélémy Vignon to design a 'Temple of Glory' dedicated to his Grand Army. After the Emperor's fall, construction slowed, but the church was finally consecrated in 1845. Inside are three-and-a-half giant domes, a striking organ and pseudo-Grecian side altars amid a sea of multicoloured marble. The painting by Ziegler in the chancel depicts the history of Christianity, the ever-modest Napoléon prominent in the foreground. Now a favourite venue for society weddings.

Palais Garnier

pl de l'Opéra, 9th (box office 08.36.69.78.68/ www.opera-de-paris.fr). M° Opéra. **Open** 10am-5pm daily. **Guided tours in English** (01.40.01.22.63) 1pm and 2pm Tue-Sun €10; €5-€9 reductions. **Admission** €6; €4 over 60s; free under 26s, students. **No credit cards**. **Map** p405 G4.

Brimming with gilt and red velvet, the opera house designed by Charles Garnier in 1862 is a monument to the Second Empire haute bourgeoisie. The cushy auditorium seats more 2,000 people and the exterior is just as opulent, with sculptures of music and dance on the facade, Apollo topping the copper dome and nymphs holding torches. Carpeaux's sculpture *La Danse* shocked Parisians with its frank sensuality; in 1869 someone threw a bottle of ink over its thunderous marble thighs. The original is now safe in the Musée d'Orsay. The Garnier hosts both lyric and ballet productions. Visitors can see the library, museum, Grand Foyer, Grand Staircase and auditorium with its false ceiling, painted by Chagall in 1964. Occasionally, there's talk of returning to the original, still underneath. (*See also chapters* **Music: Classical & Opera** and **Dance**.)

Quartier de l'Europe

While hard to picture nowadays, this area north of Opéra around Gare St-Lazare was the Impressionist *quartier*. Monet depicted the exciting new steam age in the 1870s in *La Gare St-Lazare* and *Pont de l'Europe*; Caillebotte and Pissarro painted views of the new boulevards; Monet also lived in the 'hood on rue d'Edimbourg and Manet had a studio on rue de St-Petersbourg. Today, rue de Budapest remains a thriving red light district, while rue de Rome has long been home to Paris' stringed-instrument makers. Just east of Gare St-Lazare, peruse the imposing **Eglise de la Trinité** and art nouveau brasserie Mollard.

Eglise de la Trinité

pl Estienne d'Orves, 9th (01.48.74.12.77). M° Trinité. **Open** *Sept-June* 7.15am-8pm Mon-Fri; 9am-8pm Sat; 8.30am-1pm, 4.30-8pm Sun; *July-Aug* 11am-8pm Mon-Sat; 10.30am-1pm, 2pm-6pm Sun. **Map** p405 G3.

Dominated by the tiered belltower, this neo-Renaissance church was built 1861-67 by Théodore Ballu. Composer Olivier Messiaen (1908-92) was organist here for over 30 years. Guided tours on some Sundays. *Wheelchair access (call ahead).*

The Grands Boulevards

Contrary to popular belief, the string of Grands Boulevards between Madeleine and République (des Italiens, Montmartre, Poissonnière, Bonne-Nouvelle, St-Denis, St-Martin) were not built by Haussmann but by Louis XIV in 1670, replacing the fortifications of Charles II's city wall. The boulevards burgeoned after the Revolution, as new residences, theatres and covered passages were built on land repossessed from aristocrats or the church. The Grands Boulevards still offer a glimpse of the city's divergent personalities: a walk from Opéra to République leads from luxury shops to St-Denis prostitutes. Between boulevard des Italiens and rue de Richelieu is place Boeldieu and the **Opéra Comique** (*see chapter* **Music: Classical & Opera**), where *Carmen* was premiered in 1875. Alexandre Dumas fils was born at No 1 in 1824.

The 18th-century *mairie* (town hall) of the 9th arrondissement (6 rue Drouot) was once home to the infamous 'bals des victimes', where every guest had to have had a relative who lost their head... to the guillotine. The **Hôtel Drouot** auction house stands surrounded by specialist antique shops, coin and stamp dealers and wine bar Les Caves Drouot, where auction-goers and valuers congregate. There are several grand *hôtels particuliers* on rue de la Grange-Batelière, which leads on one side down curious **passage Verdeau** and on the other back to the boulevards via picturesque **passage Jouffroy** (*see p88* **The mall's first call**) and the colourful carved entrance of the **Grévin** waxworks (*see chapter* **Museums**). Across the boulevard look for **passage des Panoramas**. Wander down cobbled Cité Bergère, built in 1825 as desirable residences; though most are now budget hotels, the pretty iron and glass portes-cochères remain. The area is home to some wonderful kosher restaurants and the

Folies-Bergère, with its rejuvenated can-can kick girls. The palatial art deco cinema **Le Grand Rex** offers an interesting backstage tour. East of here are Louis XIV's twin triumphal arches, the **Porte St-Martin** and **Porte St-Denis**.

Le Grand Rex

1 bd Poissonnière, 2nd (cinema info 08.36.68.70.23/www.legrandrex.com). M° Bonne Nouvelle. Tour Les Etoiles du Rex every 50 mins 10am-7pm Wed-Sun, public holidays, daily in school holidays. **Admission** €7.50; €6.50 under-16s; €12 tour and film; €11 under-16s. **Map** p406 J4.

Opened in 1932, the huge art deco cinema was designed by Auguste Bluysen with fantasy Hispanic interiors by US designer John Eberson. Go behind the scenes in the loony 50-minute guided tour which includes a presentation about the construction of the auditorium, a visit to the production room complete with nerve-jolting Sensurround effects. *Wheelchair access (call ahead).*

Hôtel Drouot

9 rue Drouot, 9th (01.48.00.20.20/ recorded information 01.48.00.20.17). M° Richelieu-Drouot. **Open** 10am-6pm Mon-Sat. **Map** p 405 H3.

A spiky aluminium and marble-clad concoction is the unlikely setting for the hub of France's secondary art market, though now rivalled by Sotheby's and Christie's. Inside, escalators whizz you up to small salerooms, where medieval manuscripts, 18th-century furniture, Oriental arts, modern paintings and fine wines might be up for sale. Details of forthcoming sales are published in the weekly *Gazette de L'Hôtel Drouot*, sold at newsstands. Prestige sales take place at Drouot-Montaigne. *Partial wheelchair access.*

Branches: Drouot-Montaigne, 15 av Montaigne, 8th (01.48.00.20.80); Drouot Nord, 64 rue Doudeauville, 18th (01.48.00.20.90).

Porte St-Denis & Porte St-Martin

corner rue St-Denis/bd St-Denis, 2nd/10th; 33 bd St-Martin, 3rd/10th. **Map** p406 K4.

These twin triumphal gates were erected in 1672 and 1674 at important entry points as part of Colbert's strategy to glorify Paris and celebrate Louis XIV's victories on the Rhine. Modelled on the triumphal arches of ancient Rome, the Porte St-Denis is particularly harmonious, based on a perfect square with a single arch, bearing Latin inscriptions and decorated with military trophies and battle scenes.

Les Halles & Sentier

In the 1st and 2nd arrondissements.

Once the plump, jolly belly of Paris, few places epitomise the transformation of central Paris more than **Les Halles**, the city's wholesale fruit and veg market since 1181 when the covered markets were established by King Philippe-Auguste. In 1969 the market was relocated to the southern suburb of Rungis, leaving a giant hole – nicknamed 'le trou des Halles' (a pun on bum-hole). After a long political dispute it was filled in the early 1980s by the miserably designed **Forum des Halles** shopping and transport hub. One pavilion was

Palais Garnier

saved and reconstructed at Nogent-sur-Marne (*see chapter* **Beyond the Périphérique**). The Forum is grubby; hold onto your handbag and your nose (pee and fried lamb is the *parfum maison*) and leave a trail of croissant crumbs so you can find your way out. The mayor does have plans for a revamp and has asked architects, town planners and landscape artists to produce a global project, promising 'rien ne sera interdit' (nothing will be forbidden); except maybe the disaffected suburban boys and assorted homeless that currently make Les Halles their own.

East of the Forum is place des Innocents, centred on the Renaissance Fontaine des Innocents. The structure was moved here from the city's main burial ground, nearby Cimetière des Innocents, which was demolished in 1786 after flesh-eating rats started gnawing into people's living rooms, and the bones transferred to the **Catacombes** (*see chapter* **Left Bank**). Pedestrianised rue des Lombards is a beacon for nightlife, with bars, restaurants and the **Baiser Salé**, **Sunset**, **Sunside** and **Duc des Lombards** jazz clubs (*see chapter* **Popular Music**). King Henri IV was assassinated in 1610 by Catholic fanatic François Ravaillac on ancient rue de la Ferronnerie when the royal carriage was held up in the traffic. The street has now become an extension of the Marais gay circuit so the only thing Henri would be held up for today is, perhaps, ridicule.

By the Pont-Neuf is **La Samaritaine** department store, currently metamorphosing from ugly ducking into serious luxury swan after a takeover by LVMH. It has a fantastic art nouveau staircase and verrière (glazed roof) and the Toupary restaurant and tearoom at the top also offers great views. From here the quai de la Mégisserie, thickly lined with horticultural suppliers and pet shops, leads towards Châtelet.

On the expressway fronting the river, Paris-Plage, a three-kilometre Seine of a beach, materialises in July-August when 3,000 tonnes of sand is trucked-in (*see p116* **The beach is back!**). Looming over the sun seekers is the **Eglise St-Eustache**, with Renaissance motifs inside and chunky flying buttresses without (just like the *plage*). At the western end of the gardens is the circular, domed **Bourse du Commerce**. Clues of the market past linger in the 24-hour brasserie Au Pied de Cochon, and the all-night-bistro La Tour de Montlhéry.

The area west of Les Halles is for material girls and boys: **Agnès b**'s empire – along most of rue du Jour – with streetwise outlets such as **Kiliwatch** and **Le Shop** on nearby streets. If you're in the mood for food, head east to pedestrianised rue Montorgueil and its belt of cafés, bakeries and the like. At 20 rue Etienne-Marcel, the restored **Tour Jean Sans Peur** is a strange relic of the fortified townhouse (1409-11) of Jean, Duc de Bourgogne.

The ancient easternmost stretch of the rue St-Honoré runs into the southern edge of Les Halles. The Fontaine du Trahoir stands at the corner with rue de l'Arbre-Sec. Opposite, the fine Hôtel de Truden (52 rue de l'Arbre-Sec) was built in 1717 for a wealthy wine merchant. Running towards the Seine south of the gardens, ancient little streets such as rue des Lavandiers-Ste-Opportune and narrow rue Jean-Lantier show a human side of Les Halles that has yet to be swept away.

The best Atrocities

Eglise St. Roch
Napoleonic troops put the clamp down on a royalist revolt (*see p84*).

Mur des Fédérés
Wall in Pere Lachaise against which Paris Commune members were felled (*see p115*).

rue de la Ferronnerie
Where King Henri IV met his maker while stuck in traffic – what a bitch (*see p92*).

Tour Jean Sans Peur
Jean 'the Fearless' schemed here and was creamed here (*see p93*).

Place de la Concorde
The guillotine was rolled into the centre before it rolled heads (*see p86*).

Mairie of the 9th
Invitations for fancy feasts required kinship with a beloved beheaded (*see p90*).

Hôtel de Ville
Now Delanoë's digs, it was once the seat of Robespierre (*see p97*).

Cimetière de Picpus
Resting place for 1,300 lost in one bloody week (*see p101*).

Bourse du Commerce
2 rue de Viarmes, 1st (01.55.65.78.41). M° Louvre. RER Les Halles. **Open** 9am-6pm Mon-Fri, limited access. Tours groups of up to 30, reserve in advance (01.55.65.70.18), 1 1/2hr tour, €42 per group. **No credit cards. Map** p406 J5.

Now housing some of the offices of the Paris Chamber of Commerce (*see chapter* **Directory**), a world trade centre and a commodity market for coffee and sugar, the city's former main grain market

Eglise St-Eustache

was built in 1767 by Nicolas Le Camus de Mézières. It was later covered by a wooden dome and replaced by an avant-garde iron structure in 1809 – then covered in copper, now in glass. *Wheelchair access.*

Eglise St-Eustache

rue du Jour, 1st (01.40.26.47.99). M° Les Halles/ RER Châtelet-Les Halles. **Open** 9am-7.30pm daily. Tour first Sun of every month 3pm, free (phone ahead). **Map** p406 J5.

This barn-like church (built 1532-1640) features paintings in the side chapel such as *Descent from the Cross* by Luca Giordano and John Armleder's contemporary *Pour Paintings* added in 2000. Works by Thomas Couture adorn the early 19th-century Lady Chapel. A favourite with music-lovers, the church boasts a magnificent 8,000-pipe organ (free recitals 5.30pm Sun).

Forum des Halles

1st. M° Les Halles/RER Châtelet-Les Halles. **Map** p406 J5.

This labyrinthine concrete mall and site of a major Métro/RER interchange extends three levels underground and includes the Ciné Cité multiplex, the Forum des Images and a swimming pool, as well as mass-market clothing chains, fast food outlets, branches of Fnac, Habitat and the Forum des Créateurs, a section given over to young designers. Saturdays are hell as gangs of teenagers descend on the place by RER.

Tour Jean Sans Peur

20 rue Etienne-Marcel, 2nd (01.40.26.20.28/ http://tour.jeansanspeur.free.fr). M° Etienne-Marcel. **Open** termtime 1.30-6pm, Wed, Sat, Sun; school holidays 1.30-6pm Tue-Sun. **Admission** €5; €3 7-18s, students; free under-7s. Tour 2pm; €8. **No Credit Cards**. **Map** p406 J5.

This is the remnant of the townhouse of Jean Sans Peur, Duc de Bourgogne. Jean got his nickname (the fearless) from his exploits in Bulgaria but he was also responsible for the assassination in 1407 of Louis d'Orléans, his rival and the cousin of Charles VI, which sparked the Hundred Years' War. Jean fled Paris but returned two years later to add this show-off tower to his mansion. The tower was also meant to protect him from any vengeance on the part of the widow of Louis d'Orléans (not so fearless, then?), but it seems his card was fatally marked: in 1419 he was assassinated by a partisan of the future Charles VII. Today you can climb the multi-storey tower. Halfway up is a remarkable vault carved with naturalistic branches of oak, hawthorn and hops, symbols of Jean Sans Peur and Burgundian power.

Rue St-Denis & Sentier

Sentier, Paris' garment district, has been a traditional trading area since the Middle Ages while cocky rue St-Denis has relied on trade of a different kind: strumpets and strip joints. In recent years the latter has been partly pushed back by energetic pedestrianisation and by the arrival of practitioners of another type of entrepreneurial activity prepared to do virtually anything for money – the start-ups.

The tackiness is gloriously unremitting along the traditional red-light district of rue St-Denis (and northern continuation rue du Faubourg-St-Denis), which snakes north from the Forum. Kerb-crawlers gawp at the neon adverts for 'l'amour sur scène', and size up defiantly dignified prostitutes in doorways.

Between rue des Petits-Carreaux and rue St-Denis is the site of the Cour des Miracles – a refuge where, after a day's begging, paupers would 'miraculously' regain use of their eyes or limbs. An abandoned aristocratic estate, it was a sanctuary for the underworld for decades until it was cleared out in 1667. Sentier's surrounding streets throng with porters shouldering linen bundles, while sweatshops churn out copies of catwalk creations. No surprise that the area attracts hundreds of illegal and semi-legal foreign workers. Streets such as rue du Caire, d'Aboukir and du Nil, named after Napoléon's Egyptian campaign, are connected by a maze of passages.

Beaubourg

Fbg-St-Denis to Gare du Nord

North of Porte St-Denis along the rue du Fbg-St-Denis is almost souk-like with its food shops, narrow passages and sinister courtyards. The brasserie Julien boasts one of the finest art nouveau interiors in Paris while garishly lit **passage Brady** is a surprising piece of India in Paris, full of restaurants, hairdressers and costume shops (*see p88* **The mall's first call**). Rue des Petites Ecuries was once known for saddlers but now has shops, cafés and Brasserie Flo, as well as top jazz venue **New Morning** (*see chapter* **Music: Popular Music**).

Eglise St-Vincent de Paul, at the top of rue d'Hauteville, has twin towers and cascading terraced gardens, and is about as close as Paris gets to Rome's Spanish Steps. Just behind, on rue de Belzunce, is the modern bistro Chez Michel and its offshoot Chez Casimir. On boulevard Magenta, the covered Marché St-Quentin was built in the 1860s.

Popular theatres such as the mosaic-filled neo-Renaissance Théâtre Antoine-Simone Berriau and the art deco Eldorado line up on boulevard de Strasbourg. At No 2, another neo-Renaissance creation houses Paris' last fan maker and the **Musée de l'Eventail** (*see chapter* **Museums**). Sandwiched between Gare de l'Est and Canal St-Martin stand the near-derelict remains of the Couvent des Récollets and the park of Square Villemin.

Couvent des Récollets

bd de Strasbourg, 10th. **Map** p402 L3.

This 17th-century Franciscan convent served as women's shelter, barracks and hospital after the Revolution. A glorious building, it fell into disrepear after years of neglect but in 2003 was being renovated with a view to turning it into studios for visiting international artists.

Eglise St-Vincent de Paul

pl Franz-Liszt, 10th (01.48.78.47.47). M° Gare du Nord. **Open** 8am-noon, 2-7pm Mon-Sat; 4.30-7.30pm Sun. **Map** p406 K2.

Imposingly set at the top of terraced gardens, the church was begun in 1824 by Lepère and completed 1831-44 by Hittorff. The twin towers, pedimented Greek temple portico and evangelist figures on the parapet are in classical mode. The interior has a double storey arcade of columns, murals by Flandrin, and church furniture by Rude.

Gare du Nord

rue de Dunkerque, 10th (08.91.36.20.20). M° Gare du Nord. **Map** p406 K2.

The grandest of the great 19th-century train stations (and Eurostar terminal since 1994) was designed by Hittorff in 1861-64. A conventional stone facade, with Ionic capitals and statues representing towns served by the station, hides a vast, bravura iron and glass vault. These days, the impressively light and airy refurbishment of the suburban-lines section of the station that borders the rue du Faubourg-St-Denis makes the Eurostar's glass-topped digs look a tad drab.

Beaubourg & the Marais

In the 3rd and 4th arrondissements.
Between boulevard Sébastopol and the Bastille lies Beaubourg – HQ for the **Centre Pompidou** since 1977 – and the Marais, built between the 16th and 18th centuries and now jam-packed with boutiques, museums and bars.

Beaubourg & Hôtel de Ville

Contemporary Parisian architecture began with the **Centre Pompidou**, and this international benchmark of inside-out high-tech is as much of an attraction as its contents, which include the impressive Musée National de l'Art Moderne. On the piazza is the **Atelier Brancusi**, the sculptor's reconstructed studio (*see chapter* **Museums**). On the other side of the piazza lies rue Quincampoix with its art galleries, bars and curious passage Molière. Beside the Centre Pompidou is place Igor Stravinsky and the funky Fontaine Stravinsky, designed by the late Nikki de Saint Phalle and Jean Tinguely, and the red brick **IRCAM** contemporary music institute (*see chapter* **Music: Classical & Opera**). The church of St-Merri, which has a Flamboyant Gothic facade complete with an androgynous demon leering over the doorway, sits on the south side of the square. Inside are a carved wooden organ loft, the joint contender for the oldest bell in Paris (1331) and 16th-century stained glass.

Beyond Châtelet looms the **Hôtel de Ville**, Paris' city hall and home to the mayor. The centre of municipal power since 1260, it overlooks a square of the same name, once known as place de Grève. Protestant heretics were burnt in the place during the Wars of Religion, and, rather grimly, the guillotine stood here during the Terror, when Danton, Marat and Robespierre made the Hôtel their seat of government. Revolutionaries made it their base in the 1871 Commune, but the building was set on fire by the Communards themselves and wrecked during savage fighting. It was rebuilt on a grander palatial scale in fanciful neo-Renaissance style with statues representing French cities along the facade.

Centre Pompidou

rue Beaubourg, 4th (01.44.78.12.33/ www.centrepompidou.fr). M° Hôtel de Ville or Rambuteau/RER Châtelet-Les Halles. **Open** 11am-9pm Mon, Wed-Sun. Closed 1 May. **Admission** €5.50-€8.50; €3.50-€6.50 18-26; free under 18s. **Credit** MC, V. **Map** p406 K5/K6.

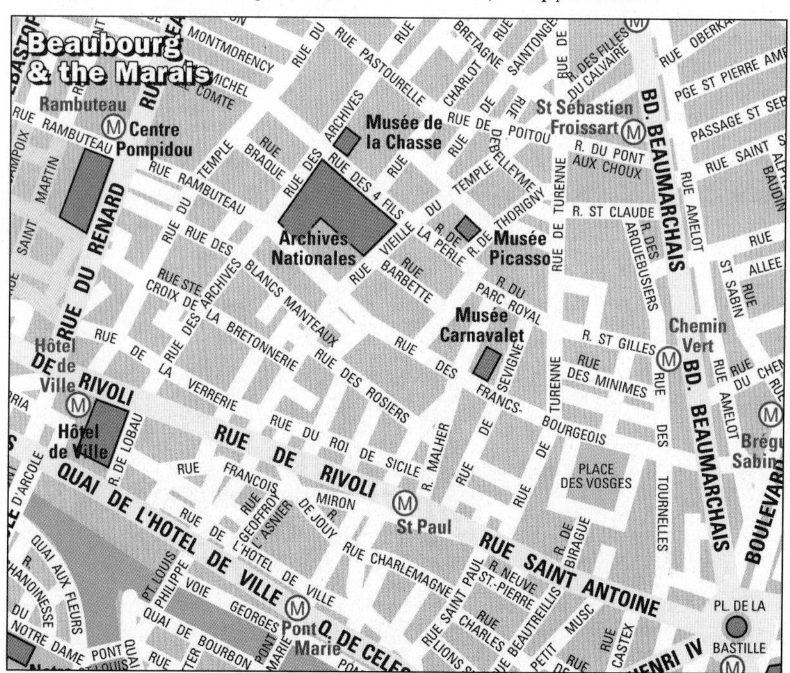

DE
Tarte

The primary colours and exposed pipes and air ducts make this one of the most recognisable buildings in Paris. Commissioned in 1968, the centre is the work of the Italo-British duo Renzo Piano and Richard Rogers. Their 'inside-out', boilerhouse approach put air-conditioning and lifts outside, leaving a freely adaptable space within. When the centre opened in 1977, its success exceeded all expectations. After a two-year revamp the centre reopened in January 2000 with an enlarged museum, renewed performance spaces, vista-rich Georges restaurant and a mission to get back to the stimulating interdisciplinary mix of old (*see chapter* **Museums**).

Hôtel de Ville

Salon d'accueil 2 rue de Rivoli, 4th (01.42.76.43.43). M° Hôtel de Ville. **Open** 10am-7pm Mon-Sat; 2-7pm Sun. Free guided tour once a week. **Map** p406 K6.
The impressive multi-purpose Hôtel de Ville is administrative centre, a place to entertain visiting dignitaries and, outside on the forecourt, a people's palace where events such as the World Cup are projected on a big screen and concert, exhibitions and trade fairs held. Small exhibitions are held in the Salon d'accueil, the rest of the building accessible only by guided tour. Mayor Delanoë himself prefers to live in a dinky, bijou pad in the Marais rather than the lofty apartment here.

Tour St-Jacques

pl du Châtelet, 4th. M° Châtelet. **Map** p406 J6.
Much-loved by the Surrealists, this solitary Flamboyant Gothic bell-tower is the remains of the St-Jacques-La-Boucherie church, built for the powerful Butchers' Guild in 1523. The statue of Pascal at the base recalls his experiments on atmospheric pressure carried out here in the 17th century. A weather station now crowns the 52-metre-high tower, which can only be admired from outside.

The Marais

The Marais, a bewitching area whose narrow streets are dotted with aristocratic *hôtels particuliers*, art galleries, fashion boutiques and stylish cafés, lies east of Roman rue St-Martin and rue du Renard. Window shop, but take the time to look up at the beautiful carved doorways and the early street signs carved into the stone. The Marais, or 'marsh', started life as piece of swampy ground inhabited by a few monasteries, sheep and market gardens. In the 16th century the elegant Hôtel Carnavalet and Hôtel Lamoignon exemplified the area's phenomenal rise as an aristocratic residential district (*see p99* **Merry Marais mansions**); Henri IV began constructing the **place des Vosges** in 1605. Nobles followed, building smart townhouses where famous literary ladies such as Mme de Sévigné and Mlle de Scudéry and influential courtesan Ninon de l'Enclos held court. The area fell from fashion a century later; happily, many of the narrow streets were essentially unchanged as mansions were transformed into industrial workshops, schools and tenements. A traditional home to minorities, it's a place where you'll see Orthodox Jews shooting the breeze alongside out-and-about gay guys; this is no kind of ghetto; it's mixed, it's cool, and, to many, represents Paris at its best.

The rue des Francs-Bourgeois, crammed with elegant mansions and unique boutiques, runs right through the Marais, and the tearoom Les Enfants Gâtés ('spoiled children') sums up its disposition. Culture buffs seek out two of Paris' most refined early 18th-century residences: Hôtel d'Albret (No 31) which is the venue for jazz concerts during the Paris quartier d'été festival (*see chapter* **Festivals & Events**) and Hôtel de Soubise (No 60), the national archives, where interiors by Boucher and Lemoine can be seen as part of the **Musée de l'Histoire de France** (*see chapter* **Museums**). On the corner of the rue des Francs-Bourgeois and rue Pavée is the austere renaissance Hôtel Lamoignon. Built in 1585 for Diane de France, Henri II's illegitimate daughter, it now houses the **Bibliothèque Historique de la Ville de Paris** (*see chapter* **Directory**).

The stunning **place des Vosges** occupies the eastern end of the street. At one corner is the **Maison de Victor Hugo** (*see chapter* **Museums**) and just over the square is the luxuriously pricey Ambroisie restaurant. An archway in the southwest corner leads to the genteel Hôtel de Sully, home to the **Patrimoine Photographique** since 1994 (*see chapter* **Museums**).

Workaday rue du Temple, once the road leading to the Templars' church, is full of surprises. Near rue de Rivoli, the **Latina** (*see chapter* **Film**) specialises in Latin American films and holds tango *bals* in the room above. At No 41 an archway leads into the former Aigle d'Or coaching inn, now the **Café de la Gare** café-théâtre, Le Studio Tex-Mex and dance studios. Further north, the Hôtel de St-Aignan at No 71 contains the **Musée d'Art et d'Histoire du Judaïsme** (*see chapter* **Museums**).

The district's two most important museums are also in sumptuous hôtels. The **Musée Carnavalet**, dedicated to the history of Paris, runs across the Hôtel Carnavalet, once home to famous letter-writer Mme de Sévigné, and the later Hôtel le Peletier de St-Fargeau. The Hôtel Salé on rue de Thorigny, built in 1656 and nicknamed after its salt tax collector owner, has been finely restored and extended to house the **Musée National Picasso**.

The Marais is also home to Paris' oldest Jewish community, dating from the 12th century, centred on rue des Rosiers, rue des Ecouffes and rue Pavée (where there's a synagogue designed by Guimard). Originally made up mainly of Ashkenazi Jews who arrived after the pogroms (many were later deported during World War II), the community expanded in the 1950s and 60s with a wave of Sephardic Jewish immigration following French withdrawal from North Africa. As a result, there are now many falafel shops alongside the Jewish bakers and delis, such as **Finkelstijn**.

The lower ends of rue des Archives and rue Vieille-du-Temple are the centre of café life and happening bars, including cutesy **Petit Fer à Cheval** and cosmopolitan café La Chaise au Plafond in the neighbouring rue du Trésor. This area is the hub of Paris' gay scene (*see chapter* **Gay & Lesbian**).

Place des Vosges

4th. M° St-Paul. **Map** p406 L6.

The first planned square in Paris was built in 1605-12 by Henri IV. Intimate, with beautifully harmonious red-brick-and-stone arcaded facades and steeply pitched roofs, it is quite distinct from the pomp of later Bourbon Paris. Moreover, it is perfectly symmetrical. Originally the place Royale, its present name dates from the Napoleonic Wars; the Vosges was the first region of France to pay its war taxes. Mme de Sévigné, salon hostess and letter-writer, was born here in 1626. At that time the garden was the scene of duels and romantic trysts; now it attracts those less hot-under-the collar – tourists, and children from the nearby kindergarten.

The Temple & Arts et Métiers

The northern, less gentrified half of the Marais towards place de la République is awash with tiny local bars, costume jewellery and rag-trade wholesalers, plus contemporary art galleries (*see chapter* **Galleries**) and recently arrived fashion designers. The Quartier du Temple was once a fortified, semi-independent entity under the Knights Templar. The round church and keep have been replaced by Square du Temple and the Carreau du Temple clothes market. The keep became a prison in the Revolution, where the royal family was held in 1792. The north-east corner of the Marais hinges on the **Musée des Arts et Metiers**, a science museum in a 12th-century chapel (*see chapter* **Museums**).

The St-Paul District

In 1559, Henri II was mortally wounded in a jousting tournament on what is now rue St-Antoine; he is commemorated by the marble *La Vierge de Douleur* by Pilon in **St-Paul-St-Louis** church. Towards the Bastille, the heavily domed church of the Visitation Ste-Marie was designed in the 1630s by Mansart. South of rue St-Antoine is a more sedate residential area known as St-Paul. The Village St-Paul, a colony of antique sellers spread across small interlinked courtyards between rues St-Paul, Charlemagne and quai des Célestins, is a promising source of 1930s and 50s furniture, kitchenware and wine gadgets (open Mon, Thur-Sun). On rue des Jardins-St-Paul is the largest surviving section of the **wall of Philippe-Auguste**. The infamous poisoner Marquise de Brinvilliers lived at Hôtel de Brinvilliers (12 rue Charles V) in the 1630s. She killed her father and brothers to inherit the family fortune and was only caught after her lover died – of natural causes.

Two of the Marais' finest mansions are on rue François-Miron: Hôtel de Beauvais, No 68, and Hôtel Hénault de Cantorbe, renovated to incorporate the **Maison Européenne de la Photographie** (*see chapter* **Museums**). At No 17 rue Geoffroy l'Asnier, the **Mémorial du Martyr Juif Inconnu** has been closed while a museum dedicated to the Holocaust is built. Down rue de Fourcy towards the river is the Hôtel de Sens, which now houses the **Bibliothèque Forney**, specialising in posters and postcards. Across from the tip of the Ile St-Louis the square Henri-Galli contains a rebuilt fragment of the Bastille prison and the **Pavillon de l'Arsenal** (*see chapter* **Museums**).

Eglise St-Paul-St-Louis

99 rue St-Antoine, 4th (01.42.72.30.32). M° Bastille or St-Paul. **Open** 9am-8pm Mon-Fri; 9-8.30pm Sat-Sun. **Map** p406 L6.

The domed Baroque Counter-Reformation church, completed in 1641, is modelled, like all Jesuit churches, on the Gesù in Rome, with its single nave, side chapels and three-storey hierarchical facade bearing (replacement) statues of Saints Louis, Anne and Catherine. The provider of confessors to the Kings of France, it was was one of the most richly endowed churches in France before Revolutionary iconoclasts broke in and stole its treasures including the hearts of Louis XIII and XIV. In 1802 it became a church again and now houses Delacroix's *Christ in the Garden of Olives*.

Fortified wall of Philippe-Auguste

rue des Jardins-St-Paul, 4th (www.philippe-auguste.com). M° Pont Marie or St-Paul. **Map** p406 L7.

King Philippe-Auguste (1165-1223), the first great Parisian builder since the Romans, enclosed the entire city within a great wall. The largest surviving section, complete with towers, extends along rue des Jardins-St-Paul. Another chunk is at 3 rue Clovis (5th) and odd remnants of towers are dotted around the Marais and St-Germain-des-Prés.

Merry Marais mansions

Imposing these posh town houses may be, but when you consider that 'marais' is French for 'swamp', well it takes the edge off a bit, doesn't it? *Swamp Mansions* may sound like a come-back CD from a dodgy 80s goth-metal band, but be warned: these joints are for aesthetes and many a literary romp has been held within. Not all the *hôtels* are open to the public (or open up), although some have official walking tours or open during the *Journées du Patrimoine* (*see chapter* **Festivals and Events**). Others can be visited as museums.

Hôtel d'Albret

31 rue des Francs-Bourgeois, 4th. Mº St-Paul. **Map** p406 L6.

In the 1650s Mme de Montespan, mistress of Louis XIV, took on Françoise d'Aubigné as governess to her eight illegitimate children. Françoise worked her way up to become the king's new official mistress, Mme de Maintenon – and she got the house.

Hôtel Carnavalet

23 rue de Sévigné, 3rd. Mº St-Paul. **Map** p406 L6.

Carnavalet's U-shaped layout set the model for the Paris *hôtel particulier*. Now, together with Mme de Sévigny's former residence, it forms the historical **Musée Carnavalet**.

Hôtel Donon

8 rue Elzévir, 3rd. Mº St-Paul. **Map** p406 L6.

This pretty *hôtel* built in 1598 gives an overall impression of verticality with its long windows, steeply pitched roof and two narrow wings. You can see its 18th-century panelled interiors as part of the **Musée Cognacq-Jay**.

Hôtel Guénégaud

60 rue des Archives, 3rd. Mº Rambuteau. **Map** p402 K5.

The Hôtel Guénégaud has been attributed to Mansart for its harmonious proportions. Now beautifully restored, it is filled with the stuffed animals of the **Musée de la Chasse**.

Hôtel Lamoignan

24 rue Pavée, 4th. Mº St-Paul. **Map** p406 L6.

This gracious *hôtel* was built in 1585 for Diane de France, illegitimate daughter of Henri II. The courtyard is magisterial, with giant Corinthian pilasters (for the first time in Paris). Now home to the **Bibliothèque Historique de la Ville de Paris**.

Hôtel Carnavalet

Hôtel Salé

5 rue de Thorigny, 3rd. Mº St-Paul. **Map** p406 L6.

Now housing the **Musée Picasso**, the *hôtel*'s name comes from the salt tax that made its original owner his fortune. A spectacular courtyard is overlooked by sphinxes.

Hôtel de Soubise/Hôtel de Rohan

60 rue des Francs-Bourgeois, 3rd. Mº Hôtel de Ville. **Map** p406 L6.

The residence was begun in 1704 for Prince and Princesse de Soubise. Architect Delamair incorporated the turreted medieval gateway of the Hôtel de Clisson into one side of the *cour d'honneur*. Rococo apartments were decorated by Boucher, Natoire, Restout and Van Loo.

Hôtel de Sully

62 rue St-Antoine, 4th (01.44.61.20.00). Mº St-Paul. **Map** p406 L7.

Designed by Jean Androuet du Cerceau in 1624, this is a perfectly restored mansion. The fine interior is closed to the public, but walk through the two beautifully proportioned courtyards, with allegorical reliefs of the seasons. Today it houses the **Mission du Patrimoine Photographique**.

The Bastille & eastern Paris

Mainly in the 11th and 12th arrondissements.
Place de la Bastille, traditionally the frontier between central Paris and the more proletarian east, has remained a potent symbol of popular revolt ever since the prison-storming that inaugurated the Revolution. While the place is still a favourite spot for demonstrations, and even hosted a son et lumière extravaganza to celebrate the memory of François Mitterrand in 2001, the influx of cafés, restaurants, galleries and bars beginning in the 1980s has made it very much the in-place to get legless.

The site of the prison itself is now a Société Générale bank while the gap left by the castle ramparts forms the present-day square, dominated by the massive, modern **Opéra Bastille**. Opened in 1989 on the bicentennial of Bastille Day, it remains controversial, but productions sell out and, along with the creation of the Port de l'Arsenal marina to the south, it has contributed to the area's rejuvenation.

The cobbled rue de Lappe typifies the Bastille's seismic shift, as the last remaining furniture workshops, the 1930s Balajo dance hall, old Auvergnat bistro La Galoche d'Aurillac and grocer Chez Teil hold out against a dizzying array of gift shops and theme bars that team with teens on weekends.

A hint of the area's old working-class flavour remains at the Sunday morning market on boulevard Richard Lenoir and in rue de la Roquette; rue du Faubourg-St-Antoine still has furniture-makers' ateliers hidden down long passageways hung with greenery. Gaudy furniture stores line the street but clothes shops and bars, including the salsa-themed Barrio Latino in an Eiffel-designed building, are making inroads. Rue de Charonne has fashionable bars, bistros and dealers in hip 60s furniture. Along with rue Keller, the patch is a focus for record shops, streetwear and, increasingly, young fashion designers. There's still something of a village spirit and the in-crowd hangs out at the Pause Café or Bistro du Peintre.

The main thoroughfares, however, reveal only half the story. Narrow street frontages hide cobbled alleys, lined with craftsmen's workshops or quirky bars and bistros that date back to the 18th century. Peruse the cours de l'Ours, du Cheval Blanc, du Bel Air (with hidden garden), de la Maison Brûlée, the passage du Chantier on Fbg-St-Antoine, the rustic-looking passage de l'Etoile d'Or and the passage de l'Homme with old wooden shop fronts on rue de Charonne. This area was originally outside the city walls on the lands of the Convent of St-Antoine (parts of which survive as the Hôpital

La Promenade Plantée. *See p103.*

St-Antoine). In the Middle Ages skilled furniture makers operating outside of the city's restrictive guilds began a tradition of free-thinking, a development which made this area a powder keg during the Revolution.

Further down rue du Fbg-St-Antoine is place d'Aligre, home to a rowdy North African vegetable market, more sedate covered market and weekend *marché aux puces*. Marketeers and locals congregate on Sunday mornings at the Baron Bouge wine bar, where you can take your *cubitainer* to fill up on cheap barrel wine. The road ends in the major intersection place de la Nation, where the guillotine was moved when the stench became too much at place de la Bastille. **Cimetière de Picpus** contains the graves of many of the Terror's victims, as well as American War of Independence hero General La Fayette.

Boulevard Beaumarchais separates rowdy Bastille from the elegant Marais, and the polygonal **Cirque d'Hiver** winter circus building, designed by Hittorff, is reminiscent of the area's animated past (*see chapter* **Cabaret, Circus & Comedy**). Further east, on rue de la Roquette, a small park and playground surrounded by modern housing marks the site of the prison de la Roquette, where a plaque remembers the 4,000 resistance members imprisoned here in World War II.

Cimetière de Picpus

35 rue de Picpus, 12th (01.43.44.18.54). M° Nation. **Open** *16 Apr-14 Oct* 2-6pm Tue-Sun; *15 Oct-14 Apr* 2-4pm Tue-Sat. **Admission** €2.50. **No credit cards**. **Map** p407 Q8.

Redolent with revolutionary associations, both French and US, this cemetery in a working convent is resting place for more than 1300 victims of the *semaine sanglante*, guillotined at the barrière du Trône (now place de l'Ile de Réunion) between 14 June and 27 July 1794. At the end of a walled garden is a graveyard of aristocratic French families. In one corner is the tomb of statesman La Fayette, who fought in the American War of Independence and had been married to a Noailles. The sites of two communal graves are marked out and you can see the doorway where the carts carrying them arrived. It was only thanks to a maid who had seen the carts that the site was rediscovered and the cemetery and adjoining convent founded by descendents of the Noailles family. In the small chapel, two tablets on either end of the transept list the names and occupation of those executed: 'domestic', 'farmer', 'employee', figure alongside 'lawyer', 'abbess' and 'prince and priest'.

Opéra Bastille

pl de la Bastille, 12th (box office 08.36.69.78.68/ guided visits 01.40.01.19.70/www.opera-de-paris.fr). M° Bastille. **Open** Guided visits only – phone for details. **Admission** €10; €8 over 60s; €5 under 26s. No credit cards. **Map** p407 M7.

Sightseeing

Opened in 1989, the Opéra Bastille has been controversial for several reasons: the cost, the scale, the architecture, and the opera productions. To some it was a stroke of genius to implant a high-culture edifice in a working-class area; others thought it typical Mitterrand skulduggery; still others found it patronising. Although it was intended as an 'opera for the people', that never materialised; opera and ballet are shared with the Palais Garnier. (*See chapters* **Music: Classical & Opera** and **Dance**.)

Place de la Bastille

4th/11th/12th. M° Bastille. **Map** p407 M7.

Nothing remains of the infamous prison which, on 14 July 1789, was stormed by the forces of the plebeian revolt. Though only seven prisoners remained, the event provided the rebels with gunpowder, and gave the insurrection momentum. It remains the eternal symbol of the Revolution, celebrated here with a lively street *bal* every 13 July. The prison was quickly torn down, its stones used to build Pont de la Concorde. Vestiges of the foundations can be seen in the Métro; there's part of a reconstructed tower at square Henri-Galli, near Pont de Sully (4th). The Colonne de Juillet, topped by a gilded génie of Liberty, is a monument to Parisians killed in the revolutions of July 1830 and 1848.

South of the Bastille

The **Viaduc des Arts**, a former railway viaduct, is now a gentrified a row of craft and design boutiques. Atop the viaduct, old ladies admire the blooms and lovers spoon among the bamboo of the **Promenade Plantée**, which continues through the Jardin de Reuilly and east to the **Bois de Vincennes**. Further along, avenue Daumesnil is fast becoming a Silicon Valley of computer outlets. No 186, **Eglise du St-Esprit**, is a curious 1920s concrete copy of Istanbul's Hagia Sophia, and while No 293, the **Musée des Arts d'Afrique et d'Océanie** is still standing, its collection is in storage and will ultimately move to the new museum under construction on quai Branly.

As late as the 1980s, wine was still unloaded off barges at Bercy but now this stretch of the Seine is firmly part of redeveloped Paris with the massive Ministère de l'Economie et du Budget and the **Palais Omnisports de Paris-Bercy** (*see chapter* **Sport & Fitness**). At the eastern edge of the park, in striking contrast to the modern **Ciné Cité** multiplex (*see chapter* **Film**), is Bercy Village. Forty-two *chais*, or brick wine warehouses, have been revamped and opened as wine bars and cafés; the result is lively, if somewhat antiseptic in a chinos-and-deck-shoes kind of way. Particularly popular is Club Med World, where the themed bars and juggling barmen are intended to put you in mind of a sun-and-sex-filled resort. A

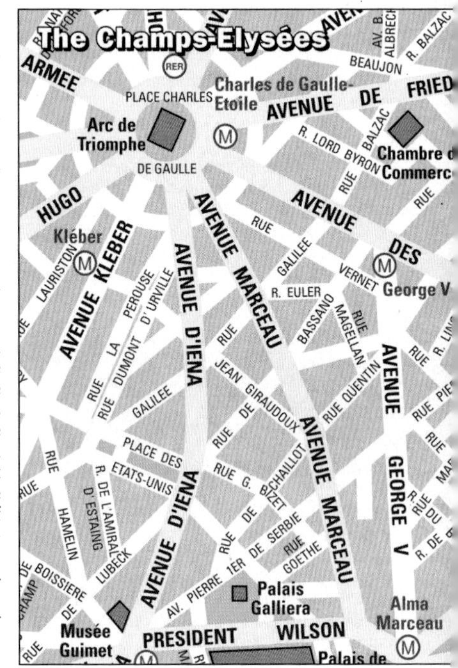

further group has been converted as the Pavillons de Bercy, containing the Musée des Arts Forains collection of fairground music and Venetian carnival salons (open to groups by appointment 01.43.40.16.22).

Bois de Vincennes

12th. M° Porte-Dorée or Château de Vincennes.

This is Paris' biggest park. Boats can be hired on the lake, there are cycle paths, a Buddhist temple, a racetrack, baseball pitch and flower gardens. It also contains Paris' main **Zoo** and the **Cartoucherie** theatre complex. The Parc Floral (01.43.43.92.95) has horticultural displays, free summer jazz and classical festivals, a picnic area, exhibition space, children's amusements and a Paris-monuments-themed crazy golf. Next to the park is the imposing Château de Vincennes (*see chapter* **Beyond the Périphérique**), where England's Henry V died in 1422. (*See also chapters* **Children** and **Theatre**).

Eglise du St-Esprit

186 av Daumesnil, 12th (01.44.75.77.50).
M° Daumesnil. **Open** 9.30am-noon, 3-7pm Mon-Fri, Sun; 9.30am-noon, 3-6pm Sat. **Map** p407 P9.

Behind a red brick exterior cladding, this 1920s concrete church follows a square plan around a central dome, lit by a scalloped ring of windows. Architect Paul Tournon was directly inspired by the Hagia Sofia cathedral in Istanbul.

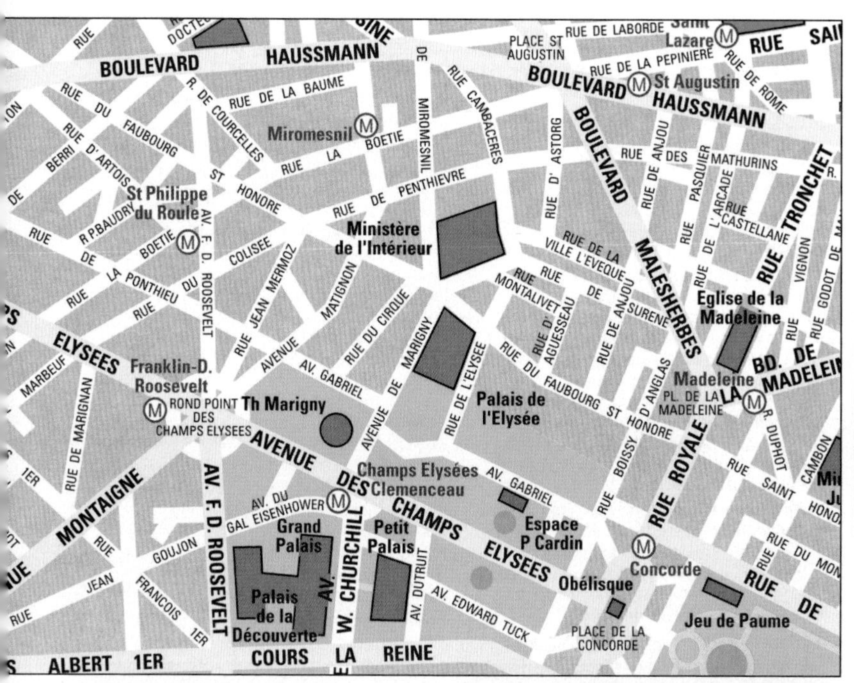

Parc de Bercy

rue de Bercy, 12th. M° Bercy or Cour St-Emilion. **Map** p407 N9/10.

Bercy park combines the French love of geometry with that of food. There's a large lawn and a grid with square rose, herb and vegetable plots, an orchard and gardens representing the four seasons.

La Promenade Plantée

av Daumesnil, 12th. M° Ledru Rollin or Gare de Lyon. **Map** p407 M8/N8.

The railway tracks atop the Viaduc des Arts have been replaced by a promenade planted with roses, shrubs and rosemary, offering a high-level view into Parisian lives. It continues at ground level through the Jardin de Reuilly and the Jardin Charles Péguy on to the Bois de Vincennes in the east. Rollerbladers are banned, but no one seems to have noticed.

Le Viaduc des Arts

15-121 av Daumesnil, 12th (www.viaduc-des-arts.com). M° Ledru-Rollin or Gare de Lyon. **Map** p407 M8/N8.

Chic glass-fronted workshops now poke out from the arches of the Promenade Plantée, providing a showroom for designers and craftspeople, including contemporary furniture and fashion designers, picture frame gilders, tapestry restorers, porcelain decorators, architectural salvage, design gallery VIA and the late-opening **Viaduc Café**.

The Champs-Elysées & west

In the 8th, 16th and 17th arrondissements.

While the 'Elysian Fields' can be a disappointment on first, tourist-filled sight, the avenue remains the symbolic gathering place of a nation – it gets positively swamped for sporting victories, New Year's Eve and displays of military might (July 14). At night, the head and tail lights of ten lanes of honking traffic form a continuous red and a white ribbon.

In the past few years the Champs-Elysées has undergone a renaissance, thanks initially to the facelift – underground car parks and granite paving – instigated by former mayor Jacques Chirac. Chi-chi shops and chic hotels have set up in the 'golden triangle' (avenues George V, Montaigne and the Champs) in recent years, including **Louis Vuitton**, **Chanel**, **Jean-Paul Gaultier**, Ladurée tearoom, Marriott and Pershing Hall hotels, while stylish restaurants such as **Spoon, Food & Wine**, **Senso** and club-combos like La Suite draw an affluent and screamingly fashionable pack. At night, crowds line up for the glitzy **Lido** cabaret, **Queen** nightclub and various cinemas, or stroll down the avenue to the floodlit **place de la Concorde** (*see p86*).

Le Fab Four: Arc de Triomphe

Imagine a monumental John Wayne standing at the end of the Champs-Elysées challenging the city's other tourist attractions to get off their horses and drink their milk. Or, seen from above, imagine Duke as the focal point of a 12-avenue Busby Berkeley choreography. Voilà the macho dominance of the rather large – 50 metres in height and 45 wide – Arc de Triomphe.

Napoléon ordered the arch's construction in 1809 as a monument to the triumph of the republican armies: he wanted to do his Julius Caesar bit, mincing at the head of his victorious armies and all that Roman Emperor jazz. Talk about tempting fate – almost immediately the empire he'd been rushing around the globe building up started to collapse – doh!

A soupçon of re-imaging later, and the Arc became a monument to the sheer *triomphe* of simply being French. It certainly fulfils that role in the civic and national psyche. In 1840, Napoléon's ashes were carried under it on their way to Les Invalides; French troops finally got to march through it victoriously to celebrate the end of the First World War; in 1921, France's Unknown Soldier was buried here; Parisians gathered here spontaneously in August 1944 when they were liberated from German occupation; when France won the soccer World Cup in 1998, the all-night party kicked off here; the annual Bastille Day procession of France's military might bgins here. No doubt, when Johnny Hallyday is finally fitted into his wooden overcoat – and may that black leather day be long, long postponed – the mourning and the funeral processions will have the Arc de Triomphe as their centre-point.

For the visitor, of course, the point of the whole thing is the view. From its viewing platform, you can admire the alignment of Haussmann's 12 avenues – you can watch the Champs-Elysées morph into the Place de la Concorde, and if you're the kind of person whose thoughts skip readily to the aesthetics of town planning, you'll find yourself lost in admiration at the imagination and practical expertise of those nineteenth-century architetectural magician dudes.

This great spine of western Paris started life as an extension to the Tuileries gardens, laid out by Le Nôtre in the 17th century. By the Revolution, the avenue had reached its full stretch, but it was more Sunday stroll territory than thoroughfare.

During the Second Empire the Champs-Elysées became a focus of fashionable society, military parades and royal processions. Bismarck was so impressed when he arrived with the conquering Prussian army in 1871 that he had a replica, the Kurfürstendamm, built in Berlin. Smart residences and hotels sprung up along its upper half, together with streetlights, pavements, sideshows, concert halls, theatres and exhibition centres. The Prussian army in 1871 and Hitler's troops in 1940 both made a point of marching down it; but jubilation accompanied the allies' victory march along the avenue in 1944.

South of the avenue, the glass-domed **Grand Palais** and **Petit Palais**, both built for the 1900 Exposition Universelle and still used for major shows, create an impressive vista across elaborate Pont Alexandre III to Les Invalides. The rear wing of the Grand Palais opening on to avenue Franklin D Roosevelt contains the **Palais de la Découverte** science museum (*see chapters* **Museums** and **Children**).

To the north are smart shops and officialdom. On circular place Beauvau a gateway leads to the Ministry of the Interior. The 18th-century Palais de l'Elysée, the official presidential residence, is situated at 55-57 rue du Fbg-St-Honoré. Nearby are the equally palatial British Embassy and adjoining ambassadorial residence, once the Hôtel Borghèse, home to Napoleon's favourite sister, Pauline.

The lower, landscaped reach of the avenue masks two theatres and haute cuisine restaurants Laurent and Ledoyen, in fancy Napoléon III pavilions. At the Rond-Point des Champs-Elysées, Nos 7 and 9 hint at the splendid mansions that once lined the avenue. From here, it's platinum cards and stick-thin women only as avenue Montaigne rolls out its array of fashion houses: Christian Dior, Chanel, Prada, Jil Sander, Loewe, Céline, Ungaro, Calvin Klein and, gulp, more. Admire the lavish **Plaza Athénée** hotel and Auguste Perret's innovative 1911-13 **Théâtre des Champs-Elysées** concert hall topped by the slick **Maison Blanche** restaurant with its view across Paris rooftops.

At the western end, the **Arc de Triomphe** towers above place Charles de Gaulle, better known as l'Etoile. Initially a project to glorify Napoléon's victories, the giant triumphal arch was later modified to celebrate the armies of the Revolution. The place was commissioned later by Haussmann. From the top, gaze upon prize Paris real estate: the swanky mansions along the grassy verges of avenue Foch or the prestige office buildings of avenues Hoche and Wagram.

Arc de Triomphe

pl Charles-de-Gaulle (access via underground passage), 8th (01.55.37.73.77). M° Charles de Gaulle-Etoile. **Open** *Apr-Sept* 10am-11pm daily; *Oct-Mar* 10am-10.30pm daily. Closed public holidays. **Admission** €7; €4.50 18-25s; free under-18s. **Credit** MC, V. Map p404 C3.
(*See p104* **Le Fab Four: Arc de Triomphe**.)

Grand Palais

av Winston-Churchill, av du Général-Eisenhower, 8th (01.44.97.78.04). M° Champs-Elysées-Clemenceau. **Map** p405 E5.
Built for the 1900 Exposition Universelle, the Grand Palais was the work of three different architects, each of whom designed a facade. The famous golden horses are currently being restored, part of a major programme of work that will keep part of the building closed until January 2005, although this remains Paris' main venue for blockbuster exhibitions and is home to the **Palais de la Découverte** science museum.

Petit Palais

av Winston-Churchill, 8th (01.44.51.19.31). M° Champs-Elysées-Clemenceau. **Map** p405 E5.
Also built for the 1900 Exposition Universelle but with a style that is rather more charmingly Rococo. The Petit Palais closed in 2001 for extensive interior renovations and is due to reopen in January 2005.

Monceau & Batignolles

Parc Monceau, with its neo-Antique follies and large lily pond, lies at the far end of avenue Hoche (main entrance bd de Courcelles). Three local museums capture the extravagance of the area when it was newly fashionable in the 19th century: the **Musée Jacquemart-André** on boulevard Haussmann, **Musée Nissim de Camondo** (18th-century decorative arts) and **Musée Cernushi** (Chinese art) (*see chapter* **Museums**). There are some nice exotic touches, too, such as the unlikely red lacquer Galerie Ching Tsai Too (48 rue de Courcelles, 8th) near the fancy wrought-iron gates of Parc Monceau, or the onion domes of the Russian Orthodox **Alexander Nevsky Cathedral** on rue Daru. Built in the mid-19th century when a sojourn in Paris was an essential part of the education of every Russian aristocrat, it is still at the heart of an émigré little Russia.

Famed for its stand during the Paris Commune, the Quartier des Batignolles to the northeast is much more working class, with the lively rue de Lévis street market, tenements lining the deep railway canyon and the attractive square des Batignolles park with its pretty church overlooking a small semi-circular place. It is, however, fast becoming fashionable. Rue des Dames contains the colourful **Eldorado** hotel, the **Lush** bar and antique bathroom shop **SBR**.

Alexander Nevsky Cathedral

12 rue Daru, 8th (01.42.27.37.34). M° Courcelles. **Open** 3-5pm Tue, Fri, Sun. **Map** p404 D3.
The edifice has enough onion domes, icons and incense to make you think you were in Moscow. This Russian Orthodox church was built 1859-61 in the neo-Byzantine Novgorod-style of the 1600s, on a Greek-cross plan by the Tsar's architect Kouzmine, architect of the St-Petersburg Beaux-Arts Academy. Services, on Sunday mornings and Orthodox saints' days, are in Russian.

Cimetière des Batignolles

rue St-Just, 17th (01.53.06.38.68). M° Porte de Clichy. **Open** Apr-Oct 8am-6pm Mon-Fri; 8.30am-6pm Sat; 9am-6pm Sun; Nov-Mar closes at 5.30pm.
Squeezed between the Périphérique and the boulevard des Amiraux lie the graves of poet Paul Verlaine, Surrealist André Breton and Léon Bakst, costume designer of the Ballets Russes.

Parc Monceau

bd de Courcelles, av Hoche, rue Monceau, 8th. M° Monceau. **Map** E2
Surrounded by grand *hôtels particuliers*, Monceau is a favourite with well-dressed children and their nannies. It was laid out in the late 18th century for the Duc de Chartres (Philippe-Egalité) in the English style that was then so fashionable, with an oval lake, spacious lawns and a variety of follies: an Egyptian pyramid, a Corinthian colonnade, Venetian bridge and ancient tombs.

Trocadéro

South of the Arc de Triomphe, avenue Kléber leads on to the monumental buildings and terraced gardens of the Trocadéro, with spectacular views across the river to the Eiffel Tower. Trocadéro's bronze and stone statues showered by powerful fountains form a dramatic ensemble with the Eiffel Tower and Champ de Mars across the river. The vast symmetrical 1930s **Palais de Chaillot** dominates the hill and houses four museums plus the **Théâtre National de Chaillot**. Across place du Trocadéro is the small **Cimetière de Passy**. To the west on avenue du Président Wilson is the **Palais de Tokyo** which harbours, in one side, the **Musée d'Art Moderne de la Ville de Paris**, and in the other, the wacky new **Site de Création Contemporaine** (*see chapter* **Museums**).

The staid area behind Trocadéro holds a few surprises. Hidden on avenue Victor-Hugo, behind a conventional-looking apartment block, is No 111, the Galerie Commerciale Argentine, a brick and cast-iron apartment block and shopping arcade, now mostly empty, designed by ever-experimental Henri Sauvage and Charles Sarazin in 1904. Pause in Champagne territory at the exclusive little bar of the Hôtel Dokhan's Trocadéro in rue Lauriston.

Cimetière de Passy

2 rue du Commandant-Schloesig, 16th (01.47.27.51.42/www.findagrave.com). M° Trocadéro. **Open** 8am-5.45pm Mon-Fri; 8.30am-5.45pm Sat; 9am-5.45pm Sun. **Map** p404 B5.
Maybe only Parisians could take an interest in matters of after-death chic but since 1874 this has been considered one of the most elegant places in Paris to be laid to rest. You'll find composers Debussy and Fauré, painters Manet and his sister-in-law Berthe Morisot, designer Ruhlmann and writer Giraudoux, as well as numerous generals and politicians.

Palais de Chaillot

pl du Trocadéro, 16th. M° Trocadéro. **Map** p404 C5.
Looming across the river from the Eiffel Tower, the immense pseudo-classical Palais de Chaillot was built by Azéma, Boileau and Carlu for the 1937 international exhibition and actually stands on the foundations of an earlier complex put up for the 1878 World Fair. It is home to the **Cinémathèque** rep cinema, **Musée de la Marine** (marine and naval history) and the **Musée de l'Homme** in the western wing (currently staging some interesting temporary exhibitions while the ethnology and anthropology sections are in storage awaiting the new museum at Quai Branly in 2005). The ex-Musée des Monuments Historiques, which used to be housed in the eastern wing, is due to reappear in 2005 as Cité de l'Architecture (*see chapter* **Museums**). The **Théâtre National de Chaillot** nests in the eastern wing.

Passy & Auteuil

West of l'Etoile, most of the 16th arrondissement is pearls-and-poodle country, dotted with avant-garde architecture and classy shops.

When Balzac lived at 47 rue Raynouard (now **La Maison de Balzac**, *see chapter* **Museums**), Passy was a country village where people came to take cures for anaemia at its mineral springs – a name reflected in the rue des Eaux. The **Musée du Vin** is of interest if only for its location in the cellars of a wine-producing monastery that was destroyed in the Revolution.

West of the Jardins du Ranelagh (originally high-society pleasure gardens, modelled on the endearingly bawdy 18th-century London version) is the Impressionist draw the **Musée**

DEPEND · DE · CELUI · QUI · PASSE
JE · SOIS · TOMBE · OU · TRÉSO
JE · PARLE · OU · ME · TAISE
ECI · NE · TIENT · QU'A · TOI
N'ENTRE · PAS · SANS · DÉSIR

Trocadéro

Abbesses

Marmottan, which features a fabulous collection of Monet's late water lily canvases, other Impressionists and Empire furniture (*see chapter* **Museums**).

Next to the Pont de Grenelle is **Maison de Radio-France**, the giant Orwellian home to the state broadcasting bureaucracy. Opened in 1963, it's a constant reminder of the pivotal role that the state still plays in people's lives. You can attend concerts or take guided tours around its endless corridors (*see chapters* **Music: Classical & Opera** and **Museums**); employees nickname the place 'Alphaville', after the Godard film. From here, in upmarket Auteuil, go up rue Fontaine, the best place to find art nouveau architecture by Hector Guimard. Despite extravagant iron balconies, Castel Béranger at No 14 was originally low-rent lodgings; Guimard designed outside and in, right down to the wallpaper and stoves. He also designed the less-ambitious Nos 19, 21 and tiny Café Antoine at No 17.

Contrastingly, around Métro Jasmin is Le Corbusier terrain. The **Fondation Le Corbusier** occupies two of his avant-garde houses in the square du Dr-Blanche. A little further up rue du Dr-Blanche, rue Mallet-Stevens is almost entirely made up of refined houses by Robert Mallet-Stevens.

West of the 16th, across the Périphérique, sprawls the **Bois de Boulogne**, a royal hunting reserve turned park which includes a boating lake and cycle paths.

Bois de Boulogne

16th. M° Porte-Dauphine or Les Sablons.

Covering 865 hectares, the Bois was the ancient Forêt de Rouvray hunting grounds. It was landscaped in the 1860s, when grottoes were created around the Lac Inférieur. The Jardins de Bagatelle (route de Sèvres à Neuilly, 16th/ 01.40.67.97.00/open 9am-5.30pm winter/8pm summer) are famous for their roses, daffodils and water lilies and contain an **Orangerie** which rings to the sound of tinkling Chopin in summer. The **Jardin d'Acclimatation** is a children's amusement park (*see chapter* **Children**). The Bois has two racecourses (Longchamp and Auteuil), sports clubs, the **Musée National des Arts et Traditions Populaires** and two restaurants. Packed at weekends with dog walkers and picnickers, at night it is transformed into a parade ground for Brazilian transsexuals, and ageing swingers.

Castel Béranger

14 rue La Fontaine, 16th. M° Jasmin. Closed to the public.

Guimard's masterpiece of 1895-98 epitomises art nouveau in Paris. Here you can see his love of brick and wrought iron, asymmetry and renunciation of harsh angles not found in nature. Along with the whiplash motifs characteristic of art nouveau, there are still many signs of Guimard's earlier taste for fantasy and the medieval: green seahorses climb up the facade and the faces on the balconies are supposedly a self portrait, inspired by Japanese figures to ward off evil spirits.

Fondation Le Corbusier

Villa La Roche, 10 square du Dr-Blanche, 16th (01.42.88.41.53/www.fondationlecorbusier.asso.fr). M° Jasmin. **Open** 1.30pm-6pm Mon; 9am-12.30pm, 1.30-5pm Tue-Fri. **Closed** Aug. **Admission** €2.40; €1.60 13-18s; free under 12s.

This house, designed by Le Corbusier in 1923 for a Swiss art collector, shows the visionary architect's ideas in practice with its strip windows, roof terraces, built-in furniture, split volumes and an unsuspected use of colour. Adjoining Villa Jeanneret – also by Le Corbusier – houses the Foundation's library.

Les Serres d'Auteuil

3 av de la Porte d'Auteuil, 16th (01.40.71.75.23). M° Porte d'Auteuil. **Open** 10am-6pm (summer); 10am-6pm (winter). **Admission** €0.80. **No credit cards**.

These romantic glasshouses were opened in 1895 to cultivate plants for Parisian parks and public spaces. Today there are seasonal displays of orchids and begonias. Best of all is the steamy tropical central pavilion with palms, birds and a pool of Japanese ornamental carp.

Montmartre & Pigalle

Mainly in the 9th and 18th arrondissements.
Montmartre, on the highest point in the city's north, is the most unabashedly romantic district of Paris. Despite the onslaught of tourists who throng **Sacré-Coeur** and place du Tertre, it's surprisingly easy to leave them all behind. Climb and descend quiet stairways, peer into little alleys and deserted squares, and explore streets like rue des Abbesses, rue des Trois Frères and rue des Martyrs with their cafés, boutiques and young, arty (but often with a nice little income from *papa*) community.

For centuries, Montmartre was a quiet, windmill-packed village. Then, when Haussmann sliced through the city centre, working-class families began to move out in search of accommodation and peasant migrants poured into an industrialising Paris from across France. Montmartre swelled. The hill was absorbed into Paris in 1860, but remained fiercely independent, and its role in the Paris Commune is commemorated by a plaque on rue du Chevalier-de-la-Barre.

Artists moved into the area from the 1880s. Toulouse-Lautrec patronised Montmartre's bars and immortalised its cabarets in his posters; later it was frequented by artists of the Ecole de Paris, Utrillo and Modigliani.

The best starting point is the Abbesses Métro, one of only two in Paris (along with Porte Dauphine) to retain its original art nouveau glass awning designed by Hector Guimard. Across place des Abbesses as you emerge from the station is the art nouveau church of St-Jean de Montmartre, with its turquoise mosaics around the door. Along rue des Abbesses and adjoining rue Lepic, which winds its way up the *butte* (hill), are many excellent food shops, wine merchants, cafés, including the heaving **Sancerre**, and offbeat boutiques. The famous **Studio 28** cinema, opened in 1928 on rue Tholozé, is where Buñuel's *L'Age d'Or* had a riotous première in 1930. It has its own dinky bar.

In the other direction from Abbesses, at 11 rue Yvonne-Le-Tac, is the Chapelle du Martyr where, according to legend, St Denis picked up his head after his execution by the Romans in the third century. Around the corner, the cafés of rue des Trois Frères are popular for an evening drink. The street leads into place Emile-Goudeau, whose staircases, wrought-iron streetlights and old houses are particularly evocative. The Bateau Lavoir, a piano factory which stood at No 13, was divided into a warren of studios in the 1890s where artists lived in penury, among them Braque, Picasso and Juan Gris. Picasso's *Demoiselles d'Avignon* was created here. The building burned down in 1970

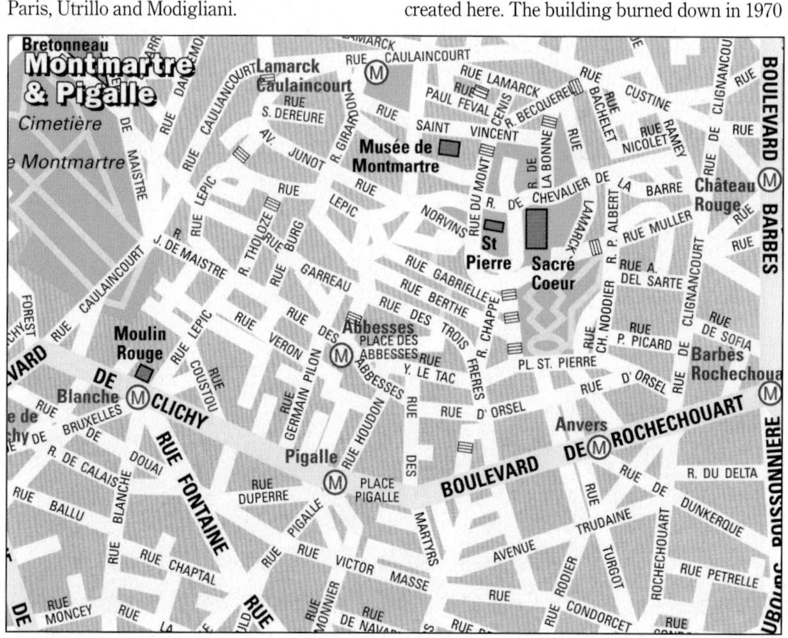

Le Fab Four: Sacré-Coeur

You can say what you like about Sacré-Coeur – Emile 'Handbags' Zola called it 'the basilica of the ridiculous', while its fans have likened it to a sculptured cloud – but where else are you going to find religious karaoke on a Sunday evening? At 5pm, a nun appears at the nave and leads an evening sing-a-long with a level of showbiz pizzazz and audience participation that evokes comparisons with Al Jolson, allegedly the world's greatest-ever entertainer.

The basilica is a lot younger than its design might have you believe. You're thinking Romano-Byzantine, right? *Mais non*: it went up in 1876 by way of striking a deal with God, as France had taken such a drubbing at the hands of the Prussians that an act of appeasement was deemed worth a try. France really was in big trouble, as was evidenced by the fact that donations and practical help to get the thing built came in from all over the country. Sacré-Coeur's raison d'être was not to beautify picture postcards (or even guide books): it was an attempt just to get a break from the shit hitting the fan. The man who won the state-run competition to design this love-means-sometimes-having-to-get-on-your-knees-and-say-you're-sorry basilica, Paul Abadie Jr, only lived long enough to see the foundation stone laid, but we think he would have liked the way they finished it off for him.

The church's interior contains a mural of Christ's passion whose beauty will relieve you of any breath you have left after the walk up the *butte* (hill) Montmartre that leads to Sacré-Coeur; and if you really do swoon and hit the deck, the image of Christ on the ceiling will knock you out. Then there are the stained-glass windows.

The basilica suffers from an unfortunate accidental built-in obsolescence. The gypsum that impregnated the exterior (no, artexing didn't originate in Essex) and that causes it to gleam so brilliantly is now gradually dissolving the outside covering.

The bell tower is occupied by the 17-ton (but it's all muscle) 'Savoyarde'; it's worth being nearby when it rings, because it makes the surroundings vibrate, and then, of course, there's the view: the dome will give you a 50-km panorama. You've got to say the whole thing worked: when was the last time Prussia won the Eurovision Song Contest, eh?

but has since been reconstructed. Further up the hill on rue Lepic are the village's two remaining windmills. The Moulin du Radet was moved here in the 17th century from its hillock in rue des Moulins near the Palais-Royal.

On top of the hill, dozens of so-called artists compete to sketch your portrait or flog lurid sunset views of Paris; **Espace Dalí** (*see chapter* **Museums**) on rue Poulbot offers a slightly more illustrious alternative. Just off the square is the oldest church in the district, St-Pierre-de-Montmartre, whose columns have grown bent with age. Founded by Louis VI in 1133, it is a fine example of early Gothic, and a contrast to its extravagant neighbour, the basilica of Sacré-Coeur.

On the north side of place du Tertre in rue Cortot is the quiet manor housing the **Musée de Montmartre** (*see chapter* **Museums**), dedicated to the area and its former inhabitants, with original Toulouse-Lautrec posters. Dufy, Renoir and Utrillo all had studios in the building. Nearby in rue des Saules is the Montmartre vineyard. The grape picking each autumn is an annual ritual (*see chapter* **Festivals & Events**).

Further down the hill amid rustic, shuttered houses is the **Lapin Agile** cabaret at 22 rue des Saules, another legendary meeting point for Montmartre. A series of pretty squares leads to rue Caulaincourt, towards the oddly romantic **Cimetière de Montmartre**. Winding down the back of the hill, the wide avenue Junot is lined with exclusive houses, among them the one built by Adolf Loos for Dadaist poet Tristan Tzara at No 15.

Cimetière de Montmartre

20 av Rachel, access by stairs from rue Caulaincourt, 18th (01.43.87.64.24/www.findagrave.com). M° Blanche. **Open** *16 Mar-5 Nov* 8am-6pm Mon-Fri; 8.30am-6pm Sat; 9am-6pm Sun and holidays; *6 Nov-15 Mar* 8am-5.30 pm Mon-Fri, 8.30am-5.30pm Sat; 9am-5.30pm Sun and holidays. **Map** p405 G1.

You can't help stumbling over the graves of the famous and infamous here. Sacha Guitry, Truffaut, Nijinsky, Berlioz, Degas, Offenbach, Feydeau, Dumas fils and German poet Heine are all buried here. Also La Goulue, the first great can-can star and model for Toulouse-Lautrec, celebrated beauty Mme Récamier, and the consumptive heroine Alphonsine Plessis, inspiration for Dumas' *La Dame aux Camélias* and Verdi's *La Traviata*. Mementoes are still left daily for scary Egyptian pop diva Dalida.

Sacré-Coeur

35 rue du Chevalier-de-la-Barre, 18th (01.53.41.89.00). M° Abbesses or Anvers. **Open** Basilica 6am-11am daily. Crypt and dome 9am-7pm daily. **Admission** free; crypt and dome €5. **Credit** MC, V. **Map** p406 J1.

(*See p110* **Le Fab Four: Sacré-Coeur**.)

Pigalle

Pigalle has long been the sleaze centre of Paris but that may be changing. A recent police blitz, instigated in response to increased tourist rip-offs and rough-ups, has shooed out the streetwalkers and many an erotic cabaret, peep show and go-go bar with them. While locals bemoan the sanitising of their atmospherically seedy neighbourhood, the up-tempo (police) beat goes on. At the end of the 19th century, of the 58 houses on rue des Martyrs, 25 were cabarets (a few such as **Michou** and **Madame Arthur** remain today); others were *maisons clos*. The **Moulin Rouge**, once the image of naughty fin-de-siècle Paris, is now a cheesy tourist draw. Its befeathered dancers still can-can across the stage but are no substitute for La Goulue and Joseph Pujol – the *pétomane* who could pass wind melodically.

Obviously that historic depth of talent fuelled Pigalle's rebirth as a bit of a trendy nightspot. The Moulin Rouge's old restaurant has become the MCM Café, while the **Folies Pigalle** cabaret is a club famed for its after-parties and drag queens. What was once the Divan Japonais, depicted by Toulouse-Lautrec, has been transformed into **Le Divan du Monde**, a nightclub and music venue, while the old **Elysée Montmartre** music hall puts on an eclectic array of pop concerts and club nights.

La Nouvelle Athènes

Just south of Montmartre and bordered by the area around Gare St-Lazare lies this mysterious, often overlooked quarter once beloved of artists of the Romantic era. Long-forgotten actresses and demi-mondaines had mansions built here and some of the prettiest can be found in tiny rue de la Tour-des-Dames, which refers to one of the many windmills owned by the once-prosperous Couvent des Abbesses. Wander through the adjoining streets and passageways to glimpse further angles of these miniature palaces and late 18th-century *hôtels particuliers*, especially on rue de La Rochefoucauld.

The area round the neo-classical Eglise Notre-Dame-de-Lorette was built up in Louis-Philippe's reign and was famous for its courtesans. From 1844 to 1857, Delacroix had his studio at 58 rue Notre-Dame-de-Lorette (next to the house, at No 56, where Gauguin was born in 1848). The painter later moved to place de Furstenberg in the 6th arrondissement (now Musée Delacroix).

Just off rue Taitbout stands square d'Orléans, a remarkable housing estate built in 1829 by English architect Edward Cresy. This ensemble of flats and artists' studios attracted the

Sightseeing

glitterati of the day, including George Sand and her lover, Chopin. The **Musée de la Vie Romantique** (*see chapter* **Museums**) in nearby rue Chaptal tastefully displays the writer's mementoes. Place Gustave-Toudouze contains pleasant tearoom **Thé Folies**, and glorious circular place St-Georges was home to the true Empress of Napoléon III's Paris, the notorious madame Païva, who lived in the neo-Renaissance No 28, thought outrageous at the time of its construction.

The **Musée Gustave Moreau**, meanwhile, is grounds alone for a visit. Fragments of *la bohème* can still be gleaned in the area, though the Café La Roche, where Moreau met Degas for drinks and rows, has been downsized to La Joconde on the corner of rues de La Rochefoucault and La Bruyère. Degas painted most of his memorable ballet scenes round the corner in rue Frochot and Renoir hired his first decent studio at 35 rue St-Georges. A few streets away in Cité Pigalle, a collection of studios, stands Van Gogh's last Paris house (No 5), from where he moved to **Auvers-sur-Oise** (*see chapter* **Trips Out of Town**). There is a plaque here, but nothing on the building in rue Pigalle where Toulouse-Lautrec drank himself to death in 1903.

The best Belle époque

Palais Royal Métro
Circa 2001, Jean-Michel Othoniel shows you can still *belle époque* it up (*see p86*).

Maxim's
Class dining room set the scene for Lehár's *Merry Widow* (*see p84*).

La Samaritaine
You can find everything here (*see p92*).

rues du Quatre-Septembre and Réaumur
Press magnates commissioned buidings on Paris' answer to Fleet Street (*see p87*).

Abbesses Métro
One of two original awnings still standing complete; a true abscess of art (*see p109*).

rue Fontaine
Guimard homage up and down the street, note Nos. 19, 21 and 17 (*see p108*).

Castel Béranger
Henri designed everything right down to the tee-pee holders (*see p108*).

Brasserie Julien
A *nouveau* jewel (*see p94*).

Lucas Carton
A Majorelle sight (*see p89 and p189*).

La Goutte d'Or

For a less orthodox Paris experience, head for Barbès-Rochechouart Métro station and the area north of it. Zola used it as a backdrop for *L'Assommoir*, his novel set among the district's laundries and absinthe cafés. These days, heroin has replaced absinthe for those who want to escape the cruel world.

Primarily an African and Arab neighbourhood, it can seem like a colourful slice of Africa or a state under perpetual siege due to the frequent police raids. Down rue Doudeauville, you'll find African music shops, rue Polonceau has African grocers and Senegalese restaurant Chez Aïda, while square Léon is the focus for la Goutte d'Or en Fête every June, which tries to harness some of the local talent (*see chapter* **Festivals & Events**). Some bands, such as Africando and the Orchestre National de Barbès, have become well known across Paris. There is a lively street market under the Métro tracks (Mon, Wed, Sat morning), with stalls of exotic vegetables and rolls of African fabrics. This area also houses the legendary bargain clothes store Tati, although Mayor Delanöe has tried to inject a bit of class by designating rue des Gardes 'rue de la mode' to encourage young designers. From here rue d'Orsel leads back to Montmartre via the Marché St-Pierre. The covered market hall is now used for exhibitions of naïve art, but in the street, outlets such as Dreyfus and Moline vie for custom with discount fabrics.

On the northern edge of the city at Porte de Clignancourt is Paris' largest flea market, the **Marché aux Puces de St-Ouen** (*see chapter* **Shops & Services**).

North-east Paris

In the 10th, 11th, 19th and 20th arrondissements.
The old working-class area north and east of République is in transition, with charming areas abreast grotty, even dangerous ones. The main tourist attraction is **Père Lachaise** cemetery, but further afield there are fascinating pockets of old Paris. Ménilmontant and Belleville, once villages where Parisians escaped at weekends, were absorbed into the city in 1860. The area also encompasses one of Paris' most beautiful and least celebrated parks, the romantic **Buttes-Chaumont**.

Parc de La Villette

Canal St-Martin to La Villette

Canal St-Martin, built 1805-25, begins at the Seine at Pont Morland, disappears underground at Bastille, then re-emerges at rue du Faubourg-du-Temple, east of place de la République. This stretch lined with shady trees and crossed by iron footbridges and locks has the most appeal, and property prices have begun to rise.

You can take a boat up the canal between the Port de l'Arsenal and the Bassin de la Villette (*see p85* **Levee Chevy**). Between the fifth and sixth locks at 101 quai de Jemmapes is the **Hôtel du Nord**, which inspired Marcel Carné's 1938 film and is now an anglophone stand-up comedy venue (*see chapter* **Cabaret, Circus & Comedy**). East of here is the Hôpital St-Louis (main entrance rue Bichat), founded in 1607 to house plague victims and built as a series of isolated pavilions to stop disease spreading. Behind the hospital, the rue de la Grange-aux-Belles housed the infamous Montfaucon gibbet, built in 1233, where victims were hanged and left to the elements. Today the street contains music cafés **Chez Adel** (No 10) and Apostrophe (No 23). Only the inconspicuous Le Pont Tournant, on the corner with quai de Jemmapes overlooking the swing bridge, still seems to hark back to canal days of old.

To the east is the Parti Communiste Français, on the place du Colonel-Fabien, a surrealistic, curved glass curtain raised off the ground on a concrete wing, built in 1968-71 by Brazilian architect Oscar Niemeyer with Paul Chemetov and Jean Deroche. To the north, place de Stalingrad was landscaped in 1989 to expose the Rotonde de La Villette, one of Ledoux's grandiose toll houses which now houses exhibitions and archaeological finds. Those of olfactory sensitivity be warned, however: it stinks. Here the canal widens into Bassin de La Villette, built for Napoléon in 1808, bordered by new housing developments, as well as some of the worst of 1960s and 70s housing. At the eastern end of the basin is an unusual 1885 hydraulic lifting bridge, the Pont de Crimée. Thursday and Sunday mornings add vitality with a canalside market at place de Joinville.

East of here, the Canal de l'Ourcq (created in 1813 to provide drinking water, as well as for freight haulage) divides: Canal St-Denis runs north through St-Denis towards the Seine, Canal de l'Ourcq runs through La Villette and suburbs east. The area has been revitalised since the late 1980s by the **Cité des Sciences et de l'Industrie** science museum, the postmodern **Parc de La Villette** and **Cité de la Musique** concert hall.

Parc de La Villette

av Corentin-Cariou, 19th. M° Porte de La Villette, or av Jean-Jaurès, 19th. M° Porte de Pantin.
Map p407 inset.

La Villette's programmes range from avant-garde music to avant-garde circus. The site of Paris' main cattle market and abattoir, it was to be replaced by

Parc des Buttes-Chaumont

a high-tech slaughterhouse (nice) but instead became the **Cité des Sciences et de l'Industrie**, a futuristic, interactive science museum. Outside are the shiny spherical **Géode** cinema and Argonaute submarine. Dotted with red pavilions or folies, the park itself is a postmodern feast (guided tours 08.03.30.63.06, 3pm Sun in summer). The folies serve as glorious climbing frames in addition to such uses as first-aid post, burger bar and children's art centre. Kiddies shoot down a Chinese dragon slide and a meandering suspended path follows the Canal de l'Ourcq. As well as the big lawns, which are used for an open-air film festival in July and August, there are ten themed gardens with evocative names such as the Garden of Mirrors, of Mists, of Acrobatics and of Childhood Fears (genuinely spooky if you lose your way en route to the **Cabaret Sauvage** circus and club venue). South of the canal are the **Zénith**, used for pop concerts, and the **Grande Halle de La Villette**, now used for trade fairs, exhibitions and the Villette Jazz Festival. It is winged by the **Conservatoire de la Musique** music school on one side and on the other the **Cité de la Musique**, designed by Christian de Portzamparc, with its concert halls, rehearsal rooms and Musée de la Musique. (*See chapters* **Festivals & Events**, **Museums**, **Cabaret, Circus & Comedy**, **Children**, **Music: Classical & Opera**, **Popular Music**, **Theatre**.)

Ménilmontant & Charonne

Mesnil-Montant used to be a few houses on a hill with vines and fruit trees, then came the bistros, bordellos and workers' housing. It became part of Paris in 1860 with Belleville, and has a similar history. Today it's a thriving centre of alternative Paris, as artists and young Parisians have moved in. Flanking boulevard de Ménilmontant, the **Cimetière du Père Lachaise** is thought to be the most illustrious burial site in Paris. South of here, rue de la Réunion ends in the deliberately unkempt Jardin Naturel.

The area mixes 1960s and 70s monster housing projects with older dwellings, some gentrified, some derelict. Below rue des Pyrénées, the Cité Leroy or Villa l'Ermitage are cobbled cul-de-sacs often housing artists' studios. At its junction with rue de Ménilmontant there is a bird's-eye view right through to the Eiffel Tower. Follow rue Julien-Lacroix to place Maurice-Chevalier and 19th-century Notre-Dame-de-la-Croix church.

While side streets still display male-only North African cafés, rue Oberkampf is home to some of the city's most humming bars. The cutting edge may be blunter of late but young international modish types have followed the artists and **Le Mécano**, **Mercerie** and **Boteco** bars have taken off on the success of **Café Charbon** and **Le Cithéa** club. Offbeat art shows happen at Glassbox, while a more cultural concentration has evolved on rue Boyer with the **Maroquinerie** literary café.

East of Père-Lachaise is Charonne, which joined Paris in 1859. The medieval Eglise St-Germain de Charonne, place St-Blaise, is the city's only church, apart from St-Pierre de Montmartre, still to have its own graveyard. The rest of Charonne, centred on rue St-Blaise, is a prettified backwater of quiet bars and bistros. Cross the Périphérique at Porte de Montreuil for the Puces de Montreuil (*see chapter* **Shops & Services**), the junkiest of the Paris fleamarkets.

Cimetière du Père Lachaise

main entrance bd de Ménilmontant, 20th (01.55.25.82.10). M° Père-Lachaise. **Open** *16 Mar-5 Nov* 8am-6pm Mon-Fri; 8.30am-6pm Sat; 9am-6pm Sun and holidays; *6 Nov-15 Mar* 8am-5.30pm Mon-Fri; 8.30am-5.30pm Sat; 9am-5.30pm Sun and holidays. **Map** p407 P5.

With thousands of tightly packed tombs arranged along cobbled lanes and tree-lined avenues, this is definitely a city of the dead. Named after the Jesuit Père de la Chaise, Louis XIV's confessor, it was laid out by the architect Brongniart in 1804. It was never meant to be 'just' a cemetery, and was designed as a place for a wander and a ponder. The presumed remains of medieval lovers Abélard and Héloïse were moved here in 1817, along with those of Molière and La Fontaine, in a bid to gain popularity for the site. Famous inhabitants soon multiplied: Sarah Bernhardt, Delacroix, Ingres, Bizet, Balzac, Proust, Chopin, Colette and Edith Piaf. Jim Morrison, buried here in 1971, still draws a flux of spaced-out pilgrims. Oscar Wilde's headstone, carved by Epstein, is a winged, naked, male angel that was considered so offensive that it was neutered by the head keeper, who used the offending member as a paperweight. The Mur des Fédérés got its name after 147 members of the Paris Commune of 1871 were lined up and shot against it. Further up the hill is a series of Holocaust memorials.

Belleville

Incorporated into the city in 1860, Belleville became both a work and leisure place for the poorer classes. Despite attempts to dissipate workers' agitation by splitting the former village between the 11th, 19th and 20th arrondissements, it was the centre of opposition to the Second Empire. Cabarets, artisans, and workers' housing typified fin-de-siècle Belleville; now it is becoming a trendy hang-out for the young Rive Droite.

On boulevard de Belleville, Chinese and Vietnamese shops rub up against Muslim and Kosher groceries, couscous and felafel eateries. On the small streets off the rue de Belleville, old buildings hide courtyards and gardens. Rue Ramponneau mixes new housing and relics of old Belleville. At No 23 an old iron smithy has become La Forge, a squat for artists, many of whom are members of La Bellevilloise association, which is trying to save the area from redevelopment and preserve its original charm. Rue Sainte-Marthe is a delightful cobbled road lined with multi-ethnic restaurants and café **Le Panier**. There is also the modern but charming parc de Belleville with its Maison des Vents devoted to birds, kites and (almost) all things airborne.

Up the avenue Simon Bolivar is the eccentric **Parc des Buttes-Chaumont**, and east of the park are a number of tiny, hilly streets lined with small houses and gardens. The FIAC art space Le Plateau just off the park attracts contemporary art zealots and, after the success (or failure, depending on whether you managed to squeeze in) of the Nuit Blanche 2002, the old Pompes Funèbres at 104 rue d'Aubervilliers are due to be turned into a multimedia art space at the end of 2004.

Parc des Buttes-Chaumont

rue Botzaris, rue Manin, rue de Crimée, 19th. M° Buttes-Chaumont. **Map** p407 N2.

Possibly the perfect meeting of nature and the artificial with its meandering paths and vertical cliffs, this park was designed by Haussmann in the 1860s. A former granite quarry, rubbish tip and public gibbit, amazingly now waterfalls cascade out of a man-made cave, which even has its own fake stalactites.

The beach is back!

For one month in 2002, Paris' Mayor, Bertrand Delanoë, converted a two-mile stretch of the Right Bank into four inner-city beaches (two sand, two pebble, 300 deckchairs, 80 palm trees – all imported, of course). It cost a mere €1.5 million of taxpayers' money, the egalitarian rationale behind it all being that it helped families who couldn't afford a proper holiday have access to some real sand and nice bit of polluted water. Karl Marx, eat your heart out.

Bertie's first beach was big success: over two million people who like their sunrays filtered through a layer of heavy pollution smeared on the tanning butter in 2002; and so last year the beach was back. And, boy, was it better than ever, sports fans! Paris-Plage Deux slinked onto the quayside with picnic tables, volley-ball, a range of Plage merchandise extending from T-shirts to hats, a Django Reinhardt tribute, tai chi, 32 world music concerts and castle competitions, *boules* and – get this – a mobile library! We're talking Sodom-and-Gomorrah-on-Sea, right?

Visitors grew to a massive three million for the month of the beach's existence, and, even now, committees are working on how they can make 2004's version better still. There's talk of more portaloos (last year there were but 18, and the occasional queue of people bent double as they grappled with bladder or colon spasms did, arguably, compromise the triumph of the exercise from a visual image point of view).

We spoke of Sodom and Gomorrah; well, to those of a divine retributionial bent, it might

not have seemed so surprising that the month of Paris-Plage coincided with a heatwave that killed countless souls, not the lissom rompers of Paris-Plage, but their lonely, elderly, infirm relatives, who spent the month literally baking to death in their flats.

Such killjoy observations aside one must doff one's kiss-me-kwik hat to the style originality of the idea of installing a beach where there was none, and while we're doing our doffing let us pray that none of Mayor Delanoë's ideas people send him any memos that begin, 'I was flying over the Himalayas the other day, and I thought what would set Paris off really nicely would be something with a bit of a peak. You know, import a few Sherpas, spray a bit of ice on the top...'

The Left Bank

Existentialists may have surrendered berets to fashion exhibitionists but this side of the Seine is still gritty, glossy, and *très (rive) gauche.*

The Latin Quarter

In the 5th arrondissement

Way back when the Sorbonne was founded here in the 13th century, students cruised the neighbourhood spouting Latin. We think 'geek', but it was the 13th-century equivalvent of the latest 50 Cent rhyme: see, you need a bit of 13th-century context. The Latin connection may be why this area east of boulevard St-Michel got its moniker; or perhaps it alludes to the vestiges of Roman Lutétia, of which it was the heart. The first two Roman streets were on the site of present-day rue St-Jacques (later the pilgrims' route to Compostella) and rue Cujas. The area boasts the city's most important Roman remains: the Cluny baths, now part of the **Musée National du Moyen Age**, and the **Arènes de Lutèce** amphitheatre, plus medieval streets and scholarly institutions.

Quartier de la Huchette

The boulevard St-Michel, at one time symbolic of student rebellion, is these days a ribbon of fast-food giants and downmarket shoe and clothing chains. Rue de la Huchette and rue de la Harpe have morphed into kebab and pizza land, although if you look past the touts and tavernas there are 18th-century wrought-iron balconies and carved masks in the latter street. Also of interest: rue du Chat-Qui-Pêche, supposedly Paris' narrowest street, and rue de la Parcheminerie, named after the parchment sellers and copyists who once lived here. Amid all the tourist paraphernalia stands Paris' most charming medieval church, the **Eglise St-Séverin**, which has an exuberant Flamboyant Gothic vaulted interior.

Across the ancient rue St-Jacques is **Eglise St-Julien-le-Pauvre**, built as a resting place for12th-century pilgrims. Nearby, opposite the *bouquinistes* (booksellers) lining the river *quais,* expats in worn tweed jackets sporting leather elbow patches gather at second-hand English bookshop **Shakespeare & Co**.

Just beyond boulevard St-Germain lies the medieval garden of the **Musée National du Moyen Age – Thermes de Cluny**. A Gothic mansion built over ruined Roman baths, the museum houses a collection of medieval art.

East of here, place Maubert, now a morning marketplace (Tue, Thur, Sat), witnessed the hanging of Protestants in the 16th century, and the little streets between here and the quais are among the city's oldest; rue de Bièvre charts the course of the river Bièvre, which flowed into the Seine in the Middle Ages. Religious foundations once abounded; remnants of the Collège des Bernardins can be seen in rue de Poissy. On quai de la Tournelle there's food for all budgets, from the illustrious **Tour d'Argent** (No 17) to the Tintin shrine café-tabac Le Rallye (No 11).

Eglise St-Julien-le-Pauvre

rue St-Julien-le-Pauvre, 5th (01.43.54.52.16). M° Cluny-La Sorbonne. **Open** 9.30am-noon, 3-6.30pm Mon-Sat; 9.30am-6.30pm Sun. **Map** p406 J7.

Once a sanctuary for pilgrims en route to Compostella, the present church is from the late 12th century, on the cusp of Romanesque and Gothic, and has capitals richly decorated with vines, acanthus leaves and winged harpies. Originally part of a priory, it became the university church when colleges migrated to the Left Bank. Since 1889 it has been used by the Greek church. One of the trees in the garden may be the oldest in Paris.

Eglise St-Séverin

1 rue des Prêtres-St-Séverin, 5th (01.42.34.93.50). M° Cluny-La Sorbonne or St-Michel. **Open** 11am-7.30pm Mon, Thur-Sat; 11am-10pm Tue, Wed; 9am-8.30pm Sun. **Map** p406 J7.

Primitive and Flamboyant Gothic styles merge here. The double ambulatory is famed for its 'palm tree' vaulting and unique double spiral column. Next door are the remains of the charnel house. The bell tower has the oldest bell in Paris (1412) while the stained glass windows are modern.

Musée National du Moyen Age – Thermes de Cluny

6 pl Paul-Painlevé, 5th (01.53.73.78.00/www.musee-moyenage.fr). M° Cluny-La Sorbonne. **Open** 9.15am-5.45pm Mon, Wed-Sun. **Admission** €5.50; €4

► For detailed museum information and opening times, turn to **Sightseeing: Museums**, starting on page 147.
► For shopping information turn to **Shops & Services**, starting on page 235.
► For information on arts events turn to **Arts & Entertainment**, starting on page 275.

18-25s, all Sun; free under-18s, CM. **Credit** (shop) MC, V. **Map** p406 J7.

The museum is famed for its Roman remains and medieval art, most notably the Lady and the Unicorn tapestry cycle. The museum itself, commonly known as Cluny, is also a rare example of 15th-century secular Gothic architecture. It was built – atop a Gallo-Roman baths complex dating from the second and third centuries – by Jacques d'Amboise in 1485-98 for lodging priests at the request of the Abbé de Cluny. With its main building behind a courtyard, it was a precursor of the Marais *hôtels particuliers*; it became a museum in 1844. The baths are the finest Roman remains in Paris: the vaulted frigidarium (cold bath), tepidarium (warm bath) and caldarium (hot bath) are visible. The medieval garden is planted with species found in medieval treatises, tapestries and paintings. (*See chapter* **Museums**.)

The Sorbonne & the Montagne Ste-Geneviève

The days of horn-rims, pipes and student goatees are long gone thanks to an influx of well-heeled residents in the 1980s, who put accommodation here beyond most students' reach. At least the intellectual tradition persists: the Montagne Ste-Geneviève is a concentration of academic institutions, from the **Sorbonne** to research centres to Grandes Ecoles such as the Ecole Normale Supérieure; students throng countless specialist book stores and the art cinemas of rue Champollion and rue des Ecoles. The district's long association with learning began in about 1100, when a number of scholars, including high-pitched Pierre Abélard, began to live and teach on the Montagne, independent of the established Canon school of Notre-Dame. This loose association of scholars came to be referred to as a university. The Paris schools attracted disciples from all over Europe, and the 'colleges' – really just student residences – multiplied, until the University of Paris was given official recognition with a charter from Pope Innocent III in 1215.

By the 16th century, the university – christened the Sorbonne, after the most famous of its colleges – had been co-opted by the Catholic establishment. A century later, Cardinal Richelieu rebuilt it, but it slid into decay. After the Revolution, when the university was forced to close, Napoléon revived the Sorbonne as the cornerstone of his new, centralised education system. The university participated enthusiastically in the uprisings of the 19th century, and was also a seedbed of the May 1968 revolt. Nowadays it is decidedly less turbulent, though there are te odd moans at prices in the canteen. The present buildings are mostly 19th century; only the Baroque Chapelle de la Sorbonne survives from his rebuilding. Contrastingly, the independent **Collège de France**, also on rue des Ecoles, was founded in 1530 by a group of humanists led by Guillaume Budé under the patronage of François 1er. Neighbouring Brasserie Balzar has historically provided fuel for philosophising.

Climb up rue St-Jacques, serpentine rue de la Montagne-Ste-Geneviève or take rue des Carmes, with its Baroque chapel (now used by the Syrian church), and rue Valette past the brick and stone entrance of the Collège Ste-Barbe, where Ignatius Loyola and later Montgolfier and Eiffel studied, to the magnificently impressive place du Panthéon.

The huge domed **Panthéon**, originally commissioned by Louis XV as a church to honour the city's patron saint, Geneviève, was converted in the Revolution into a secular temple for France's *grands hommes*. *Grandes femmes* (kicking off with Marie Curie) were only admitted for burial from 1995, suggesting, perhaps, that women's lib(erté) was not high on the list of revolutionary priorities. Alexandre Dumas was moved here in October 2002, with the kind of ceremonial hullabaloo befitting such a notorious womaniser (and author). In the surrounding square, also conceived by the Panthéon's architect, Soufflot, is the elegant mairie (town hall) of the 5th arrondissement, mirrored by the law faculty. On the north side, the Bibliothèque Ste-Geneviève university library, built 1844-50 by Labrouste, has medieval manuscripts and an iron-framed reading room. On the other side of the square is the Hôtel des Grands Hommes, where Surrealist mandarin André Breton invented 'automatic writing' in the 1920s.

Pascal and Racine, and the remains of Sainte Geneviève, are buried in **Eglise St-Etienne-du Mont**, on the northeast corner of the square. Jutting up behind it, within the illustrious and elitist Lycée Henri IV is the Gothic-Romanesque Tour de Clovis, part of the former abbey. Further along rue Clovis is a chunk of Philippe-Auguste's 12th-century city wall. Literary lord Hemingway lived on both rue du Cardinal-Lemoine and rue Descartes (plaque at No 74 rue du Cardinal-Lemoine) while James II resided at No 65 in the severe buildings of the former Collège des Ecossais, founded in 1372 to house Scottish students; James' II brain stayed on here until it was desecrated and subsequently lost by mobs ('damn, where did I put that jar?') during the French Revolution. In rue des Irlandais, the Centre Culturel Irlandais, in the renovated Collège des Irlandais, presents an intriguing programme of films, concerts, plays and spoken word events promoting Irish culture; it even has its own writer and painter in residence.

La Sorbonne

Collège de France

11 pl Marcelin-Berthelot, 5th (01.44.27.12.11). M° Cluny-La Sorbonne. **Map** p406 J7.

Founded in 1530 with the patronage of François 1er, the college's singular, and rather intruiging, purpose is to teach knowledge in the making rather than fact. Lectures – which are free and open to the public – can include such eminent names as Claude Lévi-Strauss, Emmanuel Le Roy Ladurie, Jean-Claude Pecker and Jacques Tits.

Eglise St-Etienne-du-Mont

pl Ste-Geneviève, 5th (01.43.54.11.79). M° Cardinal-Lemoine/RER Luxembourg. **Open** noon-6.30pm Mon; 8am-7.30pm Tue-Fri; 9am-noon, 2-6.30pm Sat; 9am-noon, 2.30-6.30pm Sun. **Map** p406 J8.

Ste Geneviève is credited with having saved the city from the ravages of Attila the Hun in 451 and her shrine has been a popular pilgrimage place since the Dark Ages. The present church was built in an amalgam of Gothic and Renaissance styles between 1492 and 1626, and originally adjoined the abbey church of Ste-Geneviève. The facade mixes Gothic rose windows with classical columns. The stunning Renaissance roodscreen, with its double spiral staircase and ornate stone strapwork, is the only one left in Paris and thus definitely worth a looksee, as is the ornate pulpit by Germaine Pillon. Ste Geneviève's elaborate brass-covered shrine is to the right of the choir, adorned with messages of thanks.

Le Panthéon

pl du Panthéon, 5th (01.44.32.18.00). RER Luxembourg. **Open** 10am-7.15pm daily. **Admission** €7; €4.50 18-25s; free under-18s. **Credit** MC, V. **Map** p406 J8.

Soufflot's neo-classical megastructure was the architectural *Grand Projet* of its day, commissioned by a grateful Louis XV to thank Ste Geneviève for his recovery from illness. But events caught up with its completion in 1790, and during the Revolution it was re-dedicated as a 'temple of reason' and the resting-place of the nation's great men. The austere crypt of greats includes Voltaire, Rousseau, Victor Hugo and Zola. New heroes are added rarely: Pierre and Marie Curie's remains were transferred here in 1995, she being the first woman to be interred in her own right. André Malraux, writer, Resistance hero and De Gaulle's culture minister, arrived in 1996, Alexandre Dumas in 2002. Inside, there are Greek columns and domes, as well as 19th-century murals depicting the saint's life by symbolist painter Puvis de Chavannes, a formative influence on Picasso's blue period. Up the steep spiral stairs to the colonnade there are wonderful views across the city. The reconstruction of Foucault's pendulum also hangs here. The pendulum, hung from the 'eye of God', proves that the earth does indeed spin on its axis. Therefore, while you watch the pendulum swing, the building, and you, are moving around the pendulum and not vice-

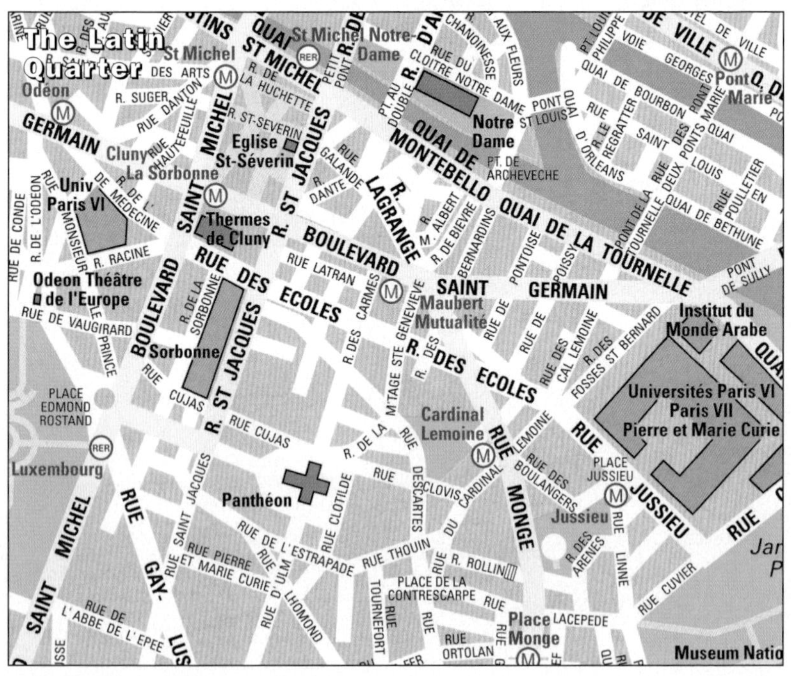

La Mosquée de Paris

versa. The central area has been cordoned off since a woman was struck by a piece of falling Panthéon à la Chicken Little.

La Sorbonne

12 rue de la Sorbonne, 5th (01.44.07.80.00/ www.sorbonne.fr). M° Cluny-La Sorbonne. **Map** p406 J7.

Founded in 1253 by Robert de Sorbon, the University of the Sorbonne was at the centre of the Latin Quarter's intellectual activity from the Middle Ages until the dramatic events of May 1968, when it was occupied by students and stormed by the CRS (riot police). The authorities subsequently splintered the University of Paris into several less-threatening outposts, but the Sorbonne remains home to the Faculté des Lettres. Rebuilt by Richelieu and reorganised by Napoléon, the present buildings mostly date from 1885 to 1900 and include a labyrinth of classrooms and quaint lecture theatres, as well as an observatory tower. The elegant dome of the 17th-century chapel dominates place de la Sorbonne; Cardinal Richelieu is buried inside. Only open to the public during exhibitions or concerts.

The rue Mouffetard area

Picturesque place de la Contrescarpe has been a famous rendezvous since the 1530s, when writers Rabelais, Ronsard and Du Bellay frequented the Cabaret de la Pomme de Pin at No 1. It still has lively cafés and people-watching galore. When George Orwell stayed at 6 rue du Pot-de-Fer from 1928-29 and detailed his experiences as a washer-upper in *Down and Out in Paris and London*, it was a place of astounding poverty; nowadays it is lined with bargain bars and restaurants, while the restored houses along rue Tournefort bear little relation to the cheap garrets in Balzac's *Le Père Goriot*. Rue Mouffetard, originally the road to Rome and one of the oldest streets in the city, winds southward swarming with cheap bistros, knick-knack shops and tourists, though the vibe as described by Hemingway – 'that wonderful narrow crowded market street, beloved of bohemians' – has somewhat changed. The busy street market (Tue-Sat and Sun morning) on the lower half seethes on weekends when the market spills on to the square and around the cafés in front of the **Eglise St-Médard**. There's also another brisk market at place Monge (Wed, Fri, Sun morning).

Beyond rue Soufflot, rue St-Jacques turns pretty. Here you'll find several ancient buildings such as the elegant *hôtel* at No 151, some good food shops as well as vintage bistro Perraudin. Rue d'Ulm houses the elitist Ecole Normale Supérieure, which was occupied by the unemployed in January 1998; in an echo of 1968, several students joined in. The outcome? Nada.

Turn off up hilly rue des Fossés-St-Jacques to discover place de l'Estrapade; in the 17th century the estrapade was a wooden tower from which deserters were dropped.

To the west, broad rue Gay-Lussac (a hotspot of May 68 and now about as revolutionary as a subscription to *The Economist*) leads to the **Jardins du Luxembourg** (*see p130*). Further down rue St-Jacques is another eminent landmark, the **Val-de-Grâce**, the least-altered and most ornate of all Paris' Baroque churches. Leading up to this, at No 6 rue du Val-de-Grâce, is the former home of Alfons Maria Mucha, the Czech art nouveau painter, most famous for his Sarah Bernhardt posters.

Eglise St-Médard

141 rue Mouffetard, 5th (01.44.08.87.00). M° Censier-Daubenton. **Open** 8am-12.30pm, 2.30-7pm Tue-Sat; 4-7pm Sun. **Map** p406 J9.

The original chapel was a dependency of the Abbaye Ste-Geneviève; rebuilding at the end of the 15th century eventually created a much larger, late-Gothic structure with elaborate vaulted ambulatory.

Eglise du Val-de-Grâce

pl Alphonse-Laveran, 5th (01.40.51.47.28). RER Port-Royal. **Open** noon-6pm, Tue, Wed, Sat, Sun. Call to arrange guided visits. **Admission** €4.60, €2.30 6-12s, free under-6s. **No credit cards**. **Map** p406 H9.

Anne d'Autriche, wife of Louis XIII, vowed to erect 'a magnificent temple' if God blessed her with a son. She got two. The resulting church and its Benedictine monastery – now a military hospital and the Musée du Service de Santé des Armées devoted to military medicine (*see chapter* **Museums**) – were built by François Mansart and Jacques Lemercier. Built over decades, this is the most luxuriously Baroque of the city's 17th-century domed churches. The swirling colours of the dome frescoes painted by Pierre Mignard in 1669 (and for which Molière wrote a eulogy) are meant to prefigure heaven.

The Jardin des Plantes district

The quieter eastern end of rue des Ecoles is a focus for Paris' Muslim community, major academic institutions and home to several Roman relics. Old-fashioned bistros on rue des Fossés-St-Bernard contrast with the brutal 1960s-70s slab architecture of Paris university's campuses VI and VII (known as Jussieu), now the subject of a major regeneration project. Between the Seine and Jussieu is the strikingly modern glass **Institut du Monde Arabe**, which has a busy programme of concerts and exhibitions and a restaurant with a great view. The Jardin Tino Rossi, along the river, contains the slightly dilapidated **Musée de la Sculpture en Plein Air** but is a favourite stop for dancing and picnicking in summer.

The Paris mosque is not far away up rue Linné, but stop off at the **Arènes de Lutèce**, the Roman amphitheatre, on the way. The central arena and many tiers of stone seating were discovered in 1869 during the building of rue Monge. Their excavation started in 1883, thanks to the archaeological zeal of Victor Hugo. The extraordinarily pretty, green-roofed **Mosquée de Paris**, partly inspired by Granada's Alhambra, was built in 1922; its beautiful Moorish tearoom has, inevitably, become a favourite with the bourgeois brigade and relaxed students, more intent on pondering their Ceylon than their Koran.

The mosque looks out on to the **Jardin des Plantes**, Paris' botanical garden. Established in 1626 as a garden for medicinal plants, it features an 18th-century maze, a winter garden brimming with rare species and the brilliantly renovated Grande Galerie de l'Evolution of the **Muséum National d'Histoire Naturelle** (*see chapter* **Museums**). There's also the Ménagerie zoo, an unlikely by-product of the Revolution, when royal and noble collections of wild animals were impounded.

Arènes de Lutèce

entrances rue Monge, rue de Navarre, rue des Arènes, 5th. M° Cardinal-Lemoine or Jussieu.
Open 8am-5.30pm winter; 8am-10pm summer.
Map p406 K8.
The Roman arena, where roaring wild beasts and glistening gladiators met their deaths, could seat

Jardin des Plantes

10,000. The site was discovered in 1869 and now incorporates a romantically planted garden. These days, it attracts skateboarders, footballers and boules players, ensuring that macho preening is alive and kicking.

Institut du Monde Arabe

1 rue des Fossés-St-Bernard, 5th (01.40.51.38.38) (www.imarabe.org). M° Jussieu. **Open** Museum 10am-6pm Tue-Sun. Library 1-8pm Tue-Sat. Café noon-6pm Tue-Sun. **Admission** roof terrace, library free. Museum €3; free under-12s. Exhibitions €6.86; €5.34 students, over-60s. **Map** p406 K7.

A clever blend of high-tech steel, glass architecture and Arab influences, this wedge-shaped Grand Projet was designed by French architect Jean Nouvel in 1980-87 with seemingly endless shuttered windows inspired by the screens of Moorish palaces; they look like and act as camera apertures according to the amount of available light. Inside is a large collection of Middle Eastern art, archaeological finds, exhibition spaces, a library and café. The Institute runs a programme of dance and classical Arab music. There is a great view from the roof.

Jardin des Plantes

pl Valhubert, rue Buffon or rue Cuvier, 5th. M° Gare d'Austerlitz or Jussieu. **Open** Main garden daily 7.15am-sunset. Alpine garden *Apr-Sept* 8-11am, 1.30-5pm. Greenhouses *Apr-Sept* 1-5pm Mon, Wed-Fri; 10am-5pm Sat, Sun. Ménagerie *Apr-Sept*, 9am-5/6pm, Mon-Sat; 9am-6.30pm Sun. Museum: Grande Galerie de l'Evolution *(01.40.79.30.00):* 10am-6pm Mon-Wed-Sun; other galleries *Apr-Sept* 10am-5pm Mon, Wed-Fri, 10am-6pm Sat, Sun. **Admission** free; greenhouses €3; Ménagerie €6, €3.50 under-18s; Grande Galerie de l'Evolution €7, €5 under-18s. **Map** p406 L8.

Although small and a tad dishevelled, the Paris botanical garden, which contains more than 10,000 species, including tropical greenhouses and rose, winter and Alpine gardens, is worth a visit. Begun by Louis XIII's doctor as the royal medicinal plant garden in 1626, it opened to the public in 1640. It also comprises the Ménagerie, a small zoo, and the Muséum National d'Histoire Naturelle, including the magnificently renovated 1880s Grande Galerie de l'Evolution. Several ancient trees on view in the gardens include a false acacia planted in 1636 and a cedar planted in 1734, while an 18th-century spiral yew maze climbs up a little hill, A plaque on the former laboratory announces that this is where Henri Becquerel discovered radioactivity in 1896. (*See also chapters* **Museums** and **Children**.)

Jardin Tino Rossi (Musée de la Sculpture en Plein Air)

quai St-Bernard, 5th. M° Gare d'Austerlitz. **Map** K8.

An open-air sculpture museum by the Seine is a fine idea – pity it's a disappointment. The concrete garden is not helped by the traffic noise from the quais, and most of the works are second-rate aside from Etienne Martin's bronze *Demeure I* and the Carrera marble *Fenêtre* by Cuban artist Careras. This area, however, hots up during those crazy summer nights when it's the venue for free salsa, tango and hip hop parties, so bring your orange shirt with the triangular, frilly sleeves.

Sightseeing

Bridge it, Jones!

Where would we be without the Seine? Residing on one mass of land just called 'The Bank'? And more crucially what would we do with all the bridges? From the golden arches of hilariously old **Pont-Neuf** to **Pont Charles-de-Gaulle** with its smooth lines of aerodynamic magic, the bridges of Paris number 36 and afford some of the most straddlingly seductive reasons to visit the city (those can-can girls aside of course). The date of the very first construction traversing the Seine is a well-guarded secret, so don't ask. What we do know is that the position of today's **Petit Pont** was established way back when the Parisii Celts were making a mint as river traders and toll-bridge operators in the 1st century BC. This said, it was not until those DIY maniacs, the Romans, arrived that things really started to get organised. Quick as a flush down the swanny, they had knocked up a cross-island thoroughfare in the guise of a reinforced **Petit Pont** and the Grand Pont (now called **Pont de Notre-Dame**) in order to create a nice, straight line of horse dung from Orléans to Belgium.

Let's focus for a moment on what really interests you, the callous reader: disaster. These bridges have been bombed, bashed to smithereens by buses, boats and barges, weather-beaten to destruction and even trampled to toppling point when, in 1634, **Pont St-Louis** collapsed beneath the weight of a religious procession. During the middle ages the handful of bridges linking the islands to its banks were lined with shops and houses – a bit of canny town planning you might think? Perhaps not considering every time the flimsy wooden constructs caught fire or got washed away their inhabitants floundered too. The **Petit Pont** sank 11 times before councillors woke up from what must have been a particularly long, boozy lunch break and banned building homes on top of bridges.

Born to save the rather rocky reputation of the Parisian bridge, the **Pont-Neuf** arrived in 1607 and, as a bastion of majestic stability, it has been standing sturdy, gargoyles a-goggle ever since. This was the first bridge to be built without buildings to encumber the

view of the river. Another first for the Neuf was the addition of a raised level of road at the edge to protect walkers from traffic and horse dung. The new-fangled 'pavement' soon caught on. (Where is the respite from the spittle, poodle poo, slaloming bladers and weak bladders that darken our glad ambling today you may well wonder?) As for the semi-circular alcoves that now provide handy smooching pit-stops they were once filled with a medley of peddlers, merchants, teeth pullers and *bouquinistes*, the second-hand book sellers that later moved on to the bank and spread their wares way down the length of the quayside.

The 19th century saw a boom in bridge building, 21 river evaders in fact, including the first suspension, steel and iron bridges. **Pont de la Concorde** famously rose from the rubble of the Bastille after the storming of 1789. Romantic **Pont des Arts** was the first solely pedestrian crossing allowing a peaceful treading of the boards since 1803 (though it was rebuilt in the 1980s). The most glitteringly exuberant would have to be the gilded torch-headed **Pont Alexandre III** to which Tsar Nicholas II laid the first stone. The most pleasingly practical is the **Pont de l'Alma** with its statue of the Zouave. This has become a popular flood level measure: when his toes get wet the state raises the flood alert and starts to close the quay-side roads; when he is fully ankle paddling it is no longer possible to navigate the river by boat. This offers some indication of how devastating the great 1910 flood must have been, when the statue disappeared up to his neck along with the rest of central Paris.

The 20th century also welcomed some parabola-tastic additions to the line-up. **Pont Charles-de-Gaulle** for example stretches resplendent like a huge aeroplane's wing and iron **Viaduc d'Austerlitz** (1905) is striking yet elegant in the way it cradles the line 5 Métro. Planned for 2006 the **Passerelle de la Bibliothèque Nationale**, as Paris' 37th bridge, has a lot to live up to. Whispers are of a low lying, cabled construction without any ground supports between the banks, and a walkway stretching 180 metres. Quay magnifico!

Institut de France

La Mosquée de Paris

1 pl du Puits-de-l'Ermite, 5th (01.45.35.97.33/ tearoom 01.43.31.38.20/Turkish baths 01.43.31.18.14/www.mosquee-de-paris.com). M° Censier-Daubenton. **Open** tours 9am-noon, 2-6pm Mon-Thur, Sat, Sun (closed Muslim holidays); tearoom 10am-midnight daily; restaurant 7.30pm-10.30pm daily; baths (women) 10am-9pm Mon, Wed, Sat; 2-9pm Fri; (men) 2-9pm Tue; 10am-9pm Sun. **Admission** €2.30; €1.50 7-25s, over-60s; free under-7s; tearoom free; baths €15-€35. **Credit** MC, V. **Map** p406 K9.

The mosque's stunning green-and-white square minaret oversees the centre of the Algerian-dominated Muslim community in France. Built in 1922-26 in Hispano-Moorish style, with elements inspired by the Alhambra and Fez's Mosque Bou-Inania, the mosque is a series of buildings and courtyards in three sections: religious (grand patio, prayer room and minaret, all of which are for serious worshippers as opposed to inquisitive tourists); scholarly (Islamic school and library); and, entered from rue Geoffroy-St-Hilaire, commercial (domed hammam or Turkish baths, relaxing Moorish tearoom and souvenir and bird-cage shop).

St-Germain-des-Prés & Odéon

To paraphrase Nile Rogers, le 6th c'est chic. The myths of Paris café society and intellectual life were born in St-Germain-des-Prés. Verlaine and Rimbaud drank here; later, Sartre, Camus and de Beauvoir scribbled and squabbled, and musicians congregated around writer, critic and trumpeter Boris Vian in Paris' postwar jazz boom. Poor old attention-seeking self-proclaimed Lizard King Jim Morrison spent most of his final days here in the summer of 1971.

Earnest types still vogue their way down the road ostentatiously bearing weighty tomes and the literati still gather on terraces – to give interviews – but the area is so expensive that any writers here are either well-established or rich. Existential questions have been replaced with pragmatic ones: 'Should I have the club sandwich or the carpaccio?' Armani took over the old Drugstore, Dior a bookshop, Cartier a classical record shop and Louis Vuitton unpacked its bags at place St-Germain; the All Jazz Club and La Villa Jazz Club closed and musicians crossed the river. It didn't happen without a fight, though it has to be said it was more a 'powder puffs at dawn' affair: in 1997 a band of intellectuals founded 'SOS St-Germain' to halt the encroaching tide of commercialism. Sonia Rykiel joined the campaigners; Karl Lagerfeld opened his own photography gallery on rue de Seine. The upshot? St-Germain now almost rivals the avenue Montaigne for designer boutiques.

From the Boulevard to the Seine

Hit by shortages of coal during World War II, Sartre descended from the ivory tower of his apartment on rue Bonaparte to save a bundle in heating bills. 'The principal interest of the Café de Flore,' he noted, 'was that it had a stove, a nearby Métro and no Germans.' Although you can now spend more on a few coffees here than on a week's heating, the **Flore** (172 bd St-

Germain) remains an arty favourite and hosts café philo evenings in English. Its rival, **Les Deux Magots**, facing historic **Eglise St-Germain-des-Prés**, on pl St-Germain-des-Prés, provides for an interesting cross-section of tourists. At No 151 is politicians' favourite **Brasserie Lipp** while art nouveau fans prefer the brasserie Vagenende (No 140); at No 170 is the late-night bookshop and intelligentsia pick-up venue **La Hune**.

St-Germain grew up around the important abbey and traces of its cloister and part of the abbot's palace remain behind the church on rue de l'Abbaye. Built in 1586 in red brick with stone facing, it prefigures the place des Vosges. The charming place Furstenberg (once the stables of the Abbot's palace), now shades upmarket furnishing fabric stores and the house and studio where the painter Delacroix lived (*see chapter* **Museums**). Ingres, Wagner and Colette lived on rue Jacob; its elegant 17th-century *hôtels particuliers* now contain specialist book, design and antiques shops, pleasant hotels and bohemian throwbacks including *chansonnier* bistro Les Assassins.

Further east, the rue de Buci hosts a street market, running into rue de Seine with lots of activity centred around the Bar du Marché and Les Etages cafés. Hôtel La Louisane, on the same road, accommodated jazz gods Chet Baker and Miles Davis and Existentialist deities Sartre and de Beauvoir. Rue Bonaparte (Manet was born at No 5 in 1832), rue de Seine and rue des Beaux-Arts are still packed with small art galleries specialising in 20th-century abstraction, tribal art and art deco furniture (*see chapter* **Galleries**). Oscar Wilde complained about the wallpaper and then checked out for good at what was then the Hôtel d'Alsace, now the renovated and fashionably over-the-top **L'Hôtel** in rue des Beaux-Arts. La Palette and Bistro Mazarin are good stopping-off points with enviable terraces on rue Jacques-Callot, while rue Mazarine, with shops of lighting, vintage toys and jewellery, also houses Conran's brasserie L'Alcazar (No 62) and hipster club **WAGG** in a former cabaret. The **Ecole Nationale Supérieure des Beaux-Arts**, Paris' main fine-arts school, occupies a former monastery at the northern end of rue Bonaparte. On the quai de Conti is the domed **Institut de France**, cleaned to within an inch of its crisp classical life. Next door stands the neo-classical Hôtel des Monnaies, formerly the mint (1777-1973) and now the **Musée de la Monnaie**, a coin museum. Opposite, the iron Pont des Arts footbridge leads across to the Louvre in a direct route to the culture palace.

Coffee made its first appearance in Paris in 1686 at Café Procope on rue de l'Ancienne-Comédie. Once frequented by Voltaire, Rousseau, Benjamin Franklin, revolutionary Danton and later Verlaine, its guests today are primarily tourists. It does, however, contain some remarkable memorabilia, including Voltaire's desk and a postcard from Marie-Antoinette. The back opens on to the twee cobbled passage du Commerce St-André, home to toy shops, jewellers, chintzy tearooms and tapas trove La Catalogne . In the 18th century, Dr Joseph-Ignace Guillotin first tested out his notorious device – designed to make public executions more humane and destined to come in more than a little handy in revolutionary Paris – in the cellars of what is now the Pub St-Germain. The first victim was reputedly a sheep. Jacobin regicide Billaud-Varenne was one of those who felt the blade of Dr Guillotin's invention. His former home (45 rue St-André-des-Arts) was an incongruous location for the first girls' lycée in Paris, the Lycée Fénelon, founded in 1883. Formerly a 'des res', today rue St-André-des-Arts is lined with gift shops, crêperies and an arts cinema. Veer off the main drag into the quiet side streets, such as rue des Grands-Augustins, rue de Savoie and rue Séguier, home to printers, bookshops and dignified 17th-century buildings. On the corner of rue and quai des Grands-Augustins, the restaurant Lapérouse has a series of private dining rooms, where gentlemen liked to entertain their demi-monde mistresses; while contemporary Les Bouquinistes is easy to peek into. The turreted Hôtel de Fécamp, at 5 rue de

The best Spiritual vibes

Eglise St-Séverin
1 rue des Prêtres-St-Séverin, 5th. See p177.
Are we talking the merging of Primitive and Flamboyant Gothic styles here, or what?

Eglise du Val-de-Grâce
pl Alphonse-Laveran, 5th. See p121.
Baroque 'n'roll heaven.

La Mosquée de Paris
1 pl du Puits-de-l'Ermite, 5th. See p123.
Religious, scholarly and welcoming. And what a minaret.

Mur Pour la Paix
Champ de Mars, 7th. See p132.
Erected in the year 2000 to celebrate the hopes for peace. You can't stop hoping.

Hautefeuille, was the medieval townhouse of the abbots of Fécamp, begun in 1292. Rue Gît-le-Coeur ('here lies the heart') is so-called, legend has it, because one of Henri IV's mistresses lived here. At No 9 is the now rather luxurious Hôtel du Vieux Paris, or the 'Beat Hotel', where William Burroughs revised *The Naked Lunch*.

Ecole Nationale Supérieure des Beaux-Arts (Ensb-a)

14 rue Bonaparte, 6th (01.47.03.52.15/ www.ensba.fr). M° St-Germain-des-Prés. **Open** courtyard 9am-5pm Mon-Fri; exhibitions Tue-Sun 1-7pm. **Admission** exhibitions €4; €2.50 students, children, free under-12s. Credit V. **Map** p405 H6.

Paris' most prestigious fine-art school resides in what remains of a 17th-century convent, the 18th-century Hôtel de Chimay and some later additions. After the Revolution, the buildings were transformed into a museum of French monuments, then in 1816 into the Ecole. Exhibitions are often held (*see chapter* **Museums**).

Institut de France

23 quai de Conti, 6th (01.44.41.44.41/www.institut-de-france.fr). M° St-Germain-des-Prés. Guided tours Sat, Sun (call ahead for times). **Admission** €3.10. **No credit cards. Map** p406 H6.

The elegant domed building, designed by Louis Le Vau in 1663-84, was originally a school for provincial children founded by Cardinal Mazarin. In 1805, the five academies of the Institut (Académie Française, Académie des Inscriptions et Belles-Lettres, Académie des Sciences, Académie des Beaux-Arts, Académie des Sciences Morales et Politiques), were transferred here. Inside is Mazarin's ornate tomb by Hardouin-Mansart, and the Bibliothèque Mazarine (open to over-18s, €15 for a one-year card with ID and two photos). The Académie Française, the overly zealous guardian of the French language was founded by Cardinal Richelieu in 1635 with the aim of preserving the purity of French from corrupting outside influences, such as English. The Immortals, as the members of the Academy are still modestly known, pluckily refuse to surrender and have never stopped trying to impose archaic rules on a language and a population that are embracing multi-cultural influences.

Eglise St-Germain-des-Prés

3 pl St-Germain-des-Prés, 6th (01.43.25.41.71). M° St-Germain-des-Prés. **Open** 8am-7.45pm Mon-Sat; 9am-8pm Sun. **Map** p405 H7.

This, ladies and gentlemen, is the oldest church in Paris. On the advice of Germain (later bishop of Paris), Childebert, son of Clovis, had a basilica and monastery built here around 543; it was originally called the Church of St Vincent and then came to be known as St-Germain-le-Doré because of its copper roof. During the Revolution the abbey was burnt and a saltpetre refinery installed; the spire was only added as part of a clumsy 19th-century restoration. Despite this, most of the present structure is 12th-century, and some ornate carved capitals and the tower remain from the 11th. Illustrious tombs include those of Jean-Casimir, deposed king of Poland, who became abbot of St-Germain in 1669, and Scottish nobleman William Douglas. Under the window in the second chapel is philosopher and mathematician René Descartes' funeral stone; his ashes (bar those from his skull) have been lodging here since 1819.

St-Sulpice & the Luxembourg

The quarter south of boulevard St-Germain between Odéon and Luxembourg, crammed with historic buildings and interesting shops, epitomises civilised Paris. Just off the boulevard lies the covered market of St-Germain, once the site of the medieval St-Germain Fair. It now houses an underground swimming pool, auditorium, food hall and a shopping arcade. There are bars and bistros along rue Guisarde, nicknamed rue de la soif (street of thirst) thanks to its regular bevy of merry carousers. Rue Princesse and rue des Canettes are a beguiling mix of gleeful bistros, including Mâchon d'Henri and Brasserie Fernand, budget eateries, Italian pizzerias and late-night haunts known to a determined – if unsteady – few: the Birdland bar, Bedford Arms pub and notoriously elitist nightspot **Club Castel**.

Pass the fashion boutiques, antiquarian book and print shops and high-class pâtisseries (note the huge queue outside Pierre Hermé, the portly Picasso of pâtisserie) and you come to **Eglise St-Sulpice**, a surprising 18th-century exercise in classical form with two uneven turrets and a colonnaded façade. The square contains Visconti's imposing, lion-flanked Fontaine des Quatre Point Cardinaux (its name is a pun on cardinal points and the statues of Bishops Bossuet, Fénelon, Massilon and Flechier, none of whom was actually a cardinal) and is the site for an antiques fair and a poetry fair each summer. The Café de la Mairie is a favourite with intellectuals and students, while amid shops of religious artefacts, the chic boutiques on place and rue St-Sulpice include Yves Saint Laurent, Christian Lacroix, **Agnès b**, **Vanessa Bruno**, Muji, Catherine Memmi, perfumier Annick Goutal and milliner **Marie Mercié**. Prime shopping territory continues west: clothes on rue Bonaparte and rue du Four and accessory and fashion shops on rue du Dragon, rue de Grenelle and rue du Cherche-Midi.

If you spot a queue in the latter street, it's most likely for **Poilâne**'s designer bread, which also graces the sandwiches at busy wine bar Au Sauvignon at the fraught carrefour de la Croix-Rouge. The chapel of St-Joseph des Carmes (70 rue de Vaugirard), once a Carmelite convent,

Eglise St-Germain-des-Prés

now hidden within the Institut Catholique, was the scene for the killing of 115 priests during the Terror in 1792. To the east lies wide rue de Tournon, lined by some grand 18th-century residences, such as the elegant Hôtel de Brancas, with figures of Justice and Prudence over the door. This street opens up to the Palais du Luxembourg, which now serves as the Senate, and its adjoining park.

Back towards boulevard St-Germain lies the neo-classical **Odéon, Théâtre de l'Europe**, built in 1779 and currently closed for renovation. Beaumarchais' *Marriage of Figaro* was first performed here in 1784. The semi-circular place in front was home to revolutionary hero Camille Desmoulins, at No 2, now La Méditerranée restaurant, designed by Jean Cocteau. Another hangout among the antiquarian bookshops on rue de l'Odéon is Le Bar Dix. Joyce's *Ulysses* was first published next door (No 12) by Sylvia Beach at the legendary Shakespeare & Co in 1922 (no relation to the Latin Quarter bookshop).

Up the street, at 12 rue de l'Ecole-de-Médecine, is the colonnaded neo-classical Université René Descartes (Paris V) medical school, and the Musée d'Histoire de la Médecine (*see chapter* **Museums**). The Club des Cordeliers cooked up revolutionary plots across the street at the Couvent des Cordeliers (No 15), and Marat, one of the club's leading lights, met an undignified end in the tub at his home in the same street when he was stabbed by Charlotte Corday. Check out at the sculpted doorway of the neighbouring *hôtel* and the domed building at No 5, once the barbers' and surgeons' guild. Climb up rue André-Dubois to rue Monsieur-le-Prince and popular budget restaurant Polidor at No 41, around since 1845 and, near the boulevard St-Michel, the arts cinema Les 3 Luxembourgs.

Eglise St-Sulpice

pl St-Sulpice, 6th (01.46.33.21.78). M° St-Sulpice.
Open 8am-7pm daily. **Map** p405 H7.

It took 120 years (starting from 1646) and six architects to finish the church of St-Sulpice. The grandiose Italianate facade with its two towers was designed by Jean-Baptiste Servandoni, although he died in 1766 before the second tower was completed, leaving one tower a good five metres shorter than the other. Three paintings by Delacroix in the first chapel: *Jacob's Fight with the Angel*, *Heliodorus Chased out of the Temple* and *St-Michael Killing the Dragon*, create a suitably sombre atmosphere. The square and fountain in front were designed in the 19th century by Visconti.

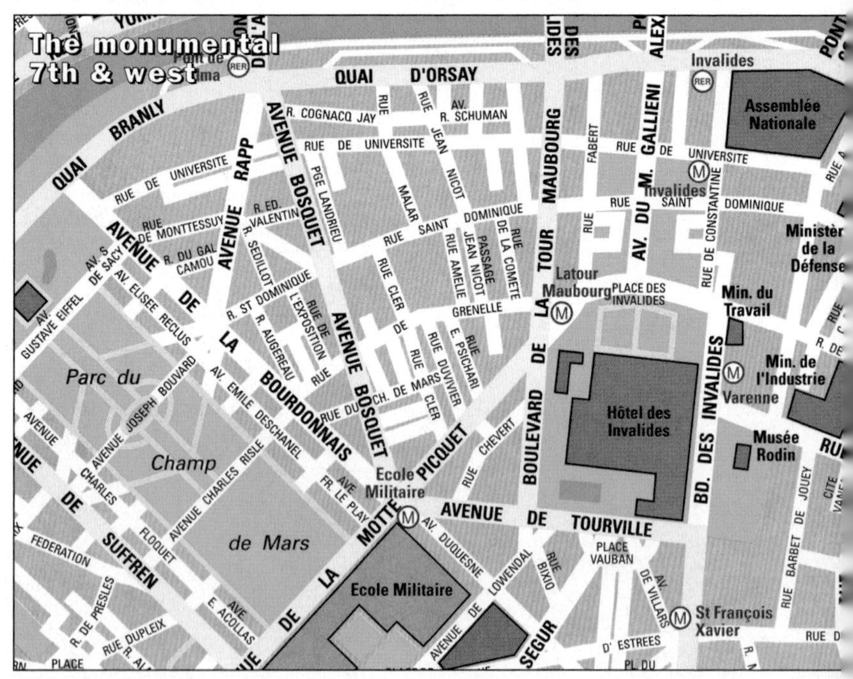

Jardins and Palais du Luxembourg

pl Auguste-Comte, pl Edmond-Rostand or rue de Vaugirard, 6th. M° Odéon/RER Luxembourg. **Open** dawn-dusk daily. **Map** p405 H8.

The palais was built in the 1620s for Marie de Médicis, widow of Henri IV, by Salomon de Brosse on the site of the former mansion of the Duke of Luxembourg. Its rustic, Italianate style was intended to remind her of the Pitti Palace in her native Florence. In 1621, she commissioned Rubens to produce for the palace the 24 huge paintings celebrating her life (in various stages of undress) that are now in the Louvre. Reworked by Chalgrin in the 18th century, the palais now houses the French parliamentary upper house, the Sénat. The gardens are the real draw: part formal, with terraces and gravel paths, part 'English garden' of lawns and mature trees, they are the quintessential Paris park. The garden is peopled with diverse sculpted dramatis personae, from the looming Cyclops on the 1624 Fontaine de Médicis, to queens of France, a mini Statue of Liberty, wild animals and a monument to Delacroix. There are orchards, containing 300 varieties of apples and pears, and an apiary where you can take courses in beekeeping. The **Musée du Luxembourg** (*see chapter* **Museums**) is used for prestigious art exhibitions, with lesser art shows in the former Orangerie. Most interesting, though, are the people: chess players, joggers in ill-advised shorts and martial arts practitioners; children on ponies, in sandpits, on roundabouts and playing with the old-fashioned sailing boats on the pond. Then, there are the choicest tennis courts on the Left Bank, *boules* pitches, a café, a bandstand and acres of park chairs. (*See also chapter* **Children**).

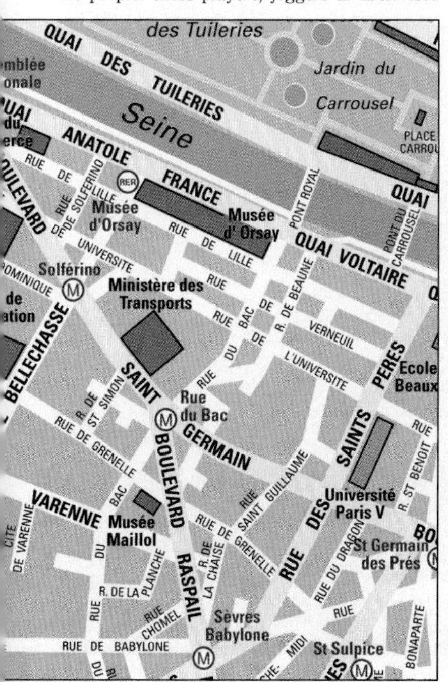

The Monumental 7th & west

Mainly 7th arrondissement, parts of 6th and 15th.

Townhouses spread out westwards from St-Germain into the profoundly establishment 7th arrondissement, as the vibrant street and café life gives way to tranquil residential blocks and government offices. The 7th easily divides into two halves: the more intimate Faubourg St-Germain to the east, with its historic mansions and fine shops and, to west of Les Invalides, windswept wide avenues and the **Eiffel Tower**.

The Faubourg St-Germain

Often written off by notorious old bore Proust as a symbol of staid, *haute bourgeoise* and aristocratic society, this area remains home to some of Paris' oldest and grandest families, though most of its 18th-century *hôtels particuliers* have now been taken over by embassies and government ministries. Glimpse their stone gateways and elegant courtyards, especially on rues de Grenelle, St-Dominique, de l'Université and de Varenne. Among the most beautiful is the Hôtel Matignon (57 rue de Varenne), residence of the Prime Minister. Used by the French statesman Talleyrand for lavish receptions, it contains the biggest private garden in Paris. The Cité Varenne at No 51 is a lane of exclusive houses with more private gardens. Fancy Hôtel Bouchardon now houses the **Musée Maillol**. You'll have to wait for the open-house *Journées du Patrimoine* (*see chapter* **Festivals & Events**) to see the decorative interiors and private gardens of others such as the Hôtel de Villeroy (Ministry of Agriculture, 78 rue de Varenne), Hôtel Boisgelin (Italian Embassy, 47 rue de Varenne), Hôtel d'Estrées (residence of the Russian ambassador, 79 rue de Grenelle), Hôtel d'Avaray (residence of the Dutch ambassador, 85 rue de Grenelle) or Hôtel de Monaco (Polish Embassy, 57 rue St-Dominique). Then there's rue du Bac where **Bon Marché**, Paris' oldest department store, lies in wait and unlikely pilgrimage spot, the **Chapelle de la Médaille Miraculeuse**.

Across boulevard St-Germain, the 'Carré Rive Gauche' – the quadrangle of streets enclosed by quai Voltaire, rues des Sts-Pères, du Bac and de l'Université – is lined with drool-inducing antiques shops. Just west of here a beaux-arts

Le Fab Four: The Eiffel Tower

Yes, of course it's an obvious thing to say, but, in purely architectural terms, in the surging, emotive power with which it breaks free from physical restraint, the Eiffel Tower resembles nothing so much as one of the late Barry White's yearning string arrangements for the Love Unlimited Orchestra. More prosaically, of course, it's a Gustave Eiffel metal girder arrangement, constructed in 1889 for the Exposition Universelle.

The boy Gustave must have been on the architectural Viagra, because he erected this 324-metre monument in less than two years, and it's been up ever since. (That said, in 1994, a group of terrorists hijacked a plane, which they were intent on flying into the Tower. Only the quick-witted air traffic controllers with whom the hijackers were in communication prevented disaster: they convinced the terrorists – falsely – that there wasn't enough fuel to reach the Tower, and the attempt was abandoned at Marseille.)

Six million people visit the Tower each year, which is why it's the only major Paris tourist monument that makes a profit, and that's despite an ingenious scam dreamt up by some of its cashiers; in a recent sting it was revealed that the computerised ticketing system kept 'breaking down' – it was actually being switched off by unscrupulous employees, who trousered vast amounts of tickets while the system was down, and sold them later at knock-down prices, to the alleged tune of €1 million. A bit naughty, that.

The summer of 2003 saw the unveiling of the Tour's new €4.3 million sparkly dress – every night for the next decade, for ten minutes per hour, 20,000 lights will be a-flash, an effect that typifies the nonchalant swagger of the world's most popular tourist monument. Some vital statistics: to get to the top, you have to climb 1665 steps (but there are three viewing levels where you can have a lie down and/or myocardial infarction while geekier friends marvel at the view; the Tower is made up of 7,300 tonnes of steel; for 2003's night-time flashing, 42 km of electrical wiring had to be fitted. Unmissable.

train station houses the unmissable art collections of **Musée d'Orsay**. Continuing westward, facing place de la Concorde across the Seine, is the **Assemblée Nationale**, the lower house of the French parliament. Beside the Assemblée is the Foreign Ministry, often referred to by its address, 'quai d'Orsay'. Beyond it a long, grassy esplanade leads up to the golden-domed **Invalides**, the vast military hospital complex and Eglise du Dôme and St-Louis-des-Invalides churches, built by Louis XIV. It now houses the **Musée de l'Armée**, as well as Napoléon's tomb inside the Eglise du Dôme. Stand with your back to the dome to survey cherubim-laden Pont Alexandre III and the Grand and Petit Palais across the river. Just beside Les Invalides, a cosier place to visit is the **Musée Rodin**, housed in the charming 18th-century Hôtel Biron and its romantic gardens. Rodin was invited to move here in 1908 on the understanding that he would give his work to the state. As a result, you can now see many of his great sculptures, including *The Thinker* and *The Burghers of Calais*.

Assemblée Nationale

33 quai d'Orsay, 7th (01.40.63.60.00/ www.assemblee-nat.fr). M° Assemblée Nationale. **Open** 8.40-11.40am, 2-5pm Mon, Fri, Sat. **Admission** free; guided tours 10am, 2pm, 3pm Sat; ID required. **Map** p405 F5.
The Palais Bourbon has harboured parliament's lower house since 1827. The palace was extended by the Prince de Condé, who added the Hôtel de Lassay, now official residence of the Assembly's president. Inside, the library is decorated with Delacroix's *History of Civilisation*. Visitors can attend debates.

Chapelle de la Médaille Miraculeuse

Couvent des Soeurs de St-Vincent-de-Paul, 140 rue du Bac, 7th (01.49.54.78.88). M° Sèvres-Babylone. **Open** 7.45am-1pm, 2.30-7pm Mon-Sat; 7.30am-2pm, 2.30-7pm Sun. **Map** p405 F7.
In 1830 saintly Catherine Labouré was visited by the Virgin, who gave her a medal which performed many miracles. Uh huh. Attracting over two million faithful every year, the kitsch chapel – a concoction of statues, mosaics and murals, and the embalmed bodies of Catherine and her mother superior – continues to be one of France's most visited pilgrimage sites. Reliefs recount the nun's story.

Les Invalides

esplanade des Invalides, 7th (01.44.42.54.52/Musée de l'Armée 01.44.42.37.67/www.invalides.org). M° Invalides. **Open** *Apr-Sept* 10am-5.45pm daily; *Oct-Mar* 10am-4.45pm daily. **Admission** courtyard free. Musée de l'Armée & Eglise du Dôme €6; €4.50 students under 26; free under-18s, CM. **Credit** MC, V. **Map** p405 E6.
Despite its imposing gilded dome, the Hôtel des Invalides was (and in part still is) a hospital. Commissioned by Louis XIV to care for the war-wounded, at one time it housed up to 6,000 invalids – hence the name. The foundations were laid in 1671 and the design is Bruand's baby. Now the *hôtel* contains the **Musée de l'Armée** (*see chapter* **Museums**), which has a staggering display of wartime paraphernalia, and Musée de l'Ordre de la Libération. Since 1840 the Baroque Eglise du Dôme has been dedicated to the worship of Napoléon, whose body was supposedly brought here from St-Helena (although now there is now some doubt about that). The church of St-Louis, known as the Church of the Soldiers, is decorated with captured flags and its crypt filled with the remains of military men. Wander the principal courtyard, with its grandiose arcades and sundials, to breathe in the power of royal patronage.

Musée d'Orsay

1 rue de la Légion d'Honneur, 7th (01.40.49.48.14/ recorded information 01.45.49.11.11/www.musee-orsay.fr). M° Solférino/ RER Musée d'Orsay. **Open** 10am-6pm Tue, Wed, Fri, Sat; 10am-9.30pm Thur, 9am-6pm Sun. **Admission** €7; €5 students, over-60s, Sun; free under-18s; free first Sun of month. **Credit** (shop) AmEx, MC, V. **Map** p405 G6.
Originally a train station (statues representing the towns originally served line the facade), designed by Victor Laloux to coincide with the 1900 Exposition Universelle. The platforms proved too short for modern trains and, by the 1950s, the station was threatened with demolition. It then became home to a theatre (the Renaud-Barrault), and Orson Welles' film of *The Trial* was shot here. It was saved in the late 1970s when President Giscard d'Estaing decided to turn it into a museum spanning the fertile art period 1830-1914, home to masterpieces by Manet, Monet, Degas, Renoir, Gauguin, Cézanne and Van Gogh among others. The painter Edouard Detaille had said it looked like a palace of fine art when it was built. Italian architect Gae Aulenti redesigned the interior. (*See also chapter* **Museums**.)

West of Les Invalides

To the west of the Invalides is the massive Ecole Militaire, the military academy built by Louis XV to educate the children of penniless officers. It would later train Napoléon. Still used by the army, it is closed to the public. Opposite its south entrance are the Y-shaped **UNESCO** building, constructed in 1958, and the Modernist Ministry of Labour. But it's not all officialdom and bureaucracy: there's one of Paris' prettiest street markets on the avenue de Saxe, old-fashioned bistro Thoumieux at 79 rue St-Dominique, and smart food shops in rue Cler.

This area was once far more industrial. The corner of rue Surcouf and rue de l'Université is the site of the Manufacture du Gros Caillou, where France's first cigarettes were made in 1845. From the north-western side of the Ecole

Militaire begins the vast Champ de Mars, a market garden converted into a military drilling ground in the 18th century. It now houses the *Mur pour la Paix*, erected in 2000 against the backdrop of the **Eiffel Tower** to celebrate the hopes for peace brought by the new millenium.

Les Egouts de Paris

entrance opposite 93 quai d'Orsay, by Pont de l'Alma, 7th (01.53.68.27.81). M° Alma-Marceau/ RER Pont de l'Alma. **Open** 11am-4pm Sat-Wed. Closed three weeks in Jan. **Admission** €3.80; €3.05 students, over 60s; €2.30 5-12s; free under 5s, CM. **Map** p404 D5.

For centuries the main source of drinking water in Paris was the Seine, which was also the main sewer. Thankfully, construction of an underground sewerage system began in 1825 under Napoléon (one of the first Frenchmen to have a bath, too). Today, the Egouts de Paris are perhaps the smelliest museum in the world; each sewer in the 2,100km system is marked with a replica of the street sign above. The Egouts can be closed after periods of heavy rain.

The best Intello spots

Montagne Ste-Geneviève

5th arrondissement. See p188.

What's the collective noun for Left Bank intellectuals? Answer: a 'goatee'. If you crammed the whole goatee into one area, it would fill Montagne-Ste-Geneviève, home to the Sorbonne, the Research Centres and the Ecole Normale Supérieure.

Collège de France

5th arrondissement. See p120.

Egalité, my friend: here's where they share out all that collidge nollidge. Lectures are open to the public. ('What shall we do tonight, dear? Go and listen to a lecture or have crazy monkey sex?' 'Fetch me my duffle coat and my horn rims.')

Institut de France

6th arrondissement. See p128.

The five academies of the Institut include the Académie Française, the protectors of the French language from outside linguistic imperialism. God only knows what the Immortals, the members of the Academy, are making of 'freedom fries'.

Rue Louise-Weiss

13th arrondissement. See p139.

The achingly contemporary galleries in this street manage to draw crowds to their *vernissages* without offering a single drop of alcohol, such is the thirst for pretentious hob-nobbing. Good for snapping up cheap collectibles, though.

Eiffel Tower

Champ de Mars, 7th (01.44.11.23.45/recorded information 01.44.11.23.23/www.tour-eiffel.fr). M° Bir-Hakeim/RER Champ de Mars Tour Eiffel. **Open** *Sept-13 June* 9.30am-11pm daily; *14 June-31 Aug* 9am-midnight. **Admission** By lift 1st level €3.70; €2.3 3-12s; 2nd level €7; €3.90 3-12s; 3rd level €10.20; €5.50 3-12s; free under-3s. By stairs (9.30am-6.30pm) 1st & 2nd levels €3.3. **Wheelchair access (1st & 2nd levels only). Credit** AmEx, MC, V. **Map** p404 C6.

(*See p132* **Le Fab Four: The Eiffel Tower**).

UNESCO

7 pl de Fontenoy, 7th (01.45.68.10.00/ www.unesco.org). M° Ecole-Militaire. **Open** 9.30am-2.30pm Mon-Fri; Tours 3pm (phone 01.45.68.16.42). **Map** p404 D7.

The Y-shaped UNESCO headquarters, built in 1958, is the work of a group of architects of three nationalities: American Marcel Breuer, Italian Pier Luigi Nervi and Frenchman Bernard Zehrfuss. It's worth visiting for the sculptures and paintings by Picasso, Arp, Giacometti, Moore, Calder and Miró, and the Japanese garden, with a contemplation cylinder by Japanese minimalist architect Tadao Ando.

Village Suisse

38-78 av de Suffren/54 av de la Motte-Picquet, 15th (01.43.06.44.18). M° La Motte-Picquet-Grenelle. **Open** 10.30am-1pm; 2-7pm Mon, Thur-Sun. **Map** p404 D7.

The mountains and waterfalls created for the Swiss Village at the 1900 Exposition Universelle are long gone, but the village lives on. Rebuilt as blocks of flats, the street level has been colonised by some 150 boutiques offering high-quality antiques and expensive collectibles.

Fronts de Seine

Downstream from the Eiffel Tower, the 15th arrondissement is a bit of a cultural wasteland. The high-tech **Maison de la Culture du Japon** stands near the Pont Bir-Hakeim on quai Branly. The riverfront, with its tower block developments, was the scene of some of the worst architectural crimes of the 1970s. Further west there is hope: the sophisticated headquarters of the Canal+ TV channel (2 rue des Cévennes) are surrounded by fine modern housing, and the **Parc André Citroën**.

Parc André Citroën

rue Balard, rue St-Charles, quai Citroën, 15th. M° Javel or Balard. **Open** dawn-6pm Mon-Fri; 9am-6pm Sat, Sun, public holidays. **Map** p404 A9.

This park is a fun, 21st-century take on a French formal garden. It comprises glasshouses, computerised fountains, waterfalls, a wilderness and gar-

Parc André Citroën

dens with different-coloured plants and even sounds. Stepping stones and water jets prove that this is a garden for pleasure as well as philosophy. There's also a panoramic Paris in miniature.

Maison de la Culture du Japon

101 bis quai Branly, 15th (01.44.37.95.00). M° Bir-Hakeim/ RER Champ de Mars Tour Eiffel. **Open** noon-7pm Tue, Wed, Fri, Sat; noon-8pm Thur. **Admission** free. **Map** p404 C6.
Built in 1996 by the Anglo-Japanese architectural partnership of Yamanaka and Armstrong, this opalescent glass cultural centre reflects Paris' large Japanese community. There is a full programme of exhibitions, theatre and film, plus a library, authentic Japanese tea ceremony and a shop.

Montparnasse & beyond

Mainly 6th and 14th arrondissements, parts of 13th and 15th.
Artists such as Picasso, Léger and Soutine fled to 'Mount Parnassus' in the early 1900s to escape the rising rents of Montmartre. They were soon joined by Chagall, Zadkine and other escapees from the Russian Revolution and by Americans, including Man Ray, Henry Miller, Ezra Pound and Gertrude Stein. Between the wars the neighbourhood symbolised modernity.

Today, Montparnasse is a less festive place. The high-rise **Tour Montparnasse** is the most visible of several atrocious projects of the 1970s; at least there are good views from the top. At its foot are the Red Light and new Amnesia nightclubs (*see chapter* **Clubs**), joined in winter by an outdoor ice rink. The old Montparnasse railway station witnessed two events of historical significance: the Germans surrendered Paris here on 25 August 1944, and in 1898 a runaway train went out of control and burst through its facade. The train station was rebuilt in the 1970s, a nondescript affair but which hides the surprising **Jardin de l'Atlantique** and the **Mémorial du Maréchal Leclerc/Musée Jean Moulin**, testifying to French wartime resistance and the Liberation, above the tracks.

As the station that speeds off to Brittany, rue du Montparnasse is clustered with crêperies. Nearby, strip joints have replaced most of the theatres on ever-saucy rue de la Gaîté, but if you don't fancy the T&A routine, boulevard Edgar-Quinet has pleasant cafés and a street market (Wed, Sat mornings), as well as the main entrance to the **Cimetière du Montparnasse**. The boulevard du Montparnasse still buzzes at night, thanks to its many cinemas and brasseries: Le Dôme at No 108, now a fish restaurant and bar; giant art deco brasserie La Coupole at No 102, which opened in 1927; and opposite, classic late-night café Le Select. Further east, literary café La Closerie des Lilas was a favourite with everyone from Lenin and Trotsky to Picasso and Hemingway. For a glimpse of Montparnasse's artistic past, wander down rue de la Grande-Chaumière. Bourdelle and Friesz taught at the venerable Académie de la Grande-Chaumière (No 14), frequented by Calder, Giacommetti and

Pompon among others, and it still offers drawing lessons today, and visit nearby **Musée Zadkine**, the sculptor's former house and studio. There are shoe, food and children's shops on rues Vavin and Bréa, which lead to the **Jardins du Luxembourg**. Stop for a coffee at Café Vavin and look at Henri Sauvage's white tiled apartment building at 6 rue Vavin, built in 1911-12. A more recent addition is the glass and steel **Fondation Cartier** designed by Jean Nouvel on boulevard Raspail, the jewellery company's HQ and an exhibition centre for contemporary art.

Cimetière du Montparnasse

3 bd Edgar-Quinet, 14th (01.44.10.86.50). M° Edgar-Quinet or Raspail. **Open** *16 Mar-5 Nov* 8am-6pm Mon-Fri; 8.30am-6pm Sat; 9am-6pm Sun; *6 Nov-15 Mar* 8am-5.30pm Mon-Fri; 8.30am-5.30pm Sat; 9.30am-5.30pm Sun. **Map** p401 G9.
(*See p137* **Bones, thugs 'n' harmony**.)

Jardin de l'Atlantique

entry from Gare Montparnasse or pl des Cinq-Martyrs-du-Lycée-Buffon, 15th. M° Montparnasse-Bienvenüe. **Open** dawn-dusk daily. **Map** p405 F9.
Perhaps the hardest of all Paris gardens to find, the Jardin de l'Atlantique, opened in 1995, takes the Parisian quest for space airbound with an engineering feat suspended 18m over the tracks of Montparnasse station. It is a small oasis of granite paths, trees and bamboo in an urban desert of modern apartment and office blocks. Small openings allow you to peer down on the trains below.

Tour Maine-Montparnasse

33 av du Maine, 15th (01.45.38.52.56). M° Montparnasse-Bienvenüe. **Open** 9.30am-10.30pm daily. **Admission** exhibition/terrace €8; €6.80 students, over-60s; €5.50 5-14s; free under-5s. **No credit cards. Map** p405 F9.
Built in 1974 on the site of the former Gare Montparnasse, this steel-and-glass monster, at 209m high, is lower than the Eiffel Tower, but more central. A lift whisks you up to the 56th floor, where you'll find a display of aerial views of Paris. Classical concerts are held on the terrace.

Denfert-Rochereau & Montsouris

The bones of six million people were transferred to the Catacombs at Denfert-Rochereau just before the Revolution, taken from overcrowded Paris cemeteries to a network of tunnels that spreads under much of the 13th and 14th arrondissements. The gloomy entrance is next to one of the tollgates of the Mur des Fermiers-Généraux built by Ledoux in the 1780s. Nearby rue Daguerre, meanwhile, is alive with cafés and a street market. A bronze lion, sculpted by Bartholdi of Statue of Liberty fame, dominates the traffic junction. One of the big draws here is the **Parc Montsouris**. On its opening day in 1878 the man-made lake inexplicably emptied and the engineer responsible committed suicide. Around the western edge of the park are small streets such as rue du Parc Montsouris and rue Georges-Braque that were built up in the early 1900s with charming villas and artists' studios. On the southern edge of Montsouris is the **Cité Universitaire**, home to 6,000 foreign students.

Les Catacombes

1 pl Denfert Rochereau, 14th (01.43.22.47.63). M° Denfert-Rochereau. **Open** 10am-6pm Tue-Sun; Closed public holidays. **Admission** €5; €3.30 over 60s; €2.50 students, 14-26s; free under-14s.
No credit cards. Map 405 H10.
These miles of dark, subterranean passages have existed since Roman times. Towards the end of the 18th century many of the old over-crowded Paris cemeteries suffered from overflow and corpses started to shoot into people's cellars. So, the bodies were transferred here. Neatly arranged stacks of bones are interspersed by tidy rows of skulls; quotations inscribed on stone tablets contribute reflections on death. There are supposedly bits of some six million people down here, including many victims of the Revolutionary Terror. Don't be deterred by the warning at the entrance to the ossuary: 'Stop! This is the empire of death!'. It's all very Vincent Price and not at all terrifying.

Cité Universitaire

bd Jourdan, 14th (www.ciup.fr). RER Cité-Universitaire.
The Cité Universitaire is an odd mix. Created between the wars in a mood of internationalism, the 40 halls of residence spread across landscaped gardens were designed in supposedly national style, some by architects of the country like the De Stijl Collège Néerlandais by Willem Dudok; others in exotic pastiche like the Asie du Sud-Est building with its Khmer sculptures and bird-beak roof. The Brits get what looks like a minor public school; the Swiss (1935) and Brazilians (1959) get Le Corbusier.

Parc Montsouris

bd Jourdan, 14th. RER Cité-Universitaire.
The most colourful of the capital's parks was laid out for Baron Haussmann by Alphand in the 19th century. It boasts sweeping, gently sloping lawns, the obligatory artificial lake and artificial cascades.

The 15th arrondissement

Centred on the shopping streets of rue du Commerce and rue Lecourbe, Paris' largest arrondissement probably has the least to offer tourists. But … it's worth making a detour to visit **La Ruche** ('beehive'), designed by Eiffel as a wine pavilion for the 1900 Exposition Universelle and resituated here as artists'

Bones, thugs 'n' harmony

When, as you will need no reminding, it prophesies in the Book of Revelation, '... and death and hell will deliver up the dead which were in them' (chapter 20, verse 13, isn't it?), there will be few better places to which you could rush with the pages of your autograph book flapping and your Polaroid primed than Paris. And how many days pass by when we don't think of Mrs Allonby and her 'when good Americans die they go to Paris'? Paris is full of dead celebs, of all nationalities, by the way, Mrs A.

The City of Light offers what must be the world's most prestigious selection of boneyard, to whit: Père Lachaise, Passy, Picpus, Montmartre and Montparnasse.

The creation of the latter in 1824 represented something of a *volte face* on the part of the authorities, who since the 1786 incident at the Cimetière des Innocents (when over-crowding of corpses and earth-subsidence had caused dead bodies or parts thereof to start popping out like torpedoes in all sorts of places) had banned the construction of new cemeteries in, or too near, the city. The failure of the one tiny element upon which the whole plan rested – that Parisians would stop dying – scuppered the whole notion. And so it came to pass that, in 1824, three farms were combined into one 1,800-acre cemetery, Montparnasse.

When it comes to the pecking order of Paris' boneyards, Montparnasse is often overshadowed by social snobbery in the minds of visitors by Père Lachaise, almost certainly because the latter contains what's left of Oscar Wilde and 'erotic politician', 'Lizard King' and singer Jim Morrison.

Cemeteries are not, of course, suitable arenas for 'mine's-bigger-than-yours' competitiveness, but consider at whose gravesides you can pause and shed a distinguished tear at Montparnasse: Frédéric Bartholdi (sculptor of the Statue of Liberty), Samuel Beckett, Tristan Tzara, Simone de Beauvoir, Constantin Brancusi, Henri Laurens, perv supreme Serge Gainsbourg, André Citroën (he of car and park fame), beloved comic Coluche, Guy de Maupassant, Man Ray, Jean-Paul Sartre, Ionesco and 'troubled' actress, Jean Seberg. One of Montparnasse's star stiffs is poet Charles Baudelaire, who'd clearly been not just at the booze but the Bible, too, as he'd scrawled a few lines about plunging into the abyss, heaven or hell. Still, not bad for a roll call, eh? Beat that, Highgate. And some of the statuary is just beautiful.

Then, of course, there is the tranquillity and the oft-overlooked benefit of reflective thought opportunities offered by the cemetery. When you feel the need for a break from the big city hurly-burly, hoi polloi and the roaring traffic, you can't beat unfurling your corned beef roll and having a bit of a pit-stop at a cemetery: it's quiet, you're unlikely to be mown down by skateboarders as you bend at the knee to tighten the laces on your Campers, and, best of all, it offers many an opportunity for a banal observation concerning our 'here-one-minute-gone-the-next' lot and the consequent need to *carpe* that *diem* as you ram the lid down on your Tuppaware with a new resolve.

Who needs theme parks? You can have a lot of good, clean fun in a graveyard like Montparnasse. Hey, and if you happen to be a satanist, well...

studios. Nearby on rue des Morillons the **Parc Georges Brassens** was opened in 1983 while Porte de Versailles, housing Paris' international exhibition centre, was created in 1923; it is now the fourth-largest exhibition space in Europe.

Parc Georges Brassens

rue des Morillons, 15th. M° Porte de Vanves. **Map** p404 D10.

Built on the site of the former Abattoirs de Vaugirard, parc Georges Brassens prefigured the industrial regeneration of parc André Citroën and La Villette. The gateways crowned by bronze bulls have been kept, as have a series of iron meat market pavilions, which house a busy antiquarian and second-hand book market at weekends. The Jardin des Senteurs is planted with aromatic species while, in one corner, a small vineyard produces 200 bottles of Clos des Morillons every year.

La Ruche

passage de Dantzig, 15th. M° Convention. **Map** p404 D10.

Peek through the grille or sneak in behind an unsuspecting resident to see the iron-framed former wine pavilion, rebuilt by philanthropic sculptor Alfred Boucher to be let out as studios for struggling artists. Chagall, Soutine, Brancusi and Modigliani all spent periods here, and the 140 studios are still much sought after by artists today.

Paris Expo

Porte de Versailles, 15th (01.43.95.37.00). M° Porte de Versailles. **Map** p404 B10.

The vast exhibition centre hosts everything from fashion to medical equipment fairs. Many are open to the public, such as the Foire de Paris, the Salon de l'Agriculture or the contemporary art fair FIAC.

The 13th arrondissement

The 13th arrondissement had its share of bad luck when grubby old industry set up digs in the 19th century, then those nasty tower blocks shot up in the 1960s, but since the late 1990s, the 13th's fortune has been changing, with the vast **ZAC-Rive Gauche** project.

Gobelins & La Salpêtrière

Its image may be of tower blocks, but the 13th also contains some historic parts, especially bordering the 5th. The **Manufacture Nationale des Gobelins**, home to the French state weaving companies, continues a tradition dating back to the 15th century. The river here was notorious for its pollution, while the slums were depicted in Hugo's *Les Misérables*. The area was finally tidied up in the 1930s.

The busy road intersection of place d'Italie has seen more developments with, opposite the town hall, the Centre Commercial Italie 2, a bizarre high-tech confection designed by Japanese architect Kenzo Tange, which contains the **Gaumont Grand Ecran Italie** cinema.

Chapelle St-Louis-de-la-Salpêtrière

47 bd de l'Hôpital, 13th (01.42.16.04.24). M° Gare d'Austerlitz. **Open** 8.30am-6.30pm daily. **Map** p406 L9

The austerely beautiful chapel was designed by Libéral Bruand in 1657-77 with an octagonal dome in the centre and eight naves in order to separate the sick from the insane, the destitute from the debauched. Around the chapel sprawls the vast Hôpital de la Pitié-Salpêtrière, founded on the site of a gunpowder factory (hence its name from saltpetre) by Louis XIV to round up vagrant and unwanted women, becoming a research centre of the insane in the 1790s. Charcot pioneered neuro-psychology here, receiving a famous visit from Freud. It is now one of Paris' main teaching hospitals, but the chapel is regularly used for contemporary art exhibitions.

Bibliothèque Nationale de France François Mitterrand

Château de la Reine Blanche

17 rue des Gobelins, 13th. M° Gobelins.
Map p402 K10.

Through a gateway you can spot the turret and first floor of an ancient house. The curious relic is named after Queen Blanche of Provence who had a château here, but was probably rebuilt in the 1520s for the Gobelin family. Blanche was also associated with the Couvent des Cordeliers (a centre of theological teaching), of which a fragment survives on the corner of rue Pascal and rue de Julienne.

Manufacture Nationale des Gobelins

42 av des Gobelins, 13th (01.44.08.52.00). M° Gobelins. **Open** guided tours only, 2pm and 2.45pm Tue-Thur (90 mins); reserve in advance on 01.44.54.19.33. **Admission** €8; €6 7-24s; under-7s free. **No credit cards. Map** p406 K10.

Named after Jean Gobelin, a dyer who previously owned the site, the factory was at its wealthiest during the *ancien régime* when tapestries were produced for royal residences under artists such as Le Brun and Oudry. Today tapestries are still woven and visitors can watch weavers work. The guided tour (in French) through the 1912 factory takes in the 18th-century chapel and the Beauvais tapestry workshops. Arrive 30 minutes before the tour.

Chinatown & La Butte aux Cailles

South of the rue de Tolbiac stretches Paris' main Chinatown, centred between the bleak 1960s tower blocks along avenues d'Ivry and de Choisy. South-East-Asia-sur-Seine is lined with restaurants, Vietnamese pho noodle bars and Chinese pâtisseries, as well as the large Tang Frères supermarket on avenue d'Ivry. There's even a Buddhist temple hidden in an underground car park beneath the tallest tower block (Autel de la culte de Bouddha, avenue

d'Ivry, opposite rue Frères d'Astier-de-la-Vigerie, open 9am-6pm daily). Traditional lion and dragon dances take place here at Chinese New Year (*see chapter* **Festivals & Events**).

In contrast to Chinatown, the villagey Butte aux Cailles is a neighbourhood of old houses, winding cobblestone streets and funky bars and restaurants. This workers' neighbourhood, home in the 1800s to many small factories, was one of the first to fight during the 1848 Revolution and the Paris Commune. The Butte has preserved its insurgent character, residents openly wearing Fidel Castro T-shirts and resisting the aggressive forces of city planning and construction companies. The cobbled rue de la Butte-aux-Cailles and the rue des Cinq-Diamants are the hub of the arty, soixante-huitard bohemian forces, where you'll find relaxed, inexpensive bistros include **Le Temps des Cérises**, run as a cooperative, **Chez Gladines** and the upmarket **Chez Paul**. The cottages built in 1912 in a mock-Alsatian style at 10 rue Daviel were one of the earliest public housing schemes in Paris. Further south, explore passage Vandrezanne, the square des Peupliers, the rue Dieulafoy and the flower-named streets of the Cité Florale.

The developing East

The staid old 13th, that was once the touchingly rhapsodic spinster of the Left Bank, is enjoying a new vivacity, thanks to two most welcome phenomena. Well, one is less of a phenomenon and more a road, namely rue Louise-Weiss, where, for no fathomable reason, a big art scene has sprung up underneath an annex of the Ministry of Finance and where some or the capital's most innovative artists are doing their thing (*see chapter* **Galleries**).

The second phenomenon goes by the name of ZAC-Rive Gauche, and things really all started with a load of old railway warehouses were standing around empty and with not much to do. What the powers that be decided to do was to transform them into the **Bibliothètheque National de France**. Nice bit of re-theming, that. Now, in the 13th arrondissement, there was also a lot of wasteland, so then-Mayor Jacques Chirac decided to kick around a few urban regereration ideas in 1991. The construction of the Bibliothèque Nationale de France breathed life into what had become the sort of place blues men wail about, a desolate area stretching the whole way from Gare d'Austerlitz to the Périphérique formerly taken up by lonesome railway yards. This project, which is now beginning to blossom after a decade's hard slog, combines office and residential developments and will culminate in the creation of a new university, the none-too-catchily named Université de Paris VII Denis Diderot. The aim is to create a 21st-century Latin Quarter. Students and faculties will co-exist with the 'real world', in the form of atelier-dwellers and businesses, who've been encouraged to move into the area in order to prevent it becoming too rarified. Whatever the genre of student it fosters, the university will cater for over 25,000 students and 4,000 teaching staff when it opens in (latest estimate) 2006. Existing industrial buildings in the area, such as Les Frigos former refrigerated warehouses (now containing artists' studios), and the majestic Grands Moulins de Paris, partly burnt down in 1996, will be incorporated. A new main street, the avenue de France, is being constructed over the railway tracks. Temporary building site it may be, but it's no dump, as grafitti artists have moved in in force and coloured the place in. It's going to be fascinating to see if the theory behind the whole project will live up to its aim; if it does, the ZAC-Rive Gauche will give the entire Left Bank a new image. The **MK2 Bibliothèque** (see pxxx) cinema complex, with its late-night bar and the flotilla of music bars and clubs – **Batofar**, Péniche Blues Café and Péniche Makara (see chapters Clubs and Popular Music) – moored on the Seine in front of the library are also providing signs of new life in the air.

Bibliothèque Nationale de France François Mitterrand

quai François-Mauriac, 13th (01.53.79.53.79/ www.bnf.fr). M° Bibliothèque or Quai de la Gare.
Open 10am-8pm Tue-Sat; noon-7pm Sun. Closed two weeks in Sept/Oct and two weeks in Aug. **Admission** day €3; annual €30; student €15. **Credit** MC, V. **Wheelchair access. Map** p406 M10.

Opened in December 1996, the new national library (dubbed 'TGB' or *Très Grande Bibliothèque*) was the last of Mitterrand's *Grands Projets* and also the most expensive. The architect, Dominique Perrault, was criticised for his curiously dated-looking design, which hides readers underground and stores the books in four L-shaped glass towers. He was also criticised for forgetting to include blinds to protect the books from sunlight; they had to be added after construction. In the central void is a garden (filled with 140 trees, uprooted from Fontainebleau at a cost of 40 million francs. Those who are interested in such minor details as the destination of tax-payers' money will be relieved to hear that nowhere near enough dosh was channelled into the prosaic activity of making things work. The research section opened in autumn 1998, whereupon the computer system failed and staff promptly went on strike. The library houses over ten million volumes, and has room for 3,000 readers. Books, newspapers and periodicals are accessible to anyone over 18. There are regular classical music concerts and exhibitions.

Beyond the Périphérique

It's not all pit bulls and attitude in the 'burbs. There's a mega-mix of art and football, castles and cathedrals; there are even parks for promenades.

Boulogne & the west

Paris' most-desirable suburbs lie to the west, where expensive properties were built between the wars. Nowadays, Anglo expats also tend to nest west. Decentralisation means that **La Défense**, Neuilly, Boulogne, Levallois and Issy-les-Moulineaux have become work locations for Parisians, notably in the advertising, media and service industries, so weekdays see an influx of business bouffants. **Neuilly-sur-Seine** is the chicest residential suburb. Smart apartment blocks have replaced the mansions around the **Bois de Boulogne**.

Boulogne-Billancourt is the main town in the region outside Paris. In 1320 the Gothic Eglise Notre-Dame was begun in tribute to a statue of the Virgin washed up at Boulogne-sur-Mer. By the 18th century, Boulogne was known for its wines and laundries and, early in the 20th century, for its artist residents (Landowski, Lipchitz, Chagall, Gris), while Billancourt was known for cars, aviation and cinema. The former Renault factory has been sitting in the Seine like a school disco wallflower since it closed in 1992, but it has a big future as the Fondation Pinault contemporary art museum, due to open in 2006. Near the Bois de Boulogne are elegant villas, and some fine examples of 1920s and 30s architecture. The **Musée des Années 30** (*see chapter* **Museums**) focuses on artists who lived in the town at the time. Across the Seine, villas surround the **Parc de St-Cloud**. South of St-Cloud is Sèvres, site of the **Musée National de Céramique** (*see chapter* **Museums**).

The **Château de Malmaison** at Rueil-Malmaison was loved by Napoléon and Joséphine. The Château de Monte Cristo (01.30.61.61.35) at Port Marly was built for Alexandre Dumas with a tiled Moorish room.

St-Germain-en-Laye is a smart suburb with a château, where Henri II lived in style with his wife Catherine de Médicis and his mistress Diane de Poitiers. Here Louis XIV was born, Mary Queen of Scots grew up, and the deposed James II lived for 12 years. Napoléon III turned the château into the **Musée des Antiquités Nationales**. The **Musée Départemental Maurice Denis** has a collection of Nabi and Post-Impressionist art in the former royal priory where painter Maurice Denis lived (*see chapter* **Museums**).

St-Denis. *See p142.*

Further west, the town of Poissy merits a visit for its Gothic Collégiale Notre Dame (8 rue de l'Eglise), much restored by Viollet-le-Duc, and Le Corbusier's avant-garde **Villa Savoye**.

Château de Malmaison

av du Château, 92500 Rueil-Malmaison (01.47.49.48.15). M° Grande Arche de la Défense/ RER La Défense. **Open** *Oct-Mar* 10am-5pm daily; *Apr-Sept* 10am-5.45pm daily. **Admission** Short visit €4; €2.50 18-25s; free under 18s; Long visit €4.50; €3.50 18-25; free under 18s. **No credit cards.**

This was Napoléon and Joséphine's love nest. Bought by Joséphine in 1799, it was the Emperor's favourite retreat during the Consulate (1800-03). After the couple's divorce, Napoléon gave the château to his ex, who died here in 1814. All that historical-romantic relevance has not gone to waste: today the château is open, not only for sightseeing purposes, but as a wedding venue, too, and not just for dwarfish megalomaniacs.

Les Jardins Albert Kahn

14 rue du Port, 92100 Boulogne-Billancourt (01.46.04.52.80). M° Boulogne-Pont St-Cloud. **Open** *May-Sept* 11am-7pm Tue-Sun; *Oct-Apr* 11am-6pm Tue-Sun. **Admission** €3.30; €2.20 13-25s, over-60s; free under-13s, disabled. **Credit** V.

With red bridges, Japanese shrines, Alsatian forests and cascading streams, the gardens created by financier Albert Kahn (1860-1940) should be twee, yet somehow never are. There's an enormous variety crammed in a small space. *Wheelchair access.*

Parc de St-Cloud

92210 St-Cloud (01.41.12.02.90). M° Pont de St-Cloud. **Open** *Mar-Apr* 7.30am-8.50pm daily; *May-Aug* 7.30am-9.50pm daily; *Sept-Oct* 7am-8.50pm daily; *Nov-Feb* 7.30am-7.50pm daily. **Admission** free; €3.50 cars. **No credit cards.**

This is another classic French park laid out by Le Nôtre, and all that remains of a royal château that belonged to 'Monsieur', brother of Louis XIV. There are complex avenues, long perspectives, a great view over Paris from the Rond-Point du Balustrade and a series of pools and fountains: most spectacular is the Grande Cascade, a multi-tiered feast of dolphins and sea beasts (spouting 2pm, 3pm, 4pm Sun in June).

Villa Savoye

82 rue de Villiers, 78300 Poissy (01.39.65.01.06). RER Poissy + bus 50: Villa Savoye or 15 min walk. **Open** *Mar-Oct* 10am-6pm Tue-Sun; *Nov-Feb* 10am-1pm, 2-5pm Tue-Sun. **Admission** €4.60; €3.10 18-25s; free under-18s. **Credit** MC, V.

Built in 1929 for a family of rich industrialists, this luxury house with its sculptural spiral staircase, *pilotis* and roof terraces is perhaps Le Corbusier's most successful work. *Wheelchair access.*

La Défense

La Défense's skyscrapers and walkways create the feeling of another world. It was named after a stand against the Prussians in 1870: in 2001, its martial associations were underlined when the tensions caused by dreadful social conditions and the failure of French society to assimilate its immigrant population erupted into a two-hour gang battle. Ironically, La Défense has been a showcase for French business since the mid-50s, when the triangular CNIT exhibition hall (01.46.92.11.11/open 9am-6pm Mon-Sat) was built for trade shows, but it was the **Grande Arche** that gave the district a true monument. More than 100,000 people work here, and another 35,000 live in the futuristic blocks of flats on the southern edge. None of the skyscrapers display any great architectural distinction, although together they make an impressive sight. Recent development westward includes a new 40-storey tower by Pei Cobb Freed and a church by Franck Hammoutène. The Info-Défense kiosk (01.47.74.84.24/open Apr-Oct 10am-6pm, Nov-Mar 9.30am-5.30pm Mon-Fri) in front of CNIT has maps and guides of the area.

La Grande Arche de la Défense

92400 Paris la Défense (01.49.07.27.57/ www.grandearche.com). M° La Défense. **Open** 10am-7pm. **Admission** €7.50; €6 6-18s, students; free under 6s. **Credit** AmEx, MC, V.

Completed for the bicentenary of the Revolution in 1989, the Grande Arche, designed by obscure Danish architect Johan Otto von Spreckelsen, is now a major tourist attraction. A stomach-churning ride in high-speed glass lifts soars up through the 'clouds' to the roof where there is a fantastic view into Paris. Outside on the giant forecourt are fountains and sculptures by artists including Miró, Serra, Calder and César's *Thumb*. *Wheelchair access.*

St-Denis & the north

Amid the suburban sprawl stands one of the treasures of Gothic architecture: the **Basilique St-Denis**, where most of France's monarchs were buried. St-Denis also boasts the innovative **Musée de l'Art et d'Histoire de St-Denis** in a scrupulously preserved Carmelite convent, a busy covered market, and some fine modern buildings, such as Niemeyer's 1989 HQ for Communist newspaper *L'Humanité* and Gaudin's extension to the town hall. Across the canal is the elegant **Stade de France**. The département of Seine St-Denis has a buzzing theatre scene (*see right*) and prestigious jazz and classical music festivals. Le Bourget, home to Paris' first airport, contains the **Musée de l'Air et de l'Espace**. North of Sarcelles, Ecouen, noted for its Renaissance château, now the **Musée National de la Renaissance**, allows glimpses of a rural past. **Enghien-les-Bains**, set around a large lake where you can hire rowing boats and pedalos, provided a pleasure haven in the 19th century with the development of its spa, a casino (the only one in the Paris region) and a racecourse. In a housing estate in the middle of Asnières is the memorial to the people who died in the World War II internment camp at **Drancy**.

Basilique St-Denis

6 rue de Strasbourg, 93200 St-Denis (01.48.09.83.54). M° St-Denis-Basilique. **Open** *Apr-Sept* 10am-6.15pm Mon-Sat; noon-6.15pm Sun. *Oct-Mar* 10am-5.15pm Mon-Sat; noon-5.15pm Sun. **Admission** €6.10; €4.10 18-25s; free under-18s. Guided tours 11.15am, 3pm Mon-Sat, 12.15pm Sun. **No credit cards.**

Legend has it that when St Denis was beheaded, he picked up his head and walked to Vicus Catulliacus (now St-Denis) to be buried. The first church, parts of which can be seen in the crypt, was built over his tomb in around 475. The present edifice was the first

Beyond the fringe theatre

Suburban theatre complexes have bubbled up all around the crown of the city, thanks to ubiquitous Maison de Culture grants (along with media attention and brandname direction). But are these establishments bringing culture to the under-privileged masses, or is it rather more that the posh are turned on by keeping culture among the elite, but in the areas where the peasants live?

Suburban theatre was born in the 1950s to cultivate inhabitants of the northern and eastern *banlieue*, areas stigmatised as uncouth and lower-class. In 1998, Stanislas Nordey, then director of the **Théâtre Gérard Philipe** (01.48.13.70.00/ www.theatregerardphilipe.com) in St-Denis, began, but never finished, a project he called 'Theatre for the Citizens', whereby he hoped to bring the art form to all audiences by offering cheap tickets and events, engaging young companies and new playwrights. There are several theories as to why his initiative failed, but the most convincing is inaccessibility of content.

Suburban productions are still considered avant-garde and international in their outlook, even by Parisians. But, despite ticket reductions for local residents, the audience make-up still appears to be dominated by metropolitan culture-vultures, making a brave venture into the suburbs as they scour for something alternative. The validity of this cynicism aside, the suburban theatres are often beautifully constructed compounds that continue to house young talent eager to create and work with renowned directors.

Before Nordey was director of the Théâtre Gérard Philipe, Daniel Mesguich established a cycle of 'residences' here, with companies and directors, setting the trend for many of the theatres today. Mesguich is currently working at **Théâtre de St-Quentin-en-Yvelines** (01.30.96.99.00/www.theatresqy.org), moulding Moliere's *Dom Juan* in his own fashion. Even Irina Brook directs here. Under new director Bruno Deschamps, a mission for the theatre has been set: to present vibrant shows, support new talent and the education of the people. In the president's letter to the audience, he states in closing, 'But above all else, our theatre's goal is to bring fitting theatre to residents of the area.'

The **Maison des Arts de Créteil** (01.45.13.1919/www.maccreteil.com), best known as a dance venue, is putting on a

bilingual interpretation of Koltès' *The Night Just Before the Forest* in 2004. **Théâtre Nanterre-Amandiers** (01.46.14.70.00/ www.tem-nanterre.com) has established itself with troupes from Algeria and Sweden, as well as works by Claude Régy (now at the Théâtre National de la Colline in Paris). They're putting on the hits with *Hamlet* in January.

But perhaps the theatre on most people's lips is the **MC93 Bobigny** (01.41.60.72.72/ www.mc93.com), under the direction of Californian magnate Peter Sellars. In 2002, he directed Euripides' *Children of Herakles*, where he cast children from surrounding schools for the performance, while the following year it was the venue for Théâtre de Complicité's excellent *Mnemonic*, where the audience was hypnotised in French then watched the play in English. In 2004, the annual festival, The Ideal Standard (11 Mar-16 Apr), whose 'ideal' is to bring linguistically mixed acts together from East and West, will include Tennessee Williams' *Forever Young* in German, *Die zehn Gebote* written by Italian native Raffaele Viviani, Hungary's classic *Liliom* in its rightful language, and Orwell's *Homage to Catalonia*, in, well, Catalan.

Peripheral vision

Highways, motorways, freeways – call them what you will – have a modern urban relevance that goes beyond that of the practical. They're in the consciousness. Think of Route 66, the M25, the road to Mandalay, ye tak the high rood an ahl tak the low rood, etc. Then there's the shameful roster of rock bands that have whinged on interminably about the rigours of life on the road. There must be some escapist appeal to it all. Then there's trucker chic (*see chapter* **Gay & Lesbian**).

In Paris, the arena in which to git yo motor runnin' and head out on the highway is called Le Périphérique, 35km of high-quality ring-road that celebrated its 30th birthday in 2003 (though its gestation period was far from brief: as far back as 1943, the Vichy Régime had the idea of surrounding Paris with a road, part of whose *raison d'être* was to make the capital just that little bit more occupiable).

The idea outlasted the Occupation, and in 1953 the construction of 8,000 flats began, replacing 19th-century fortifications on the perimeter of where the road would be, so that the less well-off would be firmly established in their hell-holes by the time the heavy-lead pollution started pouring down their lungs. The first section of road to be finished was that between Porte d'Italie and Porte de Châtillon, and by 1973 the Périphérique was born.

Such highways are, of course, irresistible to leather-clad speed freaks. Le Périphérique's most famous was the dude known only as 'the Black Prince'. This *chevalier de nos jours* (whose identity was a well-kept secret; it wasn't that anyone gave a toss who he was, but he felt the secrecy added to his mystique) famously once circumnavigated Le Périphérique at an average speed of 190kmph on his Kawasaki in full, heavy traffic conditions. Declaring that a mere practice run, and that now was the time for unleashing some real speed, the Prince remounted with a gravelly roar of his throttle. He lasted just over two minutes before a misjudgement concerning the relative speed of two lorries and his bike's ability to outstrip them via some nifty over-taking put an end to his biking and, indeed, breathing career. There's a moral there, kids: the Périphérique hasn't got any safer.

example of true Gothic architecture. Abbot Suger began the basilica in the 12th century. In the 13th, master mason Pierre de Montreuil erected the spire and rebuilt the choir, nave and transept. This was the burial place for all-but three French monarchs between 996 and the end of the *ancien régime*, so the ambulatory is a museum of French funerary sculpture. During the Revolution in 1792, the tombs were desecrated and the royal remains thrown into a pit.

Cimetière des Chiens

4 pont de Clichy, 92600 Asnières (01.40.86.21.11). M° Mairie de Clichy. **Open** *mid-Mar to mid-Oct* 10am-6pm Tue-Sun; *mid-Oct to mid-Mar* 10am-4pm, Tue-Sun. **Admission** 3; 1 6-12s. **No credit cards.**

Founded in 1899 by French feminist Marguerite Durand, this island on the Seine is the final resting place for 55,000 Parisian pooches. Some of the graves have photos of the faithful friends; others contain mementoes such as moth-eaten tennisballs or messages of devotion. A decaying neo-Byzantine entrance points to a grander past: just within lies a monument, a small girl draped over a large dog: Barry the St Bernard 'who saved the lives of 40 people. He was killed by the 41st.' RIP, Bazza.

Eglise Notre Dame du Raincy

av de la Résistance, 93340 Le Raincy (01.43.81.14.98). SNCF/RER Raincy-Villemomble. **Open** 10am-noon, 2-6pm Mon-Sat; 3-5pm Sun.

Auguste Perret's little-known modernist masterpiece was built 1922-23 as a modest war memorial. In place of conventional stained glass, the windows are glass blocks that create fantastic reflections.

Le Mémorial de la Déportation du Camp de Drancy

15 rue Arthur Fontaine, 93700 Asnières (01.48.95.35.05). M° Mairie de Clichy.

In 2001, the French government finally made the remains of Drancy, the World War II internment camp, into an historic monument. This site was originally built as a housing estate in the 1930s. In August 1941, 4,232 Jews – many of whom had fled to France hoping for refuge from oppressive regimes elsewhere in Europe – were interned at the unfinished concrete camp. From here, most of the inmates were customarily shipped to Auschwitz (a total of some 70,000 people). The internment camp was staffed by French gendarmes. A small memorial exhibition was opened in 1989, and there is a memorial sculpted by Shelomo Selinger.

Stade de France

rue Francis de Pressensé, 93200 St-Denis (01.55.93.00.00/www.stadefrance.fr). M° St-Denis Porte de Paris/RER B La Plaine-Stade de France/RER D-Stade de France St-Denis. **Open** 10am-6pm daily. **Guided visits** Cour du Stade (1hr, on the hour, visit in English 10.30am, 2.30pm) 10 adults; 8.50 students; 7 under-12s. **Credit** MC, V.

The Stade de France, designed by Zubléna, Macary, Regembal and Constantini, was built in an aston-

La Défense

1998 football World Cup triumph. Its spectacular flying saucer-like steel and aluminium roof has become a landmark. (Paris St-Germain play, of course, at Parc des Princes, sports fans). *Wheelchair access.*

Vincennes & the east

The more upmarket residential districts in the east surround the Bois de Vincennes, such as **Vincennes** with its royal château and Paris' main zoo. Joinville-le-Pont and Champigny-sur-Marne draw weekend strollers along the Marne.

Château de Vincennes

av de Paris, 94300 Vincennes (01.48.08.31.20). M° Château de Vincennes. **Open** *Oct-Mar* 10am-noon, 1.15pm-5pm daily; *Apr-Sept* 10am-noon, 1.15 - 6pm daily. **Admission** Short visit €4; €2.50 18-25s; free under 18s; Long visit €5.50; €3.50 18-25; free under 18s. **No credit cards.**

An imposing curtain wall encloses this medieval fortress. The square keep was begun by Philippe VI and completed by Charles V, who also began rebuilding the newly renovated Flamboyant Gothic Sainte-Chapelle. Louis XIII had the Pavillon du Roi and Pavillon de la Reine built by Louis Le Vau.

Pavillon Baltard

12 av Victor Hugo, 94130 Nogent-sur-Marne (01.43.24.76.76/www.pbpa.net). RER Nogent-sur-Marne. **Open** during salons/exhibitions only.

When Les Halles was demolished someone had the remarkable foresight to save one of Baltard's iron and glass market pavilions and resurrect it for the benefit of the suburbs.

Sceaux & the south

Bordering Paris, left-wing Montrouge and Malakoff house many artists. **Sceaux** was formerly the setting for a château built for Louis XIV's finance minister Colbert. Only the gardens and orangerie remain – the present building housing the Musée de l'Ile de France (01.46.61.06.71) dates from 1856. At **Châtenay-Malabry**, the 1930s Cité de la Butte-Rouge garden-city estate was a model for social housing. The south-eastern suburbs boomed during 19th-century industrialisation. Ivry-sur-Seine is famed for social policies, such as the L'Atelier housing projects, while the new town of Evry is of note for radical housing estates and the **Cathédrale de la Résurrection**.

Arcueil Aqueduct

Spanning the Bièvre valley through Arcueil and Clamart, this impressive double-decker structure brings water from Wissous to Paris. A Roman structure existed a few metres from this one. In 1609 Henri IV decided to reconstruct the aqueduct, and by 1628 it provided water for 16 Paris fountains.

Cathédrale de la Résurrection

21 cour Monseigneur Roméro, 91000 Evry (01.64.97.93.53). SNCF Evry-Courcouronnes. **Open** 10am-noon, 2-6pm Mon-Sat; 2.30-7pm Sun.

Completed in 1995, this was the first new cathedral in France since the war. Mario Botta's rather heavy, truncated, red-brick cylindrical form seeks to establish a new aesthetic for religious architecture.

paris museum pass
carte musées-monuments
paris museum pass
carte musées-monuments
3
jours
days
Valid for 1, 3 or 5 days, the Paris museum pass gives wait-free admission to see the permanent collections of 60 museums and sights in and around Paris.
On sale in museums, monuments, metro stations and at the Paris Tourist Office.
interMusées

DALÍ
ESPACE
MONTMARTRE

Museums

Find your art's desire in the city of museums, but don't forget its other collected treasures: history, medicine, literature, science and, er, sex.

Even without the plundersome talents of François 1er, Napoléon et al, Paris would have enough art to fill a whole arrondissement (a big one at that). In addition to the **Louvre**, **Musée d'Orsay**, **Musée d'Art Moderne** and the **Centre Pompidou** there are dozens of other state collections and smaller, more specialised museums covering anything from advertising to Edith Piaf.

The new buzzword from the Ministry of Culture is 'transversality' which means that the **Centre National de la Photographie** and the Jeu de Paume are to merge as a new structure devoted to photography and the image and the new **Palais de Tokyo** also faces some transversal goings-on from 2005. Meanwhile some of Paris' long-term museum projects continue: the **Musée de l'Histoire de France**, **Musée de l'Armée** and **Musée de la Marine** remain open during renovation projects, while the Institut National de l'Architecture can be found temporarily at the **Palais de la Porte Dorée** before it moves to Chaillot in 2005.

After seasons devoted to Bohemia and Algeria, this time it's the turn of China, meaning Sino-centric exhibitions of everything from antiquities at the **Grand Palais** to the latest video art at the **Maison Européenne de la Photographie**. Other major exhibitions in 2004 include Joan Miró at the **Centre Pompidou**, **Veronese** at the **Musée du Luxembourg**, Paris in the year 1400 at the **Louvre**, and exhibitions focusing on Napoléon, who was crowned emperor in 1804, and the 60th anniversary of the liberation of Paris.

PARIS CARTE MUSEES ET MONUMENTS

If you do opt for death by cultural overdose, the best-value way to do it is with the **Carte Musées et Monuments** (CM). Coming in handy one-day (€15), three-day (€30) or five-day (€45) formats, it allows entry into 70 museums and monuments all over Paris (although you have to pay extra for special exhibitions) and allows you to jump queues.

The card is available from museums, tourist offices, branches of Fnac and main Métro and RER stations. For further information, visit www.intermusees.com. In our listings CM indicates venues where the card is accepted.

The Egyptian Room at the Louvre. *See p148.*

Museums often offer a reduced rate for students, children and over-60s – bring an ID card or passport to prove your status. In any case, all the permanent collections at municipal-run museums are free and a reduced rate is usually applicable on Sundays. All national museums are completely free on the first Sunday of the month and most museums throw open their doors for the annual Printemps des Musées (Springtime of the Museums) on a Sunday in April (more information on 01.40.15.36.00/www.culture.gouv.fr). Thousands also turn out for the annual Journées du Patrimoine (national heritage days) in September for the chance to see behind the normally closed doors of some of the capital's oldest and most beautiful buildings (*see chapter* **Festivals & Events**).

Jostling with busloads of tourists and their hand-held cameras takes the joy out of the museum experience, so try to visit on weekdays, or take advantage of the *nocturnes* (late night opening) that most of the big museums offer. Pre-booking is essential before 1pm at the **Grand Palais**, and it's also possible to pre-book the **Louvre**, the **Luxembourg** and other major exhibitions. Most museums close on either Monday or Tuesday, and most ticket counters – and, more unfairly, some loos – shut 30-45 minutes before closing.

The Louvre

entrance through Pyramid, Cour Napoléon, 1st (01.40.20.50.50/recorded information 01.40.20.51.51/www.louvre.fr). M° Palais Royal.
Open 9am-6pm Thur-Sun; 9am-9.45pm Mon, Wed. Closed Tue. **Admission** €7.50 (until 3pm); €5 after 3pm, Sun; free under-18s, first Sun of month; CM. Exhibitions €3.80-€5.50. Day pass €9.50-€11.50. **Credit** MC, V. **Map** p401 G5.

The labyrinthine Louvre is the museum to end all museums: just when you think you've mastered it, you turn a corner and discover another awesome staircase or a series of rooms. Its breadth is mind-boggling but that also means that there's something for everyone (if only you can find it), including Renaissance painting, grandiose battle scenes, Antique sculpture, Egyptian mummies, medieval jewels, courtly tapestries – and that's aside from the building itself. Neck pains are the price you pay for admiring the marvellous ceiling: ornate giltwork snakes around most of the one-time royal palace, and the ceiling paintings rival anything on the walls. A circular room in Sully portrays Icarus, with the wax on his wings melting, plunging directly, seemingly, on to those of us below. The Louvre is a marvellous architectural hybrid: its intricately carved stonework gives the impression that it has been constructed entirely of custard cream biscuits, whilst the futuristic Pyramid, surrounded by gently lapping water, is the glassy-eyed sentinel.

The original Louvre was built by Philippe-Auguste in the 1190s as part of his Paris defences; by the mid-14th century it had been turned into a royal residence. Remains of walls and turrets, including the Charles V library tower, lay buried beneath the new palace for centuries. Much of it has now been unearthed and can be seen in the underground complex, including the ancient heart of Philippe-Auguste's fortress, the vaulted Salle St-Louis with its central supporting column and carved grotesque head. Subsequent rulers all had their ha'penny worth to add. In the 1540s, François 1er asked Pierre Lescot to begin a Renaissance palace (now the western wing of the enclosed Cour Carrée). Continued by his successors, the different facades are carved with royal monograms – H interlaced with C and D for Henri II, his queen Catherine de Médicis and favourite Diane de Poitiers. Suave devils, or were they trying to stir it for poor old Henri? Henri IV and Louis XIII completed the Cour Carrée and built the wing along the Seine. The pedimented facade along rue du Louvre was added by Perrault under Louis XIV. Louis brought in Le Vau and Le Brun to refurbish the interior, with a sumptuous suite for his mother Anne of Austria (which she'd be delighted to know now houses Roman antiquities). After Louis XIV's court left for Versailles, the royals abandoned the palace and the apartments were often occupied by artists and state servants. Still, people just couldn't resist touching the place up. After the Revolution, Percier and Fontaine, Napoléon's architects, added a grand stairway of which only the ceilings of the one-time landing remain (now Salles Percier and Fontaine). At the Emperor's command, they also built the galleries along rue de Rivoli, complete with imperial figures, although it was Napoléon's nephew, Napoléon III, who added the Cour Napoléon.

The art collection was first opened to the public in 1793, but the Ministry of Finance remained in the palace until the 1980s, when the ministers were dragged kicking and screaming out of their lavish apartments and over to the much less glamourous 12th *arrondissement*. The space they left enabled the Louvre's latest transformation, which began with the opening of the Richelieu Wing in 1993. I. M. Pei's glass pyramid opened in 1989 to a chorus of disapproval from traditionalists, but even they seem to have been won over now. It serves as a dramatic main entrance to one of the world's most celebrated museums.

USERS' TIPS

- The museum is divided into three wings: Denon (down the Seine side), Richelieu (down the Rivoli side), and Sully, which joins them up and runs around the Cour Carrée at the end. Pick up a plan at the information desk – you'll need it.
- Jump the worst of the queues and enter via the Carrousel from rue de Rivoli or from Palais Royal Métro (advance tickets can also be bought at the Virgin Megastore inside the Carrousel).
- Get organised: tickets can be bought in advance at Fnac, Carrefour, Auchan and Virgin ticket offices or on the web. If buying on the spot, credit card ticket machines can be quicker than the tills.
- Tickets are valid all day: you can leave the museum and re-enter if you wish.
- Staff shortages mean that some rooms are closed on a weekly basis – check on 01.40.20.51.51 or www.louvre.fr.
- Grab a bite at the elegant Café Richelieu, the Café Denon or the Café Mollien, which has an

Tribal art in The Louvre. *See p152.*

outdoor terrace in summer. Under the pyramid there's a sandwich bar, café and the Grand Louvre restaurant serving classic French cuisine. Alternatively, take a breather outside at the Café Marly, which overlooks the pyramid and serves trendy brasserie-style food. The Restorama in the Carrousel du Louvre has multiple self-service outlets, ranging from Lebanese to cheese and wine.

● Shopaholics, have your credit cards ready; the Louvre has excellent art book, postcard, poster and gift shops and a special children's art bookshop.

● Finally… don't try to see everything on one visit. Let yourself be beguiled – you're bound to get lost within the first 20 minutes, so use it as an excuse to discover the unexpected.

The Collections

Ancient Egypt

Denon: lower ground floor; Sully: lower ground, ground and 1st floors.

Announced by the Giant Sphinx in pink granite, the Egyptian department divides into two routes. The Thematic Circuit on the ground floor presents Nile culture (fishing, agriculture, hunting, daily and cultural life, religion and death); one of the biggest draws is the famous Mastaba of Akhethetep, a richly decorated burial chamber from Sakkara dating back to around 2,400BC. Six small sphinxes, a row of apes from Luxor and the lion-headed goddess Sekhmet recreate elements of temple complexes, while massive stone sarcophagi, mummies, amulets, jewellery and jars of entrails (yum!), are all part of a vivid display on funeral rites. Meanwhile, on the first floor, the Pharoah Circuit takes a chronological approach, from the Seated Scribe and other stone figures of the Ancient Empire, via the elongated painted wood figures of the Middle Empire to the New Empire with its animal-headed statues of gods and goddesses, papyrus scrolls and hieroglyphic tablets. Look out for the double statue of the God Aman protecting Tutankhamun, and the black diorite 'cube statues' of priests and attendants. The collection has its origins in Napoléon's Egyptian campaign of 1798-99 and Champollion, the French linguist and Egyptologist, who deciphered hieroglyphics in 1824.

Oriental antiquities

Richelieu: lower ground and ground floor; Sully: ground floor.

Amid Cypriot animalistic vases and carved reliefs from Byblos, there are two breathtaking palace reconstructions: the great court, *c.*713BC, from the palace of Sargon II at Khorsabad (in present-day Iraq) with its giant bearded and winged bulls and friezes of warriors and servants, and the palace of Darius I at Susa (now Iran), *c.*510 BC, with its fantastic glazed-brick reliefs depicting rows of archers, lions and griffins. The Hammurabi Code, a vital document of Babylonian civilisation in the form of a black basalt stele recording 282 laws beneath reliefs of the king and the sun god, is displayed in a new room devoted to Mesopotamia.

Greek, Roman & Etruscan antiquities

Denon: lower ground floor, ground floor; Sully: ground floor, 1st floor.

The *Winged Victory of Samothrace*, a headless Greek statue dating back to the 2nd-century BC,

David's *Sacre de Napoléon* in the Denon wing of The Louvre

stands sentinel at the top of the Daru staircase, and the rest of the Greek, Roman & Etruscan collection is no less awe-inspiring. This section is also home to the 2.3m-high *Athena Peacemaker* and the *Venus de Milo*, and is overflowing with gods and goddesses, swords and monsters. The huge collection is made up of pieces amassed by François 1er and Richelieu, plus the Borghese collection (acquired in 1808), and the Campana collection of thousands of painted Greek vases and small terracottas.

Etruscan civilisation of central Italy spans roughly the 7th century BC until submission to the Romans in the 1st century AD. The highlight is the *Sarcophagus of the Cenestien Couple*, c.530-510BC, in painted terracotta, which depicts a smiling couple reclining at a banquet. Roman antiquities include a vivid relief of sacrificial animals from a temple in Rome, intricately carved sarcophagi, mosaic floors and the Boscoreale Treasure, fabulous silverwork excavated at a villa near Pompeii.

French painting

Denon: 1st floor; Richelieu: 2nd floor; Sully: 2nd floor.
There are around 6,000 of the most famous paintings in the world on show here, and it really is exciting to see the real thing with your own eyes (over the shoulder of tourists who want to see the real thing with their own camcorder). The most impressive paintings, physically as well as aesthetically, are the massive 18th/19th-century canvases hanging in the Grand Galerie in the Denon wing. Here art meets politics with Gros' suitably dashing *Napoléon visitant le champ de bataille d'Eylau (Napoleon at the Battle of Eylau)*, David's absolutely enormous *Sacre de Napoléon* (*Coronation of Napoléon I*) and Delacroix's flag-flying frenzy, *La Liberté Guidant le Peuple* (*Liberty Leading the People*). Photojournalism has nothing on Géricault's technically beautiful but emotionally disturbing *Le Radeau de la Méduse* (*The Raft of the Médusa*): turning his artistic vision to the shocking true story of the abandoned men who resorted to cannibalism and murder after an 1816 shipwreck, he manages to contrast hope (there is a tiny hint of a boat on the horizon) with despair (the one old man who looks out of the canvas, surrounded by the dead and the dying). A little further on, but just as horrifying, is Girodet's *Le Déluge* (*The Deluge*), where a wild-eyed man tries to cling onto a woman who is being pulled down by her own children. Famous Biblical and historical scenes rub shoulders with portraits of aristocracy and grand depictions of those great moments from classical mythology, even if the Sphinx in Ingres' *Oedipus Explaining the Enigma* looks like more of a pussy cat than a man-eater.

Here you can find the earliest known non-religious French portrait (c.1350: an anonymous portrait of French king Jean Le Bon), the *Pièta de Villeneuve-les-Avignon* attributed to Enguerrand Quarton, Jean Clouet's *Portrait of François 1er* (marking the influence of the Italian Renaissance on portraiture), and works from the Ecole de Fontainebleau, including the anonymous *Diana the Huntress*, an elegant nude who bears a more than passing resemblance to Diane de Poitiers, Henri II's mistress. Poussin's religious and mythological subjects epitomise 17th-century French classicism, in works full of erudite references for an audience of cognoscenti. Don't miss Charles Le Brun's wonderfully pompous *Chancellier Seguier* and his four grandiose battle scenes, in which Alexander the Great stands in for Louis XIV. The 18th century begins with Watteau's *Gilles and the Embarkation for Cythera*. Works by Chardin include sober still lifes, but also delicate figure paintings. If you're used to the sugary images of Fragonard, don't miss the *Fantaisies*, which forego sentimentality for wonderfully fluent, broadly-painted fantasy portraits, intended to capture moods rather than particular likenesses. Also in the Sully wing are sublime Neo-Classical portraits by David, Ingres' *La Baigneuse* (*The Bather*) and *Le Bain Turc* (*Turkish Bath*), portraits and Orientalist scenes by Chassériau and landscapes by Corot.

French sculpture

Richelieu: lower ground floor, ground floor.
French sculpture is displayed in and around the two glazed sculpture courts created as part of the Grand Louvre. A tour round the different medieval regional schools takes in the *Virgins* from Alsace, 14th-century figures of Charles V and Jeanne de Bourbon that originally adorned the exterior of the Louvre and the late 15th-century *Tomb of Philippe Pot*, an effigy of a Burgundian knight carried by eight black-clad mourners. Fine Renaissance memorials, fountains and portals include Jean Goujon's friezes from the Fontaine des Innocents. In the Cour Marly, pride of place goes to Coustou's *Chevaux de Marly*, two rearing horses being restrained by their grooms, plus two slightly earlier equestrian pieces by Coysevox, all originally sculpted for the favourite royal château at Marly-le-Roi. In Cour Puget are the four bronze captives by Martin Desjardins, Clodion's Rococo frieze and Pierre Puget's twisting, Baroque *Milo of Croton*. Amid 18th-century heroes and allegorical subjects, look for Pigalle's *Mercury and Voltaire*.

Italian painting

Denon: 1st floor.
The Venetian paintings section is undergoing an overhaul at present, but Veronese's monumental, lavishly coloured *Noces de Cana* (*Wedding Feast at Cana*) still heralds your arrival. Two rooms of fragile Renaissance frescoes by Botticelli, Fra Angelico and Luini open the Italian department. Cimabue's *Madonna of the Angels*, c.1270, combines the composition of Byzantine icons with the Renaissance's modelling of form. Look out also for Fra Angelico's *Coronation of the Virgin* and Mantegna's *Calvary*, *St-Sebastian* and bacchanal scenes. Highlights of the Sienese school include Simone Martini's *Christ Carrying the Cross* and Piera della Francesa's *Portrait of Sigismondo Malatesta*. Florentine High Renaissance treasures include Raphael's *Belle*

Jardinière Virgin and Child, and two lovely small paintings depicting dragon slayers St George and St Michael. Leonardo's *Virgin of the Rocks* and *Virgin, Child and St-Anne* are also present, but needless to say it's the *Mona Lisa* (known in France as *La Joconde*), who hogs the limelight. She's almost impossible to look at for many reasons: because of her familiarity, because after all the hype she's still pretty small, because of the bullet-proof glass protecting her, because of the camera-clicking crowds ever before her… but she certainly has that *je ne sais quoi*, even though she's not what you'd call a Page Three stunna. As of December 2004, at the grand old age of 500 or so, she will finally be old enough to have her own room, which should be able to accommodate even more goggle-eyed tourists than usual. Other highlights in this section include Caravaggio's Baroque masterpiece *The Fortune Teller*, the celebrated *Fête Champêtre* attributed to Titian, and the magnificent fruit and leaf heads of Arcimboldo's *Four Seasons*, plus paintings by Tintoretto, Lotto and Bronzino.

Italian sculpture

Denon: lower ground floor, ground floor.
Michelangelo's *Dying Slave* and *Captive Slave* (sculptures originally planned for the tomb of Pope Julius II in Rome) are the real show-stealers here, but other Renaissance treasures include a painted marble relief by Donatello, Adrien de Vriesse's gleaming, elongated bronze *Mercury and Psyche* and Giambologna's *Mercury*. Benevenuto Cellini's *Nymph of Fontainebleau* relief is on the Mollien staircase.

Northern schools

Denon: first floor; Richelieu: 2nd floor.
The northern Renaissance includes Flemish altarpieces by Memling and Van der Weyden, Bosch's fantastical, proto-Surrealist *Ship of Fools*, Metsys' *The Moneylender and his Wife*, which combines a complex moral message, lively everyday detail and visual games, as well as the northern Mannerism of Cornelius van Haarlem. The Galerie Médicis is devoted to Rubens' Médicis cycle. The 24 canvases commissioned in the 1620s for the Palais de Luxembourg by Marie de Médicis, widow of Henri IV, mix historic events and classical mythology for the glorification of the queen who was not afraid to put her best features on public display. But look also at Rubens' more personal, glowing portrait of his second wife *Hélène Fourment and her Children*, along with Van Dyck's *Charles I and his Groom* and peasant-filled townscapes by Teniers.

Dutch paintings in this wing include early and late self-portraits by Rembrandt, his *Flayed Ox* and the warmly glowing nude *Bathsheba at her Bath*. There are Vermeer's *Astronomer* and *Lacemaker* amid interiors by De Hooch and Metsu, and the meticulously finished portraits and *trompe l'oeil* framing devices of Dou, plus works from the Haarlem school. German paintings in small side galleries include portraits by Cranach, Dürer's *Self-Portrait* and Holbein's *Anne of Cleves*. The rooms of Northern and Scandinavian paintings include Caspar David Friedrich's *Trees with Crows*, the sober, classical portraits of Christian Købke and pared-back views of Peder Balke. A small but high-quality British collection includes landscapes by Wright of Derby, Constable and Turner and portraits by Gainsborough, Reynolds and Lawrence. Northern sculpture (Denon, lower-ground floor), ranges from Erhart's Gothic *Mary Magdalene* to the Neo-Classical work of Thorvaldsen.

Decorative arts

Richelieu: 1st floor; Sully: 1st floor
The decorative arts collection runs from the Middle Ages to the mid-19th century, often with royal connections. Many of the finest medieval items came from the treasury of St-Denis amassed by the powerful Abbot Suger, counsellor to Louis VI and VII, among them *Suger's Eagle* (an amazing antique porphyry vase with gold mounts), a serpentine plate surrounded by precious stones and the sacred sword of the kings of France, dubbed 'Charlemagne's sword' by the Capetian monarchs as they sought to legitimise their line.

The Renaissance galleries take in ornate carved chests, German silver tankards, and the *Hunts of Maximilien*, twelve 16th-century Brussels tapestries depicting months, the zodiac and hunting scenes. 17th- and 18th-century French decorative arts are displayed in superb panelled rooms, and include characteristic brass and tortoiseshell pieces by Boulle. Later displays move on to the elaborate Rococo 'monkey commode' – fair sets the mind a-wandering, doesn't it – of Crescent and parquetry by Leleu, as well as French faïence and porcelain, silverware, watches and scientific instruments. Napoléon III's opulent apartments, used until the 1980s by the Ministry of Finance (who said France doesn't have a monarchy?), have been preserved with chandeliers and upholstery intact.

Islamic art

Richelieu: lower-ground floor.
Islamic decorative arts include early glass, fine 10th-to-12th-century dishes decorated with birds and calligraphy, traditional Iranian blue and white wares, Iznik ceramics, intricate inlaid metalwork from Syria, carpets, screens, weapons and funerary stele.

Tribal art

Denon: ground floor.
A small display in the Pavillon de Flore augurs what is to come in the future Musée du Quai Branly. Items range from Benin bronze heads from Nigeria and Polynesian carved wood statues to pot-bellied terracotta figures from Mexico. This is definitely the place to enthuse museum-weary children.

Temporary exhibitions

Temporary exhibitions are held in various galleries around the Louvre; the major shows go in the Hall Napoléon, including (Apr to mid-July) '*Paris 1400: Les arts sous Charles VI*', a display of Gothic finery.

Centre Pompidou

Other Museums

Fine art & photography

Centre Pompidou (Musée National d'Art Moderne)

rue St-Martin, 4th (01.44.78.12.33/ www.centrepompidou.fr). M° Hôtel de Ville or Rambuteau/RER Châtelet-Les Halles. **Open** 11am-9pm Mon, Wed-Sun (until 11pm some exhibitions). Closed Tue, 1 May. **Admission** €5.50; €3.50 18-26s; free under-18s; CM. Exhibitions (includes museum) €6.50-€8.50; €4.50-€6.50 18-26s; day pass €10, €8 18-26s. **Credit** MC, V. **Map** p406 K6.

The unparalleled French state collection of modern art (nearly 5,000 artists, over 50,000 works of art) is rivalled in its breadth and quality only by MOMA in New York. The sheer scale of the Centre Pompidou's holdings – and the size of many contemporary art installations – means that only a fraction can be seen at any one time, so there is a partial rehang every year. You now enter on level four with post-1960s art before going upstairs to level five, which roughly covers the period 1905-1960.

The historic section takes a journey through the making of modern art history, encompassing Primitivism, Fauvism, Cubism, dada and Surrealism right up to American Color-Field painting and Abstract Expressionists. Masterful ensembles allow you to see the span of Matisse's career on canvas and in bronze, the variety of Picasso's invention and the development of cubic orphism by Sonia and Robert Delaunay. Others on the non-stop hit list include Derain, Braque, Duchamp, Picabia, Mondrian, Malevich, Kandinsky, Dix, Ernst, Miró, Klee, Magritte, Rothko and Bacon. Don't miss the reconstruction of a wall of André Breton's studio, combining the tribal art, folk art, flea-market finds and drawings by fellow artists that the Surrealist artist and theorist had amassed. The photography collection also has an impressive roll call, including Brassaï, Kertesz, Man Ray, Cartier-Bresson and Doisneau. Inserted in smaller vitrines between the main rooms are works on paper, photography and archive material, while other galleries are devoted to design and architecture.

The latest rehang (until late 2004) of floor 4 focuses on abstraction, with a large gallery of paintings by Richter, Stella, Lavier and the newly acquired cycle *La Vie des Plantes* by Anselm Kiefer. Other thematic rooms are devoted to Anti-forme (Morris, Flanagan, Hesse, Nauman) and arte povera (Kounellis, Merz, Penone, Anselmo), while monographic displays include Hains, Frize, Opalka, Manzoni, César, Serra, Toroni and Klein. Recent acquisitions line the central corridor while installations by Boris Achour, Mathieu Mercier and Dominique Gonzalez-Foerster are in a room devoted to *nouvelle création*.

Major shows in 2004 include Non-Standard Architecture (until 1 Mar), Sophie Calle (until 15 Mar), Joan Miró (Mar-June), Guiseppe Penone (Apr-July) and Aurélie Nemours (June-Sept). The new Espace 315 focuses on the under-40 generation, including the winner of the Prix Marcel Duchamp each winter. (*See also chapters* **Architecture, Sightseeing: Right Bank**, **Children** and **Film**.)

Auditorium. Café. Children's workshops. Cinema. Guided Visits. Restaurant. Shops. Wheelchair access.

Hidden treasures

Your *Mona Lisas* and your waterlilies are all well and good if you can detach your sensibilities from the hype. However, deciding whether the great work is actually bigger, smaller, greener, more or less protected than you expected can detract from appreciation of why the greats are great in the first place. This is one reason you may want to bypass the crowds and head to works that are equally interesting but less likely to cause you, in an attempt to avoid cliché, to tell your friends how you thought the smile was on a far shallower parabola than expected.

Musée National du Moyen Age

Musée d'Orsay

You've had Manet's *Déjeuner sur l'Herbe*, now meet Whistler's mother. American-born Whistler named his work *Arrangement in Grey and Black (1871)* in order to divert attention away from the subject matter and on to the craftsmanship of the painting itself. Whistler was one of the first to champion the notion of Art for Art's Sake.

Musée du Louvre

Da Vinci's old smiler is a baby in comparison to the oldest item in the Louvre, found in the Oriental Antiquities collection. The piece is a 7,000-year-old white, flat, frontal statue made from gypsum with eyes rimmed in black bitumen. Now on long-term loan from Jordan, it lay undiscovered in Ain Ghezal until 1985.

Musée National Rodin

You've pondered *The Thinker* but have you examined the work of Rodin's model and troubled mistress Camille Claudel? Before being carted off to the lunatic asylum, Claudel was a prolific and acclaimed sculptor who had a great influence on Rodin (she even claimed he got credit for her ideas). However she was often criticised in the patriarchal art world for the emotional sensibility contained in her work – note the tortured ugliness of *Clotho* (1893) made after a break-up with Rodin.

Musée Carnavalet

Among the gruesomely popular revolution-era relics (eg prisoners' chains from the Bastille) is a lock of Marie-Antoinette's hair intertwined with that of her confidante and alleged Sapphic lover the Princess of Lamballe, who lost her life at the hands of a revolutionary mob. The Princess's pretty blonde head was then paraded on a spike before the Queen's prison window.

Musée Marmottan–Claude Monet

Having reflected on Monet's waterlilies, revel in the fresh flourishes of Berthe Morisot. Model and sister-in-law of Manet, as an artist she was faithful to the Impressionist movement. In *At the Ball* (1875) the feather-light, 'feminine' flavour is characteristic of her paintings and pastels often affectionately depicting her own family life.

Musée National Picasso

The master of pinks and blues, Picasso is less well-known for his collages. *Femmes à leur Toilette* (1938) is a massive collage covering a whole wall in the museum and is mostly made of wallpaper, as Picasso took Cubism and his love of women on to the grand scale in this boudoir scene.

Musée National du Moyen Age

Once you've seen the tapestry cycle *La Dame et la Licorne*, don't miss the beautiful Limoges enamels. The painstaking process of mixing and melting the enamel powders, combining deep opaque colours with elaborate metalwork, was a speciality of the Massif Central town and a skill that took a lifetime to perfect. Among early 11th- to 13th-century enamels is a casket representing martyr-saint Thomas à Becket.

Musée d'Art Moderne de la Ville de Paris/Couvent des Cordeliers

11 av du Président-Wilson, 16th (01.53.67.40.00/ www.paris.fr/musees). M° Iéna or Alma-Marceau. **Open** reopens Nov 2004; 10am-5.30pm Tue-Fri; 10am-7pm Sat, Sun. Closed Mon, 1 Jan, 1 May, 25 Dec. **Admission** free. Exhibitions €3-€7; free under-13s. **Credit** MC, V. **Map** p404 D5.

The monumental 1930s building that houses Paris' rich municipal collection of modern and contemporary art is currently closed for renovation (expected to reopen in late 2004). In the meantime parts of its collection, which runs from Cubism to the present, will be presented in town halls (Mairies) around Paris, along themes such as the Ecole de Paris, André Breton and the Nouveaux Réalistes. The adventurous contemporary wing ARC has temporarily crossed the river to the Couvent des Cordeliers (15 rue de l'Ecole de Médecine, 6th), where exhibitions will include Anri Sala and Annette Messager, in parallel with a programme of debates, performances and projections.

Musée Cognacq-Jay

Hôtel Donon, 8 rue Elzévir, 3rd (01.40.27.07.21). M° St-Paul. **Open** 10am-6pm Tue-Sun. Closed Mon, some public holidays. **Admission** free. Exhibitions €2.50-€3.30; free under-13s. **No credit cards. Map** p406 L6.

This intimate museum in a carefully restored *hôtel particulier* houses the collection put together in the early 1900s by Ernest Cognacq, founder of La Samaritaine, and his wife Marie-Louise Jay. Their tastes stuck mainly to the French 18th century, focusing on outstanding French Rococo artists such as Chardin, Watteau, Fragonard, Boucher, Greuze and pastellist Quentin de la Tour, although some English (Reynolds, Lawrence, Romney), Dutch and Flemish (an early Rembrandt, Ruysdael, Rubens), and a sprinkling of Canalettos and Guardis have slipped in too. Pictures are displayed in panelled rooms alongside furniture, porcelain, tapestries and sculpture of the same period.

Bookshop. Children's workshops.

Musée Départemental Maurice Denis, 'Le Prieuré'

2bis rue Maurice Denis, 78100 St-Germain-en-Laye (01.39.73.77.87/www.musee-mauricedenis.fr). RER A St-Germain-en-Laye. **Open** 10am-5.30pm Tue-Fri; 10am-6.30pm Sat, Sun. Closed Mon, 1 Jan, 1 May, 25 Dec. **Admission** €3.80; €2.20 12-25s, students, over-60s; free under-12s; CM. Exhibitions (museum included) €5.30; €3.80 12-25s, students, over-60s; free under-12s. **No credit cards.**

Out in the elegant commuterland of St-Germain-en-Laye, this former royal convent and hospital became home and studio to Nabi painter Maurice Denis, who also decorated the chapel in the garden, in 1915. This remarkable collection comprises paintings, prints and decorative objects by the Nabis – the name means 'Prophets' – who counted Sérusier, Bonnard, Vuillard, Roussel and Valloton among their number. Seeking a renewed spirituality in painting, they took inspiration from Gauguin and Toulouse-Lautrec, who also have some paintings on show here.

Bookshops. Workshops.

Musée Jacquemart-André

158 bd Haussmann, 8th (01.45.62.11.59/ www.musee-jacquemart-andre.com). M° Miromesnil or St-Philippe-du-Roule. **Open** 10am-6pm daily. **Admission** €8; €6 7-17s, students; free under-7s; CM. **Credit** MC, V. **Map** p405 E3.

The magnificent collection gathered by Edouard André and his wife Nélie Jacquemart – and the mansion they built to house it – are as worth visiting for their illustration of the life of the 19th-century *haute bourgeoisie* as for the treasures they unearthed. The ground-floor reception rooms take in the circular Grand Salon, rooms of tapestries and French furniture, Boucher mythological fantasies, the library (with Dutch paintings including Rembrandts), the smoking room hung with English portraits, and the magnificent polychrome marble winter garden with double spiral staircase. On the stairway three recently restored Tiepolo frescoes from the Villa Contarini depict the arrival of Henri III in Venice. Upstairs, what was to have been Nélie's studio became their 'Italian museum', an exceptional Early Renaissance collection that includes Uccello's *St George and the Dragon*, Mantegna's *Ecce Homo*, a superb Schiavone portrait, a Carpaccio panel and Della Robbia terracottas. Even the tea room has a Tiepolo ceiling. The free audio guide is both useful and atmospheric.

Audio guide in six languages. Bookshop. Café (11.30am-6pm). Partial wheelchair access.

Musée Marmottan – Claude Monet

2 rue Louis-Boilly, 16th (01.42.24.07.02/www.musee-marmottan.com). M° La Muette. **Open** 10am-6pm Tue-Sun. Closed Mon, 1 Jan, 1 May, 25 Dec. **Admission** €6.50; €4 8-25s, over-60s; free under-8s. **Credit** MC, V. **Map** p404 A6.

Michel Monet bequeathed 165 of his father's works, plus sketchbooks, his palette and family photos, to the Musée Marmottan, including a breathtaking series of late water lily canvases, now on display in the basement in a special circular room. The collection also contains the seminal Monet, *Impression Soleil Levant*, which gave the Impressionist movement its name. There are also canvases by Sisley, Renoir, Pissarro, Manet, Caillebotte, the 19th-century Realists, the Wildenstein collection of medieval manuscripts, and a large donation of the paintings of Berthe Morisot. The ground- and first-floor salons house smaller Monets, early 19th-century gouaches, a Sèvres porcelain geographical clock and a fabulous collection of First Empire furniture.

Shop. Wheelchair access.

Musée de l'Orangerie

Jardin des Tuileries, 1st. M° Concorde. **Open** 2005 or 2006. **Map** p403 F5.

Discovery of chunks of the Louvre's original curtain wall in the basement mean that renovation work on the Orangerie has been delayed and the museum, which houses Monet's eight, extraordinarily fresh, huge, late *Nymphéas* (water lilies), left by the artist to the nation as a 'spiritual testimony', as well as the Jean Walter and Paul Guillaume collection of Impressionism and the Ecole de Paris, is unlikely to reopen until at least 2005.

Musée d'Orsay

1 rue de la Légion d'Honneur, 7th (01.40.49.48.14/ recorded information 01.45.49.11.11/www.musee-orsay.fr). M° Solférino/RER Musée d'Orsay. **Open** 10am-6pm Tue, Wed, Fri, Sat (from 9am June-Sept); 10am-9.45pm Thur; 9am-6pm Sun. Closed Mon, 1 Jan, 1 May. **Admission** €7; €5 18-25s, all on Sun; free under-18s; CM. **Exhibitions** (museum included) €8.50; €6.50 18-25s, all on Sun; free under-18s. **Credit** (shop) AmEx, MC, V. **Map** p405 G6.

This Beaux-Arts train station, built for the 1900 Exposition Universelle, was saved from demolition to become the Musée d'Orsay, the Paris museum devoted to the pivotal years from 1848 to 1914. Italian architect Gae Aulenti remodelled the interior, keeping the iron-framed coffered roof and creating galleries off either side of a light-filled central canyon. There are some organisational drawbacks: the Impressionists and Post-Impressionists are knee-deep in tourists upstairs, while too much space is given downstairs to Couture's languid nudes or Meissonier's history paintings – but it somehow manages to maintain its open-plan feel.

The museum follows a chronological route, starting on the ground floor, running up to the upper level and finishing on the mezzanine, thus highlighting both the continuities between Impressionist painters and their forerunners, and their revolutionary use of light and colour.

Running down the centre of the tracks, a central sculpture aisle takes in monuments and maidens by artists including Rude, Barrye and Carrier-Belleuse, but the outstanding pieces are by Carpeaux, including his controversial *La Danse* for the facade of the Palais Garnier. The Lille side, on the right of the central aisle, is dedicated to the Romantics and history painters: Ingres and Amaury-Duval contrast with the Romantic passion of Delacroix's North African period, Couture's colossal *Les Romains de la Décadence* and the cupids of Cabanel's *Birth of Venus*. Further on are examples of early Degas, and works by Symbolist painters Gustave Moreau and Puvis de Chavannes, while a new photo gallery puts on changing selections from Orsay's vast holdings of early photography.

The first rooms to the Seine side of the central aisle are given over to the Barbizon landscape painters Corot, Daubigny and Millet. One room is dedicated to Courbet, with *The Artist and his Studio*, his monumental *Burial at Ornans* and his show-stopping *L'Origine du Monde* (*The Origin of the World*). This floor also covers pre-1870 works by Impressionists, including Manet's provocative *Olympia*, and their precursor Boudin.

Upstairs holds the main attraction, the Impressionists gallery, with masterpieces by Pissarro, Renoir and Caillebotte, Manet's once controversial *Déjeuner sur l'Herbe*, several of Monet's paintings of Rouen cathedral, and works by Degas. The riches continue with the Post-Impressionists. Among the boiling colours and frantic brushstrokes of Van Gogh are his *Church at Auvers* and his last painting, *Crows*. This is where you will find the primitivist jungle of the Douanier Rousseau, the gaudy, vivacious Montmartre lowlife depicted by Toulouse-Lautrec, the colourful exoticism of Gauguin's Breton and Tahitian periods, Cézanne's still lifes, landscapes and *The Card Players*, Seurat, Signac and the mystical, pastel drawings of Odilon Redon.

On the mezzanine are works by the Nabis painters – Vallotton, Denis, Roussel, Bonnard and Vuillard. Several rooms are given over to art nouveau decorative arts, including furniture by Majorelle, silverware, and Gallé and Lalique ceramics. Paintings by Klimt and Burne-Jones reside here, and there are also sections on architectural drawings and early photography. The sculpture terraces include busts and studies by Rodin, heads by Rosso and bronzes by Bourdelle and Maillol.

Exhibitions for 2004 include Dutch landscape painter Johan Barthold Jongkind.

Audioguide. Bookshop. Café-restaurant. Cinema. Guided tours. Library. Wheelchair access.

One-man shows

Atelier Brancusi

piazza Beaubourg, 4th (01.44.78.12.33 www.centrepompidou.fr). M° Hôtel de Ville or Rambuteau/RER Châtelet-Les Halles. **Open** 2-6pm Mon, Wed-Sun. **Admission** (included with Centre Pompidou – Musée National d'Art Moderne) €5.50; €3.50 18-26s; free under-18s, first Sun in month. **Credit** AmEx, MC, V. **Map** p406 K6.

When Constantin Brancusi died in 1956 he left his studio in the 15th *arrondissement* and all its contents to the state. Rebuilt outside the Centre Pompidou, the studio has been faithfully reconstructed. His fragile works in wood and plaster, including his endless columns and streamlined bird forms, show how Brancusi revolutionised sculpture.

Atelier-Musée Henri Bouchard

25 rue de l'Yvette, 16th (01.46.47.63.46/ www.musee-bouchard.com). M° Jasmin. **Open** 2-7pm Wed, Sat. Closed last two weeks of Mar, June, Sept and Dec. **Admission** €4; €2.50 students under-26; free under-6s. **No credit cards**.

Prolific sculptor Henri Bouchard had this house and studio built in 1924. Lovingly tended by his son and daughter-in-law, his dusty studio, crammed with sculptures, casts and moulds, sketchbooks and tools, gives an idea of the official art of the time. Bouchard began with Realist-style peasants and maidens, but around 1907-09 he moved to a more stylised, pared down, linear modern style, as seen in his reliefs for the Eglise St-Jean-de-Chaillot and the monumental *Apollo* at the Palais de Chaillot.

Partial wheelchair access.

Clegg & Guttman at the **Palais de Tokyo**. *See p163.*

Espace Dalí Montmartre

11 rue Poulbot, 18th (01.42.64.40.10). M° Anvers or Abbesses. **Open** *Sept-June* 10am-6.30pm daily; *July-Aug* 10am-9pm daily. **Admission** €7; €6 over-60s; €5 8-25s, students; free under-8s. **Credit** (shop) AmEx, MC, V. **Map** p405 H1.

The black-walled interior, artistically programmed lighting and specially composed soundtrack make it clear that this is a high-marketing presentation of the artist's work. Don't expect to see Dalí's Surrealist paintings; the museum concentrates on his sculptures and sketches (many from the latter end of his career) and his literary tributes to La Fontaine, Freud, de Sade, Dante and *Don Quixote*.

Fondation Dubuffet

137 rue de Sèvres, 6th (01.47.34.12.63/ www.dubuffetfondation.com). M° Duroc. **Open** 2-6pm Mon-Fri. Closed weekends, Aug, public holidays. **Admission** €4; free under 10s. **No credit cards**. **Map** p405 E8.

You literally have to travel up a (charming) garden path to reach this museum tucked away in an old three-storey mansion. Set up just a decade before his death by the master of art brut and one-time wine merchant , the foundation ensures that there is a significant body of his works permanently accessible to the public. There is a changing display of Dubuffet's playful and exuberant drawings, paintings and sculptures, plus models of the architectural sculptures from the Hourloupe cycle. The Fondation also administers the Closerie Falballa, 3D masterpiece of the Hourloupe cycle, at Périgny-sur-Yerres east of Paris (by appointment only, €8).

Archives (by appointment). Bookshop.

Musée Bourdelle

16-18 rue Antoine-Bourdelle, 15th (01.49.54.73.73/ www.paris.fr/musees/bourdelle). M° Montparnasse-Bienvenüe or Falguière. **Open** 10am-6pm Tue-Sun. Closed Mon, public holidays. **Admission** free. **No credit cards**. **Map** p405 F8.

Rodin's pupil, sculptor Antoine Bourdelle (1861-1929), produced monumental works including the Modernist relief friezes at the Théâtre des Champs-Elysées, inspired by Isadora Duncan and Nijinsky. Housed around a small garden, the museum includes the artist's apartment and a row of studios used not only by Bourdelle, but also the painter Eugène Carrière, Dalou and Chagall. A 1950s extension follows the evolution of Bourdelle's equestrian monument to General Alvear in Buenos Aires, and his masterful *Hercules the Archer*. A new wing by Christian de Portzamparc housing bronzes such as Bourdelle's studies of Beethoven in various guises that embody different aspects of creative genius.

Bookshop. Children's workshops. Reference library (by appointment). Wheelchair access.

Musée National Delacroix

6 pl Furstenberg, 6th (01.44.41.86.50/www.musee-delacroix.fr). M° St-Germain-des-Prés. **Open** 9.30am-5pm Mon, Wed-Sun. Closed Tue, 1 Jan, 1 May, 25 Dec. **Admission** €4; €2.60 18-25s, all on Sun; free under-18s, first Sun of month; CM. **Credit** MC, V. **Map** p405 H6.

Romantic painter Eugène Delacroix moved to this apartment and studio in pretty place Furstenberg in 1857 to be nearer to the Eglise St-Sulpice where he was painting murals. The Louvre and the Musée d'Orsay house his major paintings, but the collection displayed in his apartment and studio includes

Palais de Tokyo. *See p163.*

small oil paintings, among them an early self-portrait in the romantic stance of a Walter Scott hero and the *Madeleine au Désert,* some free pastel studies of skies, sketches and lithographs, the artist's palette and memorabilia from Morocco. Other displays include correspondence relating to his friendships with Baudelaire and George Sand.
Bookshop.

Musée National Hébert

85 rue du Cherche-Midi, 6th (01.42.22.23.82). M° St-Placide or Vaneau. **Open** 12.30-5.30pm Mon, Wed-Fri; 2-5.30pm Sat, Sun, public holidays. Closed Tue, 1 Jan, 1 May, 25 Dec. **Admission** €3; €2.30 18-25s; free under-18s, first Sun of month; CM. **No credit cards**. **Map** p405 F7.

Ernest Hébert (1817-1908) was a painter of Italian landscapes and figurative subjects, who started off with hilariously uptight pious portraits and lachrymose depictions of sentimental shepherdesses, before turning towards brightly coloured, Symbolist-influenced muses and Impressionist-tinged ladies. Although Hébert was fairly successful in life, for most people the watercolours and oils are unremarkable and soon begin to drag a bit. However, if nothing else, they remain an interesting testament to 19th-century taste, and the run-down house, built in 1743, has a certain (run-down) appeal.

Musée-Jardin Paul Landowski

28 av André Morizet, 92100 Boulogne-Billancourt (01.46.05.82.69/www.mairie-boulogne-billancourt.fr). M° Boulogne-Jean Jaurès. **Open** 11am-6pm Tue-Sun. Closed 15-31 Aug, some public holidays. **Admission** €4.10 (€6.20 with garden); €3.10 students; free under 16s. **Credit** MC, V.

Sculptor Paul Landowski (1875-1961) had the great good fortune to win the Prix de Rome in 1900, and thereafter was kept busy with state commissions. Landowski was not a man who thought small or sat around twiddling his chisel: most of his work treats both classical and modern themes on a monumental scale. One of his most intriguing creations is *Temple*: four sculpted walls depicting 'the history of humanity'. About a hundred sculptures are on show in this pleasant garden and studio.
Wheelchair access.

Musée Maillol

59-61 rue de Grenelle, 7th (01.42.22.59.58/ www.museemaillol.com). M° Rue du Bac. **Open** 11am-6pm Mon, Wed-Sun. Closed Tue. **Admission** €7; €5.50 students; free under-16s. **Credit** (shop) AmEx, MC, V. **Map** p405 G7.

Dina Vierny was only 15 when she met Aristide Maillol (1861-1944) and became his principal model for the next decade, idealised in such sculptures as *Spring, Air* and *Harmony.* In 1995 she opened this delightful museum over the renovated 18th-century Hôtel Bouchardon, displaying Maillol's drawings, pastels, engravings, tapestry panels, ceramics and his early Nabis-related paintings, as well as the sculptures and terracottas that epitomise his distinctive calm, modern classicism. A 20th-century treasure trove, the museum also displays works by Picasso, Rodin, Gauguin, Degas and Cézanne, a whole room of Matisse drawings, some rare Surrealist documents and multiples by Marcel Duchamp and Jacques Duchamp-Villon, and works by naive artists including Aloïse. Vierny has also championed Russian artists from Kandinsky and

Poliakoff to Ilya Kabakov, whose installation *The Communal Kitchen* recreates the atmosphere and sounds of a shared Soviet kitchen. Well-conceived monographic exhibitions are devoted to modern and contemporary artists, with Francis Bacon and Serge Poliakoff lined up for 2004.
Bookshop. Café. Wheelchair access.

Musée Gustave Moreau

14 rue de La Rochefoucauld, 9th (01.48.74.38.50). M° Trinité. **Open** 10am-12.45pm, 2-5.15pm Mon, Wed-Sun. Closed Tue, 1 Jan, 1 May, 25 Dec. **Admission** €4; €2.60 18-25s, Sun; free under-18s; CM. **Credit** MC, V. **Map** p405 G3.

Easily the looniest of all the one-man museums, this is not only where the Symbolist painter Gustave Moreau (1825-98) lived, worked and taught, but was also designated by the artist to become a museum after his death – as was almost inevitable given that the enormous double-storey studio is stuffed to the gills with his paintings, finished or otherwise. Thousands more of his drawings and watercolours can be pulled out from shutters on the walls. His mind in retreat, Moreau developed a personal mythology, filling his detailed canvases with images of St John the Baptist, St George, the divinely lascivious Salomé. Writhing maidens, mystical beasts, strange plants and fantastical architecture emerge like an outpouring of 19th-century sexual repression, especially when you see the dinky private apartment where he lived with his parents, and which he arranged symbolically in their memory.
Bookshop.

Musée National Picasso

Hôtel Salé, 5 rue de Thorigny, 3rd (01.42.71.25.21/ www.musee-picasso.fr). M° Chemin-Vert or St-Paul. **Open** *May-Sept* 9.30am-6pm Mon, Wed-Sun; *Oct-Apr* 9.30am-5.30pm Mon, Wed-Sun. Closed Tue, 25 Dec, 1 Jan. **Admission** €5.50; €4 18-25s; free under-18s, first Sun of month; CM. **Credit** (shop) AmEx, MC, V. **Map** p404 L6.

This astonishing testament to one man's bewilderingly inventive genius was acquired by the state in lieu of inheritance tax and is housed in one of the grandest Marais mansions. The collection represents all phases of the master's long and varied career, showing Picasso's continual inventiveness and life-affirming sense of humour. Masterpieces include a gaunt, blue-period self-portrait, studies for the *Demoiselles d'Avignon*, *Paolo as Harlequin*, his Cubist and classical phases, the surreal *Nude in an Armchair*, lively beach pictures of the 1920-30s, sand-covered tableaux-reliefs, portraits of his favourite models Marie-Thérèse and Dora Maar, and the unabashedly ribald artist-and-model paintings he produced in later years. The unusual wallpaper collage, *Women at their Toilette*, gets its own small room, and there are also prints and ceramics, minotaur etchings, and Picasso's collection of tribal art – juxtaposed with 'primitive' wood figures that he actually carved himself. Take the time to concentrate on his bizarrely wonderful sculptures, from the vast plaster head on the staircase and the spiky *Project for Monument to Apollinaire* to the *Girl on a Swing*. Look closely at the sculpture of an ape – its face is actually made out of a toy car. Exhibitions for 2004 include Picasso and Ingres.
Audiovisual room. Bookshop. Outdoor café May-Oct. Wheelchair access.

Musée National Rodin

Hôtel Biron, 77 rue de Varenne, 7th (01.44.18.61.10/www.musee-rodin.fr). M° Varenne. **Open** *Apr-Sept* 9.30am-5.45pm Tue-Sun (gardens 6.45pm); *Oct-Mar* 9.30am-4.45pm (gardens 5pm) Tue-Sun. Closed Mon, 25 Dec, 1 Jan, 1 May. **Admission** €5; €3 18-25s, all on Sun; free under-18s, first Sun of month; CM. Gardens only €1. **Credit** MC, V. **Map** p405 F6.

The Rodin Museum occupies the *hôtel particulier* where the sculptor lived at the end of his life. *The Kiss*, *Cathedral*, the *Walking Man*, portrait busts and early terracottas are indoors, as well as many of the individual figures or small groups that also appear on the *Gates of Hell*, accompanied by several works by Rodin's mistress and pupil, Camille Claudel. To top it off, the walls are hung with paintings by Van Gogh, Monet, Renoir, Carrière and Rodin himself. But it's the gardens that most people seem to love, perhaps because they do away with museum claustrophobia, or perhaps because they're spotted with shady trees, and full of unexpected treasures. Look out for the *Burghers of Calais*, the elaborate *Gates of Hell*, inspired by Dante's *Inferno*, the *Thinker*, *Orpheus* under a shady stretch of trees, and several unfinished nymphs emerging from their marble prison. Fans can also visit Villa des Brillants at Meudon (01.41.14.35.00; *May-Oct*, 1-6pm Fri-Sun, museum and gardens €2, gardens only €1), where Rodin worked from 1895.
Bookshop. Garden café. Partial wheelchair access. Visits for visually handicapped (by appointment).

Musée Zadkine

100bis rue d'Assas, 6th (01.55.42.77.20/ www.paris.fr/musees/Zadkine). M° Notre-Dame-des-Champs or Vavin/RER Port Royal. **Open** 10am-6pm Tue-Sun. Closed Mon, public holidays. **Admission** collection free; exhibitions €4; €3 students, over-60s; €2 under-26s; free under-13s; CM. **No credit cards**. **Map** p405 G8.

Works by the Russian-born Cubist sculptor Ossip Zadkine are displayed around the tiny house and garden near the Jardins du Luxembourg, where he lived from 1928 until his death in 1967. Zadkine's compositions include musical, mythological and religious subjects and his style varies with the materials: bronzes tend to be geometrical, wood more sensuous, flowing with the grain. Sculptures are displayed at eye level, along with drawings and poems by Zadkine and some paintings by his wife, Valentine Prax. Changing exhibitions of contemporary artists are held in the former studio, with a sound installation by Akio Suzuki and photos by Jan Dibbets in 2004.
Partial wheelchair access.

Photography

See also **Temporary exhibition centres**, **Centre Pompidou** and **Musée d'Orsay**.

Centre National de la Photographie/ Centre de l'Image Jeu de Paume

until June 2004 Hôtel Salomon de Rothschild, 11 rue Berryer, 8th (01.53.76.12.32/www.cnp-photographie.com). M° Charles de Gaulle-Etoile or George V. **Open** until June 2004 noon-7pm Mon, Wed-Sun. Closed Tue, 1 May. **Admission** €4.60; €2.30 10-25s, over-60s; free under-10s. **Credit** MC, V. **Map** p404 D3. *From July 2004 Jeu de Paume, 1 pl de la Concorde, 8th. M° Concorde.* **Map** p405 F5.

Paris' photo offering is in a state of flux as the Centre National de la Photographie is set to leave its home in the Hôtel Salomon de Rothschild in mid-2004 and move to the Jeu de Paume, redesignated the Centre National de la Photographie et de l'Image (or whatever name is eventually decided upon). The new institution promises an inter-disciplinary stance between photography, film and video.

Bookshop. Café. Cinema. Wheelchair access.

Fondation Henri Cartier-Bresson

2 impasse Lebouis, 14th (01.56.80.27.00/ www.henricartierbresson.org). M° Gaîté. **Open** 1-6.30pm Tue, Thur, Fri; 1-8.30pm Wed; 11am-6.45pm Sat. Closed Mon, Sun, Aug, public holidays. **Admission** €4; €2 students, over-60s, children. **No credit cards. Map** p405 F9.

The career of veteran French photographer Henri Cartier-Bresson (now in his 90s) has spanned the globe and much of the 20th century. In 2003, the Fondation, an initiative by Cartier-Bresson and his wife Martine Franck, opened occupying five floors of a listed 19th-century studio building in Montparnasse. As well as photos, it has his drawings, paintings, writings and films, plus the reserves of his negs, contact sheets and archives. Temporary exhibitions focus on other photographers.

Maison Européenne de la Photographie

5-7 rue de Fourcy, 4th (01.44.78.75.00/www.mep-fr.org). M° St-Paul or Pont-Marie. **Open** 11am-7.30pm Wed-Sun. Closed Mon, Tue, public holidays. **Admission** €5; €2.50 students, over-60s; free under-8s, all 5-8pm Wed. **Credit** MC, V. **Map** p406 L6.

The MEP's setting, in a restored Marais *hôtel particulier* and its minimalist modern extension, is ideal in scale for photography exhibitions. Elements of the MEP's collection focusing on photo masters from the 1950s on, such as Penn, Koudelka, Newton, Tosani, Parr and Ristelhueber, and a large hoard of Polaroids alternate with temporary exhibitions. René Burri, Marc Riboud and Chinese video art are promised for 2004. An energetic venue, it organises the citywide biennial Mois de la Photo (next in Nov 2004) and the Art Outsiders (new media art on the web) festival in September.

Auditorium. Café. Library. Wheelchair access.

Patrimoine Photographique

Hôtel de Sully, 62 rue St-Antoine, 4th (01.42.74.47.75/www.patrimoine-photo.org). M° Bastille. **Open** 10am-6.30pm Tue-Sun. Closed Mon, some public holidays. **Admission** €4; €2.50 students, under 25s, over-60s; free under-10s, under-25s, over-60s; free under-10s. **No credit cards. Map** p406 L7.

A small gallery devoted to photographic heritage, located in a stunning Marais *hôtel*. Shows usually take an historical angle (Cecil Beaton, Jacques-Henri Lartigue, Lucien Hervé), or a theme (the Egyptian pyramids, crime photography).

Temporary exhibition centres

Paris' non-museum exhibition centres have lots of advantages: the shows are often less crowded, offer a specialised look at interesting subjects, and are often significantly cheaper (or free). Most are only open to the public during exhibitions, so check listings in *Pariscope* before dropping by. Cultural centres often put on exhibitions that can make a welcome change: Centre Culturel Calouste Gulbenkian (Portugal – 51 av d'Iéna, 16th, 01.53.23.93.93). Centre Culturel Suisse (32-38 rue des Francs-Bourgeois, 3rd/01.42.71.38.38). Centre Wallonie-Bruxelles, 127 rue St-Martin, 4th, 01.53.01.96.96). Goethe Institut (Germany – 17 av d'Iéna, 16th, 01.44.43.92.30 and Galerie Condé, 31 rue de Condé, 6th/01.40.46.69.60). Institut Finlandais (60 rue des Ecoles, 5th, 01.40.51.89.09). Centre Culturel Irlandais (5 rue des Irlandais, 5th, 01.58.52.10.30). Institut Néerlandais (121 rue de Lille, 7th, 01.53.59.12.40). Maison de l'Amérique Latine (217 bd St-Germain, 7th, 01.49.54.75.00).

Bibliothèque Forney

Hôtel de Sens, 1 rue du Figuier, 4th (01.42.78.14.60). M° Pont-Marie. **Open** 1.30-8.30pm Tue-Sat. Closed Mon, Sun, public holidays. **Admission** €4; €2 students under 28, over-60s; free under-12s. **No credit cards. Map** p406 L7.

In the turrets of the oldest mansion in the Marais, the library specialises in the applied and graphic arts. A wing is given over to temporary displays, often of poster art.

Bibliothèque Nationale de France – Richelieu

58 rue de Richelieu, 2nd (01.53.79.81.26/ www.bnf.fr). M° Bourse. **Open** 9am-6pm Mon-Sat. Closed Sun, two weeks in Sept, public holidays. **Admission** €5; €4 students, 13-25s; free under-13s. Crypte free. **Credit** AmEx, MC, V. **Map** p405 H4.

Within the old Bibliothèque Nationale, the Galeries Mansart and Mazarine take in all works on paper from medieval manuscripts and historic watercolours to photography and contemporary prints. A new gallery, La Crypte, is used for contemporary and graphic art. *Wheelchair access.*

Bibliothèque Nationale de France – Richelieu

Bibliothèque Nationale de France – François Mitterrand

quai François-Mauriac, 13th (01.53.79.59.59/ www.bnf.fr). M° Bibliothèque or Quai de la Gare. **Open** 10am-7pm Tue-Sat; noon-7pm Sun. Closed Mon, two weeks in Sept, public holidays. **Admission** €5; €4 students, 13-25s; free under-13s. **Credit** MC, V. **Map** p407 M10.

The gigantic new library could not be more of a contrast to its historic parent but it shares a similarly erudite programme of exhibitions, including photography, artists' books and an ongoing cycle on writing. In 2004, an exhibition on Chinese painting and calligraphy from March to May forms part of L'Année de la Chine.

Café. Wheelchair access.

Chapelle St-Louis de la Salpêtrière

47 bd de l'Hôpital, 13th (01.42.16.04.24). M° Gare d'Austerlitz. **Open** 8.30am-6.30pm daily. **Admission** free. **Map** p406 L9.

Libéral Bruand's austere 17th-century chapel provides a fantastic setting for contemporary art, notably to date installations by Viola, Kawamata, Kapoor and Holzer for various Festivals d'Automne.

Wheelchair access.

Espace Paul Ricard

9 rue Royale, 8th (01.53.30.88.00/ www.espacepaulricard.com). M° Concorde. **Open** 10am-7pm Mon-Fri. Closed weekends, some public holidays. **No credit cards**. **Map** p405 F4.

The purveyor of *pastis* here promotes contemporary art, notably with the Prix Paul Ricard – young French artists shortlisted by an indepedent curator for an annual prize – held to coincide with FIAC each autumn. Other shows have included new German painters and contemporary design.

Fondation Cartier pour l'art contemporain

261 bd Raspail, 14th (01.42.18.56.72/recorded info 01.42.18.56.51/www.fondation.cartier.fr). M° Raspail. **Open** noon-8pm Tue, Wed-Sun. Closed Mon. **Admission** €5; €3.50 under-25s, students, over-60s; free under-10s. **Credit** AmEx, MC, V. **Map** p405 G9.

Jean Nouvel's jaw-dropping 1990s glass and steel building, which combines an exhibition centre with Cartier's offices up above, is as much a work of art as the quirky installations inside. Monographic shows by contemporary artists and photographers (Pierrick Sorin, Eggleston, Takashi Murakami) alternate with wide-ranging multicultural, century-crossing themes, such as 'Birds' or 'the Desert', with the designer Marc Newson and Congolese painter Chéri Samba programmed for 2004.

Bookshop. Wheelchair access.

Fondation EDF – Espace Electra

6 rue Récamier, 7th (01.53.63.23.45/www.edf.fr). M° Sèvres-Babylone. **Open** noon-7pm Tues-Sun. Closed Mon, public holidays. **Admission** free. **No credit cards**. **Map** p405 G7.

This former electricity substation, opened by the French electricity board as a public relations booster, is used for varied, well-presented exhibitions, from garden designer Gilles Clément to pioneer film-maker Georges Méliès.

Fondation Mona Bismarck

34 av de New-York, 16th (01.47.23.38.88). M° Alma-Marceau. **Open** 10.30am-6.30pm Tue-Sat. Closed Mon, Sun, Aug, public holidays. **Admission** free. **Map** p404 C5.

Good old Mona (née Strader, but she married well, and often): the Fondation provides a chic setting for eclectic exhibitions of everything from Etruscan antiquities to North American folk art.

Hôtel de Ville de Paris

Salon d'accueil, 2 rue de Rivoli, 4th (01.42.76.43.43). M° Hôtel de Ville. **Open** 10am-7pm Mon-Sat; 2-7pm Sun. **Map** p406 K6.

Varied exhibitions in Paris city hall vary from nostalgia trips about Piaf to contemporary African art.

Galeries Nationales du Grand Palais

3 av du Général-Eisenhower, 8th (01.44.13.17.17/ reservations 08.92.68.46.94/www.rmn.fr). M° Champs-Elysées-Clemenceau. **Open** 10am-8pm Mon, Thur-Sun; 10am-10pm Wed. Pre-booking compulsory before 1pm. Closed Tue, 1 May, 25 Dec. **Admission** €10.10 before 1pm with reservation; €9 after 1pm; €8 (before 1pm) €5.50 (after 1pm) 18-26s, all on Mon; free under-13s. **Credit** MC, V. **Map** p405 E5.

Paris' premier blockbuster venue is a striking leftover from the 1900 *Exposition Universelle*. The central hall is closed for restoration, but two other exhibition spaces remain. Highlights of 2004 include 'Le Cirque' on the circus in modern art and 'Hôtes des brumes', prize pieces from Chinese museums.

Audioguides. Shop. Café. Cinema. Wheelchair access.

Grenier des Grands-Augustins

7 rue des Grands-Augustins, 6th (01.43.54.09.00). M° St-Michel or Odéon. **Open** 3-6.30pm Mon-Fri (reserve ahead). **Admission** free. **No credit cards**. **Map** p406 H7.

Picasso's former studio, where the artist lived from 1936 to 1955 and where he painted *Guernica*, is now used for exhibitions intended to widen the audience for art. Until 15 May 2004: The tapestry of Guernica.

Halle St-Pierre – Musée d'Art Naïf Max Fourny

2 rue Ronsard, 18th (01.42.58.72.89/ www.hallesaintpierre.org). M° Anvers. **Open** 10am-6pm daily. Closed 1 Jan, 1 May, 25 Dec, Aug. **Admission** €6.50; €5 students 4-26s; free under-4s. **Credit** (shop) MC, V. **Map** p406 J2.

The former covered market in the glorious shadow of Sacré-Coeur specialises in *art brut* (a term coined by Dubuffet to describe self-taught *singuliers,* including the mentally ill, who used poor or idiosyncratic materials) and *art naïf* (self-taught artists who use more traditional techniques) from its own and other collections.

Bookshop. Café/restaurant. Children's workshops.

Musée-atelier Adzak

3 rue Jonquoy, 14th (01.45.43.06.98). Mº Plaisance. **Open** hours vary, call in advance. **Admission** free.
The eccentric house and studio built by the late Roy Adzak harbours traces of the conceptual artist's plaster body columns and dehydrations. Now a registered British-run charity, it gives (mainly foreign) artists a first chance to exhibit in Paris.
Partial wheelchair access.

Musée National du Luxembourg

19 rue de Vaugirard, 6th (01.42.34.25.95/ www.museeduluxembourg.fr). Mº St-Sulpice/RER Luxembourg. **Open** 11am-10.30pm Mon, Fri-Sun; 11am-7pm Tue-Thur. **Admission** €9; €6 students; €4 8-12s; free under 8s. **Credit** MC, V. **Map** p405 F7.
This small but imposing museum was the first public gallery in France when it opened in 1750 and was later a forerunner of the Musée National d'Art Moderne. Its current stewardship by the national museums and the French Senate has brought a more imaginative stance and some impressive coups. Following 2003's crowd-pulling shows of Modigliani and Botticelli (until end Feb 2004), 2004 promises 20th-century self-portraits and Veronese.
Café. Shop. Wheelchair access.

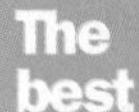

Ex-residents

See also **Atelier Brancusi, Maison de Balzac, Maison de Victor-Hugo, Musée Bourdelle, Musée Delacroix, Musée Gustave Moreau, Musée Pasteur, Musée Rodin, Musée Zadkine.**

François 1er

Frankie commissioned a palatial pad at the **Louvre**. *See p148.*

La Reine Margot

Henri IV's ex-wife led a libertine life in what's now the **Bibliothèque Forney**. *See p160.*

Cardinal Mazarin

The powerful man in red held court at the **Bibliothèque Nationale Richelieu**. *See p160.*

Mme de Sévigné

The world's greatest letter writer put quill to paper at **Musée Carnavalet**. *See p170.*

Louise de France

Louis XV's daughter led a wimpled life at **Musée de l'Art et d'Histoire de St-Denis.** *See p169.*

Suzanne Valadon

Valadon and son Utrillo's studios are now the **Musée de Montmartre**. *See p171.*

Musée du Montparnasse

21 av du Maine, 15th (01.42.22.91.96). Mº Montparnasse-Bienvenüe. **Open** 12.30-7pm Tue-Sun. **Admission** €5; €4 students under-26, over-60s; free under-12s. **No credit cards. Map** p405 F8.
The Musée du Montparnasse opened in 1998 in one of the last remaining alleys of artists' studios in the area. In the 1930s and 40s it was home to Marie Vassilieff, who opened her own academy and canteen where penniless artists – including regulars Picasso, Modigliani, Cocteau, Matisse and Zadkine – came for cheap food. Trotsky and Lenin were also among her guests. Exhibitions focus on aspects of Montparnasse's artistic heritage as well as artists still working in the area today.

Palais de Tokyo: Site de Création Contemporaine

13 av de New-York, 16th (01.47.23.54.01/ www.palaisdetokyo.com). Mº Iéna or Alma-Marceau. **Open** noon-midnight Tue-Sun. Closed Mon, some public holidays. **Admission** €5; €3 students under-26; free under-18s, art students. **Map** p404 B5.
Proclaimed 'a laboratory for contemporary art', the Palais de Tokyo opened in 2002, bringing a breath of fresh air to Paris' art institutions. The 1930s building has been stripped back to its concrete shell, revealing a skylit central hall, and permitting the coexistence of exhibitions and installations, fashion shows and performances. The late opening hours and funky café seem to have succeeded in drawing a wider, younger audience. Just as the echoing halls appeared to be getting into their stride, with intelligent shows about political activism and geographical mapping, solo shows and installations by Frank Scurti, Chen Zhen and Pierre Joseph, its future has come into doubt, with announcements by the Ministry of Culture of a more museum-like approach from 2005, reappropriating the remaining empty acres for pieces from public and private collections.
Bar. Restaurant. Shops. Wheelchair access.

Passage de Retz

9 rue Charlot, 3rd (01.48.04.37.99). Mº Filles du Calvaire. **Open** 10am-7pm Tue-Sun. **Admission** €6; €4 students under 26, over-60s; free under-12s. **Credit** (over €10) MC, V. **Map** p406 L5.
This gorgeous Marais mansion, latterly a toy factory, was resurrected as a gallery in the 1990s, to host exhibitions and installations by contemporary artists, architects, designers and photographers. Wooden floors, a glass roof and walled garden give it a relaxing vibe. Pop into the designer café, if only to see the extraordinary silver sponge bar, which looks for all the world like an enormous bosom.
Bookshop. Café. Partial wheelchair access.

Pavillon des Arts

Les Halles, Porte Rambuteau, 1st (01.42.33.82.50/ www.paris.fr/musees). Mº Châtelet-Les Halles. **Open** 11.30am-6.30pm Tue-Sun. Closed Mon, public holidays. **Admission** €5.50; €4 students, over-60s; €2.50 14-26s; free under-14s. **No credit cards. Map** p406 K5.

This gallery in the Forum des Halles hosts varied exhibitions from contemporary photography to Turner to Paris history.
Wheelchair access.

La Pinacothèque de Paris

30bis rue de Paradis, 10th (01.53.34.06.70/ www.pinacotheque.com). M° Bonne Nouvelle or Poissonnière. **Open** 10am-10.30pm Mon, Fri; 10am-7pm Tue-Thur, Sat, Sun. **Admission** €12; €8 13-25s, students; €6 8-12s; free under-12s. **Credit** MC, V. **Map** p406 H5.

This new privately funded venue opened in November 2003 (the 30th anniversary of Picasso's death) in the former Musée Baccarat. Its first exhibition (until 28 Mar) shows 100 works from the collection of Jacqueline Picasso, Picasso's second wife, many of them depicting her. Thereafter the venue will close until autumn 2004 while work is done to create 4,000m² of exhition space. Created by art historian Marc Restellini, who is responsible for bringing high-profile exhibitions like Raphael and Modigliani to the Musée du Luxembourg, its ambition is to bring over crowd-pulling exhibitions of artists such as Klimt, Munch or Renoir, often planned as partnerships with exhibition centres in Japan and the USA. There's a café overseen by the ubiquitous Alain Ducasse. On the ground floor, a room will present changing displays of works on long-term loan from private collections.
Café.

Le Plateau

corner of rue des Alouettes and rue Carducci, 19th (01.53.19.84.10/www.fracidf-leplateau.com). M° Buttes Chaumont or Jourdain. **Open** 2-7pm Wed-Fri; 11am-7pm Sat- Sun. **Admission** free.

This new contemporary art space, opened in spring 2002, has become the low-budget challenger to the Palais de Tokyo. Born out of a campaign by local associations for an arts centre in northeast Paris and the search for an exhibition space for the FRAC d'Ile de France (Fonds Régional d'Art Contemporain), the small exhibition space has addressed the diversity of current art practice taking in installation, painting and photography, complemented by experimental cinema, contemporary music and dance. Shows in 2004 include, until Feb, 20 artists from the FRAC collection; Mar-May, *'Non Lieu'* (Miriam Cahn, Laurent Pariente, Romain Pellas); June-Aug, *'Distances?'*, nine artists from Poland.

Architecture & urbanism

Musée des Années 30

Espace Landowski, 28 av André-Morizet, 92100 Boulogne-Billancourt (01.55.18.46.45). M° Marcel Sembat. **Open** 11am-6pm Tue-Sun. Closed Mon, 15-31 Aug, public holidays. **Admission** €4.10; €3.10 students, over-60s; free under-16s. **No credit cards.**

The Musée des Années 30 is a reminder of what an awful lot of second-rate art was produced in the 1930s. There are decent Modernist sculptures by the Martel brothers, graphic designs and Juan Gris still lifes and drawings, but the highlights are the designs by avant-garde architects including Perret, Le Corbusier, Lurçat and Fischer.
Guided visits 2.30pm Sun. Shop. Wheelchair access.

Palais de la Porte Dorée

293 av Daumesnil, 12th (01.44.74.84.80/recorded information 01.43.46.51.61). M° Porte Dorée. **Open** 10am-5.20pm Tue-Sun. **Admission** €4; €2.60 under-25s, students. **No credit cards.**

Until the opening of the ambitious new Cité de l'Architecture in the Palais de Chaillot in 2005, which will combine the former Musée des Monuments Nationaux and the Institut Français de l'Architecture, architectural exhibitions are being held in the now empty shell of the former Musée des Arts Africains et Océaniques. The Galerie d'Actualité covers contemporary architecture and urbanism, while other shows in 2004 include concrete maestro Auguste Perret (Jan) and *'Maisons et Jardins'* (June). The magnificent building designed for the 1931 Exposition Coloniale has an art deco bas-relief glorying in France's colonial past and two art deco rooms by Ruhlmann with murals by Ducos de la Haille. Happily for the crocodiles (some of whom arrived here from Dakar in 1948), the basement still houses its rather noisy aquarium, one of the finest collections of tropical fish in Europe.

Pavillon de l'Arsenal

21 bd Morland, 4th (01.42.76.33.97/www.pavillon-arsenal.com). M° Sully-Morland. **Open** 10.30am-6.30pm Tue-Sat; 11am-7pm Sun. Closed Mon, 1 Jan. **Admission** free. **Credit** (shop) MC, V. **Map** p406 L7.

This centre presents imaginative exhibitions on urban design and architecture, often looking at Paris from unusual perspectives, be it that of theatres, hidden courtyards or the banks of the Seine. There's a 50m² model of Paris, and a regularly updated permanent exhibition *'Paris, la ville et ses projets'* on the historic growth of the city.
Bookshop. Café.

Decorative arts

Galerie-Musée Baccarat

11 pl des Etats-Unis, 16th (01.40.22.11.00). M° Charles de Gaulle-Etoile or Iéna. **Open** 10am-7pm Mon-Sat. Closed Sun, public holidays. **Admission** €4; €3 students, under-25s. **No credit cards.** **Map** p400 C4.

The glass showrooms and museum of crystal manufacturer Baccarat have acquired an altogether more glamorous image in their new location. The *hôtel particulier* that once belonged to aristocratic art patron Marie-Laure de Noailles has been given a magical, tongue-in-cheek makeover by Philippe Starck. The museum itself has come out reduced in size but sharpened in focus. Two rooms, one of them painted with an allegory of alchemy by Gérard Garouste, pinpoint different techniques, showcasing the work of great designers, such as Georges

Chevalier and Ettore Sottsass, services made for princes and maharajahs, and monumental show-off items made for the great exhibitions of the 1800s.
Restaurant. Shop.

Musée des Antiquités Nationales

Château, pl Charles de Gaulle, 78100 St-Germain-en-Laye (01.39.10.13.00/www.musee-antiquitiesnationales.fr). RER St-Germain-en-Laye. **Open** 9am-5.15pm Mon, Wed-Sun. Closed 25 Dec, 1 Jan. **Admission** €4; €2.60 students 18-25; free under-18s, first Sun of month; CM. **Credit** (shop) MC, V.

Thousands of years spin by from one cabinet to the next in this awe-inspiring museum tracing France's rich archaeological heritage: some of the early Paleolithic animal sculptures existed long before the Ancient Egyptians. The redesigned Neolithic galleries feature statue-menhirs, female statues and an ornate tombstone from Cys-la-Commune. Exhibits are well presented and full of curiosities, like the massive antlers from a prehistoric Irish deer or the set of 18th-century cork models of ancient sites, although the gallery of artefacts from Roman Gaul is currently closed. The museum also hosts interesting temporary exhibitions.
Guided visits. Shop. Wheelchair access.

Musée National des Arts et Traditions Populaires

6 av du Mahatma-Gandhi, Bois de Boulogne, 16th (01.44.17.60.00). M° Les Sablons. **Open** 9.30am-5pm Mon, Wed-Sun. Closed Tue, some public holidays. **Admission** €4; €2.60 10-25s, students, over-60s; free under-10s, first Sun of month; CM. **Credit** MC, V.

In contrast with its setting in a 1960s building, this centre of French folk art in the Bois de Boulogne spotlights the traditions and popular culture of pre-industrial France. Rural life is depicted through agricultural tools, household objects and costumes. The liveliest sections are those devoted to customs and beliefs – a crystal ball, tarot cards, thunder stones and early medicines – and popular entertainment. If you're interested visit now – it's due to move to Marseille in 2008.
Auditorium. Library/sound archive (by appointment). Shop. Wheelchair access.

Musée des Arts Décoratifs

107 rue de Rivoli, 1st (01.44.55.57.50/www.ucad.fr). M° Palais Royal. **Open** 11am-6pm Tue-Fri; 10am-6pm Sat, Sun. Closed Mon, some public holidays. **Admission** €6; €4.50 18-25s; free under-18s; CM. **Credit** MC, V. **Map** p406 H5.

Musée National de la Céramique

This rich collection of decorative arts is currently undergoing a major facelift as part of the Grand Louvre project. So far only the Renaissance and Middle Ages galleries are open; the remaining departments are scheduled for completion in 2005. In addition to 16th-century Venetian glass and Flemish tapestries, there are two reconstructions of period rooms: a panelled Gothic Charles VIII bedchamber and a Renaissance room. The religious art collection includes a wonderful altarpiece of the life of John the Baptist by Luis Borassa.
Library. Shop. Wheelchair access (105 rue de Rivoli).

Musée National de la Céramique

pl de la Manufacture, 92310 Sèvres (01.41.14.04.20). M° Pont de Sèvres. **Open** 10am-5pm Mon, Wed-Sun. Closed Tue, public holidays. **Admission** €4; €2.60 18-25s; free under-18s, all on Sun; CM. **Credit** (showroom) MC, V.

Founded in 1738 as a private concern, the world-famous porcelain factory moved to Sèvres from Vincennes in 1756 and was soon taken over by the state. Finely painted, delicately modelled pieces that epitomise French Rococo style, together with later Sèvres, adorned with copies of Raphaels and Titians, demonstrate extraordinary technical virtuosity. The collection also includes Delftware, Meissen, Della Robbia reliefs, Hispano-Moorish pieces and wonderful Ottoman plates and tiles from Iznik.
Shop and showroom. Wheelchair access.

Musée de la Chasse et de la Nature

Hôtel Guénégaud, 60 rue des Archives, 3rd (01.53.01.92.40). M° Rambuteau. **Open** 11am-6pm Tue-Sun. Closed Mon, public holidays. **Admission** €4.60; €2.30 16-25s, students under 26, over-60s; €0.75 5-16s; free under 5s. **No credit cards**. **Map** p406 K5.

It may seem a strange thing to find in the middle of town, but housed on three floors of a beautiful 17th-century mansion designed by Mansart is a collection of objects under the common theme of hunting (nature, not counting the alarming array of stuffed animals, including an unlikely polar bear and a pair of gorillas, doesn't get much of a look-in). The highlight is the wonderfully ornate weapons: crossbows inlaid with ivory and mother-of-pearl, rifles decorated with hunting scenes, all reminders that hunting's accoutrements were important status symbols, while animals also find their way on to porcelain tureens, tea sets, console tables and ornately carved tankards. There's a huge display of bird and animal studies by France's first great *animalier* painter Alexandre-François Desportes, as well as his portrait of Louis XIV's hunting dogs *Blonde and Diane*.
Bookshop. Wheelchair access.

Musée de l'Eventail

2 bd de Strasbourg, 10th (01.42.08.90.20). M° Strasbourg-St-Denis. **Open** 2-6pm Mon-Wed. **Workshop** 9am-12.30pm, 2-6pm Mon-Fri. Closed Aug, public holidays. **Admission** €5; €2.50 under 12s. **No credit cards**. **Map** p406 K4.

The fan-making Hoguet family's collection is housed in the workshop and neo-Renaissance showroom, and you may well see fans being made (now generally for fashion shows) as you walk around. Exhibits go from 18th-century fans with mother-of-pearl and ivory sticks to early 20th-century advertising fans and contemporary designs by Karl Lagerfeld.

There's also a display on the techniques and materials used to make these luxury items – which, until the French Revolution, only the nobility were permitted to use.

Musée de la Mode et du Textile

107 rue de Rivoli, 1st (01.44.55.57.50/www.ucad.fr). M° Palais Royal. **Open** 11am-6pm Tue-Fri; 10am-6pm Sat, Sun. Closed Mon, some public holidays. **Admission** €6; €4.50 18-25s; free under-18s; CM. **Credit** MC, V. **Map** p406 H5.

Housed in the Palais du Louvre (but entered separately), the Musée de la Mode boasts the richest collection of 20th-century fashion in the world, including the entire archives of Vionnet and 5,000 original drawings by Schiaparelli, as well as some stunning historical items. The museum may be more for those who live for fashion, but it's also about fashion for life, including designs that pave the way for future wardrobe must-haves by the likes of Comme des Garçons or Junya Watanabe. The display changes once or twice a year, with Elsa Schiaparelli and handbags on the rails for 2004.

Wheelchair access.

Musée de la Mode de la Ville de Paris (Musée Galliéra)

Palais Galliéra, 10 av Pierre 1er de Serbie, 16th (01.56.52.86.00). M° Iéna or Alma-Marceau. **Open** during exhibitions 10am-6pm Tue-Sun. Closed Mon, public holidays. **Admission** (includes audioguide) €7; €5.50 over-60s; €3.50 13-26s; free under-13s. **Credit** MC, V. **Map** p404 C5.

Opposite the Musée d'Art Moderne de la Ville de Paris is this fanciful 1890s mansion housing the administrative offices of the state's vast costume collection. The two ground-floor rooms hold changing exhibitions, ranging from the history of *toile de Jouy* to the annual '*Modes à Suivre*' (early Sept), where the creations of young designers are showcased at the same time as they hit the shops.

Musée National du Moyen Age – Thermes de Cluny

6 pl Paul-Painlevé, 5th (01.53.73.78.00/www.musee-moyenage.fr). M° Cluny-La Sorbonne/RER St-Michel. **Open** 9.15am-5.45pm Mon, Wed-Sun. Closed Tue, 1 Jan, 1 May, 25 Dec. **Admission** €5.55; €4 18-25s, all on Sun; free under-18s, first Sun of month; CM. **No credit cards**. **Map** p406 J7.

Occupying the Paris mansion of the medieval abbots of Cluny and the remains of a Roman bathing establishment, the museum of medieval art and artefacts retains a domestic scale suitable for the intimacy of many of its treasures. Most famous is the mesmerising *Lady and the Unicorn* tapestry cycle: six, late 15th-century Flemish *mille-fleurs* tapestries depicting convoluted allegories of the five senses, beautifully displayed in a special circular room. Other textiles include fragile Coptic embroidery and Edward III's emblazoned saddle cloth and a cycle of the life of St Stephen. Elsewhere there are enamel bowls and caskets from Limoges, ornate gold reliquaries, stained glass, carved ivory, medieval books of hours, wooden chests and locks, Nottingham alabasters, and Flemish and German wood carving. One room is devoted to chivalry and everyday life at the end of the Middle Ages. The heads of the kings of Judah from Notre-Dame cathedral, mutilated in the Revolution under the mistaken belief that they represented the kings of France and rediscovered (minus their noses) in 1979, are the highlight of the sculpture collection, which also includes carvings from St-Denis and the original abbey of St-Germain-des-Prés. An exhibition in autumn 2004 will showcase 12th-century Catalan sculpture.

Bookshop. Concerts. Guided tours in English 2pm Wed; 11.45am Sat.

Musée Nissim de Camondo

63 rue de Monceau, 8th (01.53.89.06.40/www.ucad.fr). M° Villiers or Monceau. **Open** 10am-5pm Wed-Sun. **Admission** €4.60; €3.10 18-25s; free under-18s; CM. Closed Mon, Tue, some public holidays. **Credit** MC, V. **Map** p405 E3.

The collection, put together by Count Moïse de Camondo, is named after his son Nissim, killed in World War I. Moïse replaced the family's two houses near Parc Monceau with this palatial residence in 1911-14, and lived here in a style more in keeping with his love of the 18th century. Grand first-floor reception rooms are stuffed with furniture by leading craftsmen of the Louis XV and XVI eras, including Oeben and Reisener, huge silver services and vast services of Sèvres and Meissen porcelain, Savonnerie carpets and Aubusson tapestries. Nissim de Camondo's bedroom, the kitchens and servants' quarters are also open to the public.

Bookshop.

Musées des Parfumeries-Fragonard

9 rue Scribe, 9th (01.47.42.04.56) and 39 bd des Capucines, 2nd (01.42.60.37.14). M° Opéra. **Open** 9am-5.30pm Mon-Sat. Closed Sun, 25 Dec. (Apr-Oct rue Scribe open daily). **Admission** free. **Credit** AmEx, MC, V. **Map** p405 G4.

Get on the scent at the two museums showcasing the collection of perfume house Fragonard. The five rooms at rue Scribe range from Ancient Egyptian ointment flasks to Meissen porcelain scent bottles, while the second museum contains, among others, bottles by Lalique and Schiaparelli. Both have displays on scent manufacture and an early 20th-century 'perfume organ' (which sounds saucier than it actually is) with rows of ingredients used by 'noses' to create those stimulating concoctions.

Shop.

Musée de la Publicité

107 rue de Rivoli, 1st (01.44.55.57.50/www.museedelapub.org). M° Palais Royal. **Open** 11am-6pm Tue-Fri; 10am-6pm Sat, Sun. Closed Mon, some public holidays. **Admission** €5.40; €3.90 18-25s; free under-18s; CM. **Credit** MC, V. **Map** p405 H5.

Upstairs element of the triumvirate with the Musée des Arts Décoratifs and Musée de la Mode et du Textile, the advertising museum occupies an artfully distressed interior by Jean Nouvel. Only a small

fraction of the enormous collection of posters, promotional objects and packaging can be seen at one time; although vintage posters can be accessed through the multimedia space. Temporary exhibitions go from individual graphic designers to 20th-century Chinese posters and look at marketing, branding and corporate image. Campaigns promoting household electrical goods feature in 2004.
Archives. Shop. Wheelchair access.

Musée National de la Renaissance

Château d'Ecouen, 95440 Ecouen (01.34.38.38.50/ www.musee-renaissance.fr). SNCF from Gare du Nord to Ecouen-Ezanville, then bus 269. **Open** 9.45am-12.30pm, 2-5.15pm Mon, Wed-Sun. Closed Tue, 1 Jan, 1 May, 25 Dec. **Admission** €4; €2.60 18-25s, Sun; free under-18s, first Sun of the month, CM. **No credit cards**.
The Renaissance château built 1538-55 for Royal Constable Anne de Montmorency and his wife Margaret de Savoie is the authentic setting for a wonderful collection of 16th-century decorative arts. There are some real treasures arranged over three floors of the château (some parts only open in the morning or afternoon, so phone ahead if you have things you particularly want to see). Best of all are the original painted chimneypieces, decorated with caryatids, grotesques, Biblical and mythological scenes. Complementing them are Limoges enamels, armour, embroideries, rare painted leather wall hangings, and a magnificent tapestry cycle depicting the story of David and Bathsheba.
Bookshop. Wheelchair access (call ahead).

History & religion

Mémorial du Maréchal Leclerc de Hauteclocque et de la Libération de Paris & Musée Jean Moulin

23 allée de la 2e DB, Jardin Atlantique (above Grandes Lignes of Gare Montparnasse), 15th (01.40.64.39.44). M° Montparnasse-Bienvenüe. **Open** 10am-6pm Tue-Sun. Closed Mon, public holidays. **Admission** collection free. Exhibitions €4; €3 students, over 60s; €2 under 25s; free under 13s; CM. **No credit cards**. **Map** p405 F9.
This rooftop double museum follows World War II and the Résistance movement through Free French Forces commander General Leclerc and left-wing Résistance hero, Jean Moulin. Extensive documentary material is backed up by film archives (in the first part captions are translated into English, though the translations disappear in the Résistance room). An impressive 270° slide show relates the liberation of Paris and memorable documents include a poster exhorting Frenchmen in occupied France to accept compulsory work service in Germany – to act as 'ambassadors of French quality'. Until April 2004 an exhibition investigates plots against Hitler; other exhibitions will celebrate the 60th anniversary of the Liberation of Paris.
Bookshop. Lectures. Research centre. Wheelchair access (call ahead).

Musée de l'Armée

Hôtel des Invalides, esplanade des Invalides, 7th (01.44.42.37.72/www.invalides.org). M° Varenne or Latour-Maubourg. **Open** *Apr-Sept* 10am-6pm daily; *Oct-Mar* 10am-5pm daily. Closed first Mon of month, 1 Jan, 1 May, 1 Nov, 25 Dec. **Admission** €7; €5.50 students under 26; free under-18s, CM. **Credit** MC, V. **Map** p405 E6.
After checking out Napoléon's tomb under the vast golden dome of Les Invalides, many tourists don't bother to follow up with the army museum (included in the ticket). If you are interested in military history, the museum is a must, but even if sumptuous uniforms and armour are not your thing, the building is in itself a splendour. Besides military memorabilia, the rooms are filled with fine portraiture (don't miss Ingres' masterpiece, *Emperor Napoléon on his Throne*), some well-recreated interiors, as well as the newly reopened museum of maquettes of fortifications. The World War I rooms are particularly immediate and moving, the conflict brought vividly to life by documents and photos. The General de Gaulle wing, opened in 2000, at last gives World War II the coverage it deserves, taking in not only the Free French forces and the Résistance but also the Battle of Britain and war in the Pacific, and alternating weaponry, uniforms and curious artefacts with some blood-chilling film footage. Certain rooms in the west wing are closed as part of Athena II, a huge renovation project, but key items will be displayed in the east wing.
Café. Concerts. Films. Lectures. Shop.

Musée d'Art et d'Histoire du Judaïsme

Hôtel de St-Aignan, 71 rue du Temple, 3rd (01.53.01.86.60/www.mahj.org). M° Rambuteau. **Open** 11am-6pm Mon-Fri; 10am-6pm Sun. Closed Sat, some Jewish holidays. **Admission** €6.10; €3.80 18-26s, students; free under-18s. **Credit** (shop) AmEx, MC, V. **Map** p406 K6.
Opened in 1998 in a Marais mansion, this museum originated from the collection of a private association formed in 1948 to safeguard Jewish heritage, so much of which had been desecrated in the Holocaust. Displays bring out the importance of ceremonies, rites and learning, and show how styles were adapted across the globe through some fine examples of Jewish decorative arts: a silver Hannukah lamp made in Frankfurt, finely carved Italian synagogue furniture, a painted wooden sukkah cabin from Austria, embroidered Bar Mitzvah robes, Torah scrolls and North African dresses to name but a few. There are also documents and paintings relating to the emancipation of French Jewry after the Revolution, and the Dreyfus case, from Zola's *J'Accuse* to anti-Semitic cartoons. An impressive array of paintings by the early 20th-century avant-garde and the Ecole de Paris includes El Lissitsky, Mané-Katz, Modigliani, Soutine and Chagall. This museum does not deal with the Shoah (Holocaust), with the exception of a work by Christian Boltanski that commemorates the Jews who were living in the

Musée National du Moyen Age – Thermes de Cluny. *See p167.*

building in 1939, 13 of whom died in concentration camps; but the new Musée de la Shoah is due to open this year (*see p172*).
Auditorium. Café. Library. Shop. Wheelchair access.

Musée d'Art et d'Histoire de St-Denis

22bis rue Gabriel Péri, 93200 St-Denis (01.42.43.05.10). M° St-Denis Porte de Paris. **Open** 10am-5.30pm Mon, Wed-Fri (until 8pm Thur); 2pm-6.30pm Sat, Sun. Closed Tue, some public holidays. **Admission** €4; €2, over-60s; free under-16s. **No credit cards**.
This prizewinning museum in the suburb of St-Denis is housed around the cloister of a former Carmelite convent which in the 18th century numbered Louis XV' s daughter Louise de France among its incumbents. Although there are displays of local archaeology, prints about the Paris Commune, Modern and Post-Impressionist drawings and documents relating to poet Paul Eluard who was born in the town, the most vivid part is the first floor where items, including some fine religious art, are displayed within the nuns' austere cells.
Partial wheelchair access.

Musée du Cabinet des Médailles

58 rue de Richelieu, 2nd (01.53.79.81.26/ www.bnf.fr). M° Bourse. **Open** 1-6pm daily. Closed Sun, two weeks in Sept, public holidays. **Admission** free. **Credit** MC, V. **Map** p406 H4.
On the first floor of the old Bibliothèque Nationale is the anachronistic Cabinet des Médailles. This collection of coins and medals is actually for specialists, but efficient sliding magnifying glasses help bring exhibits to life. Probably the most interesting aspects for the general public are the museum's parallel Greek, Roman and medieval collections, where oddities include the Merovingian King Dagobert's throne and Charlemagne's chess set, nestling among Greek vases and miniature sculptures.
Shop. Partial wheelchair access.

Musée Carnavalet

23 rue de Sévigné, 3rd (01.44.59.58.58/www.paris-france.org/musees). M° St-Paul. **Open** 10am-6pm Tue-Sun. Closed Mon, some public holidays. **Admission** free. exhibitions €5.50; €4 over-60s; €2.50 14-26; free under-14s; **Credit** (shop) AmEx, MC, V. **Map** p406 L6.
An unexpected treasure in the heart of the Marais, this magnificent building houses some 140 rooms dedicated to the history of Paris, from pre-Roman Gaul to the 20th century. Built in 1548, and transformed by the celebrated architect Mansart in 1660, it became a museum in 1866 when Baron Haussmann had a twinge of conscience about all the buildings being destroyed to make way for his new boulevards. He persuaded the city to buy the Hôtel Carnavalet to preserve some of the more beautiful interiors, and the rest is history!

Displays are chronological. The original 16th-century rooms house the Renaissance collections with portraits by Clouet, and furniture and pictures relating to the Wars of Religion. The first floor covers the period up to 1789 with furniture, applied arts and paintings displayed in restored, period interiors. The bold colours, particularly in the oval boudoir from the Hôtel de Breteuil (1782), may come as a shock to those with pre-conceived ideas about subdued 18th-century taste. Interesting interiors include the

Rococo cabinet painted for engraver Demarteau by his friends Fragonard, Boucher and Huet in 1765 and the Louis XIII-style Cabinet Colbert.

The collections from 1789 onwards move into the Hôtel Le Peletier de Saint-Fargeau next door, acquired in 1989. The Revolutionary items are the best way of getting an understanding of the convoluted politics and bloodshed of the period. There are portraits of all the major players, prints, objects and memorabilia including a bone model of the guillotine, Hubert Robert's gouaches and a small chunk of the Bastille prison. Highlights of the later collections include items belonging to Napoléon, views of Paris depicting the effects of Haussmann's programme, the ornate cradle given by the city to Napoléon III on the birth of his son, the art nouveau boutique designed by Mucha in 1901 for jeweller Fouquet and the art deco ballroom of the Hôtel Wendel painted by Catalan artist José-Maria Sert. Rooms devoted to literature finish the tour with portraits and room settings, including Proust's cork-lined bedroom.

Not much remains of the original interior of the Hôtel Le Peletier except the elegant grand staircase and one antique panelled cabinet; its newly restored *orangerie*, the only surviving 17th-century one in Paris, now houses Neolithic dug-out canoes excavated at Bercy amongst other Gallo-Roman archaeological finds. The museum is well-known for its temporary exhibitions, too. 2004 includes exhibitions on Paris during the Directoire and Consulat and Paris seen by painter Alfred Marquet.

Bookshop. Guided tours. Lectures. Reference section (by appointment). Wheelchair access.

Musée de l'Histoire de France

Hôtel de Rohan, 87 rue Vieille-du-Temple, 3rd (01.40.27.60.96/www.archivesnationales.culture.gouv.fr/chan). M° Hôtel-de-Ville or Rambuteau. **Open** 10am-12.30pm, 2-5.30pm Mon, Wed-Fri; 2-5.30pm Sat, Sun. Closed Tue, public holidays. **Admission** €3; €2.30 18-25s; free under-18s. **No credit cards. Map** p406 K6.

Housed in one of the grandest Marais mansions, this museum is to be renovated with a view to new presentation that favours the plurality of historical interpretations. In the meantime, a changing selection of historical documents and artefacts cover not just major political events – the Wars of Religion, the French Revolution – but also social issues and quirky aspects of daily life, from the founding of the Sorbonne to an ordinance about umbrellas. In the autumn, a new room will open devoted to the Napoleonic myth. The adjoining Hôtel de Soubise boasts the finest Rococo interiors in Paris decorated for the Prince and Princesse de Soubise in the

Blake & Mortimer at **Musée de l'Homme**. *See p176.*

1730s with superb plasterwork, panelling and paintings by artists including Boucher, Natoire, Restout and Van Loo (visits on Sunday afternoons by reservation: call 01.40.27.62.18).
Concerts. Library. Shop. Workshops.

Musée de la Marine
Palais de Chaillot, pl du Trocadéro, 16th (01.53.65.69.69/www.musee-marine.fr). M° Trocadéro. **Open** 10am-6pm Mon, Wed-Sun. Closed Tue, some public holidays. **Admission** €6; €4 under-25s, over-60s; €3 6-18s; free under-6s; CM. Admission with exhibition: €7; €5.40 under-25s, over 60s; €3,85 6-18s; free under 6s. **Credit** (shop) AmEx, MC, V. **Map** p404 B5.
French naval history is explored, from detailed carved models of battleships and Vernet's imposing series of paintings of the ports of France (1754-65) to a model of a nuclear submarine. There's also the Imperial barge, built when Napoléon's delusions of grandeur were reaching their zenith in 1810, carved prows, old maps, antique and modern navigational instruments, ships in bottles, underwater equipment and romantic maritime paintings. A new area is devoted to the modern navy.
Shop.

Musée de la Monnaie de Paris
11 quai de Conti, 6th (01.40.46.55.35/ www.monnaiedeparis.fr). M° Odéon or Pont-Neuf. **Open** 11am-5.30pm Tue-Fri; noon-5.30pm Sat, Sun. **Admission** €3 (€8 with audioguide); €2.20 students; free under-16s, over-60s, all on first Sun of month; CM. **Credit** (shop) MC, V. **Map** p406 H6.
Housed in the handsome Neo-Classical mint built in the 1770s by Jacques-Denis Antoine, this high-tech museum tells the story of France's coinage from pre-Roman origins to the present day through a series of sophisticated displays and audiovisual presentations. Until the advent of the euro, the history of the French state was, of course, directly linked to its coinage, and the museum is informative about both.
Shop. Visit to atelier (2.15pm Wed, Fri reserve ahead).

Musée de Montmartre
12 rue Cortot, 18th (01.46.06.61.11/ www.museedemontmartre.com). M° Lamarck-Caulaincourt. **Open** 10am-12.30pm, 1.30-6pm Tue-Sun. Closed Mon, 1 Jan, 1 May, 25 Dec. **Admission** €4.50; €3.50 students, over-60s; free under-8s. **Credit** (shop) MC, V. **Map** p405 H1.
At the back of a peaceful garden, this 17th-century manor is a haven of calm after touristy Montmartre. Documents and artefacts trace the history of the historic hilltop, with rooms devoted to the reconstructed study of composer Gustave Charpentier, some original Toulouse-Lautrec posters, porcelain from the short-lived factory at Clignancourt and a tribute to the local cabaret, the Lapin Agile. 2004 sees an exhibition devoted to Impressionist painter Suzanne Valadon, who once occupied a studio above the entrance pavilion, as did, at various times, Renoir, Emile Bernard, Raoul Dufy and Valadon's son Maurice Utrillo.

Musée de la Poste
34 bd de Vaugirard, 15th (01.42.79.23.45/ www.laposte.fr). M° Montparnasse-Bienvenüe. **Open** 10am-6pm Mon-Sat. Closed Sun. **Admission** €4.50; €3; free under 12s. **Credit** V. **Map** p405 E9.
This is a tad more interesting than it sounds. Although belonging to the state postal service, this is much more than just a company museum. Amid uniforms, pistols, carriages, bicycles, letter boxes, portraits, official decrees, cartoons and fumigation tongs emerge some fascinating snippets of history: during the 1871 Siege of Paris, hot-air balloons and carrier pigeons were used to get post out of the city and *boules de Moulins*, balls containing hundreds of microfiche letters, were floated down the Seine in return, mostly never to arrive. The second section gives a survey of French and international philately – fascinating, if you go in for that sort of thing.

Musée de la Préfecture de Police
4 rue de la Montagne-Ste-Geneviève, 5th (01.44.41.52.50/www.prefecturepolice-paris.interieur.gouv.fr). M° Maubert-Mutualité. **Open** 9am-5pm Mon-Fri; 10am-5pm Sat. Closed public holidays. **Admission** free. **No credit cards**. **Map** p406 J7.
Rather spookily located upstairs in a hideous police station, the history of Paris is viewed via crime since the establishment of the Paris police force in the 16th century. You need to read French to best appreciate the assorted warrants and edicts, but there are plenty of evocative murder weapons. Among eclectic treasures are prisoners' expenses from the Bastille including those of dastardly jewel thief the Comtesse de la Motte, the exploding flowerpot planted by Louis-Armand Matha in 1894 in a restaurant on the rue de Tournon, and the gory Epée de Justice, a 17th-century sword blunted by the quantity of noble heads chopped.

Musée de la Résistance Nationale
Parc Vercors, 88 av Marx Dormoy, 94500 Champigny-sur-Marne (01.48.81.00.80/www.musee-resistance.com). RER A Champigny-St-Maur then bus 208. **Open** 9am-12.30pm, 2-5.30pm Tue-Fri; 2-6pm Sat, Sun. Closed Mon, weekends in Aug, Sept. **Admission** €4; €2 16-25s; free under-16s. **No credit cards**.
Occupying five floors of a 19th-century villa, the Résistance museum starts at the top with the pre-war political background and works down, via defeat in 1940, through German occupation and the rise of the *maquis*, to victory. Given the way the Résistance movement has captured the imaginations of people around the globe, it's slightly odd that no effort is made for foreign visitors: hundreds of photographs aside, the bulk of the material consists of newspaper archives, both from official and clandestine presses, with no translations. Three short archive films and a few solid artefacts are more accessible, with a sobering wall of machine guns and pistols, a railway saboteur's kit (cutters to chop through brake pipes, sand to pour into gearboxes

and logs to lay across tracks) and a homemade device for scattering tracts. Displays steer clear of wallowing in collaborationist disgrace and of Résistance hero tub-thumping.

Musée de la Shoah

17 rue Geoffroy-l'Asnier, 4th (01.42.77.44.71). M° St-Paul or Pont Marie. **Open** from mid 2004 ring for details. **Admission** ring for details. **Map** p405 K6.

The Mémorial du Martyr Juif Inconnu is due to reopen during 2004 as an enlarged display devoted to the memory of the Holocaust and the 76,000 Jews deported from France between 1942 and 1944.

Literary

Maison de Balzac

47 rue Raynouard, 16th (01.55.74.41.80/ www.paris.fr/musees). M° Passy. **Open** 10am-6pm Tue-Sun. Closed Mon, public holidays. **Admission** free. **No credit cards. Map** p404 B6.

Honoré de Balzac (1799-1850) rented a flat at this address in 1840 to avoid his creditors and established a password to sift friends from bailiffs. The museum is spread over several floors, and although the displays are rather dry, the garden is pretty and gives an idea of the sort of country villa that lined this street when Passy was a fashionable spa in the 19th century. A wide range of memorabilia includes first editions, letters, corrected proofs, prints, portraits of friends and Polish mistress Mme Hanska, with whom he corresponded for years before finally marrying, plus a 'family tree' of Balzac's characters that covers several walls. The study houses his desk, chair and the monogrammed coffee pot that fuelled all-night work on Balzac's sprawling, multi-novel *Comédie humaine.*

Library (by appointment). Children's trail.

Maison de Chateaubriand

La Vallée aux Loups, 87 rue de Chateaubriand, 92290 Chatenay-Malabry (01.47.02.08.62). RER B Robinson + 20 min walk. **Open** (guided tours only except Sun) *Apr-Sept* 10am-noon, 2-6pm Tue-Sun; *Oct-Mar* 2-5pm Tue-Sun. Closed Mon, Jan, 25 Dec. **Admission** €4.50; €3 students, over-60s; free under-12s. **No credit cards**.

In 1807, attracted by the quiet Vallée aux Loups, René, Vicomte de Chateaubriand (1768-1848), author of *Mémoires d'outre tombe* (*Memoirs from Beyond the Grave*), set about transforming a simple 18th-century country house into his own Romantic idyll and planted the park with rare trees as a reminder of his travels. Most interesting is the over-the-top double wooden staircase, based on a maritime design, a reminder of the writer's noble St-Malo birth, and the portico with two white marble Grecian statues supporting a colonnaded porch. Anyone familiar with David's *Portrait of Mme Récamier* in the Louvre will find the original chaise longue awaiting the sitter, who was one of Chateaubriand's numerous lovers – no doubt to the discomfort of his stern wife, Céleste. After a politically inflammatory work Chateaubriand was ruined and in 1818 had to sell his beloved valley.

Concerts/readings (spring, autumn). Shop. Tearoom.

Musée de la Vie Romantique

16 rue Chaptal, 9th (01.55.31.95.67). M° Blanche or St-Georges. **Open** 10am-5.40pm (6pm in summer) Tue-Sun. Closed Mon, public holidays. **Admission** collection free. Exhibitions €4.50, €3 over-60s, students under 26; €2.20 under-18s; CM. **Credit** AmEx, MC, V. **Map** p405 G2.

When Dutch artist Ary Scheffer lived in this villa, this area south of Pigalle was known as the New Athens because of the concentration of writers, composers and artists living here. Baronne Aurore Dupin – better known as George Sand (1804-76) – was a frequent guest at Scheffer's soirées, and many other great names crossed the threshold, including Sand's lover, Chopin, Delacroix and composers Charpentier, Liszt and Rossini. The museum is charming, with a lovely rose garden and tearoom, but literary detectives on the trail of the great George Sand, novelist and proto-feminist, might be disappointed: the watercolours, lockets and jewels she left behind reveal little of her ideas or her affairs. In the courtyard, Scheffer's studio is used for exhibitions.

Archives. Bookshop. Children's workshops. Concerts. Tearoom.

Musée Mémorial Ivan Tourguéniev

16 rue Ivan Tourguéniev, 78380 Bougival (01.45.77.87.12). M° La Défense, plus bus 258. **Open** 10am-6pm Sun; by appointment for groups during the week. **Admission** collection free. exhibitions €5.50; €2.50 12-26s; free under-12s. **Credit** MC, V.

The datcha where novelist Ivan Turgenev lived for several years until his death in 1883 was a gathering spot for composers Saint-Saëns and Fauré, divas Pauline Viardot (with whom Turgenev was in love) and Maria Malibran, and writers Henry James, Flaubert, Zola and Maupassant. Letters and editions (mainly in Russian) are on the ground floor, and above there's the music room where Viardot held court, as well as the writer's deathbed. The guided tour (in French) is worthwhile.

Bookshop. Concerts. Guided tours 5pm Sun.

Maison de Victor Hugo

Hôtel de Rohan-Guéménée, 6 pl des Vosges, 4th (01.42.72.10.16/www.paris.fr/musees). M° Bastille. **Open** 10am-6pm Tue-Sun. **Admission** €5.50; €4 students; €2.50 13-26s; free under-13s. **No credit cards**.

The intense, prolific Victor Hugo lived here from 1832 to 1848, and the house has now been turned into a museum for France's favourite son. You can see first editions of his books, nearly 500 drawings, and, more bizarrely, Vic's home-made furniture, some of which he carved with his own teeth. Terrible thing, gum splinters. The museum also holds varying exhibitions on themes related to Hugo.

Giftshop.

Musée de la Vie Romantique

Music & media

Musée Edith Piaf

5 rue Crespin-du-Gast, 11th (01.43.55.52.72). M° Ménilmontant. **Open** by appointment 1-6pm Mon-Wed; 9am-noon Thur (call two days ahead). Closed June, Sept. **Admission** donation. **No credit cards**. **Map** p407 N5.

Les Amis d'Edith Piaf run this tiny two-room museum in a part of Paris that the archetypal French singer knew well. The memorabilia on show exudes love for the 'little sparrow', her diminutive stature graphically shown by a lifesize cardboard cut-out. Her little black dress and tiny shoes are particularly moving, and letters, posters and photos provide a personal touch. There's also a sculpture of the singer by Suzanne Blistène, wife of Marcel, who produced most of Piaf's films.

Library. Shop.

Musée de la Musique

Cité de la Musique, 221 av Jean-Jaurès, 19th (01.44.84.44.84/www.cite-musique.fr). M° Porte de Pantin. **Open** noon-6pm Tue-Thur, Sat; noon-7.30pm Fri; 10am-6pm Sun. Closed Mon, some public holidays. **Admission** €6.10; €4.57 18s-25s; €2.29 6-18s; free under-6s, over-60s; CM. **Credit** MC, V. **Map** p407 insert.

Alongside the concert hall in the striking modern Cité de la Musique, the innovative music museum houses a gleamingly restored collection of instruments from the old Conservatoire, interactive computers and scale models of opera houses and concert halls. On arrival you are supplied with an audio guide in a choice of languages. Don't be a precious old luvvie and spurn this offer, for the musical commentary is an informative joy, playing the appropriate music or instrument as you approach the exhibit. Alongside the trumpeting brass, curly woodwind instruments and precious strings are more unusual items, such as the Indonesian gamelan orchestra, whose gurgling, percussive sounds influenced the work of both Debussy and Ravel. Some of the concerts in the museum's amphitheatre use historic instruments from the collection.

Audioguide. Library. Shop. Wheelchair access.

Musée de l'Opéra

Palais Garnier, 1 pl de l'Opéra, 9th (01.40.01.24.93). M° Opéra. **Open** 10am-6pm daily. **Admission** €6; €4 10-25s, students, over-60s; free under-10s. **No credit cards**. **Map** p405 G4.

The magnificently restored Palais Garnier houses small temporary exhibitions relating to current opera or ballet productions, and a permanent collection of paintings, scores and bijou opera sets housed in period cases. The entrance fee includes a visit to the auditorium (if rehearsals permit).

Guided tours in English.

Oriental & tribal art

Musée National des Arts Asiatiques – Guimet

6 pl d'Iéna, 16th (01.56.52.53.00/ www.museeguimet.fr). M° Iéna. **Open** 10am-6pm Mon, Wed-Sun. Closed Tue. **Admission** (includes temporary exhibition and free audioguide) €7; €5 students, 18-25s, Sun; free under-18s, first Sun of month; CM. **Credit** (shop) MC, V. **Map** p405 E5.

The reopened museum of Asian art was the success story of 2001, as it emerged enlarged and rejuvenated from five years of renovation. Founded by Lyonais industrialist Emile Guimet in 1889 to house his collection of Chinese and Japanese religious art, and later incorporating the Oriental collections from the Louvre, Musée Guimet boasts some 45,000 objects from Neolithic times on in a voyage to Asia that conveys the flow of religions and civilisations. Lower galleries focus on India and Southeast Asia, centred on the stunning collection of Hindu and Buddhist Khmer sculpture from Cambodia. Amid legions of calmly smiling Buddhas and the striking seventh-century Harihara, a half-Shiva, half-Vishnu figure, you can't miss the massive *Giant's Way*, part of the entrance to a temple complex at Angkor Wat, where two female demi-goddesses hold a seven-headed cobra. Upstairs, Chinese antiquities include mysterious jade discs, an elephant-shaped Shang dynasty bronze pot, lively terracotta figures, horses and camels found in tombs, fragile paintings from Dunhuang and later Chinese celadon wares and porcelain. Other rooms contain Afghan and Pakistani glassware and sculpture, Tibetan mandalas and statues, Japanese Buddhist sculpture, paintings and lacquer and ceramics, as well as Moghul jewellery, caskets, fabrics and miniatures.
Auditorium. Guided visits. Library. Restaurant. Shop. Wheelchair access.

The best Atmospheric

Musée Jacquemart-André
Edouard and Nélie slept in separate beds but shared a love of art. Their 'Italian museum' is magic. *See p155.*

Atelier-Musée Henri Bouchard
Henri Bouchard's studio, tended by his son and daughter, is just as the sculptor left it (only dustier). *See p156.*

Musée Bourdelle
Sculpture and painting studios around a small garden evoke the Montparnasse circle. *See p156.*

Musée Gustave Moreau
Mummy's boy Moreau set up his own museum for his crazed mythological outpourings. *See p159.*

Musée Zadkine
A sculpture secret garden and some enchanting poems in the home of a Russian émigré. *See p159.*

Musée Nissim de Camondo
Count Moïse de Camondo designated his collection of French national treasures as a museum in memory of his son who died in World War I. Thereafter the rest of the family perished in Auschwitz. *See p167.*

Musée Edith Piaf
Paris' most intimate museum, in two rooms in Belleville, is testament to the love still felt for the little sparrow. *See p173.*

Musée Pasteur
Poignant for those who remember school milk, Pasteur and his wife's apartment is full of family photos and scientific instruments. *See p176.*

Musée Cernuschi

7 av Velasquez, 8th (01.45.63.50.75/www.paris.fr/musees). M° Villiers or Monceau. **Open** reopens late 2004, ring for details. **Admission** collection free; exhibitions ring for details. **Map** p405 E2.

This fabulous museum of Chinese art is set to emerge spruced up and enlarged in display space by a third at the end of 2004. The hoard was amassed by erudite banker Henri Cernuschi on a long voyage to the Far East in 1871. It ranges from Neolithic terracottas and legions of Han and Wei dynasty funeral statues to refined Tang celadon wares, Sung porcelain, fragile paintings on silk, bronze vessels and jade amulets.

Musée Dapper

35bis rue Paul-Valéry, 16th (01.45.00.01.50). M° Victor-Hugo. **Open** 11am-7pm Wed-Sun. Closed Mon, Tue, some public holidays. **Admission** €5; €2.50 students, 16s-25s; free under-16s. **Credit** MC, V. **Map** p404 B4.

This small specialist museum makes a refreshing change from the conventional Paris pit stops. The Fondation Dapper began in 1983 as an organisation dedicated to preserving sub-Saharan art. Reopened in 2000 after a renovation, the new Alain Moatti-designed museum includes a performance space, bookshop and café. A glass bridge leads you into the reception area, underneath is the café, a mixture of red lacquer and brown hues. The exhibition space houses two themed exhibitions every year covering Africa and the African diaspora.
Wheelchair access.

Musée de l'Institut du Monde Arabe

1 rue des Fossés-St-Bernard, 5th (01.40.51.38.38/www.imarabe.org). M° Jussieu. **Open** 10am-6pm Tue-Sun. Closed Mon, 1 May. **Admission** €4; €3 12-25s, students, over-60s; free under-12s; CM. Exhibition prices vary. **Credit** MC, V. **Map** p402 K7.

Opened in 1987 as one of Mitterrand's *Grands Projets*, the institute of the Arab world brings together a library, cultural centre, exhibitions and the 'Museum of Arab Museums', displaying items on long-term loan from museums in Syria and

Tunisia, alongside its own permanent collection. The objects cover a huge geographical and historical span from prehistory to the present. Particularly strong are the collections of urns and masks from ancient Carthage, early scientific instruments, 19th-century Tunisian costume and jewellery and contemporary fine art. (*See also chapter* **Left Bank**.)
Bookshop. Cinema. Lectures. Library. Tearoom. Wheelchair access.

Musée du Quai Branly

quai Branly, 7th. Under construction.
President Chirac's pet project for a museum of tribal art is taking longer than originally planned. The Jean Nouvel building is now due to open in 2006; meanwhile works from the old Musée des Arts Africains et Océaniques and the Musée de l'Homme are in storage.

Science, medicine & technology

La Cité des Sciences et de l'Industrie

La Villette, 30 av Corentin-Cariou, 19th (01.40.05.80.00/08.92.69.70.72/www.cite-sciences.fr). M° Porte de la Villette. **Open** 10am-6pm Tue-Sat; 10am-7pm Sun. Closed Mon, public holidays. **Admission** €7.50; €5.50 7-16s, students under 25, over-60s; free under-7s; CM. **Credit** MC, V. **Map** p407 insert.
The ultra-modern science museum at La Villette has been riding high since its opening in 1986 and pulls in over five million visitors a year. The old slaughterhouse and meat market was originally going to be converted into a hi-tech abattoir but the project was derailed mid-construction and converted into this marvellous state-of-the-art science park instead. Explora, the permanent show, occupies the upper two floors, whisking visitors through 30,000m² of 'space, life, matter and communication', where scale models of satellites including the Ariane space shuttle, planes and robots make for an exciting journey. Experience weightlessness in the section devoted to man's conquest of space. There's an impressive array of interactive exhibits enabling you to learn about sound waves, how the vocal cords work and how we hear. In the Espace Images, try out the delayed camera and other optical illusions, draw 3D images on computer or lend your voice to the *Mona Lisa*. The hothouse 'garden of the future' investigates futuristic developments in agriculture and biotechnology, with (May-Dec) an investigation of an ecological project for the absorption of carbon in the Amazon. Other sections feature climate, ecology and the environment, health, energy, water, the ocean and volcanoes. The Automobile gallery looks at the car both as myth and technological object, with driving simulator and displays on safety, pollution and future designs. On the lower floors, temporary exhibitions include '*Climax*' (until 29 Aug), an exhibition about climatic change and the consequences of global warming. The Cité des Enfants runs workshops for children (*see chapter* **Children**). The Louis Lumière cinema shows films in 3-D, and you can also visit the Argonaute, a restored 1950s naval submarine moored next to Omnimax cinema La Géode.
Bookshop. Café. Cinema. Conference centre. Library (multimedia). Wheelchair access & hire.

Musée de l'Air et de l'Espace

Aéroport de Paris-Le Bourget, 93352 Le Bourget Cedex (01.49.92.71.99/recorded information 01.49.92.71.71/www.mae.org). M° Gare du Nord then bus 350/M° La Courneuve then bus 152/RER Le Bourget then bus 152. **Open** *May-Oct* 10am-6pm; *Nov-Apr* 10am-5pm Tue-Sun. Closed Mon, public holidays. **Admission** €7; €50 8-16s, students; free under-8s. **Credit** MC, V.
The air and space museum is a potent reminder that France is a technical and military as well as cultural power. Housed in the former passenger terminal at Le Bourget airport, the collection begins with the pioneers, including fragile-looking biplanes, the contraption in which Romanian Vivia succeeded in flying 12 metres in 1906, and the strangely nautical command cabin of a Zeppelin airship. Outside on the runway are Mirage fighter planes, a Boeing 707, an American Thunderchief with painted shark-tooth grimace and Ariane launchers 1 and 5. Within a vast hangar, walk through the prototype Concorde 001 and view wartime survivors, a Spitfire and German Heinkel bomber. Further hangars are packed with military planes, helicopters, commercial jets, bizarre prototypes, stunt planes, missiles and satellites. A section is devoted to hot air balloons, invented in 1783 by the Montgolfier brothers and swiftly adopted for military reconnaissance. Recent additions to the museum include a new and improved planetarium and the 'Espace' section, dedicated to space travel. Most captions are summarised in English.
Shop. Wheelchair access (except new 'Espace' building).

Musée des Arts et Métiers

60 rue Réaumur, 3rd (01.40.27.22.20). M° Arts et Métiers. **Open** 10am-6pm Tue, Wed, Fri-Sun; 10am-9.30pm Thur. Closed Mon, public holidays. **Admission** €6.50; €4.50 under-18s, students under-26; free under-18s. **Credit** MC, V. **Map** p406 K5.
The successful combination of a 12th-century structure (it is housed in the medieval abbey of St-Martin-des-Champs) and 21st-century technology and design reflects the museum's aim – to demonstrate the history and future of the technical arts. A new permanent exhibition looking at seven aspects of science and technology has been created from the museum's vast collection of more than 80,000 machines and models. Throughout, videos and interactive computers explain the science behind the exhibits and at the end of each section there is a workshop for budding young scientists and technophobes alike to get to grips with what is on display. Most impressive is the chapel, where an elaborate

glass and steel staircase enables you to climb right up into the nave. There, amid the stained glass, you can gaze down upon the wonders of man's invention, which include Blériot's plane and the first steam engine.

Musée de l'Assistance Publique

Hôtel de Miramion, 47 quai de la Tournelle, 5th (01.46.33.01.43). M° Maubert-Mutualité. **Open** 10am-6pm Tue-Sun. Closed Mon, Aug, public holidays. **Admission** €4; €2 students, over-60s; free under-13s, CM. **No credit cards. Map** p406 K7.

The history of Paris hospitals, from the days when they were receptacles for abandoned babies to the beginnings of modern medicine with anaesthesia, is explained in a lively fashion through paintings, prints, various grisly medical devices and a reconstructed ward and pharmacy; texts in French only. Another case presents part of the museum's huge collection of pharmacy ceramics, often in beautifully decorated earthenware, while the courtyard garden has been planted with medicinal plants.

Sightseeing

Musée d'Histoire de la Médecine

Université René Descartes, 12 rue de l'Ecole-de-Médecine, 6th (01.40.46.16.93). M° Odéon. **Open** *15 July-Sept* 2-5.30pm Mon-Fri; *Oct-13 July* 2-5.30pm Mon-Wed, Fri, Sat. Closed Sun, public holidays. **Admission** €3.50; €2.50 students; free under-8s. **No credit cards. Map** p406 H7.

The medical faculty collection covers the history of medicine from ancient Egyptian embalming tools through to a 1960s electrocardiograph. There's a gruesome array of serrated-edged saws and curved knives used for amputations, plus stethoscopes and syringes, the surgical instruments of Dr Antommarchi, who performed the autopsy on Napoléon and the scalpel of Dr Félix, who operated on Louis XIV.

Muséum National d'Histoire Naturelle

36 rue Geoffroy-St-Hilaire/2 rue Bouffon, pl Valhubert/57 rue Cuvier, 5th (01.40.79.30.00/ www.mnhn.fr). M° Gare d'Austerlitz or Jussieu. **Open** Grande Galerie: 10am-6pm Mon, Wed, Fri-Sun; 10am-10pm Thur. Other galleries: 10am-5pm Mon, Wed-Fri; 10am-5pm Sat, Sun Apr-Sep. Closed Tue, 1 May. **Admission** Grande Galerie €7; €5 5-16s, students, over-60s; free under-5s (with exhibition €9 and €5. Other galeries each €5; €3 5-16s, students, over-60s; free under-5s. **No credit cards. Map** p406 K9.

Within the Jardin des Plantes botanical garden, the brilliantly renovated Grande Galerie de l'Evolution has taken Paris' Natural History Museum out of the dinosaur age. Architect Paul Chemetov successfully integrated modern lifts, stairways and the latest lighting and audiovisual techniques into the 19th-century iron-framed structure. As you enter, you will be confronted with the 13.66m-long skeleton of a whale: the rest of the ground floor is dedicated to other sea creatures. On the first floor are the mammals, including Louis XVI's rhinoceros, stuffed on a wooden chair frame. Videos and interactive computers give information on life in the wild. Glass-sided lifts take you up through suspended birds to the second floor, which deals with man's impact on nature and considers demographic problems and pollution. The third floor traces the evolution of species, with a gallery of endangered and extinct species. The separate Galerie d'Anatomie comparée et de Paléontologie contains more than a million skeletons of virtually every creature you can imagine, and a fossil collection of world importance. The galeries of Mineralogy and Geology might not sound as exciting, but their collections of crystals and semi-precious stones are worth seeing. The butterfly gallery is currently closed. (*See also chapter* **Children**).

Auditorium. Bookshop. Café. Library. Wheelchair access (Grande Galerie).

Musée de l'Homme

Palais de Chaillot, 17 pl du Trocadéro, 16th (01.44.05.72.72/www.mnhn.fr). M° Trocadéro. **Open** 9.45am-5.15pm Mon, Wed-Sun. Closed Tue, Aug, public holidays. **Admission** €5; €3 4-16s, students under 27, over-60s. **Credit** (shop) MC, V. **Map** p404 B5.

The human arm of the Muséum National d'Histoire Naturelle considers human evolution (skulls of prehistoric man and Stone Age tools), genetic diversity and the reasons and likely consequences of the population explosion of today. (Note that the ethnology collection has gone, set to remerge in the new Musée du Quai Branly in 2005.) Much of the space is used by temporary exhibitions in build up to a long-term refurbishment. Not all anthropology is serious: until 30 Apr, comic-strip heroes Blake and Mortimer star in an exhibition amid pterodactyl skeletons, an Egyptian sarcophagus, a Peruvian mummy, medieval arms and 1950s machines.

Café. Cinema. Lectures. Library. Photo Library. Wheelchair access (call ahead).

Musée Pasteur

Institut Pasteur, 25 rue du Dr-Roux, 15th (01.45.68.82.83/www.pasteur.fr). M° Pasteur. **Open** 2-5.30pm Mon-Fri. Closed weekends, public holidays, Aug. **Admission** €3; €1.50 students. **Credit** V. **Map** p405 E9.

The apartment where the famous chemist and his wife lived for the last seven years of his life (1888-95) has hardly been touched since his death; you can still see their furniture and possessions, family photos and a room of scientific instruments. The highlight is the extravagant, Byzantine-style mausoleum on the ground floor housing Pasteur's tomb, decorated with mosaics of his scientific achievements.

Musée de Radio France

Maison de Radio France, 116 av du Président-Kennedy, 16th (01.56.40.15.16/ 01.56.40.21.80/ www.radio-france.fr). M° Ranelagh/RER Kennedy-Radio France. **Open** guided tours 10.30am, 11.30am, 2.30pm, 3.30pm, 4.30pm Mon. **Admission** €3.80; €3 8s-25s, students, over-60s. **No credit cards. Map** p404 A7.

Musée National des Arts Asiatiques – Guimet. *See p173.*

Musée de l'Erotisme

'Sex is natural, sex is fun,' sang George 'I could use a leg rub' Michael. And it is surely the appeal of some harmless fun in a world that could do with some more fun right now that has led one man to spend his life amassing enough vagina, bottom and penis paraphernalia – more than 5,000 pieces – to fill the seven floors of the Musée de l'Erotisme in the heart of garter-pinging Pigalle.

Curator Alain Plumey legitimised his private collection when his museum opened in 1998 and he has been delighting 150,000 annual visitors ever since. He says the clientele is largely female (What? Women interested in sex?) and is generally a well-behaved bunch. The museum itself is surprisingly clean, with marble floors, golden balustrades, gilt frames and German tourists, in fact in daylight hours it behaves just as a regular museum should. As natural light gives way to a neon glow (it's open till 2am) the crowd turns more libertine

Before you go in take a look in the window. The grubby faux leopardskin chair complete with a wheel of plastic tongues rotating through a hole in the seat should prepare the wary voyeur for what lies beyond the turnstyle. Don't be alarmed when advised to 'start down below then go straight to the top and work your way back to the bottom' – this is how you navigate the massive collection. In the foyer are the most precious items including pottery made by 1st-century Mochica Indians in Peru whose worship included the erotic styling of clay penises. Plumey and his partner have diligently travelled the world to ensure exotic erotica is available from every gene pool. Items harvested include a phallic Malagasy tomb statue supposed to embellish a man's reputation in the afterlife. Apart from the compilation of 1905-1935 porn films (think moustachioed fatties getting their kicks and licks from girls dressed as waitresses), it is in the basement where things start to get seriously base. A vaginal dinner plate makes for an original wedding present, accompanied by phallic cutlery and a bottle of 1982 *Côtes du Rhone Cuvée Erotique.*

The fourth floor lays bare a detailed photographic history of the early 20th-century *maisons closes* (brothels) of Paris and Marseille including snaps of a grimacing Marseille *madame* among her sailor-weary girls and an Occupation-era prostitute's ledger which details accounts from a 17-a-day workload: 'Cheveux plats' (flat hair) gets a better deal than 'Vieux sale' (dirty old man).

The freshly touched-up top floors host temporary exhibitions of contemporary pornographic art: 2004 will welcome incoming material from the sister museum in Hamburg.

Arriving at the exit you will either feel primed for action, or like we did on a rainy October morning, completely knob-numb. If the former is true, the small gift shop stocking lewd literature and jewellery to dress-up your nethers could provide a pretty gift. Or for a wider selection pop next door to Rebecca Ril's sexy supermarket complete with shopping trolleys for those with a long list. (*See p179 for opening hours and admission.*)

Degas makes a trio of tarts even less erotic than they probably were.

In the Alphaville-like setting of the Maison de Radio France audio-visual history is presented with an emphasis on French pioneers such as Edouard Branly and Charles Cros, including documentary evidence of the first radio message transmitted between the Eiffel Tower and the Panthéon. Particularly interesting is the London broadcast of the Free French with its delightfully obscure coded messages. From the museum you can see people recording radio programmes below.

Musée du Service de Santé des Armées

Val de Grace, pl Alphonse-Laveran, 5th (01.40.51.51.94). RER Port-Royal. **Open** noon-5pm Tue, Wed groups; noon-5pm Sat, Sun individuals. Closed 1 May. **Admission** €4.60; €2.30 6-12s; free under-6s. **No credit cards. Map** p406 J9.

Housed in the beautiful royal convent designed by François Mansart, and adjoining a military hospital, this museum traces the history of military medicine, via recreations of field hospitals and ambulance trains, and beautifully presented antique medical instruments. The section on World War I brings a chilling insight into the true horror of the conflict, when many buildings were transformed into hospitals and, ironically, medical science progressed in leaps and bounds. Grisly models of head wounds show developments in reconstructive plastic surgery.

Palais de la Découverte

av Franklin D Roosevelt, 8th (01.56.43.20.21/ www.palais-decouverte.fr). M° Champs-Elysées Clemenceau or Franklin D Roosevelt. **Open** 9.30am-6pm Tue-Sat; 10am-7pm Sun. Closed Mon, 1 Jan, 1 May, 14 July, 15 Aug, 25 Dec. **Admission** €5.60; €3.70 5-18s, over-60s, students under 26; free under-5s. Planetarium €3.10. **Credit** AmEx, MC, V. **Map** p405 E5.

Join hordes of schoolkids at Paris' original science museum, housing designs from Leonardo da Vinci onwards. Replicas, models, audiovisual material and real apparatus are used to bring displays to life, whilst permanent exhibits cover biology, astronomy, astophysics, chemistry, physics, earth sciences and mathematics (yes, they actually make it fun). The Planète Terre space shows developments in meteorology, while one room is dedicated to the sun. If that gets you in an astro-mood, then be sure to take in one of the various shows at the Planetarium too. There are even regular 'live' experiments (mainly Sat, Sun afternoons and school holidays), ranging from the effect of pesticides, the chemical principles behind cooking (why does an egg white go hard on cooking?), fluid science and magneticism to the literally hair-raising experience of electrostatics. The Palais even claims to be the only museum in the world where the public can actually look in on demonstrations of radioactivity and watch nuclear reactions in a particle accelerator: Homer Simpson eat your heart out. (*See also chapter* **Children**.)

Café. Experiments. Shop. Wheelchair access.

Eccentricities

Musée de la Contrefaçon

16 rue de la Faisanderie, 16th (01.56.26.14.00). M° Porte-Dauphine. **Open** 2-5.30pm Tue-Sun. Closed Mon, public holidays. **Admission** €2.50; free under-12s. **No credit cards. Map** p404 A4.

This small museum set up by the French anti-counterfeiting association puts strong emphasis on the penalties for forgery. Although the oldest known forgery is displayed (vase covers from *c*.200 BC), the focus is on contemporary copies of well-known brands – Reebok, Lacoste, Vuitton, Ray Ban – with the real thing displayed next to the fake.

Musée de la Curiosité

11 rue St-Paul, 4th (01.42.72.13.26/ www.museedelamagie.com). M° St-Paul or Sully Morland. **Open** 2-7pm Wed, Sat, Sun (longer during school holidays). Closed Mon, Tue, Thur, Fri. **Admission** €7, €5 3-12s; free under-3s. **No credit cards. Map** p405 L7.

The magic tricks start in the queue and get more complicated as you work your way through this cabinet of curiosities dedicated to the history of magic. Going as far back as Ancient Egypt, there is a broad selection of the tools of the trade, ranging from wands to boxes for cutting sequinned ladies in half. The welcome is enthusiastic and friendly, and the guides are passionate about their art.

Musée de l'Erotisme

72 bd de Clichy, 18th (01.42.58.28.73/ www.eroticmuseum.com). M° Blanche. **Open** 10am-2am daily. **Admission** €7, €5 students. **Credit** MC, V. **Map** p401 H2

See left, **Musée de l'Erotisme**.

Musée de la Franc-Maçonnerie

16 rue Cadet, 9th (01.45.23.20.92). M° Cadet. **Open** 2-6pm Tue-Sat. Closed Mon, Sun, some public holidays, July, Aug. **Admission** €2; free under-12s. **No credit cards. Map** p405 H3.

At the back of the Grand Orient de France (French Masonic Great Lodge), the history of freemasonry is traced from medieval stone masons' guilds to the present via prints of famous masons (General Lafayette and 1848 revolutionary leaders Blanc and Barbès). If you're not already in on the funny handshakes, don't expect anything to be given away.

Bookshop. Wheelchair access (call ahead).

Musée du Vin

Rue des Eaux, 16th (01.45.25.63.26/ www.museeduvinparis.com). M° Passy. **Admission** €6.50; €5.90 over-60s; €5.70 students; under 14s free. **Credit** (shop/restaurant) AmEx, DC, MC, V. **Map** p404 B6.

This museum is aptly housed in the vaulted cellars of a former wine-producing monastery. The ancient bottles, vats, corkscrews and cutouts of medieval peasants making wine are quickly seen, but at the end your patience is rewarded with a tasting.

Restaurant (noon-3pm). Shop. Partial wheelchair access.

Eat, Drink, Shop

Features

Restaurants

What the fur hat is to Moscow, the sauna to Stockholm and the sombrero to Chihuahua, cuisine is to Paris. Let us advise you on the tastiest.

The state of the Paris restaurant scene boils down to two words: tapas and terroir. Haute cuisine chefs, such as **Joël Robuchon** and **Hélène Darroze**, are making their refined fare more accessible – both financially and psychologically – by serving it finger-food-style in casual dining rooms. At the same time, great-value, regional-minded bistros such as **La Régalade** and **Chez Michel** are spawning a second generation of young chefs who are going out on their own – hence, **L'Ami Jean** and **L'Entredgeu** have enjoyed instant popularity. All of the city's best chefs share a concern for top-quality ingredients, their awareness enhanced by the food scares of recent years.

Except for the very simplest restaurants, it is wise to book ahead. This can usually be done the same day as your intended visit. More time should be allowed for haute cuisine restaurants, which need to be booked weeks in advance and confirmed the day before. On the clothing front, there is nothing wrong with either jeans or trainers, but avoid the two together – and at the really posh joints men should wear a jacket and tie, especially in the evenings, to avoid any awkwardness. All bills include the service charge, so only tip if you're bowled over. In this chapter, we use the terms *menu* and *prix-fixe* to denote set meals, where you get a starter, main and dessert for one price.

For further listings see the new book *Time Out Paris Eating and Drinking*, on sale at good bookshops or at www.timeout.com/shop.

The Islands

Bistros & brasseries

Le Vieux Bistro

14 rue du Cloître-Notre-Dame, 4th (01.43.54.18.95). M° Cité or St-Michel. **Open** noon-2.15pm, 7.30-10.15pm daily. **Average** €30. **No credit cards. Map** p406 J7.

Given its location across the street from Notre-Dame, it comes as a surprise that this long-running bistro is so good. Classic dishes include some of the best boeuf bourguignon anywhere in France and the house Bordeaux is excellent. Choose from the spacious front dining room, cosy back one where the diners are more likely to be French, or, in summer, (heatwaves permitting) the terrace.

Haute cuisine

Hiramatsu

7 quai de Bourbon, 4th (01.56.81.08.80). M° Pont Marie. **Open** noon-2pm, 8-10pm Tue-Sat. Closed Aug. **Average** €120. **Prix fixe** €95, €130. **Credit** AmEx, DC, MC, V. **Map** p406 K7.

Hiroyuki Hiramatsu has been hailed as a Japanese Alain Ducasse. In his tiny, minimalist restaurant he demonstrates a love of French produce, but without the carbohydrates. Crème de grenouille (yes, frog cream) on a truffle feuilleté, snail fricassée on a mushroom millefeuille, and salmon in a fine consommé flavoured with orange flower water, are typical of the delicate approach. Chef Hajime Nakagawa is a master of technique and the friendly staff are professional.

The Louvre, Palais-Royal & Les Halles

Bistros & brasseries

L'Absinthe

24 pl du Marché-St-Honoré, 1st (01.49.26.90.04). M° Tuileries. **Open** 12.15-3pm, 7.45-10.30pm Mon-Fri; 7.45-10.30pm Sat. Closed one week in Aug. **Average** €32. **Prix fixe** €26, €32. **Credit** AmEx, MC, V. **Map** p401 G4.

In summer, book a table on the spacious, fume-free terrace of this bar-turned-bistro on a square that's been transformed by Ricardo Bofill's glass-walled architecture. This is one of the (fainter) stars in the galaxy of chef Michel Rostang, so the menu is not without invention (on a good day) and pretension (on a bad) with dishes such as a chestnut véloute starter, scallop brochette and pear Tatin with walnut sauce. Wines are helpfully grouped by price.

Brasserie Zimmer

1 pl du Châtelet, 1st (01.42.36.74.03/ www.lezimmer.com). M° Châtelet. **Open** 9am-1am daily. Food served 11am-12.30am. **Average** €25. **Prix fixe** €18.60. **Credit** AmEx, MC, V. **Non-smoking room. Map** p406 J6.

This Costes brothers address is particularly worth knowing about in August, when many other places are closed. Try starters such as the green bean salad or tomato with mozzarella, and move on to chicken brochette, a juicy steak or pasta dishes. Earnest young waiters buzz about and enhance the lounge-attitude atmosphere.

Hiramatsu

Menu lexicon

Agneau lamb. **Aiguillettes** (*de canard*) thin slices (of duck breast). **Aïoli** garlic mayonnaise. **Aligot** mashed potatoes with melted cheese and garlic. **Aloyau** beef loin. **Anchoïade** spicy anchovy and olive paste. **Andouillette** sausage made from pig's offal. **Ananas** pineapple. **Anguille** eel. **Asperge** asparagus. **Aubergine** aubergine/eggplant.

Ballotine stuffed, rolled up piece of meat or fish. **Bar** sea bass. **Bavarois** moulded cream dessert. **Bavette** beef flank steak. **Béarnaise** sauce of butter and egg yolk. **Beignet** fritter or doughnut. **Belon** smooth, flat oyster. **Biche** venison. **Bifteak** steak. **Bisque** shellfish soup. **Blanc** breast. **Blanquette** 'white' stew made with eggs and cream. **Boudin noir/blanc** black (blood)/white pudding. **Boeuf** beef; **– bourguignon** beef cooked Burgundy style, with red wine, onions and mushrooms; **– gros sel** boiled beef with vegetables. **Bouillabaisse** Mediterranean fish soup. **Bourride** a *bouillabaisse*-like soup, without shellfish. **Brochet** pike. **Bulot** whelk.

Cabillaud fresh cod. **Caille** quail. **Canard** duck. **Cannelle** cinnamon. **Carbonnade** beef stew with onions and stout or beer. **Carré d'agneau** rack of lamb. **Carrelet** plaice. **Cassis** blackcurrants; blackcurrant liqueur. **Cassoulet** stew of white haricot beans, sausage and preserved duck. **Céleri** celery. **Céleri rave** celeriac. **Cèpe** cep mushroom. **Cervelle** brains. **Champignon** mushroom; **– de Paris** button mushroom. **Chateaubriand** thick fillet steak. **Chaud-froid** a sauce used to glaze cold dishes. **Chèvre** goat; goat's cheese. **Chevreuil** young roe deer. **Choucroute** sauerkraut, served *garnie* with cured ham and sausages. **Ciboulette** chive. **Citron** lemon. **Citron vert** lime. **Citronelle** lemongrass. **Civet** game stew. **Clafoutis** batter filled with fruit, usually cherries. **Cochon de lait** suckling pig. **Coco** large white bean. **Colin** hake. **Confit de canard** preserved duck. **Contre-filet** sirloin steak. **Coquelet** baby rooster. **Coquille** shell. **Coquilles St-Jacques** scallops. **Côte** chop; **– de boeuf** beef rib. **Crème brûlée** creamy custard dessert with caramel glaze. **Crème Chantilly** sweetened whipped cream. **Crème fraîche** thick, slightly soured cream. **Cresson** watercress. **Crevettes** prawns (GB), shrimp (US). **Croque-madame** sandwich of toasted cheese and ham topped with an egg; **croque-monsieur** sandwich of toasted cheese and ham. **En croûte** in a pastry case. **Cru** raw. **Crudités** assorted raw vegetables. **Crustacé** shellfish.

Daube meat braised in red wine. **Daurade** sea bream. **Désossé** boned. **Dinde** turkey. **Duxelles** chopped, sautéed mushrooms.

Echalote shallot. **Eglefin** haddock. **Endive** chicory (GB), Belgian endive (US). **Entrecôte** beef rib steak. **Epices** spices. **Epinards** spinach. **Escabèche** sautéed and marinated fish, served cold. **Escargot** snail. **Espadon** swordfish. **Estouffade** meat that's been marinated, fried and braised.

Faisan pheasant. **Farci** stuffed. **Faux-filet** sirloin steak. **Feuilleté** 'leaves' of (puff) pastry. **Filet mignon** tenderloin. **Fines de claire** crinkle-shelled oysters. **Flambé** flamed in alcohol. **Flétan** halibut. **Foie** liver; **– gras** fattened goose or duck liver. **Forestière** with mushrooms. **Au four** baked. **Fraise** strawberry. **Framboise** raspberry. **Fricassé** fried and simmered in stock, usually with creamy sauce. **Frisée** curly endive. **Frites** chips (GB); fries (US). **Fromage** cheese; **– blanc** smooth cream cheese. **Fruits de mer** shellfish. **Fumé** smoked.

Galette round flat cake of flaky pastry, potato pancake or buckwheat savoury crêpe. **Garni** garnished. **Gelée** aspic. **Gésiers** gizzards. **Gibier** game. **Gigot d'agneau** leg of lamb. **Gingembre** ginger. **Girolle/chanterelle** small, trumpet-like mushroom. **Glace** ice cream. **Glacé** frozen or iced. **Goujon** breaded, fried strip of fish; also a small catfish. **Gras** fat. **Gratin dauphinois** sliced potatoes baked with milk, cheese and garlic. **Gratiné** browned with breadcrumbs or cheese. **A la grècque** vegetables served cold in the cooking liquid with oil and lemon juice. **Cuisses de grenouille** frogs' legs. **Grillé** grilled. **Groseille** redcurrant. **Groseille à maquereau** gooseberry.

Haché minced. **Hachis Parmentier** shepherd's pie. **Hareng** herring. **Haricot** bean; **– vert** green bean. **Homard** lobster. **Huître** oyster.

Ile flottante whipped egg white floating in vanilla custard.

Jambon ham; **– cru** cured raw ham. **Jarret** ham shin or knuckle. **Julienne** vegetables cut into matchsticks.

Langoustine Dublin Bay prawns, scampi. **Lapin** rabbit. **Lamelle** very thin slice. **Langue** tongue. **Lard** bacon. **Lardon** small cube of bacon. **Légume** vegetable. **Lièvre** hare. **Limande** lemon sole. **Lotte** monkfish.

Mâche lamb's lettuce. **Magret** duck breast. **Maison** of the house. **Maquereau** mackerel. **Marcassin** wild boar. **Mariné** marinated. **Marmite** small cooking pot. **Marquise** mousse-like cake. **Merguez** spicy lamb/beef sausage. **Merlan** whiting. **Merlu** hake. **Meunière** fish floured and sautéed in butter. **Miel** honey. **Mignon** small meat fillet. **Mirabelle** tiny yellow plum. **Moelle** bone marrow; **os à la –** marrow bone. **Morille** morel mushroom. **Moules** mussels; **– à la marinière** cooked with white wine and shallots. **Morue** dried, salted cod; **brandade de –** cod puréed with potato. **Mousseline** hollandaise sauce with whipped cream. **Myrtille** bilberry/blueberry.

Navarin lamb and vegetable stew. **Navet** turnip. **Noisette** hazelnut; small round portion of meat. **Noix** walnut. **Noix de coco** coconut. **Nouilles** noodles.

Oeuf egg; **– en cocotte** baked egg; **– en meurette** egg poached in red wine; **– à la neige** see *Ile flottante*. **Oie** goose. **Oignon** onion. **Onglet** cut of beef, similar to *bavette*. **Oseille** sorrel. **Oursin** sea urchin.

Palourde type of clam. **Pamplemousse** grapefruit. **Pané** breaded. **En papillote** cooked in a packet. **Parfait** sweet or savoury mousse-like mixture. **Parmentier** with potato. **Paupiette** slice of meat or fish, stuffed and rolled. **Pavé** thick steak. **Perdrix** partridge. **Persil** parsley. **Petit salé** salt pork. **Pied** foot (trotter). **Pignon** pine kernel. **Pintade/pintadeau** guinea fowl. **Pipérade** Basque dish of green peppers, onions, Bayonne ham and tomatoes, often served with scrambled egg. **Poivre** pepper. **Poivron** red or green (bell) pepper. **Pomme** apple. **Pomme de terre** potato. **Pommes lyonnaises** potatoes fried with onions. **Potage** soup. **Pot-au-feu** boiled beef with vegetables. **Potiron** pumpkin. **Poulet** chicken. **Poulpe** octopus. **Pressé** squeezed. **Prune** plum. **Pruneau** prune.

Quenelle light, poached fish (or poultry) dumpling. **Quetsche** damson. **Queue de boeuf** oxtail.

Ragoût meat stew. **Raie** skate. **Râpé** grated. **Rascasse** scorpion fish. **Réglisse** liquorice. **Rillettes** potted pork, goose, salmon or tuna. **Ris de veau** veal sweetbreads. **Riz** rice. **Rognons** kidneys. **Rôti** roast. **Rouget** red mullet.

St Pierre John Dory. **Salé** salted. **Sandre** pike-perch. **Sanglier** wild boar. **Saucisse** sausage. **Saucisson sec** small dried sausage. **Saumon** salmon. **Seîche** squid. **Selle** (*d'agneau*) saddle (of lamb) **Suprême** fillets (of chicken) in a cream sauce. **Supion** small squid.

Tagine slow-cooked North African stew. **Tapenade** Provençal olive and caper paste. **Tartare** raw minced steak (also tuna or salmon). **Tarte aux pommes** apple tart. **Tarte Tatin** warm, caramelised apple tart cooked upside-down. **Timbale** dome-shaped mould, or food cooked in one. **Tisane** herbal tea. **Tournedos** small slices of beef fillet, sautéed or grilled. **Tourte** covered pie or tart, usually savoury. **Travers de porc** pork spare ribs. **Tripes** tripe. **Tripoux** dish of sheep's offal and sheep feet. **Truffes** truffles. **Truite** trout.

Vacherin cake of layered meringue, cream, fruit and ice cream; a soft, cow's milk cheese. **Veau** veal. **Velouté** stock-based white sauce; creamy soup. **Vichyssoise** cold leek and potato soup. **Volaille** poultry.

Cooking time (La cuisson)

Cru raw. **Bleu** practically raw. **Saignant** rare. **Rosé** pink (said of lamb, duck, liver, kidneys). **A point** medium rare. **Bien cuit** well done.

Le Dauphin

167 rue St-Honoré, 1st (01.42.60.40.11). M° Pyramides. **Open** noon-2.30pm, 7.30-10.30pm daily. **Prix fixe** €34. **Lunch menu** €23. **Credit** AmEx, DC, MC, V. **Map** p402 H5.

Chefs Edgar Duhr and Didier Oudill here present a pared-down version of the exciting, south-western food that wowed critics at the Café de Paris in Biarritz. Diners share starters such as rustic terrines and goose rillettes, a grill menu offers various combinations of seafood, meat and vegetables and there's also a classical carte. A meltingly tender pig's cheek, cooked for seven hours in aged Armagnac, gives a whiff of what to expect, and desserts such as a fabulous tartelette à l'orange are a strong point.

Le Petit Flore

6 rue Croix des Petits Champs, 1st (01.42.60.25.53). M° Palais Royal. **Open** 6am-8pm Mon-Sat. Food served noon-2.30pm. Closed Aug. **Prix fixe** €12. **Credit** DC, MC, V. **Wheelchair access. Map** p402 H5.

Hiding its culinary pleasures behind an unobtrusive exterior, this little restaurant offers a slap-up French menu for a wondrous €12. The starter of herring fillet with buttery, boiled potato is a rather brilliant little dish, and the entrecôte holds swarthy charcoal tastes. Almost everything comes with heaps of great chips, but puddings can be a let-down.

Le Safran

29 rue d'Argenteuil, 1st (01.42.61.25.30). M° Pyramides. **Open** noon-2.30pm, 7-11pm Mon-Fri; 7-11pm Sat. **Average** €38. **Prix fixe** €24, €38. **Lunch menu** €14.50. **Credit** AmEx, MC, V. **Wheelchair access. Map** p401 G5.

Caroll Sinclair's saffron-coloured dining room is cosy and welcoming, and the menu too features her signature spice in quite a few dishes. Flavour is key, in starters such as sautéed girolles and the saffron-tinted velouté de fruits de mer, and mains of seared tuna topped with foie gras, and the rich and tender lamb cooked for 'seven hours'. Desserts are also a deluxe take on comfort food and the short but interesting wine list yields some good quaffs.

Contemporary/trendy

Hôtel Costes

239 rue St-Honoré, 1st (01.42.44.50.25). M° Concorde or Tuileries. **Open** 7am-1am daily. **Average** €60. **Credit** AmEx, DC, MC, V. **Wheelchair access. Map** p401 G5.

The Costes, with its permanent coterie of bright young things, a little discreet lifting and a calculated air of disdain, hasn't changed a bit. Same giggle-inducing prices, same stupidly named food ('an undressed lettuce heart and two weeping tigers, please'), same snooty but breathtakingly beautiful staff and, astoundingly, the same buzz. Nooks and crannies accommodate the rich and the reclusive, but if your accessories (shoes, date, AmEx Centurion) are up to it then push for a visible table and enjoy the attention.

Lô Sushi Pont Neuf

1 rue du Pont-Neuf, 1st (01.42.33.09.09/ www.losushi.com). M° Pont-Neuf or Châtelet. **Open** 11am-midnight daily. **Happy hour** 6-8pm. **Average** €25. **Credit** AmEx, MC, V. **Map** p402 J6.

A computer screen is installed at each of the 65 places around the sushi conveyer belt, allowing you to send messages to fellow diners while keeping a beady eye on the goodies circulating on their different coloured saucers. The creamy-white plastic counter, dove-grey oak and leather stools with low backs give this Lô Sushi a softer, gentler feel than the original branch. The selection of maki and rolls goes beyond the standard cucumber or tuna; there are also crunchy Japanese green beans in their pods and a tasty seaweed salad.

Branch: 8 rue de Berri, 8th (01.45.62.01.00).

Macéo

15 rue des Petits-Champs, 1st (01.42.97.53.85). M° Bourse or Opéra. **Open** 12.30-2.30pm, 7-11pm Mon-Fri; 7-11pm Sat. **Average** €48. **Prix fixe** €35, €38 (dinner only). **Lunch menu** €29, €34. **Credit** MC, V. **Map** p402 H5.

Spacious, high-ceilinged salons with large windows and Second Empire mouldings are given a clever update by sculptural bronze and twig light-fittings. at this British owned sibling to Willi's Wine Bar chef Jean-Paul Deyries gives southwest-tinged French cuisine a contemporary, cosmopolitan lift, as seen in a succulent lamb and aubergine main course, and cod roasted on its skin, accompanied by a garam masala spice reduction and a solid dollop of split green pea purée with chunks of bacon.

Haute cuisine

L'Espadon

Hôtel Ritz, 15 pl Vendôme, 1st (01.43.16.30.80/ www.ritzparis.com). M° Madeleine or Concorde. **Open** noon-2.30pm, 7.30-10.30pm daily. **Average** €180. **Prix fixe** €160 (dinner only). **Lunch menu** €68. **Credit** AmEx, DC, MC, V. **Map** p401 G4.

From the minute you tread the plush carpet towards the dining room it is impossible to find flaw at the Ritz's restaurant. The €68 menu is not bad value. Enjoy such decadent starters as oysters marinated with orange, pineapple and fennel, and silky green asparagus purée with beautifully cooked spiced langoustines. Prix fixe mains are essentially bistro classics refined – meltingly tender duck breast with carved turnip and caramelised spring onions, sole in cockle-cream sauce – but you still get star service.

International

Cambodian: La Mousson

9 rue Thérèse, 1st (01.42.60.59.46). M° Pyramides. **Open** noon-2.30pm, 7.15-10.30pm Mon-Sat. Closed 25 Dec, Aug. **Average** €25. **Prix fixe** €16.50, €21.10. **Lunch menu** €12.40, €16.80. **Credit** MC, V. **Map** p402 H5.

The tiny cook here, known to her faithful customers as Lucile, moved to Paris in 1975 and has been recreating Khmer flavours ever since. Won ton soup is prepared in the Cambodian way with lettuce and prawns in a subtle broth. Authentic main courses include amok, a soothing steamed fish dish made with coconut milk, galangal, lemongrass, lemon zest and kaffir lime leaf, and giant prawns in their shells with a mild tomato and chilli sauce. Ta peir – fermented black rice – for dessert, is an acquired alcoholic taste, or try the squishy, sweet coconut cakes.

Japanese: Kinugawa

9 rue du Mont-Thabor, 1st (01.42.60.65.07). Mº Tuileries. **Open** noon-2.30pm, 7-10pm Mon-Sat. Closed 24 Dec-7 Jan. **Average** €60. **Prix fixe** €86-€108 (dinner only). **Lunch menu** €26, €52. **Credit** AmEx, DC, MC, V. **Non-smoking room. Map** p401 G5.

Everything at Kinugawa breathes excellence, from the decor to the the crockery and gentle, assiduous service. The food follows the highly refined kaiseki-ryori tradition, embodying the quintessential Japanese virtues of wabi (simplicity) and sabi (unstudied elegance). The €86 menu comprises nine courses plus dessert. From the classic, stunningly fresh sashimi to the original lime-scented fish consommé, every fascinating combination of texture and flavour will have you swooning.

Branch: 4 rue St-Philippe-du-Roule, 8th (01.45.63.08.07).

Vegetarian

Foody's Brunch Café

26 rue Montorgueil, 1st (01.40.13.02.53). M° Châtelet or Les Halles. **Open** 11.30am-5pm Mon-Sat. Closed first three weeks of Aug. **Average** €9. **Prix fixe** €8-€12.50. **Credit** MC, V. **Wheelchair access. Map** p402 J5.

This is a pleasant place to grab a quick lunch at a good price. Salads are the house speciality. Help yourself to a tray and a bowl (small or big) and fill it up with whatever in the buffet catches your eye. Greek, pasta, red beans and artichoke heart are some of the ten or so salads you can choose from (there is even some token ham for carnivores). There is also a soup and a plat du jour.

The best Delicacies

Hiramitsu
Mmmm, dig that puréed frog. *See p182.*

Pierre Gagnaire
Veal mixed with frog: divine. *See p198.*

Le Pré Verre
Ravioli stuffed with snail goo. *See p203.*

La Table de Michel
Snails, foie gras, ceps... and tagliatelle? *See p204.*

Café Max
Go on: treat yourself to that bucket of foie gras! *See p208.*

Maison Blanche
Sea urchins and caviar. *See p198.*

Opéra & the Grands Boulevards

Bistros & brasseries

L'Alsaco

10 rue Condorcet, 9th (01.45.26.44.31). Mº Poissonnière. **Open** 8-10.30pm Mon, Sat; noon-2pm, 8-10.30pm Tue-Fri. **Average** €30. **Prix fixe** (dinner only) €20, €30. **Credit** DC, MC, V. **Map** p402 J2.

This cosy place serves as a de facto showcase for one of the country's best regional cuisines. Let friendly Alsatian owner Claude Steger choose a wine for you then sample some presskopf (head cheese) or delicious Black Forest ham. Next, go with the best choucroute garnie in Paris. The full works means grilled pork knuckle, smoked pork, bacon and sausages. In the unlikely event that you can manage a dessert, finish up with a slice of seasonal fruit tart.

The Kitchen

153 rue Montmartre, 2nd (01.42.33.33.97/ www.thekitchen.fr). M° Grands Boulevards or Bourse. **Open** 9am-midnight Mon-Thur; 9am-1.30am Fri; 11.30am-1.30am Sat; noon-4pm Sun. **Average** €13 (lunch), €23 (dinner). **Lunch menu** €9.50, €10.50. **Brunch** (Sat, Sun) €16.50. **Credit** MC, V. **Non-smoking room** (lunch only). **Map** p402 J4.

Recently opened by Irishman Bennet Holmes, The Kitchen looks like a design-junkie's dream kitchen, and exudes delicious home-cooking smells. Chunky terrine and organic bread, vast bowls of hearty vegetable soup and apple crumble better than Mum makes make this place special. The staff are laid-back and, taking the concept of a kitchen-supper to its logical conclusion, always offer seconds.

Aux Lyonnais

32 rue St-Marc, 2nd (01.42.96.65.04). Mº Bourse or Richelieu-Drouot. **Open** noon-2pm, 7.30-11pm Tue-Fri; 7.30-11pm Sat. **Average** €45. **Prix fixe** €28. **Credit** AmEx, MC, V. **Map** p402 H4.

Bistro-lovers should be relieved that this restaurant is now owned by Alain Ducasse and Thierry de la Brosse, two wealthy and passionate defenders of French culinary tradition. The menu of modernised Lyonnais, Bressane and Beaujolais classics is enough to warm anyone's heart, with first courses of charcuterie from Sibilla (the best charcutier in

La Paprika. See p191.

Lyon), and luscious suckling pig meat confit with foie gras and mains such as quenelle (perch dumpling) with crayfish, and good steaks.

Mimosa

44 rue d'Argout, 2nd (01.40.28.15.75). M° Sentier. **Open** noon-4pm Mon-Fri (evenings for private parties by arrangement). **Lunch menu** €12, €14. **Credit** MC, V. **Map** p402 J5.

Business is booming in this increasingly popular local canteen where a solid crew of regulars are faithful to Thierry Soulat's good home cooking and the gentle warmth of the welcome. Daily specials might include rump-steak with pepper sauce, grilled andouillette (tripe sausage), and black pudding with apples. Save room for Thierry's desserts: chocolate mousse with orange flower water, or castagnaccio, an airy Corsican cake made with chestnuts.

Casa Olympe

48 rue St-Georges, 9th (01.42.85.26.01). M° St-Georges. **Open** noon-2pm, 8-11pm Mon-Fri. **Prix fixe** €34. **Credit** AmEx, MC, V. **Map** p402 H3.

Dominique Versini has left her jet-setty past behind her to create this superb bistro just off the place St-Georges. The attractive mustard-coloured room is a must, and service is well-paced and friendly. Main courses such as guinea hen with a single, large, wild-mushroom-stuffed ravioli, and pork fillet with sauerkraut are satisfying; desserts are exceptional.

Haute cuisine

Lucas Carton

9 pl de la Madeleine, 8th (01.42.65.22.90/ www.lucascarton.com). M° Madeleine. **Open** 8-10.30pm Mon, Sat; noon-2.30pm, 8-10.30pm Tue-Fri. Closed Aug. **Average** €200. **Lunch menu** €76. **Credit** AmEx, DC, MC, V. **Map** p401 F4.

Cosseted in a merlot-coloured banquette, looking out through art nouveau partitions with glass encased dragonflies, and a glass of 1995 Dom Pérignon – it's lunchtime heaven on a plate. The 'déjeuner affaires' is good value and doesn't feel in any sense like second-best, with offerings such as tender green asparagus with an emerald asparagus 'cappuccino'; plump little just-cooked scallops studded with shell-topped toothpicks threaded with pink pickled ginger; and a standout main of featherweight tempura of sole and peppery celery leaves, lightly flavoured with curry. Alain Senderens is passionate about marrying wine with food, thus each dish has a suggested tipple.

What a corking good *vin* plan

Even though none of us wants to commit the old 'I'll have half a pint of the white Burgundy' gaffe, let's face it – pairing wine with food isn't brain surgery: it's more common sense. Anyone who denies that is either a *bona fide* wine expert (you don't meet many of them) or a cultural snob (you meet more than enough of them). Forget the old standard white-with-fish and red-with-meat and just go with your instincts. Provided, that is, that those instincts don't insist on port with oysters or Sauternes with mustardy kidneys, or – let us not skirt the issue – drinking the entire bottle before the guests turn up. But then again, taste is subjective and, unfortunarely, received social conformity is not. This best answer is, as ever, to keep it simple.

Start by choosing a wine that you want to drink, and don't be cheap. Mediocre wine is rarely improved by good food, even if the bottle shop bod insists otherwise. Balance the wine with the food; don't mix the weight divisions – herd the heavyweights and line up the lightweights. OK, so things have changed a tad since all whites were fruity and light and all reds were clarety and heavy, but just wade right in there and give it a go.

Of course, you don't want to make yourself look a prat, France being the grape outdoors and all that. Its dazzling array of wine styles can lead an average quaffer into playing pin the tail on the drunken donkey with a mere average wine list. It doesn't help that the French don't pop the helpful monikers of '*chardonnay*' or '*cabernet*' or handy suggestions like '*goes nice with burgers*' on their bottles. No, they base their wine marketing on where the wine's made rather than what it's made of. And, they don't do it just to be different. No: it's a philosophy, born out of a belief in the sacred '*terroir*' (the effect of the environment and the soils).

But's let's not disappear up our own corkscrews. Hearty food needs a hearty wine: roast lamb works a treat with a Bordeaux while a red Burgundy suits roast beef. Marinated beef goes with a red Bordeaux or a Côtes du Rhône while marinated chicken teams well with Beaujolais.

There's also the 'if it ain't broke' school: remember, classic pairings such as oysters and Muscadet, caviar and Champagne, foie gras and sugary Sauternes haven't become classic pairings for nothing.

Alsace's Gewürztraminer is great with Munster cheese and, at the other end of the range, Thai food. Dry Rieslings pair with shellfish and goose.

Bordeaux reds partner rabbit, venison, duck and roast lamb with ease. Sweet whites are good with chicken liver pâté and Roquefort cheese.

Burgundy reds are ideal with coq au vin and boeuf bourguignon, as well as game and duck. The whites are a dream with lobster, salmon and frogs' legs.

Champagne is usually an apéritif, but locals insist it goes with everything! Try it with oysters or sole. Loire Valley Sancerre is a delight with seafood and stinky cheese while the reds are good with charcuterie. Rhône Valley reds suit pork, duck, pheasant and casseroles. Languedoc-Rousillon and Provençal wines' soulmate is Mediterranean-style food (grilled fish and olive oil-laced roast veg).

Finally, wine from a particular region will usually pair well with food from the same area: Riesling with choucroute or Madiran with cassoulet. And, if you're a home on the range cooker, just throw in some of the wine that you're planning to serve. The tastes are sure to match then, *non*?

Fish

Iode

48 rue d'Argout, 2nd (01.42.36.46.45). Mº Sentier. **Open** noon-2.45pm, 8-11.30pm Mon-Fri; 6pm-11.30pm Sat. Closed 10 days in Aug. **Lunch menu** €15. **Average** €35. **Credit** MC, V. **Map** p402 J5.

Appetisers might include rocket salad with shaved parmesan and lightly breaded and pan-fried langoustines, and an ample plate of marinated calamari with sweet onions. Mains are no less spectacular: grilled sea bass fillet atop preserved lemon, courgette and aubergine, dressed with a verjus sauce, and a seared tuna steak with basil and parsley tempura. Follow with fruit or sorbet.

International

Hungarian: Le Paprika

28 av Trudaine, 9th (01.44.63.02.91/www.le-paprika.com). Mº Anvers or Pigalle. **Open** 9.30am-11pm daily. **Prix fixe** (dinner only) €20, €29. **Lunch menu** €15, €29. **Credit** AmEx, MC, V. **Wheelchair access. Map** p402 J2.

An appealing old-world bonhomie prevails at this restaurant, where the diners are as likely to be Polish, Romanian or Czech as Hungarian. Try the good-value menus, which include starters of paprika cheese, thin slices of the famous salami or poached egg with crayfish. Savoury main courses include tender goulash served with spätzle (nubby egg noodles), duckling roasted in cabbage and sautéed foie gras. Desserts are delicious.

Indian: Gandhi-Opéra

66 rue Ste-Anne, 2nd (01.47.03.41.00/ www.restaurant-gandhi.com). Mº Quatre-Septembre. **Open** noon-2.30pm, 7-11.30pm Mon-Sat; 7-11.30pm Sun. **Average** €27. **Prix fixe** €23, €27.50 (dinner only). **Lunch menu** €11-€19.70. **Credit** AmEx, DC, MC, V. **Wheelchair access. Map** p402 H4.

The clientele is largely French but instead of pandering to the Gallic fear of spices the chef has taken one of the plusses of the French respect for tradition – excellent quality meat – and used it in authentic tasting dishes. A speciality is the tandoori grill, including a hot, minty chicken starter and twin tandoori quail. The delicious, sizzling Bombay-style chicken is a highlight of the mains, and be sure to order the paneer sag side dish. After this, a rose sorbet will take you to heaven.

Beaubourg & the Marais

Bistros & brasseries

L'Ambassade d'Auvergne

22 rue du Grenier St-Lazare, 3rd (01.42.72.31.22/ www.ambassade-auvergne.com). Mº Rambuteau. **Open** noon-2pm, 7.30-10.30pm daily. Closed Sun 14 July to 15 Aug. **Average** €40. **Prix fixe** €27. **Credit** MC, V. **Non-smoking room. Map** p402 K5.

Cured ham comes as two hefty, plate-filling slices; salads are chock full of green lentils cooked in goose fat, studded with bacon bits and shallots. Follow with 'rôti d'agneau' or luscious Salers beef in red wine sauce. These dishes come with the Ambassade's flagship aligot (an elastic mash and cheese concoction). There is a comprehensive selection of the region's gluggable wines.

Ma Bourgogne

19 pl des Vosges, 4th (01.42.78.44.64). Mº St-Paul or Bastille. **Open** noon-1am daily. Closed Feb. **Average** €33. **Prix fixe** €32. **No credit cards. Map** p406 L6.

The terrace, under the arcades of beautiful place des Vosges, is the main point here and it's a great place to soak up the cosmopolitan atmosphere of the Marais. The food is acceptable if uninspiring: charcuterie plates, sarladaise salad (a bit short on foie gras) and Lyonnais sausage provide a sometimes insipid taste of eastern France, but the house speciality steak tartare is well seasoned and excellent.

Le Petit Marché

9 rue de Béarn, 3rd (01.42.72.06.67). Mº Chemin Vert. **Open** noon-3pm, 8pm-midnight Mon-Fri; noon-4pm, 8pm-midnight Sat; noon-5pm, 8pm-midnight Sun. **Average** €30. **Lunch menu** €13. **Brunch** (Sun) €17. **Credit** MC, V. **Map** p406 L6.

Just north of place des Vosges, this new bistro is hugely popular. What everyone really loves is the fact that it stays open until midnight, serving generous salads such as spinach topped with Parma ham, hearty main dishes including duck breast with ginger, steak tartare and calf's liver, and soothing desserts such as rice pudding. There is also a pleasant little terrace.

Le Trumilou

84 quai de l'Hôtel de Ville, 4th (01.42.77.63.98). Mº Pont Marie or Hôtel de Ville. **Open** noon-3pm, 7-11pm daily. Closed two weeks in July or Aug, 25 Dec. **Average** €25. **Prix fixe** €13.50, €16.50. **Credit** MC, V. **Wheelchair access. Map** p406 K6.

The food is dependable and copious, and by sticking to the traditional and eschewing more adventurous dishes, you'll be treated to well-executed French classics such as magret de canard, hearty stews, and generous steaks, though desserts are below-par. Although not ideal for a tête-à-tête, with its cloud of smoke and alcohol fumes, punctuated by gales raucous laughter, the Trumilou is nonetheless deservedly popular.

International

Jewish: Pitchi Poï

7 rue Caron, 9 pl Marché Ste-Catherine, 4th (01.42.77.46.15/www.pitchipoi.com). M° St-Paul. **Open** 10.30am-3pm, 6-10.30pm daily. Sunday brunch noon-4pm. **Average** €20.50. **Sunday brunch** €24. **Credit** AmEx, DC, MC, V. **Wheelchair access. Non-smoking room. Map** p406 L6.

A terrace like this – on a charming cobbled square with a couple of trees and no traffic – is rare in Paris, and hopeful diners hover about waiting for the next available table. Much of the vast menu is Eastern European, accompanied by ice-cold vodkas. The popular Sunday brunch kicks off with smoked salmon and sour cream, served with fluffy blinis and a paprika-sprinkled scrambled eggs, followed by an 'à volonté' (all-you-can-eat) buffet – smoked herring, calf's liver, herring mousse, minced eggs, crudité salad, Pinkel ham et al. Quite simply a feast.

North African: Chez Omar

47 rue de Bretagne, 3rd (01.42.72.36.26). M° Temple or Arts et Métiers. **Open** noon-2.30pm, 7-11.30pm Mon-Sat; 7-11.30pm Sun. **Average** €30. **No credit cards**. **Map** p402 L5.

Omar doesn't take reservations and by 9pm the queue stretches the length of the long zinc bar and out the door. Everyone is waiting for the same thing: couscous. Prices range from €11 (vegetarian) to €24 (royale); otherwise there is a selection of French classics (duck, fish, steak). Affable, overstretched waiters magically slip through the crowds with mounds of semolina, steaming vats of vegetable-laden broth, and steel platters heaving with meat and more meat – best of all are the spicy merguez sausages.

Vegetarian

La Verte Tige

13 rue Ste-Anastase, 3rd (01.42.77.22.15). M° St-Sébastien-Froissart or St-Paul. **Open** noon-2.30pm, 7.30-10.30pm Tue-Sat; 12.30-4pm Sun. Closed Aug. **Average** €20. **Prix fixe** €18 (evenings and weekends). **Credit** MC, V. **Map** p406 L6.

Unusually for a vegetarian restaurant the menu here is overflowing with alcoholic drinks, including cheap pichets of wine and organic cider. The chef conjures up original and appealing vegetarian dishes based on Iranian cuisine. Espinada is a tasty starter of spinach, garlic, fried onions and yoghurt; viridis an avocado and garlic spread served with bread. Meat substitutes appear, such as smoked vegetarian sausages with couscous, and soy protein sautéed with nuts and prunes.

Piccolo Teatro

6 rue des Ecouffes, 4th (01.42.72.17.79/ www.piccoloteatro.com). M° St-Paul or Hôtel de Ville. **Open** noon-3pm, 7-11.30pm daily. **Average** €20. **Prix fixe** €15.10, €21.50 (dinner only). **Lunch menu** €8.90-€14.70. **Credit** AmEx, DC, MC, V. **Map** p406 K6.

Exposed stone walls, dark wooden beams and candlelight combine to produce an intimate and relaxed one-room restaurant. There are salads and soups to start with, and Piccolo Teatro's house speciality is the filling gratin: a mix of vegetables cooked with cream and finished off with a layer of gruyère. There is a range of yoghurt-based desserts, and a delicious and filling rhubarb Charlotte. Service, by a single waiter, is impressively professional.

The Bastille & eastern Paris

Bistros & brasseries

Astier

44 rue Jean-Pierre-Timbaud, 11th (01.43.57.16.35). M° Parmentier. **Open** noon-2pm, 8-10.15pm Mon-Fri. Closed Easter, Aug, 25 Dec. **Prix fixe** €25. **Lunch menu** €20.50. **Credit** MC, V. **Wheelchair access** (ring in advance). **Map** p403 M4.

The unmistakable smell of fine French cooking, the look of unbridled contentment on the crimson faces of the local businessmen, both tell you that this is a serious bastion of traditional food. Homemade terrines lead the way, including chicken liver and seafood versions. Follow with firm yet tender lamb sweetbreads and sinfully good gratin dauphinois or monkfish in an unctuous, buttery sauce, then a smooth nougat glacé enriched by morsels of marrons glacés. Amazingly this three-course feast costs a mere €20.50 at lunch– book ahead.

C'Amelot

50 rue Amelot, 11th (01.43.55.54.04). M° Chemin Vert. **Open** 7-10.30pm Mon, Sat; noon-2pm, 7-10.30pm Tue-Fri. **Prix fixe** €33 (dinner only). **Lunch menu** €16, €23. **Credit** AmEx, MC, V. **Map** p407 M6.

Didier Varnier is one of a group of young bistro chefs who relish the contrast of serving inventive and refined food in low-key settings. The dining room has a countrified feel with its panelling and bare wood tables. The lunch menu, with two options for each course, is particularly good value, offering such seasonal dishes as lentil soup with foie gras, lamb chops in poivrade (white wine) sauce with polenta and prunes in spiced wine.

A la Biche au Bois

45 av Ledru Rollin, 12th (01.43.43.34.38). M° Gare de Lyon. **Open** noon-2.30pm, 7-11pm Mon-Fri. Closed first three weeks in Aug. **Average** €23. **Prix fixe** €21.60. **Credit** AmEx, DC, MC, V. **Wheelchair access**. **Map** p407 M8.

Among the big brasseries and tourist traps that surround the Gare de Lyon is this bistro buzzing with authenticity – great for a rib-sticking pre-Eurostar meal. The prix fixe is good value, served in hearty portions. The real event here is the stews, including game in season, served in enormous casserole dishes and the ripe cheeses and genuine versions of puds such as crème caramel are satisfying too.

Paris Main d'Or

133 rue du Fbg-St-Antoine, 11th (01.44.68.04.68). M° Ledru-Rollin. **Open** noon-3pm, 8pm-midnight Mon-Sat. Closed Sun, Mon in Aug. **Average** €30. **Lunch menu** €11. **Credit** MC, V. **Map** p407 M7.

The attraction of dinner at this popular Corsican owes as much to the waiters' non-stop banter as to the cooking itself. All of the island's specialities are here – various starters feature the soft cheese brocciu, including a plump cannelloni oozing with

Le Souk

the stuff. There's cabri (kid) served in the pot and and filling storzapretti, dumplings made from yet more brocciu and sprinkled with the Corsican herb nepita, which tastes like a cross between mint and marjoram. At lunchtime, Corsican food takes a back seat to a good value standard French menu.

Le Square Trousseau

1 rue Antoine-Vollon, 12th (01.43.43.06.00). M° Ledru-Rollin. **Open** Tue-Sat noon-2.30pm, 8-11.30pm. Closed Aug. **Average** €40. **Lunch menu** €20, €25. **Credit** MC, V. **Map** p407 N7.

This restaurant would be worth visiting for its superb 1900s interior alone, but what makes the place a must is its joie de vivre, as white-aproned waiters bustle around a fashion and media crowd. Silky-textured smoked salmon and candied lemon timbale and a tomato, cucumber and avocado mille-feuille with mozzarella are exemplary starters, and main courses include plump farm chicken served with a mini, creamy risotto and tender strips of duck in a delicious cherry sauce.

Le Temps des Cerises

31 rue de la Cerisaie, 4th (01.42.72.08.63). M° Sully Morland or Bastille. **Open** 7.30am-8pm Mon-Fri. Food served 11.30am-2.30pm. Closed Aug. **Average** €18.50. **Lunch menu** €12.50. **No credit cards. Map** p406 L7.

A warm greeting is dispatched by the flamboyantly moustached Mr Vimard, while Madame might be chatting with the regulars or helping the waitress clear off the tables. The good-value three-course lunch menu consists of salads, egg with mayonnaise, saucisson, chicken and chips, marinated fish, roasts, crème caramel and fruit tarts – nothing is spectacular, but this place worth coming back to.

International

Cuban: Calle 24

13 rue Beautreillis, 4th (01.42.72.38.34). M° Bastille. **Open** 6pm-11.30pm Mon-Fri, Sun; 6pm-midnight Fri, Sat. **Average** €22. **Prix fixe** €18. **Credit** MC, V. **Map** p402 L3.

This tiny Cuban bar-restaurant on a side-street near Bastille exudes the sunny personality of its manageress, Mechy. There are only five tables, and a bar where you can perch to drink some of the best mojitos in town. The excellent-value prix fixe starts with a selection of beautifully presented and piquant tapas, followed by such delights as tiny cod-stuffed squid in their ink or spicy, marinated lamb chops accompanied by okra ratatouille, fluffy rice and quimbombo, a kind of black bean stew.

North African: Le Souk

1 rue Keller, 11th (01.49.29.05.08). M° Ledru-Rollin or Bastille. **Open** 7.30-midnight Tue-Fri; noon-2.30pm, 7.30pm-midnight Sat; noon-2.30pm, 7.30-11pm Sun. Tea room 3-7pm. **Average** €27. **Prix fixe** €31, €35. **Credit** MC, V. **Wheelchair access. Map** p407 N7.

The pungent aromas that assail you on lifting the kilim at the entrance to this Moroccan restaurant are a quick fix for winter blues. Once settled at one of the mosaic tables, choose a full-bodied Algerian wine and nibble on the little dishes of spicy carrots and olives before ordering. The specialities here are sizzling hot, rich tagines and towering pots of couscous. The simple chicken tagine (stewed with dates and onions) is better than some of the more sumptuous sounding versions. There are two sittings at dinner – book ahead.

The Champs-Elysées & west

Bistros & brasseries

Le Boeuf sur le Toit

34 rue du Colisée, 8th (01.53.93.65.55). M° St-Philippe du Roule. **Open** noon-3pm, 7pm-1am daily. **Average** €38. **Prix fixe** €31. **Credit** AmEx, DC, MC, V. **Non-smoking room. Map** p401 E4.

Le Boeuf sur le Toit started out as a lively cabaret in the 1920s. Taken over by Groupe Flo in the mid-1980s, the brasserie was restored and enlarged, but echoes of 'les années folles' remain in the decor and the bubbly crowd. The huge bank of oysters is one of the highlights here, but there are also some satisfying Mediterranean-style dishes à la carte, alongside brasserie classics such as the andouillette de Troyes. The wine list offers a good choice, including carafes, and a range of prices.

Chez Léon

32 rue Legendre, 17th (01.42.27.06.82). M° Villiers. **Open** noon-2pm, 7.30-10pm Mon-Fri. Closed Aug. **Average** €40. **Prix fixe** €29. **Credit** AmEx, MC, V. **Map** p401 E2.

This old-fashioned spot is charming for its sincerity, fly-in-amber decor and carefully made, generous, rare bistro classics. The €29 prix fixe offers stunning value for money since it includes a better-than-decent half bottle of wine. What a treat to find homemade jambon persillé so full of taste. Main courses of smoked herring with an aubergine timbale and rumpsteak with chips are also excellent, and the waiters express an existential resignation worthy of a boulevard comedy.

Les Ormes

8 rue Chapu, 16th (01.46.47.83.98). M° Exelmans. **Open** 12.15-2pm, 7.45-10pm Tue-Sat. Closed Aug, first week in Jan. **Average** €45. **Prix fixe** €40.50 (dinner and Sat lunch). **Lunch menu** €26, €30. **Credit** AmEx, MC, V.

It's worth the trip to discover the cooking of talented young chef Stéphane Molé, whose delicious cooking is at once lusty and refined. The good-value prix fixe – three courses plus cheese from the fromagerie Alléosse – changes almost daily but typical dishes include quenelles de brochet (pike-perch dumplings) with sauce américaine, and boneless veal knuckle with gnocchi. Desserts are excellent, too.

Restaurant GR5

19 rue Gustave Courbet, 16th (01.47.27.09.84). M° Trocadéro. **Open** noon-3pm, 7-11pm Mon-Sat. **Average** €17. **Prix fixe** €20 (dinner only). **Lunch menu** €13.60, €16. **Credit** AmEx, MC, V. **Map** p400 B4.

Incongruously located among the chic boutiques of the 16th is this mock mountain refuge, named after the long-distance footpath that winds through the Jura to the Alps. The welcome is warm, and rib-sticking cheese and potatoes are the key ingredients in Savoyarde fare such as fondue queyrassienne (€35 for two people) – a three-cheese version of the Alpine classic with bacon and onions – raclette valaisienne, or tartiflette, a cheese, potato, and bacon concoction that will give you the energy, if you can get up from the table, to climb Mont Blanc.

Restaurant L'Entredgeu

83 rue Laugier, 17th (01.40.54.97.24). M° Porte de Champerret. **Open** noon-2pm, 8-10.15pm Tue-Sat. **Prix fixe** €28. **Lunch menu** €20. **Credit** MC, V. **Map** p400 C2.

This snug little bistro has been packed ever since it opened thanks to its excellent food at very reasonable prices. Young chef Philippe Tredgeu mastered this sure-fire formula while heading the kitchen at Chez Casimir. The blackboard menu changes daily, and might feature scallops cooked in their shells with salted butter and crumbled cauliflower, chewy, flavourful roast pork with braised chicory and lamb stuffed with foie gras. Homely desserts run to caramelised bananas and apple crumble.

Le Scheffer

22 rue Scheffer, 16th (01.47.27.81.11). M° Trocadéro. **Open** noon-2.30pm, 7.30-10.30pm Mon-Sat. Closed Sat in July and Aug, 25 Dec-2 Jan. **Average** €24. **Credit** AmEx, MC, V. **Map** p400 B5.

A stone's throw from busy Trocadéro, Le Scheffer is a tourist-free haven for French family-style dining. OK, so the French Sloanes with immaculate *enfants* aren't your average family, but their palates are reassuringly classical. Slather os à moëlle (unctuous marrow bone) on bread and follow with crispy confit de canard or salmon grilled à l'unilatéral (on one side). A mound of profiteroles or fluffy île flottante vie for top sweet. Be sure to book ahead.

Contemporary/trendy

Le 16 au 16

16 av Bugeaud, 16th (01.56.28.16.16). M° Victor Hugo. **Open** noon-2.30pm, 7.30-10.30pm Tue-Sat. **Average** €80. **Lunch menu** €35. **Credit** AmEx, DC, MC, V. **Wheelchair access. Map** p400 B4.

Ghislaine Arabian's former restaurant has been adroitly reinvented and even improved by the team she left behind. Chef Frédéric Simonin has a sassy creativity and excels in seasoning and timing, as shown in the fillet of beef in a rich shallot and red wine reduction with ratte potatoes, and sea bass with white beans and thyme. Dessert thrills include sublime figs poached in wine with pine nuts, and the assiette 16 sur 16, a spectacular study in chocolate and caramel. There's a brilliant wine list with a good selection of foreign bottles, and a buzzy crowd.

L'Envue

39 rue Boissy d'Anglas, 8th (01.42.65.10.49) M° Madeleine or Concorde. **Open** 8am-11pm Mon-Sat. Closed Aug. **Average** €35. **Credit** AmEx, DC, MC, V. **Map** p401 F4.

Even if you have an aversion to fashion restaurants, make an exception for this place, since the decor, food and service are really good in a part of Paris that desperately needed an option between the plastic corner café and haute cuisine. The menu is ideal for grazing, since you can order a tasting plate of seafood – sea bass sashimi, salmon tartare and rillettes, brandade and green beans – and a similar all-in veg plate, or go à la carte with a cheese-and-chive soufflé or tomatoes stuffed with chèvre, followed by steak tartare, chicken in lemon-saffron sauce, or langoustine risotto with mango.

Flora

36 av George V, 8th (01.40.70.10.49). M° George V. **Open** noon-2pm, 8-10.30pm Mon-Fri; 8-10.30pm Sat. Closed two weeks in Aug. **Average** €40. **Credit** AmEx, MC, V. **Wheelchair access. Map** p400 D4.

Engaging chef Flora Mikula runs this stylish new restaurant with floral-upon-floral wallpaper and 1940s-style glass wall sconces. Mikula, one of the best Provençal chefs in Europe, has broadened her horizons to include an international version of the south that visits Morocco, Turkey, India and Vietnam. Starters such as a croustillant de crabe in tomato soup, a main of lobster with broad beans and girolles in a jus of its own coral, and desserts including a macaroon in rose syrup with lime sorbet, are all wonderful, and the hospitality is southern too.

The best For brunch

Foody's Brunch Café

Does exactly what it says on the tin, in a very nice environment, too. *See p188.*

The Kitchen

Home-made grub to see off that morning-after queasiness. *See p188.*

Le Petit Marché

Scores high on relaxing atmosphere. See *p191.*

Pitchi Poï

A nice Jewish-food nosh-up to set you up for the day. Or week. *See p191.*

Maison Blanche

15 av Montaigne, 8th (01.47.23.55.99/ www.maison-blanche.fr). M° Alma-Marceau.
Open daily noon-2.30pm, 8pm-midnight. **Average** €100. **Lunch menu** €75. **Credit** AmEx, MC, V. **Map** p400 D5.

The Pourcel twins have done a brilliant job at reviving this trendy spot over the Théâtre des Champs-Elysées. The decor is slick and the menu is superb. It's the starters that star, with dishes as visually interesting as they are appetising: sea urchins stuffed with dressed crab and garnished with caviar; tarte Tatin of shallots with grilled red mullet, and mains such as sea bass baked with preserved lemons and roast duck fillet with a 'pastilla' of carrots and apricots. Desserts are brilliant, too.

Spoon, Food & Wine

14 rue de Marignan, 8th (01.40.76.34.44/ www.spoon.tm.fr). M° Franklin D. Roosevelt.
Open noon-2pm, 7-11pm Mon-Fri. Closed 14 July, last week in July and first three weeks in Aug. **Average** €75. **Prix fixe** €37 (dinner only). **Lunch menu** €37, €43. **Credit** AmEx, DC, MC, V. **Map** p401 E4.

While others have come and gone Spoon, with its mix-and-match menu, has stayed much the same, though it's not chock-full as it used to be and prices are decidedly cheeky. The Speedy Spoon, a recently introduced 40-minute lunch menu, draws on a different continent every day, providing a kind of upmarket TV dinner. The Spoon Top Five desserts include great cheesecake and nougat ice cream.

Haute cuisine

Alain Ducasse au Plaza Athénée

Hôtel Plaza Athénée, 25 av Montaigne, 8th (01.53.67.65.00/www.alain-ducasse.com). M° Alma-Marceau. **Open** 8-10.30pm Mon-Wed; 1-2.30pm, 8-10.30pm Thur, Fri. Closed last two weeks in Dec, mid-July to mid-Aug. **Average** €220. **Prix fixe** €190, €280. **Credit** AmEx, DC, MC, V. **Map** p400 D5.

Ducasse's spectacular cuisine continues to shine, and the service is probably the most professional, engaging and precise of any restaurant in Paris. From amuse-bouches of perfectly poached langoustines topped with caviar, and spider crab served in its orange shell beneath a bubbly foam of coral, through sautéed Breton lobster with asparagus tips and morels in a light sauce of its own cooking juices, a superb plate of cheeses and desserts that are an operatic triumph, this address provides an unforgettable dining experience. Book well ahead.

Le V

Hôtel Four Seasons George V, 31 av George V, 8th (01.49.52.70.00/www.fourseasons.com). M° George V. **Open** noon-2.30pm, 6.30-11pm daily. **Average** €180. **Prix fixe** €90, €190. **Lunch menu** €70. **Credit** AmEx, DC, MC, V. **Wheelchair access. Map** p400 D4.

A look at the menu replete with lobster, truffles, caviar, Bresse chicken, turbot and sea bass and you could believe it to be simply a roll-call of grandeur. Not so. Philippe Legendre does indeed produce luxury fare, but combined with precise execution, well-judged service and just a whiff of invention. The undoubted highlight is the lobster, wood-smoked in its shell and surrounded by a delicate, frothy morel sauce. The cheese trolley is full of well-aged specimens, among them the fabulous venaco de Corse.

Pierre Gagnaire

6 rue Balzac, 8th (01.58.36.12.50/ www.pierre-gagnaire.com). M° Charles de Gaulle-Etoile or George V. **Open** noon-2pm, 7.30-10pm Mon-Fri; 7.30-10pm Sun. Closed one week in Feb, last two weeks in July. **Average** €150. **Prix fixe** €195. **Lunch menu** €90. **Credit** AmEx, DC, MC, V. **Wheelchair access. Map** p400 D3.

There is only one Pierre Gagnaire. The man is a creative genius, and a meal here is a breathtaking adventure. Dishes are made up of several elements, served separately, which attempt to tell the story of a particular ingredient: 'la langoustine', for instance, featuring a pan-fried version with a lime tuile, a mousseline with lemongrass, a tartare with apple and ginger, and grilled, with thyme nougatine. Others illustrate surprising complementarities (veal and frogs, for example). The prix fixe offers an ideal introduction, with some nine separate courses. Book well ahead at this top table.

International

Japanese: Kifuné

44 rue St-Ferdinand, 17th (01.45.72.11.19). M° Argentine. **Open** 7-10pm Mon; noon-2pm, 7-10pm Tue-Sat. Closed two weeks in Aug, two weeks in winter. **Average** €35. **Lunch menu** €23.50. **Credit** MC, V. **Map** p400 C3.

The sleepy street is not very easy to find but that doesn't stop this small, understated restaurant from filling up with an entirely Japanese crowd. Starters include a sublime crab and prawn salad – real crab claws with squeaky fresh prawns and ever-so-thin marinated cucumber slices – and richly flavoured miso soup with clams. Sushi and sashimi are expensive but the quality is equivalently high.

Montmartre & Pigalle

Bistros & brasseries

Café Burq

6 rue Burq, 18th (01.42.52.81.27). M° Abbesses.
Open 8pm-midnight Tue-Sun. Closed Aug. **Average** €25. **Credit** MC, V. **Map** p401 H1.

Frédéric Peneau and Patrick Bouin have replaced the rustic decor of the former Moulin à Vins with minimalist shiny black tables, translucent plastic lighting fixtures and a framed jigsaw puzzle. Starters are more impressive than the mains –

competent meat-and-potatoes classics which can lack dominant flavour. But the point here is less about the food than the neighbourhoody scene.

A la Cloche d'Or

3 rue Mansart, 9th (01.48.74.48.88). M° Blanche. **Open** noon-2.30pm, 7pm-4am Mon-Fri; 7pm-4am Sat; 7pm-1.30am Sun. Closed Aug, Christmas. **Average** €35. **Prix fixe** €22 (dinner only), €25. **Lunch menu** €14, €20. **Credit** MC, V. **Map** p401 G2.

Actress Jeanne Moreau's parents opened the restaurant in 1928 and the boozy, smoky smell of decades of late-night revelry still hangs in the faux-rustic decor. The homemade French fare is all reliable – starters of snails, lamb's lettuce with warm chicken livers and the house chicken liver pâté; soothing confit de canard and zesty steak tartare.

L'Entracte

44 rue d'Orsel, 18th (01.46.06.93.41). M° Abbesses or Anvers. **Open** noon-2pm, 7-10.30pm Wed-Sat; noon-2pm Sun. Closed Aug. **Average** €40. **Credit** MC, V. **Map** p402 J2.

Stepping into this little bistro near the Sacré-Cœur, you can expect a local atmosphere. Start with a bowl of onion soup or a small salad and then move on the steak au poivre with a sauce so good it'll make your spine tingle. Soak that up with the homemade fries and move right on to the cheese. Then try the mousse au chocolat and a quick expresso and you should be on your way. Reserve or starve.

Le Petit Caboulot

6 pl Jacques-Froment, 18th (01.46.27.19.00). M° Guy-Moquet. **Open** noon-2pm, 8-11pm Mon-Fri; noon-2:30pm, 8-11pm Sat. Closed two weeks in Aug. **Average** €25. **Lunch menu** €10. **Credit** MC, V. **Wheelchair access**.

With all the trappings of a neighbourhood bistro you'll wish this were your local. A huge curved bar and a vast collection of old enamel adverts evoke a bygone era. Brik de chèvre aux pommes, a crisp pastry of apple and melting goat's cheese on a bed of salad; foie gras maison; succulent duck confit and haddock brandade are 100% comfort food. You'll think it can't get better until the tarte Tatin arrives.

Fish

La Table de Lucullus

129 rue Legendre, 17th (01.40.25.02.68). M° La Fourche or Guy Môquet. **Open** 12.30-2pm, 8-11pm Tue-Fri; 8-11pm Sat. Closed Aug, first week in May. **Average** €55. **Lunch menu** €20. **Credit** AmEx, DC, MC, V. **Wheelchair access. Non-smoking room. Map** p401 F1.

Self-taught Nicolas Vagnon brings a rare enthusiasm and inventiveness to French cuisine. Try an entire meal, for instance, themed around a particular fish. Eel is a Vagnon favourite or choose the variations on the sea bream: first a steaming cup of bouillon, then a very complex and fine dish of crusty bream belly with edible fins which taste like crisps. Mains are a lesson in simplicity, accompanied by choice vegetables and sublime olive oil. Inventive desserts include one creation that combines lemon peel, pear, olive oil, almonds and curry.

L'Envue. *See p197.*

International

African: Marie Louise

52 rue Championnet, 18th (01.46.06.86.55). M° Simplon. **Open** noon-4pm, 6pm-midnight Tue-Sat. **Average** €17. **Credit** MC, V.

Malik and Aïda took over a cryogenically-preserved bistro in 2002 and transformed it into this newcomer to the Senegalese food scene. Overflowing West African hospitality combines with generous portions of all the standard dishes – yassa, maffé, thieb'oudjen. More unusual dishes include kandia, a lamb, smoked fish and okra soup with a spicy, palm oil base (served Fridays only).

Indian: Les Jardins de Shalamar

174 rue Ordener, 18th (01.46.27.85.28). M° Guy Môquet. **Open** 11am-2.30pm, 6.30-11pm daily . **Average** €20. **Prix fixe** €17, €20. **Lunch menu** €9.15, €10.60. **Credit** MC, V.

On the dark side of Montmartre lies this little gem of an Indo-Pakistani eatery. The menu at first glance seems ordinary, but even the humble vegetable fritters and handmade samosas are exquisite, while freshness and vivid colours infuse cinnamony dahl, tangy green aubergine bagan bartha, and tender chicken jalfrezi stewed with tomatoes, green peppers and coriander. Finish with authentic puddings such as badam halwa, a mild, bright-orange semolina cake, and cardamom-flavoured Shalamar tea.

Portuguese: O Por do Sol

18 rue de la Fontaine-du-But, 18th (01.42.23.90.26). M° Lamarck-Caulaincourt. **Open** noon-2pm, 7-10:30pm Mon, Tue, Thur, Fri, Sun; 7-10:30pm Sat. Closed Aug. **Average** €25. **Prix fixe** €18.50. **Lunch menu** €10. **Credit** MC, V. **Map** p401 H1.

The Portuguese call bacalhau (salted cod), 'fiel amigo', faithful friend, and in José and Elesia's tiny dining room you'll find out why. You'll be hard pressed to imagine anything better than the morue du chef: cod layered with roasted onion, pepper, tomato and potato in a heaving casserole. Finish with pasteis de nata, delicious custard tarts.

Vegetarian

Au Grain de Folie

24 rue de la Vieuville, 18th (01.42.58.15.57). M° Abbesses. **Open** 12.30pm-2.30pm, 7.30-11.30pm Mon-Sat; noon-11pm Sun. **Average** €15. **Prix fixe** €8, €12, €15. **No credit cards. Map** p401 H1.

Seating just 14, Le Grain may not be the smallest restaurant in Paris, but there can't be too many other places where adult strangers can get this intimate without breaking the law. The menu, like the floor space, is limited but very cleverly and efficiently organised. Starters, such as avocat au roquefort, are nicely seasoned, and the potage de légumes is a heart-warming mini-meal, the constituent vegetables changing with the season. Main courses are dominated by salads.

North-east Paris

Bistros & brasseries

Bistro des Capucins

27 av Gambetta, 20th (01.46.36.74.75). M° Père-Lachaise or Gambetta. **Open** 12.15-1.45pm, 7.30-9.45pm Tue-Sat. Closed three weeks in Aug, one week at Christmas. **Prix fixe** €20, €25. **Credit** AmEx, MC, V. **Map** p400 D5.

Just across the street from Père Lachaise cemetery, this bistro has rapidly become one of the best in the area, attracting young arty types with its convivial buzz. Chef Gérard Fouché combines south-western heartiness with precision and creativity in dishes such as rabbit compote, an excellent gâteau of marinated sardines and aubergines, Aubrac steaks in shallot sauce and liver deglazed with sherry vinegar. Delicious desserts and reasonably priced wines make this a great destination.

La Cave Gourmande

10 rue du Général-Brunet, 19th (01.40.40.03.30). M° Botzaris. **Open** 12.15pm-2.30pm, 7.30-10.30pm Mon-Fri. Closed one week in Feb, three weeks in Aug. **Prix fixe** €32 (dinner only). **Lunch menu** €25. **Credit** MC, V.

American chef Mark Singer has cultivated a loyal following at this quiet address near the Buttes Chaumont with its obligatory three-course prix-fixe. Singer has an imaginative flair that makes each mouthful a discovery. Typically, a sensual marriage of flavours in the terrine d'artichauts with roast almonds and a zesty lemon sauce, and concentrated Provençal tastes in the red pepper and pesto garnish of the pintade, wrapped in thin slices of aubergine.

L'Hermitage

5 bd de Denain, 10th (01.48.78.77.09). M° Gare du Nord. **Open** noon-2.30pm, 7-11pm Mon-Fri; 7-11pm Sat. Closed two weeks in Aug. **Prix fixe** €23. **Credit** AmEx, DC, MC, V. **Non-smoking room. Map** p402 K2.

This bistro, hidden among the chains around Gare du Nord, contains the refined and surprisingly ambitious cooking of chef François Déage. The menu alone will have you salivating, and tastes don't disappoint in dishes such as a pressé of rosy foie gras interleaved with tender figs and house terrine of venison marinated in Muscadet. Mains include both standards and more adventurous choices – scallops with a dash of Egyptian pepper and steamed spinach and watercress, anyone? Make sure you save room for one of the prettily presented desserts.

Contemporary/trendy

Le Martel

3 rue Martel, 10th (01.47.70.67.56) M° Château d'Eau. **Open** noon-2.30pm, 8-11pm Mon-Fri; 8-11.30pm Sat. **Average** €30. **Lunch menu** €17. **Credit** DC, MC, V. **Map** p402 K3.

Anyone looking for proof that the formerly shabby 10th arrondissement is surfing a new wave of hip need go no further than this hybrid French-Algerian bistro. Amidst a decor of globe lamps, framed photos, soft lighting and bare wood tables and floors, the hip crowd runs to photographer Peter Beard, Vivienne Westwood and John Galliano, along with models, stylists. journalists and wannabes. Wannabes like us, for example.

Favela Chic

18 rue du Fbg-du-Temple, 11th (01.40.21.38.14/ www.favelachic.com). M° République. **Open** Mon-Sat 8pm-2am. **Average** €30. **Credit** MC, V. **Wheelchair access. Map** p402 L4.

Be sure to get to this Brazilian cantina early as Favela Chic doesn't take reservations and is permanently packed. The shabby chic interior full of foliage, flowers and kitsch artefacts is welcoming if a little overwhelming, while the buzz in the open-plan kitchen contributes to the frenetic atmosphere. The menu has recently been scaled back to just three dishes (beans and rice, chicken and vegetarian lasagne). But the food isn't really the point; Favela Chic is more about shaking your booty (not too much, otherwise you'll get hiccups). To this end, the blinding mojitos are indispensable.

International

North America: Blue Bayou

111-113 rue St-Maur, 11th (01.43.55.87.21/ www.bluebayou-bluebillard.com). M° Parmentier. **Open** restaurant 7.30pm-2am, bar 11am-2am, daily. **Average** €26. **Prix fixe** €15-€24. **Credit** AmEx, MC, V. **Wheelchair access**. **Map** p403 M5.

With 13 tons of tree trunks and one giant stuffed alligator, eating here is like a trip to a hospitable log cabin on the Mississippi Delta. Cajun cuisine is famous for its hearty one-pot meals. The jambalaya is a fiery mix of crawfish, spiced sausage, chicken, peppers, rice and many more ingredients; the gumbo (seafood and game soup) deliciously spiced with okra and ground sassafras leaf.

Caribbean: Chez Dom

34 rue de Sambre et Meuse, 10th (01.42.01.59.80). M° Colonel Fabien. **Open** noon-2.30pm, 7pm-midnight Tue-Fri; 7pm-midnight Sat, Sun. **Credit** MC, V. **Map** p403 M3.

Like a little beach shack, Chez Dom is decked out with strawberry-print tablecloths, fruit-drop lights and yellowing school maps. The entrance is through the kitchen, where two luscious, big-haired ladies work behind an array of fruits preserved in rum. The cooking drifts somewhere between Senegal and the French Caribbean – don't miss the fabulous, spicy gambas and the slow-cooked, African maffé that falls off the bone right onto your orgasm gland. 'Sexy chocolate' more than lives up to the promise of its name. It's sexy, and it's made from chocolate.

The Latin Quarter & the 13th

Bistros & brasseries

L'Avant-Goût

26 rue Bobillot, 13th (01.53.80.24.00). M° Place d'Italie. **Open** noon-2pm, 7.30-11pm Tue-Fri. Closed one week in Jan, one week in May, three weeks in Aug/Sept. **Prix fixe** €26. **Lunch menu** €12. **Credit** MC, V.

This is one of the best and most generous modern bistros on the Left Bank. Chef Christophe Beaufront and his wife run the restaurant like a sort of all-comers party every night, but service is commendably professional and prompt. With starters of tuna tartare with roasted vegetables, herby cold spinach soup garnished with poppyseed-coated croutons, Beaufront's signature dish of pot-au-feu de cochon you really can't go wrong, and there are some delicious wines to accompany it.

Chez Gladines

30 rue des Cinq-Diamants, 13th (01.45.80.70.10). M° Corvisart. **Open** noon-2.30pm, 7pm-midnight Mon-Fri; noon-2.30pm, 7pm-1am Sat, Sun. Closed Aug. **Average** €15. **Lunch menu** €10. **No credit cards**.

Chez Gladines is in the Butte-aux-Cailles – a series of villagey streets hidden among the huge housing blocks south of Place d'Italie. In this little oasis, you could almost pretend to be somewhere in the Pays Basque, with its regional food, drinks and flag on the wall. Most diners go for the giant salads served in earthenware bowls with a choice of ingredients including jambon de Bayonne and just about every duck part imaginable. Desserts are reasonable. This is a no-frills experience, but completely enjoyable.

Chez Paul

22 rue de la Butte-aux-Cailles, 13th (01.45.89.22.11). M° Place d'Italie or Corvisart. **Open** noon-2.30pm, 7.30pm-midnight daily. Closed Christmas. **Average** €35. **Credit** MC, V. **Wheelchair access**.

Chez Paul is a beacon to professional types who lurk in the quirky 13th arrondissement, its white-cloth-and-wood approach offering a chic alternative to other offbeat spots along the strip. Tradition takes pride of plate (pot-au-feu, beef knuckle, bone marrow – in fact, bones galore) and you can eat your way from one end of a beast to the other. Seafood also makes an appearance on the blackboard menu.

Le Pré Verre

8 rue Thénard, 5th (01.43.54.59.47). M° Maubert-Mutualité. **Open** 7.30-10.30pm Mon; noon-2pm, 7.30-10.30pm Tue-Sat. Closed first two weeks in Aug. **Prix fixe** €24 (dinner only). **Lunch menu** €12. **Credit** MC, V. **Non-smoking room. Map** p406 J7.

As soon as you've tucked into a superb starter you'll understand why this new bistro-à-vins has become a roaring hit. The blackboard menu changes daily, but might include ravioli stuffed with snails in a

La Table de Michel

green aniseed-spiked cream sauce, roast suckling pig and a succulent veal steak accompanied by a purée of celeriac, potato and almonds. Desserts are lovely to behold and delicious.

Restaurant Marty

20 av des Gobelins, 5th (01.43.31.39.51/ www.marty-restaurant.com). M° Les Gobelins. **Open** noon-midnight daily. **Average** €40. **Prix fixe** €35. **Credit** AmEx, DC, MC, V. **Non-smoking room. Map** p406 K10.

Marty is a pure art deco brasserie, with luxurious curves, leopardskin-print chairs and murals. Were it not for the food and efficient staff you might think this was a Prohibition-era jazz club. A fishy menu includes a rich crabmeat and avocado starter, salmon and cod brochette with corn cake, and a mixed grill of tuna, sea bream and salmon – all competently prepared, and the creamy, fresh fruit-topped rice pudding is big enough to share.

La Table de Michel

13 quai de la Tournelle, 5th (01.44.07.17.57). M° Maubert-Mutualité. **Open** 7-11pm Mon; noon-2.30pm, 7-10.30pm Tue-Sat. Closed Aug. **Average** €35. **Prix fixe** €27. **Lunch menu** €19. **Credit** AmEx, MC, V. **Non-smoking room. Map** p406 K7.

Chef Michel does a personal take on Franco-Italian fusion cuisine. An artistic tomato and mozzarella salad and a luscious feuilleté d'escargots are successful starters. Mains include a pungent cep risotto and a winning tagliatelle au foie gras, served in a filo pastry basket. Brie stuffed with roquefort and walnuts is a clever variant on the Italian mascarpone/gorgonzola version, or there's the classic creamy panna cotta with a bitter cherry coulis.

Fish

L'Huître et Demie

80 rue Mouffetard, 5th (01.43.37.98.21). M° Place Monge. **Open** noon-2pm, 7-11pm daily. **Average** €46. **Prix fixe** €17, €28. **Credit** AmEx, DC, MC, V. **Non-smoking room. Map** p406 J8.

The €28 menu is no half-hearted effort here – it includes a choice of nine oysters, in keeping with the restaurant's name. Non-oyster eaters might enjoy the seafood salad, a generous heaping of prawns arranged on greens, with an unusual and tasty kiwi sorbet. Just as satisfying are main courses such as scallops roasted with garlic and olive oil, and salmon and monkfish cooked with butter and cream.

Haute cuisine

La Tour d'Argent

15-17 quai de la Tournelle, 5th (01.43.54.23.31/ www.tourdargent.com). M° Pont Marie or Cardinal Lemoine. **Open** 7.30-9pm Tue; noon-1.30pm, 7.30-9pm Wed-Sun. **Average** €180. **Lunch menu** €65. **Credit** AmEx, DC, MC, V. **Wheelchair access. Non-smoking room. Map** p406 K7.

Aside from the thrill of being handed a numbered postcard if you order the signature mallard, La Tour can boast a fabulous view over the Seine. The €65 lunch menu makes this just about affordable, too, with dishes such as quenelles de brochet (fluffy pike-perch dumplings), and caneton rôti Pierre Elby – duck à l'orange served on apple compote, with a spinach-and-cream feuilleté on the side. Desserts are a highlight here.

International

American: Breakfast in America

17 rue des Ecoles, 5th (01.43.54.50.28/ www.breakfast-in-america.com). M° Cardinal Lemoine. **Open** 8.30am-midnight Mon-Wed; 8am-2am Thur-Sat; 9am-5pm Sun. **Average** €10. **Prix fixe** €11.50 (lunch only), €13.95 (weekend brunch only). **Credit** MC, V. **Map** p406 J7.

the perfume of frying fat infuses the air, and the waiter swings by to ask if you'd like a coffee refill: yep, this could almost be a truck stop somewhere off the Interstate. For breakfast (until 3pm), choose from bagels and cream cheese, eggs any style with bacon and hash browns, pancakes and a crispy French toast (both available with real maple syrup). For lunch there are club sandwiches and burgers.

Chinese: Tricotin

15 av de Choisy, 13th (01.45.84.74.44). M° Porte de Choisy. **Open** 9am-11pm daily. **Average** €15. **Credit** MC, DC, V. **Wheelchair access**.

Tricotin's twin dining rooms – either side of a passageway – have an air of downtown Singapore. Windows lined with racks of whole glazed ducks are a promising start, but better by far are the dim sum, great-value meal-in-one soups and vermicelli salads. Across the way, the Malaysian/Thai half of the operation serves a fine choice of Thai curries, satays and fish dishes. Don't miss the oh-so-Asian drinks – sweet red beans mashed in milk, or fresh coconut milk.

Greek: Mavrommatis

5 rue du Marché des Patriarches, 5th (01.43.31.17.17/ www.mavrommatis.fr). M° Censier Daubenton. **Open** noon-2.15pm, 7-11pm Tue-Sun. Closed Aug. **Average** €37. **Prix fixe** €28.50. **Lunch menu** €18.50. **Credit** AmEx, MC, V. **Wheelchair access**. **Map** p406 J9.

If you've tasted the fabulous modern cooking you can find in parts of Athens, you'll appreciate what the Mavrommatis brothers have been doing for some time now in the Latin Quarter. Here you'll find the best dolmades ever tasted, along with sophisticated takes on Greek classics such as aphelia with a sweet fruity sauce topped with a thin slice of salty kaseri cheese from Metsovo.

Seychelles: Au Coco de Mer

34 bd St-Marcel, 5th (01.47.07.06.64). M° St-Marcel or Les Gobelins. **Open** 7.30-10.30pm Mon; 11.30am-2.30pm, 7.30-10.30pm Tue-Sat. Closed two weeks in Aug. **Average** €37. **Prix fixe** €30. **Credit** AmEx, MC, V. **Wheelchair access**. **Map** p406 K9.

This small enclave of the Seychelles sends you home with joy in your stomach and the beach in your shoes – the wooden beach cabin room out front has a carpet of luxuriously soft sand. Seated among the bourgeois diners you'll be swept away to paradise by the potent rum cocktails and fresh, tangy dishes such as tuna tartare with grated ginger and lime juice, filet de bourgeois (a tropical fish), and octopus in a gentle coconut milk curry.

Couldn't stand the heat

On 13 February 2003 the *Guide Gault-Millau: France 2003*, a well-known restaurant guide, was published. One of the restaurants reviewed, the Côte d'Or in Burgundy, was owned by Bernard Loiseau, a star chef-cum-businessman who also owned three restaurants in Paris. The Côte d'Or was awarded 17 points out of a possible 20. Its review noted that it was 'a great old favourite, but nothing more'. Twelve days later, Loiseau shot himself.

Cue an outbreak of self-dramatising feyness that shows you the high regard in which star chefs hold themselves here (funnily enough, bus drivers who fall on their swords don't seem to attract the same sort of publicity as suicidal cooks). Loiseau's fellow restaurateur Paul Bocuse was in no doubt about why he had pulled the trigger. '*Gault-Millau* killed him', he whimpered, before adding that the publicity resulting from the suicide certainly wouldn't harm the guide's sales profile. What a comfort Bocuse's verdict (and its message that *Gault-Millau* ratings meant more to Loiseau than his family) must have been to the wife and children left behind.

Loiseau's death was not caused by the *Gault-Millau* guide. It may have been a result of the way the restaurant game has evolved in France. Big business is taking over, and the kind of skills involved in whipping up a *soufflé* aren't necessarily accompanied by the psychological firepower needed to keep shareholders at bay. Loiseau was involved in a big way. His hotel, restaurant and publishing group *'Loiseau – Art de vivre et gastronomie'* was quoted on the French stock exchange.

Recently the business had started to wobble. Loiseau worked himself ceaselessly trying to keep everybody – the customers, the shareholders and the critics – happy. It wasn't *Gault-Millau* that killed him, so much as the system of which that guide is a small part. Indeed, Loiseau gave an indication of his concerns just a couple of weeks before he died when he said, 'I'm OK with the frogs' legs – it's the stock exchange I can't handle'. Being a restaurateur in Paris these days ain't no piece of cake.

Vegetarian

Le Grenier de Notre-Dame

18 rue de la Bûcherie, 5th (01.43.29.98.29/ www.legrenierdenotredame.com). M° St-Michel or Maubert-Mutualité. **Open** noon-2.30pm, 7.30-11pm Mon-Thur; noon-2.30pm, 7.30-11.30pm Fri, Sat; noon-3pm Sun. Closed New Year. **Average** €22. **Prix fixe** €14.50 (dinner only). **Lunch menu** €12.50. **Credit** MC, V. **Non smoking. Map** p406 J7.

Plants intertwined around the spiral staircase give this place a welcoming feel. If you think vegetarian food is all lentils and chickpeas you'll be pleasantly surprised. Take starters of tempura-style vegetable fritters and miso soup (though it bears little resemblance to true Japanese miso). Main dishes include ratatouille with wheat kebab, and seasonal vegetables fried with soya, tofu and white beans. Light desserts are good and there's organic Côtes du Rhône by the pitcher (€7.10 for 50cl).

Les Quatre et Une Saveurs

72 rue du Cardinal-Lemoine, 5th. (01.43.26.88.80). M° Cardinal-Lemoine. **Open** noon-2.30pm, 7-10.30pm Mon-Thur, Sun; noon-2.30pm Fri; 7-10.30pm Sat. Closed Aug. **Average** €22. **Prix fixe** €25. **Credit** MC, V. **Non smoking. Map** p406 K8.

This is healthy eating at its most serious; they don't use microwaves or freezers, they filter the table water and though they do serve fish, they steer clear of farmed fish – and eating here is a treat. Organic vegetables, juices and soups are delicious and mains come as beautiful displays of colours and textures that taste equally good. Each protein, be it fish, tofu, tempeh or seitan (vegetable meat substitute) comes with plenty of vegetables.

St-Germain & Odéon

Bistros & brasseries

Allard

41 rue St-André-des-Arts, 6th (01.43.26.48.23). M° Odéon or RER St-Michel. **Open** noon-2.30pm, 7-11pm Mon-Sat. Closed three weeks in Aug. **Average** €50. **Prix fixe** €30.50. **Lunch menu** €22.90. **Credit** AmEx, DC, MC, V. **Map** p406 H7.

Allard has a delicious pre-war feel, and its kitchen sends out the kind of glorious Gallic grub that everyone dreams of finding in Paris. Lyonnais sausage studded with pistachios, served with potato salad, roast shoulder of lamb, roast Bresse chicken with ceps or roast duck with olives are superb classics. Finish up with the tarte fine aux pommes.

La Bastide Odéon

7 rue Corneille, 6th (01.43.26.03.65/www-bastide-odeon.com). M° Odéon. **Open** 12.30-2pm, 7.30-10.30pm Tue-Sat. Closed three weeks in Aug, 25 Dec-2 Jan. **Average** €38. **Credit** AmEx, MC, V. **Wheelchair access. Map** p406 H7.

Gilles Azuelos' stylish and reliable modern cooking skims along the Mediterranean seaboard from Spain to Italy using herbs that recall the perfumes of the maquis. Gazpacho laced with ricotta and anchovy and avocado bruschetta are typical starters. For the mains there is plenty of fish and a pasta option that will keep non-meat eaters happy, while carnivores can salivate over the lapin confit or poulet fermier with baby potatoes in their skins. Desserts are fruity and fashionable. Service is friendly and relaxed.

Brasserie Lipp

151 bd St-Germain, 6th (01.45.48.53.91). M° St-Germain-des-Prés. **Open** noon-1am daily. **Average** €40. **Credit** AmEx, DC, MC, V. **Non-smoking room. Map** p406 H7.

Saunter in with boundless confidence, a whiff of metropolitan attitude and a sense of humour, and odds are you'll get a good table in the see-and-be-seen downstairs front portion of this legendary brasserie. You'll eat well too: pistachio-studded pâté en croûte, steak tartare and steaks are excellent, the wine list offers a nice treat or two.

L'Epi Dupin

11 rue Dupin, 6th (01.42.22.64.56). M° Sèvres-Babylone. **Open** 7-10.30pm Mon; noon-2.30pm, 7-10.30pm Tue-Fri. Closed Aug. **Prix fixe** €29.80. **Lunch menu** €19.80. **Credit** MC, V. **Map** p405 G8.

Owner-chef François Pasteau is still on form, combining terroir with invention. For mains, a 'mille-feuille' of excellent-quality sea bream sandwiched with tangy black pudding on a bed of savoy cabbage works remarkably well. Desserts are satisfying, too: salivate over the combination of orange ice cream and a gently caramelised spiced pain perdu. The tables are a bit crammed-in, but staff are friendly and the price is unbelievable for the quality.

Le Petit Saint-Benoît

4 rue St-Benoît, 6th (01.42.60.27.92). M° St-Germain-des-Prés. **Open** noon-2.30pm, 7-10.30pm Mon-Sat. Closed Aug. **Average** €16. **No credit cards. Map** p405 H6.

Budget fare in St-Germain? There's hope for civilisation. Layers of paint on the wainscoting, a brazen refusal to take credit cards or reservations, and a bent coat hanger holding open the door prove Le Petit Saint-Benoît has not given in to fashion. You'll find all the old-school French favourites: hard-boiled egg and mayonnaise, rabbit terrine, roast chicken and fruit clafoutis and there's even a bell that rings when the food is ready to be unceremoniously plopped before you.

Contemporary/trendy

Le Bélier

13 rue des Beaux-Arts, 6th (01.44.41.99.01/www.l-hotel.com). M° St-Germain-des-Prés. **Open** 12.30-2.15pm, 7.30-10.15pm Tue-Sun. Closed Aug. **Average €55. Lunch menu** €24.50. **Credit** AmEx, DC, MC, V. **Map** p405 H6.

In the lush Jacques Garcia decor of L'Hôtel, where Oscar Wilde expired, this intimate restaurant is a clubby hit with surprisingly excellent food. The lavishly upholstered Napoléon III room is populated by neighbourhood editors and art and antiques dealers at noon, and well-heeled locals in the evening. Expect high-quality French comfort food, with the odd cosmopolitan touch – Iberian ham with fresh tomato-rubbed bread, or gazpacho.

Ze Kitchen Galerie

4 rue des Grands-Augustins, 6th (01.44.32.00.32). M° St-Michel. **Open** noon-2pm, 7-11pm Mon-Fri; 7-11pm Sat. **Average** €39. **Lunch menu** €21-€32. **Credit** AmEx, DC, MC, V. **Wheelchair access. Map** p405 H6.

William Ledeuil's contemporary space feels a bit like a bachelor's loft. His beautifully presented dishes subtly draw on ingredients from around the globe. The three-course €32 menu with a glass of wine and coffee is the way to go: crab-and-prawn-filled cucumber with green mango and papaya matchsticks, salmon marinated in rice vinegar with a passion fruit vinaigrette and scorpion fish a la plancha are typical of the refreshing approach.

Fish

La Méditérranée

2 pl de l'Odéon, 6th (01.43.26.02.30/ www.lamediterranee.com). M° Odéon. **Open** noon-2.30pm, 7.30-11pm daily. Closed 25 Dec, 1 Jan. **Average** €50. **Prix fixe** €25, €29. **Credit** AmEx, DC, MC, V. **Non-smoking room. Map** p405 H7.

Opened in the 1940s by artist-loving Jean Subrenat, La Méditérranée has Cocteau doodlings on the dinner plates and murals by Vertès and Bérard. A young team is at the helm and the good prix fixe includes delicacies such as a petit tian niçois de légumes, golden-crusted merlu (hake) and a satisfying bouillabaisse. Finish with the cooling nougat ice cream with mango sauce.

International

Italian: Il Vicolo

34 rue Mazarine, 6th (01.43.25.01.11). M° Mabillon or Odéon. **Open** 12.30-2.30pm, 8-11pm Mon-Sat. **Average** €40. **Lunch menu** €21. **Credit** AmEx, MC, V. **Map** p405 H6.

Antonio Procopio's restaurant, now run by his Tuscan sous-chef, continues to pull in an arty and international crowd. The dining room feels a bit clubby, but service is prompt and polite. The homemade spaghetti with pesto sauce, green beans and potato slivers, a Genoan classic, is delicious, as is the tuna steak cooked in balsamic vinegar. All the pastas are freshly made and perfectly sauced.

Spanish: La Catalogne

4-8 cour du Commerce St-André, 6th (01.55.42.16.19/ www.catalogne.infotourisme.com). M° Odéon. **Open** noon-3pm, 7-11pm Tue-Fri; noon-3pm, 7-11pm Sat. Closed Aug. **Average** €25. **Prix fixe** €14, €18. **Lunch menu** €11. **Credit** AmEx, DC, MC, V. **Map** p405 H7.

Tapas are weighted towards the potato; better is the main menu with starters of warm spinach sautéed with raisins and a delicious if splashy salad of tiny broad beans, young salad leaves and serrano ham. 'Land and sea' is a delicious concoction of stewed, jointed chicken, tiny octopus, mussels and a giant prawn in a thick, orange fish sauce begging to be sopped up by the mashed potato. Helpings are vast.

The 7th & the 15th

Bistros & brasseries

L'Ami Jean

27 rue Malar, 7th (01.47.05.86.89). M° Invalides. **Open** noon-2pm, 7pm-midnight Tue-Sat. Closed Aug. **Average** €35. **Prix fixe** €28. **Credit** MC, V. **Map** p404 D6.

This long-running Basque address has suddenly become a huge hit after the arrival of La Régalade's former sous-chef, Stéphane Jégo. Starters are heavenly. Among the mains, tender veal shank comes de-boned with a lovely side of baby onions, and house-salted cod is soaked, sautéed and doused with an elegant vinaigrette. Desserts and cheeses aren't quite as good, still, there is a great wine list. A party atmosphere sets in as the night grows long.

Au Bon Accueil

14 rue Monttessuy 7th (01.47.05.46.11). M° Alma-Marceau. **Open** noon-2.15pm, 7.30-10.30pm Mon-Fri. **Average** €40. **Prix fixe** €29. **Lunch menu** €25. **Credit** MC, V. **Map** p404 D6.

Jacques Lacipière's bistro is one of the good deals of the 7th arrondissement. The pleasantly redone dining room, with big windows and a stone satyr, provides the setting for an updating of French classics such as raw marinated sardines sandwiched between tiny, new spring leeks, rosé veal kidneys on a bed of fresh spinach, and a rich braised beef cheek in deep red wine sauce. A relaxed atmosphere and courteous staff make this an address to cherish.

Café Max

7 av de la Motte Picquet, 7th (01.47.05.57.66). M° La Tour-Maubourg. **Open** 7.30-11pm Mon; noon-2.30pm, 7.30-11pm Tue-Sat. Closed Aug. **Prix fixe** €16, €20 (dinner only). **No credit cards. Wheelchair access. Map** p405 E6.

Perhaps the only genuine resident of the area, Max, originally from the south-west, believes food should be served with gushing love. Shouldn't, when you think about it, everything? The solid €20 menu lands you a huge bucket salad full of foie gras, tuna, apples and tomatoes draped in a tangy curry dressing, and an entire duck terrine from which you hack off your own portion. The grilled Lyonnais sausage with creamy, nutmeggy potatoes and the stocky cassoulet are enough to feed a football team, and a ladies' one at that.

Au Bon Accueil

Le Clos des Gourmets

16 av Rapp, 7th (01.45.51.75.61). M° Alma-Marceau/RER Pont de L'Alma. **Open** 12.15-2pm, 7.15-11 pm Tue-Sat. Closed Aug. **Average** €30. **Prix fixe** €30 (dinner only). **Lunch menu** €24, €27. **Credit** MC, V. **Map** p400 D5.

This small, elegant address three minutes from the Eiffel Tower takes its food very seriously. Pompous it's not, however. Fresh market salad tossed in walnut oil, and hare terrine are appetising starters; mains might include roast sea bass on a bed of puréed potatoes and black truffles, or spring chicken topped with pine nuts, mushrooms and crunchy roast potatoes. Avocado millefeuille in a tangy orange sauce is an unusual dessert surprise.

Le Père Claude

51 av de la Motte-Picquet, 15th (01.47.34.03.05). M° La Motte-Picquet-Grenelle. **Open** noon-2pm, 7.30-10.30pm daily. **Average** €50. **Prix fixe** €24, €29. **Lunch menu** €20 (Mon-Fri). **Credit** AmEx, MC, V. **Non-smoking room. Map** p404 D7.

The sleekness of the decor at this executive favourite (Chirac's photo is on the wall with Gregory Peck, Jospin was spotted lunching here) belies basic if well-executed bistro food, some of it roasted right behind the zinc-and-marquetry bar. The mixed grill of chicken, beef, pork and boudin, and the poulet rôti moelleux, are both accompanied by silky mashed potatoes. The green apple sorbet makes a suitably light dessert and the light-filled, glassed-in terrace jutting on to the pavement reserved for non-smokers is a real plus.

Contemporary/trendy

L'Atelier de Joël Robuchon

5 rue de Montalembert, 7th (01.42.22.56.56). M° Rue du Bac. **Open** 11.30am-3pm, 6.30pm-midnight daily. **Average** €55. **Credit** MC, V. **Wheelchair access. Non smoking. Map** p405 G6.

The best-known gastronaut in France is back with a Parisian take on a New York coffee shop-cum-sushi bar. The assortment of the little tasting plates is the most inventive part of the menu, including veal sweetbreads skewered with a bay leaf twig and a tart of mackerel fillet, parmesan and olives. Robuchon's formula of 'la convivialité d'abord' is mainly working, but the system of having to turn up early to bag a table for later on has been known to cause angst among the ardent foodies who come here.

Quinze

8 rue Nicolas-Charlet, 15th (01.42.19.08.59). M° Pasteur. **Open** noon-2.30pm, 7.30-10.30pm Mon-Thur; noon-2.30pm, 7.30-11.30pm Fri, Sat. Closed ten days in Aug. **Average** €37. **Lunch menu** €26. **Credit** AmEx, MC, V. **Map** p405 E9.

Linen-dressed tables, food photos on cocoa-coloured walls and dark wood chairs are the decor, and though the dance soundtrack is a bit too agitated for a relaxed meal, the menu is very appealing. Scallops on a bed of cabbage in a sauce of 'smoked' milk, and John Dory cooked with calf's foot, both accompanied by a bowl of mashed ratte potatoes, are first-rate.

R

8 rue de la Cavalerie, 15th (01.45.67.06.85) M° La Motte-Piquet-Grenelle. **Open** noon-2.30pm, 8-11.30pm Mon-Sat; brunch 11am-4.30pm Sun. **Average** €40. **Credit** AmEx, MC, V. **Map** p404 D7.

The welcome at this hip new spot in a penthouse space is warm and the service good. The Eiffel Tower view adds some real drama to a very attractive setting with stone walls, moulded pedestal chairs and white laminate tables. Chef Eric Danel does a seasonal menu with dishes such as sautéed girolles to start, a fine navarin of lamb with preserved lemons and imaginative desserts

Thiou

49 quai d'Orsay, 7th (01.45.51.58.58). M° Invalides. **Open** noon-2pm, 8-10.30pm Mon-Fri; 8-10.30pm Sat. Closed Aug. **Average** €60. **Credit** AmEx, MC, V. **Map** p401 E5.

The owner-chef of this modish Thai subscribes to a simple mantra: super-fresh, high-quality ingredients prepared with care and flair. Start with juicy, peanutty chicken satay or a prawn soup heavy with lemongrass, and follow with kae phad prik wan, tender cubes of lamb sautéed with red and green pepper, or grilled John Dory fillets with spinach and bean sprouts. The wine list is reasonable, the service attentive and polite, and the setting cosy.

Branch: Le Petit Thiou, 3 rue Surcouf (01.40.62.96.70).

Fish

Le Divellec

107 rue de l'Université, 7th (01.45.51.91.96/www.le-divellec.com). M° Invalides. **Open** noon-2pm, 7.30-9.30pm Mon-Fri. Closed 25 Dec-1 Jan, 1 May, Aug. **Average** €110. **Lunch menu** €50, €65. **Credit** AmEx, DC, MC, V. **Non-smoking room. Map** p401 E5.

Often in restaurants of this calibre, you get the proverbial fish eye when you opt for the cheapest prix fixe – not here. Delicious appetisers of tiny grey North Sea shrimp, fresh marinated sardine and accras (salt cod fritters) are whisked to the table before you choose from a menu that includes an excellent fish soup, Cancale oysters, impeccably cooked fish mains and superb desserts.

Haute cuisine

L'Arpège

84 rue de Varenne, 7th (01.45.51.47.33/www.alain-passard.com). M° Varenne. **Open** 12.30-2pm, 8-10pm Mon-Fri. **Average** €250. **Prix fixe** €300. **Credit** AmEx, DC, MC, V. **Map** p405 F6.

Alain Passard's devotees are willing to overlook the surprisingly cramped conditions for his unique way with food. Passard prefers pared-down simplicity to culinary acrobatics, but he is a genius. Is his now-famous beetroot, baked in a pyramid of coarse grey Guérande sea salt, worth €60 for two golf-ball-sized roots? That depends on how much €60 means to you. This is a cult address for those who take their food very seriously indeed.

International

Iranian: Cheminée Royale

22 bis rue de l'Ingénieur-Robert-Keller, 15th (01.45.79.44.22). M° Charles Michel. **Open** daily noon-3pm, 7.30pm-midnight. **Average** €30. **Lunch menu** €13 (Mon-Fri). **Credit** AmEx, MC, V. **Map** p404 B8.

A magnet for Iranian émigrés, the Cheminée Royale has two menus – the one in Farsi serving exotic dishes such as fesenjan (poultry in pomegranate and walnut sauce) and gormeh sabzi (meat stew packed with fresh herbs) – ask for them, even if you don't speak the language. Otherwise, the hearty meat brochettes are served with out-of-this-world fluffy Iranian rice.

Spanish: Bellota-Bellota

18 rue Jean-Nicot, 7th (01.53.59.96.96). M° Pont de l'Alma or La Tour Maubourg. **Open** Tue-Fri 10am-3.30pm, 5.30-11pm; Sat 10am-11pm. Closed two weeks in Aug. **Average** €40. **Credit** DC, MC, V. **Map** p405 E6.

A bellota is an acorn in Spanish, a reference to the preferred food of the black, free-grazing Iberico race of pig, which produces this ham. The restaurant serves five different Bellota-Bellota (their trademark) hams from four different regions of Spain. The ham is served, along with manchego ewe's milk cheese from La Mancha province, anchovies, olives, pickled garlic and pimentos, and tuna, as part of various tasting platters. A first-rate assortment of Spanish wines is served by the bottle or glass.

The best Newcomers

Aux Lyonnais
Rescued from ruin by Alain Ducasse. *See p188.*

Le Pré Verre
Spiced-up French fare. *See p203.*

L'Ami Jean
Basque-ing in renewed glory. *See p208.*

L'Atelier de Joël Robuchon
Worth the queue. *See p211.*

R
Stylish setting, stunning Eiffel Tower view. *See p211.*

Bellota-Bellota
Hamming it up, Spanish-style. *See p212.*

Apollo
Comfort food in space-age surroundings. *See p213.*

Montparnasse & beyond

Bistros & brasseries

L'O à la Bouche

124 bd du Montparnasse, 14th (01.56.54.01.55). M° Vavin. **Open** noon-3pm, 7-11pm Tue-Thur; noon-3pm, 7pm-midnight Fri, Sat. Closed three weeks in Aug. **Average** €50. **Prix fixe** (dinner only) €26-€31. **Lunch menu** €16, €19. **Credit** AmEx, MC, V. **Non-smoking room. Map** p405 G9.

Guy Savoy-trained Franck Paquier was one of the pioneers of the modern bistro movement. Seasonality is at the heart of his cooking with a reasonably-priced menu-carte – winter brings a satisfying chestnut soup with lots of ceps and truffle oil, a homely lamb shank braised with rosemary, tomatoes, Tarbais and coco beans and a pineapple cake with banana sorbet and rum-infused raisins. Fish ranges from the fashionable to the classical.

La Régalade

49 av Jean-Moulin, 14th (01.45.45.68.58). M° Alésia. **Open** 11am-2pm, 7-11pm Mon-Thur; 11am-2pm, 7pm-midnight Fri, Sat. Closed Aug. **Prix fixe** €30. **Credit** MC, V.

It still takes a substantial effort to secure a booking at Yves Camdeborde's rustic, convivial bistro, but you'll be rewarded with some of the best cooking in the city. Camdeborde's approach is characterised by generosity (the terrine with cornichons appetiser served à volonté), and exuberance. Dishes on the €30 prix fixe include the likes of a black pudding gratin, a carpaccio of calf's head, and tiny squid cooked like elvers with a squid ink risotto. Desserts are just as exciting, and wines decently priced.

Au Rendez-Vous des Camionneurs

34 rue des Plantes, 14th (01.45.42.20.94). M° Alésia. **Open** noon-2.30pm, 7-9pm Mon-Fri. Closed Aug. **Average** €15. **Prix fixe** €12.50. **No credit cards.**

At this locals' restaurant the €12.50 set menu is limited, but served generously by Monique as Claude toils in the kitchen. Starters can be forgettable but mains (from a choice of three) are tastier – of note, the tender pork sauté cooked in a hearty sauce. An endless supply of fresh homemade bread, a good, cheap carafe of Côtes du Rhône and friendly conversation between tables adds to the bonhomie.

Aux Saveurs de Claude

12 rue Stanislas, 6th (01.45.44.41.74). M° Vavin. **Open** noon-2pm, 7.45-10.15pm Mon-Sat. Closed two weeks Aug, one week Christmas, one week Easter. **Average** €30. **Prix fixe** (dinner only) €25, €30.

Le Père Claude. *See p211.*

Lunch menu €20, €26. **Credit** AmEx, MC, V. **Non-smoking room. Map** p405 G8.
The charming and talented young couple who run this sweet mini-bistro sincerely want you to have a good meal (and you will). Recent dishes on the blackboard have included a fine fricassée of wild mushrooms, tiny ravioli filled with yellow chanterelles, entrecôte with bordelaise sauce and puréed potato, and veal kidneys sautéed with wild mushrooms and chestnuts. Desserts include a first-rate tarte Tatin.

Contemporary/trendy

Apollo

3 pl Denfert-Rochereau, 14th (01.45.38.76.77) M° Denfert-Rochereau. **Open** noon-3pm, 8-11pm daily. Closed 24 Dec. **Average** €40. **Lunch menu** €16. **Credit** AmEx, DC, MC, V. **Wheelchair access. Map** p405 H10.
This high-design new restaurant in the former RER offices of Denfert-Rochereau takes a leaf from the original 1970s RER design, with white leatherette banquettes, tomato-coloured chairs and oval mirrors. The menu is a modern take on comfort food: herring caviar and potatoes, blanquette de coquilles St-Jacques and braised beef with carrots.

Fish

Bistrot du Dôme

1 rue Delambre, 14th (01.43.35.32.00). M° Vavin. **Open** 12.15-2.30pm, 7.30-11pm daily. Closed Sun and Mon in Aug. **Average** €36. **Credit** AmEx, MC, V. **Non-smoking room. Map** p405 G9.
At this offspring of the brasserie Le Dôme, staff, dressed in black and white, are thoroughly professional yet will even take pity on budget diners by filling wine glasses practically to the brim. Each fish is prepared conservatively but expertly.
Branch: 2 rue de la Bastille, 4th (01.48.04.88.44).

La Cagouille

10-12 pl Constantin-Brancusi, 14th (01.43.22.09.01/ www.la-cagouille.fr). M° Gaîté. **Open** 12.30-2.30pm, 7.30-10.30pm daily. **Average** €45. **Prix fixe** €23, €38. **Credit** AmEx, MC, V. **Map** p405 F9.
Gérard Allemandou is one of the capital's great fish cooks, and this is one of the rare Paris fish houses to stay open all summer. Griddle-cooked mussels are a classic starter, and the small squid with onions, parsley and garlic are light and flavourful.

Vegetarian

Aquarius

40 rue de Gergovie, 14th (01.45.41.36.88). M° Pernety or Plaisance. **Open** noon-2.15pm, 7-10.30pm Mon-Sat. Closed last two weeks in Aug. **Average** €15. **Prix fixe** €12 (dinner only). **Lunch menu** €11. **Credit** AmEx, DC, MC, V. **Wheelchair access. Non-smoking room. Map** p405 F10.
Master of ceremonies (the originally Scottish) Richard Leigh maintains a steady stream of hilarious, off-the cuff commentary on his own personal beauty, the foibles of his clients and the state of world affairs. The cuisine can be a bit bland – crudités, salads, grain quinoa (a cross between bulgur wheat and rice) and biryani but the tarts, clafoutis, puddings, cakes and creams are great. Och aye.

Bars, Cafés & Tearooms

After doing museums and churches trying to look thrilled, one needs to stash the camera away, ease one's buns into a bar stool and sink a livener or three.

In no other city will lingering in a public establishment for 14 hours at a stretch be encouraged, or rather, expected. Noxious fumes lick the tobacco-stained walls, often fabricating 'my life is a novel' euphoria. You are just as likely to sit next to a bearded freak in a Che T-shirt rolling his own fags as you are to a skeletal fashionista with her sweater-clad lapdog. Though plenty of old-school zinc bars remain, trendy watering holes *à la* New York are springing up for the Parisian smart set. This is a welcome wave to those bemoaning the staid stables, yet, as always, this is seen as a threat to the timelessness of the lifestyle. Café culture here is a spectator sport: those chairs coyly joined side-to-side assure premium stadium seating and serve doubly as a shooting gallery for those on the outside looking in. Bars can range from quiet cocktail lounges to dance-on-the-tables joints, especially after midnight. A *demi* of beer can range from thin on the ground to expensive (and is most always cheaper at the bar). For the peckish, most cafés serve *tartines* (open sandwiches), *croques* (toasted cheese with ham) and salads. It's your round, we believe! For more information see the new book *Time Out Paris Eating & Drinking 2004*, on sale in good bookshops and from the website timeout.com/shop

The Islands

Cafés

Le Flore en l'Isle

42 quai d'Orléans, 4th (01.43.29.88.27).
M° Hôtel de Ville or Pont-Marie. **Open** 8am-2am daily. **Credit** MC, V. **Map** p406 K7.
Le Flore en l'Isle is particularly popular on hot summer afternoons as the dessert menu includes ice creams and sorbets from the famous *glacier* Berthillon. The rest of the rather expensive menu consists of dressed-up, mostly meaty traditional fare. Dark wood panelling and obscure classical music create a sombre atmosphere inside, but most customers come to enjoy the terrace and the view. Great for the kind of chicks with blue-rinsed poodles and pink-rinsed perms.

The Louvre, Palais-Royal & Les Halles

Cafés

Le Café des Initiés

3 pl des Deux-Ecus, 1st (01.42.33.78.29).
M° Louvre-Rivoli or Les Halles. **Open** 7.30am-1am Mon-Sat. **Credit** AmEx, MC, V. **Map** p406 H5.
After a recent transformation from traditional Paris corner bistro to designer hangout, this café has retained only its long zinc bar. Now the room is lined with ergonomic red banquettes, and sleek black articulated lamps peer down from the ceiling. Dotted around the windowsills are tall, slender vases filled with fresh, scented lilies. The friendly staff and central location make this an excellent place to meet for a drink or a quick bite, either inside or out.

Le Dénicheur

4 rue Tiquetonne, 2nd (01.42.21.31.01).
M° Etienne-Marcel. **Open** 12.30-3.30pm, 7pm-midnight Tue-Sat; 12.30-3.30pm Sun. **Map** p402 J5.
The row of garden gnomes standing to attention in the window give the game away: Le Dénicheur doesn't take itself too seriously. Even better, a few steps from the tourist-fleecing joints of Les Halles, it's a place where you can pick up a very affordable light lunch or supper, such as a huge plate of very fresh salad followed by a crunchy homemade apple crumble. There's also a Sunday brunch.

Pubs & bars

Le Fumoir

6 rue de l'Amiral-de-Coligny, 1st (01.42.92.00.24/ www.lefumoir.com). M° Louvre-Rivoli. **Open** 11am-2am daily. **Credit** AmEx, MC, V. **Map** p402 H6.
At this elegant bar directly opposite the Louvre, neo-colonial fans whirr lazily, oil paintings adorn the walls and even the bar staff seem to have been included in the interior decorator's sketches. A sleek crowd sipping martinis or browsing the papers at the long mahogany bar (originally from a Chicago speakeasy), gives way to young professionals in the restaurant and pretty young things in the library. It can make you feel like going berserk with a fire extinguisher. But don't do it, kids.

The World Bar. *See p217.*

Hemingway Bar at the Ritz

Hôtel Ritz, 15 pl Vendôme, 1st (01.43.16.30.31/ www.ritzparis.com). M° Madeleine or Concorde. **Open** 6.30pm-2am Tue-Sat. Closed 25 July-25 Aug. **Credit** AmEx, DC, MC, V. **Map** p401 F5.

This is simply one of the loveliest places in Paris to do cocktail hour. The dark wood, muffled laughter, black-and-white photos of the Old Man and the old-school charm of Colin the barman make the bar a cocoon from the horrors of the outside world. Pulling in its fair share of characters, honeymooners and expense-account nerds, it's also a wonderful place to people-watch. The cocktails are as near to alcoholic Nirvana as possible, in particular the raspberry martini, a divine blend of raspberries and vodka. A mere €22 for something this good? It's a snip!

Wine bars

Juveniles

47 rue de Richelieu, 1st (01.42.97.46.49). M° Palais Royal or Pyramides. **Open** noon-midnight Mon-Sat. **Credit** AmEx, MC, V. **Map** p402 H4.

Tim Johnston is an eccentric and genial host, a humorous Scot with attitude. Foodwise, simple dishes and tapas make fine accompaniments to interesting wines. Munch on feather-light, crisp celeriac chips and an apéritif glass of 1999 Pieropan Soave Classico at €4 and follow with mains such as Duval sausages and mash with chutney, and nicely cooked salmon with lots of vegetables. We recommend the surprisingly supple 1995 Rioja from Marques de Murrieta (€40).

Wine and Bubbles

3 rue Française, 1st (01.44.76.99.84/ www.wineandbubbles.com). M° Etienne Marcel. **Open** 6pm-2am Mon-Sat. **Credit** AmEx, MC, V. **Non-smoking room. Map** p402 J5.

This wildly successful wine-shop-cum-wine-bar is all clean lines and good lighting, with the wine beautifully displayed by region and country. The bar continues in the same vein – spindly modern tables and chairs, low lights and funky music. One of the secrets of its success seems to be a very reasonable corkage fee of €3 which is added to the shop price for bottles consumed on the premises. Wines run to the delicious and original La Motte Millennium from South Africa. The charcuterie plates are rather basic but served with good bread and cornichons.

Opéra & the Grands Boulevards

Cafés

The World Bar

Level 5, Printemps de l'Homme, 64 bd Haussmann, 9th (01.42.82.78.02). M° Havre-Caumartin. **Open** noon-10pm Mon-Wed, Sat, Sun; 9.30am-10pm Thur. **Credit** AmEx, DC, MC, V. **Map** p401 G3.

This Paul Smith-designed café provides a suitable setting for fashion-conscious shoppers to take stock of their latest acquisitions. Breezeblock walls are plastered with yellowing newspapers dating from Paul Smith's birth and a velvet Union Jack hangs decadently above the bar as house music pulses around the room. Food, provided by the ubiquitous Flo Group, is a continental version of modern pub grub that mixes French standards such as confit de canard with favourites from abroad.

Pubs & bars

Footsie

10-12 rue Daunou, 2nd, (01.42.60.07.20). M° Opéra. **Open** noon-2.30pm, 6pm-2am Mon-Thur; noon-2.30pm, 6pm-4am Fri, Sat. **Credit** AmEx, MC, V. **Map** p401 G4.

This is such a plummy idea it should be floated on the stock market: bar prices modelled on shares which rise and fall every four minutes depending on how many people buy them. (Tip: popular brews go up, pensioners' tipples stay cheap.) Footsie goads you into mixing your drinks and playing City whiz-kids till dawn. A whisky can fluctuate between €5.80 and €10.50 in seconds. Yet among the throng, few drinkers seem to be looking up at the screens, scanning for bargains. Prices 'crash' occasionally, encouraging yet more windfall boozing.

Le Général Lafayette

52 rue Lafayette, 10th (01.47.70.59.08). M° Poissonière. **Open** 10am-4am daily. **Credit** AmEx, DC, MC, V. **Map** p402 J3.

This attractive spot with a belle époque decor serves up nine different beers on tap, including several Belgian abbey brews and a variety of other quaffs by the bottle. The crowd runs from financial toffs to scruffy artists, giving the place a nice buzz. The food is good, too, including trout with bacon, cep omelettes and andouillette, making this ideal for a one-stop night out.

Beaubourg & the Marais

Cafés

L'Etoile Manquante

34 rue Vieille du Temple, 4th (01.42.72.48.34/ www.cafeine.com). M° Hôtel de Ville or St-Paul. **Open** 9am-2am daily. **Credit** MC, V. **Map** p406 K6.

One of five venues that Xavier Denamur owns on the same street, L'Etoile Manquante shows that he is fully in tune with local café culture. The salads are delicious and filling, the cocktails punchy and the decor both trendy and comfortable. As ever with Denamur's places, no visit is complete without a trip to the loo. An electric train runs between cubicles, starlight beams down from the ceiling and a hidden camera films you washing your hands. Don't worry, though, the images aren't bound straight for TF1 – just the small screen on the wall behind you.

Stringfellows
London Paris

Grizzli Café

7 rue St-Martin, 4th (01.48.87.77.56). M° Châtelet. **Open** 9am-2am daily. Closed 1 Jan, 1 May, 25 Dec. **Credit** AmEx, MC, V. **Map** p406 K6.

The pedestrian streets around the Centre Pompidou are sometimes too crowded for comfortable people-watching. So snag yourself a table at this modish café/bistro off rue de Rivoli. Order the Grizzli, a huge salad topped with duck and sliced apples, or the equally good antipasti salad, and watch the pretty people stroll by. The sun hits the terrace at just the right angle, even in the cooler months, so order another glass of wine and linger. In winter, sit inside and tuck into one of the heartier main courses.

Pubs & bars

Andy Wahloo

69 rue des Gravilliers, 3rd (01.42.71.20.38). M° Arts et Métiers. **Open** noon-2am Mon-Sat. **Credit** AmEx, DC, MC, V. **Map** p402 K5.

Andy Wahloo – created by the people behind its neighbour 404 and London's Momo – is Arabic for 'I have nothing'. But it does, and bundles of it. From head to toe, it's a beautifully designed venue with a wide, swooping bar, Moroccan artefacts, and enough colours to fill a Picasso. Quiet early, the atmosphere heats up later on. The cocktails are good and the snacks fresh in from next door.

Le Trésor

7 rue du Trésor, 4th (01.42.71.35.17). M° St-Paul. **Open** 11.30am-2am daily. **Credit** AmEx, MC, V. **Map** p406 K6.

This modish bar/restaurant has come out of refurb with an eye-catching scheme of luminous pink, green, white and grey, and fairground-tastic concave mirrors. None of this, however, deters the mixed crowd of trendies. The food and wine have a distinct Franco-Italian twist, and the loos are definitely worth a gander, with live goldfish swimming in the cisterns. Don't worry, you can't flush them away.

Wine bars

Les Enfants Rouges

9 rue de Beauce, 3rd, (01.48.87.80.61). M° Temple or Arts et Métiers. **Open** noon-3pm Tue-Sat; 7pm-2am Thur, Fri. Closed three weeks in Aug. **Credit** MC, V. **Map** p402 L5.

This bar is a new venture from the couple who brought us the now-defunct Moulin à Vins in Montmartre. The selection of wines by the glass is limited, but the 1999 Côtes du Rhône Viognier from Gaillard makes an aromatic and silky apéritif and, of course, there are many treats to follow. Familiar faces in the wine glitterati take up their places at this wine bar to watch, quaff and then, no doubt, be disparaging in their Sunday column. To accompany the wine list are enjoyable French mainstays such as pink duck magret with lentils and faux-filet steak with exemplary homemade chips on the side.

Polichinelle Café

The Bastille & eastern Paris

Cafés

Polichinelle Café

64-66 rue de Charonne, 11th (01.58.30.63.52) M.° Ledru-Rollin. **Open** 10am-1am daily. Food served noon-3.30pm, 7.30-11.30pm; Sun brunch noon-5pm. Beer €2.50. **Credit** MC, V. **Map** p407 N7.

What makes Polichinelle our favourite spot for a long lunch in Paris? Is it the charming Hélène, the 1950s mosaic floor, or the banquettes for winter and sunny terrace for summer? The food delivers every time. Go for the meaty options – succulent bavette d'alloyau with red onion jam or magret de canard with pain d'épices sauce – or, for those who prefer fish, salmon with a tapenade vinaigrette. The fruits in the crumble taste as if they have just been picked.

T pour 2 Café

23 cour St-Emilion, 12th (01.40.19.02.09). M° Cour St-Emilion. **Open** 11am-midnight daily. **Credit** AmEx, DC, MC, V. **Map** p407 P10.

This fashionable modern café, restaurant and bar in the renovated Bercy wine district offers a vast selection of teas and coffees ranging from the traditional (lapsang souchong) to the exotic (Guadeloupe bonifieur) and the just plain amusing (grand jasmin monkey king). The atmosphere is relaxed – big comfy chairs, mugs of coffee and Fashion TV and M6 playing. There is a selection of light foods including desserts, sandwiches and salads (around €12).

Pubs & bars

Pop In

105 rue Amelot, 11th (01.48.05.56.11). M° St-Sébastien-Froissart. **Open** 6.30pm-1.30am Tue-Sun. Closed Aug. **Credit** MC, V. **Wheelchair access. Map** p402 L5.

Any bar that hosts a Christian Dior after-show party has got to be cool, right? Wrong. At best, the Pop In reminds you of a London squat covered in a carcinogenic cloud – not the sort of place you'd expect to find yer Hugh Grant types stammering over a G&T. But what this higgeldy-piggeldy bar lacks in finesse is more than made up for by the down-to-earth staff, cheap drinks, chilled punters and cellar that alternates between an open mike night and a club for DJs. As you fight your way to the bar check out what is probably the most comprehensive collection of bad haircuts you will ever see in Paris.

China Club

50 rue de Charenton, 12th (01.43.43.82.02/ www.chinaclub.cc). M° Ledru-Rollin or Bastille. **Open** 7pm-2am Mon-Thur, Sun; 7pm-3am Fri, Sat. Closed July-Aug. **Credit** AmEx, MC, V. **Map** p407 M7.

With huge Chesterfields, low lighting and a sexy long bar, it's impossible not to feel glamorous here. In fact, if you've had a few, it's hard not to drop into a gentle snooze. Yes, this is the land of the extremely relaxed gentleman's club with a distinctly colonial Cohibas-and-cocktails feel. They take their martinis seriously and you can't go wrong with a well-made Champagne cocktail. This is ideal seduction territory – though alcoholic impotence is a risk for the ones who strike it lucky – but it's an equally good venue for a venomous gossip session about your friends, particularly during the inhibition-demolishing happy hour (7-9pm).

Impala Lounge. *See p223.*

Wine bars

Chai 33

33 cour St-Emilion, 12th (01.53.44.01.01/ www.chai33.com). M° Cour St-Emilion. **Open** noon-midnight Mon, Sun; noon-2am Tue-Sat. Lounge bar 7pm-2am. **Credit** AmEx, DC, MC, V. **Wheelchair access. Map** p407 P10.

This recent offering from the team behind B*fly, Buddha Bar and Barrio Latino combines lounge bar, restaurant, terrace bistro and wine shop in a converted wine warehouse in Bercy. Wine comes first, but design has not been forgotten, from the stainless steel vats to pink-satin boudoir-style ladies. Upstairs sit along the bar or recline in Indonesian deckchairs over an unusual wine cocktail. If *grands crus* are your thing, venture into the 'Paradis' caves where you can purchase fine vintages to drink in for far less than a standard restaurant mark-up.

The Champs-Elysées & west

Cafés

Le Dada

12 av des Ternes, 17th (01.43.80.60.12/ www.dada-bar.com). M° Ternes. **Open** 6am-2am Mon-Sat; 6am-midnight Sun. **Credit** AmEx, MC, V. **Map** p400 C3.

Perhaps the hippest café on this classy avenue, Le Dada is best known for its well-placed, sunny terrace, but the kookily dada-influenced two-floor interior is ideal for lunch. Standard brasserie dishes, brought out by efficient but obviously overworked waiters, are placed on wood-block carved tables, and the red walls provide a warm atmosphere for the Parisian crowd. If terracing is your thing, you could probably spend a whole summer afternoon here.

Pubs & bars

Atelier Renault

53 av des Champs-Elysées, 8th (01.49.53.70.00/ www.atelier-renault.com). M° Franklin D. Roosevelt. **Open** 8am-2am daily. **Credit** AmEx, DC, MC, V. **Credit** MC, V. **Map** p401 E4.

Upstairs, American elm, glass and steel provide surroundings that take their cue from a ship's cabin. There's a bar with armchairs and low tables, while five footbridges crossing the space give the 200-seat restaurant views over conceptual cars below and genuine traffic (jams) on the avenue. Food is modern/international (Moroccan-glazed roast lamb, spicy scampi with Chinese ravioli), or you can stop by anytime for snacks and ice cream sundaes.

Bindi

63 av Franklin-Roosevelt, 8th (01.53.89.66.66). M° Franklin D. Roosevelt. **Open** 8-11pm Mon, Sat; noon-3pm, 8pm-2am Tue-Fri. **Credit** AmEx, DC, MC, V. **Map** p401 E4.

Rumour has it that Bindi's decor was modelled on the Buddha Bar, and you can see why. This likeable underdog has all the trappings of its more illustrious peer, though, thankfully, none of the gold-chained punters to tarnish the furniture. It's essentially a classy Indian restaurant with a bar at the back – a hybrid of Oriental bric-a-brac and neo-kitsch – which plays host to relaxed trendsetters, smitten couples and simpler folk who believe that bars are basically about decent drinks and genuine service. Perched above the lounge, DJs spin a cocktail-sipping blend of ambient and downtempo sounds.

Le V

Hotel Four Seasons George V, 31 av George V, 8th (01.49.52.70.00). M° George V. **Open** 9am-2am daily. **Credit** AmEx, DC, MC, V. **Wheelchair access. Map** p400 D4.

The swanky V bar (read 'cinq') is the place to indulge any oil magnate fantasies. Dark wood, a roaring fire, amazing floral displays and utterly loaded punters

Eat, Drink, Shop

combine to make it a must for bling-bling beverages, although we weren't quite brave enough to go for the mysterious 'monkey's gland'. The martini list is superb, the purple being the best. A barman appears at your table to make like Tom Cruise and shake it just for you, the parma-violet-flavoured drink is then poured into a stemless crystal triangle, resting in a bowl of crushed ice, all lovingly cocooned on a posh silver tray. Looks and tastes divine but more than two and the stemless glass becomes tricky.

Impala Lounge

2 rue de Berri, 8th (01.43.59.12.66). M° George V. **Open** 9.30am-2.30am Mon, Tue; 9.30am-3am Wed, Thur; 9.30am-5am Fri, Sat. **Credit** AmEx, DC, MC, V. **Map** p400 D4.

Dubbed the 'African Bar' by regulars, this trendy escapade hams up the colonial with zebra skins, tribal masks and a throne hewn out of a tree trunk. Beer, wine, tea and coffee can all be found here, but best beverages are the cocktails, one of which claims to boost a waning libido with its mystery mix of herbs and spices. DJs rock Sunday afternoon away.

Bar Panoramique

Hôtel Concorde La Fayette, 3 pl du Général-Koenig, 17th (01.40.68.51.31). M° Porte Maillot. **Open** 4pm-3am daily. **Credit** AmEx, DC, MC, V. **Map** p400 B3.

Perfect for lovers or the alone and pensive, Bar Panaromique comes up tops with visual therapy, gazing from the 33rd floor onto the Eiffel Tower, Arc de Triomphe and La Défense. At night, the mirrored 70s interior and city skyline create a soft-lens glamour, enjoyed by American business travellers, cupped in the tiers of leather banquettes. Beware the 9pm watershed, when the piano bar hoicks all drinks up to €19.50, from Champagne to coffee. Crafty, that, especially if you're too elated to care.

Petit Défi de Passy

18 av du Président-Kennedy, 16th, (01.42.15.06.76/ www.defidepassy.com). M° Passy. **Open** 10am-midnight Mon, Tue; 10am-2am Wed-Sat; 11am-midnight Sun. **Credit** AmEx, MC, V. **Non-smoking room. Map** p404 B6.

Tucked into the viaduct below Passy station, this refreshingly no-fuss bar-restaurant challenges the local chichi rule, jollying along friendly students and English teachers through happy hour in a distinct whiff of late adolescence. For the occasional Thursday night live, DJs, Hooray Henris and pretty gals come out in force, pogoing and whooping on the makeshift dance floor to 80s French pop, sans irony and sans *beaucoup de chance* of getting ones *jambe* over. But then that's most discos.

Wine bars

L'Evasion

7 pl St-Augustin, 8th (01.45.22.66.20/ www.levasion.net). M° St-Augustin. **Open** 8am-1am Mon-Fri; 11am-1am Sat. **Credit** AmEx, DC, MC, V. **Map** p401 F3.

Take one corner café, give it a lick of yellow paint and cover the walls with little blackboards listing the food and wines on offer. It seems that was deemed necessary at L'Evasion to turn the place around, but the real changes are in glass and plate. For the wines we are talking natural, simply natural, bio-dynamic growers: Crozes Hermitage from Dard et Ribo, Morgon from Jean Foillard, Domaine Gramenon in Côtes du Rhône. To eat: top saucisson sec or thinly shaved Parma ham, pan-fried guinea fowl flank, steak with marrow, cod, or veal kidneys.

Caves Pétrissans

30bis av Niel, 17th (01.42.27.52.03). M° Ternes or Péreire. **Open** 10am-10.30pm Mon-Fri. **Credit** AmEx, MC, V. **Non-smoking room. Map** p400 C2.

A classic turn-of-the-20th-century wine-merchant-cum-restaurant, Caves Pétrissans is split in three: the corniced main dining room; another smaller room which serves as the shop; and a tiny, booth-like corner room. Epicurean locals get down to some serious eating and drinking at the tightly packed tables. A three-course menu of robust classics is available at €31, and à la carte offerings include foie gras and steamed chicken with a creamy tarragon sauce. The weekly-changing wines by the glass are irreproachable, and you can also choose from hundreds of bottles at shop price plus €16 corkage.

Montmartre & Pigalle

Cafés

Le Chinon

49 rue des Abbesses, 18th (01.42.62.07.17). M° Abbesses. **Open** 7am-2am daily. **No credit cards. Map** p402 H1.

Many of the bars and restaurants in Montmartre are filled entirely with tourists, but in this stretch of the road the atmosphere is more Parisian. With trendy tables and chairs worthy of a collector, this café can almost be forgiven for serving wine that may disappoint, such as the vieilles vignes Chinon. As long as you stick to coffee or beer, like the mostly French clientele, you should be fine.

Branch: Le Troisième Chinon, 56 rue des Archives, 4th (01.48.87.94.68).

Francis Labutte

122 rue Caulaincourt, 18th (01.42.23.58.26). M° Lamarck-Caulaincourt. **Open** 8.30am-2am Mon-Sat; 9am-2am Sun. **Credit** MC, V. **Map** p401 H1.

Bypass the tourist-flooded cafes near the Sacré-Cœur and take a stroll down the backside of the *butte* to marvel at the Montmartrois architecture and this convivial café. The interior vibrates with colours but the heated terrace (covered in winter) is where it's at – a funky crowd of all ages convenes here in any season for drinks or salads. Good croque monsieur and vegetarian tarts fill the menu, plus a range of mojito-family cocktails (€6.50) for when things turn bar-like.

Pubs & bars

3 Pièces Cuisine

25 rue de Chéroy/100 rue des Dames, 17th (01.44.90.85.10). M° Rome or Villiers. **Open** 8am-2am Mon-Fri; 9.30am-2am Sat, Sun. **Credit** MC, V. **Map** p401 G1.

This Batignolles bar looks like a scruffy old neighbourhood caff that's been taken in hand by a young *Elle Déco* reader. Red flock wallpaper and green study lamps create an intimate parlour at the back, with a few salvaged cinema seats thrown into the picture for boho credibility. Staff are cheery, but the clientele keep their voices pretty low – you get the impression that talk is more Serge Gainsbourg than Johnny Hallyday. Try the chocolate milkshake – it has far more ice cream in it than your mum would ever have allowed.

Lush

16 rue des Dames, 17th (01.43.87.49.46/ www.lushbars.com). M° Place de Clichy. **Open** 4pm-2am Mon-Fri; noon-2am Sat, Sun. Closed 25-28 Dec. **Happy hour** 4-7pm. **Credit** MC, V. **Map** p401 G1.

At a prime address in upwardly mobile Batignolles, this recently opened bar is a sleek lair for chilled-out drinking. Soft grape purples and comfy banquettes provide a suitable setting for inexpensive pints, well-chosen New World wines and delicious cocktails. Premiership football and rugby on big-screen TV – cue the stampede, ladies.

Doudingue

24 rue Durantin, 18th (01.42.54.88.08). M° Abbesses. **Open** 6pm-2am Mon-Fri; 11am-2am Sat, Sun. **Credit** AmEx, DC, MC, V. **Map** p402 H1.

This bar is just how one might imagine Antony and Cleopatra's pad to have looked had things worked out, with lots of indulgent, palatial details (big plumplicious cushions, cherubs on the ceiling and dainty chandeliers). The food, such as tuna steak with wild rice, is generally delicious and often commendably healthy. And the atmosphere and music swing to the right side of the wannabe meridian. Would Tony and Cleo wait an hour for their drinks to arrive? Not likely, but us mere mortals could do a lot worse.

Le Sancerre

35 rue des Abbesses, 18th (01.42.58.47.05). M° Abbesses. **Open** 7am-2am daily. **Credit** MC, V. **Map** p402 H1.

Bohemia is alive and well in this fashionably dishevelled café on the slopes of Montmartre. Don't let the scruffy appearance fool you. Service is efficient and the kitchen serves up salads, sandwiches and appetisingly runny omelettes. On busy evenings, you can bypass the terrace and get among the throng inside. The people-watching possibilities are just as good and you're less likely to be jostled by sightseers. There's even music on Sundays 6-10pm: it's like the Paris you see in the films.

Froth and mania

Philippe Bloch rarely goes into cafés in France. It's too dangerous. 'If I'm sitting at a café terrace raising my hand ten times for a waiter who never comes, I quite simply want to kill him.'

This businessman's homicidal impulses towards sniffy Gallic serving staff reflect an underlying feeling of public revolt against the tradition of the sneering French waiter. It's a subject Bloch addressed in his best-selling, co-written book *Service Compris*: a call-to-arms-cum-handbook for better French customer services. And in his subsequent venture – the Columbus Café chain – he hopes to do further damage to the antiquated 'shrug-and-slam' approach to serving coffee in France.

The Columbus Café is an American-style coffee shop modelled on, Bloch insists, a certain Cooper's Coffee on New York's Columbus Avenue. The emphasis is on quality products served in bright, clean, surroundings. His own chain is a set of discreet, smilingly efficient places in which to slurp. Unsurprisingly they are now dotted all over France like frontier stations.

The traditional French café is in decline (from 300,000 in 1900 to 43,000 today) but Bloch fervently believes that his cafés have no real effect on the phenomenon. If neighbourhood cafés are closing, he claims, it is because they offer nothing to the customer, who is often alienated by rude service and crappy coffee.

Crucially for Bloch the Columbus chain's success is due to the fact that at its inception it filled a gap, nay chasm, nay grand canyon in the market. Until recently, as a genre they have stood alone on French streets. Come early 2004, however, they will have to contend with the first French outposts of the mighty Starbucks empire. Luckily for Bloch, Columbus has already cornered the lion's share of the market and he predicts that all those buccaneers of the zingo juice can do is set up a flagship store or two.

Columbus will be seeing some marketing changes in the near future, moving from ambivalently Franco-American to a more Gallic style, from froth to bottom if you will. And if the traditional French cafés don't like it, they'll just have to put up with it. Even in a republic, the customer is *roi*.

North-east Paris

Cafés

Chez Prune

71 quai de Valmy, 10th (01.42.41.30.47).
M° République. **Open** 8am-2am Mon-Sat; 10am-2am Sun. Closed between Christmas and New Year. **Credit** MC, V. **Map** p402 L4.

Should the producers of *Friends* (OK, it's a big should) ever decide to relocate shooting to Paris, Chez Prune would be the hangout chosen by Chandler et al to replace Central Perk. At lunch the dining room and terrace reverberate with indescribably vile screenplays being pitched across the packed tables, while in the evenings a laid-back crowd checks each other out from behind their mojitos. Sadly, brunch doesn't start till noon.

La Kaskad'

2 pl Armand-Carrel, 19th (01.40.40.08.10).
M° Laumière. **Open** 9am-1am daily. **Credit** MC, V. **Wheelchair access**. **Map** p403 N2.

Named after the impressive manmade waterfall in the Buttes-Chaumont opposite, La Kaskad' has been a real hit with the local glitz and those who have just climbed over the railing after being locked in the park at night. Pose on the terrace and watch the limos roll up for wedding pictures in the park, or sit in the stylish taupe and mahogany interior and sip a cocktail to nu-jazz sounds. The food is delicious, including mains such as luscious pork cheeks and steaks, and huge salads for €10.40; if you're feeling flush there are some serious wines on the list.

Pubs & bars

L'Atmosphère

49 rue Lucien-Sampaix, 10th (01.40.38.09.21).
M° Gare de l'Est or Jacques Bonsergent. **Open** 6pm-midnight Mon; 10am-2am Tue-Sat; noon-9pm Sun. **No credit cards**. **Map** p402 L3.

Despite having lost its evening live music permit after years of push and pull with neighbours and the mayor's office, L'Atmosphère remains at the centre of the Canal St-Martin renaissance. Parisians of all kinds chat, read and people-watch on the canal-side terrace while, within, the simple, tasteful interior, animated conversation and cheapish drinks provide spectacle enough for locals. Drop in for world and experimental music Sundays 5-7pm.

De La Ville Café

34 bd Bonne-Nouvelle, 10th (01.48.24.48.09).
M° Bonne Nouvelle. **Open** 11am-2am daily. **Credit** MC, V. **Map** p402 J4.

Grotty meets naughty in the remains of the old Marguerit brothel, with leftover crystal sconces and marble as proof. Pass under (uninvited) flying pigeons in the warehouse-like foyer, to oversized second-date wicker love seats facing the 'food and sex', mural, then to the summer cocktail terrace dotted

Lou Pascalou

with orange plastic chairs where flirty waiters weave between tables and the ripped-tee-and-tattoo brigade on their way to Rex and Pulp. The virginal adjoining restaurant through the hole in the wall, complete with a romantic imported Italian mosaic ceiling and long bar, has two lounges and a 'butterfly room' for those more intimate moments.

Lou Pascalou

14 rue des Panoyaux, 20th (01.46.36.78.10).
M° Ménilmontant. **Open** 9am-2am daily. **Beer** 25cl €2-€2.30. **Cocktails** €5.50. **Credit** AmEx, DC, MC, V. **Map** p403 P5.

Dress down for a visit to this Ménilmontant mainstay, where a bohemian crowd spills on to the pavement on clement evenings. Chess matches roll on for hours as regulars settle scores over a *pression* or two (sets and a board are available from behind the bar). Guinness and Kilkenny (pint €5.80) are not much cop, but the selection of cocktails is remarkable.

Wine bars

Le Vin de Zinc

25 rue Oberkampf, 11th (01.48.06.28.23).
M° Oberkampf or Filles du Calvaire. **Open** noon-2pm, 8-11pm Tue-Sat. Closed Aug. **Credit** MC, V. **Map** p403 M5.

This spacious bar is a welcome newcomer, with simple red Formica tables and blackboards listing the day's specials. Starters such as lovely, clean-tasting piquillo peppers stuffed with goat's cheese and little,

fat snail ravioli with minced vegetables are winners – mains are less successful. The wine is all very new-school: lots of unsulphured and naturally produced bottles. A glass of Vire Clesse 1999 from Vergé had a delicate taste of star anise. The Morgon Côte de Py from Foillard is gorgeous and concentrated, though the *patronne* can be frosty.

The Latin Quarter & the 13th

Cafés

Les Pipos

2 rue de l'Ecole-Polytechnique, 5th (01.43.54.11.40/ www.lespipos.com). M° Maubert-Mutualité. **Open** 8am-midnight Mon-Sat. Closed three weeks in Aug. **No credit cards. Map** p406 J8.

When crowded a visit to the ancient, atmospheric Les Pipos can be smoky and uncomfortable with all the tables taken and very little room to manoeuvre at the tiny bar. But, on a warm afternoon in early spring, it has another vibe completely: the door wide open and all quiet except for a few solitary literary types, scribbling away. A clique of eccentric regulars provide excellent entertainment and there's a surprisingly modern selection of wines available as well as simple, cheap cheese and charcuterie plates (€5-€9.90) and hearty plats du jour, all under €15.

Pubs & bars

The Bombardier

2 pl du Panthéon, 5th (01.43.54.79.22/ www.bombardier.com). M° Maubert-Mutualité/ RER Luxembourg. **Open** noon-2am daily. Food served noon-3pm Mon-Sat; noon-4pm Sun. **Credit** MC, V. **Map** p406 J8.

Snuck into a niche opposite the Panthéon, the Bombardier is a convincing recreation of a home counties pub (minus the retired colonels), with Bombardier beer on tap from Bedford brewery (and proprietor) Charles Wells. Despite the swirly glass and olde worlde tapestry, it's a lot less hardcore Anglo than most English pubs in Paris, managing to pull in healthy measures of pretty young French things. Great for a pint over the Sunday papers, the weekend footie or a raucous rugby session.

Le Pantalon

7 rue Royer-Collard, 5th (no phone). RER Luxembourg. **Open** 11am-2am Mon-Sat. **No credit cards. Map** p406 J8.

The neighbourhood bar you always wished was your local, Le Pantalon is at once deeply familiar and utterly weird. The strange vacuum-cleaner sculpture and disco-light loos give a clue to the madcap nature of the place, but it's the regulars and staff who tip the balance firmly into eccentricity. Friendly and seriously funny French grown-ups and international students chat away in a mish-mash of accents and languages. Happy hours are fantastic, but drinks here are always cheap enough to get happily tipsy without worrying about a cash hangover.

Connolly's Corner

12 rue de Mirbel, 5th (01.43.31.94.22). M° Censier-Daubenton. **Open** 4pm-2am daily. **No credit cards. Map** p406 K9.

This cosy pub is unabashedly Irish. Revellers from the nearby rue Mouffetard join staunch regulars to knock back stout and generous measures of Paddy or Breton beer Coreff at beer-barrel tables. The live music on Tuesday, Thursday and Sunday at 7.30pm, while charming, takes up half the main bar.

Le Couvent

69 rue Broca, 13th (01.43.31.28.28). M° Les Gobelins. **Open** 9am-2am Mon-Fri; 6pm-2am Sat. **Credit** MC, V. **Map** p406 J10.

For an address that might well read: 'middle of nowhere', this heavily beamed bar creates a delightful hideaway. It first appeared in Pierre Gripari's novel *Contes de la rue Broca*, but has come a long way since those dingy days. Nowadays it's the chouchou of uni students and thirtysomething couples, especially at concert time when live chords get feet tapping. Always busy, always smoky.

Le Merle Moquer

11 rue de la Butte-aux-Cailles, 13th (01.45.65.12.43). M° Place d'Italie or Corvisart. **Open** 5pm-2am daily. **Credit** MC, V.

Le Merle Moquer fits perfectly into the bucolic Butte-aux-Cailles. It's basically a 'no' bar: no frills, no tables, no waiters, just get up there and order. The bamboo and kiddies' paintball attempts are intentionally tacky but no one cares, as most eyes are focused on the colourful lights refracted by the fruity punches or the barmaid's generous chest. Come here if you want to see that rarest of sights: French people letting go of their inhibitions.

Wine bars

Les Papilles

30 rue Gay-Lussac, 5th (01.43.25.20.79/ www.lespapilles.fr). RER Luxembourg. **Open** 10am-8pm Mon, Wed, Fri, Sat; 10am-10pm Tue, Thur. **Credit** MC, V. **Wheelchair access. Map** p406 J8.

Decorated in the style of a Provençal kitchen, Les Papilles ('tastebuds') is all about eating and drinking well. It's run by two couples dedicated to gastronomy – Brigitte and Julie look after the food while their husbands Gérard and Pierre trawl the countryside looking for new wines. The regularly changing menu emphasises seasonal cooking. Regulars lap up the excellent wines of the week selection including an excellent red from Corsica. Jams, vinegars, olive oils, pasta, whiskies and vintage Ports are all there to take home, and shelves of wine await, like a fine library, to be perused, and picked out for an evenings indulgence though it must be said it's a challenge to get pissed on a book.

St-Germain & Odéon

Cafés

Bar de la Croix-Rouge

2 carrefour de la Croix-Rouge, 6th (01.45.48.06.45). M° Sèvres-Babylone or St-Sulpice. **Open** 6am-9pm daily. Food served all day. **No credit cards. Map** p405 G7.

On a sunny afternoon you'd be hard-pushed to bag one of the pavement tables on the compact terrace. The dark brown interior is fairly cramped but buzzing, and the simple food is good value. Choose from a range of cheese or cold meat platters, or one of the deservedly famous Poilâne tartines.

Au Petit Suisse

16 rue de Vaugirard, 6th (01.43.26.03.81). M° Odéon. **Open** 7am-11pm Mon-Fri; 8am-1pm Sat, Sun. **Credit** MC, V. **Map** p405 H7.

Named after Marie de Médicis' Swiss guards, the compact Au Petit Suisse has an enviable location next to the Jardins du Luxembourg. The bilingual menu offers a range of predictable but generally decent food, served by old-school waiters.

Le Rostand

6 pl Edmond-Rostand, 6th (01.43.54.61.58). RER Luxembourg. **Open** 8am-midnight daily. **Map** p406 H8.

You certainly can't deny that it has a superlative view of the Jardins du Luxembourg and the inside is classy and clean with Orientalist paintings, long mahogany bar and wall-length mirrors. The brasserie menu is pricey, but the café selection offers generous, fluffy omelettes, salads and great fruit tarts and there are lots of beers, whiskies and cocktails.

Pubs & bars

Fu Bar

5 rue St-Sulpice, 6th (01.40.51.82.00). M° Odéon. **Open** 5pm-2am daily. **Credit** MC, V. **Map** p405 H7.

It looks tiny, but there's plenty of extra seating upstairs and anyone who's ever tasted one of the apple martinis would happily cram in at the bar anyway. The cosmopolitan is glorious and the 'suite tart' would make even the bed-weary *Sex and the City* girls squirm.

Hôtel Lutétia

45 bd Raspail, 6th (01.49.54.46.46/www.lutetia.com). M° Sèvres-Babylone. **Open** 10.30am-1am daily. **Credit** AmEx, DC, MC, V. **Map** p405 G7.

The decor is a colourblind interior designer's folly, the over-dressed waiters are uptight, and fatigued cigar-smoking businessmen are perhaps not the funkiest company, but the Lutétia's trio of bars is as popular as ever, thanks to its range of potent cocktails. The main attraction is the fabulous low-lit and louche Ernest bar, where ladies-who-shop become ladies-who-down-vodkas.

La Taverne de Nesle

32 rue Dauphine, 6th (01.43.26.38.36). M° Odéon. **Open** 6pm-4am Mon-Thur, Sun; 6pm-6am Fri, Sat. **Credit** MC, V. **Map** p406 H6.

La Taverne has three distinct drinking areas: a zinc bar at the front, a sort of Napoléonic campaign tent in the middle and a trendily-lit ambient area at the back, encouraging a gradual progression to the horizontal state. Among the hundred or so brews you'll find the best of Belgian, but it's the choice of French beers that really sets it apart. Don't miss the house special L'Epi, brewed in three different versions: Blond (100% barley), Blanc (oats) and Noir (buckwheat), or Corsican Pietra on tap.

The 7th & the 15th

Cafés

Le Café du Marché

38 rue Cler, 7th (01.47.05.51.27). M° Ecole-Militaire. **Open** 7am-midnight Mon-Sat; 7am-5pm Sun. **Credit** MC, V. **Map** p405 D6.

For an in-the-action location amid the 7th's most lively market street, you can't do much better than Le Café du Marché, which serves as a hub of neighbourhood activity but is equally comfortable welcoming tourists and the just plain curious. Big salads at €9.50 and classic French main dishes at €10 (confit de canard, poulet rôti, entrecôte) are bargains for the hungry, though the quality tends to vary, depending on the dish.

Fu Bar

Au Dernier Métro

70 bd de Grenelle, 15th (01.45.75.01.23/ www.auderniermetro.com). M° Dupleix. **Open** 6am-2am daily. **Credit** AmEx, MC, V. **Map** p404 C7.

This adorable café makes you feel at home. The walls are covered with colourful memorabilia and a football game plays on the small TV behind the bar. Lots of the Basque-influenced dishes tempt – such as the juicy fish brochettes served with saffron rice or one of the big salads, both made with care. There's a bit of pavement seating (heated in winter) and the big windows open right up. Beer is a bargain for the neighbourhood and service could not have been friendlier nor more attentive – where else might the waiter address two less-than-beauteous diners as 'my angels'?

Pubs & bars

Le Bréguet

72 rue Falguière, 15th (01.42.79.97.00). M° Pasteur. **Open** 5pm-4am Mon-Sat. **Credit** V. **Map** p405 E9.

No prizes for the location nor the decor, but the vibe is relaxed and the drinks surprisingly eclectic. As well as the usual beers on tap, there are Strongbow cider, commendably smooth Guinness, vodkas and some exotic quaffs like limoncello.

Montparnasse & beyond

Cafés

Café de la Place

23 rue d'Odessa, 14th (01.42.18.01.55). M° Edgar-Quinet. **Open** 7.30am-2am Mon-Sat; 10am-11pm Sun. **Credit** MC, V. **Map** p405 G9.

At Café de la Place, you can choose between the homely, dark-wood-panelled interior, the glassed-in terrace or, during warmer weather, the pavement under a canopy of green trees. Go for the giant Poilâne-bread croques: the vegetarian tomato and cheese version is served atop a huge pile of salad. At the edge of the famous cemetery, you'll feel miles away from Montparnasse mania.

Tearooms for the Noëls and Gerties

Not everyone's a drug-crazed clubber, looking for a discotheque in which to get mashed, do the twist and then locate a wicked after to come down from all the Vitamin C they've ingested to keep them going. There are, thank God, many venues in Paris in which latterday Noël Cowards and Gertrude Lawrences in search of a stylish cuppa can nibble, sit and be witty.

Angelina (226 rue de Rivoli, 1st/ 01.42.60.82.00) is a place where Nollie might have whispered saucy secrets into Gertie's ear. The neo-rococo salon was originally known as Rumpelmeyer's and the cakes still have an Austrian gooeyness. This also partly explains the excellence of the hot chocolate, made with African cocoa (6.20).

If you hope to mingle with royalty and rock 'n' roll over dinky sandwiches, it's hard to do better than the luxury hotel tea room at **Le Plaza Athénée** (25 av Montaigne, 8th/ 01.53.67.66.65). People-gazing, however, is a very minor pleasure compared to the Plaza's superb teas and dessert trolley. Try the *fraisier*, a strawberry and pistachio cream cake that is close to perfection. As for the teas, don't miss the mélange Plaza, a masterly blend of fig, hazelnut, quince and grape. Don't get it all over your housecoat.

The tea room at the swish hotel **Le Bristol** (112 rue du Fbg-St-Honoré, 8th/ 01.53.43.43.00) attracts connoisseurs with its carefully chosen list, exemplified by the excellent grand Foochow fumé pointes blanches and Assam doomou. Cross the apricot marble foyer and trip down the steps to the right to a vast lounge complete with marble columns, magnificent floral arrangements and a view across the lawns. The accompanying little sandwiches of tuna, smoked salmon and cheese are deliciously buttery, although the absence of thinly-sliced cucumber wouldn't have pleased Sir Noël.

Mariage Frères (13 rue des Grands Augustins, 6th/01.40.51.82.50) has established itself in the past 150 years as the city's leading tea purveyor. After taking the stairs to the elevated seating area at this St-Germain branch, let white-tailed waiters guide you through the menu cataloguing 500 teas from across the globe. Choosing a pastry requires only one eye on the dessert tray, the work of Philippe Langlois.

Confirmed snobs shouldn't forget the original branch of **Ladurée** (16 rue Royale, 8th/01.42.60.21.79), where staff have perfected the art of avoiding someone's eye when they're desperately seeking yours. The reward for your patience will be Proustian cakes – it's the macaroons that regulars devour by the mound, whether coffee (arguably the best), coconut, chocolate, pistachio or mint. Wonderfully aromatic teas soothe the senses, too. Divine!

Shops & Services

Diehard shoppers take note. Whether you want rare vinyl, unusual chocolate or a key designer outfit, Paris can satisfy even the most difficult punter.

An hour in the Musée d'Orsay is nothing compared to the joy of mooching around the *grands boulevards* and back streets of the chicest city on earth. As the birthplace of couture, Paris has all the usual designer suspects, but the luxury on offer on avenue Montaigne or rue du Faubourg-St-Honoré remains just a small slice of what's out there. If you want to have your cake, eat it and then invest in a larger pair of trousers, real Paris shopping reveals itself in trendy boutiques, mouth-watering food shops and *belle-époque* department stores with roof top views.

Practically everything is split into distinguishable areas. Classic clusters of shops include antiques in the 7th, second-hand and rare books in the 5th. Street chic and lifestyle outlets live side by side in the Marais and around rue Etienne-Marcel, while quirky newcomers settle in Abbesses or near Canal St-Martin. Those with a shoe fetish should teeter to rue du Cherche-Midi (6th) and rue de Grenelle (7th); foodies to Bon Marché (7th) and Fauchon (8th). Designer labels are scattered all over the 1st, 6th and 8th. Specialist enclaves include motorbikes and cameras on boulevard Beaumarchais and porcelain and crystal on rue de Paradis, while the flea markets at Vanves, Montreuil and Clignancourt are well worth getting out of bed for at weekends.

The listings for shops in this chapter include major branches, but not every outlet. Don't be worried about meandering off the tourist track, but, as always, the further you venture away from the main road, the less you should look like a tourist. Whether an old book is your forte, or you prefer things prêt-à-porter, Paris can kit you out with something really special without necessarily denting the old bank balance.

One-stop Shopping

Concept stores

Paris just can't seem to get enough of these designerish one-stop shops. With their fusion of art, fashion and other creative pursuits they result in a cool alternative to the traditional high brow designer boutiques. Now there's even an anti-concept, concept store.

Spree. *See p236.*

Castelbajac Concept Store

31 pl du Marché-St-Honoré, 1st (01.42.60.41.55). M° Tuileries or Pyramides. **Open** 10.30am-7.30pm daily. **Credit** AmEx, DC, MC, V. **Map** p401 G5.

Aristo designer Jean-Charles de Castelbajac's humorous, colourful world of fashion is showcased in a 230m^2 gleaming white concept store. As well as his own eclectic fashion collections (men and women) and accessories, there is funky furniture and objects by invited artists and designers.

Colette

213 rue St-Honoré, 1st (01.55.35.33.90/ www.colette.fr). M° Tuileries. **Open** 10.30am-7.30pm Mon-Sat. **Credit** AmEx, DC, MC, V. **Map** p401 G4.

Six years on, the original concept/lifestyle store is still the most cutting-edge and still frighteningly minimalist. 'Must Have' accessories are displayed well away from sticky fingers inside clinical glass cases, while hipster books, media, Sony cameras, fancy Nokias and the and the hair and beauty brands själ, Kiehl's or uslu airlines are scattered amid the ultra-cool reviews, magazines and photo albums on the ground floor and mezzanine. Upstairs has a selection of 'in' clothes (think: Tess Giberson or Generra), and accessories such as the Chrome Hearts line. Lunch, with a global selection of mineral water, can be had in the basement Water Bar.

Surface to Air

46 rue de l'Arbre-Sec, 1st (01.49.27.04.54). M° Pont-Neuf. **Open** 11am-7.30pm Mon-Sat. **Credit** MC, V. **Map** p402 J6.

Seven guys created this indefinable, non-concept concept store, which also acts as a photo and fashion production company. The cult clothing selection takes in cute T-shirt dresses, Sila and Maria's trashy tank tops, Tatty Devine's hair accessories and mens' space-invaders customised Surface to Air sweats. Chill on the sofa and check out the mags and Surface to Air's limited-edition book *Pour la Victoire*.

Espace Lab 101

44 rue de La Rochefoucauld, 9th (01.49.95.95.85). M° Pigalle or St-Georges. **Open** 12.30-7.30pm Tue-Sat. **No credit cards. Map** p401 H2.

An off-shoot of creative clubbers Project 101, Espace Lab has a changing collection of local and international streetwear labels (check out the customised military jackets by Super Sapin), as well as cutting-edge electronic music on independent labels, DVDs and fanzines.

Gravity Zero

30 rue de Charonne and 1 rue Keller, 11th (01.43.14.06.39/www.gravityzero.fr). M° Ledru-Rollin. **Open** 4-7.30pm Mon; 11am-1pm, 2-7.30pm Tue-Thur; 11am-7.30pm Fri, Sat. **Credit** MC, V. **Map** p407 N7.

This concept store brings fashion, music, photography and art together. Three floors of the Charonne store play host to the upper end of the fashion market with collections including Yu Feng, Chez Twin Ceric and funky shoes by Chez Babouche and Manuel Canovas. At rue Keller, the look is more playful streetwear plus there is an eclectic selection of electronic music.

View on Fashion

27 rue des Taillandiers, 11th (01.43.55.05.03/ www.viewonfashion.com). M° Bastille. **Open** noon-7.30pm Mon-Sat. **Credit** DC, MC, V. **Map** p407 M7.

This is one of Paris' most recent recruits to the 'concept' bandwagon, targeting sprightly young 15-35 year-olds with its affordable designer urban wear and an archly modern philosophy behind the counter. Three floors of accessories, footwear, men's streetwear and women's wear including Kulte, Kanabeach, Aem Kei, Djam, New York Industrie and Accostages are supplemented by international fashion mags, CDs and club flyers. Then have a drink on the terrace and examine your purchases.

Spree

16 rue de La Vieuville, 18th (01.42.23.41.40). M° Abbesses. **Open** 10am-7.30pm Tue-Sat. Closed Aug. **Credit** MC, V. **Map** p402 H1.

Run by Bruno Hadjadj and Roberta Oprandi (artist/ artistic director and fashion designer respectively) with a distinctly Montmartre vibe, Spree mixes fashion, design and contemporary art. Here you'll find a 60s chair draped in the latest fashions by designers such as Preen or Isabel Marant.

Department stores

The revamped *grands magasins* are upping the fashion ante and introducing new, cutting-edge designers and luxury spaces to lure the young, rich, pretty things away from concept stores and independent designer boutiques.

La Samaritaine

19 rue de la Monnaie, 1st (01.40.41.20.20/ www.lasamaritaine.com). M° Pont Neuf. **Open** 9.30am-7pm Mon-Wed, Fri, Sat; 9.30am-10pm Thur. **Credit** AmEx, DC, MC, V. **Map** p402 J6.

This venerable store underwent a massive face-lift in 2003, with one part let out to high-street shops such as Sephora (see perfume and makeup) and the remaining building promoting beauty, decoration, leisure and designer fashion. The elaborate turquoise and gold wrought-ironwork and peacock mosaics around the glass roof still make it one of the best preserved jewels of the *belle époque*. The restaurant and top-floor café have a fabulous view.

BHV (Bazar de l'Hôtel de Ville)

52-64 rue de Rivoli, 4th (01.42.74.90.00/ www.bhv.fr). Tile shop 14 rue du Temple (01.42.74.92.12); DIY hire annexe 40 rue de la Verrerie (01.42.74.97.23). M° Hôtel de Ville. **Open** 9.30am-7pm Mon, Tue, Thur, Sat; 9.30am-8.30pm Wed, Fri. **Credit** AmEx, MC, V. **Map** p401 G5.

DIY fiends spend hours in the basement of this hardware heaven, drooling over hinges, screws, nuts and bolts or dithering over paint colours upstairs. There is even a Bricolage Café, decked out like an old tool shed, offering salads and a computer to surf DIY sites. The store has a good range of men's outdoor wear, women's underwear, surprisingly upmarket bedlinen and a 2,000m^2 space devoted to every type of storage utility.

Le Bon Marché

24 rue de Sèvres, 7th (01.44.39.80.00/ www.bonmarche.fr). M° Sèvres-Babylone. **Open** 9.30am-7pm Mon-Sat. **Credit** AmEx, DC, MC, V. **Map** p405 G7.

Paris' oldest department store is also the most swish and user-friendly, thanks to an extensive redesign by LVMH. The prestigious Balthazar men's section offers a cluster of designer 'boutiques', while the Theatre of Beauty provides a comfort zone for women. Seven luxury boutiques from Dior to Chanel take pride of place on the ground floor. Escalators

John Galliano. *See p242.*

designed by Andrée Putman take you up to the fashion floor, which includes the store's well-cut, own-label cotton shirts. The Grande Epicerie food hall (01.44.39.81.00/www.lagrandeepicerie.fr; open 8.30am-9pm Mon-Sat) is in the adjacent building along with an antiques gallery, bar and restaurant.

Galeries Lafayette

40 bd Haussmann, 9th (01.42.82.34.56/fashion shows 01.42.82.30.25/fashion advice 01.42.82.35.50/ www.galerieslafayette.com). Cigar cellar 99 rue de Provence. M° Chaussée d'Antin/RER Auber. **Open** 9.30am-7.30pm Mon-Wed, Fri, Sat; 9.30am-9pm Thur. **Credit** AmEx, DC, MC, V. **Map** p401 H3.

This substantial department store has recently revamped its fashion, beauty and accessories sections and, in hot competition with Printemps, opened a new lingerie department on the 3rd floor. Le Labo and Trend on the first floor have introduced progressive international creators, while 90 established designers are spread over the remainder of the first and second floors. The store has five fashion and beauty consultants to guide you through the sartorial maze and the new men's fashion space on the third floor of Lafayette Homme is a must, with its natty designer corners and 'Club' space with fax and Internet access. On the first floor, Lafayette Gourmet offers plenty of places to snack and the second biggest wine cellar in Paris. On the other side of boulevard Haussmann, the old M&S building is being turned into 10,000m^2 of Art de Vivre decor for the home, opening end of March 2004. Don't forget to photograph the exquisite domed ceiling in the main shop or have a rooftop coffee.

Printemps

64 bd Haussmann, 9th (01.42.82.50.00/ www.printemps.com). M° Havre-Caumartin/ RER Auber. **Open** 9.35am-7pm Mon Wed, Fri, Sat; 9.30am-10pm Thur. **Credit** AmEx, DC, MC, V. **Map** p401 G3.

Printemps is the home of superlatives, with the largest shoe department in Paris on the men's fifth floor, and- wait for it- the biggest beauty department in the world, opened last autumn with nearly 200 brands. The new lingerie department is the stuff of fantasy too, stocked with luxury brands such as Eres and far-out frillies from Gaultier and Pucci. There are six floors of fabulous fashion in both the men's and women's stores. On the second floor of Printemps de la Mode, discover cutting-edge favourites, where French designers such as APC and Zadig et Voltaire sit side by side with the likes of Dolce e Gabbana and Moschino. The fifth floor Miss Code targets the teen miss and offers a huge selection of jeans and sportswear. Check out, too, the Printemps de la Maison store, with its well-stocked home decoration and furnishings departments and the more conceptual 'function floor', where knives, saucepans and coffee machines are set out on steel shelving. Zoom to the 9th-floor terrace restaurant and take in the art nouveau cupola.

Tati

4 bd de Rochechouart, 18th (01.55.29.52.50/ www.tati.fr). M° Barbès-Rochechouart. **Open** 10am-7pm Mon-Fri, 9.15am-7.15pm Sat. **Credit** MC, V. **Map** p402 J2.

Huge financial difficulties have threatened this Parisian shopping institution for the past year, but providing it's open, you will find anything from T-shirts and tights to wedding dresses, as well as jewellery and household goods. Almost unbeatable in its cheapness, but don't expect high quality. Good bargains can be found if you can get past the hordes who flock like vultures to the bins which proclaim the promise of 'only €2.99'. (*See p240* **Tati bye?**)

Branches: 172 rue du Temple, 3rd (01.42.71.41.77); 68 av du Maine, 14th (01.56.80.06.80).

Monoprix

Branches all over Paris (www.monoprix.fr). **Open** generally 8am-8pm Mon-Sat; some branches open till 10pm including Roquette, Commerce and Opéra (Champs-Elysées until midnight). **Credit** MC, V.

Every arrondissement has a couple of these practical stores stocking everything from paper clips to pâté. Bigger food stores have a wet fish counter,

The best For bobos

For that French bourgeous-bohemian look hang out around the Canal St-Martin (10th), observe well, then apply your credit card.

Spree
Most bobo of the concept stores – don't forget to mention your friends in the artists' squat up the road. *See p236.*

Abou d'Abi Bazar
Colour-coded racks of floaty things make mixing and matching a breeze. *See p244.*

Antoine et Lili
All bobo needs catered for in a bon-bon-coloured dream. *See p246.*

Ginger Lyly
Funky bags and jewellery to complement the look. *See p246.*

Come On Eileen
Vintage cool. *See p250.*

Caravane Chambre 19
Look like you've just been to Morocco and have taste. *See p261.*

Artazart
Canalside source of artful reading matter to take to Chez Prune. *See p263.*

Tati bye?

For over half a century Tati has been the only store where cheap is chic. Selling everything from discount underwear to inexpensive holidays, it has monopolised the cut-price market, holding its own in the face of changing consumer trends, trendier shops and even a bomb in 1986. This veritable shopping legend, with its 'tatty' pink gingham carrier bags, has primed the popularity polls to such an extent that nobody has ever questioned whether Tati will be around for ever. That was until now.

The Ouaki family tearfully announced the possible 'death' of their company in summer 2003. Bad market conditions and poor marketing are the culprits, as well as over-diversification into areas where the cheap and cheerful should never roam: eyewear and bridal dresses for example. It would appear that every one of their 27 stores has made massive losses and that the French government may not (unlike with France Télécom, Air France and Alstom) bail them out. This is a bit of a bugger really. Especially when you think that they've just opened a flagship store in New York to commemorate 50 years of Tati existence. The laws of Sod are clearly afoot. Should we not mobilise ourselves and campaign for continued existence in half-price heavens? Should we not chain ourselves to the railings in front of the five Tati buildings at Barbès-Rochechouart? Nah. But if it's still open by the time you visit, get buying. It will probably be your last chance. Just remember to keep your carrier bags. They might be worth money as an antique one day. (*See p239.*)

cheese and charcuterie displays, bread shop and decent wine department. Some branches carry only clothes and homeware in a separate store, though larger stores (Champs-Elysées for example) are all-encompassing. Some surprisingly good purchases can be made with decent middle-of-the-range underwear, an extensive range of sexy, coloured stockings and tights by DIM, tasteful clothes and the funky Bala Boosté jewellery range. And the question on every mum's lips: do they indeed stock Petit Bateaux? They do! Look in the kids' undies section. Check out bargain bins for belts, bags and baubles.

Fashion & Beauty

Collected designerwear

Kabuki Femme

25 rue Etienne-Marcel, 1st (01.42.33.55.65). M° Etienne Marcel. **Open** 10.30am-7.30pm Mon-Sat. **Credit** AmEx, DC, MC, V. **Map** p402 J5.

On the ground floor there's intrepid footwear and bags by Costume National, Miu Miu and Prada, along with Fendi's cult creations. Burberry belts and Miu Miu sunglasses are also stocked here. Upstairs houses no-flies-on-me suits by Helmut Lang and Véronique Leroy, Prada and Costume National.

Maria Luisa

2 rue Cambon, 1st (01.47.03.48.08). M° Concorde. **Open** 10.30am-7pm Mon-Sat. **Credit** AmEx, DC, MC, V. **Map** p401 G4.

Venezuelan Maria Luisa Poumaillou was one of Paris' first stockists of Galliano, McQueen and the Belgian fashion elite, and has an unflagging eye for rising stars. An ever-expanding series of shops covers fashion (Olivier Theyskens, Diego Dolcini, Ona Selfa, Rick Owens), accessories (Manolos and Pierre Hardy shoes, Carel & Rubio's gloves at 4 rue Cambon), mixed streetwear (38 rue du Mont-Thabor) and menswear (19bis rue du Mont-Thabor).

Kokon To Zai

48 rue Tiquetonne, 2nd (01.42.36.92.41). M° Etienne Marcel. **Open** 11.30am-7.30pm Mon-Sat. **Credit** AmEx, DC, MC, V. **Map** p402 J5.

Spot-on for uncovering the latest designer creations, Kokon To Zai is sister to the London version of this cutting-edge style emporiette. The neon lights and club atmosphere of the tiny, mirrored space are in keeping with the dark glamour of its designs. Unique pieces straight off the catwalk share space with creations by Alexandre et Matthieu, Marjan Peijoski and up-and-coming Norwegian designers.

L'Eclaireur

3ter rue des Rosiers, 4th (01.48.87.10.22/ www.leclaireur.com). M° St-Paul. **Open** 11am-7pm Mon-Sat. **Credit** AmEx, DC, MC, V. **Map** p406 L6.

Set in a dandified warehouse with iron girders, L'Eclaireur contains the most uncompromising of

Shine

the über labels' designs, including pieces by Comme des Garçons, Martin Margiela, Dries Van Noten and Junior Watanabe. New in stores are the Victorian-style designs of Paul Harden, and Carpe Diem.
Branches: 10 rue Herold, 1st (01.40.41.09.89); men 12 rue Malher, 4th (01.44.54.22.11); 26 av des Champs-Elysées, 8th (01.45.62.12.32).

Onward

147 bd St-Germain, 6th (01.55.42.77.56).
M° St-Germain-des-Prés. **Open** 11am-7pm Mon, Sat; 10.30am-7pm Tue-Fri. **Credit** AmEx, DC, MC, V. **Map** p405 G6.
Onward has a rapid turnover of young talent who seem to compete to see who can make the most far-out and priciest design. It currently stocks over 20 established and up-and-coming designers including Hussein Chalayan, The People of the Labyrinths and Martin Margiela. Accessories, too, are well chosen – try funky pieces by Tatty Devine, Pièce à Conviction and Yazbukey on for size.

Camerlo

4 rue de Marignan, 8th (01.47.23.77.06).
M° Franklin D Roosevelt. **Open** 11am-1pm, 2-7pm Mon-Sat. **Credit** AmEx, DC, MC, V. **Map** p401 E4.
Exuberant dressers who frequent this swanky area rely on Dany Camerlo to fit them out in head-turning style. Hence her selection of wild ideas from Russian duo Seredin et Vassiliev or Frenchman Laurent Mercier. For more low-key happenings she might suggest Pascal Humbert, Alberta Ferretti or Van der Straeten, with sleek shoes by Bruno Frisoni.

Shine

30 rue de Charonne, 11th (01.48.05.80.10).
M° Bastille. **Open** 11am-7.30pm Mon-Sat. **Credit** AmEx, DC, MC, V. **Map** p407 M7.
If you are looking for a funkier, more youthful batch of cutting-edge clothes than at Maria Luisa (*see left*), then Vinci d'Helia has just what you need: sexy T-shirts with unusual detailing, Luella's chunky knits and Earl Jeans trousers and jackets. A plethora of original if pricey accessories are there for the picking and you could end up sharing shop space with the likes of Laetitia Casta and Emma de Caunes.

Designer focus

Barbara Bui

23 rue Etienne-Marcel, 1st (01.40.26.43.65/ www.barbarabui.fr). M° Etienne Marcel.
Open 1-7.30pm Mon; 10.30-7.30pm Tue-Sat.
Credit AmEx, DC, MC, V. **Map** p402 J5.
Businesswomen who like to cut to the chase have a sartorial ally in Barbara Bui. Dressed in her lean, impeccably cut trousers, figure-hugging shirts and jackets and dagger heels, your wish is the board's command. Bui has also branched out into her own loungey CDs. But if you want to fit into your new purchases, though, hold back on the delicious world food served in her next-door café.
Branches: 43 rue des Francs-Bourgeois, 4th (01.53.01.88.05); accessories 12 rue des Sts-Pères, 6th; 35 rue de Grenelle, 7th (01.45.44.05.14); 50 av Montaigne, 8th (01.42.25.05.25).

A-poc

John Galliano

384-386 rue St-Honoré, 1st (01.55.35.40.40). M° Concorde. **Open** 11am-7pm Mon-Sat. **Credit** AmEx, DC, MC, V. **Map** p401 G4.

Designed by the architect Jean-Michel Wilmotte, whose CV includes stores for Cartier and Chaumet, this was the most exciting store to open in Paris in 2003. It is John Galliano's first-ever boutique, putting him firmly on the map and confirming his reputation as Britain's most original designer. Passers-by view the small but diverse collection of well-cut delights through the showcase window. Once inside, Louis XVI-style leather chairs complement the leather flooring in the changing room, and the divine hand-embroidered wall panels of Japanese cherry blossoms in the candle-scented loos.

Marcel Marongiu

203 rue St-Honoré, 1st (01.49.27.96.38/ www.marcel-marongiu.com). M° Tuileries. **Open** 10.30am-7.30pm Mon-Sat. **Credit** AmEx, MC, V. **Map** p401 G4.

As if expressing his roots, this part-French, part-Swedish designer's clothes mix sensuality with spareness. He is fascinated by opposites, seen in his ineffably poised jersey wool dresses with a jagged hemline. Most impressive are his black evening bustier dresses made of dozens of organza squares.

Martin Margiela

25bis rue de Montpensier, 1st (01.40.15.07.55). M° Palais Royal. **Open** 11am-7pm Mon-Sat. **Credit** AmEx, DC, MC, V. **Map** p402 H5.

The first Parisian boutique for the J D Salinger of the fashion world (he refuses to be photographed and only gives interviews by fax) is an immaculate white, unlabelled space. His clothes, which also bear a blank label, recognisable by external white stitching, are rapidly gaining respect on worldwide catwalks. Here you can find the entire line 13, 0- and 0-10 accessories for men and women; line 6 (women's basics), line 10 (menswear), magazines and shoes.

Jean-Paul Gaultier

6 rue Vivienne, 2nd (01.42.86.05.05/ www.gaultier.fr). M° Bourse. **Open** 10am-7pm Mon-Fri; 11am-7pm Sat. **Credit** AmEx, DC, MC, V. **Map** p402 H4.

King of couture, Jean-Paul Gaultier has restyled his original boutique as a modern boudoir with trapunto quilted, peach-taffeta walls. Men's and women's ready-to-wear, accessories and the cheaper JPG Jeans lines are sold here, with haute-couture upstairs (by appointment 01.42.97.48.12).

Branch: 40 av George V, 8th (01.44.43.00.44).

A-poc

47 rue des Francs-Bourgeois, 4th (01.44.54.07.05). M° St-Paul. **Open** 10.30am-7.30pm Tue-Sat. **Credit** AmEx, DC, MC, V. **Map** p406 L6.

Short for 'A Piece of Cloth', Issey Miyake's lab-style boutique designed by Erwan and Ronan Bouroullec takes a conceptual approach to clothes manufacture. Alongside ready-to-wear cotton-Lycra clothes are great rolls of seamless tubular wool jersey which is cut *sur mesure*. Miyake's assistants will advise you on a unique ensemble. The original Issey Miyake shop at 3 place des Vosges houses the creations of Naoki Takisawa, his latest design protégé.

Plein Sud

21 rue des Francs-Bourgeois, 4th (01.42.72.10.60). M° St-Paul. **Open** 11am-7pm Mon-Sat. **Credit** AmEx, MC, V. **Map** p406 L6.

Fayçal Amor's glove-tight designs are meant for the super-waifs of this world, but don't let that faze you if you're into spiky stilettos, skirts slit to show off your fishnets and a very black, or brown, wardrobe. **Branches:** 2 pl des Victoires, 2nd (01.42.36.75.02); 70bis rue Bonaparte, 6th (01.43.54.43.06).

Amin Kader

2 rue Guisarde, 6th (01.43.26.27.37). M° Mabillon. **Open** 2-7.30pm Mon; 10.30am-7.30pm Tue-Sat. **Credit** AmEx, MC, V. **Map** p406 H7.

This tiny boutique has been the fashion pros' best-kept secret – they keep coming back for the Berber couturier's superbly soft Arran-knit cashmere pullovers, fluid crêpe-de-chine trousers, raincoats dripping with elegance and hand-stitched travel bags. Kader also stocks the divine beauty products sold at the Florentine church Santa Maria Novella.

Lagerfeld Gallery

40 rue de Seine, 6th (01.55.42.75.51). M° Odéon. **Open** 11am-7pm Tue-Sat. **Credit** AmEx, MC, V. **Map** p407 H6.

Andrée Putman helped create this shrine to King Karl's world of stylish minimalism, where his creations and photography are exhibited. You could, of course, just sneak in to browse the latest fashion, beauty and art press scattered over the handsome round table at the front of the gallery.

Sonia Rykiel

175 bd St-Germain, 6th (01.49.54.60.60/ www.soniarykiel.fr). M° St-Germain-des-Prés. **Open** 10.30am-7pm Tue-Sat. **Credit** AmEx, DC, MC, V. **Map** p406 G6.

Even if her fabrics aren't as super-soft as they once were, the queen of stripes is still producing skinny rib knitwear evoking the Left Bank babes of Sartre's time. Menswear is across the street, while two recently opened boutiques feature the younger, more affordable 'Sonia by Sonia Rykiel' collection (59 rue des Sts-Pères) and children's wear (6 rue de Grenelle – the site of her original 1966 shop).

Martine Sitbon

13 rue de Grenelle, 7th (01.44.39.84.44). M° Rue du Bac or Sèvres Babylone. **Open** 10.30am-7pm Mon-Sat. **Credit** AmEx, MC, V. **Map** p405 G7.

The scent of orange and mimosa lures you into Sitbon's vault-like store. Beneath the vast ceiling, few pieces hang on the railings, but each appears to have a secret history, born of the originality of the fabric and cut and its singular harmony, often inspired by modern art. The men's clothes will tickle you pink, too. If the prices are out of your reach, she has cute accessories and candles for under €50.

Yohji Yamamoto

3 rue de Grenelle, 7th (01.42.84.28.87). M° Sèvres Babylone or St-Sulpice. **Open** 10.30am-7.30pm Mon-Sat. **Credit** AmEx, DC, MC, V. **Map** p405 G7.

One of the few true pioneers working in the fashion industry today, Yohji Yamamoto's masterful cuts and finish are greatly inspired by the kimono and traditional Tibetan costume. His dexterity with form makes for unique shapes and styles, largely in black, but when he does colour, it's a blast of brilliance. **Branches:** 47 rue Etienne-Marcel, 1st (01.45.08.82.45); Y's 25 rue du Louvre, 1st (01.42.21.42.93); 69 rue des Sts-Pères, 6th (01.45.48.22.56).

Comme des Garçons

54 rue du Fbg-St-Honoré, 8th (01.53.30.27.27). M° Madeleine or Concorde. **Open** 11am-7pm Mon-Sat. **Credit** AmEx, DC, MC, V. **Map** p400 D3.

Rei Kawakubo's juxtaposed design ideas and revolutionary mix of materials have greatly influenced fashion over the past two decades and are superbly showcased in this fire-engine red, fibreglass store. Exclusive perfume lines get a futuristic setting at Comme des Garçons Parfums (23 pl du Marché-St-Honoré, 1st/01.47.03.15.03).

Parisian chic

Agnès b

2, 3, 6, 10, 19 rue du Jour, 1st (women 01.45.08.56.56/men 01.42.33.04.13). M° Les Halles or Etienne-Marcel. **Open** 10am-7pm Mon-Wed, Fri, Sat; 10am-9pm Thur. **Credit** AmEx, MC, V. **Map** p402 J5.

Fashions come and go but Agnès b rarely wavers from her own design vision: pure lines in excellent quality cotton, merino wool and silk. Best buys are shirts, pullovers and cardigans that keep their shape for years. The cool plan is to tour her mini-empire of women, men, children, travel and accessories outlets, and the new sportswear shop.
Branches: (baby/child) 83 rue d'Assas, 6th (01.43.54.69.21); (women) 13 rue Michelet, 6th (01.46.33.70.20); (children) 22 rue St-Sulpice, 6th (01.40.51.70.69); (women/beauty/children/men) 6, 10, 12 rue du Vieux-Colombier, 6th (01.44.39.02.60); (women/men) 17, 25 av Pierre 1er de Serbie, 16th (01.47.20.22.44/01.47.23.36.69).

Bali Barret

36 rue du Mont-Thabor, 1st (01.49.26.01.75/ www.balibarret.com). M° Concorde. **Open** 2.30pm-7.30pm Mon; 10.30am-7.30pm Tue-Sat. **Credit** AmEx, MC, V. **Map** p401 G5.

This French label opened its first boutique in 2002, featuring four different-colour stories each season and offering an androgynous take on classic styles, with a sexy twist. This year's easy-to-wear collection features bright primaries. Look out for the funky belts and bags and the matching stripey knickers, stockings and cotton polo necks. With a mini-menswear collection added in 2001, there are also some great soft, logoed sweatshirts.

Claudie Pierlot

1 rue Montmartre, 1st (01.42.21.38.38). M° Les Halles **Open** 11am-7pm Mon-Sat. **Credit** AmEx, MC, V. **Map** p402 H4.

For true Parisian chic a black beret is essential, and Claudie Pierlot can always oblige no matter what the season. Wear it with her simple, elegant tank tops and cardigans and little black suits that are so right for the office.

Branch: 23 rue du Vieux-Colombier, 6th (01.45.48.11.96).

Corinne Cobson

6 rue du Marché-St-Honoré, 1st (01.42.60.48.64). M° Tuileries. **Open** noon-7.30pm Mon; 11am-7.30pm Tue-Sat. **Credit** AmEx, MC, V. **Map** p401 G4.

This mirror-covered boutique is frequented by Paris darlings. Cobson favours simple lines combined with graphic prints. Check out her anti-racism and pro-environment plunge-neck T-shirts and sumptuous chunky jumpers. Photos by her partner, Tanguy Loisance, provide the decor, and humorous designs by Samuel Lebaron take pride of place in the shop window.

Et Vous

42 rue Etienne-Marcel, 2nd (01.55.80.76.10). M° Etienne Marcel. **Open** noon-7pm Mon; 10.30am-7pm Tue-Sat. **Credit** AmEx, MC, V. **Map** p402 J5.

Fashionable, mid-upmarket womenswear in muted, neutral colours are the cornerstone of the Et Vous label. Its latest branch is ultra-minimal, with the collection displayed on pale, plywood units. The shop also sells Diesel jeans.

Pinko

36 rue Etienne-Marcel, 2nd (01.40.13.92.26). M° Etienne Marcel. **Open** 10.30am-7.30pm Mon-Sat. **Credit** AmEx, MC, V. **Map** p402 J5.

The only standalone store of the Italian Pinko label in France, this small boutique sells sexy, dressy eveningwear inspired by the 70s and 80s dance scene. Look out for the gold sequinned vest tops, frilly mini skirts, black bustiers and acrylic tops that ooze chic for late Parisian evenings.

Abou d'Abi Bazar

10 rue des Francs-Bourgeois, 3rd (01.42.77.96.98). **Open** 2-7.15pm Mon; 10.30am-7.15pm Tue-Sat; 2-7pm Sun. **Credit** AmEx, MC, V. **Map** p401 G4.

Racks of trendy, feminine attire from the likes of Vanessa Bruno, Stella Forest and Tara Jarmon are organised by colour, making pick 'n' mix fun. The only downside is the paucity of changing rooms, but you may turn heads if you opt to strip off mid-store.

Zadig & Voltaire

42 rue des Francs-Bourgeois, 3rd (01.44.54.00.60). M° St-Paul or Hôtel de Ville. **Open** 11am-8pm Tue-Sat; 2-8pm Sun; 1.30-7.30pm Mon. **Credit** AmEx, MC, V. **Map** p406 K6.

This new Marais store is the sixth Zadig & Voltaire branch in Paris. Suffused with natural light and with a ceiling striped with beams, it stocks a hip, relaxed collection. Popular separates include cotton tops, cashmere jumpers and faded jeans.

Branches: 9 rue du 29 Juillet, 1st (01.42.92.00.80); 4 12 rue Ste-Croix-de-la-Bretonnerie, 4th (01.42.72.09.55/01.42.72.15.20);1 rue du Vieux-Colombier, 6th (01.43.29.18.29).

Stella Cadente

4 quai des Célestins, 4th (01.44.78.05.95). M° Sully-Morland or Saint Paul. **Open** 11am-7.30pm daily. **Credit** AmEx, MC, V. **Map** p406 L7.

Giving on to a cobbled courtyard, this romantic and spacious designer boutique – with baby-pink walls, white curtains and a modern design – is a haven of tranquillity. Designed by Australia's Stanislassia Klein, this ultra-feminine, chic label is known for its floral, chiffon dresses and exquisite accessories.

Branch: 93 quai de Valmy, 10th (01.42.09.27.00).

Yvonne Börjesson

7 rue Aubriot, 4th (01.42.71.02.13). M° St-Paul. **Open** 1-7pm Tue-Sat; 2-7pm Sun. **Credit** AmEx, MC,V. **Map** p406 L7.

This beautiful boutique is home to Swedish designer Yvonne Börjesson, who brings a refreshing Nordic streak to the Parisian fashion scene with her sophisticated, avant-garde designs that warp Swedish folklore into highly wearable and desirable, futuristic creations. Fabric is a mix of traditional Swedish materials and modern synthetics resulting in well thought-out, feminine items. Her accessories such as reindeer skin bracelets are also worth a splash.

Zadig & Voltaire

APC

3, 4 rue de Fleurus, 6th (01.42.22.12.77). M° St-Placide. **Open** 10.30am-7pm Mon-Sat. **Credit** AmEx, MC, V. **Map** p405 G8.

Think of Muji crossed with a rough-cut Agnès b and you get an idea of why APC Jean Toutou's gear is much sought after by the Japanese in-crowd. Men's clothes are at No 4, along with quirky accessories; cross the road to No 3 for the women's collection.

Comptoir des Cotonniers

59ter rue Bonaparte, 6th (01.43.26.07.56). M° St-Germain-des-Prés. **Open** 11am-7pm Mon; 10am-7.30pm Tue-Sat. **Credit** MC, V. **Map** p405 H6.

Sturdy cotton and wool basics for mothers and daughters who like to keep in step with fashion. Trendy touches on trousers and skirts include ruffles, lacy borders, artily distressed seams and asymmetric cutting at prices that won't break the bank.

Branches include: 29 rue du Jour, 1st (01.53.40.75.77); 18 rue St-Antoine, 4th (01.40.27.09.08); 53 rue de Passy, 16th (01.42.88.06.30).

Diapositive

42 rue du Four, 6th (01.45.48.85.57). M° Sèvres Babylone. **Open** 10.30am-7pm Mon-Sat. **Credit** AmEx, MC, V. **Map** p406 H7.

A practical yet soigné range of grown-up business suits and evening wear that is good value (suits around €380). For a touch of glamour, there are gold lamé-speckled fine wool pullovers and sequin-patterned, long-sleeved T-shirts.

Branches: 12 rue du Jour, 1st (01.42.21.34.41); 33 rue de Sèvres, 7th (01.42.44.13.00); 20 av des Ternes, 17th (01.43.80.05.87).

Irié Wash

8 rue du Pré-aux-Clercs, 6th (01.42.61.18.28). M° Rue du Bac or St-Germain-des-Prés. **Open** 10.15am-7pm Mon-Sat. Closed three weeks in Aug. **Credit** MC, V. **Map** p405 F7.

Elegantly avant-garde Parisians love this Japanese designer, who is constantly researching new methods and materials, including laser cutting, hologram prints and most recently a polyester and Elastane mix, like an ultra-supple suede (€190 for a dress).

Vanessa Bruno

25 rue St-Sulpice, 6th (01.43.54.41.04). M° Odéon. **Open** 10.30am-7pm Mon-Sat. **Credit** AmEx, DC, MC, V. **Map** p406 H7.

Bruno's feminine and very individual clothes have a cool and steady Zen-like quality that no doubt comes from her stay in Japan. She also makes great bags to be seen hanging from the wrists of much of the (female) Parisian cool brigade.

Branch: 12 rue de Castiglione, 1st (01.42.61.44.60).

Corinne Sarrut

4 rue du Pré-aux-Clercs, 7th (01.42.61.71.60). M° Rue du Bac or St-Germain-des-Prés. **Open** 10am-7pm Mon-Sat. **Credit** AmEx, MC, V. **Map** p405 F7.

Fans of *Amélie* will be charmed by the work of Corinne Sarrut, who dressed Audrey Tautou for the

High street chic

Paris shopping does not have to be all designer labels and selective boutiques. In addition to pan-European brands such as Zara and Mango, the French high street has its fair share of Gallic cheapies, offering affordable versions of upper-end trendsetters. Most have multiple branches, of which we have listed just a few, and concentrations can be found in certain areas. One of the best places to go for a choice of high street shops is Le Forum des Halles (1st). It may not be known for its savoury frequentation, but it does have a massive concentration of French shops, as well as cafés and a cinema for the down time. Above ground rue de Rivoli virtually replicates the selection. Also try bd St-Michel (5th) or the La Défense shopping mall where the trek out there is made up for by a crowd-free environment.

First off is **Jennyfer** (Forum des Halles, 1st/01.40.2.01.23; 35 bd St-Michel, 5th/ 01.56.81.05.53). Teenie-bopper friendly, this place is filled to the brim with cheap and trendy items influenced by the clothes worn by French trash-TV stars. In the same genre is **Pimkie** (Forum des Halles, 1st/01.40.39.90.47; 25 bd St-Michel, 5th/01.44.27.06.02) where lots of throw-away essentials such as groovy T-shirts and faded jeans will just about see you through the season's fashion requirements. **Naf Naf** (Galeries Lafayette, 9th/01.42.82.34.56) and **Sinéquanone** (Forum des Halles, 1st/ 01.42.36.71.23) take things up a notch with well-priced catwalk knockoffs, while **Promod** (110 rue de Rivoli, 1st/ 01.40.39.09.24), **La City** (Forum des Halles, 1st/01.40.26.35.89) and **1.2.3.** (146 rue de Rivoli, 1st/ 01.40.20.97.01) cater for young things searching for a more classical look.

For a truly French look **An'ge** (Forum des Halles, 1st/01.42.36.27.22) always has plenty of funky feminine frocks and **Côte à Côte** (15 bd St-Michel, 5th/ 01.46.33.17.53) has its own line of inexpensive separates and sportswear. On the upper-end of the scale is tasteful **Caroll** (138 rue de Rivoli, 1st/ 01.40.41.11.68). From sexy sequinned eveningwear to well-tailored suits, clothing is made to last and well worth the extra few euros.

part. Anyone with a weakness for the 1940s silhouette will love her trapeze creations in silky viscose. **Branches:** (previous season) 24 rue du Champ de Mars, 7th (01.45.56.00.65); 7 rue Gustave-Courbet, 16th (01.55.73.09.73); (wedding and evening) 42 rue des Sts-Pères, 7th (01.45.44.19.92).

ICB

46 rue de Grenelle, 7th (01.45.44.40.45). M° Rue du Bac. **Open** 11am-7pm Mon; 10.30am-7pm Tue-Sat. **Credit** AmEx, MC, V. **Map** p405 G6.
This pristine pale grey and white store, where the shiny aluminium drawers reflect the products like mirrors, is the first of the Japanese ICB label in France. Clothes are elegant and aimed at the working woman with collections in mostly neutral black, beiges and whites. Look out for the sleek handbags and gorgeous multi-striped umbrellas.

Paul et Joe

62 rue des Sts-Pères, 7th (01.40.28.03.34). M° Rue du Bac or St-Germain-des-Prés. **Open** 11am-7.30pm Mon-Sat. **Credit** AmEx, DC, MC, V. **Map** p405 G6.
Fashion victims have taken a great shine to Sophie Albou's weathered 40s-style creations (named after her sons), so much so that she has opened a menswear branch and this new flagship, with its out-to-be noticed bubblegum pink gramophone. **Branches:** 46 rue Etienne-Marcel (01.40.28.03.34); (men) 40 rue du Four, 6th (01.45.44.97.70).

Antoine et Lili

95 quai de Valmy, 10th (01.40.37.41.55). M° Gare de l'Est. **Open** 1am-7pm Mon; 11am-8pm Tue-Fri; 10.30am-8pm Sat; 11.30am-7.30pm Sun. **Credit** AmEx, DC, MC, V. **Map** p402 L3.
These fuschia-pink and apple-green shops, reflected in the canal on a fine day, are a colour therapist's dream. Vibrant jumpers and neo-hippy skirts hang amid Mexican shrines, Hindu postcards and all sorts of miscellaneous kitsch. The three-shop Canal St-Martin 'Village' has an equally colourful home decoration outlet, florist and self-service café. **Branches:** 51 rue des Francs-Bourgeois, 4th (01.42.27.95.00); 87 rue de Seine, 6th (01.56.24.35.81); 7 rue d'Alboni, 16th (01.45.27.95.00); 90 rue des Martyrs, 18th (01.42.58.10.22).

Ginger Lyly

33 rue Beaurepaire 10th (01.42.06.07.73). M° République. **Open** 11.30am-7.30pm Mon, Thur-Sat; 2-7.30pm Wed; 3–7.30pm Sun. **Credit** MC, V. **Map** p402 L4.
On a side road just off the Canal St-Martin, Ginger Lyly draws in a hip crowd searching for unusual clothes and accessories to compliment their attractively calculated bohemian–bourgeois look. Bright colours and funky bags are the trademark, along with funky chintzy jewellery.

Isabel Marant

16 rue de Charonne, 11th (01.49.29.71.55). M° Ledru-Rollin. **Open** noon-7pm Mon; 10.30am-7.30pm Tue-Sat. **Credit** AmEx, MC, V. **Map** p407 M7.
Marant's clothes are easily recognisable by their ethno-babe brocades, blanket-like coats and decorated sweaters in luxurious materials, and the in-crowd is in hot pursuit.
Branch: 1 rue Jacob, 6th (01.43.26.04.12); 3 passage St-Sébastien, 11th (01.49.23.75.40).

Ladies & Gentlemen

4 passage Charles-Dallerey, 11th (01.47.00.86.12). M° Ledru-Rollin. **Open** noon-7pm Tue-Sat; 2-7pm Sun. **Credit** AmEx, DC, MC, V. **Map** p407 N7.
Amid paintings and minimalist techno beats, red dummies are lovingly swathed in the classic yet slightly surreal creations of designers Isabelle Ballu (women's) and Moritz Rogorsky (men's). Most of the clothes are temptingly hidden away in special alcoves – seek them out.

Street & club wear

These establishments serve the upwardly mobile youths who come to buy the vibe-dunkin' 'Must Haves' of the street scene.

Agnès b Sport

10 rue du Jour, 1st (01.45.08.49.89). M° Etienne Marcel. **Open** 10am-7.30pm Mon-Sat. **Credit** AmEx, MC, V. **Map** p402 J5.
With its swirling blue graffiti frescoes by New York's Rostarr, Agnès b Sport cuts a very different image to the label's mixed menswear and womenswear store down the same road. Appealing to a younger, more street-led clientele, the new store sells plain and striped sportswear in an urban, hip-hop inspired setting. Worth noting are the one-off hats by graffiti artists.

Boutique M Dia

6-7 pl des Innocents, 1st (01.40.26.03.31). M° Châtelet/RER Châtelet-Les Halles. **Open** 1-8pm Mon; 11am-8pm Tue-Sat. **Credit** AmEx, MC, V. **Map** p406 J6.
Mohammed Dia, the ultimate urban rebel from Paris' insalubrious Sarcelles suburb, went to America and came back with an idea to get him out of the ghetto -clothes design. €20 million later he has his own line of men and women's urban sports clothes and a shoe line called Tariq (worn by the Dallas Maverick basketballers). This, his first boutique, is a shrine to his success with everything in the Dia range available to anyone streetwise enough to go in.

Kanabeach

78 rue Jean-Jacques-Rousseau, 1st (01.40.26.41.66). M° Etienne Marcel. **Open** 11am-7.30pm Mon-Sat. **Credit** MC, V. **Map** p402 J5.
With its mini waterfall, astroturf garden, mini caravan and changing rooms resembling beach cabins, this French youthwear store gives off a campsite atmosphere that'll make you think Babs Windsor. The autumn/winter men's and women's collections include Jacquard check red and apricot coats, navy and cream trousers, and colourful separates.

Le Vestibule

3 pl Ste-Opportune, 1st (01.42.33.21.89). M° Châtelet. **Open** 10.30am-7pm Mon-Sat and one Sun in every month. **Credit** AmEx, DC, MC, V. **Map** p402 J5.

An eye-popping showcase for the wildest creations of the vintage street wear and club gear genre, including exhibits by mainstream labels such as Dolce e Gabbana and Castelbajac. For effortless flash and panache, Cultura, Diesel StyleLab, Replay and its Coca-Cola Ware label are hard to beat.

Kiliwatch

64 rue Tiquetonne, 2nd (01.42.21.17.37/ www.kiliwatch.tm.fr). M° Etienne Marcel. **Open** 2-7pm Mon; 11am-7pm Tue-Thur; 11am-8.30pm Fri; 11am-7.30pm Sat. **Credit** AmEx, MC, V. **Map** p402 J5.

The original protagonist of the Etienne-Marcel revival is filled to bursting with hoodies, casual shirts and washed-out jeans. Featured brands such as G-Star, Kulte and Diesel accompany a huge selection of pricey but decent-condition second-hand clothes (Adidas tracksuit tops and mini-kilts especially) for that ultimate retro-chic look.

Le Shop

3 rue d'Argout, 2nd (01.40.28.95.94). M° Etienne Marcel. **Open** 1-7pm Mon; 11am-7pm Tue-Sat. **Credit** MC, V. **Map** p402 J5.

Street-savvy teenagers hang out at this sprawling covered market with its collection of around 25 brands. Male hip-hoppers go for Homecore, Tribal, Body Cult and Triiad (also at 7 rue de Turbigo, 1st), while the girls slip into Lady Soul, Misolka and Oxyde (also at 12 rue de Turbigo).

Tokyoïte

12 rue du Roi de Sicile, 4th (01.42.77.87.01). M° St-Paul. **Open** 1.30-8.30pm Tue-Sun. **Credit** MC, V. **Map** p406 K6.

For some Tokyo-living in Paris, check out this cute and kitschy Goldorak-fronted boutique which specialises in Japanese imports. Ideal for Converse fans (it stocks lots of models you can't get anywhere else in Paris) and rare Evisu bags.

Marithé et François Girbaud

7 rue du Cherche-Midi, 6th (01.53.40.74.20.). M° Sèvres-Babylone. **Open** noon-7pm Mon; 10am-7pm Tue-Sat. **Credit** AmEx, DC, MC, V. **Map** p402 J5.

The *soixante-huitard* couple are as pioneering as ever, producing complex street wear in high-tech fabrics using laser cutting and welding. This new shop has four light-filled floors and a vertical garden of 250 plants.

Branches: 38 rue Etienne-Marcel, 2nd (01.53.40.74.20); 20 rue Mahler, 4th (01.44.54.99.01); 8 rue de Babylone, 7th (01.45.48.78.86); 49 av Franklin-Roosevelt, 8th (01.45.62.49.15).

Stealth

42 rue du Dragon, 6th (01.45.49.24.14). M° St-Germain-des-Prés or St-Sulpice. **Open** 2-7.30pm Mon; 10.30am-7.30pm Tue-Sat. **Credit** AmEx, MC, V. **Map** p406 H7.

New York record producer and designer Marcus Klossock is the mastermind behind this cool boutique. His men's label Aem Kei (the phonetic rendering of his initials) melds US street style with European refinement, and his women's line Aem Aya has fresh ideas. Other urban underground

Kanabeach

labels to discover here include Tsumori Chisato, Fake London, Haseltine and the hilariously named Poetry of Sex.

Stocks and Marques

65 rue de Lancry, 10th (01.42.00.00.46). M° Jacques Bonsergent. **Open** 11am-7.30pm Mon-Thur; 11am-3.30pm Fri; 1-7.30pm Sun. **Credit** MC, V. **Map** p402 L3.

Despite its uninspiring name, this is actually quite an inspiring shop with its crushed Coke can facade and discount designer wear on sale inside. The labels are all foreign and concentrate on funky avant-garde street wear. Brands include lesser-known English label, Pink Soda and Italian, Edwin.

Menswear

Over the past few years, the French men's fashion market has really taken off. For that Parisian chic look check out the shirts in Vercourt and Berteil, or Phist and Alain Figaret. Le Bon Marché and Galeries Lafayette give a good international overview, and Agnès b, Sonia Rykiel, and Marithé et François Girbaud add an exciting European strain.

Madelios

23 bd de la Madeleine, 1st (01.53.45.00.00). M° Madeleine. **Open** 10am-7pm Mon-Sat. **Credit** AmEx, DC, MC, V. **Map** p401 G4.

A 4,500m² one-stop-shop for men's fashion over two floors. The decor is rather boring but then it's the clothes that matter, including suits by Paul Smith, Dormeuil, Givenchy and Kenzo and casuals from Diesel and Levi's, plus shoes and accessories.

Ron Orb

39 rue Etienne-Marcel, 1st (01.40.28.09.33). M° Etienne Marcel. **Open** 11am-7pm Mon-Sat. **Credit** AmEx, MC, V. **Map** p402 J5.

Forward-looking synthetic fabrics for the techno generation come courtesy of the Breton designer. French Touch fans should check out his wide range of jackets, many with myriad useful pockets.

Thierry Mugler

54 rue Etienne-Marcel, 2nd (01.42.33.06.13). M° Etienne Marcel. **Open** 11am-7pm Mon; 10.30am-7pm Tue-Sat. **Credit** AmEx, DC, MC, V. **Map** p402 J5.

After closing his small store on place des Victoires, Thierry Mugler has moved to a larger space down the road with a high-tech, highly masculine design to display the classic menswear and accessories. Sombre casual clothing and suits in black, beige, brown, navy and grey predominate. Slick accessories include wallets, card holders and travel bags.

Nodus

22 rue Vieille-du-Temple, 3rd.(01.42.77.07.96). M° St-Paul or Hôtel de Ville. **Open** 2pm-7.30pm Mon, Sun; 10.30am-7.30pm Tue-Sat. **Credit** MC, V. **Map** p406 K6.

Free "P" Star

This cosy men's shirt specialist is a must-visit for any self-respecting male. Under the wooden beams are neatly arranged rows of striped, checked and plain men's shirts, stylish silk ties with subtle, graphic designs and silver-plated crystal cufflinks.

Slip's Home

6 rue du Grenier-St-Lazare, 3rd (01.42.77.53.23). M° Rambuteau. **Open** 2-7.30pm Mon; noon-7.30pm Tue-Sat. **Credit** AmEx, MC, V. **Map** p402 K5.

Gone are the days of the harvest festival (all is safely gathered in) but there'll be thanksgiving when you see this store that devotes 85m² to men's underwear. The pants range from the G-string to the boxer, with brands such as Tom Robinn (his cosmetics line is also on sale here). Adi Hodzic's jewellery creations can be snapped up here as well as belts and other stylish accessories. Important lingo: Y-fronts are 'slip kangourou'. No peeping joeys, OK?

L'Eclaireur Homme

12 rue Malher, 4th (01.44.54.22.11). M° St-Paul. **Open** 11am-7pm Mon-Sat. **Credit** AmEx, DC, MC, V. **Map** p406 L6.

Among the exposed ducts of this former printing works you'll find the usual designer suspects: Prada, Comme des Garçons, Dries Van Noten, Martin Margiela. The star label, though, is Italian Stone Island, whose radical technical clothing features parkas with a 'steel outer shell' to fight off pollution or the bank manager.

Jack Henry

54 rue des Rosiers, 4th (01.44.59.89.44). M° St-Paul. **Open** 2.30-8pm daily. **Credit** AmEx, DC, MC, V. **Map** p406 K6.

This thirtysomething New Yorker has been honing his sartorial skills in Paris for over a decade. His spare, dark suits offer a fine, elongated silhouette, enhanced by chest-hugging knitwear. The look is inspired by US combat gear, but this means discipline in hidden details rather than pockets in unlikely places.

Branch: (women) 1 rue Montmartre, 1st (01.42.21.46.01).

Façonnable

9 rue du Fbg-St-Honoré, 8th (01.47.42.21.18.04). M° Concorde. **Open** 10.30am-7pm Mon-Sat. **Credit** AmEx, DC, MC, V. **Map** p401 F4.

The Nice-based label may be largely the domain of the BCBG male, but its timeless city-slicker suits, striped shirts and country-gent cords are of too good a quality to be bypassed. Soft suede jackets and checked shirts are particularly tempting.

Lanvin

15 rue du Fbg-St-Honoré, 8th (01.44.71.33.33). M° Concorde. **Open** 10am-6.45pm Mon-Sat. **Credit** AmEx, DC, MC, V. **Map** p401 G4.

Where have all the beautiful people gone? Why here of course, to buy a luxurious-number-of-ply cashmere sweaters. This is heady, rocking posh-wear for those infuriating executive dudes who get all the best chicks. The range has recently been revamped to celebrate the arrival of Albert Elbaz but still slants towards suits with a statement to make.

Loft Design by

12 rue du Fbg-St-Honoré, 8th (01.42.65.59.65). M° Madeleine or Concorde. **Open** 10am-7pm Mon-Sat. **Credit** AmEx, DC, MC, V. **Map** p401 F4.

Fourteen years ago, a certain likely lad named Patrick Frêche hit upon the idea of producing clothes that were colour-coordinated with the Paris skyline – that is to say, heavy on the grey and black. This turned out to be not such a dullsville idea: Loft Design by now has a cult following with the Paris media and fashion crowd.

Branches include: 12 rue de Sévigné, 4th (01.48.87.13.07); 56 rue de Rennes, 6th (01.45.44.88.99).

Vintage, designer cast-offs & discount fashion

The craze for vintage fashion has seen second-hand clothes shops flourish, though demand ensures that bargains are rare, so you'll need to be hell-bent on good deal hunting.

Didier Ludot

19, 20 23, 24 galerie Montpensier, 1st (01.42.96.06.56/www.didierludot.com). Little black dress 125 galerie Valois, 1st (01.40.15.01.04). M° Palais-Royal. **Open** 11am-7pm Mon-Sat. **Credit** AmEx, DC, V. **Map** p402 H5.

Didier Ludot's series of mini-temples to vintage haute couture have been so successful that he now has concessions in Printemps, Harrods and Barneys New York, plus his own line of little black dresses, a perfume and book. Ludot's prices are exorbitant, but then again he has stunning pieces – Molyneux, Balenciaga, Fath, Dior, Pucci, Féraud, Stern and of course Chanel, from the 1920s onwards.

Son et Image

87 rue St-Denis, 1st (01.40.41.90.61). M° Châtelet. **Open** 10.30am-7.30pm Mon-Sat. **Credit** AmEx, MC,V. **Map** p406 J6.

This popular little second-hand clothes store in the heart of the St-Denis red light district, is filled with well-priced vintage leather, fur coats and hats, old jeans and hip boots.

L'Habilleur

44 rue de Poitou, 3rd (01.48.87.77.12). M° St-Sébastien-Froissart. **Open** 11am-8pm Mon-Sat. **Credit** MC, V. **Map** p402 L5.

Urban warriors prowl this slick store for its severely cut men's and women's wear by Dries Van Noten, Helmut Lang, John Richmond, Plein Sud, Martine Sitbon and Bikkembergs, and dagger-toed shoes by Patrick Cox. All the pieces, which are end-of-line or off-the-catwalk, are 50-70% off.

Alternatives

18 rue du Roi-de-Sicile, 4th (01.42.78.31.50). M° St-Paul. **Open** 11am-1pm, 2.30-7pm Tue-Sat. Closed 15 July-15 Aug. **Credit** V. **Map** p402 K6.

This stylish, if rather cramped, boutique is worth a rummage for designer cast-offs in surprisingly good condition. You might find a man's Burberry coat for around €375, women's Miu Miu high heels €120, along with wearable togs by Jean-Paul Gaultier, Comme des Garçons and Dries Van Noten.

Free "P" Star

8 Ste-Croix de la Bretonnerie, 4th (01.42.76.03.72). M° St-Paul. **Open** noon-11pm Mon-Sat; 2-11pm Sun. **No credit cards**. **Map** p406 K6.

This Aladdin's cave of retro glitz, 1960s-80s glad rags and ex-army jackets is perhaps the most reasonably priced of the bargain basements. Find that old skool coat and cardie, look up to find the fur coats and hats, old jeans and hip footwear, or wind down the rickety staircase to get to the farrago of outdoor-wear frivolities.

Le Depôt-Vente de Buci-Bourbon

6 rue de Bourbon-le-Château, 6th (01.46.34.45.05). M° Mabillon. **Open** 11am-8pm daily. **Credit** MC, V. **Map** p405 H7.

These two side-by-side boutiques boast an exuberant cocktail of high-quality vintage jewellery, coffee services, wild 1950s shades and men's ties in the first, and good-condition women's retro couture, second-hand modern designer clothes and shoes in the shop next door.

Le Mouton à Cinq Pattes

19 rue Grégoire-de-Tours, 6th (01.43.29.73.56). M° Odéon. **Open** 10.30am-7.30pm Mon-Fri; 10.30am-8pm Sat. **Credit** AmEx, MC, V. **Map** p406 H7.

Designer vintage and last season's collection in mint condition: Vittadini, Klaus Thierschmidt, Buscat, Donn Adriana, Chanel and Lagerfeld. Stock turnover is very quick, so this is no time to have an indecision crisis. Labels are cut out, so make sure you know what you're buying.

Branches: 15 rue Vieille-du-Temple, 4th (01.42.71.86.30); 138 bd St-Germain, 6th (01.43.26.49.25).

Come On Eileen

16-18 rue des Taillandiers, 11th (01.43.38.12.11). M° Ledru-Rollin. **Open** 11.30am-8.30pm Mon-Fri; 4-8pm Sun. **Credit** AmEx, DC, MC, V. **Map** p407 M7.

The owners of this three-floor vintage wonderland have an eye for what's funky, from cowboy gear to 60s débutantes' frocks. With clients like Kylie Minogue, they can afford to be pricey (Hermès scarves average €100), but the stock is well-sourced and in good condition. Bet you won't go in and ask for a pair of midnight runners.

Doursoux Michel

3 passage Alexandre, 15th (01.43.27.00.97). M° Pasteur. **Open** 10am-7.30pm Tue-Sat. **Credit** MC, V. **Map** p405 E9.

This place is a heaven for 'Village People' fans and something of a classic in Paris' army surplus community. The stock is quite small but provides good quality necessities such as coats, boots and gloves, as well as nifty items to wear on your Vespa.

Lingerie & swimwear

Alice Cadolle

14 rue Cambon, 1st (01.42.60.94.94/www.cadolle.fr). M° Concorde. **Open** 9.30am-1pm Mon-Sat. **Credit** AmEx, MC, V. **Map** p401 G4.

Five generations of lingerie by appointment are embodied in this boutique, founded by Hermine Cadolle, the inventor of the brassière. Her great, great, granddaughter, Poupie Cadolle, continues the tradition on the *belle époque* third floor. Poupie's ready-to-wear speciality is bodices and corsets so soigné that Christian Lacroix and Thierry Mugler have made them an intrinsic part of their collections.

Fifi Chachnil

26 rue Cambon, 1st (01.42.60.38.86). M° Madeleine. **Open** 11am-7pm Mon-Sat. **Credit** AmEx, MC, V. **Map** p401 G4.

Fifi Chachnil offers a modern take on frou-frou underwear in the pin-up and Agent Provacateur tradition. Her chic colour mixes, such as deep red silk bras with boudoir pink bows and pale turquoise girdles with orange trim, will have you purring with pleasure. Transparent black babydoll negligées with an empire-line bust are another favourite.

Princesse Tam Tam

52 bd St Michel, 6th (01.42.34.99.31). M° Cluny-La Sorbonne. **Open** 1-7pm Mon; 10am-7pm Tue-Sat. **Credit** AmEx, MC, V. **Map** p406 J7.

Quality but inexpensive underwear and swimwear brand favoured by the BCBG contingent has launched out with provocative traffic-stopping ads. Bright colours, sexy transparent and sporty are the season's story. Not for well-endowed girls, however.

Branches include: 10 rue de l'Arc en Ciel, 1st (01.44.76.89.98); 9 rue Bréa, 6th (01.55.42.14.72).

Sabbia Rosa

73 rue des Sts-Pères, 6th (01.45.48.88.37). M° St-Germain-des-Prés. **Open** 10am-7pm Mon-Sat. **Credit** AmEx, MC, V. **Map** p405 G7.

Settle yourself on the soft green leather sofa in this lingerie heaven and let Moana Moatti slip on feather-trimmed satin mules or spread before you satin, silk and chiffon negligées in delicious shades of tangerine, lemon, mocha, pistachio. All sizes are medium, others are made *sur mesure*; prices are the cheap side of extortionate for a slice of exquisite luxury.

Erès

2 rue Tronchet, 8th (01.47.42.28.82). M° Madeleine. **Open** 10am-7pm Mon-Sat. **Credit** AmEx, DC, MC, V. **Map** p401 G4.

Don't be misled by the demure interior of this boutique: the label's beautifully cut, minimalist bikinis and swimsuits are red-hot and designed to make a

Jacques Le Corre

splash. A big advantage for the natural woman is that the top and bottom can be purchased in different sizes, or you can buy just one piece of a bikini – should decide you don't want all your bases covered.
Branches: 4bis rue du Cherche-Midi, 6th (01.45.44.95.54); 40 av Montaigne, 8th (01.47.23.07.26); 6 rue Guichard, 16th (01.46.47.45.21).

Izka

140 rue du Fbg-St-Honoré, 8th (01.43.59.07.07). M° St-Philippe du Roule. **Open** 10am-7pm Mon-Sat. **Credit** AmEx, MC, V. **Map** p400 D3.
Launched in 1999, Gérard Petit's sporty, seamless lingerie has already been snapped up by Warners. The ten skimpy sets of bras and pants in microfibre (one is tempted to buy the whole collection, for fear of being caught short) have accompanying vests and you can mix and match the colours and models to cause gasps of admiration.
Branch: 74 rue de Rennes, 6th (01.45.49.25.85).

Etam

21 rue Tronchet, 8th (01.40.06.05.93/www.etam.fr). M° Havre Caumartin. **Open** 10am-7pm Mon-Sat. **Credit** AmEx, MC, V. **Map** p401 G3.
This high street shop has recently closed down many of its daywear branches in favour of its underwear shops (its original specialty). The result is all round underwear and swimsuits, catered to all tastes from sex kitten to cotton candies on a budget.
Branches: 18/22 rue du Commerce, 15th (01.45.77.27.71); 120 rue du Fbg-St-Honoré 12th, (01.43.44.77.93).

Eyewear

Turn up with your prescription and you can get some French specs made up to wow your friends back home. Visit an *opthamologiste* for an eye test.

Traction

6 rue du Dragon, 6th (01.42.22.28.77). M° St-Germain-des-Prés. **Open** 2-7pm Mon; 10.30-7pm Tue-Sat. **Credit** AmEx, DC, MC, V. **Map** p406 H7.
This brand, owned by the Gros family, marries four generations of know-how with a keen sense of modernity. Try the heavy metal specs that are super-light when worn, or the conversation-making frames with quirky details on the shaft (always a good ice-breaker).

Alain Mikli

74 rue des Sts-Pères, 7th (01.53.63.87.40). M° Sèvres-Babylone. **Open** 10am-7pm Mon-Sat. **Credit** AmEx, DC, MC, V. **Map** p405 G7.
This cult French designer was among the first to inject some vroom into prescription peepers. His signature material is cellulose acetate, a wood and cotton mix sliced from blocks. The Starck-designed boutique has a glass counter where the frames are laid out like designer sweeties, while upstairs 'travel wear' is displayed in an 18th-century setting.
Branch: 1 rue des Rosiers, 4th (01.42.71.01.56).

Lafont

11 rue Vignon, 8th (01.47.42.25.93). M° Madeleine. **Open** 10am-7pm Mon-Sat. **Credit** AmEx, MC, V. **Map** p401 G4.
Philippe Lafont carries on the impeccable, hand-finished work of his grandfather. The speciality of Philippe's designer wife (that's as in: wife who works as a designer) Laurence is small oval frames that tilt upwards like cat's eyes, perfect, of course, for those small, elfin faces.
Branches: 2 rue Duphot, 1st (01.42.60.01.02); 17 bd Raspail, 7th (01.45.48.24.23).

Hats

Jacques Le Corre

193 rue St-Honoré, 1st (01.42.96.96.40). M° Tuileries. **Open** 10am-7pm Mon-Sat. **Credit** AmEx, MC, V. **Map** p401 G4.
This flamboyant Breton experiments with textures and pigments to create daywear hats and berets in unusual fabrics. Some of his large lambskin bags have bead patterns stamped on them like Braille; others are dyed in fiery red or warm terracotta.

Philippe Model

33 pl du Marché-St-Honoré, 1st (01.42.96.89.02). M° Pyramides. **Open** 10am-7pm Mon-Sat. **Credit** AmEx, DC, MC, V. **Map** p401 H5.
With his exuberant colours and two-tone designs, Model is your man if you're determined to stand out in the wedding, racing or boating crowd. Prices from around €50 for a beret to over €3,000 for a sumptuous, made-to-measure headdress.

Marie Mercié

23 rue St-Sulpice, 6th (01.43.26.45.83). M° Odéon. **Open** 11am-7pm Mon-Sat. **Credit** AmEx, DC, MC, V. **Map** p405 H7.
Mercié's inspirations make you wish you lived in an era when hat-wearing was *de rigueur*. What fun to step out in a creation shaped like curved fingers complete with shocking-pink nail varnish and a pink diamond ring, or a beret like a face with huge turquoise eyes and red lips. Ready-to-wear starts at around €30. *Sur mesure* takes ten days.

Tête en l'Air

65 rue des Abbesses, 18th (01.46.06.71.19). M° Abbesses. **Open** 10.30am-7.30pm Mon-Sat. Closed Aug. **No credit cards. Map** p402 H1.
You know what they say: if you can't fight, wear a big hat. Couture duo Thomas and Anana have been creating hats for attention-seeking Parisians for a decade now. Among Anana's favourite creations is a Bacchus-style, overflowing goblet worn by a client at Longchamp. Prices start at around €50.

Jewellery

In this city of artisans there is certainly no lack of jewellery designers. Here is a small selection of the best to suit all tastes and pockets.

Cherry Chau

Showroom at 87 passage de Choiseul, 2nd (01.55.35.00.40) M° Quatre-Septembre. **Open** by appointment only. Stands in Galéries Lafayette and La Samaritaine (*see p236 & 239*). **Map** p401 H4.
Designer Cherry René-Bazin has invented her own range of neo-fairytale hair jewellery. All of her beautiful pieces, adorned with feathers and jewels (with sparklers by Swarovski), are limited edition but without the hefty price tag usually attached to one-offs. She also designs made-to-measure hair-deco for weddings and other special occasions.

Cécile & Jeanne

215 rue St-Honoré 1st (01.42.61.68.68/ www.cecilejeanne.com) M° Palais Royal. **Open** daily 11am-8pm. **Credit** AmEx, MC, V. **Map** p402 H5.
This small boutique offers costume jewellery with a distinct neo-ethnic feel. Lots of pretty, shiny things in unusual shapes and sizes are ideal for jazzing up any outfit without breaking the bank.
Branches: 10 rue du Vieux Colombier 6th. (01.45.48.79.16) plus Galeries Lafayette, Printemps and Bon Marché (*see p236*).

Cerize

380 rue St-Honoré, 1st (01.42.60.84.84). M° Concorde. **Open** 10am-7pm Mon-Sat. **Credit** AmEx, DC. MC V. **Map** p401 G4.
Behind the gaudy window displays, this boudoir-pink boutique has impressively crafted costume jewellery. Look out, too, for the embroidered evening bags by François Lesage, embroiderer to all the star couturiers, and some seriously eye-popping T-shirts.

Satellite

10 rue Dussoubs, 2nd (01.55.34.95.70). M° Réaumur-Sébastopol. **Open** 10am-7pm Mon-Sat. **Credit** AmEx, MC, V. **Map** p402 K5.
Stylist Sandrine Dulon uses only the best-quality material from the Czech Republic and Bavaria. The brilliance of the stones and intricacy of the work result in enchanting earrings, bracelet and necklace ensembles. Prices range from €9 to €660.
Branches: 23 rue des Francs-Bourgeois, 4th (01.40.29.45.77); 15 rue du Cherche-Midi, 6th (01.45.44.67.06).

La Licorne

38 rue Sévigné, 3th (01.48.87.84.43). M° St-Paul. **Open** noon-6.30pm daily. **Credit** AmEx, DC, MC, V. **Map** p406 L6.
The musty smell at La Licorne is perhaps not surprising given it harbours the contents of a costume jewellery factory dating from 1925-30s. Besides the abundance of art deco Bakelite, there is a veritable treasure trove of 50s diamanté, as well as some 19th-century jet. One word of warning – if you're coming from afar, it's always best to ring first.

Galerie Hélène Porée

1 rue de l'Odéon, 6th (01.43.54.17.00). M° Odéon. **Open** 11am-7pm Tue-Sat. **Credit** AmEx, MC, V. **Map** p406 H7.
Around 40 international ultra-minimalist designers are represented in this starch-white gallery. The French contingent includes Chavent, with his trompe l'oeil pieces, and Schotard, who creates an intriguing mousse-like effect using precious metals.

Irina Volkonski

45 rue Madame, 6th (01.42.22.02.37). M° St-Sulpice. **Open** 10am-7pm Mon-Sat. **Credit** AmEx, MC, V. **Map** p405 G7.
This young Russian in Paris creates affordable costume jewellery with a surreal flair, using materials ranging from Plexiglass to wood harvested after the great gale to resin sushi.

Kathy Korvin

13 rue de Tournon, 6th (01.56.24.06.66) M° Odéon. **Open** 10am-7pm Mon-Fri; 11am-7pm Sat. **Credit** AmEx, MC, V. **Map** p406 H7.
This Franco-American jeweller specialises in spider's web-thin silver necklaces and bracelets encircling semi-precious stones, feathers and Swarovski crystals. Her necklaces with nests of fine crocheted gold or silver are particularly elfin. Prices start at around €23 for simple silver earrings.

La Reine Margot

7 quai de Conti, 6th (01.43.26.62.50). M° Pont Neuf. **Open** 10.30am-1pm, 2-7pm Mon-Sat. **Credit** AmEx, DC, MC, V. **Map** p406 H6.
Gilles Cohen, proprietor of this beautiful antiques gallery, invites international jewellers to create modern pieces using ancient stones, amulets and seals. This approach results in some truly exquisite pieces designed by masters of their craft and prices are surprisingly reasonable.

Shoes & bags

Printemps' luxury floor is an excellent source of designer labels, including Hermès shoemaker Pierre Hardy, now making a name solo. Rue du Dragon in the 6th is crammed with boutiques offering young designers' creations.

Christian Louboutin

19 rue Jean-Jacques-Rousseau, 1st (01.42.36.05.31). M° Palais Royal. **Open** 10.30am-7pm Mon-Sat. Closed Aug. **Credit** AmEx, DC, MC, V. **Map** p402 J5.
Each of Louboutin's creations, with their hallmark red soles, are displayed in individual frames, like Cinderella's slipper. His Trash mules – incorporating used Métro tickets, glitter, torn letters and postage stamps – are particularly coveted.
Branch: 38 rue de Grenelle, 7th (01.42.22.33.07).

Rodolphe Menudier

14 rue de Castiglione, 1st (01.42.60.86.27). M° Concorde or Tuileries. **Open** 10.30am-7.30pm Mon-Sat. **Credit** AmEx, MC, V. **Map** p401 G5.
This silver and black cylinder of a boutique is a perfect setting for Menudier's racy designs, which mix moods and materials. Dozens of open, silver-handled drawers display his stilettos laid flat in profile. Top

Rodolphe Menudier

of the range are outrageous thigh-high boots with Plexiglass soles, but the more demure customer can opt for the ballerina pumps. Stock up, too, on exclusive hosiery made by Gerbé and Chantal Thomass.

Alain Tondowski

13 rue de Turbigo, 2nd (01.42.36.44.34). M° Etienne Marcel. **Open** 10.30am-7.30pm Mon-Sat. **Credit** AmEx, MC, V. **Map** p402 J5.
No clumpy poo-squishers here: Tondowski's shoes bring to mind the footnotes of a fashion illustration – a few perfectly executed squiggles. His super-elegant designs (from around €300) have a taut, urban edge, highlighted by the boutique with shoes framed in polished metal and Plexiglass.

Lollipops

60 rue Tiquetonne, 2nd (01.42.33.15.72). M° Etienne Marcel. **Open** 11am-7pm Mon-Sat. **Credit** AmEx, MC, V. **Map** p402 J5.
This fast-growing bag maker caters for virtually every possible taste, colour and material. There are Manga-inspired retro shoppers with Lichtenstein car prints, crunchy green leather purses and lacy red clutch bags for extra Moulin Rouge flounce. It also has great jewellery and spangle brooches.

Mandarina Duck

36 rue Etienne-Marcel, 2nd (01.40.13.02.96). M° Etienne Marcel. **Open** 11am-7pm Mon-Sat. **Credit** MC, V. **Map** p402 J5.
Mandarina Duck is a byword for sleek, trendy monotone handbags. This new, yellow and white geometric store also sells the Italian brand's wallets, luggage, watches, sunglasses and key rings.

Patrick Cox

62 rue Tiquetonne, 2nd (01.40.26.66.55). M° Etienne Marcel. **Open** 10.30am-7.30pm Mon-Sat. **Credit** AmEx, MC, V. **Map** p402 J5.
If the slipper fits it'll probably be one of Cox's. Elegance straight off the catwalk is his forte with plenty of ultra-feminine designs and mixes of fabric. Even if you're not bobo, BCBG or stinkingly wealthy, Patrick's stiletto boots and kitten heels will have your feet feeling like a million euros.

Gelati

6 rue St-Sulpice, 6th (01.43.25.67.44). M° Odéon. **Open** 10am-7pm Mon-Sat. **Credit** MC, V. **Map** p405 H7.
If you want your feet to be always in vogue but can't afford designer prices, then go for Gelati. The once-Italian (now French) company offers a stylish range of court and evening shoes in the hippest shapes and colours. Prices start at around €120.

Hervé Chapelier

1 rue du Vieux-Colombier, 6th (01.44.07.06.50). M° St-Sulpice. **Open** 10.15am-7pm Mon-Fri; 10.15am-7.15pm Sat. **Credit** AmEx, MC, V. **Map** 405 G7.
Number-one stop for the ultimate classic in chic, hard-wearing, bi-coloured totes. Often copied, but never quite equalled, they are available in pretty much every colour under the sun. Choose from a dinky purse at €22, moving up the size and price range to a stonking weekend bag at €130.

Hervé Chapelier

Peggy Huyn Kinh

11 rue Coëtlogon, 6th (01.42.84.83.83). M° St-Sulpice. **Open** 10am-7pm Mon-Sat. **Credit** AmEx, MC, V. **Map** p405 G7.
This street may not scream fashion, but that does not deter Peggy Huyn Kinh, former creative director for Cartier and other luxury heavyweights, whose bags may use boarskin or python. She does minimalist silver jewellery, too.

Robert Clergerie

5 rue du Cherche-Midi, 6th (01.45.48.75.47). M° St-Sulpice. **Open** 10am-7pm Mon-Sat. **Credit** AmEx, MC, V. **Map** p405 G7.
Clergerie has thankfully settled back into designing his exquisitely practical daywear. The maestro has even revived the two-tone loafer he created at the start of his career in 1981. Not that he is out of the fashion ring: his stylised 'boxing trainer' knocks the socks off other models.
Branches: 46 rue Croix-des-Petits-Champs, 1st (01.42.61.49.24); 18 av Victor-Hugo, 16th (01.45.01.81.30).

Iris

28 rue de Grenelle, 7th 01.42.22.89.81). M° Rue du Bac. **Open** 10.30am-7pm Mon-Sat. **Credit** AmEx, MC, V. **Map** p405 F7.

Iris is the Italian manufacturer of shoes by Marc Jacobs, Ernesto Esposito, Alessandro Dell'Acqa and Véronique Branquinho: their entire footwear range is in this dazzling white boutique. Esposito's pieces are recognisable by their flower patterns.

Jamin Puech

61 rue de Hauteville, 10th (01.40.22.08.32). M° Poissonnière. **Open** 10am-2pm, 3-7pm Mon-Sat. **Credit** MC, V. **Map** p402 K3.

The full collection of Isabelle Puech and Benoît Jamin's dazzling handbags, which use everything from tapestry and raffia to sequins, are on show in a boho setting complete with antler-horn chairs.

Sandrine Léonard

5 passage Charles-Dallery, 11th (01.47.00.09.94). M° Ledru-Rollin. **Open** 2-7pm Tue-Sat. **Credit** AmEx, MC, V. **Map** p407 M7.

Slightly off the beaten track, this boutique houses Léonard's classic feminine line and her streetwear offshoot DUP (Déplacements Urbains de Proximité), featuring colourful nylon shoppers and primary-coloured wool bags with wood handles and contrasting detailing, which will brighten any outfit.

Perfume & make-up

By Terry

21 passage Véro Dodat, 1st (01.44.76.00.76). M° Palais Royal. **Open** 10.30am-7pm Mon-Sat. **Credit** AmEx, MC, V. **Map** p402 H5.

Terry de Gunzburg, the alchemist behind Yves Saint Laurent's cosmetics for 15 years, offers exclusive made-to-measure 'haute couleur' make-up, concocted upstairs by a team of chemists and colourists, who combine high-tech treatments and hand-finished precision. There's also a prêt-à-porter line.

Branches: 1 rue Jacob, 6th (01.46.34.00.36); 10 av Victor-Hugo, 16th (01.55.73.00.73).

Galérie Noémie

17 rue du Cygne, 1st (01.44.76.06.26/ www.galerienoemie.com). M° Etienne Marcel. **Open** 1-7.30pm Tue-Sat. **Credit** DC, MC, V. **Map** p402 J5

You can tell Noémie is a painter, not just by the name of the boutique but by the way all the make-up is set out in palettes – a handy aid to putting your slap on artfully. The products don't just look pretty; they actually do their funky stuff. Little pots of gloss (a very reasonable €7.50) in myriad colours triple as lip gloss, eyeshadow or blusher.

Stéphane Marais

217 rue St-Honoré, 1st (01.42.61.73.22). M° Tuileries. **Open** 10.30am-7.30pm Mon-Sat. **Credit** AmEx, MC, V. **Map** p401 G5.

The first boutique of the acclaimed make-up artist to the designers may be a bit painfully self-conscious for the casual shopper. These are the risks one takes. Architect-designed, original tubes, pots and compact holders vie for attention with an eclectic selection of contemporary art.

L'Artisan Parfumeur

24 bd Raspail, 7th (01.42.22.23.32). M° Rue du Bac. **Open** 10.30am-7pm Mon-Sat. **Credit** AmEx, DC, MC, V. **Map** p405 G7.

Among scented candles, potpourri and charms, you will find the best vanilla perfume Paris can offer – Mûres et Musc, a bestseller for over 20 years.

Editions de Parfums Frédéric Malle

37 rue de Grenelle, 7th (01.42.22.77.22). M° Rue de Bac. **Open** 11am-7pm Mon-Sat. **Credit** AmEx, MC, V. **Map** p405 F6.

Choose from eight perfumes made for Frédéric Malle, former consultant for Lacroix, Chaumet and Hermès. This is minimalism taken to the extreme.

Guerlain

68 av des Champs-Elysées, 8th (01.45.62.52.57/ www.guerlain.fr). M° Franklin D Roosevelt. **Open** 10.30am-8pm Mon-Sat; 3-7pm Sun. **Credit** AmEx, MC, V. **Map** p401 E4.

This bijou boutique recalls the golden age of the Champs-Elysées. Although the family sold the company to LVMH some years ago, the 'maison' still produces outstanding creations and old favourites like Samsara, Habit Rouge and Vetiver.

Make Up For Ever Professional

5 rue La Boétie, 8th (01.42.66.01.60). M° Miromesnil. **Open** 10am-7pm Mon-Sat. Closed Sat in Aug. **Credit** AmEx, DC, MC, V. **Map** p401 E3.

With glitter, nail varnish, lipstick, fake eyelashes and stick-on tattoos, prepare for a colour explosion from this outfit beloved of catwalk make-up pros.

Branch: 22 rue de Sèvres, 7th (01.45.48.75.97).

Parfums Caron

34 av Montaigne, 8th (01.47.23.40.82). M° Franklin D Roosevelt. **Open** 10am-6.30pm Mon-Sat. **Credit** AmEx, DC, MC, V. **Map** p401 E4.

In its elegant art deco boutique, Caron sells re-editions of its classic favourites from 1911-54.

Sephora

70 av des Champs-Elysées, 8th (01.53.93.22.50/ www.sephora.fr). M° Franklin D Roosevelt. **Open** 10am-midnight Mon-Sat; noon-midnight Sun. **Credit** AmEx, MC, V. **Map** p401 E4.

The flagship of the cosmetic supermarket chain carries 12,000 French and foreign brands of scent and slap. Sephora Blanc (14 cour St-Emilion, 12th/ 01.40.02.97.79) features ethnic beauty products. Sephoras are popping up all over town so for a full list check out their website above.

Detaille 1905

10 rue St-Lazare, 9th (01.48.78.68.50/ www.detaille.com). M° Notre-Dame de Lorette. **Open** 3-7pm Mon; 10am-1.30pm, 3-7pm Tue-Sat. **Credit** MC, V **Map** p401 H3

Step back in time when entering this shop, opened, as its name, testifies, in 1905. Six key fragrances, three for women and three for men are made using, as far as possible, the original recipes. Truly Parisian.

Vinyl fantasy

Paris doesn't spring to mind as a prime spot for feeding your vinyl addiction, however there are specialist shops lurking in back streets (rue des Taillandiers and rue Keller in the 11th are the best bets) which merit a browse and could lead to some surprising finds.

Drum 'n' bass, breaks

Black Label (25 rue Keller, 11th/ 01.40.21.92.44) finds D&B enthusiasts hanging out and exchanging 'bons plans'. **Beep ah Fresh** (41 rue St-Sauveur, 2nd/ 01.40.39.09.43) is run by an Englishman with a penchant for British hip-hop, broken beats and nu breakz.

Funk, soul, hip-hop

DMC (2 bd Richard-Lenoir, 11th/ 01.43.38.00.00) has everything a future DMC champion could need as well as a quality house selection. For a fine choice of French and US hip-hop head to **Urban Music** (22 rue Pierre Lescot, 1st/01.40.13.99.28).

Electronica & oddities

Wave (36 rue Keller, 11th/01.40.21.86.98) is an electronica nerd's paradise with an overwhelming choice of noise, bleeps, post rock and field recordings on vinyl and CD.

Hardcore sounds

At **Hokus Pokus** (32 bd Richard Lenoir, 11th/ 01.43.55.42.89) you can find out where the next free party is being held as well as every hardcore genre under the BPM sun. **Sphénoïde** (30 rue St-Ambroise, 11th/ 01.48.07.05.47) Hardcore, tek-step and electro are all catered for.

House, techno, electro

12inch (18 rue de Turbigo, 2nd/ 01.40.13.90.00) is central, massive and even has a chill-out lounge where girlfriends can take the weight off bored feet. Get down to the sweaty cellar of **Techno Import** (16 rue des Taillandiers, 11th/01.48.05.71.56) for the hoard of listening posts which mean you never have to queue. Trance, techno and house are classified by label. At **Phat Beatz** (57 rue St-Maur, 11th/01.48.06.08.81) a constant flow of new electro, house and techno accompany the smoker accessories. **Katapult** (2 rue Franche Comté, 3rd/ 01.42.76.93.93) is the place to find German techno, minimal house and electro. The shop label Karat puts French artists on the map.

Reggae, ragga world music & jazz

Black Rain Musik (55 bis rue Jean-Pierre-Timbaud, 11th/01.40.21.92.44) contains a surpising number of ragga and reggae 45s straight from Jamaica. **Moby Disques** (9 rue des Déchargeurs, 1st/01.43.29.70.51) is a jazz specialist's dream with a great collection of 50s and 60s pressings.

Rock, new wave and metal

Born Bad (17 rue Keller, 11th/ 01.43.38.41.78) is run by true rockers and has everything metal and rock fans could ever desire, plus punk, ska and soul.

Vintage & collectables

Time-rich collectors wade through thousands of 45s and albums at **Gibert Joseph Musique** (26 bd St Michel, 6th/01.43.29.37.06), which sells new and second-hand discs. Rare punk, ska, chanson française, new wave and rock records come at reasonable prices at **Plus de Bruit** (35 rue de la Rochefoucauld, 9th/01.49.70.08.70), while **Disco Puces** (102 bd Beaumarchais, 11th/01.43.57.88.55) is the place to rummage for that Bee Gees LP.

Black Label

Children

Children's clothes & shoes

Stroll through St-Germain and you'll see toddlers decked out in designer gear (Agnès b, Bill Tornade Enfants, Bonpoint) that has never been anywhere near a sandbox. If it's cheap and cheerful you seek, you'll find plenty of funky fashions at the chains Du Pareil au Même, Sergeant Major and Tout Compte Fait. Look for small boutiques with their own style, too, such as Carabosse. There are clusters of children's shops on rue du Fbg-St-Antoine (12th), rue Bréa (6th) and rue Vavin (6th).

Carabosse

11 rue de Sévigné, 4th (01.44.61.05.98). M° St-Paul. **Open** 11am-7pm Tue-Sat; 3-7pm. **Credit** MC, V. **Map** p406 L6.
Stripes are the theme at this boutique, where you'll find fun, eye-catching outfits in durable fabrics for babies and children.

Jean Bourget

167 rue St-Jacques, 5th (01.44.07.03.48). RER Luxembourg. **Open** 10am-7pm Mon-Sat. **Credit** MC, V. **Map** p406 J8.
Stylish, well-made clothes for children under 15, with plenty of the fancy buckles, funky pockets, Velcro and clever details that appeal to kids.

Bill Tornade Enfants

32 rue du Four, 6th (01.45.48.73.88). M° St-Germain-des-Prés. **Open** 10.30am-7pm Mon-Fri; 10.30am-7.30pm Sat. Closed Aug. **Credit** AmEx, MC, V. **Map** p405 H7.
Designer Sylvia Rielle's sophisticated children's wear in shiny modern fabrics is more for trendy parties than everyday rolling around on the floor.
Branch: 1 rue de Turbigo, 3rd (01.42.21.35.52).

Jacadi

76 rue d'Assas, 6th (01.45.44.60.44/www.jacadi.fr). M° Vavin. **Open** 10am-7pm Mon-Sat. **Credit** MC, V. **Map** p405 G8.
Jacadi's well-made child and babywear – pleated skirts, smocked dresses, dungarees and fair isle knits – are a favourite with well-to-do parents, and there's some funkier party stuff too.
Branches include: 9 av de l'Opéra, 1st (01.49.27.06.29); 4 av des Gobelins, 5th (01.43.31.43.90).

Miki House

74 rue Bonaparte, 6th (01.46.33.77.55). M° St-Sulpice. **Open** 10am-7pm Mon-Sat. **Credit** AmEx, MC, V. **Map** p405 H7.
These cheerful Japanese-brand clothes depart from bourgeois stereotypes; prices, however, are sobering.

Petit Bâteau

26 rue Vavin, 6th (01.55.42.02.53). M° Vavin. **Open** 10am-7pm Mon-Sat. **Credit** MC, V. **Map** p405 G8.
Petit Bâteau is the place for the comfy, well-made cotton T-shirts, vests and other separates in myriad colours and cuts so coveted by Channel-hopping mums. Their teen range is also currently seen adorning rich and famously thin grown-ups.
Branches: 81 rue de Sèvres, 7th (01.45.49.48.38); 116 av des Champs-Elysées, 8th (01.40.74.02.03).

Honoré

38 rue Madame, 6th (01.45.48.96.86). M° St-Placide. **Open** 10.30am-7pm Mon-Sat. **Credit** AmEx, DC, MC V. **Map** p405 G8.
This Marseille-based designer has set up an oh-so-chic boutique in St-Germain-des Prés, where families can invest in trendy matching ensembles for *maman, papa* and *bébé*.

Pom d'Api

28 rue du Four, 6th (01.45.48.39.31). M° St-Sulpice. **Open** 10am-7pm Mon-Sat **Credit** AmEx, MC, V. **Map** p405 H7
A pair of toddler shoes here will set you back €85 to €100. Is it worth it? You certainly get quality and adorable, up-to-the-minute design from this French footwear company. Lucky is the receiver of cast-offs.

Bonton

82 rue de Grenelle, 7th (01.44.39.09.20). M° Rue du Bac. **Open** 10am-7pm Mon-Sat. **Credit** AmEx, DC, MC, V. **Map** p401 F6.
A new kind of concept store for kids and their trendy parents has been set up by Irène and Thomas Cohen. T-shirts, skirts and trousers come in rainbow colours, but the prices are a little steep. There is also a selection of kids' furniture, gadgets, bedlinen, and hair accessories, plus a children's hairdresser on site.

Six Pieds Trois Pouces

223 bd St-Germain, 7th (01.45.44.03.72). M° Solférino. **Open** 10am-7pm Mon-Sat. Closed Mon in Aug. **Credit** AmEx, V. **Map** p405 F6.
An excellent range of children's and teens' shoes goes from classics by Startrite, Aster and Little Mary to trendy Reeboks and Timberlands, as well as shoes under its less-expensive own label.
Branches include: 85 rue de Longchamp, 16th (01.45.53.64.21); 78 av de Wagram, 17th (01.46.22.81.64).

Du Pareil au Même

15-17 rue des Mathurins (Maison at 23), 8th (01.42.66.93.80). M° Havre-Caumartin/RER Auber. **Open** 10am-7pm Mon-Sat. **Credit** MC, V. **Map** p401 G3.
Colourful, cleverly designed basics (three months to 14 years) at low prices. DPAM Bébé, with stylish accessories and clothing for 0-23 months, makes gifts that look more expensive than they are. The musical cuddly chicken is changing-time godsend.
Branches include: 122 rue du Fbg-St-Antoine (Maison at 120), 12th (01.43.44.67.46); 6 rue de l'Ouest (Maison at 15), 14th (01.43.20.59.51).

Toy & book shops

Cosy traditional toyshops abound in Paris. Department stores all provide animated windows and gigantic toy floors at Christmas. The best sources of children's books in English are **W H Smith** and **Brentano's** (*see p263*).

La Grande Récré

27 bd Poissonnière, 2nd (01.40.26.12.20).
M° Grands Boulevards. **Open** 10am-7.30pm Mon-Sat. **Credit** AmEx, MC, V. **Map** p402 J4.
The French toy supermarket (local rival to Toys 'R' Us) may lack the charm of more trad compatriots but its shelves are packed high: pink and plastic for girls, guns and cars for boys, plus craft sets and Playdoh, Gameboys, Pokémon spin-offs and the like.

Arche de Noé

70 rue St-Louis-en-l'île, 4th (01.46.34.61.60).
M° Pont Marie. **Open** 11am-7pm daily. **Credit** AmEx, MC, V. **Map** p406 K7.
Far from the madness of the *grands magasins*, Arche de Noé on the Ile St-Louis is the perfect place for Christmas shopping, with Czech wooden toys, plenty of puzzles and games, Babar paraphernalia and finger puppets.

Pylones

57 rue St-Louis-en-l'Ile, 4th (01.46.34,05.02).
M° Pont Marie. **Open** 10.30am-7.30pm daily. **Credit** AmEx, MC, V. **Map** p406 K7.
Hilarious gadgets and knick-knacks for kids and kids-at-heart. Furry pencil cases, painted bike bells, watches for toddlers and funky painted rattles.

Les 2 Tisserins

35 rue des Bernardins, 5th (01.46.33.88.68).
M° Maubert-Mutualité. **Open** 10am-7pm Tue-Fri; 10am-1pm, 3pm-7pm Sat. Closed two weeks before Christmas in Dec. **Credit** MC, V.
Map p406 K7.
This treasure trove has everything you could hope to find in a traditional toy shop: gorgeous stuffed animals, whimsical puppets, wooden toys (including handmade pinball machines) and its own line of colourful clothing. Staff are particularly helpful.

Chantelivre

13 rue de Sèvres, 6th (01.45.48.87.90). M° Sèvres-Babylone. **Open** 1-7pm Mon; 10am-7pm Tue-Sat. **Credit** MC, V. **Map** p405 G7.
This specialist children's bookshop leads from teen reads to picture books and a baby section. There are publications on children's health and psychology for parents, a small English-language section, plus CDs, videos, paints, stationery and party supplies.

Fnac Junior

19 rue Vavin, 6th (01.56.24.03.46). M° Vavin.
Open 10am-7.30pm Mon-Sat. **Credit** AmEx, MC, V. **Map** p405 G8.
The Fnac group has turned its hand to books, toys, videos, CDs and CD-roms for under-12s. Many things take an educational slant but there are fun basics, too. The shop lays on storytelling and activities (mainly Wed, Sat) for three-year-olds and up.
Branches: cour St-Emilion, 12th (01.44.73.01.58); 148 av Victor-Hugo, 16th (01.45.05.90.60).

Pain d'Epices

29 passage Jouffroy, 9th (01.47.70.08.68).
M° Grands Boulevards. **Open** 12.30-7pm Mon; 10am-7pm Tue-Thur; 10am-9pm Fri, Sat. **Credit** MC, V. **Map** p402 H4.
Everything a self-respecting doll would need, from cutlery to toothpaste. There are also dolls' house kits or the finished thing, and trad dolls and teddies.

Apache

84 rue du Fbg-St-Antoine, 12th (01.53.46.60.10/ www.apache.fr). M° Ledru-Rollin. **Open** 10am-8pm Mon-Sat. **Credit** MC, V. **Map** p407 M7.
The shape of toyshops to come. A brightly lit, colourful two-storey space with an activities studio and cyber-café. Equally colourful goodies go from marbles and soft toys to fancy dress, space hoppers and videos. There's also furniture and bath gear.

La Maison du Cerf-Volant

7 rue de Prague, 12th (01.44.68.00.75). M° Ledru-Rollin. **Open** 10am-7pm Tue-Sat. **Credit** V.
Map p407 M7.
Every kind of kite: dragons, galleons, scary insects and acrobatic stunt kites. If it flies, it's here.

Les Cousines d'Alice

36 rue Daguerre, 14th (01.43.20.24.86). M° Denfert-Rochereau. **Open** 10am-1.30pm, 2.30-7.15pm Mon; 10am-7.15pm Tue-Sat; 11am-1pm Sun. Closed three weeks in Aug. **Credit** MC, V. **Map** p405 G10.
This shop is crammed with soft toys, well-selected books and construction games. There are also plenty of inexpensive pocket-money treats.

Home & Gifts

Antiques & flea markets

Knowing who specialises in what is essential for antique buying in Paris, so here are a few tips. Classy traditional antiques can be found in the Louvre des Antiquaires (1st), Carré Rive Gauche (6th), Village Suisse (*see chapter* **The Left Bank**) and Fbg-St-Honoré (1st), art deco in St-Germain-des-Prés (7th), 50s-70s retro around rue de Charonne (11th), antiquarian books and stamps in the covered passages, in the *bouquinistes* along the *quais*, or at Parc Georges Brassens (*see chapter* **The Left Bank**). As well as flea markets (*see p260*), don't forget auction house **Drouot** (recorded information on 01.48.00.20.17), as well as Sotheby's and Christie's. There are also frequent *brocantes* and *braderies* – antiques and collectors' markets, especially in spring and autumn.

Pylones

Louvre des Antiquaires

2 pl du Palais-Royal, 1st (01.42.97.27.00/ www.louvre-antiquaires.com). Mº Palais Royal. **Open** 11am-7pm Tue-Sun. Closed Sun July-Aug. **Map** p406 H5.

This upmarket antiques centre behind the facade of an old *grand magasin* houses some 250 antiques dealers. Just the place for Louis XV furniture, tapestries, Sèvres and Chinese porcelain, silver and jewellery, model ships and, of course, tin soldiers.

Le Village St-Paul

rue St-Paul, rue Charlemagne and quai des Célestins, 4th. Mº St-Paul. **Open** 10am-7pm Mon-Sat. **Map** p406 L7.

This colony of antique sellers, spread across small interlinked courtyards between rues St-Paul, Charlemagne and quai des Célestins, is a promising source of 1930s and 50s furniture, kitchenware and wine gadgets.

Marché aux Puces d'Aligre

pl d'Aligre, 12th. Mº Ledru-Rollin. **Open** 9am-noon Tue-Sun. **Map** p407 N7.

This flea market has origins going back before the Revolution, when it was set up to provide old clothes for the poor. Remaining true to its junk tradition, you'll find a handful of *brocanteurs* peddling books, kitchenwares and knick-knacks at what seem optimistically astronomical prices. Be ready to bargain.

Marché aux Puces de Vanves

av Georges Lafenestre and av Marc-Sangrier, 14th. Mº Porte de Vanves. **Open** 7.30am-6pm Sat, Sun.

The smallest and friendliest of the Paris flea markets is good for collectors of dolls, 1950s costume jewellery, glass, crystal, old photographs, magazines, eau de cologne bottles, lace, linens and buttons – lots of small gems you can fit in your suitcase.

Marché aux Puces de St-Ouen (Porte de Clignancourt)

17 av de la Porte de Clingnancourt. Mº Porte de Clignancourt, 18th. **Open** 7am-6pm Mon, Sat, Sun.

This enormous market, reputedly the largest flea market in Europe – with over 2,000 stands and ten miles of walkways – is made up of arcades of semi-permanent shops as well as stands. There are, in theory, rare and quality items to be found here, but the market is overrun with tourists, hence the steep prices. It's divided into ten different markets, each heaving with treasures from 18th-century commodes and art deco lighting to retro ballgowns.

Marché aux Puces de Montreuil

93100 Montreuil-sous-Bois. Mº Porte de Montreuil. **Open** 7.30am-6pm Sat, Sun, Mon.

Like one vast car boot sale, this market disgorges mountains of second-hand clothing, parts for cars, showers and sundry machines, and a jumble of miscellaneous rubbish from its dusty, grungy bowels. You'll find little pre-1900, but there are fun collectables like branded *pastis* water jugs.

Design, furniture & tableware

Astier de Villatte

173 rue St-Honoré, 1st (01.42.60.74.13). Mº Madeleine. **Open** 11am-7.30pm Mon-Sat. **Credit** AmEx, MC, V. **Map** p401 G4.

Once home to Napoléon's silversmith Biennet, this ancient warren of small rooms now houses white and platinum ceramics inspired by 17th-and 18th-century designs, created by the Astier de Villatte siblings and handmade in their Bastille workshop. Also hand-made glass and Moroccan furniture.

Christophe Delcourt

125 rue Vieille-du-Temple, 3rd (01.42.78.44.97). Mº Filles du Calvaire. **Open** 10am-7pm Mon-Fri; 11am-7pm Sat. **Credit** V. **Map** p402 L6.

Delcourt's art deco-influenced geometrical lines are given a contemporary edge by their combination of stained wood with waxed black steel.

Bô

8 rue St-Merri, 4th (01.42.72.84.64). Mº Hôtel de Ville. **Open** 11am-8pm Mon-Sat; 2-8pm Sun. **Credit** AmEx, MC, V. **Map** p406 K6.

Pared-back contemporary style: candlesticks, vases, unusual lights, new-agey incense burners and elegant grey Limoges porcelain. All *très bô.*

Caravane Chambre 19

Sentou Galerie

18 and 24 rue Pont Louis-Philippe, 4th (01.42.71.00.01). M° Pont Marie. **Open** 11am-7pm Tue-Sat **Credit** AmEx, MC, V. **Map** p406 K7.
Favoured by *Marie Claire Maison*, this is the trend-setting shop for tableware and furniture. There are lots of eye-catching colours at the moment, with painted Chinese flasks, wiggly vases and a lime-green accordion bench.

Yves Delorme

8 rue Vavin, 6th (01.44.07.23.14). M° Vavin. **Open** noon-7pm Mon; 10.30am-1.30pm, 2.30-7pm Tue-Sat. **Credit** AmEx, MC, V. **Map** p405 G8.
Extravagant thread-counts with prices to match. The ludicrously soft sheets in tastefully muted tones are ideal for four-posters and futons alike.
Branch: 96 rue St-Dominique, 7th (01.45.55.51.10).

Kartell Flagship Shop

242 bd St-Germain, 7th (01.45.48.68.37). M° Rue du Bac. **Open** 10am-1pm, 2-7pm Tue-Sat. **Credit** MC, V. **Map** p405 G6.
The Italian plastic furniture pioneer stocks stuff by such names as Philippe Starck, Piero Lissoni and Antonio Citterio; office lines are displayed upstairs and lollipop-colours downstairs.

CFOC

170 bd Haussmann, 8th (01.53.53.40.80). M° St-Philippe-du-Roule. **Open** 10am-7pm Mon-Sat. **Credit** AmEx, DC, MC, V. **Map** p401 E3.
La Compagnie Française de l'Orient et de la Chine is full of eastern promise, from Chinese teapots and celadon bowls, to Iranian blown glass.
Branches include: 163, 167 bd St-Germain, 6th (01.45.48.00.18); 65 av Victor-Hugo, 16th (01.45.00.55.46).

Le Bihan

41 rue du Fbg-St-Antoine, 11th (01.43.43.06.75). M° Bastille. **Open** 2-7pm Mon; 10am-7pm Tue-Sat. **Credit** AmEx, V. **Map** p407 M7.
In case you thought the Faubourg was now entirely clothes shops or mock Louis XV, check out this three-floor 800m² showcase for the best of modern design. Furniture and lighting from Perriand, Gray and Mies Van der Rohe to Pesce, Santachiara, Pillet, Morrison, Arad et al. It also organises sporadic exhibitions and other happenings.

Caravane Chambre 19

19 rue St-Nicolas, 12th (01.53.02.96.96/www.caravane.fr). M° Ledru-Rollin. **Open** 11am-7pm Mon-Sat. **Credit** AmEx, MC, V. **Map** p407 M7.
This offshoot of Françoise Dorget's original Marais shop makes you want to pack your bags and move in. The goodies found here include exquisite hand-sewn quilts from West Bengal, crisp cotton and organdie tunics, Berber scarves and deep lounging sofas and daybeds. There are also chic travel accessories such as silk sheet sleeping bags and stripey neckrests with matching eyemasks.
Branch: 6 rue Pavée, 4th (01.44.61.04.22).

Florists

Au Nom de la Rose

87 rue St-Antoine, 4th (01.42.71.34.24). M° St-Paul. **Open** 9am-9pm Mon-Sat 9am-2pm Sun. **Credit** AmEx, MC, V. **Map** p406 L7.
Specialising in the most eloquent of flowers, this is the place to go for your wedding bouquet – even if staff can seem a bit vague – or indeed an impromptu bouquet. The shop also has its own line of rose-based beauty products and candles.

Christian Tortu

6 carrefour de l'Odéon, 6th (01.43.26.02.56). M° Odéon. **Open** 10am-8pm Mon-Sat. Closed two weeks in Aug. **Credit** AmEx, DC, MC, V. **Map** p405 H7.
Paris' most celebrated florist is famous for combining flowers, twigs, bark and moss into still lifes. You can buy his vases at 17 rue des Quatre-Vents, 6th.

Kitchen & bathroom

E Dehillerin

18 rue Coquillière, 1st (01.42.36.53.13). M° Les Halles. **Open** 9am-12.30pm, 2-6pm Mon; 9am-6pm Tue-Sat. **Credit** MC, V. **Map** p402 J5.
Suppliers to great chefs since 1820, this no-nonsense warehouse has the kind of kitchen utensils found in the *Larousse Gastronomique*. A saucepan from Dehillerin is for life.

Bains Plus

51 rue des Francs-Bourgeois, 4th (01.48.87.83.07). M° Hôtel de Ville. **Open** 11am-7.30pm Tue-Sat; 2.30-7.30pm Sun. **Credit** AmEx, MC, V. **Map** p406 K6.
The ultimate gents' shaving shop: duck-shaped loofahs, seductive dressing gowns, chrome mirrors, bath oils and soaps.

Résonances

13 cour St-Emilion, 12th (01.44.73.82.82). M° Cour St-Emilion. **Open** 11am-9pm daily. **Credit** AmEx, MC, V. **Map** p407 P10.
Résonances stocks an eclectic but well-chosen array of supplies and gadgets in timeless designs for the home. DIY enthusiasts will appreciate the tape measures, paints and brushes (get a life, guys) and interior design books; sybarites will dig the bath products. Most items are under €20, making this ideal stocking-filler territory.

Kitchen Bazaar

11 av du Maine, 15th (01.42.22.91.17). M° Montparnasse-Bienvenüe. **Open** 10am-7pm Mon-Sat. **Credit** AmEx, MC, V. **Map** p405 F8.
A festival of chrome gadgetry and modish accessories, Kitchen Bazaar is perfect for luxury items. Its sister shop Bath Bazaar Autrement (6 av du Maine, 15th/01.45.48.89.00), across the street, sells bathroom goodies.
Branches: 23 bd de la Madeleine, 1st (01.42.60.50.32).

Leisure

Books

See also p265 **Fnac** and **Virgin Megastore**.

Galignani

224 rue de Rivoli, 1st (01.42.60.76.07). M° Tuileries. **Open** 10am-7pm Mon-Sat. **Credit** MC, V. **Map** p401 G5.

Opened in 1802, Galignani was reputedly the first English-language bookshop in Europe, and at one point even published its own daily newspaper. Today it stocks fine and decorative arts books and literature in both French and English.

W H Smith

248 rue de Rivoli, 1st (01.44.77.88.99/ www.whsmith.fr). M° Concorde. **Open** 9am-7.30pm Mon-Sat; 1-7.30pm Sun. **Credit** AmEx, MC, V. **Map** p401 G5.

If you're feeling homesick, this is just like being back in Blighty; over 70,000 titles and a huge crush around the magazine section. Upstairs stocks quality English language videos, DVDs and story tapes. The homesick ex-pat staff actually know their stuff though, which may be different from back home.

Brentano's

37 av de l'Opéra, 2nd (01.42.61.52.50). M° Opéra. **Open** 10am-7.30pm Mon-Sat. **Credit** AmEx, MC, V. **Map** p401 G4.

A good address for American classics, modern fiction and bestsellers, plus an excellent array of business titles. The children's section is in the basement and the French part at the back. Dinky gifts are also available next to the wide range of greetings cards.

The Red Wheelbarrow Bookstore

13 rue Charles V, 4th (01.42.77.42.17). M° St-Paul. **Open** 9.30am-7pm Mon-Sat. **Credit** MC, V. **Map** p406 L7.

Literature lords it over pulp fiction in this small but sincere book-lined cranny, which has a well-stocked kiddies' corner.

Bouquinistes

Along the quais, especially quai de Montebello, quai St-Michel, 5th. M° St-Michel. **Open** times depend on stall, Tue-Sun. **No credit cards. Map** p406 J7.

The green boxes along the quais selling second-hard books are one of Paris' oldest institutions. Ignore the nasty postcards and rummage through the stacks of ancient paperbacks for something existential. Be sure to haggle, it would be rude not to.

Librairie Gourmande

4 rue Dante, 5th (01.43.54.37.27). M° St-Michel. **Open** 10am-7pm Mon-Sat. **Credit** DC, MC, V. **Map** p406 J7.

Chefs from all over hunt out Geneviève Baudon's bookstore dedicated to cooking, wine and, of course, 'table arts'.

Shakespeare & Co

37 rue de la Bûcherie, 5th (01.43.26.96.50). M° Maubert-Mutualité/RER St-Michel. **Open** noon-midnight daily. **No credit cards. Map** p406 J7.

George Whitman founded this Paris institution in 1951. His eccentric creation consists of three floors of books stuffed into every nook and cranny. The struggling ex-pat writers who live in the upstairs rooms in exchange for working in the shop calmly play chess while you browse in their bedrooms.

La Chambre Claire

14 rue St-Sulpice, 6th (01.46.34.04.31). M° Odéon. **Open** 10am-7pm Tue-Sat. **Credit** MC, V. **Map** p406 H7.

A hommage to Barthes, this bookshop/gallery specialises in photography and also holds exhibitions.

Gibert Joseph

26, 30 bd St-Michel, 6th (01.44.41.88.88). M° St-Michel. **Open** 10am-7.30pm Mon-Sat. **Credit** MC, V. **Map** p406 J7.

Best known as a bookshop for the Left Bank learning institutions, as well as a place to flog text books; Gibert Joseph also has stationery, office supplies and CD/DVD emporia further up the street.

La Hune

170 bd St-Germain, 6th (01.45.48.35.85). M° St-Germain-des-Prés. **Open** 10am-11.45pm Mon-Sat; 11am-7.45pm Sun. **Credit** AmEx, MC, V. **Map** p405 G7.

A Left Bank institution, La Hune boasts an international selection of art and design books and a suberb collection of French literature and theory.

Tea and Tattered Pages

24 rue Mayet, 6th (01.40.65.94.35) M° Duroc. **Open** 11am-7pm Mon-Sat; noon-6pm Sun. **Credit** MC, V. **Map** p405 F8.

A gentle and friendly American-style tea salon-cum-bookshop where you can browse through 15,000 second-hand, mainly paperback, books in English whilst sipping a steaming-hot cuppa. (Watch out for spillages if you have an unsteady hand.)

Village Voice

6 rue Princesse, 6th (01.46.33.36.47). M° Mabillon. **Open** 2-8pm Mon; 10am-8pm Tue-Sat; 2-8pm Sun. **Credit** AmEx, DC, MC, V. **Map** p406 H7.

The city's best selection of new fiction, non-fiction and literary magazines in English. It also holds literary events and poetry readings if you fancy a game of spot the luvvie.

Bookstorming

24 rue de Penthièvre, 8th (01.42.25.15.58/ www.bookstorming.com). M° Miromesnil or Champs-Elysées-Clemenceau. **Open** 1-7pm Tue-Sat and by appointment. **Credit** MC, V. **Map** p401 E3.

This recent arrival on the arts scene boasts an impressive space – more than 280m^2 of books and catalogues on contemporary art, including limited editions, plus a collection of 300 videos.

Shakespeare & Co

Institut Géographique National

107 rue La Boétie, 8th (01.43.98.85.00). M° Franklin D Roosevelt. **Open** 9.30am-7pm Mon-Fri. **Credit** AmEx, MC, V. **Map** p401 E4.

Paris' best cartographic shop stocks international maps, detailed guides to France, wine, cheese, walking and cycling maps and historic maps of Paris.

Artazart

83 quai de Valmy, 10th (01.40.40.24.00/ www.artazart.com) M° Jacques-Bonsergent. **Open** 11am-8pm Mon-Fri; 2-7pm Sat, Sun. **Credit** MC, V. **Map** p402 L4.

A bright yellow beacon along trendy Canal St-Martin, this bookshop and gallery has cutting-edge publications on fashion, art, architecture and design.

Gifts & eccentricities

See also p264 **Only in Paris**.

Métro et Bus Paris, objets du Patrimoine boutique

In the Salle des échanges at RER Châtelet-les Halles, next to the entrance to the line 4 and Pl Carrée exit, 1st. **Open** 8am-7.30pm Mon-Fri. **Credit** MC, V. **Map** p402 J5.

Métro-focussed souvenirs for those who don't have to take it every day include T-shirts with the Métro map or a bath towel which looks like a large, fluffy Métro ticket.

Nature et Découvertes

Carrousel du Louvre, 99 rue de Rivoli, 1st (01.47.03.47.43). M° Palais Royal. **Open** 10am-8pm daily. **Credit** AmEx, MC, V. **Map** p401 H5.

Camping and stargazing accessories, musical instruments, art supplies, divining rods and games. Kids' play space, and workshops Wed afternoon.
Branches include: Forum des Halles, 1st (01.40.28.42.16).

Papeterie Moderne

12 rue de la Ferronnerie, 1st (01.42.36.21.72). M° Châtelet. **Open** 9am-12.30am, 1.30-6.30pm Mon-Sat. **No credit cards. Map** p402 J5.

This is the source of those enamel plaques that adorn Paris streets and forbidding gateways ('Attention: chien bizarre' – ideal Chrimbo present for the mother-in-law) for less than €10.

Velvet

9 rue Royale, 1st.(01.49.24.05.77). M° Concorde. **Open** 10.30am-6.30pm Tue-Sat. **Credit** MC, V. **Map** p401 F4.

If you have some spare sapphires and diamonds that you'd like set in a custom-made ink-pen, this is where to go. Hidden in the rue Royale gallery, the dimly lit, polished boutique sells ink-pens starting at €300.

L'Art du Bureau

47 rue des Francs-Bourgeois, 4th (01.48.87.57.97) M° St-Paul. **Open** 10.30am-7.30pm Mon-Sat; 2-6.30pm Sun. **Credit** Amex, CD, MC, V. **Map** p406 L6.

This boutique in the Marais sells sleek and modern desk accessories, including some sexy ones that bring a whole new meaning to the term 'stress balls'.

Litchi

4 rue des Ecouffes, 4th.(01.44.59.39.09). M° Saint Paul. **Open** noon-8pm Tue-Sat; 1.30-7pm Sun. **Credit** MC, V. **Map** p406 L6.

Only in Paris

In the days before Bonne Maman jam and Poulain chocolate had made it to your local Sainsbury's, finding the perfect gift for a friend back home was as easy as going to Monoprix. Now that everything has gone global, you'll need inside knowledge to track down something uniquely Parisian.

Food

L'Epicerie (*see p270*), on the Ile St-Louis, sells little jewel-toned jars of jam (try the blackcurrant with violet or Périgord strawberries), flavoured mustards and vinegars, and spiced salts and sugars. Wooden gift boxes make even a simple jar of tarragon mustard seem luxurious.

Gadgets

Tiny **Le Passe-Partout** (21 rue St-Paul, 4th/01.42.72.94.94), in the Village St-Paul's collection of antique shops, specialises in rare corkscrews, most of them French, dating from the gadget's invention in the 18th century. For cooking enthusiasts, the professional kitchenware shop **E Dehillerin** (*see p261*), stocks carbon-steel knives and nifty plastic pastry cutters stamped with its name.

Beauty

Champagne-slugging Brits in the know swear by UPSA Vitamine C, an effervescent Aspirin-based medicine available in any pharmacy, as a miracle hangover cure. At the other end of the price scale, order a custom-made negligée at **Sabbia Rose** (*see p250*), luxury lingerie supplier to many a Paris *maîtresse*.

Jewellery

The **Tati Or** branch at 19 rue de la Paix (01.40.07.06.76) sells bold knock-offs of Chanel, Cartier and other nearby prestige jewellers. For jewellery by up-and-coming French designers, visit **Diamantissimo** (28 rue du Four, 6th/01.42.22.66.31).

Paris mementos

Métro fans will fall for the T-shirts and bath towels at the **Métro et Bus Paris** boutique (*see p263*). Museum boutiques (especially the big one at the Louvre) and **Paris-Musées** (*see right*) are great sources of art books (including many for children), ceramics and classy reproductions.

Brighten up your living room with Bollywood-inspired paraphernalia. Colourful and kitsch, this small gift shop overflows with floral candles, vases, gilt framed pictures of Indian actors, ornaments, beaded jewellery and floral bags.

Paris-Musées

29bis rue des Francs-Bourgeois, 4th (01.42.74.13.02). M° St-Paul. **Open** 2pm-7pm Mon; 11am-7am Tue-Sat; 11am-6.30pm Sun. **Credit** AmEx, DC, MC, V. **Map** p406 L6.

Run by Ville de Paris museums, this shop showcases funky lamps and ceramics by young designers, along with reproductions from the city's museums.

Robin des Bois

15 rue Ferdinand-Duval, 4th (01.48.04.09.36). M° St-Paul. **Open** 10.30am-7pm Mon-Sat; 2-7.30pm Sun. **Credit** MC, V. **Map** p406 L6.

Robin Hood is linked to an ecological organisation of the same name. Everything is made with recycled or ecologically sound products.

Diptyque

34 bd St-Germain, 5th (01.43.26.45.27). M° Maubert-Mutualité. **Open** 10am-7pm Mon-Sat. **Credit** AmEx, MC, V. **Map** p405 G6.

Diptyque's divinely scented candles in 48 different varieties are the best you'll ever come across.

Deyrolle

46 rue du Bac, 7th (01.42.22.30.07). M° Rue du Bac. **Open** 10am-6.45pm Mon-Sat. **Credit** AmEx, MC, V. **Map** p405 G6.

Established in 1831, this dusty shop overflows with taxidermied animals. Have your own pet stuffed (€500 for a cat) or even hire a beast for a few days.

Madeleine Gély

218 bd St-Germain, 7th (01.42.22.63.35). M° Rue du Bac. **Open** 9.30am-7pm Tue-Sat. **Credit** AmEx, MC, V. **Map** p405 G6.

Short or long, plain or fancy, there's an umbrella or cane here to suit everybody, including 400 styles of walking sticks. Umbrellas can also be made to order.

Sennelier

3 quai Voltaire, 7th (01.42.60.72.15/ www.sennelier.fr). M° St-Germain-des-Prés. **Open** 2-6.30pm Mon; 9.30am-12.30pm, 2-6.30pm Tue-Sat. **Credit** AmEx, DC, MC, V. **Map** p406 H6.

Old-fashioned colour merchant Sennelier has been supplying artists since 1887. Oil paints, water-colours and pastels include rare pigments, along with primered boards, varnishes and paper.

Paris Accordéon

80 rue Daguerre, 14th (01.43.22.13.48). M° Denfert-Rochereau or Gaîté. **Open** 9am-noon, 1-7pm Tue-Fri; 9am-noon, 1-6pm Sat. **Credit** AmEx, MC, V. **Map** p405 G10.

This joint brims with accordions, from simple squeeze-boxes to the most beautiful tortoise-shell models, both second-hand and new.

Music & CDs

See p256 **Vinyl fantasy** for specialist record shops aimed at those happy few with a turntable to call their own.

Monster Melodies

9 rue des Déchargeurs, 1st (01.40.28.09.39). M° Les Halles. **Open** 11am-7pm Mon-Sat. **Credit** MC, V. **Map** p402 J5.

The owners will help you hunt out treasures, and with over 10,000 second-hand, well-priced CDs of all species, it's just as well.

Papageno

1 rue de Marivaux, 2nd (01.42.96.56.54). M° Richelieu-Drouot. **Open** 1.30-7.30pm Tue-Fri, 11am-7.30pm Sat. **Credit** MC, V. **Map** p402 H4.

This classical music shop specialises in rare opera finds on vinyl, some of which date back to the beginning of the century, as well as the usual large selection of CDs.

Blue Moon Music

84 rue Quincampoix, 4th (01.40.29.45.60). M° Rambuteau. **Open** 11am-7pm Mon-Sat. **Credit** V. **Map** p406 J6.

Specialising in reggae and ragga, this is the place to come for some authentic Jamaican sounds as it receives new imports on a weekly basis.

Madeleine Gély

Paul Beuscher

15-17, 23-29 bd Beaumarchais, 4th (01.44.54.36.00) M° Bastille. **Open** 2-7pm Mon; 10.15am-7pm Tue-Sat. **Credit** V. **Map** p406 M6.

Music superstore stocking guitars, pianos, percussion and accessories. North of the river, there are instruments to hire and a music school; while on the Left Bank, you'll find a musical bookshop with sheet music and lots of teaching material.

Branch: 66 av de la Motte-Piquet, 15th.

Crocodisc

40-42 rue des Ecoles, 5th (01.43.54.47.95). M° Maubert-Mutualité. **Open** 11am-7pm Tue-Sat. Closed two weeks Aug. **Credit** MC, V. **Map** p406 J7.

An excellent, albeit slightly expensive, range includes pop, rock, funk, African, North-African country music and classical. For jazz, blues and gospel you should try its specialised branch Crocojazz (64 rue de la Montagne Ste-Geneviève, 5th/ 01.46.34.78.38).

La Flute de Pan

49, 53, 59 rue de Rome, 8th (01.44.70.91.68). M° Europe. **Open** 10am-6.30pm Mon, Tue, Thur-Sat; 2.30-6.30pm Wed. **Credit** MC, V. **Map** p401 E1.

Here you'll find sheet music for strings, wind and orchestra, plus learning material at number 49; brass, sax, percussion and jazz at number 52 and piano, organ, harpsichord and singers at number 59.

Fnac

74 av des Champs-Elysées, 8th (01.53.53.64.64/ www.fnac.com). M° George V. **Open** 10am-midnight Mon-Sat; noon-midnight Sun. **Credit** AmEx, MC, V. **Map** p400 D4.

Fnac's musical range is tame but wide-reaching – the African section being particularly reliable. Fnac also stocks books, computers, stereo, video and photography equipment, as well as being Paris' main concert box office.

Branches: Forum des Halles, 1st (01.40.41.40.00); 136 rue de Rennes, 6th (01.49.54.30.00); 4 pl de la Bastille, 12th (01.43.42.04.04) music only.

Virgin Megastore

52-60 av des Champs-Elysées, 8th (01.49.53.50.00). M° Franklin D Roosevelt. **Open** 10am-midnight Mon-Sat; noon-midnight Sun. **Credit** AmEx, DC, MC, V. **Map** p401 E4.

The luxury of perusing the latest CDs till midnight makes this a choice spot. Not only that, but the listening system allows you to play any CD by its barcode. Videos and books are also on offer.

Branches: Carrousel du Louvre, 99 rue de Rivoli, 1st (01.49.53.50.00); 15 bd Barbès 18th (01.56.55.53.70).

Bimbo Tower

5 passage St-Antoine, 11th (01.49.29.76.70). M° Ledru-Rollin. **Open** 2pm-7pm Mon-Sat. **No credit cards**. **Map** p407 M7.

Bimbo stocks all manner of new underground, counter-culture music from concrete music to sonic poetry and performance, rare discs, independent labels, auto-produced records and Japanese imports.

Virgin Megastore. *See p265.*

Sport & fitness

For general sports equipment and clothes, the chains **Go Sport** and **Décathlon** really can't be beaten. For more specialised needs Paris also has an array of sporting boutiques where you can get kitted out, even if your sporting intentions mean you only want to look the part.

Clery Brice

11 rue Pierre-Lescot, 1st (01.45.08.58.70). M°/RER Les Halles. **Open** 11am-1pm, 2-7pm Mon-Sat. **Credit** MC, V. **Map** p402 J5.

Here you pay lofty prices to get limited editions of the coolest trainers six months before the rest of the world finds out they should be wearing them.

Go Sport

Forum des Halles, 1st (01.53.00.81.70/www.go-sport.com). RER Châtelet-Les Halles. **Open** 10am-7.30pm Mon-Sat. **Credit** AmEx, MC, V. **Map** p406 J6.

Everything and anything is catered for in this reasonably priced chain, be it a home exercise machine, saddle wax or a wet suit. Classic labels such as Nike and Adidas are on offer along with Go Sport's cheaper own range.

Au Vieux Campeur

Main shop 48 rue des Ecoles, 5th (01.53.10.48.48/ www.au-vieux-campeur.com). M° Maubert-Mutualité. **Open** 11am-7.30pm Mon-Tue, Thur-Fri; 11am-9pm Wed; 9.30-7.30pm Sat. **Credit** AmEx, MC, V. **Map** p406 J7.

A Parisian institution, Au Vieux Campeur runs 19 specialist shops between rue des Ecoles and the bd St-Germain. The group deals with just about all sports you can do in public, from scuba diving to skiing – except golf, which it considers too bourgeois. Despite such rampant thought policing, staff are knowledgeable and friendly with experts ready to kit you out for climbing those higher limits.

Chattanooga

53 av Bosquet, 7th (01.45.51.76.65). M° Ecole Militaire. **Open** 10.30am-7.30pm Tue-Sat. **Credit** MC, V. **Map** p404 D6.

Old school to the new cool – founded in 1978, Chattanooga looks to the evolution of the skateboard. Alongside boards and wheels are clothing labels Quiksilver, Eastpak, Carhartt and Billabong if you want to look the grungy part.

L'Esprit du Sud Ouest

108 rue St-Dominique, 7th (01.45.55.29.06). M° Ecole Militaire. **Open** 10.30am-1pm, 3-8pm Tue-Sat. **Credit** MC, V. **Map** p404 D6.

At this shop dedicated to the hearty spirit of the south-west, rugby shirts of French and overseas teams form part of a scrummage with confit de canard and foie gras – well, the players have to get meaty somehow.

Boutique PSG

53 av des Champs-Elysées, 8th (01.56.69.22.22). M° Franklin D Roosevelt. **Open** 10am-9.45pm Mon-Sat; noon-9.45pm Sun. **Credit** AmEx, MC, V. **Map** p401 E4.

Fans of Paris' number one football team stock up on memorabilia and match tickets, along with a small range of international club and country shirts. With its prime location, the boutique is also the venue for special signings.

Décathlon

26 av de Wagram, 8th (01.55.31.74.00/ www.decathlon.fr). M° Charles de Gaulle-Etoile. **Open** 10am-8pm Mon-Fri; 9am-8pm Sat. **Credit** MC, V. **Map** p400 C3.

The B&Q of the sporting world has a comprehensive catalogue and helpful staff to ensure you're decked out with the right equipment at a competitive price. The range is awesome: think garden ping-pong to pro-tennis. It is also a camper's heaven.

Equistable

177 bd Haussmann, 8th (01.45.61.02.57). M° St-Philippe-du-Roule. **Open** 11am-7pm Mon-Fri; 10am-6pm Sat. **Credit** AmEx, DC, MC, V. **Map** p401 E4.

Camillas are in heaven at this shop full of quality equine gear, from Hermès saddles to horsey trinkets.

Citadium

50-55 rue Caumartin, 9th (01.55.31.74.00). M° Havre Caumartin. **Open** 10am-8pm Mon-Wed, Fri, Sat; 10am-9pm Thur. **Credit** AmEx, DC, MC, V. **Map** p401 G3.

This is one of France's biggest sports' emporiums, and it's fast gaining cult status. The latest surf 'n' skater vids blast out into the four themed circular floors ('urban street', 'glide', 'athletic' and 'outdoor'), all of which are manned by expert staff. Citadium stocks everything from designer watches to cross-country skis and travel books.

Subchandlers – Plongespace

80 rue Balard, 15th (01.45.57.01.01/ www.subchandlers.com). M° Balard. **Open** 2.30-7.30pm Mon; 10.30am-7.30pm Tue-Sat. **Credit** MC, V. **Map** p404 A9.

Big Blue fans gather here before heading south. These Europe-wide diving experts can provide all the basic apparatus, plus underwater cameras, DVDs, books, and monthly soirées on photography, film and all things aquatic.

Nike Town

12-14 Rond-Point des Champs-Elysées, 16th (01.45.62.57.57). M° Champs-Elysées-Clemenceau. **Open** 10.30am-8.30pm Mon-Wed; 10.30am-8pm Thur-Sat; noon-8pm Sun. **Credit** AmEx, MC, V. **Map** p400 C3.

Nike's French flagship store opened in April 2003. Covering three floors, where huge video screens diffuse Nike's most recent ads, it stocks the sports brand's multiple collections of menswear, womenswear and childrenswear.

Nauti Store

40 av de la Grande-Armée, 17th (01.43.80.28.28). M° Argentine. **Open** 11am-7pm Mon; 10am-7pm Tue-Sat. **Credit** AmEx, MC, V. **Map** p400 C3.

This shop is far less Nauti than it sounds with a vast range of sailing clothes and shoes from labels such as Helly Hansen and Sebago. A bookshop provides guidance before you set sail. Chandlers congregate in the Breton-influenced Montparnasse area.

Food Shops

In an ever-more-expensive world, a lovingly aged chèvre, a pristine pain au chocolat or a dinky little jar of raspberry-flavoured vinegar are among the few luxuries that remain within reach. Probably nowhere will you find more edible ways to spoil yourself than in Paris. Neighbourhood fromagers and charcutiers have lost some ground to supermarkets, but recent industrial food scandals have led to a renewed interest in 'terroir', the idea that each food has its season and its place.

Bakeries

Poilâne

8 rue du Cherche-Midi, 6th (01.45.48.42.59/ www.poilane.com). M° Sèvres Babylone or St-Sulpice. **Open** 7.15am-8.15pm Mon-Sat. **No credit cards. Map** p405 F8.

Poîlane the international brand lives on despite Lionel's demise in a helicopter crash. The famous pain au levain is at its freshest in this tiny, old-fashioned boutique, where bakers toil around the clock before a wood-burning oven in the cellar. Equally divine are the buttery apple tarts.

Branch: 49 bd de Grenelle, 15th (01.45.79.11.49).

Moisan

5 pl d'Aligre, 12th (01.43.45.46.60). M° Ledru-Rollin. **Open** 7am-1.30pm, 3-8pm Tue-Sat; 7am-2pm Sun. **No credit cards. Map** p407 N7.

An organic baking pioneer, Michel Moisan lovingly turns out crunchy boules de levain, fragrant petits pains, gorgeous orange-scented brioches and flaky apple tarts, all of it stunningly fresh.

Branch: 4 av du Général Leclerc, 14th (01.43.22.34.13).

Max Poilâne

87 rue Brancion, 15th (01.48.28.45.90/www.max-poilane.fr). M° Porte de Vanves. **Open** 7.30am-8pm Tue-Sat; 10am-7pm Sun. **No credit cards. Map** p404 D10.

Using the venerable Poilâne family recipe, the lesser-known Max produces bread that easily rivals that of his more famous brother, the late Lionel.

Branches: 29 rue de l'Ouest, 14th (01.43.27.24.91); 42 pl du Marché-St-Honoré, 1st (01.42.61.10.53).

Moulin de la Vierge

166 av de Suffren, 15th (01.47.83.45.55). M° Sèvres-Lecourbe. **Open** 7am-8pm Mon-Sat. **No credit cards. Map** p404 C6.

Basile Kamir learned breadmaking after falling in love with an old abandoned bakery. His naturally leavened country loaf is dense and fragrant.

Branches include: 82, rue Daguerre, 14th (01.43.22.50.55); 105 rue Vercingétorix, 14th (01.45.43.09.84); 15 rue Violet, 15th (01.45.75.85.85).

Cheese

Fromagerie 31
64 rue de Seine, 6th (01.43.26.50.31). M° Mabillon. **Open** 10am-8pm Tue-Sat; 10.30-1.30pm Sat. **Credit** AmEx, MC, V. **Map** p405 H7.
This recently opened cheese shop has modern tasting space behind a glass partition where you can sample some perfectly aged specimens, aided by a glass of wine.

Marie-Anne Cantin
12 rue du Champ-de-Mars, 7th (01.45.50.43.94/ www.cantin.fr). M° Ecole Militaire. **Open** 8.30am-7.30pm Mon-Sat. **Credit** MC, V. **Map** p404 D6.
Cantin, a vigorous defender of unpasteurised cheese, is justifiably proud of her dreamily creamy st-marcellins, aged chèvres and nutty beauforts. The cheeses are ripened in her cellars.

Alléosse
13 rue Poncelet, 17th (01.46.22.50.45). M° Ternes. **Open** 9am-1pm, 4-7pm Tue-Thur; 9am-1pm, 3.30-7pm Fri, Sat; 9am-1pm Sun. **Credit** MC, V. **Map** p400 C2.
People cross town for these cheeses – wonderful farmhouse camemberts, delicate st-marcellins, a choice of chèvres and several rarities.

Fromagerie Dubois et Fils
80 rue de Tocqueville, 17th (01.42.27.11.38). M° Malesherbes or Villiers. **Open** 9am-1pm, 4-8pm Tue-Fri; 9am-1pm Sat, Sun. Closed first three weeks in Aug. **Credit** MC, V. **Map** p401 E2.
Dubois, who stocks some 80 varieties of goat's cheese plus prized, aged st-marcellin and st-félicien, is a darling of the superchefs.

Fromagerie Bocquet
32 rue des Abbesses, 18th (01.42.52.96.27). M° Abbesses. **Open** 9am-1pm, 4-8pm Tue Sat; 9am-noon Sun. **Credit** MC, V. **Map** p402 H2.
This is not the most famous fromagerie in Paris, but Marie Bocquet's lovingly selected cheeses, most of them aged on the premises, are exemplary. She has a penchant for goat's cheese, but the real farmers' camemberts are also exceptional.

Chocolate

Christian Constant
37 rue d'Assas, 6th (01.53.63.15.15). M° St-Placide. **Open** 8.30am-9pm Mon-Fri; 8am-8.30pm Sat; 8.30am-7pm Sun. **Credit** MC, V. **Map** p405 G8.
A master chocolate maker and traiteur, Constant is revered by *le tout Paris* and scours the globe for new and delectable ideas. Ganaches are subtly flavoured with verbena, jasmine or cardamom.

Jean-Paul Hévin
3 rue Vavin, 6th (01.43.54.09.85). M° Vavin. **Open** 10am-7.30pm Mon-Sat. Closed three weeks in Aug. **Credit** MC, V. **Map** G8.
Jean-Paul Hévin dares to fill his chocolates with potent cheeses, to be served with wine as an apéritif. Even more risqué are his aphrodisiac chocs.
Branches: 231 rue St-Honoré, 1st (01.55.35.35.96); 16 and 23bis av de La Motte-Picquet, 7th (01.45.51.77.48).

Debauve & Gallais
30 rue des Sts-Pères, 7th (01.45.48.54.67/ www.debauve-et-gallais.com). M° St-Germain-des-Prés. **Open** 9am-7pm Mon-Sat. **Credit** DC, MC, V. **Map** p405 G7.
This former pharmacy, with a facade dating from 1800, once sold chocolate for medicinal purposes. Its intense chocolates filled with tea, honey or praline do, indeed, heal the soul.
Branch: 33 rue Vivienne, 2nd (01.40.39.05.50).

Richart
258 bd St-Germain, 7th (01.45.55.66.00/ www.richart.com). M° Solférino. **Open** 10am-7pm Mon-Sat. **Credit** AmEx, MC, V. **Map** p405 F6.
Each chocolate ganache has an intricate design, packages look like jewel boxes and every purchase comes with a tract on how best to savour chocolate.

La Maison du Chocolat
89 av Raymond-Poincaré, 16th (01.40.67.77.83/ www.lamaisonduchocolat.com). M° Victor-Hugo. **Open** 10am-7pm Mon-Sat. **Credit** AmEx, MC, V. **Map** p400 B4.
Robert Linxe opened his first Paris shop in 1977 and has been inventing new chocolates ever since. Using Asian spices, fresh fruits, herbal infusions and most recently wine, he has won over the most demanding chocolate-lovers.
Branches: 19 rue de Sèvres, 6th (01.45.44.20.40); 225 rue du Fbg-St-Honoré, 8th (01.42.27.39.44); 52 rue François 1er, 8th (01.47.23.38.25); 8 bd de la Madeleine, 9th (01.47.42.86.52).

International

Kioko
46 rue des Petits-Champs, 2nd (01.42.61.33.65). M° Pyramides. **Open** 10am-8pm Tue-Sat; 11am-7pm Sun. **Credit** V. **Map** p401 H4.
Everything you need to make sushi (or good ready-made sushi for the lazy), plus sauces, snacks, sake, Japanese beer, tea and kitchen utensils. Staff will point you to the ingredient you're looking for.

Pasta Linea
9 rue de Turenne, 4th (01.42.77.62.54). M° St-Paul. **Open** 11am-9pm Tue-Fri; Sat 11am-8pm Sun. **Credit** MC, V. **Map** p406 L6.
Artichoke ravioli with truffle cream sauce or fresh linguine with tomato and rocket are among the heavenly hot pastas you might find here, or buy top-quality dried pasta, rice and sauce to eat at home.

Mexi & Co
10 rue Dante, 5th (01.46.34.14.12). M° Maubert-Mutualité. **Open** noon-11pm daily. **Credit** MC, V. **Map** p406 J7.

Moulin de la Vierge. *See p267.*

Everything you need for a fiesta, includes marinades for fajitas, dried chillies, South American beers, cachaça and tequilas.

Petrossian

18 bd de la Tour-Maubourg, 7th (01.44.11.32.32). M° Invalides. **Open** 8.30am-7pm Mon-Sat. **Credit** AmEx, DC, MC, V. **Map** p405 E6.
High-quality smoked salmon doesn't come cheap, so you might as well blow the budget entirely at this luxury delicatessen, where fans say it's the best in the universe. It's also the place to stock up on caviar.

Jabugo Iberico & Co

11 rue Clément-Marot, 8th (01.47.20.03.13). M° Alma-Marceau or Franklin D Roosevelt. **Open** 10am-8pm Tue-Sat. **Credit** MC, V. **Map** p401 E4.
This shop specialises in Spanish hams with the Bellota-Bellota label, meaning the pigs have feasted on acorns. Manager Philippe Poulachon compares the complexity of his cured hams (at €95 a kilo) to the delicacy of truffles.

Sarl Velan Stores

87 passage Brady, 10th (01.42.46.06.06). M° Château d'Eau. **Open** 8.30am-9.30pm Mon-Sat. **Credit** AmEx, DC, MC, V. **Map** p402 K4.
Nestled in a run-down arcade of Indian cafés and shops, plus restaurants whose waiters try to tempt you in, this is an emporium of spices, vegetables and saris shipped from Kenya and India.

Les Délices d'Orient

52 av Emile-Zola, 15th (01.45.79.10.00). M° Charles-Michels. **Open** 7.30am-9pm Tue-Sun. **Credit** MC, V. **Map** p404 B8.
Supplying the local Lebanese community, this shop brims with houmous, stuffed aubergines, halva, Lebanese bread, felafel, olives and all manner of Middle Eastern delicacies.
Branch: 14 rue des Quatre-Frères Peignot, 15th.

Merry Monk

87 rue de la Convention, 15th (01.40.60.79.54). M° Boucicaut. **Open** 10am-7pm Mon-Sat. Closed Aug. **Credit** V. **Map** p404 B9.
As tidy as your granny's larder, this shop stocks British ex-pats' essentials and loose tea, along with a section dedicated to South Africa.

Pâtisseries

Finkelsztajn

27 rue des Rosiers, 4th (01.42.72.78.91). M° St-Paul. **Open** 11am-7pm Mon; 10am-7pm Wed-Sun. Closed Aug. **No credit cards. Map** p406 L6.
Filled with poppy seeds, apples or cream cheese, the dense Jewish cakes in this motherly shop pad the bones for the Parisian winter.

Pierre Hermé

72 rue Bonaparte, 6th (01.53.67.66.65). M° St-Sulpice. **Open** Tue-Sun 10am-7pm. Closed Aug. **Credit** AmEx, DC, MC, V. **Map** p405 G7.
The Ganesh of pastry chefs, Pierre Hermé attracts the crème de la crème of St-Germain. Highlights of his autumn/winter 2003 'collection' included the surprise kawaii, a giant meringue bonbon filled with orange compote, pain d'épices and lemon mousse, and the PH3, three orbs of white chocolate with complex fillings ranging from sweet to tart.

Sadaharu Aoki

35 rue de Vaugirard, 6th (01.45.44.48.90/ www.interq.or.jp/gold/sada/). M° St-Placide. **Open** 11am-1.30pm, 2.30-7pm Tue-Sun. **Credit** DC, MC, V. **Map** p405 G8.
This discreet yet dashing Japanese pastry chef, who opened his minimalist boutique in 2001, has achieved perfection with his innovative éclairs (try the green tea or blackcurrant-chestnut version) and the Japon, ethereal layers of génoise, Chantilly and heavenly – scented strawberries.

Peltier

66 rue de Sèvres, 7th (01.47.34.06.62). M° Duroc or Vaneau. **Open** 9am-7.30pm Mon-Sat; 9am-6.30pm Sun. **Credit** AmEx, MC, V. **Map** p405 F7.
Philippe Conticini has whisked this historic pastry shop into the 21st century. Alongside conventional cakes are sultry mousses filled with pear chutney or dried-apricot jam.
Branch: 6 rue St-Dominique, 7th (01.47.05.50.02).

Markets

Street markets are some of the best places to buy fresh, seasonal food, as well as to chat to stall-owners and get recipe tips. Most *arrondissements* have three or four, either daily markets (open Tue-Sat 8am-1pm, 4-7pm; Sun 8am-1pm) or roving ones which set up once or twice a week from 8am-2pm then disappear in a flurry of green cleaning trucks (see www.paris.fr/markets for a full list). Of note are the **Marché des Enfants Rouges** (39 rue de Bretagne, 3rd), Paris' oldest market, dating back to 1615, and serving all sorts of treats from foreign soils as well as French specialities, and, for atmosphere, **avenue de Saxe** (7th), where Parisians parade their poodles and buy olives to a backdrop of the Eiffel Tower. **Marché Place Baudoyer** (4th) is the first roving market to open in the afternoons (3-8pm Wed), with a great free range egg stall, charcuterie and fish. Don't miss beautifully presented **Marché Mouffetard** (rue Mouffetard, 5th) with its elaborate displays of fruit and veg. Organic food fans should head to the **Marché Biologique** on Sundays on boulevard Raspail (14th).

Treats & traiteurs

Torréfacteur Verlet

256 rue St-Honoré, 1st (01.42.60.67.39). M° Palais Royal. **Open** shop 9.30am-7pm Mon-Sat; tea room 9.30am-6.30pm daily. Closed Aug. **Credit** MC, V. **Map** p401 G5.
The freshly roasted coffee in this gem of a shop smells as heavenly as the priciest perfume. Eric Duchaussoy roasts rare beans to perfection – sip a *petit noir* at a wooden table, or treat yourself to what is probably the city's best coffee at home.

L'Epicerie

51 rue St-Louis-en-l'Ile, 4th (01.43.25.20.14). M° Pont Marie. **Open** 11am-8pm daily. Closed 25 Dec, 1 Jan. **Credit** MC, V. **Map** p406 K7.
Perfect for the condiment-crazy, this shop is crammed head to toe with beautiful bottles of vinegar with flavours ranging from rose to tomato-tarragon, spiced salts (such as turmeric and ginger or Sichuan pepper), a multitude of mustards and a joyous selection of jams, including blackcurrant-violet and bitter orange with chocolate.

Jean-Paul Gardil

44 rue St-Louis-en-l'Ile, 4th (01.43.54.97.15). M° Pont Marie. **Open** 9am-12.45pm, 4-5.45pm Tue-Sat; 9am-12.30pm Sun. **Credit** MC, V. **Map** p406 K7.
Rarely has meat looked so alluring as in this fairy-tale shop, where geese hang in the window and a proliferation of plaques confirm the butcher's skill in selecting the finest meats, such as milk-fed veal and lamb, coucou de Rennes chickens, free-range Barbary ducklings, and Bresse poulard and geese.

Da Rosa

62 rue de Seine, 6th (01.40.51.00.09). M° Mabillon. **Open** 10am-10pm daily. **Credit** AmEx, MC, V. **Map** p405 H7,
José Da Rosa travelled the world for a decade seeking out ingredients for top Paris restaurants before opening his own boutique, designed by Jacques Garcia. Each product – whether it be Spanish ham, spices from Breton chef Olivier Roellinger or truffles from the Luberon – comes with a 'fiche technique' describing how Da Rosa discovered it.

Huilerie Artisanale Leblanc

6 rue Jacob, 6th (01.46.34.61.55). M° St-Germain-des-Prés. **Open** 2.30-7.30pm Mon; 11am-7.30pm Tue-Sat. Closed two weeks in Aug. **No credit cards**. **Map** p405 H6.
The Leblanc family started out making walnut oil from its family tree in Burgundy and selling to its neighbours before branching out skilfully to press pure oils from hazelnuts, almonds, pine nuts, grilled peanuts, pistachios and olives.

Fauchon

26-30 pl de la Madeleine, 8th (01.47.42.60.11). M° Madeleine. **Open** 9.30am-7pm Mon-Sat. **Credit** AmEx, DC, MC, V. **Map** p401 F4.
Paris' most famous food store is like every specialist deli rolled into one. There's a prepared-food section, cheese, fish and exotic fruit counters, an Italian deli, fine wines in the cellar, chocolates and a plush tea room for refreshment. All it lacks, sadly, is soul.

Hédiard

21 pl de la Madeleine, 8th (01.43.12.88.88/ www.hediard.fr). M° Madeleine. **Open** 8.30am-9pm Mon-Sat. **Credit** AmEx, DC, MC, V. **Map** p401 F4.
The first to introduce exotic foods to the Parisians, Hédiard specialises in rare teas and coffees, unusual spices, imported produce (this is the place to go for cherries in December), jams and candied fruits, all

Prêt
du Musée de l'Oie et
du Canard
de Thiviers,
en Périgord Vert .
ENCHAUD DE PORC

Fauchon

Posh spice and vanilla *paradis*

Anyone who has ever tried to find a decent curry in Paris knows that the French have an uneasy relationship with spices. It hasn't always been that way: Taillevent, the country's first celebrity chef, wrote in the 14th century that no respectable pantry would be complete without ginger, cinnamon, cloves, cardamom, chilies and peppercorns, cinnamon flower, saffron, nutmeg, bay leaves, cumin and a few now-obsolete flavourings. By the 19th century, however, the French were turning up their noses at spice, and most of the classics of the past 100 years call for nothing more exotic than salt, pepper, nutmeg and bay leaf.

If the worst condemnation of a dish is still the words '*trop épicé*', several chefs have now come out of the spice closet, notably Pascal Barbot at L'Astrance. William Ledeuil at Ze Kitchen Galerie, Philippe Delacourcelle at Le Pré Verre and the mad scientist of haute cuisine, Pierre Gagnaire (*see chapter* **Restaurants**). Paris might not be the world spice capital, but at a few shops that are well-known among chefs such as these you'll find nutmeg, Espelette pepper, Moroccan ras-el-hanout, supple organic vanilla pods and unusual flavourings such as tonka bean.

Leading the way is Jean-Marie Thiercelin of **Goumanyat** (3 rue Dupuis, 3rd/ 01.44.78.96.74), whose family has been in the spice business since 1809. The Goumanyat story started with saffron, which few people know was cultivated near Orléans until the end of the 19th century. Six generations later, Thiercelin continues to sell top-quality saffron from countries such as Iran and Spain, carefully screening the product for authenticity. Among the other cook's treasures to be found in the antique chemists' drawers at Goumanyat are long pepper, an Indian variety used in stews and preserves; Indonesian cubebe pepper found in Arab spice mixes; nutmeg so fresh it looks polished; and *fleur de sel*, salt skimmed from the surface of the sea and used to add the finishing touch to meat, fish and salads.

More souk-like is the long-established **Izraël** in the Marais (30 rue François-Miron, 4th/ 01.42.72.66.23), where sacks overflow with ochre and rust-red powders, beans, lentils, rice and gleaming candied fruit. This is the place to come for ready-made spice mixes, Hungarian paprika, Espelette pepper (dried or puréed), the pepper grinder of your dreams and gift boxes for the spice enthusiast.

Few scents are more irresistible than vanilla, and a visit to **La Maison de la Vanille** (18 rue du Cardinal-Lemoine, 5th/ 01.43.25.50.95; *pictured*) is a feast for the nose. A shop and tea room serving vanilla-perfumed savoury dishes and desserts, plus heartening hot chocolate, it stocks top-quality Bourbon vanilla from Reunion Island, available whole in various sizes (for crème anglaise and ice cream), powdered (for cakes) or in syrup (to use in cold drinks or desserts). You'll also find giant shavings of headily perfumed wild cinnamon bark.

For Asian cooking, head to Belleville (20th) or the larger Chinatown in the 13th, where big Asian supermarkets stock dried spices and mushrooms, ready-made sauces, and fresh ingredients such as lemongrass, red-hot chilli peppers and (harder to find) galangal. The biggest and best-known is **Tang Frères** (48 av d'Ivry, 13th/ 01.45.70.80.00), supplier to most Asian restaurants, but smaller shops can be a good source of hard-to-find ingredients and fun to look around.

Your cupboard stocked with these essentials, there is only one danger – that French people will declare your cooking '*trop bon*'.

packaged in their smart red-and-white tins and boxes. The original shop, dating from 1880, has a posh tea room upstairs.
Branches include: 126 rue du Bac, 7th (01.45.44.01.98); 31 av George V, 8th (01.47.20.44.44); 70 av Paul-Doumer, 16th (01.45.04.51.92); 106 bd des Courcelles, 17th (01.47.63.32.14).

La Maison de la Truffe

19 pl de la Madeleine, 8th (01.42.65.53.22/ www.maison-de-la-truffe.fr). M° Madeleine. **Open** 9am-9pm Mon-Sat. **Credit** AmEx, DC, MC, V. **Map** p401 F4.
Here, at one of a cluster of gourmet specialist shops around the Madeleine, sniff out truffles priced like precious jewels or for more affordable truffle oils and vinegars that make fine gourmet presents.

Allicante

26 bd Beaumarchais, 11th (01.43.55.13.02/ www.allicante.com). M° Bastille. **Open** 10am-7.30pm daily. **Credit** AmEx, DC, MC, V. **Map** p407 M6.
A paradise of oily delights, including rare olive oils from Liguria, Puglia and Greece as well as a broad French selection, fragrant pine nut, pistachio and almond varieties, and oils extracted from apricot, pumpkin and avocado seeds and pits. Wow your guests with pricey argania oil, pounded by hand by Berber women in Morocco.

Poissonerie du Dôme

4 rue Delambre, 14th (01.43.35.23.95). M° Vavin. **Open** 8am-1pm, 4-7pm Tue-Sat; 8am-1pm Sun. Closed Aug. **Credit** MC, V. **Map** p405 G9.
Jean-Pierre Lopez's tiny shop is probably the best fishmonger in Paris. His fish are individually selected, many coming straight from small boats off the Breton coast. Each one is bright of eye and sound of gill. Try the drool-inducing (but bank-breaking) turbot, the giant crabs or the scallops, when in season.

Wine, beer & spirits

Legrand Filles et Fils

1 rue de la Banque, 2nd (01.42.60.07.12). M° Bourse. **Open** 11am-7pm Mon, Wed-Fri; 10am-7.30pm Thur; 10am-7pm Sat. **Credit** AmEx, MC, V. **Map** p402 H4.
This fourth-generation shop offering fine wines and brandies, chocolates, teas, coffees and bonbons now has a wine bar and showroom for its huge selection of tasting glasses and gadgets. It's a good source of wine books too, and stocks the now-available (non-hallucinogenic) French absinthe.

Julien, Caviste

50 rue Charlot, 3rd (01.42.72.00.94). M° Filles du Calvaire. **Open** 9.30am-8.30pm Tue-Sat; 10am-1.30pm Sun. **Credit** MC, V. **Map** p402 L5.
This up-and-coming *caviste* near the Marché des Enfants-Rouges overflows with enthusiasm for the small producers he has discovered. He speaks English with a London accent, so ask him about his latest finds in rhyming slang.

La Dernière Goutte

6 rue de Bourbon-le-Château, 6th (01.43.29.11.62). M° Mabillon. **Open** 4-9pm Mon; 10am-1.30pm, 3-8.30pm Tue-Fri; 10am-8.30pm Sat. **Credit** AmEx, MC, V. **Map** p405 H7.
Run by the bilingual team behind the wine bar Fish, this clubby little shop has estate-bottled wines for every budget, starting at less than €3.

Ryst Dupeyron

79 rue du Bac, 7th (01.45.48.80.93/ www.dupeyron.com). M° Rue du Bac. **Open** 12.30-7.30pm Mon; 10.30am-7.30pm Tue-Sat. Closed one week in Aug. **Credit** AmEx, MC, V. **Map** p405 F7.
The Dupeyron family has sold Armagnac for four generations. You'll find bottles dating from 1868 in this listed shop, plus collectors' bottles to be offered as personalised gifts. Treasures include some 200 fine Bordeaux, vintage Port and rare whiskies.

Les Caves Augé

116 bd Haussmann, 8th (01.45.22.16.97). M° St-Augustin. **Open** 1-7.30pm Mon; 9am-7.30pm Tue-Sat. Closed Mon in Aug. **Credit** AmEx, MC, V. **Map** p401 E3.
The oldest wine shop in Paris – Marcel Proust was a regular customer – is serious and professional, with sommelier Marc Sibard advising.

Les Caves Taillevent

199 rue du Fbg-St-Honoré, 8th (01.45.61.14.09/ www.taillevent.com). M° Charles-de-Gaulle-Etoile or Ternes. **Open** 2-7.30pm Mon; 9am-7.30pm Tue-Fri; 9am-7.30pm Sat. Closed first three weeks in Aug. **Credit** AmEx, DC, MC, V. **Map** p400 D3.
Half a million bottles make up the Taillevent cellar, supervised by three head sommeliers.

La Maison du Whisky

20 rue d'Anjou, 8th (01.42.65.03.16/ www.whisky.fr). M° Madeleine. **Open** 9.30am-7pm Mon; 9.15am-8pm Tue-Fri; 9.30am-7.30pm Sat. **Credit** AmEx, V. **Map** p401 F4.
Jean-Marc Bellier is fascinating as he explains which whisky matches which food, waxing lyrical about different flavours such as honey and tobacco. He also hosts a whisky club.

Bières Spéciales

77 rue St-Maur, 11th (01.48.07.18.71). M° St-Maur. **Open** 10.30am-1pm, 4-9pm Tue-Sat. **Credit** AmEx, DC, MC, V. **Map** p403 M3.
Single bottles and cans from 16 nations (at last count) neatly cover the walls. Belgium might dominate but you'll also find Polish, Scottish, Corsican, Portuguese and Chinese brews.

Les Domaines qui Montent

136 bd Voltaire, 11th (01.43.56.89.15). M° Voltaire. **Open** 10am-8pm Mon-Sat. Lunch served noon-2.30pm. **Credit** MC, V. **Map** p403 M5.
This is not only a wine shop but a convivial place to have breakfast, lunch or tea. Wines cost the same as they would at the producer's. Saturday tastings with up-and-coming winemakers are held in the shop.

Bal du
Moulin Rouge
Féerie
Kris Gautier

Arts & Entertainment

Features

Festivals & Events

Chocolate, jazz and Jesus: all three get the Parisian glitter ball turning. But you can also witness some exemplary jumping, warbling and Beaujolais drinking.

The panoply of French *fêtes* is frighteningly well-stacked. In Paris, the phrase 'Fête de la...' often ends with a byword for a good time (e.g. music) although sometimes the object of celebration can be as obscure as bookbinding. Anniversaries, too, are fervently observed by the cultural agenda-setters, unrelentingly reminding us of great Gauls' birthdays and deathdays. This year marks 60 years since the Liberation of Paris and even though much flag flying, speeches and quaffing of the freedom juice is expected, at the time of going to press no concrete plans had been made.

The pro-active reign of Mayor Delanoë has done much to refresh the capital's diary. 'Paris-Plage', an urban beach installed on the banks of the Seine for the hot summer months, and 'Nuit Blanche', an autumnal, all-night culture fest, have been high-profile successes. Last year the Mairie de Paris bought the city another can of cultural Red Bull with the introduction of the 'Soirée du Patrimoine', a recreation of a period party to go with the annual opening of historic buildings to the public.

In terms of cultural seasons, Paris really only gets stuck in from October, keeping busy until the beginning of summer, when the entire arts scene sods off down South. What's left are some lovely outdoor festivals, and a substantial wait for those who won't get out of bed for less than Peter Brook's finest. Sporting events take place throughout the year, with the exception of July and August.

The *Time Out Paris* section inside *Pariscope* covers events each week. Selected museum shows are previewed in the **Museums** chapter; further annual events and festivals are covered in the **Arts & Entertainment** chapters.

Public holidays

On *jours feriés* banks, many museums, most shops and some restaurants close; public transport runs as on Sunday. New Year, May Day, Bastille Day and Christmas are the most fully observed holidays. Full list: New Year's Day (Jour de l'An); Easter Monday (Lundi de Pâques); May Day (Fête du Travail); VE Day (Victoire 1945) 8 May; Ascension Day (Jour de l'Ascension); Whit Monday (Lundi de Pentecôte); Bastille Day (Quatorze Juillet) 14 July; Feast of the Assumption (Jour de l'Assomption) 15 Aug; All Saints' Day (Toussaint) 1 Nov; Remembrance Day (L'Armistice 1918) 11 Nov; Christmas Day (Noël).

Spring

14 Feb-17 April: Six Nations' Cup

Stade de France, rue Francis de Pressensé, 93210 St-Denis (0892.700.900/www.stadedefrance.fr).
France and England are still set to be the strongest contenders in the European rugby clash – they meet on 27 March, with France-Ireland on 14 February.

9-15 Feb: Tennis Open Gaz de France

Stade Pierre de Coubertin, 82 av Georges-Lafont, 16th (0825.811.812). M° Porte de St-Cloud.
Women tennis stars compete at this indoor event.

28 Feb-7 Mar: Salon de l'Agriculture

Paris-Expo, pl de la Porte de Versailles, 15th (01.49.09.60.00/www.salon-agriculture.com). M° Porte de Versailles. **Admission** €7-€11.
France's farmers meet to show off beautiful beasts and prize crops. There's also regional food and wine.

mid-Mar: Les Festins d'Aden

Various venues. **Information** http://aden.lemonde.fr.
Le Monde's savvy arts supplement *Aden* invites big names and hot tips for a week of damn fine music.

5, 6 Mar: International Showjumping

Palais Omnisports Paris/Bercy, 8 bd Bercy, 12th (01.46.91.57.57/www.ticketnet.fr). M° Bercy.
The world's best jumpers unite at Bercy.

Mar-Apr: Banlieues Bleues

Seine St-Denis area **Information** 01.49.22.10.10/ www.banlieuesbleues.org. **Admission** €11-€15.
Five weeks of French and international jazz, blues, R&B, soul, funk, flamenco, world and gospel.

20-21 Mar: La Nuit des Publivores

Grand Rex, 1 bd Poissonnière, 2nd. M° Bonne-Nouvelle. **Information** 01.44.88.98.00. **Admission** €34.
This all-night ad-fest elevates commercial breaks to cult status. A pantomime atmosphere pervades.

end Mar-early May: Foire du Trône

pelouse de Reuilly, 12th (01.46.27.52.29). M° Porte Dorée. **Admission** free; rides €1.50-€4.
France's biggest funfair boasts stomach-churning rides, bungee jumping, freak shows and candyfloss.

Good Friday: Le Chemin de la Croix

square Willette, 18th. M° Anvers or Abbesses. **Information** Sacré-Coeur (01.53.41.89.00).
Crowds follow the Archbishop of Paris from the bottom of Montmartre up the steps to the Sacré-Coeur, as he performs the stations of the cross.

Le Chemin de la Croix

29 Mar-6 Apr: Festival du Film de Paris

Various venues. **Information** 01.45.72.96.40/ www.festivaldufilmdeparis.com. **Admission** €6-€7.
Public previews of international films, plus mingling with directors, actors and technicians.

1 Apr: Poisson d'Avril

Watch your back as pranksters attempt to stick paper fish on to each other as an April Fool's gag.

4 Apr: Marathon de Paris

starts around 9am, av des Champs-Elysées, first runners finish around 11am, av Foch. **Information** 01.41.33.15.68/www.parismarathon.com.
The Paris marathon takes in many of the city's personal bests. There's also a half-marathon in March to get in training.

18 Apr: Prix du Président de la République

Hippodrome d'Auteuil, Bois de Boulogne, M° Porte d'Auteuil. **Information** www.france-galop.fr.
Usually more chasers than steeples at this world renowned horse racing event.

beg May: Foire de Paris

Paris-Expo, pl de la Porte de Versailles. M° Porte de Versailles. **Information** 01.49.09.60.00/ www.comexpo-paris.com. **Admission** €9.15.
This enormous lifestyle salon includes world crafts and foods, plus the latest health and house gizmos.

1 May: Fête du Travail

Labour Day is ardently maintained. All museums and sights (except the Eiffel Tower) close, while unions stage a colourful march through working-class eastern Paris via the Bastille. Lilies of the valley are sold on street corners and given to mum.

14-17 May: Belleville open studios

Information www.ateliers-artistes-belleville.org. **Admission** free.
Belleville is artsville as painters, sculptors and other artists open up their studios to the public.

mid May-end July: Paris Jazz Festival

Parc Floral de Paris, Bois de Vincennes. M° Château de Vincennes. **Information** 01.55.94.20.20/ www.parcfloraldeparis.com. **Admission** park €1.50.
Free outdoor jazz concerts on hot weekend afternoons, in the charming Parc Floral.

mid May-end June: Festival de St-Denis

Various venues in St-Denis. M° St-Denis Basilique. **Information** 01.48.13.06.07/www.festival-saint-denis.fr. **Admission** €9-€55.
The Gothic St-Denis Basilica and other historic buildings host classical concerts.

Summer

24 May-6 June: French Tennis Open

Stade Roland Garros, 2 av Gordon-Bennett, 16th (01.47.43.48.00/www.frenchopen.org). M° Porte d'Auteuil. **Admission** €21-€53.
Showbiz stars fill the stands at the glitzy Grand Slam tournament to watch the balls fly.

end May-beg June: Quinzaine des Réalisateurs

Forum des Images, Porte Saint-Eustache, Forum des Halles, 1st. M° Les Halles. **Information** 01.44.76.62.00/ www.forumdesimages.net. **Admission** €5.50.
As soon as the dust has settled on the Croisette, Cannes' Director's Fortnight is shown to Paris.

5, 6 June: Le Printemps des rues

Information 01.47.97.36.06/ www.leprintempsdesrues.com. **Admission** free.
Annual street-theatre fest celebrates the Year of China with acts along a lantern-lit Canal St-Martin.

beg June: Journées de la Maison Contemporaine

Various venues. **Information** 01.53.90.19.30/ www.maisonscontemporaines.com. **Admission** free.
Modern architects open their sleek abodes for the public to ooh and aah.

beg June: Les Cinq Jours de l'Objet Extraordinaire

rues du Bac, Sts-Pères, de l'Université, quai Voltaire, 7th. M° Rue du Bac. **Information** 01.42.60.70.10/ www.carrerivegauche.com. **Admission** free.
Chic antique dealers each showcase one exciting find.

5 June-6 July: Foire St-Germain
pl St-Sulpice and other venues in St-Germain-des-Prés, 6th. Mº St-Sulpice. **Information** 01.43.29.61.04/www.foiresaintgermain.org.
Concerts, theatre, lectures and workshops. In the square there's an antiques fair and poetry salon.

13 June: Prix de Diane Hermès
Chantilly (30 minutes from Gare du Nord). **Information** *03.44.62.41.00/www.france-galop.com*
French equivalent of the Derby draws high society and horse racing enthusiasts.

11-14 June: L'Art du Jardin
Domaine National de St-Cloud. Mº Boulogne/Pont de St-Cloud. **Information** 01.49.09.64.14/www.art-du-jardin.com. **Admission** €10.
Stylish garden salon digs deep for the latest looks and species.

mid June-mid July: Festival Chopin à Paris
Orangerie de Bagatelle, parc de Bagatelle, Bois de Boulogne, 16th. Mº Porte Maillot, then bus 244. **Information** 01.45.00.22.19/www.frederic-chopin.com. **Admission** €16-€31.
The romance of the piano is promised, with candle-lit evening concerts complementing the mood.

21 June: Fête de la Musique
All over France. **Information** 01.40.03.94.70/www.fetedelamusique.fr. **Admission** free.
Dancing in the streets as free concerts invade the city. The music is incredibly varied.

26 June: Gay Pride March
Information Centre Gai et Lesbien (01.43.57.21.47/www.fiertes-lgbt.org).
Outrageous floats and costumes parade towards Bastille. Followed by an official *fête* and club events.

beg July: La Goutte d'Or en Fête
square Léon, 18th. Mº Barbès-Rochechouart. **Information** 01.46.07.61.64/www.gouttedorenfete.org. **Admission** free.
Established names play raï, rap and reggae alongside local talent in the up-and-coming, largely Arab and African Goutte d'Or neighbourhood.

beg-mid July: Paris Cinéma
Various venues. **Information** www.pariscinema.org. **Admission** varies.
Premières, tributes and restored films make up the programme of the Mairie de Paris' summer film-going initiative.

beg July-end Aug: Le Cinéma en Plein Air
Parc de La Villette, 19th (01.40.03.76.92/www.la-villette.com). Mº Porte de Pantin. **Admission** free.
Settle back in a deckchair as night falls over the park and take in classic films projected onto the inflatable big screen.

13, 14 July: Le Quatorze Juillet (Bastille Day)
A national holiday commemorates the storming of the Bastille prison on 14 July 1789, (*see chapter* **History**). On the evening of 13 July, Parisians dance

Gay Pride March

at place de la Bastille. At 10am on the 14th, crowds line the Champs-Elysées as the President reviews a military parade. (Note: Métro stops on the Champs are closed.) Thousands gather on the Champ de Mars for fireworks. Party on at firemen's balls or the big gay ball on quai de la Tournelle (5th).

14 July: Miss Guinguette

38 quai Victor Hugo, Ile du Martin Pêcheur, Champigny sur Marne. RER Champigny sur Marne. **Information** 01.49.83.03.02. **Admission** €7.50.
A hunt to find the light-footed queen of the open-air dance hall scene, on this river island venue.

mid July-mid Aug: Paris, Quartier d'Eté

Various venues. **Information** 01.44.94.98.00/ www.quartierdete.com. **Admission** free-€15.
A lively series features classical and jazz concerts, dance and theatre performances in outdoor venues.

mid July-mid Aug: Paris-Plage

quai Henri IV to quai des Tuileries. M° Sully Morland. **Information** 08.20.00.75.75/www.paris.fr. **Admission** free.
During this city-to-seaside metamorphosis, sun gods laze by the Seine on (France's smallest) beaches, under the shade of fake palm trees. Rollerbladers, cyclists and walkers have free run of the quais.

July: Le Tour de France

finishes av des Champs-Elysées, 8th. **Information** 01.41.33.15.00/www.letour.fr.
Spot the yellow jersey as cyclists speed along the Champs-Elysées to the finish line .

Aug: Cinéma au clair de lune

Various venues. **Information** 01.44.76.62.18/ www.forumdesimages.net. **Admission** free.
Reels on wheels provide open-air screenings of films set in Paris, near the locations where they were shot, at this atmospheric film fest.

15 Aug: Fête de l'Assomption

Cathédrale Notre-Dame de Paris, pl Notre-Dame, 4th (01.42.34.56.10). M° Cité. **Admission** free.
Notre-Dame again becomes a place of religious pilgrimage for Assumption Day, with a parade around the Ile de la Cité behind a statue of the Virgin. A national holiday.

end Aug-beg Sept: L'Etrange Festival

Forum des Images, Porte Saint-Eustache, Forum des Halles, 1st. M° Les Halles. **Information** 01.44.76.62.00. **Admission** €4.50-€6.
Get your freak on with this celebration of weird celluloid, including all-night 'Nuits Freakshows'.

End Aug: Festival Silhouette

Parc des Buttes-Chaumont, 19th. M° Buttes-Chaumont. **Information** www.association-silhouette.com.
Open-air projections of short films in the gorgeous parc des Buttes-Chaumont.

Autumn

mid Sept: Jazz à La Villette

211 av Jean-Jaurès, 19th (08.03.07.50.75/ 01.44.84.44.84/www.la-villette.com). M° Porte de Pantin. **Admission** €13-€16.
One of Paris' best jazz fests. The slick line-up is a thoughtful cross-section of talents.

mid Sept: Techno Parade

Information 01.42.47.84.76/www.technopol.net.
BPM junkies get their annual headrush with this parade (usually finishing at place de la Bastille). Marks the start of Rendez-vous Electroniques.

mid-Sept: Rendez-vous Electroniques

Information www.technopol.net.
Paris becomes a magnet for all things electronic. Most clubs put on some kind of event, there's also VJing, films and multimedia installations.

3rd weekend in Sept: Journées du Patrimoine + Soirée du Patrimoine

All over France. **Information** www.jp.culture.fr.
Embassies, ministries and corporate headquarters open their doors to queues of snooping punters. In 2003, the Mairie introduced the Soirée du Patrimoine, a lavishly authentic recreation of a period knees-up, taking place on the first Journée du Patrimoine. *Le Monde* and *Le Parisien* publish info.

mid-Sept to Dec: Festival d'Automne

Various venues. **Information** 156 rue de Rivoli, 1st (01.53.45.17.00/www.festival-automne.com). **Admission** €9-€30.
Keeping Paris at the cutting edge, this festival features challenging contemporary theatre, dance and modern opera, and is committed to bringing non-Western culture into the French consciousness.

Sept: En ville sans ma voiture

The French leave their cars at home for a day in an attempt to save the environment.

end Sept: Portes Ouvertes à la Garde Républicaine

18 bd Henri IV, 4th (01.49.96.13.26). M° Sully-Morland. **Admission** free.
The public is allowed a rare glimpse of the uniforms, arms and gleaming mounts of the Presidential Guard.

end Sept-Oct: Open Studios

Génie de la Bastille 01.40.09.84.03); Ménilmontant, 11th, 20th (01.40.03.01.61); 13ème Art, 13th (01.45.86.17.67). **Admission** free.
Artists open their studios to the public around the Bastille, Ménilmontant and the 13th.

early Oct: Fête des Vendanges à Montmartre

rue des Saules, 18th. M° Lamarck-Caulaincourt. Mairie du 18ème, 1 pl Jules-Joffrin, 18th.

M° Jules-Joffrin. **Information** 01.46.06.00.32.
Music, speeches, locals in costume and a parade celebrate the Montmartre grape harvest.

beg Oct: Prix de l'Arc de Triomphe
Hippodrome de Longchamp, Bois de Boulogne, 16th (01.49.10.20.30/www.france-galop.com). M° Porte d'Auteuil, plus free shuttle bus. **Admission** free-€8.
France's richest flat race attracts the elite of horse racing amid much pomp and ceremony.

early Oct: Nuit Blanche
Various venues. **Information** 08.20.00.75.75/www.paris.fr. **Admission** free.
Delanoë's initiative keeps the city up all night with culture by moonlight. Galleries and museums host one-off installations, and swimming pools, bars and clubs stay open late.

end Oct: Salon du Chocolat
Venue to be confirmed (01.45.03.21.26/ www.chocoland.com). **Admission** €5-€10.
Choc and awe as the world's best chocolate-makers gather to show off their mastery.

end Oct: FIAC
Paris-Expo, Porte de Versailles. 15th. M° Porte de Versailles. **Information** OIP (01.41.90.47.80/ www.fiaconline.com). **Admission** €14.
Well-respected international contemporary art fair.

1 Nov: All Saints' Day
1 Nov is an important date for traditionalists – a day for visiting cemeteries and remembering the dead.

early Nov: Tennis Masters series
Palais Omnisports Paris/Bercy, 8 bd Bercy, 12th 01.46.91.57.57/www.ticketnet.fr). M° Bercy.
Top-ranking international men's tennis tournament.

early Nov: Festival Inrockuptibles
Various venues. **Information** www.lesinrocks.com. **Admission** varies.
Originally indie-centred, Inrocks has lately admitted trance, techno and trip hop. Still the place to discover the Next Big Thing.

11 Nov: Armistice Day
Arc de Triomphe, 8th. M° Charles de Gaulle-Etoile.
Remembering the dead of the World Wars, wreaths are laid by the President at the Tomb of the Unknown Soldier under the Arc de Triomphe. The *bleuet* (cornflower) is worn.

mid Nov: Paris Photo
Carrousel du Louvre, 99 rue de Rivoli, 1st. M° Palais Royal. **Information** 01.41.90.47.70. **Admission** €14.
Over 100 cutting-edge galleries from all over the globe show old and new photography.

18 Nov: Fête du Beaujolais Nouveau
The arrival of Beaujolais Nouveau on the third Thursday in November sees bars, cafés and wine bars throng (some from midnight on Wednesday) as customers 'assess' the new vintage.

Winter

end Nov-early Dec: Salon du Cheval
Paris-Expo, 1 pl de la Porte de Versailles, 15th (08.92.69.76.87/www.salon-cheval.com). M° Porte de Versailles. **Admission** €11 adults; €8 under-13s; free under-6s.
Displays of rare breeds and evening equine spectacles including a weekend of dressage competitions (Concours Hippique International).

Dec-Mar: Paris sur glace
pl de l'Hôtel de Ville, 4th. M° Hôtel de Ville; pl Raoul Dautry, 15th. M° Montparnasse-Bienvenüe; pl de la Bataille de Stalingrad, 19th. M° Stalingrad.
Information 08.20.00.75.75/www.paris.fr.
Admission free (skate hire €4.50).
Take to the ice on the fir-tree-lined outdoor rink in front of the city hall. Watch out for the pros.

end Dec: Africolor
Various venues, St-Denis (01.47.97.69.99/ www.africolor.com). M° St-Denis Basilique.
Admission €13.
Festival of African music both traditional and modern, with a spirited end-of-festival party.

24, 25 Dec: Christmas
Christmas is a family affair in France, with a dinner on Christmas Eve, normally after mass, that traditionally involves foie gras or oysters, goose or turkey and a rich Yule log (*bûche de Noël*). Notre-Dame cathedral is packed for the 11pm service.

31 Dec: New Year's Eve
On the Réveillon, or Fête de la St-Sylvestre, thousands crowd the Champs-Elysées and let off bangers. Nightclubs and restaurants put on expensive soirées. More foie gras and bubbly. On 1 Jan La Grande Parade de Paris sees colourful floats, giant balloons, bands and dancers parade the streets.

6 Jan: Fête des Rois (Epiphany)
Pâtisseries sell *galettes des rois*, cakes with frangipane filling in which a fêve or tiny charm is hidden. Whoever finds it becomes king or queen for a day, gets to wear the crown, choices a consort and is subject to speculation about his sex life.

Jan: Commemorative Mass for Louis XVI
Chapelle Expiatoire, 29 rue Pasquier, 8th (01.42.65.35.80). M° St-Augustin.
On the Sunday closest to 21 January, anniversary of the beheading of Louis XVI in 1793. France's aristocracy, die-hard royalists and other far-right crackpots gather to mourn the end of the monarchy.

Jan/Feb: Nouvel An Chinois
Around av d'Ivry and av de Choisy, 13th. M° Porte de Choisy or Porte d'Ivry.
Lion and dragon dances and martial arts demonstrations in celebration of the Chinese New Year. Some restaurants offer special menus.

Nuit Blanche

Cabaret, Circus & Comedy

If frou-frou, feathers and men in tutus don't sugar your boat, how about some avant-garde circus, satirical cabaret or, ahem, English stand-up?

There is more to Paris cabaret than the get-your-glitz-out-for-the-boys genre. The joyous throngs (and thongs) of glamour cabarets are in abundance, but a purer, less pretentious type of cabaret is still working its way around the circuit in good old-fashioned café-théâtres. Here for an all-in fee, many venues serve up satire, songs, plays or sketches with a meal and inhibition-loosening drinks.

The French may not be known for their wicked sense of humour, but ze' old funny bone is not as dried up as it may seem. Paris is littered with venues for a Gallic giggle, from plays to stand-up and satirical singing. For those less gifted in the language department, Laughing Matters provides a ripe choice of anglophone comedians fresh off the show boat.

All things circus are lapped up big-top style in Paris. The Parc de La Villette alone boasts several ground-breaking circus extravaganzas each year. Fans of the more traditional circus number fear not: it's all on offer in what is fast becoming the circus capital of the world.

Cabaret & café-théâtre

Glitzy cabaret

La Belle Epoque

36 rue des Petits-Champs, 2nd (01.42.96.33.33). M° Opéra or Quatre Septembre. **Dinner** 9pm daily, **Shows** 10.30pm daily, dancing from midnight. **Tickets** €52 Champagne and show; €70-€100 dinner and show. **Credit** AmEx, DC, MC, V **Map** p401 H4.

This ex-music hall may have lost a tad of class in recent years but it remains one of the only ritzy cabarets where you can have a boogie at the end of the evening. After-dinner singers and an interesting lasso act join the semi-naked girlies.

Crazy Horse Saloon

12 av George V, 8th (01.47.23.32.32). M° Alma-Marceau or George V. **Shows** 8.30pm, 11pm Tue-Fri, Sun; 7.30pm, 9.45pm, 11.50am Sat. **Tickets** €69-€90 for two drinks & show; €20 extra for Champagne. **Credit** AmEx, DC, MC, V. **Map** p400 D4.

Since the 1950s this ode to the female form has entertained punters with curvaceous dancers whose names (Choo-choo Night Train and Looky Boop) are as fitting as their costumes are non-existent. Don't worry about taking the family though – the girls are 'clothed' in 70s swirly light patterns instead.

Le Lido

116bis av des Champs-Elysées, 8th (01.40.76.56.10/ www.lido.fr). M° George V. **Dinner** 7.30pm. **Shows** 9.30pm Mon-Thur, Sun; 9.30pm & midnight Sat. **Tickets** €70-€90 Champagne & show; €130-€160 dinner & show; €25 under-12s. **Credit** AmEx, DC, MC, V. **Map** p400 D4.

Booby shaking is *à la carte* in this classy show where impressive special effects and 60 Bluebell Girls decorate the stage with explosive panache. Big-name chef Paul Bocuse revolutionised the menu a few years back ensuring top nosh for those who eat. *Wheelchair access.*

Moulin Rouge

82 bd de Clichy, 18th (01.53.09.82.82/ www.moulin-rouge.com). M° Blanche. **Dinner** 7pm. **Shows** 9pm, 11pm daily. **Tickets** €82-€92 Champagne & show; €130-€160 dinner & show. **Credit** AmEx, DC, MC, V. **Map** p401 G2.

Kitsch has lost its cool in this birthplace of the can-can, but as a renowned Pigalle venue it is still the most traditional of the glamour cabarets. With three shows a night you may feel rushed, but the 60 Dorriss girls do provide all the necessary trimmings of feathers, breasts and lashings of sequins.

Café-théâtre

Au Bec Fin

6 rue Thérèse, 1st (01.42.96.29.35). M° Pyramides. **Shows** 7pm, 8.30pm, 10pm daily, matinées for children 2.30pm, 4pm during school holidays. Closed Aug. **Tickets** €14; €12 students; €9 children; €36 dinner & show. **Credit** MC, V. **Map** p401 H5.

The oldest café-théâtre venue in Paris claims a 300-year-old pedigree. Dine on French cuisine, then head upstairs to see everything from Oscar Wilde to a cheesy version of Robin Hood for the little 'uns.

Le Tartuffe

46 rue Notre-Dame-de-Lorette, 9th (01.45.26.21.37). M° St-Georges or Pigalle. **Shows** 7.30pm Mon-Sat. **Tickets** dinner and all three shows €26-€29; €16 with a drink after 9pm. **Credit** MC, V. **Map** p402 H3.

Le Tartuffe is a cheesy place where true comic cabaret combines with a great atmosphere. Three acts a night culminate in audience participation and unavoidable embarrassment.

Chez Michou

80 rue des Martyrs, 18th (01.46.06.16.04). M° Pigalle. **Dinner** daily 8.30pm. **Show** 11pm approx (ring to check). **Admission** €95 dinner

& show; €35 show and one drink. **Credit** MC, V. **Map** p402 H2.
Larger-than-life incarnations of Tina Turner and French *chanson* diva Dalida will have you launching into unruly fits of belly laughter at Michou's. There's even a drag-queen Brigitte Bardot. Book ahead if you want to dine.

Au Lapin Agile

22 rue des Saules, 18th (01.46.06.85.87). M° Lamarck Caulaincourt. **Shows** 9pm-2am Tue-Sun. Show and one drink €24. **Credit** MC, V. **Map** p402 H1.
This quaint pink building remains a platform for young *chanson* writers to test their wares. Tourists outnumber the locals, but it still harbours an echo of old 'authentic' Montmartre.

Comedy & fringe theatre

Caveau de la République

1 bd St-Martin, 3rd (01.42.78.44.45/www.caveau.fr). M° République. **Show** 8.30pm Tue-Thur; 4.30pm Sat; 3.30pm Sun. **Admission** €25 Tue-Thur; €32 Fri-Sun; €16 students. Closed in Aug. **Credit** V. **Map** p402 L4.
Hours of French fun can be had here, one of the last remaining 'chansonniers' on the block. Artists, young and old, sing Brel, Brassens and their own compositions and dole out monologues of a political-satirical nature. Laughs are squeezed out from any current scandal so this is not for those who are new to French language and culture.

Life is a cabaret, *mon pote*

While 1930s Britain was revelling in the delights of early Hollywood exports (barber shop quartets and dancing girl movies), pre-war France was already whooping it up with its own answer to American culture – 'le music hall'. One presenter and 12 acts would strut their stuff twice daily and make sure everyone knew the French could dazzle and laugh just as well as their straight-toothed counterparts. From this were born stars such as Charles Trenet and Edith Piaf. After World War II, music hall gave way to a new model of cabaret. Cradled in Germany, it was leagues away from the glitzy boob-wobbling associated with the word today. Often politically rebellious, it rolled out barrels of humorists such as Pierre Dac, and boosted the careers of musicians including Brassens and Brel.

Recently the old style of cabaret has undergone a revival, proving that if you can't teach an old dog new tricks, you can give the old dogma new acts. One of the most successful shows is husband-and-wife duo Achille Tonic, whose stage personas are the chuckle-worthy cousins **Shirley and Dino** (*pictured*). Situated somewhere between music hall and cabaret, they invite artists to put on original sketches, songs and circus acts, interspersed with comical capers of their own. This mish-mashed extravaganza has earned them a Molière comedy award, prime time TV and chart topping DVDs, as well as a sell-out show at the Théâtre de Paris.

Another Molière award winner on the new-wave cabaret circuit is **Le Quatuor**. Four musicians, heavily endowed in the string department, hit the spot with parodies from jazz, classical music, film soundtracks and musicals. Their barking bonanza, *Le Quatuor, Sur la Corde Rêve*, is out on DVD.

Look out for smaller, more intimate gigs for real cabaret flavour. **Forceps Italia** performs regular one-offs at the **Hôtel du Nord** where four comical bright sparks (alias an old bully, a perverted pianist, a seductive tenor and an English nymphomaniac) whisk you off to a place of farcical refinement, with music from Nino Rota, Verdi and Dalida. Call to check dates and venues (Compagnie des Bavardages 01.44.64.11.45).

Le Quatuor twangs the G-string. *See p283.*

Café de la Gare

41 rue du Temple, 4th (01.42.78.52.51/ www.cafe-de-la-gare.fr.st). M° Hôtel de Ville or Rambuteau. **Shows** 7.30pm, 9pm Mon, Tue, Sun; 8pm, 10pm Wed-Sat. **Tickets** €10-€20. **Credit** MC, V. **Map** p406 K6.

Up and running since the revolutionary days of 1968, this atmospheric venue has 300 stage-hugging seats and hosts quality French stand-up and raucous, irreverent comedies in the 'Carry On' line.

Le Point Virgule

7 rue Ste-Croix-de-la-Bretonnerie, 4th (01.42.78.67.03). M° Hôtel de Ville. **Shows** 7.30pm, 9pm, 10pm daily. **Tickets** €15, €12 students. **No credit cards. Map** p406 K6.

This small Marais theatre is a breath of fresh air for French comedy. The crowds are animated, the acts well polished, and they are not afraid of offering precious stage space to up-and-coming performers.

Le Zèbre

63 bd de Belleville, 20th (01.43.55.55.55). M° Père Lachaise. **Open** varies. **Tickets** vary. **Map** p403 N4.

Impressario Francis Schoeller rescued the art deco Zèbre cinema in 2002. After forays in various directions it has chosen to remain true to the Parisian tune of satirical cabaret and chirruping *chanson*.

Comedy in English

Laughing Matters

Info (01.53.19.98.88/www.anythingmatters.com). *Shows normally take place at the Hôtel du Nord, 102 quai de Jemmapes, 10th. M° République or Jacques Bonsergent.* **Tickets** €20; €17 students. **No credit cards. Map** p402 L4.

Seemingly the only guy Anglophone mirthsters will cross the sea for, promoter Karel Beer hauls in performances from many a big comedy shark. In 2004 look out for Ardal O'Hanlon, Greg Proops, Ross Noble and Daniel Kitson.

Circus

Traditional circuses generally only come to Paris during the winter months, while avant-garde circuses are more prevalent in the summer. For full listings consult 'Cirque' in the children's section of *Pariscope* which has up to date info on where to spot the Big Tops.

Cirque d'Hiver Bouglione

110 rue Amelot, 11th (01.47.00.12.25/ www.cirquedhiver.com). M° Filles du Calvaire. **Shows** vary. **Tickets** €10-€35. **Credit** V. **Map** p402 L5.

The beautiful winter circus was built by Hittorff in 1852. The Bouglione family dynasty, who owns it, puts on an extravaganza twice a year with animals, cabaret and international performers. The rest of the time it is used by visiting troupes.

Cirque Pinder

37 rue de Coulagnes, 94370 Sucy-en-Brie (01.45.90.21.25/www.cirquepinder.com). RER Sucy Bonneuil. Pelouse de Reuilly, Bois de Vincennes, 12th. M° Porte Doré or Porte de Charenton. **Open** all year; Pelouse de Reuilly generally mid-Nov to early Jan. **Tickets** €12-€36; free under-twos. **Credit** AmEx, DC, MC, V.

One of the oldest circus giants around, Pinder usually heaves up its glittering tent pegs from its permanent address 40km out of Paris and heads into town for Christmas at the Pelouse de Reuilly.

Contemporary circus venues

Cabaret Sauvage

Parc de La Villette, 19th (01.42.09.01.09/ www.cabaretsauvage.com). M° Porte de La Villette. **Shows** vary. **Tickets** €12-€20. **Credit** MC, V. **Map** p403 inset.

Housed in an old circus venue, a mixture of tent, Western saloon and hall of mirrors provides a stage for jugglers, acrobats and other performers, plus concerts, bals and club nights.

Espace Chapiteaux

Parc de La Villette, 19th (01.42.09.01.09/ www.villette.com). M° Porte de Pantin or Porte de La Villette. **Shows** Wed-Sat 8.30pm; Sun 4pm. **Tickets** €17; €14 students, under 25s; €8 under 12s. **Credit** MC, V. **Map** p403 inset.

Parc de La Villette's impressive tent pitch boasts a jam-packed calendar. Cirque Plume are regulars and 2004 promises a vibrant array of new acts.

Children

A baby – even if it's got a face like a gargoyle that just dropped off Notre-Dame – will delight any Parisian. In their element then, kids will find loads to do here.

Paris has a thriving population of under-16s, and Parisians enjoy parading *en famille* (witness the orderly tartan crocodiles promenading on Sundays at Versailles, or rainbow-clad toddlers atop the shoulders of Bastille protestors). But this isn't Italy or Spain. State inducements make serial parenthood an attractive career option, but kids have a hard life before stumbling, exhausted, into the 35-hour week. French babies are frequently *crêched* out before they reach nursery school, aged three, when they enjoy an eight-hour day starting around 8.30am, followed by judo, pony, chess, tennis, piano and homework. No hand-wringing over Literacy Hour *ici*. Worse, the French kids themselves are (like their parents) generally quieter and better-behaved, less media-crazed and, yes, thinner, than their stroppy, chocolate-smeared Anglo-Saxon counterparts. Hmmm….

There is plenty for kids to do, and every chance to offload them on to someone else, provided you sign the forms. Central Paris is wonderfully well-supplied with carousels and play areas (*see p287*), and puppet shows, theatre productions, museum workshops and the like are part of every Paris childhood. Popular family events include the 13th *arrondissement*'s spectacular Chinese New Year celebrations in February, and the *Fête de la Musique* (21 June), Jack Lang's midsummer *carte blanche* to street musicians (avoid the crush around the big stages and sample events at quartier level). Bastille Day (14 July) features a truly cracking firework display, and Hallowe'en is huge nowadays (shiver your timbers with Cap'n Hook and the other bad guys at Disneyland Paris). At Christmastime, outdoor ice-rinks feature at the Hôtel de Ville and Montparnasse.

Some tips for travellers with tikes: watch out for Wednesdays, when school's out for under-16. Remember that the Gallic combination of no-nonsense parenting and underdeveloped political correctness can rattle tender Anglo-Saxon sensibilities. Zoos are Real Zoos (you won't be singing *Born Free*), circuses mostly feature exotic wildlife electro-prodded onto its hind legs. They love it.

Paris is a high-density city, but hi-energy youngsters can still go for the burn. For the over-10s, **The Roller Squad Institut** (01.56.61.99.61/www.rsi.asso.fr) organises beginners' roller tours from the Esplanade des Invalides (Métro Invalides) on Sundays at 2.45pm. There are great outdoor pools (*see chapter* **Sport & Fitness**), and the favourite, Paris Plage (*see chapter* **Right Bank**) featured sandcastle workshops and a children's splash basin in 2003, downstream from the Pont au Change (M° Châtelet). If the weather's iffy, hit indoor Aquaboulevard (4 rue Louis Armand, 15th/01.40.60.10.00), or ice-rink at the Palais Omnisports (www.bercy.fr, click on Patinoire).

For listings and events, get Pariscope (www.pariscope.fr). Free advice and leaflets are dispensed at the mairie (town hall) of any arrondissement, and the **Espace du Tourisme** in the **Carrousel du Louvre**. The website www.iledenfance.com is good for ideas, as is the bi-monthly *Paris-Mômes* supplement, with the newspaper *Libération* (call 01.49.29.01.21 for more details).

A miniature masterpiece

See France in a day! No wonder **France Miniature** attracts an enthusiastic crowd. Europe's biggest miniature park (er...) is a five-hectare scale model of France, complete with mountains, rivers and 139 splendid, architecturally-accurate models of the country's best buildings, dotted with thousands of tiny little model visitor-ettes, and all intertwined with the world's longest outdoor miniature railway, plus – get this – fully-operational TGV. This being France, wonders of industry and engineering like the A6 motorway (with a lovingly recreated miniature car crash) and the Michelin tyre factory at Clermont-Ferrand rank proudly alongside medieval Carcassonne. Your kids will love it, but resist the urge to give them an architectural history lesson ('You see, the Stade de France is actually a suspended structure...'). Grown-ups find it hard to resist, too – the cathedrals are stunning ('Look at the flying buttresses on that....'), as are the best bits of Paris, including the Arc de Triomphe and place de la Concorde. There's a clear, signposted circuit, but monument fatigue inevitably leaves you stumbling around after a time, unsure whether you're looking at the Corderie Royale de Rochefort, or the Abbatiale Saint Philibert-de-Grand-Lieu. A visit to the waiter-service restaurant will now be in order; it's all freshly-cooked, soigné and delicious, in keeping with the general mission to uphold things Traditional, Regional and French. There are some masterpieces of miniature: a Japanese temple, a Lyon brasserie, Maxim's art nouveau dining-room. Others provide a peepshow into places abandoned or forgotten: an empty corridor in a modern apartment block, a derelict theatre, the bottom of a grubby, white-tiled municipal swimming baths. Ohlmann's tiny slices of life transferred here after years in Lyon. This is Zen and the art of model-making.

Getting there

25 route du Mesnil, bd André Malraux, 78990 Elancourt, Saint-Quentin-en-Yvelines (01.30.16.16.30/www.franceminiature.com). **Open** *Apr to mid-Nov* 10am-7pm daily; *July, Aug* 10am-11.30pm Sat. **By train** SNCF La Verrière from Gare Montparnasse, then bus 411. **By car** France Miniature is a 10-minute drive from Versailles. A13, then A12 direction St-Quentin-en-Yvelines/Dreux, then Elancourt Centre. **Admission** €13 adults and over 15s; €9 4-14s; free under-4s. Train/admission tickets available from all Paris stations: €18.50 adults, over-15s, €15.70 10-14s; €10.80 4-9s; free under-4s. **Credit** AmEx, MC, V.

Getting around

Public transport

After the London Tube, the Métro is comparative heaven, but pushchairs won't attract eager helpers, and as for those gnashing automatic double doors at the Sortie… If you absolutely must, travel between 10am and 5pm, and try the new, central, driverless Line 14 (Madeleine to Bibliothèque F. Mitterand). Parisian kids love to sit up front, hurtling headling down the tunnels. The mostly overground Line 6 (Nation-Charles de Gaulle-Etoile) and Line 2 (Nation-Porte Dauphine) offer attractive views, and Paris's excellent bus service remains a pleasant. Under-fours travel free on public transport, while four-to-ten-year-olds qualify for a half-price carnet (ten tickets) valid on the Métro, RER and buses, including the Montmartrobus minibus, the funicular and the Balabus, which takes in everything from the Grande Arche de La Défense to the Gare de Lyon, on Sundays and bank holidays.

Taxis

Like their vehicles, Parisian cabbies are less accommodating than their London counterparts. Three passengers is usually the limit, but they may take a family of four, provided someone is under ten (they count as half). There may be a small cover charge (around €1) for a foldable pushchair.

Did you know?

The Batobus (01.44.11.33.99/www.batobus.com) is a regular boat route linking eight prime sights along the Seine, including Notre-Dame (from the quay on the Left Bank), the Louvre and the Eiffel Tower. (Apr-Nov, boats every 20 minutes. Two-day unrestricted ticket €12.50, under 12s €6.50).

Help & babysitting

The American Church

65 quai d'Orsay, 7th (01.40.62.05.00/ www.americanchurchparis.org). M° Invalides.
Open 9am-noon, 1-10.30pm Mon-Sat; 9am-2pm, 3-7.30pm Sun. Sunday worship at 9am and 11am.**Map** p401 E5.

The free noticeboard in the basement is a major source of information on recommended English-speaking baby-sitters and au pairs.

Baby Sitting Services

01.46.21.33.16/www.babysittingservices.com.
Open 24-hrs daily. Babysitting for up to 2 children: €6.30/hr 8am-10pm + €10.90 tax Mon-Sat; €7/hr + €15.90 tax Mon-Sat 10pm-8am, Sun and bank holidays. €1/hr supplement for each extra child. **Credit** MC, V.

This is a most useful, customer-friendly service as baby-sitting can be arranged at short notice, plus accompanied visits to museums and cinemas, so the guilt factor's not too awaful while you're out raving. Also tuition, activities and children's parties.

Inter-Service Parents

(01.44.93.44.93). **Open** 9.30am-12.30pm, 1.30-5pm Mon, Tue, Fri; 9.30am-12.30pm Wed; 1.30-5pm Thur.
Free state-funded advice service lists babysitting agencies as well as giving advice on schools, child psychologists and family lawyers.

Message

info@messageparis.org/www.messageparis.org.
A non-profit English-speaking support network for international mothers and mothers-to-be in Paris, Message dispenses advice, classes, leisure activities and a useful book, ABCs of *Motherhood in Paris* (€18 to non-members, €12 members).

Swings & roundabouts

Many public gardens offer mini playgrounds, concrete ping-pong tables, poodle-poop-free sandpits etc – there's a handy one alongside Notre Dame, facing the Left Bank, and even the posh place des Vosges has slides and rocking horses. On Wednesdays and weekends, puppet shows feature Guignol, with a groovy pony tail (*Derrière vous!*). Paris park-keepers still think grass dies if touched, so don't in places like the Luxembourg, Tuileries, Monceau and Palais-Royal. The Bois de Vincennes and Bois de Boulogne offer freedom, natural woodland, picnic areas, boating lakes and cycle paths.

Jardin d'Acclimatation

Bois de Boulogne, 16th, (01.40.67.90.82/ www.jardindacclimatation.fr). M° Les Sablons. **Open** *June-Sept* 10am-7pm daily; *Oct-May* 10am-6pm daily. **Map** p398. **Admission** €2.50.

A much-loved feature of every Paris childhood, the *'Clim'* opened as a family venue in 1900, after an abortive first life as a zoo (the inmates were eaten during the Siege of 1870…). Its gentle attractions include boat-rides, a Chinese dragon rollercoaster, the Enchanted House for two-to-fours (where you can leave them to romp, supervised, around the ball-pool and game consoles), the Petits Chevaux (fairground horses that carry you off into the greenery), and the more futuristic Explor@dome, packed with interactive multimedia gadgetry. If your children don't get upset by this sort of thing. There are three bears, and a Normandy farm and an aviary.

Parc des Buttes-Chaumont

19th (01.42.02.91.21). M° Buttes Chaumont or Botzaris. **Open** *Oct-June* 7am-9pm; *15 June-15 Jul* 7am-10pm daily. *15 July-1 Oct* 7am-11pm daily.
Map p403 N2

Could there possibly be a better place these days for exploring, especially now that the Makolo tribe has largely been done? The view from here is arguably even better than from Sacré Coeur – fewer tourists get in the way as you scuttle in with your disposable camera. Temples, suspension bridges, grottoes and waterfalls complement the usual puppet shows, donkey rides and playgrounds.

Jardins du Luxembourg

pl Edmond-Rostand, pl Auguste-Comte, rue de Vaugirard, 6th (01.42.34.20.00/www.mairie-paris.fr). RER Luxembourg/M° Odéon or St-Sulpice. **Open** *winter* 8am-one hour before sunset; *summer* 7.30am-one hour before sunset. **Map** p405 H8.

Besides the folding chairs and mainly inaccessible grass, there's a small, well-equipped adventure playground, swing boats, an adorable old-fashioned merry-go-round, a toy boating-pond, pony rides and marionette shows.

Parc de la Villette

211 av Jean-Jaurès, 19th (01.40.03.75.03/www.villette.com). M° Porte de Pantin or Porte de la Villette. **Open** 6am-1am daily. **Map** p403 inset.

Part of the re-developed Villette canal basin, this series of themed parks includes Le Jardin des Miroirs – a walk through a strange reflected landscape – and the even weirder Jardin des Frayeurs Enfantines ('Garden of Childish Terrors'), which uses spooky music to recreate a fairy-tale forest.

Museum mayhem

Egyptian mummies at the **Louvre**, Surrealist fun with Salvador at the **Espace Dalí**, unicorns at the **Musée National du Moyen Age**, magnificent flying machines at the **Musée de l'Air et de l'Espace** (at Le Bourget airport), the Planetarium at the **Palais de la Découverte**... There's plenty to capture children's imagination, and under-18s can usually get in free, or almost (*see chapter* **Museums**). Many places provide free activity sheets (ask at the *Accueil*) and children's activities (though mostly in French) on Wednesdays and weekends. The Louvre's impressive programme is led by artists, architects, film-makers, etc. (01.40.20.51.77), **Musée Rodin** organises kids' clay modelling workshops in August (01.44.18.61.24), and **Musée Picasso** offers family visits on Sundays, with children-only workshops on Wednesday afternoons during the school year, exploring animal sculptures and pictures by the Old Goat himself (01.42.71.25.21).

Have the words 'all French state museums-except Orsay are closed on Tuesdays' carved into your cortex.

Centre Pompidou – Galerie des Enfants

4th (01.44.78.49.13/www.centrepompidou.fr). M° Hôtel de Ville/RER Châtelet-Les Halles. **Open** 11am-7pm Mon, Wed-Sun; workshops most Wed and Sat afternoons. Museum entry includes the Galerie des Enfants: €5.50; €3.50 under 25s/students; under-18s free. **Workshop & exhibition** €8. **Map** p402 K5.

Beautifully thought-out exhibitions by top artists and designers introduce children to modern art, design and architecture, with hands-on workshops for six-to-12s, and family visits one Sunday a month (11.15am-12.30pm). Close by, kids love the colourful, animated Stravinsky fountain by Tinguely and Nikki de St Phalle; less well-known is the animated clock in the *Quartier de l'Horloge* on the piazza's north side. Every hour, the plucky bronze Defender of Time fights off a crab, a dragon or a cockerel (and all three at midday and 5pm), but remains happily unscathed since his installation in 1979.

Grévin

10 bd Montmartre, 9th (01.47.70.85.05/www.musee-grevin.com). M° Grands Boulevards. **Open** 10am-6.30pm Mon-Fri (last admission 6pm), 10am-7pm Sat-Sun, school and public holidays (last admission 6pm) **Admission** €16; €13.80 students; €9 children 6-14. **Map** p402 H4.

Star-struck kids will enjoy Zinédine Zidane or Lara Croft but this spectacular waxworks museum is educational too, with heads of state, artists, writers, and prominent French historical figures. Recent arrivals include French teen pop sensation Lorie, who gets to rank alongside Madonna and Our Elton...

Musée de la Curiosité

11 rue St-Paul, 4th (01.42.72.13.26). M° St-Paul or Sully-Morland. **Open** 2-7pm Wed, Sat, Sun and school summer hols (1 July,-31 Aug); daily during other school holidays (October, Christmas, February, Easter). **Admission** €7; €5 3-12s; free under-3s. **Map** p406 L7.

Kids will even love queueing for this wonderful museum of magic and illusions – a magician is on hand to pull scarves out of ears. There's conjuring, and a strictly hands-on approach to optical illusions.

Muséum National d'Histoire Naturelle

36 rue Geoffrey-St-Hilaire/2 rue Bouffon, pl Valhubert/57 rue Cuvier, 5th (01.40.79.30.00/www.mnhn.fr). M° Gare d'Austerlitz or Jussieu. **Open** 10am-6pm (last admission 5.15pm) Mon, Wed-Sun. **Admission** €5-€7 (*see chapter* **Museums** *for full details*). **Credit** MC, V. **Map** p406 K9.

Not one museum but several, gathered within the Jardin des Plantes. The awe-inspiring Grande Galerie de l'Evolution, with its famous Noah's Ark-like stream of animals, is an imaginative re-installation of the museum's impressive collection of stuffed creatures and skeletons (they even have a rhinoceros that belonged to Louis XV), and children will enjoy the microscopes and interactive games in the small Espace Découverte. The Gallery of Comparative Anatomy and Paleontology will capture the imagination of older children, with its jars of eerie pickled samples. The giant crystals and hunks of meteorite in the Gallery of Mineralogy, Geology and Paleobotany are also popular.

Musée de la Poupée

Impasse Berthaud, 3rd (01.42.72.73.11). M° Rambuteau. **Open** 10am-6pm Tue-Sun (closed public hols). **Admission** €6; €4 students; €3 3-18s. **No credit cards. Map** p402 K5.

Parc Astérix. See p290.

This museum hosts a collection of 300-plus dolls, some over 150 years old, featuring a wealth of minutely-detailed clothes, furniture and accessories.

Cité des Enfants

Level One, Cité des Sciences et de l'Industrie, 30 av Corentin-Cariou, 19th (01.40.05.80.00/www.cite-sciences.fr). M° Porte de La Villette. **Open** for 90-minute visits, 9.45am, 11.30am, 1.30pm, 3.30pm Tue, Thur-Fri; 10.30am, 12.30pm, 2.30, 4.30pm, Wed and Sat-Sun. Times vary in school holidays. **Admission** €5 per session. **Credit** MC, V. **Map** p403 inset.

Two vast hands-on discovery zones cater for under-fives, and 5s-to-12s. A must for every school outing within a 100-km radius since it opened in the mid-1980s, the Cité can look a little tired, though the tots' area has aged far better than the 'senior' section. Highlights for the under-fives include the endlessly-fascinating water cascades (switch the 'points' and watch the wheels spin round), and a massive building-site with foam blocks, working cranes, wheelbarrows and pulleys. 5-to-12s can try interacting in a 'working' TV studio, or train a robot builder. You'll want to try the walk-in ant-hill, too.

Did you know?

Nicolas Flamel, Albus Dumbledore's old mate in the first Harry Potter book, was a real-life Parisian alchemist who actually claimed to have discovered the Philospher's Stone, and the secret of eternal life. Kids visiting the **Musée du Moyen Age** (*see chapter* **Museums**) can hunt for his tombstone, featuring secret alchemical symbols (it's on the left wall of a flight of stairs towards the end, but don't tell them…). There's also a rue Nicolas Flamel (north off rue de Rivoli opposite the Tour St Jacques, which he helped to pay for), and in the heart of the Marais, Flamel's house (the oldest in Paris, to boot) is now a restaurant: Auberge Nicolas Flamel, 51 rue de Montmorency (01.42.71.77.78). Magic!

Animal magic

Aquarium at the Palais de la Porte Dorée

293 av Daumesnil, 12th (01.44.74.84.80). M° Porte Dorée. **Open** Mon, Weds-Sun 8.30am-5pm. **Admission** €4 adults, €2.60 4-25s, under-4s free. **Credit** (shop) MC, V.

Formerly home to the Musée des Arts d'Afrique et d'Océanie, this splendid art deco palace still holds the Paris aquarium's fine displays of colonial crocs (brought from Dakar in 1948).

Ferme du Piqueur

Domaine National de St-Cloud, 92210 St-Cloud (01.46.02.24.53). M° Boulogne-Pont de St-Cloud/RER Garches-Marne la Coquette. **Open** 10am-12.30pm, 1.30-5.30pm Sat, Sun, school holidays and daily in Aug. Children's workshops for 4-12s, 10am, 2pm, 4pm on Wed (advance bookings only). **Admission** €2. **No credit cards**.

Small kids will enjoy the farm's cows, chickens, pigs and rabbits, within the Parc de St-Cloud. Let's hope the rabbits restrain themselves.

La Ménagerie

57 rue Cuvier, 5th (01.44.05.72.72). M° Gare d'Austerlitz or Jussieu. **Open** *winter* 9am-5.30pm daily; *summer* 9am-6.30pm. **Admission** €6; €3.05 4-18s, students, over-60s; free under-4s. **No credit cards. Map** p406 K8.

Paris zoo is over 200 years old, and it ain't no safari park, but the scale is just right for younger kids. An added attraction is the Microzoo, a unique look at the weird and wonderful mini-universe visible only through a microscope.

Musée Vivant du Cheval

60631 Chantilly (03.44.57.13.13/www.musee-vivant-du-cheval.fr). SNCF Chantilly from Gare du Nord. By car 40km from Paris by A1, exit 7. **Open** *Apr-Oct* 10.30am-5.30pm Mon, Wed-Sun (plus 2-5pm Tue *July-Aug*, and from 10.30am Tue, *May-June*); Nov-Mar 2-5pm Mon, Wed, Fri; 10.30am-5.30pm Sat, Sun. **Admission** €8; €7.50 students; €6.50 13-17s; €5.50 4-12s; free under-4s. **Credit** MC, V.

As its name implies, over 40 breeds live at the historic stables of the Château de Chantilly – a real treat for horse-and-pony-mad youngsters. Daily demonstrations at 11.30am, 3.30pm and (in summer) 5.15pm, explain dressage (you'll soon know your piaffe from your passage), and children can stroke the animals. Note that Chantilly's bi-annual international fireworks competition, the Nuits de Feux, will take place here on 18-19 June 2004.

Parc de Thoiry

78770 Thoiry-en-Yvelines (01.34.87.52.25/ www.thoiry.tm.fr). By car A13, A12 then N12 direction Dreux until Pont Chartrain, then follow signs. 45km west of Paris. **Open** *winter* 11am-5pm daily; *summer* 10am-6pm daily. **Admission** park €17.80; €16 over-60s; €13 3-12s, students under 26; château €4.30; €3.50 3-12s. **Credit** MC, V.

One of Europe's first and best safari parks, Thoiry allows zebras to smear their noses all over your windscreen, while lions laze and bears amble down a forest track (no T-Rexs yet, but stay in your vehicle even so…).

Theme parks outside Paris

Disneyland® Paris/Walt Disney Studios Park

Marne-la-Vallée (01.60.30.60.30); from UK 0990 030 303. RER A or TGV Marne-la-Vallée-Chessy. By car 32km by A4 Metz-Nancy exit 14.
Open *Apr-June* 9am-8pm daily; *July, Aug* 9am-11pm daily; *Sept-Mar* 10am-6pm Mon-Fri; 9am-8pm Sat, Sun. **Admission** 1-day passport €39; €29 3-11s; 3-day passport €107 adults; €80 3-11s. Free under-3s **Credit** AmEx, DC, MC, V.

Perhaps it was always meant to be: perhaps the world just wasn't ready until the 1990s. The original plans for the park at Versailles famously form an instantly-recognisable, schematised, big-eared mouse… Today, Disneyland® Paris and its companion studio complex form a magic kingdom for kids of all ages (although over-60s might think twice before stepping aboard Space Mountain). Rides range from gentle to gut-wrenching (Fantasyland and Adventureland are the best all-rounders), and the 3D interactive movie, *Honey I Shrunk the Audience*, is unmissable. A second park, Walt Disney Studios, takes young film buffs behind the scenes, with an interactive Animation Courtyard, special effects and stunts on the Back Lot, and Flying Carpets Over Agrahbah, in which a real-life Aladdin Genie (we don't think it's really Robin Williams…) directs a film starring the kids themselves. Paris can't compete with the Florida weather (unless you count the summer of 2003), but the park comes into its own at Hallowe'en and Christmas: great times to visit, with loads of extra themed attractions.

Une Journée au Cirque

Cirque de Paris, 115 bd Charles de Gaulle, 92390 Villeneuve la Garenne (01.47.99.40.40). M° Porte de Clignancourt + Bus 137 (Zone Industriel Nord) or RER St Denis + bus 261. **Open** *Oct-June* 10am-5pm Wed, Sun. Shows 3pm circus performance. **Tickets** (full day) €36.50-€41 adults, over-11s; €29-€34.50 3-11s; (show only) €11-€24 adults, over-11s; €7-€14.50 3-11s. **Credit** MC, V.

From 10am, children can try tightrope-walking, juggling, clowning and dressage (not lion taming, strangely), followed by lunch with the stars, a tour of the menagerie and the fairground museum, and finally, at 3pm, the show itself!

La Mer de Sable

La Mer de Sable, 60950 Ermenonville (03.44.54.18.44/48/www.mer-de-sable.com). By car A1, exit 7, direction Ermenonville. RER B CDG1 Roissy, then special shuttle (10.30am, return 6.10pm Apr, May, Jun, Sep; 10am and 11.20am, return 5.25pm and 6.45pm Jul, Aug). **Open** *Apr-Sep* 10.30am-6.30pm *Mon-Fri*, 10.30am-7pm Sat-Sun, but call or check the website (Calendrier tarifs) for the numerous exceptions. **Admission** €15.50; €13.50 3-11s. **Credit** AmEx, MC, V.

Kids and adults alike enjoy this popular Wild West theme park in a natural geological curiosity (the sea of sand) in the heart of the forest of Ermenonville. The live shoot-outs and equestrian acrobatics are fabulous, and there's a great range of rides.

Parc Astérix

60128 Plailly (03.44.62.34.34/www.parcasterix.fr). RER B Roissy-Charles de Gaulle 1, then shuttle (9.30am-1.30pm, 4.30pm-closing time). By car A1 exit Parc Astérix. **Open** *Apr to mid-Oct* 10am-6pm daily; July, Aug 9.30am-7pm daily. Closed mid Oct-Mar; call or check the website calendar to check extra closures. **Admission** €30; €22 3-11s; free under-3s. **Credit** AmEx, MC, V.

The feisty little Roman-basher has his own theme park - predictably pédagogique, with historical zones covering Ancient Greece, the Roman Empire, the Middle Ages and 19th-century Paris. Children can meet Asterix, Getafix (known as Panoramix in French, though heaven knows why) and Obelix (we

Swingin' from the trees

2004 (or thereabouts) will go down in the history of the French leisure industry as the year people took a fresh look at forests. *Accrobranches* is a new-ish craze (think office outings and swanky kids parties) combining tree-hugging with mountaineering, to get you grappling up the south face of a sycamore, or abseiling between the branches faster than you can say 'Cedar of Lebanon'. The tree-hugging part introduces climbers to the varieties they are about to assail, after which everyone dons hard hats and crotch-compressing harnesses (you get the picture regarding office outings) to either shin straight up, working in pairs, or follow one of the graded parcours (pre-installed circuits). Children from as young as five can take part, and it's a great way to coax them out for some fresh air. Accrobranches action has, seemingly, not yet hit the Bois de Boulougne or the Bois de Vincennes, but several sites are easily reached from Paris.

Forest Jump *Le Moulin du Perthuis, 45700 Conflans-sur-Loing (02.38.94.66.26/ www.forestjump.fr).* **Open** 10am-8pm daily, three-hour session €17 (adults and over-11s), €12 8-11s, €8 5-8s. **By car** (about 90mins): A6 direction Lyon, exit Nevers-Montargis, then A77 exit Montargis. Follow the ringroad direction Châtillon-Coligny (D93), to Conflans-sur-Loing. An excellent centre south of Paris with seven trails including a Kids route for 5s and up. Booking strongly recommended.

Parcours Lémurien de Graville *Chemin de Graville, 77670 Vernou (01.60.39.07.04/ www.tipiks.com).* **Open** *14 Feb-13 Jun & 13 Sept-14 Nov* 9.30am-6pm Wed, Sat-Sun, public holidays and school holidays; *14 Jun-12 Sept* 9.30am-8pm Mon, Tue-Sun. **Admission** €18 adults and over-14s, €14 9-13s, €10 5-8s. **By car** (about 1hr): A5 direction Troyes, exit 17 (Forges), then D210 direction Samoreau, and left on D39. A popular site with two new trails opening for 2004 (seven in all).

Léz'art Café *Fontainebleau (01.64.22.38.14/ www.lezart-cafe.fr).* **Open** pool *Jun-Aug* 10am-7pm daily. **By train** Trains run direct to Fontainebleau from Gare de Lyon (35 mins), about every 40 minutes. **By car** (50 mins): A6 direction Lyon, exit Fontainebleau, follow Centre Ville, then Gare SNCF. Three minutes walk from Fontainebleau SNCF station (atop the slope above the main road), this snazzily-revamped 1930s lido on the edge of Fontainebleau forest combines a café-bar with activities including a circus school and accrobranches (leave 'em to it while you enjoy a swim and a massage...). A two-hour session costs €17 (1pm-3pm, Sat-Sun), with Wednesday sessions from Apr-Sept. Booking advisable.

CAPS *41 rue Liancourt, 14th (01.45.87.13.63/ www.caps-adventure.org).* **By train** RER C to Chaville-Vélizy, or suburban lines from Montparnasse and St-Lazare. **By car** Porte de St-Cloud, the direction pont de Sèvres, N118 exit Chaville, or A 86 exit Vélizy. A collective of adventure professionals offers accrobranches sessions (advance group bookings only) in the Forêt de Meudon at Chaville, west of Paris. On summer nights, after a hard day's tree-climbing and abseiling, try relaxing in a treetop hammock 15m from the ground (still wearing your harness, of course)... Children are welcome from age 8; individual bookings by arrangement in the summer months.

don't think it's really Gérard Depardieu) in the topsy-turvy Gaulish village. Rides include Goudurix, a terrifying loop-the-loop, or the log flume frenzy *La Petite Tempête*; the *Déscente du Styx*, a water journey through the Greek Underworld, is inevitably much calmer... Minimum height restrictions apply for the more challenging rides.

Entertainment

Fairytales, La Fontaine's fables and, more recently, folk stories from Francophone Africa, have become force-fed favourites for the numerous childrens shows at theatres and *café-théâtres*, especially on Wednesdays and weekends (details in *Pariscope*). Productions for the very young, involving music, clowning puppets and dance can be enjoyed with little or no French, while older linguists may enjoy Ecla Théâtre's performances of Molière and other classics (01.40.27.82.05/www.ecla-theatre.com). Théâtre Dunois, at 7 rue Louise Weiss in the 13th (01.45.84.72.00) features adventurous theatre, dance and musical creations – perfect for little luvvies. France's venerable circuses often pass through Paris, especially at Christmas (*see chapter* Cabaret, Comedy & Circus), while the annual *Foire du Trône* funfair hits town from April-June (Métro line 8, Porte Dorée or Liberté). Proto-clubbers can try the monthly Sunday afternoon *'Bal grenadine'* at the Divan du Monde (*see chapter* Clubs). Children's movies are mostly dubbed into French, but you can catch *VO* (original version) screenings of the latest hits at the Champs-Elysées and Odéon, after 6pm. Alternatively, look out for children's showings and talks on Wednesdays at the Forum des Images (01.44.76.63.44.47/www.forumdesimages.net). French is not required for the Théâtre du Châtelet's Pochette Surprise cinema club, featuring silent classics., with live piano accompaniment (01.42.56.90.10 for details). Two Imax cinemas – the Dôme (La Défense/ 08.36.67.06.06) and the Géode (La Villette/ 01.40.05.79.99/www.lageode.fr) – will keep kids goggle-eyed; for more of the same, plus some truly amazing 3D computer animations-cum-rides, try the Futuroscope, a spectacular futuristic park near Poitiers, a mere 80 mins direct from Paris Montparnasse by TGV, and worth it (www.futuroscope.com).

The American Library

10 rue du Général-Camou, 7th (01.53.59.12.60/ www.americanlibraryinparis.org). M° Ecole Militaire/ RER Pont de l'Alma. **Open** 10am-7pm Tue-Sat (Aug noon-6pm Tue-Fri; 10am-2pm Sat). Membership €150 family; €45 under-12s. **No credit cards. Map** p404 D6. Absolutely spell-bending storytelling sessions in English for members and their children.

Une Journée au Cirque. See p290.

Concerts du Dimanche Matin

Châtelet, Théâtre Musical de Paris, 1 pl du Châtelet, 1st (01.40.28.28.40/children's programme 01.42.56.90.10/www.chatelet-theatre.com). M° Châtelet. **Tickets** €10 children, €20 adults; workshops free. **Credit** AmEx, MC, V. **Map** p406 J6. While parents attend the 11am classical concert on Sundays, 4-to-12-year-olds can take part in music workshops (4-7s), and (for 8-12s) a children's choir run by American leader Scott Alan Prouty, or 'electronic' music sessions using computers to mix synthesized and natural sounds to make a univers sonore. Book ahead for these (not the concerts).

La Croisière Enchantée

Bateaux Parisiens, Port de la Bourdonnais, 7th (01.44.11.33.44). M° Bir-Hakeim. **Trips** *Oct-June* 3.45pm Weds, Sat-Sun, public holidays (except Dec 25 and Jan 1); daily at 1.45pm and 3.45pm during Paris school holidays. **Admission** €9.50 (€8 per person for groups of four or more). **Credit** MC, V. **Map** p404 C6. Booking not required.
Two elves take three-to-ten-year-olds and (yes!) their parents on an enchanted Seine cruise, complete with songs and games.

Clubs

Clubbing may never again reach the hedonistic heights of dancing with a banana-clad Josephine Baker, but you can still strut your all 'neath the Paris glitterball.

Paris clubbing has a different style to that of London and Berlin, and while it might not be so full-on, the advantage has long been that you can easily move from club to after party on foot. Recently, however, clubbing has started decentralising. Small local scenes are growing away from the Parisian spotlight; look out for the new hip-hop scene springing out of Versailles, the ever-popular local drum 'n' bass, and hardcore collectives organising semi-legal outdoor 'teknivals' all over France. (The clamp-down on naughty dance raves and up-all-night clubbers introduced by Interior Minister Nicolas Sarkozy [*see p29*] has seen itself so outnumbered by law-breakers that a legalisation-with-police security policy is in the process of being tested.) House music has become mainstream, with fashionable venues such as **Batofar**, **Pulp**, **Rex**, **La Scène** and **Nouveau Casino** programming more rock and electro-influenced nights. House fans can still find events with quality local and international DJs at Batofar, Rex, **Wagg**, **Elysée Montmartre**, Nouveau Casino and **Studio 287**, mainly on Saturdays. The most pumping and modern house music can be found at the various Sunday morning after parties at venues such as **Red Light**, **Batofar** and various bars. Interestingly, although hip-hop and R'n'B are reaching skyscraper sales, it can be difficult to find quality events. **Queen** has launched its new Gift on Wednesdays (combining house and R'n'B), **Senso** has become the place for the more monied enthusiasts, as has Be Fly on Wednesdays at **Les Bains**, with an undress-to-impress policy. Trance fans should look out for nights organised by Gaia as well as Wednesday and Friday nights at **Gibus**. Drum 'n' bass, or 'drum', is linked closely with the hardcore scene, although there are more purist nights such as Massive (first Wednesday of every month) at Rex, Meet at **Glaz'art** and Break it Up at Batofar. Those who like their BPMs over 160 gather at **La Flèche d'Or** on Wednesdays and at one-offs in hired venues.

USEFUL ADVICE

Parisian clubs don't really get going until 2am as people often have a drink in a DJ bar beforehand. Many clubbers visit several clubs in one night and finish their evening at an after party on Sunday morning. This can be expensive but free passes can often be found hidden among flyers in shops or handed out outside clubs. On weekdays, clubs often hold free nights with quality DJs so going out in Paris need not be expensive.

CLUBBING COMMANDMENTS

1) Trainers are often used as a pretext to deny entrance, so if in doubt wear proper shoes.
2) Avoid baseball caps and tracksuit bottoms unless you are Jennifer Lopez, as for a bouncer this spells trouble.
3) A total look or a killer accessory such as anything colourfully customised can help procure instant access.
4) Don't arrive in a group unless you are a group of girls (un)dressed to kill, in which case you may even get in for free.
5) Speak English loudly in the queue: tourists mean easy money.

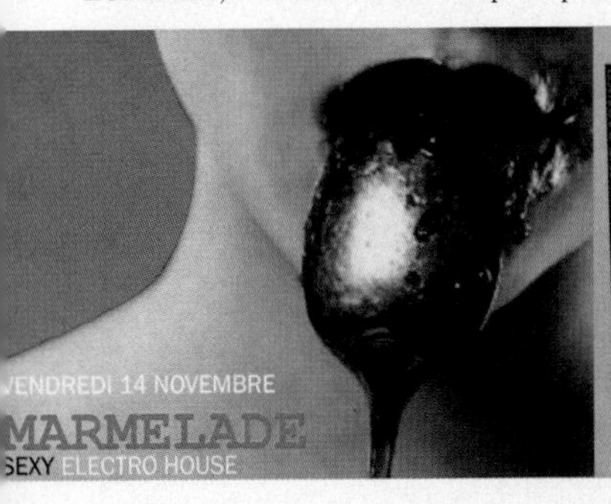

Ain't no doubt, we are here to party

Those among you who think that Paris has such a monopoly of cool that you dare not approach a dancefloor without possessing iron-clad cred on the latest clubbing trends could not be more misguided. Do you ever dream of re-donning your hen-night glad rags or your ill-fitting Travolta suit and shaking your booty like you just don't care, like you could in fact be the mayor of Funky Town? Everyone knows the best nights are often had when it's not all about toned calves, hair extensions and syncopated head nodding. Well, you can – shock – have a laugh in Paris. Of course you can, here's our selection of where to go if you just wanna kick back and push pineapple.

A big hit with 30-something crazies is the Thursday night soirée **Seven 2 One** (161 rue Montmartre, 2nd/01.43.18.38.68. M° Grands Boulevards. 7pm-1am. €8). Based on the concept of '*le after-work*' (Translation: early-bird special) it has a buzzing atmosphere as young professionals do a bit of crotch-thrusting on the dancefloor before getting the last Métro home.

Weaving the old smart-casual magic, **Le Globo** (8 bd de Strasbourg, 10th/ 01.42.41 55.70. M° Strasbourg St Denis. 11pm-dawn Fri only. €15) knows red velvet curtains are a winner. The dancefloor fills with Friday-night revellers as DJ Philippe Roux mixes house, garage and 80s. At **Le Saint** (7 rue St-Séverin, 5th/01.43.25.50.04. M° St-Michel. Open 11.30pm-dawn Tue-Sat; €15) you can shimmy your blue suedes to hip-hop, house, disco and funk. Jig and giggle at the **New Riverside** (7 rue Grégoire de Tours, 6th/01.43.54.46.33. M° Odéon. Free for women Mon-Thur and before midnight Fri, Sat. Fellas €12 weekdays, €15 Fri, Sat), where 90s and contemporary hits please a youngish crowd. For a wider appreciation of your moon-walking grooves (don't foget to pack your white socks), head to lively **Bar Three** (3 rue de l'Ancienne-Comédie, 6th/01.43.25.78.01. M° Odéon. Open 9pm-4am, Wed-Sun. Free-€2) a few streets away. It is very popular, pulling in international students with €5 pints and cocktails at €6 during happy hour (9pm-2am Wed-Thur; 9pm-midnight Fri-Sun).

There is always a chance you may fancy your hand at *le rock français*. If so, get down to the **Slow-Club** (130 rue de Rivoli, 1st/ 01.42.33.84.30. M° Châtelet. Open 10pm-4am Tue-Sat) for swing, be-bop and rock'n' roll following the club's live jazz concerts. The dancefloor talent ranges from 20- to 70-year-olds. On the other side of the river is intimate hot-spot **Le Club Zed** (2 rue des Anglais, 5th/01.43.54.93.78. M° Maubert Mutualité. Open 11pm-5am Thur-Sat. €8-€16), which has been rockin' and rollin' since 1973. Pictures of Elvis, Brigitte Bardot and Liza Minnelli adorn the walls above the gold glittery tables.

Tap your tootsies to happy house, funk, disco, R 'n' B and hip-hop at **Le Réservoir** (16 rue de la Forge Royale, 11th/01.43.56.39.60. M° Faidherbe Chaligny. Open 8pm-2am Tues-Fri; till 4am Sat. Free-€15), a restaurant which stages weekend concerts before turning into a club. Its friendly vibe and distressed decor are typical of the 11th arrondissement. Next door is **Le Casbah** (18-20 rue de la Forge Royale, 11th/01.43.71.04.39. M° Faidherbe Chaligny. Open 8pm-2am Tue,Wed; Thur-Sat 8pm-5am. €16), a charming Moroccan restaurant with a club downstairs. Amid mosaic walls and lattice partitions, weave away to funky world music.

6) If you're a model walk right in; if not, find one.
7) Look confident as you enter.
8) Order a bottle of spirits at the door of any posey club; this can mean free entrance, VIP treatment and your own table. Though prices are astronomical it works out the same as a couple of rounds of drinks if you are in a group.
9) Find out the *phsyionomiste* (door person)'s first name and kiss them hello as you walk in.
10) As you leave say ta-ta and thank you to the bouncers and '*physio*': they'll be so surprisied, they might remember who you are next time.

INFO AND GETTING HOME

The best way to know what's going on is through flyers, prime flyer spots being **Le Shop**, **Hokus Pokus** and **Techno Import** – www.flyersweb.com scans them into a day-to-day agenda. Other useful web sites are www.novaplanet.com, www.radiofg.com house and www.lemonsound.com for house and techno events. Radio FG 96.2FM and Radio Nova 101.5 FM give regular listings. Getting home between the last (around 12.45am) and first Métro (5.45am) is difficult. Get a taxi.

Posh & posey

Le Cab

2 pl du Palais Royal, 1st (01.58.62 .56 .25). M° Palais-Royal. **Open** 11.30pm-5am Wed-Sat. **Admission** free Wed; €15 Thur; Fri; €20 Sat. **Drinks** €13-€20. **Credit** AmEx, MC, V. **Map** p406 H5.

The Cabaret has now not only been shortened to 'Cab' but has had an interior face-lift by young Franco-Japanese designer Ora Ito, making it look remarkably like the Milk Bar in Kubrick's *Clockwork Orange*. Sadly, the music remains rather dated with 80s revival nights, R'n'B and commercial house.

Les Bains

7 rue du Bourg-l'Abbé, 3rd (01.48.87.01.80). M° Etienne-Marcel. **Open** 11pm-5am Mon-Sat. **Admission** €16-€20. **Drinks** €14. **Credit** AmEx, MC, V. **Map** p402 J5.

This club has lost its credibility with Paris trend-setters, although it still remains the place for star spotting and model spotting, especially during the Wednesday night Supafly.

La Suite

40 av George V, 8th (01 53 57 49 49). M° George V. **Open** 8pm-4am Tue-Sat (often closed for private parties). **Admission** free. **Drinks** €20. **Credit** AmEx, MC, V. **Map** p400 D4.

Cathy and David Guetta, who made their name with Les Bains, have launched this new venture with a dance floor and lounge area attracting unusually tall women with smaller-than-average men.

Nirvana

3 av Matignon, 8th (01.53.89.18 91). M° Franklin D Roosevelt. **Open** 8am-4am daily. **Admission** free. **Drinks** €12-€16. **Credit** AmEx, MC, V. **Map** p401 E4.

Opened by Buddha Bar disc compiler Claude Challe, Nirvana has a vague eastern theme with the music varying from lounge to up-front house. Sunday's Sunny Day attracts breakdancers who perform to a slightly wary-looking crowd.

Le VIP

78 av des Champs-Elysées, 8th (01.56.69.16.66). M° George V. **Open** Tue-Sun midnight-5am. **Admission** free. **Drinks** €20. **Credit** AmEx, DC, MC, V. **Map** p400 D4.

Run by personality Jean Roch, this club has become the place for launch parties and celebrity birthdays. The atmosphere resembles a family party straight out of *The Sopranos* – which is meant, of course, in the most complimentary sense.

Le Hammam

94 rue d'Amsterdam, 9th (01.55.07.80.00). M° Place de Clichy. **Open** 11.30pm-5am daily. **Admission** €16 Mon-Thur; €20 Sat, Sun. **Drinks** €13. **Credit** MC, V. **Map** p401 G2.

This Arabian-Nights-inspired venue has a restaurant serving lavish North African cuisine . The music volleys between the latest R'n'B and raï, attracting the gilded youth of second and third-generation North Africans, young film stars, fashion designers and TV personalities.

L'Amnesia

33 av Maine, 15th (01.56.80.37.37). M° Montparnasse-Bienvenüe. **Open** 10pm-6am Mon-Sat; 6pm-2am Sun. **Admission** €15 Mon-Thur (ladies free Thur); €20 Fri, Sat; €10 Sun . **Drinks** €10. **Credit** MC, V. **Map** p405 F9.

Tireless rock singer Johnny Hallyday opened this nightclub with a media bang last year.

L'Etoile

12 rue de Presbourg, 16th (01.45.00.78.70). M° Charles de Gaulle-Etoile. **Open** Mon-Sat 11.30pm-5am. **Admission** free Mon, Tue; €20 Wed-Sat. **Drinks** €12-€19. **Credit** AmEx, DC, MC, V. **Map** p400 C3.

Don't bother turning up if you don't own an Armani suit, as the door policy is very strict. Being a model or having one on your arm helps.

Mainstream

La Scala

188bis rue de Rivoli, 1st (01.42.22.78.56). M° Palais Royal. **Open** 10.30pm-6am Tue-Sun. **Admission** €12 Tue-Thur; €15 Fri, Sat. **Drinks** €10. **Credit** MC, V. **Map** p401 H5.

This huge central club has plenty of potential with its lasers and ample dancefloor. However, the music remains charty, commercial and dated and the clientele wet behind the ears.

Club Med World

39 cour St-Emilion, 12th (08.10.81.04.10). M° Cour St- Emilion. **Open** 11am-2am Tue-Thur; 11am-6am Thur-Sat. **Admission** €15 Tue, Wed; €20 Thur-Sat. **Drinks** €10. **Credit** AmEx, MC, V. **Map** p407 N10.

This huge venue in the recently created Bercy Village hosts popular disco and 80s nights at the weekends for those who don't actually like night clubs but like to strut their stuff, dance-wise.

Queen

102 av des Champs-Elysées, 8th (01.53.89.08.90/ www.queen.fr). M° George V. **Open** midnight-dawn daily. **Admission** €10-€20. **Drinks** €8-€18. **Credit** AmEx, MC, V. **Map** p400 D4.

Queen was once a top-notch gay club but has become rather commercial and unimaginative. The music is often poor unless an international DJ is invited to play, and the crowd is a combination of tourists, gym queens and business school students.

Bus Palladium

6 rue Fontaine, 9th (01 53 21 07 33). M° Blanche. **Open** 11pm-5am daily. **Admission** €20. **Drinks** 13€. **Credit** AmEx, MC, V. **Map** p401 H2.

After several revamps, 'Le Bus' remains a prime chat-up spot for suits and young well-to-do girls dressed in their mothers' clothing, especially on Tuesdays when girls get in – and drink – for free.

La Loco

90 bd de Clichy, 18th (01.53.41.88.88/ www.laloco.com). M° Place de Clichy. **Open** 11pm-5am Tue-Sun. **Admission** €10-€16. **Drinks** €8-€16. **Credit** AmEx, MC, V. **Map** p401 G2.

After an attempt at attracting gay and fashion conscious clubbers La Loco has gone back to a more mainstream policy with a strong teenage and *banlieue* following. The three dancefloors feature house, dance and chart music on weekends with regular metal and gothic concerts during the week.

Cool clubs

Most are mixed gay and heterosexual although some nights are essentially gay. Trainers are acceptable, although some racist bouncers use this as a pretext for denying entrance.

Pulp

25 bd Poissonnière, 2nd (01.40.26.01.93). M° Grands Boulevards. **Open** midnight-5am Wed-Sat. **Admission** free Wed-Thur; €12 Fri, Sat. **Drinks** €5-€9. **Credit** MC, V. **Map** p402 J4.

Essentially a lesbian club, this venue has opened its doors to a more mixed crowd on Wednesdays and Thursdays, when free entrance creates an atmosphere midway between a late-hours bar and a club. Watch out for top international DJs passing through.

Rex

5 bd Poissonnière, 2nd (01.42.36.10.96). M° Bonne Nouvelle. **Open** 11.30pm-dawn Thur-Sat, and some Weds. **Admission** free-€16. **Drinks** €5-€12. **Credit** MC, V. **Map** p402 J4.

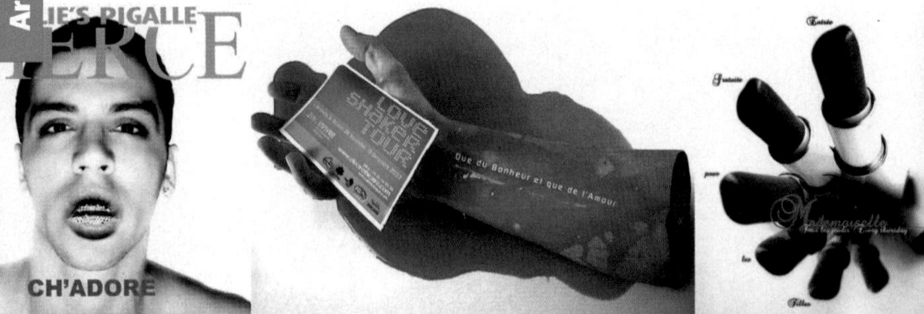

Arts & Entertainment

La Loco

The Rex has held its reputation as a prime venue for electronic music for over ten years. It is Laurent Garnier's home-from-home, where he gives spectacular perfomances of up to 12-hour sets. Friday favours techno, Wednesdays and Thursdays are often free. Saturdays feature house with residencies by DJs such as Charles Schillings and Dan Ghenacia.

Le Triptyque

142 rue Montmartre, 2nd (01.40.28.05.45/ www.letriptique.com). M° Grands Boulevards. **Open** 8.30pm-2am Tue-Sun. **Admission** €5-€15. **Drinks** €3-€8. **Credit** AmEx, MC, V. **Map** p402 J4.

Eclectic programming ranging from jazz to trance means this brand new central club means that it has yet to make its mark, but it has now started doing mid-month Sunday morning afters.

Wagg

62 rue Mazarine, 6th (01.55.42.22.00). M° Odéon. **Open** 11pm-5am Wed-Sun. **Admission** €5-€12. **Drinks** €9-€15. **Credit** AmEx, DC, MC, V. **Map** p406 H7.

The former Whisky Go Go, where Jim Morrison hung out when he was in Paris, is now a club part-owned by Fabric in London but hasn't quite found its place. The music is primarily house with regular nights featuring local labels such as F Com and Dialect, and the crowd definitely Left Bank.

Folies Pigalle

11 pl Pigalle, 9th (01.48.78.25.26/www.folies-pigalle.com). M° Pigalle. **Open** midnight-dawn Tue-Sat; 6pm-midnight Sun. **Admission** €8-€16. **Drinks** €10-€16. **Credit** V. **Map** p401 G2.

After a recent clamp-down resulting in a three-month closure, 'Les Folies' has kept a low profile and ditched its famous after parties, though the regular Miss Transsexual competitions remain. The venue attracts Pigalle's underbelly as well as accidental tourists.

Bateau Concorde Atlantique

facing 25 quai Anatole-France, 7th (01.47.05.71.03). M° Assemblée Nationale. **Open** 11pm-5am Mon-Sat. **Admission** €10-€15. **Drinks** €4-€8. **Credit** MC, V. **Map** p401 F5.

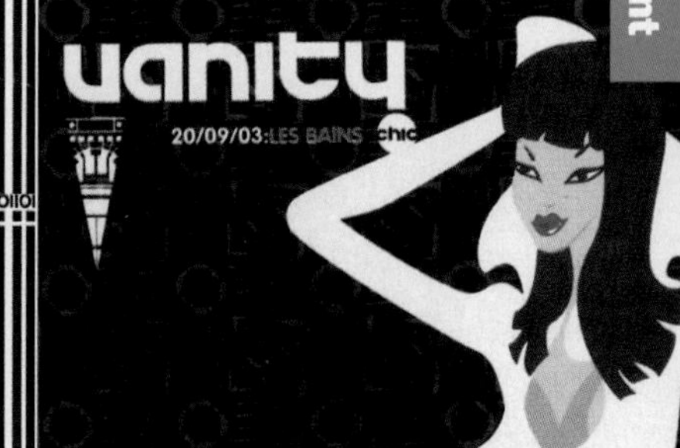

Titz & glitz: the British are coming!

Since that repercussive day in the Garden of Eden, we have all had to confront some harsh facts about the nature of humanity: that certain people judge others by race or appearance; that the stronger will inevitably exploit the weaker, and that, to some, there is no finer sight on God's earth than a topless woman in a crap wig sliding her perineum up and down a pole, ideally, in close proximity to other spectators fighting their way through a plate of so-so nosh.

Aesthetics is, of course, all about subjectivity, and one can hardly imagine the late Sir Harold Acton spraying his dining companions with a gob full of half-chewed *boeuf*, commenting, 'Look at the Dutch Alps on that, lads.' But these places do seem popular. Especially, and unsurprisingly, among Anglo-Americans, and thus the increasing internationalisation of Paris has seen a cultural invasion, led by Britain's own (surely soon 'Sir') Peter Stringfellow. His aim is 'to give Paris back its sexuality'. What Stringers means is that he wants to conserve French culture by reviving a Parisian tradition: until the 1950s strip clubs were everywhere.

Feminism and all that other subjective stuff rather did for Parisian stripping in the 1960s. However, 30 years later the King arrived, golden mullet gloriously a-flap, to put the 'Ooh' back in 'Ooh la la' and he's chosen a great venue for it (27 avenue des Ternes', near the Champs-Elysées). The place is far from tacky, it's even rather *belle-époque*.

This column is not the place for comment on the relative pulchritude of the dancers, but we cannot miss an opportunity to comment on the terpsichorean talents of the titz 'n' glitz on offer at Stringfellows: terrific; Nureyevian. Those poles they glide down down up and down on must have been mighty righteous in a previous life. Nay. Instead we shall focus on what was discovered when two *Time Out* journalists pooped along incognito to test the place. Here's why it will be a success.

The hedonistic atmosphere, coupled with our professional instinct to blend in by drinking rivers upon rivers of booze, did not mix well with the unusually potent level of testosterone unleashed within our M&S imported slacks. In brief, and inner-ear science remains hazy on this, our balance was affected and one of us managed to knock the table over as we got up to leave. In London, this would be enough to have you slung out. But not in Stringfellows Paris – we were dusted down and asked if we were OK. One felt like David Niven. The other grappled for public-school niceties learnt in short trousers at Sedbergh. On the way out, one of us had to be fireperson-lifted up the staircase. The obliging bouncer made it seem like it was the least he could do, a real pleasure. When, two steps from the top, all three of us overbalanced and executed a slapstack tumble back down, his reaction was one of *bonhomie*. We all looked at each other and laughed. As we said, this is not told for reasons of anecdote: it illustrates Stringfellows' brilliant cultural understanding of French glamour, the English sense of the ridiculous, impeccable French *politesse* and everyone's appreciation of how a fine set of knockers can fell international barriers.

Stringfellows Paris

22 av des Ternes, 17th (01.47.66.45.00). M° Ternes. **Open** 8.30pm-4am Mon-Sat. **Admission** €25 Mon-Sat; €16 students. Closed in Aug. **Credit** V. **Map** p402 L4.

Stringfellows Paris

This two-level boat has become the clubbers' spot during the summer with its terrace and voluminous dancefloor. From July until September the Respect team hold a popular weekly Wednesday night bash with free admission before 10pm.

Le Gibus

18 rue du Fbg-du-Temple, 11th (01.47.00.78.88/ www.gibus.fr). M° République. **Open** midnight-dawn Wed-Sat. **Admission** free-€18. **Drinks** €9-€11. **Credit** AmEx, DC, MC, V. **Map** p402 L4.

This 80s punk hot spot has gone through plenty of different styles, settling on house and disco at the weekends, R'n'B on Thursday nights and trance every Wednesday and Friday. Despite efforts to attract Paris' movers and shakers, the crowd is essentially non-Parisian and remarkably mellow.

Nouveau Casino

109 rue Oberkampf, 11th (01.43.57.57.40). M° Parmentier. **Open** Sun 9pm-2am Mon-Wed; 9pm-5am Thur-Sat. **Admission** €7-€15. **Drinks** €5-€11. **Credit** MC, V. **Map** p403 M5.

The Café Charbon's backyard has not only become a prime concert venue with an emphasis on rock, but also features club nights from Wednesday to Saturday inviting local collectives and international names. The music varies from dub to techno with almost everything in between. Regular nights such as Minimal Dancing attract a loyal crowd.

La Scène

2bis rue des Taillandiers, 11th (01.48.06.50.70/ www.la-scene.com). M° Bastille. **Open** 8pm-5am Wed-Sat. **Admission** €10-€15. **Drinks** €5.50-€9.50. **Credit** AmEx, MC, V. **Map** p407 M7.

This Bastille restaurant/bar/club complex holds regular concerts as well as club events from Thursday to Saturday. There's an alternative gay emphasis on Fridays; when popular nights such as Eyes Need Sugar attract a very fashionable crowd.

Batofar

opposite 11 quai François-Mauriac, 13th (01.56.29.10.00/www.batofar.org). M° Quai de la Gare. **Open** 9pm-2am Mon-Wed; 9pm-3am Thur; 9pm-5am Fri-Sat; 5am-noon Sun. **Admission** €3-€12. **Drinks** €3-€8. **Credit** MC, V. **Map** p407 N10.

Some jumped ship while a new crowd embarked after a change in management at the light-house boat. Monday's are now jazz, Wednesdays live concerts, Thursdays drum'n' bass, dub and reggae, Fridays more underground dance music and Saturdays are 100% house. During the summer clubbers chill on the quayside while DJs play on deck.

Red Light

34 rue du Départ, 14th (no phone). M° Montparnasse-Bienvenüe. **Open** 11pm-2am Fri, Sat. **Admission** €20. **Drinks** from €10. **Credit** AmEx, MC, V. **Map** p405 F9.

House mecca with a handful of local and international DJs spinning harder house music. Fridays rotate around monthly nights BPM and XX and Saturdays attract a very preened gay clientele for events such as King$ with resident DJ David Guetta.

Elysée Montmartre

72 bd de Rochechouart, 18th (01.44.92.45.38). M° Anvers. **Open** midnight-6am Fri, Sat. **Admission** €10-€18. **Drinks** €7-€12. **Credit** AmEx, DC, MC, V. **Map** p402 J2.

Although more of a concert venue than a club, promoters hire it out for big nights such as the monthly Open House and Panic nights, which attract over 1,000 clubbers at weekends.

Studio 287

33 av de la Porte d'Aubervilliers, 18th (01.48.34.00.00). **Open** 11pm-5am Tue-Sat; 6am-noon Sat, Sun. **Admission** €10-€16. **Drinks** €8-€16. **Credit** AmEx, MC, V.

After a nine-month closure by authorities, this vast superclub has reopened with a bang, offering Ibiza-style clubbing en masse.

Le Glaz'art

7-15 av de la Porte de La Villette, 19th (01.40.36.55.65). M° Porte de La Villette. **Open** 8.30pm-2am Thur (sometimes Weds); 10pm-5am Fri, Sat. **Admission** €8-€12. **Drinks** €5-€9. **Credit** MC, V. **Map** p403 inset.

The converted Eurolines station is a little out of the way but its strong live programming and theme nights attract a loyal crowd. Watch out for regular dub, techno and drum 'n' bass nights.

Arts & Entertainment

Latino, world & rock'n'roll

Caveau de la Huchette

5 rue de la Huchette, 5th (01.43.26.65.05). M° St-Michel. **Open** 9.30pm-2.30am Mon-Thur; 9.30pm-3.30am Fri, Sat. **Admission** €10-€13. **Drinks** from €4.60. **Credit** MC, V. **Map** p406 J7.

A popular haunt for fun-seeking divorcées and veterans not ready to settle down quite yet. Music varies from funky jazz to rock'n'roll classics

Les Etoiles

61 rue du Château d'Eau, 10th (01.47.70.60.56). M° Château d'Eau. **Open** 9pm-4am Thur-Sat. **Admission** €10. **Drinks** €3-€6. **Credit** V. **Map** p402 K3.

A quality live salsa band electrifies the dancefloor every weekend. Anyone looking a little uncertain will be swept into a frenzy of footwork with free advice dished out to the less adept.

La Chapelle des Lombards

19 rue de Lappe, 11th (01.43.57.24.24). M° Bastille. **Open** 10.30pm-dawn Thur-Sat; concerts Thur 8.30pm. **Admission** €15-€18.50. **Drinks** €5-€12. **Credit** AmEx, MC, V. **Map** p407 M7.

Tourists, Latinos and Africans sweat it out in this friendly venue specialising in world music with a combination of zouk, salsa, soukous' and raï.

Le Cabaret Sauvage

59 bd MacDonald, 19th (01.42.09.03.09/ www.cabaretsauvage.com). M° Porte de La Villette. **Open** (depends) 8pm-dawn. **Admission** €10-€20. **Drinks** €4-€10. **Credit** AmEx, MC, V. **Map** p403 inset.

This circus venue is hired out for all sorts of nights, the most popular dedicated to North African music.

Bar-clubs

La Mezzanine de L'Alcazar

62 rue Mazarine, 6th (01.53.10.19.99). M° Odéon. **Open** 7pm-1am daily. **Admission** free. **Drinks** €10. **Credit** AmEx, DC, MC, V. **Map** p405 H7.

The stylish mezzanine bar owned by Terence Conran has an impressive DJ line-up attracting Parisian yuppies. They aren't really there for the music, which can get quite pumping past midnight.

Le Purgatoire

14 rue Hautefeuille, 6th (01.43.54.41.36). M° Odéon. **Open** 6pm-2am Mon-Wed; 6pm-5am Thur-Sat. **Admission** free. **Drinks** €3.5-€7. **Credit** MC, V. **Map** p406 J7.

Purgatory is the first DJ bar of its kind in touristy St-Michel. Wednesdays and Thursdays are dedicated to electronic live sets and electro, while the weekend remains commercial.

Le Man Ray

34 rue Marbeuf, 8th (01.56.88.36.36). M° Franklin D Roosevelt. **Open** 6pm-2am Mon-Thur; 6pm-5am Fri, Sat; 7pm-2am Sun. **Admission** free Mon-Thur, Sun; €20 after 12.30am Fri, Sat. **Drinks** €15. **Credit** AmEx, MC, V. **Map** p400 D4.

This be-seen restaurant continues to attract the crowds who willingly slide on to le dancefloor. Local and international DJs spin house on the weekends.

Senso

16 rue La Trémoille, 8th (01.56.52.14.14). M° Alma-Marceau. **Open** 10pm-2am Wed-Sat. **Admission** free. **Drinks** €10-€15. **Credit** AmEx, MC, V. **Map** p400 D4.

This new hotel bar, also Conran-owned, prides itself on catering for chic lovers of hip-hop and R'n'B. Bling clad B boys squeeze into the tiny lounge area next to the sleek contemporary restaurant and sip Coca-Cola while eyeing the ladies.

L'Ile Enchantée

65 bd de La Villette, 10th (01.42.01.67.99) M° Colonel Fabien. **Open** noon-2am Mon-Fri; 5pm-2am Sat, Sun. **Admission** free. **Drinks** €3.50-€6.50. **Credit** MC, V. **Map** p403 M3.

This popular bar has invested in a mini club area upstairs where Paris' new electro generation hand out flyers and exchange gossip.

La Fabrique

53 rue du Fbg-St-Antoine, 11th (01.43.07.67.07). M° Bastille. **Open** 11am-5am daily. **Admission** free Mon-Thur; €10 Fri, Sat. **Drinks** €3.50-€9. **Credit** AmEx, DC, MC, V. **Map** p407 M7.

So popular is this DJ bar/club restaurant that it has opened an annexe in Japan. Local house DJs spin to a trendy Bastille crowd. Getting past the bouncers can be a little trying.

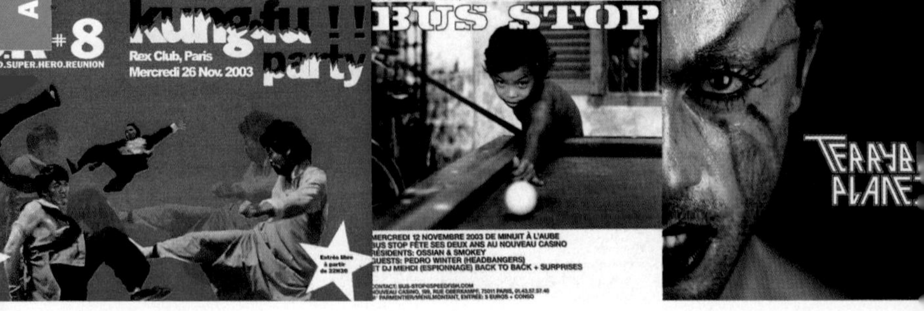

Dance

Contemporary? Paris is positively futuristic in its devotion to dance. And for those who want to vogue it for themselves, the parquet's a-glistening.

When it comes to dance, Paris is a real *pointe*-scorer. Avant-garde movers and shakers flock to the city's very serious, and very impressive, contemporary scene; there is also much creativity shuttling back and forth between Paris and Brussels. Crucially, there is an audience out there prepared to vote with its feet. An appearance by Pina Bausch is treated like a state visit; stalwarts such as the Nederlands Dans Theater and William Forsythe are regularly in town. The *événement* of 2004 will be the long-awaited ribbon-cutting of the **Centre National de la Danse** just outside the city in Pantin (*see p302*).

And although you wouldn't know it by some of the lamentable shape-throwing on Paris' dancefloors, this is a capital teeming with dance classes. The Buena Vista-inspired Latino phenomenon holds strong, too, with a plethora of salsa and tango clubs, bars and classes. Summer dancing on the *quais* near the Institut du Monde Arabe has become an institution: take your pick from tango, salsa, capoeira and rock 'n' roll and and drop a few *sous* in a hat for the loan of the ghetto-blaster.

Some of the most exciting contemporary dance is to be found at festivals. Some to look out for, all of which feature big names alongside lesser known experimentalists, are Paris Quartier d'été (www.quartierdete.com, July-Aug), the Festival d'Automne (www.festival-automne.com, Sept-Dec), Rencontres Chorégraphiques de Seine-St-Denis (www.rencontreschoregraphiques.com, May-June), the Agora festival at Centre Pompidou's Ircam (www.ircam.fr, June), the Onze Bouge season (www.festivalonze.org, June) and street-dance led Rencontres at La Villette (www.villette.com, Oct-Nov).

Major dance venues

Théâtre du Châtelet

1 pl du Châtelet, 1st (01.40.28.28.00). M° Châtelet. Closed July-Sept. **Tickets** €9-€75. **Credit** AmEx, MC, V. **Map** p402 J5.

Châtelet plays host to touring international ballet corps, as well as inviting French regional ballets to strut their stuff. Occasional cabaret-style dance-musicals are usually top-notch and usually well worth booking ahead for.

Théâtre de la Ville

2 pl du Châtelet, 4th (01.42.74.22.77/ www.theatredelaville-paris.com). M° Châtelet-Les Halles. **Box office** 11am-7pm Mon; 11am-8pm Tue-Sat; telephone bookings 11am-7pm Mon-Sat. Closed July-Aug. **Tickets** €11-€29. Tickets jeunes for students and under 27s. **Credit** MC, V. **Map** p406 J6.

Paris' leading contemporary dance forum is still at the cutting edge. This season, book well in advance for the return of both Anne Teresa De Keersmaeker (Apr, May) and the inimitable Pina Bausch (4-22 June). Its sister, **Théâtre des Abbesses** (31 rue des Abbesses, 18th) programmes mainly ethnic dance. *Wheelchair access.*

Théâtre des Champs-Elysées

15 av Montaigne, 8th (01.49.52.50.50/ www.theatrechampselysees.fr). M° Alma-Marceau. **Box office** 1-7pm Mon-Sat; phone bookings 10am-noon, 2-6pm Mon-Fri. Closed mid-July, Aug. **Tickets** €10-€55. **Credit** AmEx, MC, V. **Map** p400 D5.

This elegant hall made famous by free dance pioneer Isadora 'Scarf Face' Duncan and 'Nails' Nijinsky's riotous first performance of *Rite of Spring* is now largely devoted to classical music. The dance agenda includes annual big box officer the *Gala des Etoiles du XXIe siècle*.

Ballet de l'Opéra National de Paris

Palais Garnier, pl de l'Opéra, 9th. M° Opéra. (08.92.89.90.90/www.opera-de-paris.fr). **Box office** 11am-6.30pm Mon-Sat. Closed 15 July-Aug. **Tickets** €6-€67. **Credit** AmEx, MC, V. **Map** p407 M7.

Palais Garnier still treads carefully between tutu classics and new creation. Highlights this season include a modernist triple-bill with old pieces by Bronislava Nijinska and Paul Taylor, plus a new work, *La Septième Lune*, by Davide Bombana. Mats Ek's 80s re-working of *Giselle* and Nureyev's colourful take on *Don Quichotte* get new airings in May. Ballet is also mounted at the **Opéra Bastille** (*see chapter* **Music: Classical & Opera**). *Wheelchair access (call ahead on 01.40.01.18.08).*

Théâtre National de Chaillot

1 pl du Trocadéro, 16th (01.53.65.30.00/ www.theatre-chaillot.fr). M° Trocadéro. **Box office** 11am-7pm Mon-Sat; 11am-5pm Sun; telephone bookings 9am-7pm Mon-Sat; 11am-5pm Sun. Closed July-Aug. **Tickets** €9.50-€30. **Credit** MC, V. **Map** p400 C5.

Chaillot has the clout to snag big names, but also keeps an eye on home-grown talents. Cherry-picks this year include La Fontaine's fables choreographed for children by Dominique Hervieu,

Béatrice Massin and Dominique Rebaud (end April-May); the Nederlands Dans Theater with a new choreography by Mats Ek (6-15 May), and the Paris premiere of *The Art of Urban Dance*, Niels Robitzky's history of hip-hop (24-27 June). Rounding off the season is William Forsythe's swansong as head of the Ballet Frankfurt (30 June-3 July). *Wheelchair access.*

Centre National de la Danse

1 rue Victor-Hugo, 93507 Pantin (01.42.74.06.44/ www.cnd.fr). M° Hoche/RER Pantin. **Tickets** €9-€13.
Housed in a specially converted concrete office block next to the Canal de l'Ourcq, this centre will put one roof over studios, stages, offices and a vast dance médiathèque. The building opens this summer with a weekend (18, 19 June) of free performances from the likes of Robyn Orlin. First billing goes to the *enfant terrible* of dance, Boris Charmatz and his Association Edna (5-9 July).

Maison des Arts de Créteil

pl Salvador Allende, 94000 Créteil (01.45.13.19.19/www.maccreteil.com). M° Créteil-Préfecture. **Box office** 1-7pm Tue-Sat. Closed July-Aug. **Tickets** €7-€18. **Credit** MC, V.
It may be in the *banlieue*, but this arts centre is firmly on the international dance map, hosting the prestigious EXIT festival and drawing big feet such as Merce Cunningham.

Other dance spaces

Studio CND

15 rue Geoffroy-l'Asnier, 4th (01.42.74.44.22/ www.cnd.fr). M° Pont Marie or St-Paul. **Box office** 2-7pm Mon-Fri. **Tickets** €9; €8 under-26s. **No credit cards. Map** p406 K6.
The studio of the Centre National de la Danse concentrates on young choreographers; the more established (eg Georges Momboye) also pass through.

Ménagerie de Verre

12/14 rue Léchevin, 11th (01.43.38.33.44/ www.ifrance.com/menagerie-de-verre). M° Parmentier. **Box office** 1 hr before show. Closed end July-Aug. **Tickets** €13. **No Credit. Map** p403 N5.
This multidisciplinary hothouse is firmly rooted in the avant-garde, but also receives established names such as Mathilde Monnier. It holds the biannual dance festival Les Inaccoutumés, and offers contemporary dance masterclasses led by the likes of Mark Tompkins.

Théâtre de la Bastille

76 rue de la Roquette, 11th (01.43.57.42.14/ www.theatre-bastille.com). **Box office** 10am-6pm Mon-Fri; 2-6pm Sat. Closed July-Oct. **Tickets** €12.50-€19. **Credit cards** MC, V. **Map** p407 M6.
Split between dance and drama, this small theatre has a penchant for ribald experimentalism. Boris Charmatz revisits a decade-old choreography in *Les Disparates* (17-28 May).

If the slipper fits

It's not unusual for big ballet productions to call on the services of well-known couturiers to tog up the dancers. The lower ranks of the dance world are, of course, hardly on the same sartorial pegging, but as fashion borrows from ballet wardrobes and vice versa, light feet are stepping out in greater style.

Your first Parisian ballet booty call has to be at the legendary ballet store **Repetto** (22 rue de la Paix, 2nd, 01.44.71.83.12), part of a chain started by 'Madame Repetto' (mother to dance star Roland Petit). The full leg-warming, body-hugging caboodle can be found here in quality materials for all ages and sizes; colours are mainly plain or pastel. What the fashionistas all flock to the shop to snaffle up is of course the shoes. Shoes? Calling this lot shoes is like calling Burberrys bum-freezers. Pointes commence at €5, and demie-pointes at €13. Repetto-owned **Côté Danse** (24 rue Châteaudun, 9th, 01.53.32.84.84) stocks the label's pointes, demie-pointes and togs, as well as Gamba salon shoes; upstairs is a discount section, including basic pumps for €7.62.

The staff match the name at dance specialists **Attitude Diffusion** (12 rue de Clichy, 9th, 01.42.81.44.87) – great for playing spot the assistant – but there is nevertheless a large label choice, including Pietragalla & Merlet, Gamba, Chacott and Col P Dansco. Clothes styles range from classic pastel frou-frou frocks to more jazz-contemporary numbers.

Paris Menkes (12 rue Rambuteau, 3rd, 01.40.27.91.81), certainly not named after the fashion editor of the *Herald Tribune*, sells a combination of flamenco shoes and clothing and drag queen platforms – a bizarre mix, but great for Almoldóvar fans. And drag queens.

Even more zany is the tap shoe specialist **Swingtap** (21 rue Keller, 11th, 01.48.06.38.18/www.swingtap.com), run by Victor 'the talking feet of Paris' Cuno. Don't be surprised to see a chorus line in the shop itself – seven levels of classes are taught in between flogging steel-tipped clogs and trainers, and baby if you ain't got that swing after that... well, you ain't got that swing (classes: €25 membership, three-month *carnets* €150-€360).

Ballet de l'Opéra National de Paris. *See p301.*

Théâtre de la Cité Internationale
21 bd Jourdan, 14th (01.43.13.50.50/ www.theatredelacite.ciup.fr). RER Cité Universitaire. **Box office** 2-7pm Mon-Sat. Closed July-Aug. **Tickets** €18; €12.50 concessions; €9.50 under-26s and Mon. **Credit** MC, V.
The theatre of the Cité-U hosts performances from the Festival d'automne and is an established contemporary dance venue.

L'Etoile du Nord
16 rue Georgette-Agutte, 18th (01.42.26.47.47). M° Guy-Môquet. **Box office** 1-6pm Mon-Fri. Closed July-Aug. **Tickets** €19; €13 students, over 65s; €8 under-26s. **Credit** MC, V.
This theatre provides a much-needed platform for the contemporary multi-media dance scene. Deconstructionist choreographer-in-residence Gabriel Hernandez's carte blanche will see him dancing in the street (audience in toe) to the Mains d'Oeuvre (18, 28, 29 May). (*See chapter* **Music: Popular Music**).

Le Regard du Cygne
210 rue de Belleville, 20th (01.43.58.55.93/ http://redcygne.free.fr). M° Télégraphe. **Box office** Closed Aug. **Tickets** €5-€15. **No credit cards. Map** p403 Q3.
Created in 1983 to promote choreographic research, this remains one of the few truly alternative spaces in Paris. During Spectacles Sauvages, for a symbolic fee (nearly) anybody can present a ten-minute piece to the public.

Dance classes

Paris is so footloose it has classes in virtually any dance you can think of. Explanation is found in the seduction success enjoyed in the city by salsa kings and queens, African dance teachers (they only have to say 'Momboye' and the chics come flocking) and, believe it or not, rock'n'rollers. Here's just a small selection.

La Casa del Tango
11 allée Darius-Milhaud, 19th (01.40.40.73.60/ www.lacasadeltango.net). M° Ourcq or Laumière. **Map** p407 P2.
New centre devoted to all things tango in a space reminiscent of Buenos Aires.

Centre de Danse du Marais
41 rue du Temple, 4th (01.49.23.40.43/ www.parisdanse.com). M° Rambuteau. **Map** 402 K5.
One of the 'famous three' dance schools in Paris. Big-name choreographers and teachers flock here.

Centre Mandapa
6 rue Wurtz, 13th (01.45.89.01.60). M° Glacière. **Map** p406 J10.
This space hosts visiting companies and has some excellent classes in classical Indian dance.

Centre Momboye
25 rue Boyer, 20th (01.43.58.85.01/ www.ladanse.com/momboye). M° Gambetta.
Only centre in France to devote itself entirely to African dance (which, in Momboye's book, includes hip-hop). Classes are taught to live drumming.

Espace Oxygène
168 rue St-Maur, 11th (01.49.29.06.77). M° Goncourt or Belleville. **Map** p403 M4.
An exotic range of classes from capoeira to Egyptian.

Flamenco en France
33 rue des Vignolles, 20th (01.43.48.99.92). M° Avron or Buzenval. **Map** p407 Q7.
Right next to the Socio-Anarchist Party is this very authentic school, where La Juana will show you how to put some olé into your dance moves.

Smoking et Brillantine
13 rue Guyton de Morveau, 13th (01.45.65.90.90/ www.smoking-brillantine.com). M° Corvisart.
Specialists in partner dance, including rock 'n roll, acrobatic rock, salon dances, salsa and tango.

Film

Paris is a movie-able feast. If you are an art house aficionado, a Hollywood-head or simply in need of a second-date distraction, the city is pictures perfect.

'Is cinema more important than life?' François Truffaut was fond of asking. If the position of film both in the French capital and the nation's heart is anything to go by, the answer would be a resounding '*Mais, oui*'.

The silver screen cops a lot of love here. In early 2003, the Mayor unveiled the results of his blockbusting brief '*Mission: cinéma*'. They were: financial aid for independent picture houses, a new July festival 'Paris Cinéma', and funding for children's film education projects. Two questions: where else would the *septième art* receive such attention? And why?

Perhaps it is because the feisty Gaul has always been fiercely proud of anything he had a hand in. After all, Paris can claim that cinema was born here, with the first public screening of the brothers Lumière's *La Sortie des Usines Lumière à Lyon* in 1875. Then there's the fact that the French, and Parisians especially, are movie maniacs. They go to the pictures more than any other Europeans, frequently enough in fact to sustain not only the spawning multiplexes, massive art deco auditoriums and all the tiny 100-seat independents in the capital, but also a hoard of specialist venues such as the chain of three **Action** cinemas that screen almost exclusively 1940-50s Americana.

Every Wednesday up to 17 new releases appear, ranging from short films (*courts métrages*) from Iran to Tinseltown's latest and everything in between: third world, documentary and gay cinema are on offer, usually at an art cinema such as **L'Entrepôt** or one of the **Cinémathèques**. Nostalgia features highly, too, with weekly retrospectives dedicated to a particular director or actor.

To the envy of film makers all over the globe, the French state and television companies who largely aid the 150-plus films churned out every year. Recent home-grown hits have been few, however. The dream started by *Amélie Poulain* faded to reality when French product did not even get a look-in at Cannes 2003. Some say the problem lies in the sheer quantity of films being made: with over 160 new French releases in one year, competition for press coverage and ticket sales is fierce. Others blame the industry's

Ciné Cité Bercy

Arts & Entertainment

current nervousness to Vivendi's withdrawal of a sizeable flake of the cash croissant. Perhaps it's time to fly the moneyed nest that has for years resulted in a fecund environment for new talent and experimentalism and wake up to the scary world where the box office dictates.

So, a crisis in French cinema? Isn't there always, you might yawn. André Téchiné, director of one of the rare successes of the year, *Les Egarés*, believes, 'If there was never the occasional crisis nothing would get done.' Let's hope he's right; the French are at their best when driving full-throttle away from the commercial Hollywood formula. At the end of 2002, for example, lining up in the starting blocks with such filmic Olympians as *Harry Potter* and *Lord of the Rings*, the French candidate that went on to win over audiences and critics worldwide was called *Etre et Avoir*, a documentary set in a rural primary school. Touché, French film: just never change.

Ciné showcases

Le Grand Rex

1 bd Poissonnière, 2nd (08.36.68.05.96). M° Bonne Nouvelle. **Tickets** €9; €7 students, over-60s; €5.95 under-12s. **Map** p406 J4.

The blockbuster programming of this huge art deco cinema matches the vast screen. Listed as a historic monument, this is the place if you hanker after the 1930s cinema experience complete with plush red carpets and roll-down screen. *Wheelchair access.*

Max Linder Panorama

24 bd Poissonnière, 9th (01.48.24.88.88/ 08.36.68.50.52). M° Grands Boulevards. **Tickets** €8.50; €6 Mon, wed, Fri, students, under-12s. **Map** p406 J9.

A state-of-the-art screening facility (THX sound). The walls and seating are all black, to prevent even the tiniest twinkle of reflected light distracting the audience from what's happening on the screen. Look out for all-nighters and one-offs such as rare vintage films. *Wheelchair access.*

UGC Ciné Cité Bercy

2 cour St-Emilion, 12th (08.36.68.68.58). M° Cour St-Emilion. **Tickets** €8.90; €6.50 students, over-60s; €5.50 under-12s. **Map** p407 N10.

This ambitious 18-screen development screens art movies as well as mainstream, and holds meet-the-director screenings. The Les Halles version (7 pl de la Rotonde, Nouveau Forum des Halles, 1st/ 08.92.70.00.00/M° Les Halles) offers the same mix, and the *UGC Illimitée* card provides unlimited access for €16.46 per month. *Internet café. Wheelchair access.*

Gaumont Grand Ecran Italie

30 pl d'Italie, 13th (08.92.69.69.69). M° Place d'Italie. **Tickets** €9.50 (big screen); €8 (other screens); €5.50 under-12s. **Map** p406 J10.

Speedy bon car-chase

'At the age of 37, she realised she'd never ride, through Paris in a sports car, With the cool wind in her hair.' The Ballad of Lucy Jordan, sung by Marianne Faithful.

Cheer up, love! Claude Lelouch's cult short *C'était un rendezvous* will put the wind in your hair and then some. Described as the ultimate car chase, putting scenes from *Bullitt* to shame, the film has for three decades only been available on poor-quality pirate copies owned by misty-eyed car enthusiasts. That was until a London-based film maker got hold of a second generation VHS version and decided it deserved a wider audience. The film was made in 1976 when Lelouch, still giddy from the success of *Un homme et une femme*, strapped a camera to the bonnet of his Ferrari 275 GTB and went for a spin. The result is a death-defying, fascinating nine-minute dash through the streets of Paris from Porte Dauphine to the steps of the Sacré Coeur taking in all the sights between at a jaunty 110mph flyby. Not clever, kids, but entertaining to watch. What distinguishes it as a car nut's pornography is the fact it was made without any special effects or roadblocks, and thus it qualifies as the rawest form of *cinéma vérité*. Rumours abound as to the making of the film. Was it the director himself driving or a hired Fomula One racer? Was Lelouch really arrested when it was first shown? Was the car fuelled with petrol or a distilled form of Lelouch's own ego?

A century of French film

When it comes to wielding a camera, those garlic-munchers have never been less than pioneering. They started it, and they're bloody good at it – just ask them. Here are some they prepared earlier.

La Sortie des Usines Lumière à Lyon

(Louis Lumière, 1895)
Cinema was born when the Lumière brothers charged a one-franc entrance fee for a minute-long projection of workers leaving a factory in Lyon. Louis Lumière saw no future for the invention beyond that of fair-ground novelty. However, among the spectators was theatre-owner Georges Méliès.

Un Chien Andalou

(Luis Buñuel, 1929)
Buñuel teamed up with Salvador Dalí in Paris to create this nine-minute succession of Surrealist images: a woman's eye is slit, a priest is pulled along by a piano. In the hands of these masters, cinema became a medium for artistic expression and the truly weird.

La Règle du Jeu

(Jean Renoir, 1939)
Son of the painter, Renoir had to sell some of his dad's work to fund his early career. His recklessness paid off: he is now considered one of the first great cinema *auteurs*, praised for his set design, use of natural scenery and social critique. This masterpiece was a commercial flop when first released, however.

A Bout de Souffle

(Jean-Luc Godard, 1959)
New Wave directors marked a break with the past with a cinema where anything seemed possible. Challenging the convention of the staid studio-bound film of the 40-50s, Godard famously made his actors improvise and used hand-held cameras around the streets of Paris to achieve an infinitely fresher product.

Jules et Jim

(François Truffaut, 1962)
A foreigner's idea of the typical French movie: manic laughing, poetics and a love triangle. Truffaut, like his New Wave colleagues, was an innovator. Sound, montage and pace receive a thorough shake-down. So does the traditional woman's role, as Jeanne Moreau behaves like a raving coquette and gets away with it – as raving coquettes do.

Subway

(Luc Besson, 1985)
Besson and his peers exploited techniques used in television commercials and music clips to create a polished, fast-moving style that was popular with the kids but despised by traditionalist critics. The emphasis on 'look' over substance is forgivable at a first glance of Jean Reno with hair.

Les Amants du Pont-Neuf

(Leos Carax, 1991)
Les Amants was made at the breaking crest of the '*cinéma du look*' wave where style and production costs were becoming dangerously Americanised. To get the ambitious Hollywood-sized project finished involved not only the building of a replica Pont-Neuf bridge on a lake in Montpellier, but also the united support of just about the whole country.

Le Fabuleux Destin d'Amélie Poulain

(Jean-Pierre Jeunet, 2001)
The *Amélie* phenomenon injected a shot of pure glucose into the flagging energies and confidence of the French film industry. A winner in all categories: it has the brunette, kooky beauty, the stunning Parisian backdrop and the stellar international career. Just don't mention the Oscars.

Truffaut directing *Jules et Jim*

Arts & Entertainment

This impressive complex designed by Japanese architect Kenzo Tange is the place to see your favourite actor emblazoned across the vast 24m x 10m screen – the biggest in Paris. *Wheelchair access.*

MK2 Bibliothèque

128-162 av de France, 13th (08.92.68.14.07). M° Bibliothèque or Quai de la Gare. **Tickets** €8.50-€9; €6.50 students, 12-18s (Mon-Fri before 6pm); €5.50 under-12s; €4.90 before noon; €18 monthly pass. **Map** p407 M10.

This latest addition to the MK2 chain offers an all-in-one night out, with 14 screens, three restaurants, a bar that stays open till 5am at weekends and two-person 'love seats' (why not three, the prudes?). MK2 is a paradigm of imaginative programming that aims to bring arthouse to the masses. The Carte Le Pass offers unlimited access for €18 per month at any MK2. *Wheelchair access.*

Le Cinéma des Cinéastes

7 av de Clichy, 17th (01.53.42.40.20). M° Place Clichy. **Tickets** €6.60; €5.40 Wed, students, under-12s, over-60s. **Map** p401 G2.

Decorated to evoke old-fashioned film studios, this three-screen showcase of world cinema holds meet-the-director sessions and festivals of classic, foreign, gay and documentary films. *Cartes illimitées* (season tickets). *Bar-restaurant. Wheelchair access.*

La Géode

26 av Corentin-Cariou, 19th (08.92.68.45.40). M° Porte de la Villette. **Tickets** €8.75; €6.75 students. **Credit** MC, V. **Map** inset p407.

The OMNIMAX cinema is housed in a glorious, shiny geodesic dome at La Villette. The 1000m^2 hemispheric screen lets you experience 3-D plunges through natural scenery or animated adventures where the characters zoom out to greet you. *Wheelchair access (reserve ahead).*

MK2 Quai de Seine

14 quai de la Seine, 19th (08.36.68.14.07). M° Stalingrad. **Tickets** €8.20-€8.50; €6.50 students, under-18s (Mon-Fri before 6.30pm); €5.50 under-12s; €5.50 before noon. **Map** p407 M2.

MK2's flagship before it was superceded (if, that is, you think size matters – you do?) by the Bibliothèque site, the stylish six-screen complex also has a canal-side restaurant and exhibition space. *Wheelchair access.*

Art cinemas

Le Latina

20 rue du Temple, 4th (01.42.78.47.86/ www.lelatina.com). M° Hôtel de Ville. **Tickets** €7; €5.50 Mon, Tue, students, under-20s. **Map** p406 K6.

Representing 'the crossroads of Latin cultures', programming ranges from Argentinian to Romanian films. You can also do the Fred and Ginger to salsa or tango music with the €16 film-dinner-dancing deals on Monday and Wednesday evenings. *Restaurant.*

La Pagode. See p308.

Accattone

20 rue Cujas, 5th (01.46.33.86.86). M° Cluny La Sorbonne/RER Luxembourg. **Tickets** €6.50; €5.50 Wed, students, under-20s. **Map** p406 J8.

Named after Pasolini's first film, this tiny Latin Quarter cinema has a clear preference for old Italian art house flicks. However, there is plenty of room on the rolling weekly programme of around 30 films for the likes of Roeg, Oshima, Buñuel and Ken Russell.

Action

Action Ecoles *23 rue des Ecoles, 5th (01.43.29.79.89). M° Maubert-Mutualité.* **Tickets** €6.50; €5 students, under-20s. **Map** p406 J8.
Grand Action *5 rue des Ecoles, 5th (01.43.29.44.40). M° Cardinal-Lemoine.* **Tickets** €7; €5.50 students, under-20s. **Map** p406 K8.
Action Christine *4 rue Christine, 6th (01.43.29.11.30). M° Odéon.* **Tickets** €7; €5.50 students, under-20s. **Map** p406 J7.

A Left Bank feature since the early 80s, the Action group is renowned for screening new prints of old movies. Heaven for those nostalgic for 1940s and 50s Tinseltown classics and American independents.

Le Cinéma du Panthéon

13 rue Victor-Cousin, 5th (01.40.46.01.21). RER Luxembourg. **Tickets** €7; €5.50 Mon, Wed, students, 13-18s; €4 under-13s. **Map** p406 J8.

Paris' oldest surviving movie house (founded in 1907 in the Sorbonne gymnasium) is still a place to catch new, often obscure international films.

La Pagode

57bis rue de Babylone, 7th (01.45.55.48.48). M° St-François-Xavier. **Tickets** €7.30; €5.80 Mon, Wed, students, under-21s. **Map** p405 F7.

Wowser, what a cinema: two screens housed in a 19th-century replica of a Far Eastern pagoda that was given historic monument status in 1986.

Le Balzac

1 rue Balzac, 8th (01.45.61.10.60/ www.cinemabalzac.com). M° George V. **Tickets** €7; €5.50 Mon, Wed, students, under-18s, over-60s. **Map** p400 D4.

Built in 1935 with a mock ocean-liner foyer, Le Balzac scores high for design and programming.

Le Denfert

24 pl Denfert-Rochereau, 14th (01.43.21.41.01). M° Denfert-Rochereau. **Tickets** €6.50; €5 Mon, Wed, students, over-60s; €4.60 under-15s. **Map** p406 H10.

An eclectic repertory selection ranges from François Ozon and Kitano to short films and new animation, as well as new foreign films. *Wheelchair access.*

L'Entrepôt

7-9 rue Francis de Pressensé, 14th (08.36.68.05.87/ www.lentrepot.fr). M° Pernéty. **Tickets** €6.70; €5.40 students, over-60s; €4 under-12s. **Credit** MC, V. **Map** p405 F10.

Documentary, shorts, gay, Second and Third World cinema are preferred to the mainstream. A debate or a chance to meet the director often accompanies the film. *Café. Restaurant.*

Studio 28

10 rue Tholozé, 18th (01.46.06.36.07). M° Abbesses. **Tickets** €7; €5.80 students, under-12s. **Map** p405 H1.

Montmartre's historic Studio 28 was the venue for Cocteau's scandalous *L'Age d'Or*. Today it offers a decent repertory mix of classics and recent movies.

Public repertory institutions

Auditorium du Louvre

Musée du Louvre, 99 rue de Rivoli, 1st (01.40.20.51.86/www.louvre.fr). M° Palais Royal. **Tickets** €5; €3 under-26s. **Map** p406 H5.

This 420-seat auditorium was designed by IM Pei. Film screenings are sometimes related to the exhibitions; silent movies with live music are regulars.

Forum des Images

2 Grande Galerie, Porte St-Eustache, Forum des Halles, 1st (01.44.76.62.00/www.forumdesimages.net). M° Les Halles. **Open** 1-9pm Tue, Wed, Fri-Sun; 1-10pm Thur. Closed two weeks in Aug. **Tickets** €5.50 per day; €4.50 students, under-30s, membership available. **Map** p406 J5.

This archive is dedicated to Paris on celluloid. The Forum also screens the Rencontres Internationales du Cinéma (*see below*), the trash treats of L'Etrange Festival and films from the critics' selection at Cannes.

Centre Pompidou

rue St-Martin, 4th (01.44.78.12.33/ www.centrepompidou.fr). M° Hôtel de Ville. **Tickets** €5; €3 students. **Map** p406 K6.

Themed series, experimental and artists' films and a weekly documentary session give a flavour of what's on. This is the venue for the *Cinéma du Réel* festival in March which, for 25 years, has been promoting documentary film. *Wheelchair access.*

La Cinémathèque Française

Palais de Chaillot, 7 av Albert-de-Mun, 16th (01.56.26.01.01/www.cinemathequefrancaise.com). M° Trocadéro. **Tickets** €4.73; €3 students. **Map** p404 C5.

Salle Grands Boulevards, 42 bd Bonne-Nouvelle, 10th (01.56.26.01.01). M° Bonne Nouvelle. **Tickets** €4.73; €3 students, membership available. **Map** p404 J4.

The Cinémathèque was vital in shaping the New Wave directors in the late 1950s.

Festivals & special events

Côté Court

Ciné 104, 104 av Jean Lolive, 93500 Pantin (01.48.46.95.08). M° Eglise de Pantin. **Dates** Mar-Apr.

A great selection of new and old short films.

Festival international de films de femmes

Maison des Arts, pl Salvador-Allende, 94040 Créteil (01.49.80.38.98). M° Créteil-Préfecture. **Dates** Mar-Apr.

A selection of retrospectives and new international films by female directors. *Wheelchair access.*

Rencontres internationales du cinéma

Forum des Images (see above). **Dates** Oct-Nov.

A global choice of new independent features, documentary and short films, many screened in the presence of their directors.

Paris Cinéma

Various locations (01 55 25 55 25/ www.pariscinema.org). **Dates** July.

The Mairie is funding this new celebration of the silver screen. Its debut year was innovative, including short, documentary, experimental and animated films along with a host of avant-premières and stars.

Cinéma au clair du lune

Various locations (01.44.76.62.18/ www.forumdesimages.net). **Dates** Aug.

At this atmospheric festival you can sit and picnic under the stars in the location of the film projected on the giant open-air screen before you.

Le Cinéma en plein air

Parc de la Villette, 19th (01.40.03.76.92/www.la-villette.com). M° Porte de Pantin. **Dates** mid-July to mid Aug.

Thousands turn up to see their favourite flicks projected on to an inflatable screen as they lounge decadently on the grass.

Galleries

Knitting, empty bottles, poetry and torn posters: not the contents of a hermit's Portakabin, just the usual kind of stuff you find in a Paris gallery.

Stumble down a dark flight of stairs to a barely flickering screen of light, tiptoe across a floor of crunchy lava, shiver in front of a billowing curtain... Heat, smell and sound can all feature in artworks today, but then equally so can installation, video, sculpture and, yes, even, painting and drawing. Confused? You might be, but then that's one of the reactions the artist probably wants – to get you wondering what it's all about with references that range from popular culture to the long annals of art history.

If the French art scene lacks the outlandish showbiz antics of London or the commercial weight of New York and Cologne, head inside the city's numerous art galleries and you'll discover an eclectic and highly international scene. 2003 sadly saw the demise of the adventurous Galerie Jennifer Flay, but **Galerie Yvon Lambert**, **Chantal Crousel** or **Almine Rech** remain places to watch, and new galleries, such as **Cosmic**, **Maisonneuve** and **Jean Brolly**, continue to pop up, as do more alternative and artist-run spaces.

For innovative work and international names head for the northern Marais and the streets near the Centre Pompidou, where historic *hôtels particuliers* may well be the haven for video and installation art, or to 'Louise', the nucleus of young galleries in the 13th. Galleries in St-Germain-des-Prés, home of the avant-garde in the 1950s and 60s, largely confine themselves to traditional sculpture and painting, those near the Champs-Elysées present big modern and contemporary names. The international art fair FIAC in early October gives a quick fix on the gallery scene, both French and international; Paris-Photo in mid November draws specialists in classic and contemporary photography.

French art magazines include monthlies *Beaux Arts*, *L'Oeil*, bilingual *Art Press* and the fortnightly *Journal des Arts*. *Galeries Mode d'Emploi* (Marais/Bastille/Louise-Weiss/ www.artsiders.com) and *Association des Galeries* listings foldouts (Left and Right Bank/ suburban cultural centres) and flyers can be picked up inside galleries. Best info on the web is on www.paris-art.com, which also publishes the comprehensive free *paris-art* booklet every two months. Most galleries close on Monday, and from late July to early September and over Christmas. Admission to all is free.

Beaubourg & the Marais

Galerie Jean Brolly

16 rue de Montmorency, 3rd (01.42.78.88.02). M° Rambuteau. **Open** 11am-7pm Tue-Sat. **Map** p402 K5.

Collector Jean Brolly opened his gallery in 2002. He shows mainly painting, such as nostalgic images by Adam Adach and conceptual, manipulated canvases by Claude Rutault and Stephen Parrino.

Galerie Chantal Crousel

40 rue Quincampoix, 4th (01.42.77.38.87/ www.crousel.com). M° Rambuteau/RER Châtelet-Les Halles. **Open** 11am-7pm Tue-Sat. **Map** p406 J6.

Crousel features some of the hottest names today, including Rikrit Tiravanija, Thomas Hirschhorn, Graham Gussin and rising French stars Albanian-born Anri Sala and Melik Ohanian. An on-going series entitled 'Géographies' explores notions of homelands, migrations and frontiers.

Galerie Cent 8

108 rue Vieille-du-Temple, 3rd (01.42.74.53.57). M° Filles du Calvaire. **Open** 10.30am-1pm, 2.30-7pm Tue-Sat. **Map** p406 L5.

Stimulating, varied shows take in all media from paintings of Rémy Zaugg and Jugnet & Clairet, photographer Esko Männikki or the genetics/anthropological explorations of Christine Borland.

Cosmic Galerie

76 rue de Turenne, 3rd (01.42.71.72.73). M° Filles du Calvaire. **Open** noon-7pm Tue-Sat. **Map** p402 L5.

Matt Collishaw and Vanessa Beecroft lead the hip brigade at this spacious gallery which opened in 2002 over three floors of a Marais building

Galerie de France

54 rue de la Verrerie, 4th (01.42.74.38.00). M° Hôtel de Ville. **Open** 11am-7pm Tue-Sat. **Map** p406 K6.

This is one of the rare galleries that runs through the whole 20th century and beyond, often featuring singular figures who don't fit neatly into any movement, such as painter Eugène Leroy or the mechanical contraptions of Rebecca Horn.

Galerie Frank

7 rue St-Claude, 3rd (01.48.87.50.04/ www.galeriefrank.com). M° St-Sébastien-Froissart. **Open** 2-7pm Tue-Sat. **Map** p402 L6.

Shows here might feature the painted Tergal colour scapes of Cécile Bart, wordworks by Charles Sandison, drawings and knitting by Pierrette Bloch and a batch of Finnish artists.

Galerie Marian Goodman

79 rue du Temple, 3rd (01.48.04.70.52). M° Rambuteau. **Open** 11am-7pm Tue-Sat. **Map** p406 K6.

The New York gallerist has an impressive Paris outpost in a 17th-century mansion. Alongside established names like Jeff Wall and Lothar Baumgarten, she has snapped up brilliant Brit videomaker Steve McQueen and fab Finn Eija-Liisa Ahtila.

Galerie Karsten Greve

5 rue Debelleyme, 3rd (01.42.77.19.37). M° Filles du Calvaire. **Open** 11am-7pm Tue-Sat. **Map** p402 L5.

The Cologne gallery's Paris outpost is the venue for retrospective-style displays of top-ranking artists. Jannis Kounellis, Louise Bourgeois, Pierre Soulages and Jean Dubuffet have all featured in recent years.

Galerie Yvon Lambert

108 rue Vieille-du-Temple, 3rd (01.42.71.09.33). M° Filles du Calvaire. **Open** 10am-1pm, 2.30-7pm Tue-Fri; 10am-7pm Sat. **Map** p402 L5.

Probably France's most important gallery (with a New York offshoot since 2003), Lambert pulls out all the stops, whether it's the latest production by a major international name, such as Nan Goldin or Christian Boltanski, new installation by Claude Levêque or Carlos Amorales, or the pick of the young video generation.

Galerie Nelson

40 rue Quincampoix, 4th (01.42.71.74.56/ www.galerie-nelson.com). M° Châtelet or Rambuteau. **Open** 2-7pm Tue-Sat. **Map** p406 J6.

Nelson was the first gallery in France to show Thomas Ruff, Thomas Schutte and Rodney Graham, and also features rising French artists Guillaume Paris and Stéphane Calais, as well as representing the late Fluxus maverick Robert Filliou.

Galerie Nathalie Obadia

3 rue du Cloître-St-Merri, 4th (01.42.74.67.68). M° Rambuteau. **Open** 11am-7pm Tue-Sat. **Map** p406 K6.

Nathalie Obadia recently moved to spacious new premises. Jean-Marc Bustamente, Manuel Ocampo and Pascal Pinaud are regulars, as are many female artists, including Fiona Rae, Carole Benzaken and Jessica Stockholder.

Gilles Peyroulet & Cie

80 rue Quincampoix, 3rd (01.42.78.85.11). M° Rambuteau or Etienne Marcel. **Open** 2-7pm Tue-Sat. **Map** p402 K5.

Peyroulet is strongest with photo-based artists including Marin Kasimir and Nick Waplington, but he also cleverly bridges the gap between fine art and design, with items commissioned from young designers, such as Frédéric Ruyant and Matali

Will Cotton at **Galerie Templon**

Crasset, and archival-type shows of 20th-century pioneers such as Eileen Gray and Alvar Aalto.

Galerie Thaddaeus Ropac
7 rue Debelleyme, 3rd (01.42.72.99.00/ www.ropac.net). M° St-Sébastien-Froissart or St-Paul. **Open** 10am-7pm Tue-Sat. **Map** p402 L5.
The Austrian-owned gallery is strong on American Pop, neo-Pop and neo-Geo (Warhol, Tom Sachs, Alex Katz), but also features major artists Ilya Kabakov, Gilbert & George, Anthony Gormley, Sylvie Fleury, and quirky theme shows.

Galerie Templon
30 rue Beaubourg, 3rd (01.42.72.14.10). M° Rambuteau. **Open** 10am-7pm Mon-Sat. **Map** p402 K5.
Templon mainly shows well-known painters, which is perhaps why his gallery is a favourite with the French art establishment. David Salle, Jean-Marc Alberola, Claude Viallat, Vincent Corpet are regulars along with eternally youthful Raymond Hains and he's recently added some young German artists.

Galerie Chez Valentin
9 rue St-Gilles, 3rd (01.48.87.42.55). M° Chemin Vert. **Open** 2.30-7pm Tue-Sat. **Map** p407 L6.
A sense of urban angst pervades the work here. Look for the creeping detritus installations and videos of Véronique Boudier, photos by Nicolas Moulin, videos by François Nouguiès and the projects of 2003 Prix Duchamp winner Mathieu Mercier.

Galerie Anne de Villepoix
43 rue de Montmorency, 3rd (01.42.78.32.24/ www.annedevillepoix.com). M° Rambuteau. **Open** 10am-7pm Tue-Sat. **Map** p402 K5.
In her spacious quarters near the Centre Pompidou, Anne de Villepoix's generational mix takes in established US names Sam Samore and Chris Burden or Austrian Erwin Wurm, and a younger conceptual set including Franck Scurti, Gillian Wearing, Jean-Luc Moulène and Valérie Jouve.

Galerie Zurcher
56 rue Chapon, 3rd (01.42.72.82.20). M° Arts et Métiers. **Open** 11am-7pm Tue-Sat; 2-6pm Sun. **Map** p402 K5.
Young artists with a new take on painting and video include Camille Vivier, Gwen Ravillous, Philippe Hurteau and Dan Hays.

Bastille & northeast Paris

Galerie Alain Gutharc
47 rue de Lappe, 11th (01.47.00.32.10). M° Bastille. **Open** 2-7pm Tue-Fri; 11am-1pm, 2-7pm Sat. **Map** p407 M7.
Gutharc talent-spots young French artists. Check out Delphine Kreuter's fetishistic, colour-saturated slice-of-life photos, quirky text pieces by Antoinette Ohanassian and the videos by Joël Bartolomméo and former fashion stylist François-Xavier Courrèges. There's also an annual design show.

Galerie Maisonneuve
24-32 rue des Amandiers, 20th (01.43.66.23.99/ www.saintmonday.net). M° Père Lachaise. **Open** 2-7pm Tue-Sat. **Map** p403 P5.
Its location on the fifth floor of a block of modern flats immediately gives this gallery a somewhat out-of-the-ordinary atmosphere. The programme tends to involve installation/happenings from artists such as Claudia Triozzi and Jan Kopp, or Jota Castro, whose *Love Hotel* could be rented for the night.

Champs-Elysées

Galerie Lelong
13 rue de Téhéran, 8th (01.45.63.13.19). M° Miromesnil. **Open** 10.30am-6pm Tue-Fri; 2-6.30pm Sat. **Map** p401 E3.
Lelong shows bankable, post-1945, international names including Alechinsky, Bacon, Hockney, Kounellis, Scully. Branches in New York and Zurich.

Galerie Jérôme de Noirmont
38 av Matignon, 8th (01.42.89.89.00/ www.denoirmont.com). M° Miromesnil. **Open** 10am-1pm, 2.30-7pm Mon-Sat. **Map** p401 E4.
The location could arouse suspicions that Noirmont sells purely business art. Not a bit of it – eye-catching shows by A.R. Penck, Clemente, Jeff Koons, Pierre et Gilles, Shirin Neshat and Bettina Rheims make this gallery worth the trip.

St-Germain-des-Prés

Galerie 1900-2000
8 rue Bonaparte, 6th (01.43.25.84.20/ www.galerie1900-2000.com). M° St-Germain-des-Prés. **Open** 2-7pm Mon; 10am-12.30pm, 2-7pm Tue-Sat. **Map** p406 H7.
Marcel and David Fleiss show a strong predilection for Surrealism, dada, Pop art and Fluxus, with works on paper by anyone from Breton and De Chirico to Lichtenstein, plus the occasional photo show.

Galerie Jeanne Bucher
53 rue de Seine, 6th (01.44.41.69.65). M° Mabillon or Odéon. **Open** 9am-6.30pm Tue-Fri; 10am-12.30pm, 2.30-6pm Sat. **Map** p406 H7.
Based on the Left Bank since 1925, Bucher specialises in postwar abstract (De Staël, Viera da Silva, Rebeyrolle) and Cobra painters.

Galerie Loevenbruck
40 rue de Seine, 6th (01.53.10.85.68/ www.loevenbruck.com). M° Mabillon. **Open** 2-7pm Tue-Sat. **Map** p405 H6.
New and funky with a taste for visual jokes from artists including Virginie Barré, Bruno Peinado, Alain Declerq and Olivier Blanckart.

Galerie Maeght
42 rue du Bac, 7th (01.45.48.45.15/ www.galeriemaeght.com). M° Rue du Bac. **Open** 10am-6pm Mon; 9.30am-7pm Tue-Sat. **Map** p405 G6.

The gallery founded by Aimé Maeght in 1946 is now run by his grandchildren, but pales against a past that included Léger, Chagall, Giacometti and Miró.

Galerie Denise René

196 bd St-Germain, 7th (01.42.22.77.57/ www.deniserene.com). M° St-Germain-des-Prés or Rue du Bac. **Open** 10am-1pm, 2-7pm Tue-Fri; 11am-1pm, 2-7pm Sat. **Map** p406 H7.

Denise René is a Paris institution and has remained committed to kinetic art, Op art and geometrical abstraction ever since Tinguely first presented his machines here in the 1950s.

Branch: 22 rue Charlot, 3rd (01.48.87.73.94).

Galerie Darthea Speyer

6 rue Jacques-Callot, 6th (01.43.54.78.41). M° Mabillon or Odéon. **Open** 11am-12.45pm, 2-7pm Tue-Fri; 11am-7pm Sat. **Map** p406 H6.

Colourful, representational painting and sculpture and naïve artists are the speciality here. It can be kitsch, but at best features the political expressionism of Golub or American dreams of Paschke.

Galerie G-P et N Vallois

36 rue de Seine, 6th (01.46.34.61.07). M° Mabillon or Odéon. **Open** 10.30am-1pm, 2-7pm Mon-Sat. **Map** p406 H7.

G-P & N Vallois sticks out as the only truly contemporary gallery left in St-Germain, but is worth the detour for *nouveau réaliste* torn-poster veteran Jacques Villeglé, and a clutch of young artists: installations by Gilles Barbier, urban interventions by Alain Bublex, polders by Tatiana Trouvé.

Galerie Lara Vincy

47 rue de Seine, 6th (01.43.26.72.51). M° Mabillon or St-Germain-des-Prés. **Open** 2.30-7.30pm Mon; 11am-12.30pm, 2.30-7.30pm Tue-Sat. **Map** p406 H7.

Lara Vincy is one of the few characters to retain something of the old St-Germain spirit and sense of 1970s Fluxus-style 'happenings'. Interesting theme and solo shows include master of the epigram, Ben, and artists' text, music, performance-related pieces.

Scène Est: rue Louise-Weiss

&:

10 rue Duchefdelaville, 13th (gb agency 01.53.79.07.13; in SITU 01.53.79.06.12; Christophe Daviet-Thery 01.53.79.05.95). M° Chevaleret. **Open** 11am-7pm Tue-Sat. **Map** p407 M10.

This gallery is shared in rotation between gb agency (which works mainly with young artists), Fabienne Leclerc's in SITU (whose artists include Mark Dion, Gary Hill, young painter Bruno Perramant plus Florence Paradeis and Patrick Corillon), and artists' book publisher Christophe Daviet-Thery.

Air de Paris

32 rue Louise-Weiss, 13th (01.44.23.02.77/ www.airdeparis.com). M° Chevaleret. **Open** 2-7pm Tue-Sat. **Map** p407 M10.

This gallery is named after Duchamp's famous bottle of air. Shows tend to be highly experimental and neo-conceptual, if not somewhat chaotic. A young international stable includes Liam Gillick, Pierre Joseph, Carsten Höller, Bruno Serralongue, Sarah Morris, muralist Lily van der Stokker and fashionista Inez van Lamsweede.

Galerie Almine Rech

127 rue du Chevaleret, 13th (01.45.83.71.90/ galeriealminerech.com). M° Chevaleret. **Open** 11am-7pm Tue-Sat. **Map** p407 M10.

A varied but classy programme includes light maestro James Turrell, installations by Ugo Rondinone and films by Ange Leccia. Annelies Strba, Serge Comte and Bruno Rousséaud feature in 2004.

Jousse Entreprise

24 & 34 rue Louise-Weiss, 13th (01.53.82.13.60/ www.jousse-entreprise.com). M° Chevaleret. **Open** 11am-1pm, 2-7pm Tue-Sat. **Map** p407 M10.

Philippe Jousse shows contemporary artists, such as Matthieu Laurette and Thomas Grünfeld, with the 1950s avant-garde furniture of Jean Prouvé and lighting of Serge Mouille as a sideline.

Galerie Kréo

22 rue Duchefdelaville, 13th (01.53.60.14.68). M° Chevaleret. **Open** 11am-7pm Tue-Sat. **Map** p407 M10.

The *bricoleurs*

An anarchic spirit is flourishing alongside the glossy production values and advanced technology of videos and Cibachrome photos. Works by the José Bovés of the art world may look homespun but, just as with the leader of the Confédération Paysanne, recycled materials and a DIY-aesthetic hide some sophisticated organisation. Thomas Hirschhorn (Chantal Crousel) is a master of *bricolage,* in staggering installations composed largely of packing tape, tin foil and sheets of polythene – with a few crucial additions, such as Chanel handbags – that take on officialdom, capitalism and institutions like Nato. Christelle Familiari crochets with coloured wire from defunct TVs, in works about the body. Mathieu Mercier (Chez Valentin) makes ambitious architectural constructions. Alain Bublex (G-P & N Vallois) drives his customised Renault 5 into madcap urbanisation schemes. AAA Corp, a cooperative from the depths of central France, cobbles together broadcasting antennae and power stations. Malachi Farrell's clattering, Heath-Robinson-esque contraptions might be about pollution or the war in Iraq. Whoever said political activism was dead?

Design gallery Kréo combines retrospectives and an agency commissioning limited-edition pieces. Look for international names Ron Arad, Marc Newson and Jasper Conran, as well as native Radi Designers, Martin Szekely and the still-hotshot boys to beat, the Bourrellec brothers.

Galerie Emmanuel Perrotin

5 & 30 rue Louise-Weiss, 13th (01.42.16.79.79/ www.galerieperrotin.com). M° Chevaleret. **Open** 11am-7pm Tue-Sat. **Map** p407 M10.

A very influential gallery, this. Perrotin is the place to catch up on the provocative young Japanese generation, including Noritoshi Hirakawa, manga maniac Takashi Murakami and glossy cyber-punkette Mariko Mori. Sophie Calle and Bernard Frize head the native talent.

Galerie Praz-Devallade

28 rue Louise-Weiss, 13th (01.45.86.20.00). M° Chevaleret. **Open** 11am-7pm Tue-Sat. **Map** p407 M10.

A varied selection includes the crazy drawings of Los Angeles artist Jim Shaw and the elaborate food-meets-feminism photos of Natacha Lesueur, so you certainly can't fault them on variety.

Photography

Photoworks of all sorts are now an integral part of contemporary art and can be found in many of the above galleries, and at branches of Fnac. The biannual Mois de la Photo (next in Nov 2004) covers both historic and contemporary work, as does Paris Photo salon in November.

Galerie Anne Barrault

22 rue St-Claude, 3rd (01.44.78.91.67). M° St-Sébastien-Froissart. **Open** 2-7pm Tue-Sat. **Map** p402 L6.

A small space, featuring the work of mainly French and Italian photographers, which all makes for an intriguing visit.

Galerie Michèle Chomette

24 rue Beaubourg, 3rd (01.42.78.05.62). M° Rambuteau. **Open** 2-7pm Tue-Sat. **Map** p402 K5.

Classical and experimental photography. Regulars Alain Fleischer, Eric Rondepierre, Lewis Baltz, Felten & Massinger, Bernard Plossu are shown alongside historic masters.

Galerie Kamel Mennour

60 rue Mazarine, 6th (01.56.24.03.63/ www.galeriemennour.com). M° Odéon. **Open** 10.30am-7.30pm Mon-Sat. **Map** p405 H6/H7.

An oh-so fashionable, often provocative (but is it any good?), list includes Nobuyoshi Araki, Peter Beard, Kriki, David LaChapelle and filmmaker Larry Clark.

Galerie Françoise Paviot

57 rue Ste-Anne, 2nd (01.42.60.10.01). M° Quatre Septembre. **Open** 2.30-7pm Tue-Sat. **Map** p402 H4.

Paviot presents contemporary and historic photographers with an emphasis on the great Surrealists.

Guillaume Paris at **Galerie Nelson**. See p310.

Artist-run & alternative spaces

Chez Robert Electron Libre

59 rue de Rivoli, 1st. M° Châtelet. **Open** 1-7pm Mon-Sat. **Map** p406 J6.

This daisy-decked art squat is a hive of paint-spattered activity. As well as looking in on the inhabitants' individual studios and living spaces, it also has a gallery putting on temporary shows.

Galerie Eof

15 rue St-Fiacre, 2nd (01.53.40.72.22). M° Bonne-Nouvelle. **Open** call for details. **Map** p402 J4.

This space puts on shows that vary from solo show to multi-media collaborations.

Glassbox

113bis rue Oberkampf, 11th (01.43.38.02.82/ www.icono.org/glassbox). M° Parmentier. **Open** 2-7pm Wed-Sat. **Map** p403 N5.

Politically oriented shows have included art, poetry, design and exchanges with other artists' collectives.

Immanence

21 av du Maine, 15th (01.42.22.05.68/www.art-immanence.org). M° Montparnasse-Bienvenüe. **Open** 2-7pm Thur-Sat. **Map** p405 F8.

Created by two artists in 2000 in a picturesque alley of old Montparnasse artists' studios, Immanence features installations and photo shows.

Public

4 impasse Beaubourg, 3rd (01.42.71.49.51). M° Rambuteau. **Open** times vary. **Map** p402 K5.

An experimental programme of sculptures, installations, short video projects and debates.

Gay & Lesbian

Paris' pink portals are pert and perfectly penetrable, and 2004 is even seeing some new sapphic rendezvous.

How do you put the gay back into a Paree that's gone just un peu drab over recent years? Openly gay Bertrand Delanoë's election as Mayor in 2001 did no harm, and neither has the Mairie's attempt at pulling in more pink tourists. Some say, however, that the Paris scene has hit a plateau. A couple of old favourites have shut up shop: Le Scorp is no more, and the outrageous Black Beur Blanc gay night at Folies Pigalle is gone. Even the notoriously sniffy door whores at Le Queen seem to let anyone in these days.

Happily, the sapphic scene is burgeoning. Paris' famously reclusive dykes have come out of hiding and the whole homosexual scene is, of course, all the better for it. Classic bars like **Le Champmeslé** and **Les Scandaleuses** have been shored up by some new-comers and, more importantly, a newly confident attitude.

A healthy bit of cross-pollination has taken place as Londoners have finally woken up to the fact that Paris is open later than home. If you fancy a change of scene, try Eurostar's cheapo clubbers' specials – you catch the last train from Waterloo, alight in Paris, spend Saturday night on the tiles and sleep it off on the first train back early Sunday morning.

For the latest goings-on, pick up a copy of the free mags, like e-m@il or illico, found in most gay bars in the 3rd and 4th – or buy a copy of the excellent gay magazine *Têtu* from pretty much any news kiosk in the city. Below, all listings are in order of arrondissement.

Bars & cafés

Banana Café

13 rue de la Ferronnerie, 1st (01.42.33.35.31/ www.bananacafeparis.com). M° Châtelet. **Open** 5.30pm-7am daily. **Credit** AmEx, MC, V. **Map** p402 J5.

One of Paris' only open-all-night gay bars – which guarantees a steady throng of cruisers craning to watch the go-go boys gyrating on the bar-top. The worse-for-wear head downstairs, to sing-a-long show tunes around the piano. *Wheelchair access.*

Eleven Café

11 rue de la Ferronnerie, 1st (01.42.36.42.66). M° Châtelet. **Open** noon-2am Mon-Sat. **Credit** MC, V. **Map** p402 J5

Friendly, trad terrace café with gay leanings (and not-very-gay wicker seats) in the pedestrianised heart of Les Halles. It's a good daytime spot for a heel-cooling coffee or a lunch spent admiring the catwalk show of cuties promenading with their shopping bags. The Saturday lunch (prix fixe 11) attracts muscle couples and Marianne Faithful lookalikes. During happy hour (7-9pm), you buy one drink get one free.

Le Tropic Café

66 rue des Lombards, 1st (01.40.13.92.62). M° Châtelet. **Open** noon-5am daily. **Credit** AmEx, MC, V. **Map** p405 G6.

This bright, upbeat café-bar is where young clubbers fuel up around midnight on filling Frenchified tapas in between cocktails and shots: plates of goat's cheese in breadcrumbs and the like from 3.50, served up by shorts-wearing staff. The noisy techno terrace is heated in winter. Le Tropic also has possibly the longest happy hour in gay Paree, from 6pm till 9pm nightly. *Wheelchair access.*

Amnesia

42 rue Vieille-du-Temple, 4th (01.42.72.16.94). M° Hôtel de Ville. **Open** 11am-2am daily. **Credit** DC, MC, V. **Map** p406 K6.

This ambient bar is the height of cosiness. Stools at the bar for a drink *tout seul*, mirrored walls, leather armchairs in secluded corners for relaxing with mates; here, comfort is guaranteed. The DJs remove the bass so you don't have to shout. It's a different story as the night wears on and the clientele slope into the basement sweatbox. Un must.

Le Central

33 rue Vieille-du-Temple, 4th (01.48.87.99.33). M° Hôtel de Ville. **Open** 4pm-2am Mon-Fri; 2pm-2am Sat, Sun. **Credit** MC, V. **Map** p406 K6.

One of the oldest gay bars in Paris, and she's feeling her age (30-plus years), now the bright young things have moved on to sprucer joints. Small, and handy for a quick *pression* in the Marais but during a slow night you'll rattle around, the silence punctuated only by the scrape of bar stools.

Le Coffee-Shop

3 rue Ste-Croix-de-la-Bretonnerie, 4th (01.42.74.24.21). M° Hôtel de Ville. **Open** 10am-2am daily. **No credit cards**. **Map** p406 K6.

Mini-landmark snack bar that's been keeping the Marais boys in café au lait and gossip for more than two decades, morning, noon and night.

Le Cox

15 rue des Archives, 4th (01.42.72.08.00). M° Hôtel de Ville. **Open** 1pm-2am daily. **No credit cards.** **Map** p406 K6.

QG

Despite the kitsch baroque style – what were they thinking with that animal mural? – this is one of the Marais' hottest outposts, a gay zoo that sure packs them in. Afternoons are sedate, but after dark out come the nighthawks. In the summer, they're spilling out on the street by 8pm. Make sure you stop by the animal house.

Le Duplex

25 rue Michel-le-Comte, 3rd (01.42.72.80.86). M° Rambuteau. **Open** 8pm-2am daily. **Credit** MC, V. **Map** p402 K5.

Despite all the trappings of a philo-café – art on the walls (changed every month), an educated crowd of students, professors and saloon politicos, a permanent smoky fug – this small split-level bar doubles up as a championship cruising ground. Pull up a stool and get, er, philosophical.

Okawa

40 rue Vieille-du-Temple, 4th (01.48.04.30.69). M° Hôtel de Ville. **Open** 10am-2am daily. **Credit** MC, V. **Map** p406 L6.

Impossible to miss this low-lit corner café-bar done out in lumberjack chic. It's an undressy, straight-friendly place with a fifty-fifty gay-lesbian split, and there are always a few high-backed stools and soft poufs free, except during fortune-telling sessions.

Open Café

17 rue des Archives, 4th (01.42.72.26.18). M° Hôtel de Ville. **Open** 11am-2am Mon-Thur, Sun; 11am-4am Fri, Sat. **Credit** MC, V. **Map** p406 K6.

A magnetic corner bar where many gay boys meet up before a night out. The spectacular, gender-free WCs are a talking point: the urinals comprise a 'weeping wall' running with water, and there's a presumably ironic squat loo, too. The management also runs the Open Bar Coffee Shop at 12 rue du Temple.

Quetzal

10 rue de la Verrerie, 4th (01.48.87.99.07/ www.quetzalbar.com). M° Hôtel de Ville. **Open** 5pm-5am daily. **Credit** MC, V. **Map** p406 K6.

The cruisiest bar in the Marais, with a posey front bar popular with beur boys, and a dancier back area full of muscle men. Pick up, or move on to a club.

Le Thermik

7 rue de la Verrerie, 4th (01.44.78.08.18). M° Hôtel de Ville. **Open** 7pm-2am daily. **No credit cards. Map** p406 K6.

An intimate, nicely rough-at-the-edges friends' drinking bar. Popular with a harder crowd looking for a pre-club warm-up, it belies its tough-nut credential by playing Stock, Aitken and Waterman 12-inch mixes.

Restaurants

L'Amazonial

3 rue Ste-Opportune, 1st (01.42.33.53.13). M° Châtelet. **Open** noon-1pm, 6pm-2am daily (last orders 1.30am). **Credit** AmEx, MC, V. **Map** p402 J6.

Paris' largest gay restaurant features decent French cuisine but this place is more about the tight T-shirted waiters than the dishes set before you.

Pig'z

5 rue Marie-Stuart, 2nd (01.42.33.05.89/www.pigz.fr) M° Etienne Marcel or Sentier. **Open** noon-midnight Tue-Sun. **Credit** MC, V. **Map** p402 J5 .

Where gay gourmets pig out on a classic fusion menu including Scottish salmon with lemon vinaigrette as a starter, Oriental-influenced chicken, and ravioli stuffed with button mushrooms.

Aux Trois Petits Cochons

31 rue Tiquetonne, 2nd (01.42.33.39.69/ www.auxtroispetitscochons.com). M° Etienne Marcel. **Open** 8.30pm-1am daily. Closed Aug. **Credit** AmEx, MC, V. **Map** p402 J5 .

Three Little Pigs eschews international boystown cuisine in favour of a tasty, daily-changing menu.

Maison Rouge

13 rue des Archives, 4th (01.42.71.69.69). M° Hôtel de Ville. **Open** noon-3pm, 8pm-midnight daily. **Credit** MC, V. **Map** p406 K6.

It's all space-creating mirrors, acres of chrome, and white, white walls. Besides the adventurous French menu interpreted by an Italian chef, it offers ringside seats for the catwalk along rue des Archives; the windows swing open for almost-terrace dining.

Au Tiborg

29 rue du Bourg-Tibourg, 4th (01.42.74.45.25). M° Hôtel de Ville. **Open** 7pm-midnight daily. **Credit** MC, V. **Map** p406 K6.

A beamed roof, glazed terracotta jugs and walls covered with framed paintings – hallmarks of many a timewarped French restaurant. Only in this one, in a Marais side-street opposite a gay sauna, there are gay and lesbian couples on every table. Besides the meaty dishes of the day and à la carte options there's a vegetarian *formule* for 15.

Le Trésor

5-7 rue du Trésor, 4th (01.42.71.35.17). M° Hôtel de Ville. **Open** noon-2am daily. **Credit** MC, V. **Map** p406 K6.

Looking to justify a peek at the 'destination' toilets at Rocco de Rubiens' white and red wonderland, that's more VIP lounge than Marais restaurant? How about the tuna in sesame crust, the 32 set menu, or the cold-cut brunch at weekends? Magic.

Men-only clubs

Le Transfert

3 rue de la Sourdière, 1st (01.42.60.48.42). M° Tuileries or Pyramides. **Open** midnight-7am Mon-Sat, 4-11pm certain Sundays. **Credit** AmEx, MC, V. **Map** p401 G5.

Small leather and SM bar mostly frequented by dedicated regulars, though trainers fetishists also get their kicks here at a special Sunday nighter. At other times, it only ever gets going in the wee hours.

La TV en rose

Would you pay €9 a month for a gay and lesbian cable channel? The producers of France's rose-tinted station know the answer has to be *oui*, if Pink TV is to survive.

Launched in November 2003, Pink TV is devoted to round-the-clock gay programming. Subscribers get pink-friendly news, dramas, films and music clip shows. You get it: a kind of CNN meets HBO meets TCM meets MTV but with a gay-lesbian-bisexual-transgender twist. Cute, maybe, but is it enough?

'We want to give gays innovative programmes that will inspire,' says Pascal Houzelot, head of Pink TV. 'European documentaries, arthouse films, and – why not? – a month dedicated to the movies of Brad Pitt'. Pink TV has an annual budget of €11.5m and a commitment to plough 23.5% of its turnover into French-based broadcasting.

This is not, Houzelot stresses, a community station, but 'gay television for the whole public. I want it to be a de-ghettoiser. It mustn't be sectarian, aggressive or leave a nasty taste.'

Pink and fluffy it may be, but it's also – controversially – a little blue, too. Before launching, the channel announced its intention to carry 'les films-X' (up to 208 porn programmes a year). The decision, says Houzelot, was commercial. 'My channel will not be a porn channel,' he insists, 'but there will be four X-rated films a week. This represents a few hours of the schedule. Porn is an integral part of gay culture, and the economics of a gay station requires it'.

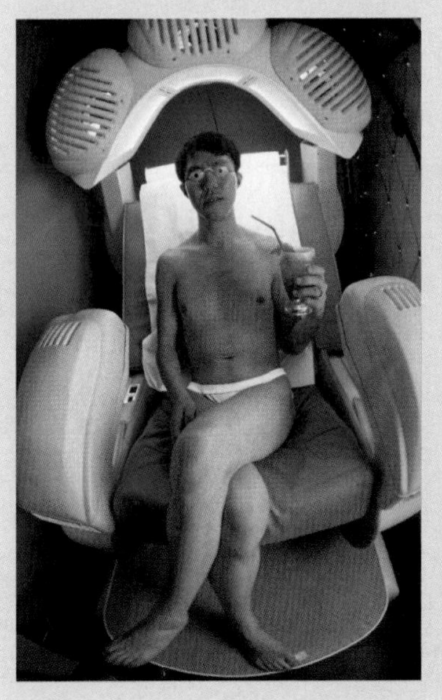

The porn thing is a sticking point. The licence for Pink TV to carry hardcore content was granted within strict parameters: such material can only be shown between midnight and 5am, and must be double-encrypted. Subscribers must be given the option of declining to take the hardcore elements. Regulators also insist that Pink TV not be allowed into cable packages offering programming for children and teenagers.

Houzelot admits he had another problem with the porn – sourcing good lesbian stuff. 'Most films do not meet the needs of lesbians,' he says. 'They are hetero fantasies. I want films to satisfy the lesbian public, and there aren't many of them'.

His decision to fight for the right to peddle pornography after hours was steeled by the fate of the world's first cable channel devoted to gay programming, Canada's PrideVision TV. Launched in 2001, it attracted only 22,000 subscribers before being sold.

However, for gay broadcasting success stories, Houzelot need not look far from home. Paris' gay radio station, Fréquence Gai, launched in the 1980s, became so popular that in 1999 it broke free from its gay roots and turned into an urban station *non segmentante*. Still pumping out dance, it's now called Radio FG and gone are the raunchy same-sex personal ads that spiced up the late-night airwaves. Since it dropped its gay tag, FG's audience figures have risen, by 2.6 per cent in 2002 to almost 250,000.

The gay press has a healthy glow. Launched in 1995, *Têtu* – which mixes high fashion with agit-prop community politics – saw its sales rise by more than a quarter in 2002; more than 40,000 copies are now shifted each month. Its biannual travel spin-off, *Têtu Plage*, is as prized a feature on trendy coffee tables as *Wallpaper*. Chic femmes-about-town can be spotted with it, and Paris' newstands give it pride of place in their displays. So how will Pink TV fare in town? By 2007, it needs to have around 200,000 subscribers, ten times what PrideVision TV managed. Here's hoping.

Le Dépôt

10 rue aux Ours, 3rd (01.44.54.96.96).
M° Rambuteau. **Open** noon-7am daily. **Admission** 10 Mon-Thur, Sun; 12 Fri, Sat (includes one drink). **Credit** MC, V. **Map** p402 K5.

Your basic sex disco, cutely positioned next to a police station. The decor is jungle netting and exposed air ducts, the dancefloor surrounded by video screens for idle cruising. Most of the action goes on in the never-ending network of backrooms.

QG

12 rue Simon-le-Franc, 4th (01.48.87.74.18/ www.qgbar.com). M° Rambuteau. **Open** 4pm-8am daily. **Credit** V. **Map** p406 K6.

There's no entrance fee, but instead there's one of the strictest dress codes in town to negotiate: only the hardest set (and door staff favour military gear) are guaranteed entry. Those who make it in earn a free drink and can join the boys in the backroom, playing in the slings, cabins and (gulp!) the bath. Get naked on Saturday nights and Sunday afternoons, and wear underwear-only on Sundays.

Full Metal

40 rue des Blancs-Manteaux, 4th (01.42.72.30.05).
M° Rambuteau. **Open** 5pm-4am Mon-Thur, Sun; 5pm-6am Fri, Sat. **Credit** V. **Map** p406 K6.

At this basement drinking den, the brickwork's decorated with netting and handcuffs, while the cute beur barstaff wear black armbands and open-ended chaps. Grab a handful of condoms at the bar and take your drinks through to the cabins (each comes with a lube dispenser), and wait. Home to regular theme events, including Paris' only night for skins.

The best Grooves

Gay stay

Looking for digs in the Marais in which to conduct that tear-stained why-didn't-I-pull post-mortem? Try the rooms in the period-perfect **Caron de Beaumarchais** or beautifully modern **Axial Beaubourg** (*see chapter* **Where to Stay**).

Gay gym

Surprisingly, Paris has no stand-alone gay gym. To work out in company that isn't menopausal and blue-rinsed, head for the gyms inside gay saunas (the one at **Univers** is most business-minded). The municipal **Fitness Quartier Latin** (*see chapter* **Sport & Fitness**) is also JGE (Just Gay Enough).

Gay cruising spots

In the summer, trunk-wearing boys and old queens in corsets are out in force along the **Quai des Tuileries,** just renamed Quai François Mitterrand (or '*boeuf plage*' – think Muscle Beach). Take a towel and join them in the sun. At night, the **Bois de Boulogne** (*see chapter* **Right Bank**) comes gaily alive, but do be warned: it can be dangerous, even to the most hardened cruiser.

Gay saunas

Univers Gym

20-22 rue des Bons Enfants, 1st (01.42.61.24.83).
M° Palais Royal. **Open** noon-2am Mon-Sat; 6pm-2am Sun. **Credit** AmEx, DC, MC, V. **Map** p402 .

More sauna than gym – despite the serious-minded buff guys working out during their *cinq-à-sept* – it's the busiest in Paris, attracting some of the best-looking Frenchmen you won't ever see in the clubs. Lubes are available on tap.

IDM

4 rue du Fbg-Montmartre, 9th (01.45.23.10.03). M° Grands-Boulevards. **Open** noon-1am Mon-Thur, Sun; noon-2am Fri, Sat. **No credit cards Map** p402 J4.

Near the Virgin Megastore, the city's largest gay sauna is modern, split over four floors, with a small gym and plenty of cabins and corridors to prowl.

Euro Mens Club

10 rue St-Marc, 2nd (01.42.33.92.63). M° Bourse or Grands-Boulevards. **Open** noon-9pm Mon-Sat; 1-9pm Sun. **Credit** DC, MC, V. **Map** p402 H4.

Oddly located in a rum shopping arcade, this sauna for older guys (50+) has a decent-sized swimming pool and pleasant Jacuzzi (if you can find space away from the wandering hands). Definitely one for those who like to look but not touch.

Key West

141 rue Lafayette, 10th. (01.45.26.31.74). M° Gare du Nord. **Open** noon-1am Mon-Thur, Sun; noon-2am Fri, Sat. **Credit** DC, MC, V. **Map** p402 K2.

Clean, modern and cruisy four-floor sauna, with a small pool, Jacuzzi, sauna and steam, plus – alongside the usual cabins – a number of cages for bad boys. Popular with off-scene Parisians and Eurostar passengers making the most of the proximity to Gare du Nord. Bring your kit and you can work out in the three-room multigym, too.

Gay shops and services

Space Hair

10 rue Rambuteau, 3rd (01.48.87.28.51).
M° Rambuteau. **Open** noon-10pm Mon; 9am-11pm Tue-Fri; 9am-10pm Sat. **Credit** DC, MC, V. **Map** p402 K5.

This flamboyant Marais barber, with its house music and starry decor, is an institution on the Paris gay scene. It is actually split into two salons, Cosmic and Classic. The nimble staff will do your short back and sides in ten minutes, or take their time over a decent dye job.

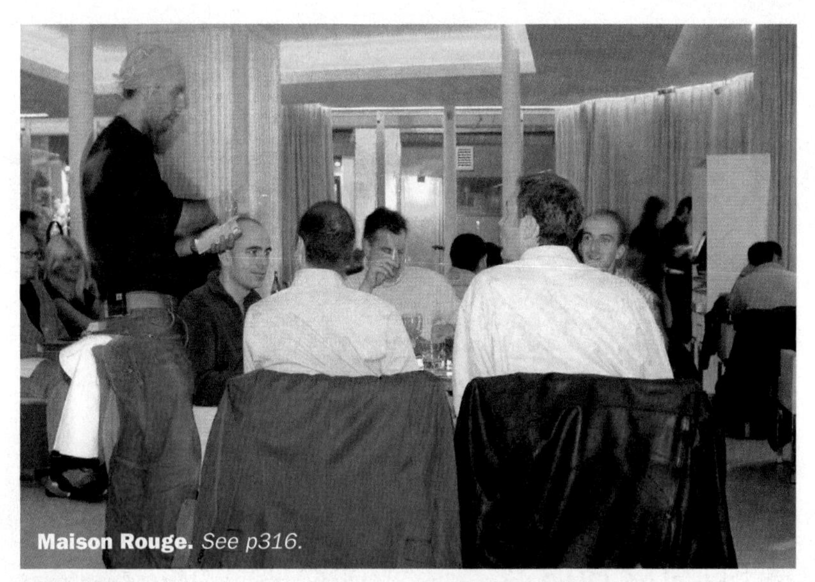
Maison Rouge. *See p316.*

Agora Press

19 rue des Archives, 4th (01.41.74.47.24). M° Hôtel de Ville. **Open** 8am-8.20pm Mon-Sat. **Credit** AmEx, DC, MC, V. **Map** p406 K6.

This eminently browsable newsagent is temptingly pitched opposite Open Café (*see p316*). It stocks plenty of international newspapers, with a permanent window display of the latest gay magazines. Browse and cruise in one spot.

Boy'z Bazaar

5 rue Ste-Croix-de-la-Bretonnerie, 4th (01.42.71.94.00). M° Hôtel de Ville. **Open** noon-8.30pm Mon-Thur; noon-10pm Fri, Sat; 2-8pm Sun. **Credit** AmEx, DC, MC, V. **Map** p406 K6.

A one-stop shop for your basic tight tees, sportswear and winningly winsome classics, plus a wing devoted to the likes of Vivienne Westwood, Bikkenberg and Evisu. A second store at No 38 (01.42.71.80.34) specialises in entertainment – titillating videos mostly, but also good for lube, hi-NRG CDs and rainbow-painted homo-tat.

Eric Filliat

24 rue Vieille-du-Temple, 4th (01.42.74.72.79). M° Hôtel de Ville. **Open** 11am-1.30pm, 2-7.30pm daily. **Credit** DC, MC, V. **Map** p406 K6.

Tiny but terrific boutique with tight racks (something we all hope for, yeah) of chic sportswear, tops and trews for gay clubbing (though just you try finding a kilt suitable for the gay gordons), and a window full of funky pumps (DKNY, W< etc). It also stocks a range of marginally less expensive gear than the rest of the Marais boutiques.

Les Mots à la Bouche

6 rue Ste-Croix-de-la-Bretonnerie, 4th (01.42.78.88.30). M° Hôtel de Ville. **Open** 11am-11pm Mon-Sat; 2-8pm Sun. **Credit** MC, V. **Map** p406 K6.

Well into its third decade serving the gay community, this book shop and meeting space stocks gay-interest literature from around the world. There's also an excellent English-language section.

IEM

208 rue St-Maur, 10th (01.42.41.21.41/www.iem.fr). M° Goncourt. **Open** 10am-7.30pm Mon-Sat. **Credit** AmEx, MC, V. **Map** p403 M4.

Hypermarket of sex, with emphasis on the harder side of gay life. Scores of videos, clothes, gadgets and condoms. Upstairs has all things leather and rubber. **Branches:** 43 rue de l'Arbre-Sec, 1st (01.42.96.05.74); 33 rue de Liège, 9th (01.45.22.69.01); 16 rue Ste-Croix de la Bretonnerie, 4th (01.42.74.01.61.).

Gay hotels

Hôtel Saintonge

16 rue de Saintonge, 3rd (01.42.77.91.13). M° Filles du Calvaire. **Rates** single 105; double 115. **Credit** AmEx, DC, MC, V. **Map** p402 L5.

Although this hotel is open to everyone, its owners cultivate a gay clientele. All rooms have a shower, hairdryer, minbar, safe and TV.

Hôtel Central Marais

33 rue Vieille-du-Temple, 4th (01.48.87.56.08). M° Hôtel de Ville. **Rates** double 87; apartment 110- 122; breakfast 7. **Credit** MC, V. **Map** p406 K6.

Paris' only strictly gay hotel (above gay bar Le Central) has seven rooms (no private bathrooms spoiling the fun), plus an apartment (100- 122). Book in advance. English is spoken and each room has double glazing and a telephone.

Useful addresses

Centre Gai et Lesbien

3 rue Keller, 11th (01.43.57.21.47/www.cglparis.org). M° Ledru-Rollin. **Open** 4-8pm Mon-Sat. **Map** p406 L7.

An anachronistic pre-liberation relic in these days of gay abandon – or a cherished community meeting space and information centre? You decide. It's a place to pore over the gay press (*Illico*) and Paris listings guides (*Zurban*) in peace, if nothing else.

SNEG (Syndicat National des Entreprises Gaies)

59 rue Beaubourg, 3rd (01.44.59.81.01). M° Rambuteau. **Open** 2-6pm Mon-Fri. **Map** p402 K5.

A gay and lesbian business group, uniting more than 1,000 companies across France.

Lesbian Paris

Fresh off the Eurostar, feeling butch and yet not sure where to start? You won't find much info in the free, unremittingly male gay press, so the best thing to do is fix yourself up with an aperitif at La Champmeslé and get chatting to lesbian scene stalwart, Josy. She's seen new bars come and go, but she'll tell you that Le Pulp (*see Chapter* **Clubs**) is still the lesbian club of choice, and that these days on Wednesdays the girls take their turn at the glory holes in Le Dépôt (*see p318*). *Incroyable*!

Lesbian bars & cafés

Le Boobsbourg

26 rue de Montmorency, 3rd (01.42.74.04.82). M° Rambuteau or Arts-et-Métiers. **Open** 5.30pm-2am Tue-Sat. **Credit** V. **Map** p402 K5.

Scuffed, slightly off-scene and nicely old-fashioned neighbourhood dyke bar with Marais prices (3.80 for a *vin rouge*). Named by ex-pat ex-pop star Tanita Tikaram, who noticed how American tourists mispronouced Beaubourg. There's a kitchen serving *assiettes* of cheese and charcuterie – go on, treat your girlfriend – plus an upstairs dancefloor that's also used for monthly film clubs.

La Champmeslé

4 rue Chabanais, 2nd (01.42.96.85.20). M° Bourse or Pyramides. **Open** 2pm-2am Mon-Sat. **No credit cards**. **Map** p402 H4.

The oldest girl bar in town – it opened in 1979 – this pillar of the lesbian community is a welcoming, neighbourhoody retreat for sapphic out-of-towners. It's also an unofficial part of the city's Lady Di tour – this is where the princess' driver Henri Paul was reportedly drinking before he chauffered her car into the fateful pillar underneath the Pont de l'Alma. Freakadelic! There are great imported beers on draught, regular cabaret (the Fetish Fantasm theme night is a highlight) and art shows.

Unity Bar

176-178 rue St-Martin, 3rd (01.42.72.70.59). M° Rambuteau. **Open** 4pm-2am daily. **No credit cards**. **Map** p402 K5.

This raucous pool bar near the Centre Pompidou (look for the subtle spray-painted graffiti sign and huge windows), attracts a cruisy female crowd, hard-smoking, hard-drinking and militant but non-threatening. Chalk up a cue, or try the more sedate Sunday nights, when out come the board games and decks of cards.

Bliss Kfé

30 rue du Roi-de-Sicile, 4th (01.42.78.49.36). M° St-Paul. **Open** 5pm-2am daily. **Credit** MC, V. **Map** p406 K6.

Laidback lezza lounge that offers a slice of (wo)Manhattan inside an old patisserie. For cocktails, apéros, and at weekends discothequing, too. When the high times come this good, expect to share air with a fair smattering of male bodies.

Le Mixer

23 rue Ste-Croix-de-la-Bretonnerie, 4th (01.48.87.55.44). M° Hôtel de Ville. **Open** 5pm-2am daily. **Credit** MC, V. **Map** p406 K6.

Not strictly women only, but a noisy pre-clubing joint where girls get their party started and fellows might feel a bit surplus to the old requirements. It's happy hour from 6pm to 8pm. Once in a while, the open decks events pull in some notable bedroom DJs.

Les Scandaleuses

8 rue des Ecouffes, 4th (01.48.87.39.26). M° St-Paul or Hôtel de Ville. **Open** 6pm-2am daily. **Credit** MC, V. **Map** p406 K6.

The Marais' prime lesbian outpost – gold-painted, no less, and packed out with handsome flirtysomethings. There's TV screens and clusters of bar stools upstairs, and hilariously naff dancing to be had in the basement. In the summer, Les Scandaleuses spill on to the street to whoop at the topless dykes on bikes roaring around the block. Good Lord, where will it all end?

Associations

Les Archives, Recherches, Cultures Lesbiennes (ARCL)

Maison des Femmes, 163 rue de Charenton 12th (01.46.28.54.94/01.43.43.41.13). M° Reuilly-Diderot. **Open** 7-9.30pm Tue. Closed Aug. **Map** p407 N8.

ACRL produces audio-visual documentation and bulletins on lesbian and women's activities with archives of lesbian and feminist documents.

Music: Classical & Opera

Will angry piano shifters and shaking batons continue into 2004? Optimistically looking forward, here are the highlights of the season and where to find them.

2003 will be remembered as the year strikes by *les intermittents du spectacle* brought the French musical festival season to its knees. The reason for the discontent was proposed changes to the status of part-time theatre workers. The generous provision, which allows three months work to qualify for nine months unemployment benefit, has been exploited by many who rarely see the interior of a theatre. The number of *intermittents* has soared, deficits have risen and the government has decided to clamp down. Naturally enough the legitimate artists and technicians are eager to preserve their hard-won rights. Hopefully there will be a quick resolution to the problem.

Gérard Mortier, who takes over at the **Opéra National de Paris** next season, is not known for his union diplomacy and his opening season will be a test of nerves. However, few doubt the need for a new broom. The national house's contribution to the Berlioz celebrations was lightweight, but happily the same can not be said of the **Théâtre du Châtelet** or the **Orchestre de Paris** whose 'Berlioz, 2003' series was one of the year's highlights.

Contemporary musical creation is a vibrant part of the city's musical make up, climaxing in the tonal abstraction of Pierre Boulez, the brains behind the **Ensemble InterContemporain**, **IRCAM** and the **Cité de la Musique**. These solid roots have now borne their fruits in composers such as Philippe Manoury, Pascal Dusapin and Peter Eötvös.

One of the city's strongest musical suits remains the early music movement led by William Christie's **Les Arts Florissants**, this season performing operas at the **Opéra National de Paris**, the **Châtelet** and the **Théâtre des Champs-Elysées**. Lines are, however, becoming pleasantly blurred with Jean-Claude Malgoire conducting Mahler last season and Rossini's *La Cenerentola* being performed on authentic instruments as part of the excellent season at the **Théâtre des Champs-Elysées**.

Lovers of church music in an authentic setting will be happy to discover the Festival d'Art Sacré (01.44.70.64.10), which celebrates religious music in the weeks before Christmas. Les Grands Concerts Sacrés (01.48.24.16.97) and Musique et Patrimoine (01.42.50.96.18) offer concerts at various churches, while music in Notre-Dame is taken care of by Musique Sacrée à Notre-Dame (01.44.41.49.99/tickets 01.42.34.56.10).

In summer, music tends to move out of concert halls into festival settings (*see p276,* **Festivals & Events**). Outside Paris, the Centre de Musique Baroque de Versailles produces early music, the Festival de l'Orangerie de Sceaux is also worth checking out, and St-Denis has a fine early summer festival in the basilica.

Information and resources

For listings, see *Pariscope* and *L'Officiel des Spectacles*. The monthly *Le Monde de la Musique* and *Diapason* also list classical concerts, while *Opéra International* provides the best coverage of all things vocal. *Cadences* and *La Terrasse*, two free monthlies, are distributed outside concerts and listings can be found on the Internet at www.arpeggione.fr and www.concertclassic.com. Many venues and orchestras offer cut-rate tickets to students (under 26) an hour before curtain up. Free concerts take place at the **Maison de Radio France**, the **Conservatoire de Paris** and certain churches.

Orchestras & ensembles

Les Arts Florissants

(01.43.87.98.98/www.arts-florissants.com).
France's most highly regarded early music group, led by William Christie, has set the standard in Rameau and Lully. A recent initiative is 'Le Jardin des Voix', which trains and promotes young artists. This season includes performances of Rameau's *Les Paladins* at the **Châtelet** in May 2004.

Ensemble InterContemporain

(www.ensembleinter.com). Based at the Cité de la Musique, Bouffes du Nord, Centre Pompidou, Musée d'Orsay and Théâtre Mogador.
The world-famous contemporary music ensemble, now directed by Jonathan Nott, spiritually remains the creation of its founder Pierre Boulez. The standard of the 31 soloists who make up the band remains consistently high. June 2004 finds them joining forces with the Orchestre de Paris for an evening of Schreker, Schönberg and Bruckner.

Ensemble Orchestral de Paris

(www.ensemble-orchestral-paris.com). Based at the Théâtre des Champs Elysées.

American John Nelson presides over this vastly improved chamber orchestra, which celebrated 25 years of music-making in 2003. This season, guest conductors include Spanish specialist Jesus Lopez Cobos for an evening of de Falla and Brahms in May.

Orchestre Lamoureux

(01.58.39.30.30/www.orchestrelamoureux.com). Based at the Théâtre des Champs-Elysées.

Rising from near extinction, the Lamoureux has found a new home in the prestigious **Théâtre des Champs-Elysées**, and a much-improved standard of playing to match. It is all the more distressing that its very existence is under threat through lack of sufficient government or private funding.

Orchestre National de France

(01.40.28.28.40/www.radiofrance.fr). Based at the Maison de Radio France and Théâtre des Champs-Elysées.

Kurt Masur has changed the profile of this prestigious orchestra: performances of the core symphonic repertoire now match the best in the world. This season sees some tempting Brahms in April 2004 with pianist Garrick Ohlsson as soloist, and a visit from legendary maestro Bernard Haitink for a Mahler evening on 30 June with baritone Mathias Goerne.

Orchestre de Paris

(01.45.61.65.60/www.orchestredeparis.com). Based at Théâtre Mogador.

Christoph Eschenbach leads the orchestra from strength to strength. The ensemble is currently based in the outdated **Théâtre Mogador**, but in May 2004 the orchestra will be in the pit for Offenbach's *Les Contes d'Hoffmann* in the **Bercy** stadium. The regular programming includes a series of free lunchtime concerts called 'Croq'notes'.

Orchestre Philharmonique de Radio France

(www.radio-france.fr). Based at the Maison de Radio France, Théâtre des Champs Elysees, Cité de la Musique.

Myung-Whun Chung's work with the orchestra has yet to produces the spectacular results the conductor seems to demand. However his work in the Romantic repertoire is reliably fine, and includes a Strauss cycle this season. There are some exciting Bartok concerts in May 2004, conducted by composer Peter Eötvös at the Cité de la Musique.

Les Talens Lyriques

(www.lestalenslyriques.com).

Harpsichordist Christophe Rousset took the name of his ensemble from Rameau's *Les Fêtes d'Hébé*. The group, which is now more than ten years old, specialises in the 17th and 18th century French and Italian repertoire and returns to the **Châtelet** in June 2004 for Tommaso Traetta's *Antigona*.

Opéra National de Paris Bastille

Venues

Opera

Opéra Comique/Salle Favart

pl Boïeldieu, 2nd (01.42.44.45.40/reservations 08.25.00.00.58/www.opera-comique.com). M° Richelieu-Drouot. **Box office** 14 rue Favart 10am-6pm Mon-Sat; telephone 11am-6pm Mon-Sat. **Tickets** €7-€50. **Credit** AmEx, DC, MC, V. **Map** p402 H4.

Jérôme Savary has done well here, which played such an important role in French musical history. Sadly, government, or indeed private, funding has not matched popular success, and the director finds himself skating on the thinnest of financial ice. Alongside Savary's own review-style shows such as his occupation musical *Zazou*, which are obviously a box office necessity, there are also some genuine opéra comique rarities being performed this season such as Adolphe Adam's *Le Toréador*, and *L'Amour Masqué* by André Messager to a libretto by Sacha Guitry. *Wheelchair access.*

Opéra National de Paris Garnier

pl de l'Opéra, 9th (08.92.89.90.90/www.opera-de-paris.fr). M° Opéra. **Box office** 11am-6.30pm Mon-Sat/telephone 9am-7pm. **Tickets** opera €7-€114; concerts €6-€55. **Credit** AmEx, MC, V. **Map** p401 G4.

The restored Palais Garnier is the jewel in the crown of Parisian music making, but the Opéra National

favours the high-tech technology of the **Bastille** (*see below*) for most new productions. May 2004 sees the completion of the restoration of the grand foyer, just in time to make a glittering backdrop for Robert Carsen's new production of *Capriccio* by Richard Strauss in June, starring diva of the decade Renée Fleming. *Wheelchair access (01.40.01.18.08, strictly two weeks in advance). See chapters* **Right Bank**, **Museums** and **Dance**.

Théâtre du Tambour-Royal

94 rue du Fbg-du-Temple, 11th (01.48.06.72.34). M° Belleville or Goncourt. **Box office** 6.30-8pm Tue-Sat; telephone 10am-8pm Mon-Sat. **Tickets** €13-€20. **Credit** MC, V. **Map** p402 M4.

This small theatre is a good place to hear the potential stars of tomorrow, but as always with such ventures standards can be hit and miss. Operatic productions are often double or triple cast, so the chances of spotting the next Pavarotti are limited.

Opéra National de Paris Bastille

pl de la Bastille, 12th (08.92.89.90.90/www.opera-de-paris.fr). M° Bastille. **Box office** 130 rue de Lyon 11am-6.30pm Mon-Sat/telephone 9am-6pm. **Tickets** €10-€142; concerts €7-€70. **Credit** AmEx, MC, V. **Map** p407 M7.

The modern building everybody loves to hate, from the disused main entrance to the unfinished *salle modulable* via the falling fascia tiles, all evoke a poor international airport rather than a theatre. A curiously unflattering acoustic is the jewel in the crown; even so operatic shows do sell out. Under Hugues Gall's steady hand and James Conlon's baton, superstars have strutted their stuff to international standards, but not always to convincing artistic ends. All may change when controversial director Gérard Mortier produces his first season in the autumn of 2004. One's breath is bated, but the waiting isn't easy. (*See also chapter* **Dance**.)

Wheelchair access (call 01.40.01.18.08, strictly two weeks in advance).

Péniche Opéra

facing 42afMuti quai de la Loire, 19th (01.53.35.07.76/ www.penicheopera.com). M° Jaurès. **Box office** 10.30am-6.30pm Mon-Fri/telephone 01.53.35.07.77. **Tickets** phone for details; no credit cards sales by telephone **Credit** MC, V. **Map** p403 M1.

An enterprising boat-based opera (land-lubbers, fear not: it's never more than millpondy) company producing a programme of chamber-scale rarities, directed by the indefatigable Mireille Larroche. Bigger shows come ashore to the **Opéra Comique**, as for this season's Honegger opera *Les Aventures du roi Pausole*. Aboard ship there is much educational work and chamber concerts featuring the excellent Carpe Diem ensemble.

Concert halls

Châtelet - Théâtre Musical de Paris

1 pl du Châtelet, 1st (01.40.28.28.40/ www.chatelet-theatre.com). M° Châtelet. **Box office** 11am-7pm daily; telephone 10am-7pm Mon-Sat. Closed July-

Aug. **Tickets** €8-€106. **Credit** AmEx, MC, V. **Map** p406 J6

Jean-Pierre Brossmann's reign at the Châtelet continues with imaginative programming in a vibrant atmosphere of discovery. This year the season is entitled 'From Berlioz to Broadway', which opened with a rare chance to see *Les Troyens* in its massive entirety, and will feature *Fosse, the Musical* as the Broadway contribution. The theatre also finds time to produce an excellent series of chamber music and symphonic concerts, including visits from mighty maestri Wolfgang Sawallisch, Riccardo Muti and Bernhard Haitink, with among the soloists pianists Brendel and Pollini and singers Jessye Norman and Thomas Hampson. *Wheelchair access*

IRCAM

1 pl Igor-Stravinsky, 4th (01.44.78.48.43/ www.ircam.fr). M° Hôtel de Ville. **Open** phone for details. **Tickets** phone for details. **Credit** AmEx, MC, V. **Map** p406 K5.

The underground bunker designed to create electronic microtonal music for the new century is looking less redundant nowadays with a full programme of conferences and courses. The showcase festival of contemporary artistic dialogue, 'Agora', now in its fifth year, features contemporary dance too. Concerts are now performed both here and next door in the Centre Pompidou.

Théâtre de la Ville

2 pl du Châtelet, 4th (01.42.74.22.77/ www.theatredelaville-paris.com). M° Châtelet. **Box office** 11am-7pm Mon; 11am-8pm Tue-Sat; telephone 11am-7pm Mon-Sat. **Tickets** €15. **Credit** MC, V. **Map** p406 J6.

The concerts in this vertiginously raked concrete amphitheatre feature hip classical outfits like the avant-garde Kronos Quartet and Fabio Biondi, as well as more conventional groups such as the Beaux-Arts trio. *Wheelchair access.*

Salle Gaveau

45 rue La Boétie, 8th (01.49.53.05.07/ www.sallegaveau.com). M° Miromesnil. **Box office** 11am-6pm Mon-Fri. **Tickets** €20-€50. **Credit** AmEx, MC, V. **Map** p401 E3.

The atmospheric Salle Gaveau is finally profiting from its recent facelift. In addition to chamber music it is now able to accommodate full orchestral concerts, without losing its essential intimacy. 2004 sees concerts from the legendary pianist Martha Argerich, as well as a long series of shows by popular French singer Juliette.

Salle Pleyel

252 rue du Fbg-St-Honoré, 8th (01.45.61.53.01). M° Ternes. **Map** p400 D3.

The Salle is currently closed for renovation (*see below* **Pleyel or played out?**).

Pleyel or played out?

Restoration of the Salle Pleyel should be completed sometime in 2004, but the newly restored hall looks set to be sidelined by the creation of a new concert space for the city. The need for a new venue has been emphasised by the residence of the Orchestre de Paris in the Théâtre Mogador during the work on Pleyel. Much ink and ill will have been spilt over the government failing to purchase and renovate Pleyel, instead allowing the hall to fall into private hands, and ushering in a future that by necessity will be more geared to profit than philanthropic artistic horizons. The new hall will in theory be built as an extension of the Cité de la Musique complex, focusing still further the city's musical activity on La Villette. Salle Pleyel will then only be needed by orchestras on an occasional basis, putting an end to a long and venerable history of music making.

The Salle Pleyel gets its name from Ignace Pleyel, a renowned composer and friend of Haydn with over 40 symphonies to his name. He set up his first music shop in 1795, and from 1807 until his death in 1831 he dedicated himself to providing ever more sophisticated instruments for the musicians of Europe. It is to Pleyel that we owe the first iron-frame piano and the rich sonority of today's concert grands. His son Camille was himself a great pianist and also a notable patron of the arts; his salons quickly became 19th-century showcases for the most gifted performers and composers of the time. He launched Chopin's career in 1832 and the Polish composer gave his last concert for Pleyel just before his death in 1849.

As salon life gave way to the need for larger venues accessible to a bigger public, the 2000-seater Salle Pleyel opened on the rue du Fbg-St-Honoré in 1927. It was one of the first and largest concert halls in Europe at the time, a truly holistic arts centre. Since that time the hall, and its two smaller performance spaces, the Salle Chopin and the Salle Debussy, have lost their lustre and no longer fulfil the expectations of dynamic young concertgoers of the 21st century. However, concert halls are notoriously difficult buildings to get absolutely right, and as old Ignace Pleyel said, 'When music is one's vocation perfection is a constant quest.'

Théâtre des Champs-Elysées

15 av Montaigne, 8th (01.49.52.50.50/ www.theatrechampselysees.fr). M° Alma-Marceau. **Box office** 1pm-7pm Mon-Sat; telephone 10am-noon, 2-6pm Mon-Fri. **Tickets** €5-€135. **Credit** AmEx, MC, V. **Map** p400 D5.

This beautiful theatre, with bas-reliefs by Bourdelle, witnessed the première of Stravinsky's *Le Sacre du Printemps* in 1913. Director Dominique Meyer is proud of its unsubsidised status and has continued the high-quality programming. This season includes visits the Vienna Philharmonic conducted by Mariss Jansons and Bernhard Haitink; also Seiji Ozawa with the Saito Kinen Orchestra. June 2004 sees a revival of the successful version of Mozart's *Marriage of Figaro* conducted by René Jacobs with crack authentic band Concerto Köln in the pit.

Théâtre Mogador

25 rue Mogador, 9th (08.92.70.26.04/ www.mogador.net). M° St Lazare. **Tickets** phone for details. **Map** p401 G3.

With the closing of the Salle Pleyel for renovations the Théâtre Mogador came to the rescue as a serious venue for classical music. Originally a music hall built by the Englishman Sir Alfred Butt Loue as a celebration of the entente cordial, the theatre became a rival to the Châtelet in its heyday. But even with 'enhanced' acoustics it does not make an ideal concert hall, and strengthens the case for those demanding a major new music venue in the capital.

Théâtre des Bouffes du Nord

37 bis bd de la Chapelle, 10th (01.46.07.34.50/ www.bouffesdunord.com). M° La Chapelle. **Box office** 11am-6pm Mon-Sat. **Tickets** €12-€18.50. **Credit** AmEx, MC, V. **Map** p402 L2.

Peter Brook and Stéphane Lissner's eclectic musical programming is becoming increasingly adventurous. Last year saw Philippe Manoury's new chamber opera, *La Frontière*, and chamber music with top artists ranging from veteran harpsichordist Gustav Leonhardt via string quartets Prazác and Talich, piainist Maria João Pires, but also finding time for French Rock groups such as Les Têtes Raides.

Maison de Radio France

116 av du Président-Kennedy, 16th (01.42.20.42.20/ www.radiofrance.fr). M° Passy/RER Kennedy Radio France. **Box office** 11am-6pm Mon-Sat. **Tickets** free-€20. **Credit** MC, V. **Map** p404 A7.

State radio station France Musiques programmes an impressive range of classical concerts, operas and ethnic music here. The main venue within the cylindrical building is the rather charmless Salle Olivier Messiaen, but the quality of music making compensates, featuring two of the capital's leading orchestras: the Orchestre National de France and the Orchestre Philharmonique de Radio France. Under-26s can obtain a Passe Musique, which gives admission to four concerts for the bargain price of €18. Watch out for frequent free events, recorded live. *Wheelchair access.*

Salle Cortot

78 rue Cardinet, 17th (01.47.63.85.72). M° Malesherbes. **No box office. Tickets** phone for details. **Map** p400 D2.

This intimate and beautiful concert hall in the Ecole Normale Supérieure de Musique has an excellent acoustic for occasional chamber music events.

Cité de la Musique

221 av Jean-Jaurès, 19th (reservations 01.44.84.44.84/www.cite-musique.fr). M° Porte de Pantin. **Box office** noon-6pm Tue-Sun/telephone 11am-7pm Mon-Sat, 11am-6pm Sun. **Tickets** €4-€33; reduced prices under 26s, over-60s. **Credit** MC, V. **Map** p403 inset.

Exciting, energetic programming focuses on contemporary creation and Baroque rediscovery, but takes in a vast non-classical repertoire, including exciting excursions into ethnic music and jazz. This year sees imaginative cycles juxtaposing the work of the late Luciano Berio and Bach, as well as a series of concerts entitled 'Espaces', which manages to embrace both Pink Floyd and Richard Wagner. The museum has a smaller amphitheatre-style concert space for demonstrating instruments from the collection (*see chapter* **Museums**), such as its wonderful original harpsichords, while the adjacent Conservatoire (01.40.40.46.46) is host to world-class performers and professors, and features many free concerts. *Wheelchair access.*

Music in museums

Auditorium du Louvre

Entrance through Pyramid, Cour Napoléon, 1st (reservations 01.40.20.55.00/www.louvre.fr). M° Palais-Royal. **Box office** 9am-5pm daily. **Tickets** €18-€23. **Credit** MC, V. **Map** p401 H5.

A fine series is proposed at the Louvre, not only musical presentations of great silent films, but a full season of chamber music and lunchtime concerts, too. This year a cycle entitled Le Violon features concerts by some top exponents of the instrument. *Wheelchair access.*

Musée National du Moyen Age - Thermes de Cluny

6 pl Paul-Painlevé, 5th (01.53.73.78.00). M° Cluny-La Sorbonne. **Tickets** phone for details. **No credit cards. Map** p406 J7.

The museum presents medieval concerts that are in keeping with the collection, in a setting that inspires authenticity.

Musee d'Orsay

62 rue de Lille, 7th (014049 48 14/www.musee-orsay.fr). M° Solférino/RER Musée d'Orsay. **Tickets** €18-€23. **Credit** MC, V. **Map** p405 G6.

A full and stimulating series of concerts sometimes uses exhibitions such as the Vuillard show as a musical stimulus, but also explores the origins of the avant-garde, women composers, and a series dedicated to the great voices of today.

Music: Popular Music

Mass-appeal music? It's a living thang: *chanson* regenerates (while staying the same), pop pulsates, jazz is jumping and even metal's in the finest fettle.

When the Cramps hit town in the autumn of 2003, Lux Interior observed in that winning way he has that what Paris needs to do is 'kill all its politicians and take some drugs'. Mr Interior speaks purely for himself, of course, but it is true that the law to which he was so subtly alluding – the one that says that bands can't play too loud – does echo Paris' reputation as being too quaint to be a rock'n'roll town.

But soft; that's not the way it is. Live music is thriving and the emergence of new bands in France speaks volumes about the creativity of young artists: but certainly quantity does not equal quality. Up-and-coming artists mingle and mix media at **Mains d'Oeuvres** and talented rookies showcase at open-mike nights at venues like **The House of Live**. And if jazz is your beat, crawl down to one of the cellars and put your ear under the high hat, as there is a revolving door of talent that passes through town. Pick up a free bi-monthly publication, *Lylo* at the FNAC or in bars, which details genres, venues and concert times.The streets are alive with a musical diversity that would satisfy the most obstinate music snob. Homebrewed homeboys of *chanson* are revered, but so are the others who bring their talents into the Gallic hexagon. Paris is a major tour destination for US and UK outfits, and, even more enrichingly, the city benefits from international acts from all continents, from the Americas to Africa and from Far East to Eastern-European folksters.

On the home front, open minds of the new school of *chanson* show a willingness to absorb influences and experiment with pop *chanson* and ethnic takes to liven up what could have been a dying art. Acts like Sanseverino's *Le Tango des Gens* allow gypsy spirits to dance with the traditional, and *chanson* cherub Benjamin Biolay's release *Négatif* revives 60s experimentation, transporting listeners back to the days of Melody Nelson (*see p328* **Sleaze me, please me**). And the ever expanding kingdom of plastic'n'wax Johnny Hallyday proved that the old guy can still do it at 60.

Today's pop culture crackles with mechanically-engineered, TV-created stars. Each one is more disposable than the next. The universe from which these stars burst forth consists of TV horrors such as *Star Academy*, *Popstars* and *Pop Idol* (newly '*A la recherche de la nouvelle star*'), which have produced brand differentiation but not talent.

For more real sounds, give a listen to French rap, strongly influenced by Africa and breaking heavily on to the music beat. Check out IAM's *Marseille*, released in autumn 2003. They have collaborated with 15-rapper collective K1FFR, who also unleashed a compilation, *La Cerise sur le ghetto* ('the cherry/icing on the ghetto'). 113 and gangster rap Rohff have new material worth a listen. Look for NTM's third album *Arsenik* and the sensitive girly gangsters, Diam's.

Gig prices tend to range from the price of a beer to a big chunk of change (above €90, higher if we're talking the Stones or Hallyday). For ticket agencies, *see chapter* **Directory**.

Le Réservoir. *See p329.*

Stadium venues

Palais Omnisports de Paris-Bercy

8 bd de Bercy, 12th (08.92.69.23.00/www.bercy.fr). M° Bercy. **Box office** 11am-6pm Mon-Sat. **Credit** MC, V. **Map** p407 N9.

Heavy-hitters such as Peter Gabriel and Macca make dates at this sports arena. *Wheelchair access.*

Zénith

211 av Jean-Jaurès, 19th (01.42.08.60.00/ www.le-zenith.com). M° Porte de Pantin. **No box office**. **Credit** MC, V. **Map** p403 inset.

Good vistas from every vantage point and good acoustics make this a solid venue. Massive Attack and the Roots were on in 2003.

Rock venues

For **Nouveau Casino**, *see chapter* **Clubs**.

L'Olympia

28 bd des Capucines, 9th (01.55.27.10.00/ reservations 08.92.68.33.68/www.olympiahall.com). M° Opéra. **Box office** 9am-9pm (9.30pm concert nights) Mon-Sat. **Credit** MC, V. **Map** p401 G4.

The queue has stretched halfway down the block for the Beatles, the Stones, Quo, Hendrix, Sinatra and Piaf, these days replaced by Placebo and Blur.

Le Bataclan

50 bd Voltaire, 11th (01.43.14.35.35). M° Oberkampf. **Box office** 10.30am-7pm Mon-Fri, 11am-7pm Sat. **Concerts** 8pm. Closed two weeks in Aug. **Credit** MC, V. **Map** p403 M5.

A charming old theatre hosts a mixed bag of seated or standing concerts and innovative ciné-theatre. Recent acts have included Zazie, Metallica, Vincent de Lerm and Gotan Project. *Wheelchair access.*

Café de la Danse

5 passage Louis-Phillipe, 11th (01.47.00.57.59/ www.chez.com/cafedeladanse). M° Bastille. **Box office** noon-6pm Mon-Fri. Closed July, Aug. **Concerts** 8pm. **No credit cards**. **Map** p407 M7.

This former dance hall gives way to *chanson*, pop/rock, world and the occasional (read: rare) dance party when seats are removed to make way for moving parts. The venue may be closed during summer 2004 for renovation. *Wheelchair access.*

Sleaze me, please me

Coincidence? We think not. Handsome 31-year-old crooner Benjamin Biolay has announced his candidature for the office of the Governor of French *chanson*, the musical throwback that evolution forgot to make extinct. This, of course, means stepping into the brothel creepers of Serge Gainsbourg, the pervatollah of *chanson*, the guy they think made the whole genre cool. Thus the question is – as it would be be with any pretender to Serge's commode – is Biolay talented enough and dirty enough to draw the sword from the stone? Time for some comparative sleaze-ology.

Serge Gainsbourg (né Lucien Ginsburg), a womaniser (four wives) and a drunk, with a face only a mother could love, stands as, arguably, France's most influential musical export. President Mitterrand once called him 'our Baudelaire', and his de Sade lifestyle and constant high-profile controversy perpetuated the living legend until he career-moved into a dead legend in 1991.

Both Biolay and Gainsbourg share musical lineages, falling into the scene through the push of artistic fathers. Both leaned on them for entrées: Gainsbourg got piano gigs, Biolay got gigs at the Conservatory. Similarly, early struggles to find their sound were solved by writing for others. It was a collaboration with Keren Ann and Henri Salvador, producing the hit ballad 'Jardin d'hiver' that placed Benji on the map. Gainsbourg, on the other hand, wrote hits for *chanson* and cinema babes France Gall, Brigitte Bardot, Jane Birkin, Françoise Hardy and Catherine Deneuve, advancing their careers more than his own.

In 1968 Gainsbourg made headlines with 'Je t'aime, moi non plus' with lover Bardot (and then again with wife Jane Birkin in 69). It was the 'anti-baise' (anti-fuck) song complete with live orgasm that ruffled many a feather and ended up banned in several countries. Biolay's career mirror? Pulling his reluctant siren wife, Chiara Mastroianni, to the microphone, in the love-hate 'Je ne t'ai pas aimé'. Here his lyrics are as ambiguous as his predecessor's, but lack the vampiric bite that Serge enjoyed inflicting on his women.

Part of Serge's success was his ability to genre-surf and experiment with foreign influences and lyrics. On *Négatif*, Biolay cross-pollinates country, rock, culture and poetry with blues, folk and pop, sampling tracks with American references like 'Little Darlin', a hick and a Buick to boot. And sex, with such erotathons as 'Glory Hole'.

Biolay's work is indebted to Gainsbourg's 1971 Nabokovian overture 'l'Histoire de Melody Nelson'. Melody, at 15, is red-headed jailbait in white cotton panties. 'Love is dirty,' philosophised Gainsbourg, 'the dirtier love is, the more beautiful it is.' This was certainly true of 'Gainsbarre', his drunken sleazy alter-ego. Gainsbarre burned a 500F note on TV and told Whitney Houston on a live music awards show that he'd like to fuck her (it was the booze talking). This kind of bad-boy behaviour is where Gainsbarre makes love like a woman, and Biolay breaks like a little girl.

Big Ben is not exactly a vision of rebellion against evolutionary French pop; rather, he moulds perfectly to the tradition, taking in his stride the lessons and successes of those who have come before him. 'Careerism' is a word that springs to mind. If advice from the heavens could rain down, Gainsbarre would disapprove. BB says he's cutting out the smokes, but Gains would surely give the nod to Biolay's marriage to beautiful blonde actress Chiara, the daughter of Catherine Deneuve. And if you listen to untitled track 14 on *Négatif*, you can hear the faint moans of a woman in pleasure. And while Gainsbarre would most certainly chortle a knowing 'Bravo' to that, the marketing guys at his label, Virgin, will be soiling their pinstriped little panties with glee.

La Cigale/La Boule Noire

120 bd de Rochechouart, 18th (01.49.25.89.99/ www.lacigale.fr). M° Pigalle. **Box office** noon-7pm Mon-Sat. Closed 15 July-15 Aug. **Map** p402 H2.

This big vaudeville theatre wraps around reliable acts and 1,900 punters. Downstairs La Boule Noire makes one of the best rooms for up-coming headliners like The Faint and old ones like Evan Dando.

Le Divan du Monde

75 rue des Martyrs, 18th (01.55.79.09.52). M° Pigalle. **Concerts** 7.30pm Mon-Sat; 5pm Sun. **No credit cards**. **Map** p402 H2.

A healthy dose of world music, a twist of electro-dance, a dollop of hip-hop and a sprinkle of indie rock/pop keeps this venue at the cutting edge.

Elysée Montmartre

72 bd de Rochechouart, 18th (01.55.07.06.00/ www.elyseemontmartre.com). M° Anvers. **Concerts** 6.30-10.30pm. Closed Aug. **No credit cards. Map** p402 J2.

Chanson, tango, techno, electro, reggae, metal and rock all join the team in this sizeable venue. The Libertines and Thievery Corporation brought their sagas and grooves and The Flaming Lips brought dancing animals. *Wheelchair access.*

Le Trabendo

211 av Jean-Jaurès, 19th (01.49.25.89.99). M° Porte de Pantin. **Concerts** from 8pm, days vary. **No credit cards**. **Map** p403 inset.

The Trabendo has widened its sphere to underground rock, world and electro-jazz. Among recents artists are The YeahYeahYeahs and Jon Spencer. *Wheelchair access.*

Mains d'Oeuvres

1 rue Charles Garnier, 93400 St-Ouen (01.40.11.25.25/www.mainsdoeuvres.org). M° Garibaldi or Porte de Clignancourt. **Concerts** 8.30pm. **No credit cards**.

A hotbed for new artists: 4,000m² of incestuous space for performance, dance, exhibition and recording. Invitations are extended to fringe rock, rap, electronica and jazz to add new talent. *Wheelchair access.*

Rock in bars

Unless marked otherwise, there is no admission charge to hear live music in the following bars.

Le Who's Bar

13 rue du Petit-Pont, 5th (01.43.54.80.71). M° St-Michel. **Bar** 8pm-5am Mon-Sat daily. **Concerts** 10.30pm. **Credit** MC, V. **Map** p406 J7.

Lots of acoustic solo acts cranking Creep, and small rock/pop bands crackling into the wee hours to entertain you and friendly guzzlers.

House of Live

124 rue La Boétie, 8th (01.42.25.18.06). M° Franklin D Roosevelt. **Bar/restaurant** 9am-5am daily. Gospel concerts 11.30pm Tue-Thur; noon Fri, Sat. **Credit** AmEx, DC, MC, V. **Map** p401 E4.

Music can seem secondary to bizarre mating rituals (as it should be); however, the card here does run from quiffed-up rock and posey pop to Sunday blues and soulful gospel.

Le Réservoir

16 rue de la Forge-Royal, 11th (01.43.56.39.60/ www.reservoirclub.com). M° Ledru-Rollin. **Bar** 8pm-2am Mon-Thur; 8pm-dawn Fri, Sat; noon-5pm Sun (jazz brunch). Closed one week Aug. **Concerts** 11pm. **Credit** MC, V. **Map** p407 N7.

Live acts range from soul, funk, groove to world, reggae, trip hop and house. This venue boasts celebrity visits and a juicy Sunday jazz brunch.

La Scène

2bis rue des Taillandiers, 11th (01.48.06.50.70/ reservations: 01.48.06.12.13/www.la-scene.com). M° Ledru-Rollin. **Bar/restaurant** 8pm-2am Tue-Sat. Closed Aug. **Concerts** 9pm Tue-Sat. **Admission** €10. **Credit** AmEx, DC, MC, V. **Map** p407 M7.

With split-level action, the newly vamped restaurant and snack bar/lounge is scene-y indeed. 'I need sugar' gay nights twice a month. *Wheelchair access.*

The Wild Geese

140 bd Richard-Lenoir, 11th (01.48.06.14.36). M° République. **Bar** 5pm-2am Mon-Sat; noon-2am Sun (brunch). **Concerts** 9pm. **Credit** V. **Map** p407 M6.

This unremarkable Irish bar pulls folk, rock and blues. On Tuesdays, the open mike gathers amiable Anglos and shy'uns front and centre.

La Flèche d'Or

102bis rue de Bagnolet, 20th (01.43.72.42.44/ www.flechedor.com). M° Gambetta. **Bar/restaurant** 6pm-2am Tue-Sun. **Concerts** 9pm. **Admission** €2-€6. **Credit** MC, V. **Map** p407 Q6.

Though it almost went belly-up, this converted train station narrowly managed to stay on its rails and continues to chug along as a popular spot for *chanson*, world, ska, electro and reggae. Open mike nights on Tuesdays. *Wheelchair access.*

Le Gambetta

104 rue de Bagnolet, 20th (01.43.70.52.01/ www.gambetta-bar.com). M° Gambetta. **Bar** 10am-2am daily. **Concerts** 9pm. **Admission** free-€5. **Credit** MC, V. **Map** p407 Q6.

This unpretentious rock and rumble haunt has an edgy student-union feel and bands that thump and rattle. Punk, rock, alternative electric guitar, plus regular world music nights.

Chanson

Now that every long-haired loverboy clinging to the zinc claims to be a *chansonnier* you can be assured that at least some of the performers will be under 65. The following venues offer an eclectic mix of singer-songwriters, jazz, gypsy music and slam poetry. Unless otherwise stated there is no entrance fee – drop a note into the hat (one of the old franc ones always pisses 'em off).

Sentier des Halles

50 rue d'Aboukir, 2nd (01.42.61.89.96). M° Sentier. **Concerts** 8pm, 10pm Mon-Sat. Closed Aug. **Admission** €9-€12. **No credit cards. Map** p402 J4.
This celebrated cellar seats 120 people for a wide variety of acts (many of them big cheeses), from *chanson* to camembert reggae and roquefort rap.

Le Limonaire

18 cité Bergère, 9th (01.45.23.33.33/ http://limonaire.free.fr). M° Grands Boulevards. **Bar** 6pm-2am Tue-Sun. **Concerts** 10pm Tue-Sat; 7pm Sun. **Credit** MC, V. **Map** p402 J4.
This bistro à vins takes its *chanson* seriously – don't come for a drink and a chat as the room becomes wrapped in reverence while the artistes perform.

Chez Adel

10 rue de la Grange-aux-Belles, 10th (01.42.08.24.61). M° Jacques Bonsergent or République. **Bar** noon-2.30pm; 5pm-2am Mon-Fri; noon-2am, Sat, Sun. **Concerts** 5pm. **Credit** MC, V. **Map** p402 L3.
What a place to whoop it up. Great sangria, frescoed walls, good-value meals (homemade Syrian at weekends) and a cosy audience. French, folk and gypsy tunes add to the warm and vibe. *Wheelchair access.*

Le Magique

42 rue de Gergovie, 14th (01.45.43.21.32/ www.aumagique.com). M° Pernéty. **Bar/restaurant** 8pm-2am Wed-Sun. Closed Aug. **Concerts** 9.30pm Wed, Thur; 10.30pm Fri, Sat. **No credit cards. Map** p405 F10.
Resident artiste Marc Havet plays politically incorrect *chanson* for a song (cheap eats and suggested €5 minimum donation). Bi-monthly detective novel readings and swaps keep the place on its toes.

Le Pataquès

8 rue Jouye-Rouve, 20th (01.46.36.44.93). M° Pyrénées. **Bar** 2pm-2am Mon, Wed-Sun. **Concerts** 8pm Fri, Sat. **No credit cards. Map** p403 N4.
Bobo Belleville locals gather regularly for slam-poetry nights, debates and experimental theatre. The recent addition of a telephone will make it easier to find out when their famous fêtes are feasting.

Le Vieux Belleville

12 rue des Envierges, 20th (01.44.62.92.66/ www.levieux-belleville.com). M° Pyrénées. **Bar** noon-2.30pm Mon-Wed; noon-2.30pm, 8pm-2am Thur-Sat. **Concerts** 9pm Thur. **Credit** MC, V. **Map** p403 N4.
Perched with a spectacular view of Paris, here you can make new friends over gingham tablecloths during *chanson*, accordion and organ-grinder *bals*. Audience participation appreciated.

Barges

See also **Batofar**, *chapter* **Clubs**.

La Balle au Bond

(01.40.46.85.12/www.laballeaubond.fr). (Oct-Mar) 55 quai de la Tournelle, 5th, M° Maubert-Mutualité; (Apr-Nov) quai Malaquais, 6th. M° Pont Neuf. **Bar** 11am-2am daily. **Concerts** 9pm. **Admission** €7. **Credit** AmEx, MC, V. **Map** p402 K7.
Mainstream commotion on mid-river. Come over all 'hello, sailor' as you swing and sway to the party-honk of rock, pop, jazz, blues and *chanson*.

La Guinguette Pirate

11 quai François Mauriac, 13th (01.43.49.68.68/ www.guingettepirate.com). M° Bibliothèque or Quai de la Gare. **Bar** 7pm-2am Tue-Sat. **Concerts** 9pm Wed-Sat. **Admission** €8-€12. **No credit cards. Map** p407 N10.
This hip seamen's (note: seamen = exotic rashes) stop sways on the Seine to folk, rock, punk, reggae, jazz, electro and *chanson*; DJs take over late into the night. You can listen for free from the lively snack bar along the quai in summer.

Blues bars

Utopia

79 rue de l'Ouest, 14th (01.43.22.79.66). M° Pernéty. **Concerts** 10pm Mon-Sat. Closed Aug. **Admission** €8-€11. **Credit** MC ,V. **Map** p401 F10.
Bluesmen from home and away dig deep into the soulful territory of their predecessors. Country blues, Delta blues, swing and blues rock are laid down with gusto as any considerations of Gallic cool are swept aside by the power of the form.

Quai du Blues

17 bd Vital-Bouhot (Ile de la Jatte), 92200 Neuilly sur Seine (01.46.24.22.00). M° Pont de Levallois. **Bar/ restaurant** 8.30pm-2am. **Concerts** 10.30pm Fri, Sat. Closed July, Aug. **Admission** €20; €39 dinner & show. **Credit** AmEx, V.
This atmospheric refurbished garage invites only genuine Afro-American artists to grace its stage. Koko Tyler and well-known feminist Ike Turner were recent visitors.

World & traditional music

Théâtre de la Ville

(01.42.74.22.77/www.theatredelaville-paris.com). 2 pl du Châtelet, 4th. M° Châtelet. 31 rue des Abbesses, 18th. M° Abbesses. **Box office** 11am-7pm Mon; 11am-8pm Tue-Sat; 11am-7pm Mon-Sat (telephone). **Concerts** 8.30pm Mon-Fri; 5pm, 8.30pm Sat. Closed July-Aug. **Credit** MC, V. **Map** p402 J6.
Artists of the highest calibre in traditional music and dance visit the Châtelet theatre and its Abbesses offshoot. Look out for the Festival de l'Imaginaire programme in spring. *Wheelchair access.*

Institut du Monde Arabe

1 rue des Fossés-St-Bernard, 5th (01.40.51.38.38/ www.imarabe.org). M° Jussieu. **Box office** 10am-5pm Tue-Sun; 7.30-9pm show nights. **Concerts** 8.30pm Fri, Sat. **Credit** AmEx, MC, V. **Map** p402 K7.
A quality auditorium with wonderful, lounge-like leather seats. The institute has sufficient cred to be able to attract a great number of top-class performers from the Arab world.

Quai du Blues. *See p330.*

La Vieille Grille

1 rue du Puits-de-l'Hermite, 5th (01.47.07.22.11/ http://vieille.grille.free.fr). M° Place Monge. **Restaurant** 7 30pm-12.30am Tue-Sat. **Bar** 6pm-1am Tue-Sun. **Concerts** 9pm Tue-Sat; 5pm Sun. **No credit cards. Map** p402 K8.

A cute, café-théâtre style niche. Regular Latin and klezmer nights alternate with traditional jazz, world music, *chanson* and text readings (ah well, that's Paris) at weekends.

Kibélé

12 rue de l'Echiquier, 10th (01.48.24.57.74). M° Bonne Nouvelle. **Restaurant** noon-3pm, 7pm-2am Mon-Sat. **Concerts** 9.30pm Wed-Sat. **Admission** €5-€10. **Credit** MC, V. **Map** p402 K4.

Dine in the Turkish restaurant and then hit the cellar and harken to rap poetry. Drift to the sounds of Brazilian crooning and North African beats.

Satellit' Café

44 rue de la Folie-Méricourt, 11th (01.47.00.48.87/ www.satellit-cafe.com). M° Oberkampf. **Bar** 8pm-4am Tue-Thur; 10pm-6am Fri-Sat. **Concerts** 9pm Tue-Thur. **Admission** €10. **Credit** MC, V (for two or more tickets). **Map** p403 M5.

Orbit around Afro blues and Algerian raï, meet like-minded martians and easy-going earthlings. *Wheelchair access.*

Cité de La Musique

221 av Jean-Jaurès, 19th (01.44.84.44.84/ www.cite-musique.fr). M° Porte de Pantin. **Concerts** Tue-Sat, times vary. **Credit** MC, V. **Map** p403 inset.

The auditorium at the La Villette complex attracts first-class world, jazz and classical musicians and, during the Rendezvous Electroniques, electro music and video too. *Wheelchair access.*

La Maroquinerie

23 rue Boyer, 20th (01.40.33.30.60). M° Gambetta. **Restaurant** 11.30am-1.30am Mon-Sat. **Bar** 11am-1am. Closed Aug. **Concerts** 8.30pm. **Map** p403 Q5.

A happening locale for world, rock, jazz and country, poetry and debate. That's right: debate.

Jazz

Le Baiser Salé

58 rue des Lombards, 1st (01.42.33.37.71). M° Châtelet. **Bar** 5pm-6am daily. **Concerts** 7pm, 10pm daily. **Tickets** €13-€20. **Credit** AmEx, DC, MC, V. **Map** p406 J6.

The 'Salty Kiss' (not 'the dirty fucker' as some have mistranslated) joneses for world, *chanson*, vocal jazz and regular pop rock. Listen to the likes of Mokhtar Samba pucker up.

Duc des Lombards

42 rue des Lombards, 1st (01.42.33.22.88). M° Châtelet. **Bar** 7.30pm-2am Mon-Sat. Closed two weeks in Aug. **Tickets** €13-€20. **Credit** MC, V. **Map** p406 J6.

Plenty of atmosphere. You're practically on top of the many jazz acts, hence a great vibe.

Le Petit Opportun

15 rue des Lavandières-Ste-Opportune, 1st (01.42.36.01.36). M° Châtelet. **Bar** 9pm-5am Tue-

Sat. **Concerts** 6pm, 10.30pm Tue-Sat. **Tickets** €13-€16. **No credit cards. Map** p406 J6.
Top French jazzers go for the high notes in this tiny medieval cellar that's atmospheric when it's packed.

Le Slow Club

130 rue de Rivoli, 1st (01.42.33.84.30). M° Châtelet. **Bar** 10pm-3am Tue, Thur; 10pm-4am Fri, Sat. **Concerts** 10pm. **Tickets** €9-€13. **Credit** MC, V. **Map** p406 J6.
A little cellar with big beat boogie-woogie orchestras, R&B, washboard jazz and swing bands.

Le Sunset/Le Sunside

60 rue des Lombards, 1st (01.40.26.46.60 Sunset/01.40.26.21.25 Sunside). M° Châtelet. **Bar** 8.30pm-2am daily. **Concerts** 10pm Sunset; 9pm Sunside. **Tickets** €8-€25. **Credit** MC, V. **Map** p406 J6.
The frosted Sunset side of this major venue likes electric jazz and world music while the wheaty Sunside appreciates acoustic acts like Brad Mehldau and Henri Texier. *Wheelchair access (Sunside only).*

Les 7 Lézards

10 rue des Rosiers, 4th (01.48.87.08.97/ www.7lezards.com). M° St-Paul. **Bar** 6pm-2am daily. **Concerts** 10pm daily. **Tickets** €11-€16. **No credit cards. Map** p406 L6.
A jazz hubbub of locals, ex-pats and visiting US maestros (Shiela Jordan, Bayard Lancaster). Prepare yourself for the frenzy of the bippidy-boppidy fury.

Les 7 Lézards

Caveau de la Huchette

5 rue de la Huchette, 5th (01.43.26.65.05). M° St-Michel. **Concerts** 9.30pm daily. **Tickets** €10.50-€13. **Credit** MC, V. **Map** p406 J7.
Set in the tourist-trap part of the Latin Quarter but worth every euro. The venue is a hit in itself.

Le Bilboquet

13 rue St-Benoît, 6th (01.45.48.81.84). M° St-Germain-des-Prés. **Concerts** 9.30pm-1.30am Tue-Sun. Dinner 7pm. **Tickets** €15 (incl one drink). **Credit** AmEx, MC, V. **Map** p405 H6.
Its 50s heyday may be over but it still attracts the likes of David Bowie and ZZ Top.

Caveau des Oubliettes

52 rue Galande, 5th (01.46.34.23.09) M° Maubert Mutualité. **Concerts** jam sessions 10pm-2am Mon-Thur, Sun; concerts 10pm Fri, Sat. **Admission** free. **Credit** AmEx, MC, V. **Map** p406 J7.
Explore the secret passage under St-Michel or jump up on stage for an improvised jazz sesh.

New Morning

7-9 rue des Pétites-Ecuries, 10th (01.45.23.51.41/). M° Château d'Eau. **Box office** 3.30pm-7.30pm Mon-Fri. Closed Aug. **Concerts** 9pm daily. **Tickets** €15-€20. **Credit** V. **Map** p402 K3.
This prestigious venue attracts a rapt audience with top-end jazz, blues and world music artists from Norway to Iran.

Parc Floral de Paris

Bois de Vincennes, 12th (01.55.94.20.20/ www.parcfloraldeparis.com). M° Château de Vincennes. **Concerts** May-July 4.30pm Sat, Sun. **Admission** €1.50. **No credit cards.**
Well-known names make the annual pilgrimage to the 'wood' for summer's open-air jazzing.

Petit Journal Montparnasse

13 rue du Commandant-Mouchotte, 14th (01.43.21.56.70/www.petitjournal-montparnasse.com). M° Gaité. **Concerts** 10pm daily. Dinner 8pm daily. Closed mid-July to mid-Aug. **Tickets** €17-€22 (with drink); €48-€50 (with dinner). **Credit** MC, V. **Map** p405 F9.
This jazz brasserie offers R&B, soul-gospel, Latin and Afro-fusion in a harmonious atmosphere.

Lionel Hampton Jazz Club

81 bd Gouvion-St-Cyr, 17th (01.40.68.30.42/ www.jazzclub-paris.com). M° Porte Maillot. **Bar** 7am-2am daily. **Concerts** 10.30pm, 2am Mon-Sat; 10pm Sun. **Tickets** €23-€25 (incl one drink). **Credit** AmEx, DC, MC, V. **Map** p400 B2.
Here you'll find R&B, soul and gospel. 75% of acts are from America, but local talent gets to swing, too.

Jawad K-Fé

114 rue de Bagnolet, 10th (01.43.67.73.35). M° Gambetta or Porte de Bagnolet. **Bar** 7am-2pm, 7pm-2am daily. **Concerts** 9pm Wed-Sun. **Admission** free. **Credit** MC, V. **Map** p407 Q6.
Tiny lights dangle and dazzle to jazzy beats and quality quartets in this neighbourhood niche.

Phallic cymbals: Paris' metal scene

Euh, *les headbanguers* en France? When asked, the majority of the French will wag a finger and tsk-tsk the existence of such a genre of music here, despite the fact that most Parisiennes over 50 look like they emerged from exactly the same part of the gene swamp as Alice Cooper. Pose that question in the right places, though, and you'll find black-clad, whey-faced compatriots who will beg to differ, muzzerfuckeur. *Vive ze evvy metal*, Paris style.

The French are proud of their culture and are content that, by law, 40% of radio noise has to come from within their country. Picture the French popular music scene, then, as a tweedy virgin who needs to be protected from brutish incursions. Given that temptation, the odd pillaging raid by the Anglo-Viking musical cosh that is metal is inevitable; the adaptation of some kind of bat-biting stage screamer was bound to slip through at some point. And given the genre's macho posture and essential conservatism, it's not surprising that such music thrives in the French culture.

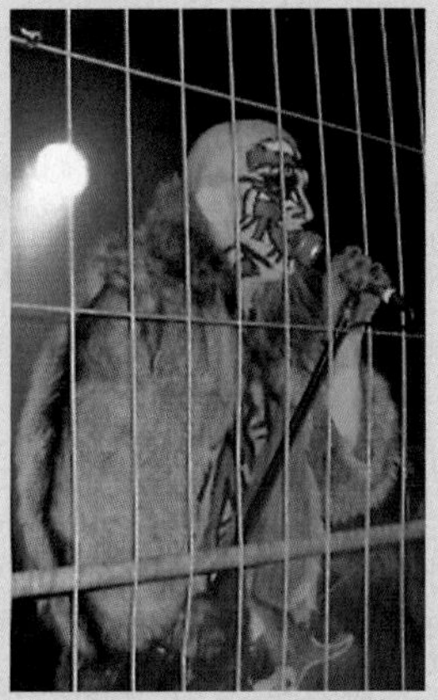

Goth and metal wear the same cloak here. Lud'o, contributor for *Metal France* (www.metalfrance.net) explains that both groups are seen as misfits (no!) who cling to black, affect ghoulish faces and chant romantic poetry. The rarity of the species means that the two sub-genres cling together like the last Cheerios in a bowl of milk. Death (pronounced 'def') metal is shunned as being too 'extreme', promoting the values of fascism, not at all in line with traditional socialistic ideals. Well, roll over Karl Marx, coz David St Hubbins is in town.

The tour stops of Iron Maiden and the queue for the three sold-out concert series by Metallica show that the classics reign absolute. Parisian mosh pits might writhe more politely, but venues like **Elysée Montmartre**, **Le Loco** (*see chapter* **Clubs**), **La Boule Noir** and **Le Divan du Monde** (*see p329*) try to accommodate crowd-sucking movement. True, French band Watcha had the crowd at **Olympia** into pogo (vertical dance, one can only imagine), but how can the French combat such stage antics as Gene Simmons' glam-licking stars? By getting naked, of course. The band Gronibard did. It's one way to distract attention from the music.

One outfit to watch is Pleymo, who have toured with Slipknot. They've cribbed sounds from Korn, NTM, Prodigy and the Deftones, melding their rap, metal, hardcore and trash sound into something, well, into something. Other French notables are Lofofora (named after peyote) and Gojira (Japanese for Godzilla – 'God help us' would be more appropriate).

What to do if you're strung out on Slayer or in need of a little 'Zep? Visit one of Paris' three main metal bars. At **Kata Bar** (37 rue Fontaine,18th, 01.40.16.12.13/ www.katabar.com), locals will happily confirm that French metal is *merde*. Punters come to hear industrial, goth, metal goth, doom and batcave. Check out the downstairs graveyard. **The Black Dog** (26 rue des Lombards, 4th, 01.42.77.66.85/ www.blackdog-bar.com), opened a year ago for migratory metalheads who prefer the centre of the city. **Les Furieux** (74 rue de la Roquette, 11th, 01.47.00.78.44/ www.lesfurieux.fr) hosts friendly sessions and lots of hooks on which to hang the black leather jacket your mum bought you.

Looking to buy your own copy of *Black Bomb A*? Of course you are, and worry not, there are secret corners of Paris where metal and vinyl meet. **Planet Rock** specialises in metal/hard rock (18 rue de Douai, 9th, 01.44.53.95.11/ www.planetrockstore.com). Heavy regulars and the occasional German tourist seeking a rare Ramstein platter can be seen rubbing elbows. **Monster Melodies** (9 rue des Déchargeurs, 1st, 01.40.28.09.39/ www.monstermelodies.com), Paris' original metal source, has a heady whiff of vinyls and though they have had to diversify their selection, they continue to shelve plenty of scream. So come on. Feel the noise. And smell the glove.

Sport & Fitness

Being in Paris doesn't mean you have to neglect your baton twirling. This is a sporty town, so pack your tankini, get your goose grease and let's get sweaty.

The possibilities for Parisian sport extend far beyond a bunch of boozed-up, rotund baldies (and that's just the chicks) tossing their *boules* argumentatively around a patch of dust. The French are a very energetic nation, or, perhaps more precisely, they do have a passion for watching sport: case in point the **Tour de France**, the event that isn't really reckoned, by certain cynical observers, to have had a vintage year unless a couple of riders have died on a vertical mountainside or OD'd on a cocktail of performance-enhancers. In 2003, millions massed at the Champs-Elysées to see Lance Armstrong claim his fifth yellow shirt. *Pas mal*, pal.

For Parisians who go in for participatory sports other than smoking, queue hopping and 'self-dating' to Sunday-night soft porn, the capital has a fantastic sporting infrastructure. So, ha! You've got no excuse. Participation in anything from hockey to hooplah is possible and the city is jumping with glorious stadiums. In terms of organisation and facilities, the staging of the 2003 World Athletics Championships did Paris proud. Let's just hope that the unruly noises coming from the home crowd has not ruined Paris' candidacy for the 2012 Olympics.

The best source of information for sport in Paris is the *Guide du Sport à Paris* (in French, of course, but a groin strain's a groin strain in any lingo), published by the Mairie de Paris and available from each arrondissement's town hall. To use certain sports centres, you will need a *carte* for which you must show an identity card or passport (take an extra photo, too), and sometimes insurance. For the major sports invents, *see chapter* **Festivals & Events**.

Spectator sports

For international events, the usual venue is the Stade de France (rue Francis de Pressensé, 93210 St-Denis, 0892.700.900/www.stadedefrance.fr for tickets, programme and visits/RER La Plaine - Stade de France). Alternatively, the Palais Omnisports de Paris-Bercy (8 bd de Bercy, 12th/0892.692 300/www.popb.fr for reservations/M° Bercy) hosts everything from martial arts to indoor jet skiing. Tickets are available online or at branches of Fnac, Virgin Megastore and Galeries Lafayette.

Basketball

Paris Basket Racing

Stade Pierre de Coubertin, 82 av Georges Lafont, 16th (01.45.27.79.12/www.ifrance.com). M° Porte de St-Cloud.

Basketball is very popular in France, and the French first division, the Pro A, is of an admirable level – by European standards, that is. Paris Basket Racing is a consistent mid-table performer, whose ultimate moment of glory so far has been – steady yourself – making the final of the 1956 French cup. They just need to build on that.

Football

Paris St-Germain

Parc des Princes, 24 rue du Commandant-Guilbaud, 16th (01.42.30.03.60/www.psg.fr). M° Porte d'Auteuil.
Tickets by Internet or phone (08.25.07.50.78). Prices range from €9-€83.

Paris' only top-division football team has had difficulty in living up to its fans' expectations. Matches are held at the fabulous 48,000-seat Parc des Princes, funding is copious and the success-starved fans are loyal. As the 2003-2004 season swung into action, the vexed and eternal question remained: so why aren't they any good, then?

Horse racing

There are seven racecourses in the Paris area. *France Galop* publishes a full racing list (01.49.10.20.30/www.france-galop.com) in its *Calendrier des Courses*. **Auteuil**, Bois de Boulogne, 16th (01.40.71.47.47/M° Porte d'Auteuil), steeplechasing. **Chantilly** (41km from Paris/03.44.62.41.00/train from Gare du Nord), flat racing. **Enghien** (18km from Paris/01.34.17.87.00/train from Gare du Nord), steeplechasing and trotting. **Longchamp**, Bois de Boulogne, 16th (01.44.30.75.00/M° Porte d'Auteuil, then free bus), flat racing. **Maisons-Laffitte** (1 av de La Pelouse, 78600 Maisons-Laffitte/01.39.12.81.70/RER A Maisons-Laffitte and then bus), flat racing. **St-Cloud** (1 rue du Camp Canadien, 92210 St-Cloud/01.47.71.69.26/RER A Rueil-Malmaison), flat racing. **Paris-Vincennes** Bois de Vincennes, 12th (01.49.77.17.17/M° Vincennes/RER Joinville le Pont), trotting.

Rollerblading

One- (or two-)session gyms

Paris equals temptation: temptation equals immediate collapse of resolve and, for the neurotic, waves of self-hatred. For some, national salvation lies in a quick visit to the gym, and in Paris there are plenty of places to have a one-off (or two-off if you're really hedonistic), cleansing sesh.

Not far from the bustle of Les Halles is **Espace Vit'Halles** (48 rue Rambuteau, 3rd, 01.42.77.21.71/www.vit-halles.com/ Mº Rambuteau), a well-liked, sunken-level health club. If you're not intimidated by thumping music, a handful of preening male models and super-exuberant instructors who are clearly just waiting to be talent-spotted, you'll like it here. As well as clean, if quite small, locker rooms and good weight-training equipment, it's got some of the best classes in Paris – Step and RPM classes (stationary bicycling) are very popular. Try Cécile's RPM class – it can get pretty raucous. Espace Vit'Halles has a flexible pricing policy and is open seven days a week. A ten-entry passbook costs €149, a single visit €20.

Just off the boulevard St-Germain in the 5th lies the venerable **Club Quartier Latin** (19 rue de Pontoise, 5th/01.55.42.77.88/ Mº Maubert Mutualité), home to the Piscine Pontoise. Two floors above the water you'll find the fitness facility. The gym is a no-frills place, though, and it scores exceptionally highly on atmosphere: there are no lockers, some of the weight machines look like they might date back to the Industrial Revolution and you may even spot a few die-hard smokers sacreligiously puffing away at the small bar downstairs. Students and families alike dig the place for the reasonable prices, for the gorgeous, multi-laned pool, for the location and the camaraderie. The price for a single session is €20.

The heavyweight on the health club scene is **Club Med Gym** (numerous branches, (www.clubmedgym.fr). One visit costs €30. The chain has the advantage of around a dozen locations in Paris alone, so you're never far from guilt. No excuses: there's a Stairmaster here with your name on it, and if you're lucky you'll snag one by a giant window so you can watch the world go by. Overall, the gyms are clean, well-lit and have good equipment, as well as prime locations.

La Compagnie Bleue has two super-clean, convenient locations in Paris (12 rue de l'Eglise, 15th/01.40.59.49.10/

Mº Commerce and 100 rue du Cherche-Midi, 6th/01.45.44.47.48/Mº Duroc). While they offer the whole spectrum of cardio-classes-weights, they really excel in yoga, relaxation and stretching classes. A one-month membership costs €122.

If you go to **La Gym Suédoise** sweaty with visions of blonde, buxom be-plaited Scandinavians you're definitely going to be disappointed. That said, the club offers its own unique gym method, fresh from Sweden, mixing simple exercises with music (34 bd de Reims, 17th/Mº Porte de Champerret; 11 rue Pierre-Villers, 7th/01.45.00.18.22/ www.lagymsuedoise.asso.fr/Mº Solferino). An individual session will set you back €10.

If you find the private clubs too intimidating or too expensive, the city is also dotted with municipal gymnasiums, where you may be able to negotiate a one-off. The best resource for information on all the municipal facilities is the annual *Parisports – Le Guide du Sport à Paris* available for free at any Mairie. And, after all, walking down to the Town Hall and lugging a copy of that back equals exercise. Well, you don't want to go mad, do you, especially if you need to carry your poodle back to the Eurostar?

Rugby

Stade Français CASG

Stade Jean-Bouin, 26 av du Général-Sarrail, 16th (01.46.51.00.75/www.stade.fr). M° Porte d'Auteuil.
Tickets €5-€35.

Le Stade Français has put Paris on the national rugby map. In June 2003, under the management of South African Nick Mallett, the Parisian team smackeroonied Toulouse 32-18 and won the championship. Triumph has had a strange effect on the team members, though, as late 2003 has seen calendars featuring the lads in a series of poses that they insist are not meant to be homoerotic, but have been snapped up – and not just by the ladies.

Activities & team sports

All-round sports clubs

The **Standard Athletic Club** (Route Forestière du Pavé de Meudon, 92360 Meudon-la-Forêt/01.46.26.16.09/www.standac.com) is a private club aimed at English-speakers living in Paris. Full membership is €625 per year, plus an initial joining fee. It fields a cricket eleven, hockey and football teams. There are eight tennis courts, two squash courts, a heated outdoor pool and billiards table. Some top-level French clubs also run teams in various sports, such as **Racing Club de France** (01.45.67.55.86/www.racingclubdefrance.org), **Paris Université Club** (01.44.16.62.62/ www.puc.asso.fr) and **Le Stade Français** (01.40.71.33.33).

American football

Though there are no teams in Paris itself, there are 15 teams in the area. Many teams have some Americans in them, whether players or coaches. Contact the **Fédération Française de Football Américain** (01.43.11.14.70/ www.ffa.org or www.efafofficiating.org for those interested in learning how to referee) to find the club nearest you.

Athletics & running

Paris has many municipal tracks (including eight indoor ones) which are generally of a good standard. To find the track nearest you, consult the *Guide du Sport* or call Paris Infos Mairie. For an open-air run, the **Bois de Boulogne** and the **Bois de Vincennes** are the only large green expanses in Paris, although most of the parks (try Buttes-Chaumont in the 19th) as well as the banks of the Seine and the canals attract a fair number of joggers. Be aware that the Bois de Boulogne is a cruising spot.

Baseball

Baseball clubs are predictably Americanised and many of the players are English-speakers. The best way to find a team near you is to contact the **Fédération Française de Baseball, Softball et Cricket** (01.44.68.89.30/www.ffbsc.org). Whatever happened to rounders, one wonders?

Basketball

Basketball is very popular in Paris, and virtually every municipal sports centre has a court and club, whose standard will usually be high. The **Comité Parisien de Basketball** (01.53.94.27.90/www.basketfrance.com) lists clubs, public and private, including **Racing Club de France** and **Paris Université Club**. There are also a number of public courts in the city where anyone can play. Popular spots include two courts under the Métro tracks near the Glacière stop in the 13th arrondissement and at M° Stalingrad in the 19th.

Bowling & boules

The Paris region has more than 25 ten-pin bowling centres. The two we list below are among the most pleasant; both rent out shoes and have restaurants, games rooms and late hours. There are eight lanes at the centrally located and lively **Bowling-Mouffetard** (73 rue Mouffetard, 5th/01.43.31.09.35/ M° Place Monge/open 3pm-2am Mon-Fri, 10am-2am Sat, Sun). The **Bowling de Paris** (Jardin d'Acclimatation, Bois de Boulogne, 16th/01.53.64.93.00/M° Les Sablons/open 9am-3am Mon-Fri; 9am-5am Sat, Sun) has 24 lanes, pool, billiards and video games. Bear in mind that you have to pay €2.50 to get into the Jardin d'Acclimatation before you get to the centre.

You can play *boules* or *pétanque* in most squares. There are also some *boulodromes* in the **Jardins du Luxembourg**.

If you feel like shooting some balls of the coloured kind, then the **Cercle Clichy Montmartre** (84 rue de Clichy/01.48.78.32.85/ www.academie-billard.com/M° Place de Clichy) is a superb place to come, with frescoes, bars and tables a-plenty. Young and old mingle from 10am-6am. Prices range from €7.90 per hour for pool to €10 for American billiards. The largest pool hall, at 1,200m², is **Academy Billard** (32 rue Linois, 15th/ 01.45.79.67.23/www.academy-billard.com/M° Charles-Michels). Open until 5am at the weekend, it lets you pot your balls to the banging' tunes of a live DJ – get your grooviest waistcoat out of mothballs.

Climbing

The wall at the **Centre Sportif Poissonnier** (2 rue Jean-Cocteau, 18th/01.42.51.24.68/ M° Porte de Clignancourt) is the largest municipal facility (there are six others in Paris). To use any of the state-owned facilities, you need to get a personal ID card. To get one, take a photo, your passport, proof of valid insurance and €3 per month to the centre you want to use. For more of a workout, there is the privately run **Mur Mur** (55 rue Cartier Bresson, 93500 Pantin/01.48.46.11.00/M° Aubervilliers-Pantin Quatre Chemins), said to be the best climbing wall in Europe, with 1,500m² of wall, 10,000 holds and an even greater number of ways of falling off. It costs €6-€12 for adults, €3-€6 for under-12s per session, though there is a joining fee of €24 for adults and €12 for under-12s. There is kit for hire and tuition on offer. Newly added is a section to practise ice-climbing (or 'dry-tooling', as they so picturesquely call it).

If you prefer real rock, you can train on the huge, slightly surreal boulders strewn around the forêt de Fontainebleau. Contact **l'Association des amis de la Forêt de Fontainebleau** (01.64.23.46.45/www.aaff.org). You might also want to check out the **Club Alpin Francais** (01.42.18.20.00/ www.clubalpin.com) who organise climbing excursions within the Ile de France every weekend and occasional trips away.

Cycling

Bike lanes have been expanded by Mayor Delanoë, and increasing numbers of cyclists are mounting their choppers and taking to the streets. In fact, every Sunday and on public holidays many areas are shut off to cars to allow pedestrians and cyclists free wheel. The quais de Seine and the Canal St-Martin are the nicest, but the Bois de Boulogne and the Bois de Vincennes also offer good cycling.

Paris has many cycling clubs, both in the competition-based and more leisurely categories. You can find your nearest club by phoning the **Fédération Française de Cyclotourisme** (01.44.16.88.88/www.ffc.fr). The **Stade Vélodrome Jacques-Anquetil** (Bois de Vincennes, 12th/01.43.68.01.27) is a functional racing track open to cyclists on a regular basis. The **Maison du Vélo** (11 rue Fénélon, 10th/01.42.81.24.72) sells and repairs all types of bikes. There are also companies offering bike tours in and around Paris and the **MDB** (01.43.20.26.02/www.mdb-idf.org) (movement for the defence of the bicycle) organises rides for its members. Membership costs €10 for the year.

Diving

For a diving shop, try **Plongespace** (80 rue Balard, 15th/01.45.57.01.01). The **Club de Plongée du 5ème Arrondissement** (01.43.36.07.67) is a club where you can train for the French licence. It organises trips to the Med and meets at the **Piscine Jean-Taris**. There are well-qualified, friendly and experienced instructors at **Surplouf** (06.14.10.26.11/ 01.42.21.18.14), which offers courses in English.

Fencing

Many of the city gyms organise fencing classes or play host to fencing clubs. For a full list of clubs consult www.escrime-ffe.fr. The **Racing Club de France**'s (5 rue Eblé, 7th, 01.45.67.55.86/www.racingclubdefrance.org) fencing section is a good bet for leisure or competition with 12 fencing masters and 18 pistes, leaving you ample room to practise those *flèches.* All levels, weapons and ages are catered for. The **Association Sportive de la Préfecture de Police (ASPP)** (4 rue de la Montagne-Ste-Geneviève, 5th/01.42.34.54.00) is worth checking out too.

Football

Those expecting to find a grass pitch for a kickabout will be disappointed. The city's 80 public pitches tend to be either dirt, artificial turf, or a place where grass once grew. To find a pitch near you, consult the *Guide du Sport* or call Paris Infos Mairie. To find an amateur team to play for, call the **Ligue Ile de France de Football** (01.42.44.12.12/www.ffr.fr) and ask for a contact number in your arrondissement.

Golf

There are no courses in central Paris, but scores in the Paris region. For a full list, contact the **Fédération Francaise de Golf** (68 rue Anatole France, 92309 Levallois Perret/ 01.41.49.77.00/www.ffg.org). The **Golf Clément Ader** (Domaine du Château Péreire, 77220 Gretz Armainvilliers/01.64.07.34.10/ SNCF Gretz Armainvilliers) is challenging. The **Golf Disneyland Paris Marne-la-Vallée** (77700 Marne-la-Vallée/01.60.45.68.90/ www.disneylandparis.com/RER Marne-la-Vallée-Chessy then taxi) has everything. Closer to central Paris is the **Académie de Golf de Paris** at the Paris Country Club, Hippodrome de St-Cloud (1 rue du Camp Canadien, 92210 St-Cloud/01.47.71.39.22/SNCF Surèsnes Longchamp), which has a nine-hole course within its horse-racing track.

Ice skating at Hôtel de Ville

Horse riding

Both the Bois de Boulogne and the Bois de Vincennes are beautiful riding areas. Excellent clubs to join are: **La Société d'Equitation de Paris** (01.45.01.20.06), the **Centre Hippique du Touring** (01.45.01.20. 88) or the **Cercle Hippique du Bois de Vincennes** (01.48.73.01.28). Beginners can learn in the unpretentious **Club Bayard Equitation** (Bois de Vincennes, Centre Bayard/UCPA de Vincennes, av de Polygone, 12th/01.43.65.46.87). Membership runs for three months (€220) or you can do a five-day course in July or August (€250). The **Haras de Jardy** (bd de Jardy, 92430 Marnes-la-Coquette/01.47.01.35.30) is a lovely equestrian centre near Versailles, which organises group rides. **ACBB** (212-214 rue Gallieni, 92100 Boulogne Billancourt/ 01.48.25.59.80/www.acbb.equitation.free.fr) offers courses and competitions for all levels. Prices for non-residents are pretty steep, however: it costs €125 to join the club, plus a €120 annual fee, €208 per trimester, and an additional €46 per hour of instruction.

Ice skating

In winter the **place de l'Hôtel de Ville** is transformed into an open-air ice rink. If temperatures drop extremely low, there is skating on the Lac Supérieur in the **Bois de Boulogne**. Indoor all-year-round rinks include the **Patinoire de Boulogne** (1 rue Victor Griffuelhes, 92100 Boulogne Billancourt/ 01.46.08.09.09/M° Marcel Sembat) and the **Patinoire d'Asnières-sur-Seine** (bd Pierre de Coubertin, 92600 Asnières/01.47.99.96.06/ M° Gabriel Péri/Asnières-Gennevilliers). The **Sonja Henie** rink (Palais Omnisports de Paris-Bercy, 01.40.02.60.60) was opened to the public in October 2002. It was previously only available for shows and to various clubs. Protection, helmets and skates are all available for hire (€6) and admission starts at €4.

Off-beat sports

Jorkyball is the new sex. The sport mixes racquets, squash and soccer. Two two-player teams face off in an enclosed court with a synthetic grass floor and Plexiglass-and-foam walls. The object is to to put the ball in the other team's goal, using the walls to pass and shoot. Enthusiasts hail the game as a faster, funnier version of football. There are now over 200 Jorkyball courts in France, Italy, Spain and England, but only one as of yet in Ile-de-France. **Jorkyball Parisien** (160 chaussée Jules César, 95130 Le Plessis Bouchard (01.34.44.04.34/ www.jorkyball.org).

Shooting paintballs while running around like a loon is a rebellion against Parisian decorum that could get many Anglophones active. **CAMP**, Europe's leading paintball organisation, has 25 hectares of forest 45 minutes from Paris at Pomponne, in which to play war (CAMP PaintballVision/01.42.68.10.00/www.paintballcamp.com/over-16s only, €29-40 per person, plus extra forre-loading).

You can live out your Tarzan fantasies 15m up in the tree canopy on a '*randonnée arboricole*' – literally, a walk in the trees. **Aye-Aye Environment** will teach you how to travel from tree to tree with ropes and pulleys across the 250 hectare nature reserve of Espace Rambouillet. After the 3½ hour training session (open to anyone over eight, €53.36), you can sign up to spend the night in a hammock in the trees (Espace Rambouillet/01.44.52.11.21/ www.ayeaye.org/SNCF Rambouillet from Montparnasse, then 6km by foot/taxi).

Finding ice-hockey too easy these days? Play it under water. Underwater hockey – or octapushy – is a growing sport in France. Using a lead puck and a hydrodynamic, curved wooden stick, it is played in swimming pools wearing masks, snorkels, flippers and ear-protecting hats. You might think the water would make it a slow and ponderous game – the flippers make it orgasmic. *Le hockey sub-aquatique* is played in pools in the 5th, 10th, 12th, 15th and 18th arrondissements (see the Mairie de Paris' *Parisports* guide) and at the **Piscine de Louvrais** at Pointoise, headquarters of the national team. (01.30.32.98.79/http://chspc.free.fr).

Rollerblading

Simply everybody's doing it. Parisian skaters have been braving both the potential disgrace of a spectacular fall and the wrath of infringed pedestrians for several years now. If, on a Friday evening stroll, you notice traffic at a standstill and rabid drivers honking their horns, you'll be witnessing the effects of 40,000 roller maniacs on their Friday Night Fever run. The Pari Roller team staff in their bright yellow T-shirts are on hand at all times to deal with mishaps. The starting point is at Gare Montparnasse at 10pm and the run finishes there three hours later. The route is announced on Thursday on the Pari Roller website: www.pari-roller.com (01.43.36.89.81).

A more sedate beginner's skate takes place every Sunday at 2.30pm, organised by **Roller et Coquillage** and meeting at the **Nomades** shop just off place de la Bastille (37 bd Bourdon, 4th/M° Bastille/01.44.54.94.42/ www.rollers-coquillages.org). The nervous neophyte is accorded as much respect as some Nureyev-on-wheels. **The Roller Squad Institute** (www.rsi.asso.fr) organises lessons for young and old, beginners and advanced alike. To book a place, call 01.42.74.70.00 48 hours in advance. For renting skates, the best place to go is **Vertical Line** (01.47.27.21.21/www.vertical-line.com), where they have 350 pairs from size 28 to 48. They also do repairs and custom-made skates. Not to be missed is **Rollerparc Avenue** (01.47.18.19.14/www.rollerparc.com), in Vitry-sur-Seine, the largest indoor roller centre in Europe with 6,000m² full of different tracks. Entrance is €10 and skate hire €4.

Rowing & watersports

You can row, canoe and kayak (Wed, Sat; equipment is provided) in the 600m x 65m basin at the **Base Nautique de la Villette** (15-17 quai de la Loire, 19th/01.42.40.29.90/M° Jaurès). You need to reserve a week in advance and have proof of your residence in Paris. Waterskiing, wakeboarding and the like are all possible at the **Club Nautique du 19ème** (28 av Simon-Bolivar), Sun 3-6.30pm. Prices start at €8. Call 01.42.03.25.24 or 06.03.91.96.92 to reserve. La Défense-based **Société Nautique de la Basse Seine** (26 quai du Président Paul Doumer, 92400 Courbevoie/01.43.33.03.47) has both competitive and recreational sections; or you can hire boats on Lac Daumesnil and Lac des Minimes in the **Bois de Vincennes** or on Lac Supérieur in the **Bois de Boulogne**.

Rugby

Top-level rugby goes on at **Racing Club de France**. For a good club standard try the **Athletic Club de Boulogne** (Saut du Loup, route des Tribunes, 16th), which fields two teams. The **British Rugby Club of Paris** (58-60 ave de la Grande Armée, 17th/01.40.55.15.15) fields two teams in the corporate league.

Skateboarding

Paris is a skateboarder's dream. There are always skaters a-plenty by the fountain near **Les Halles** (1st) shopping centre, but the standard of talent generally doesn't offer much

The crawl of nature

Every Monday and Wednesday night, a surprising metamorphosis occurs in the changing rooms of Piscine Roger Le Gall. Some have likened it to a return to the Garden of Eden; others have, perhaps more accurately, compared it to a return to the water feature of the Garden of Eden.

What happens is that potential swimmers go into the changing rooms, the day's constricting apparel comes off. And nothing replaces it. That's right: they emerge from the locker room in, to quote the poet, the naughty naked nude.

For the **Association des Naturistes de Paris**, the birthday suit is the swimming suit of choice, but of course it's all about naturism, not voyeurism. As the Association is keen to stress, these in-the-buff pool sessions have nothing to do with mere aqueous orgies.

As with any kind of naturism, nudity is seen as completely natural, a total '*non-événement*'. Naked is no big deal, giggling is frowned upon and comments – be they admiring or derogatory – are definitely not appreciated.

The naturists are realistic enough to know that the nature of their association is often open to misunderstanding. So, before a prospective member is accepted into the group, three trial sessions are required to ensure that both novice and association are happy to take the plunge.

That said, bare bathing is accepted by the Association as having connotations wider than the simple thrill of the skinny dip. This being France, a pseudo-psychological element has to rear its head one way or another, and the Association's Freudians see the participants as swimming in a kind of chlorinated amniotic fluid. Yuck. (And surely a nice long bath would be more the thing if that were the case.)

Paris' rather strict bathing-apparel rules for municipal – and even some private – pools can indeed be something of a cold shower. They insist for example that, for chaps, nut-huggers and nut-huggers alone can be worn – turn up in loose, Bermuda-style trunks and you'll be denied admission. What's more, both sexes are obliged don the swimming cap (all for admirable, hygienic reasons, to be sure, but it certainly does sod-all for your posing cred or your afro).

Thus, the opportunity to enjoy 20 lengths liberated from those constricting Speedos or that Nosferatu millinery has undoubted allure.

But let us be clear about one thing: the watery gatherings of which we treat are for genuine naturists, committed naturists, those who, during the colder months, are unable to submit their bits to the shrivelling bite of the sea without fear of a massive cardiac arrest – or, indeed, a civil one.

It's all about extending the possibilities of the French ideal of *liberté*: imagine the liberating sensation of gliding along in the fast lane, your body hair trailing behind like the lank, over-permed mane of a sea urchin.

So do overcome your nerves: it's only natural to be a tad timid when everyone's in the buff, but you'll soon forget your shyness when you're flapping around just as Mother Nature intended.

Association des Naturistes de Paris

(01.47.78.18.78/www.naturistes-paris.org or e-mail info@naturistes-paris.org. **Meetings** *Piscine Roger le Gall, 34 bd Carnot, 12th (01.44.73.81.12). Mº Porte de Vincennes*. Sept-July, Mon, Wed 9-11pm. Annual membership costs €60 (€22 for 18-26-year-olds).

in the way of a challenge. Other popular spots to strut your stuff in front of admiring tourists are **Palais-Royal** (1st) and the esplanade at **Trocadéro** (16th) where there are ramps available. **Bercy** (12th) is extremely popular because it is so huge and has some excellent flights of steps. The 17-hectare **Centre Sportif Suzanne Lenglen** (2 rue Louis-Armand, 15th/ 01.44.26.26.50/M° Balard/ 8am-10pm Mon-Fri; 8am-7pm Sat, Sun) has two outdoor ramps to accommodate skaters, skateboarders and mountain-bikers.

Squash

You can play at **Club Quartier Latin** or the **Standard Athletic Club**, or try **Squash Montmartre** (14 rue Achille-Martinet, 18th/ 01.42.55.38.30/M° Lamarck-Caulaincourt). Membership is €540 per year or €140 for three months, or you can pay each time you visit (€15 per hour).

Swimming

If you were planning on making an entrance in style, forget it. You will usually have to contend with the fetching addition of a swim cap: these can usually be bought from a vending machine or borrowed from the lifeguards. Nut-hugging trunks rather than bermudas are also *de rigueur* for blokes (with notable exceptions, *see p341* **The crawl of nature**). Paris' municipal pools are however clean and cheap. Private pools offer extra attractions, and are open longer. Night swimming to music has become an integral part of the Nuit Blanche.

Piscine Suzanne-Berlioux

Forum des Halles, 10 pl de la Rotonde, 1st (01.42.36.98.44). M° Les Halles. **Admission** €3.80. **Map** p402 J5.
This 50m pool with its own tropical greenhouse attracts a young, hip clientele.

Piscine Jean-Taris

16 rue Thouin, 5th (01.55.42.81.90). M° Cardinal Lemoine. **Admission** €2.40, €1.35 residents, under-26s. **Map** p406 J8.
Look on to a sloping garden from this 25m-pool.

Piscine Pontoise Quartier Latin

19 rue de Pontoise, 5th (01.55.42.77.88). M° Maubert-Mutualité. **Admission** €3.80 plus €0.45 for locker, €3.35 plus €0.45 for locker students. **Map** p406 K7.
This art deco 33m pool has music and underwater lighting by night.

Piscine du Marché St-Germain

12 rue Lobineau, 6th (01.43.29.08.15). M° Mabillon. **Admission** €2.40, €1.35 residents, under-26s. **Map** p405 H7.
A hip, underground 25m pool in St-Germain.

Piscine Butte-aux-Cailles

5 pl Paul-Verlaine, 13th (01.45.89.60.05). M° Place d'Italie. **Admission** €2.40, €1.35 residents, under-26s.
This complex has one main pool (33m) and two outdoor pools built in the 1920s.

Piscine Didot

22 av Georges-Lafenestre, 14th (01.45.39.89.29). M° Porte de Vanves. **Admission** €2.40, €1.35 residents, under-26s.
This 25m pool welcomes diving clubs and practitioners of aquagym as well as individual swimmers.

Aquaboulevard

4 rue Louis-Armand, 15th (01.40.60.15.15). M° Balard. **Admission** six hours in peak periods €20, under-11s €10. **Map** p404 H5.
This extravagant indoor-outdoor complex is great fun for kids. Dig the sandy beach, the whirlpool and the mini-golf. For an extra charge you get access to a steam bath and three saunas of varying intensity.

Piscine Emile-Anthoine

9 rue Jean-Rey, 15th (01.53.69.61.59). M° Bir-Hakeim. **Admission** €2.40, €1.35 residents, under-26s. **Map** p404 C6.
This large, modern pool has a fabulous view of the Eiffel Tower.

Piscine Georges-Hermant

4-6 rue David d'Angers, 19th,(01.42.02.45.10) M° Danube. **Admission** €3.35, €2.90 under-16s.
This is Paris' biggest pool, at 50m x 20m. It's uncovered in summer and there's a great atmosphere.

Tennis

The **Jardins du Luxembourg** (6th/ 01.43.25. 79.18/M° Notre-Dame-des-Champs/ RER Luxembourg) is a great place to play. The **Centre Sportif La Falguère** (route de la Pyramide, Bois de Vincennes, 12th/ 01.43.74.40.93/M° Château de Vincennes) has 21 acrylic courts. **Centre Sportif Henry-de-Montherlant** (30-32 bd Lannes, 16th/01.40.72.28.33/M° Porte-Dauphine) has seven hard courts. To demonstrate your prowess on these courts you need to get hold of the Paris tennis card. Then you only pay for the time spent on court (€5.75 per hour for a court – there are no indoor courts). The private **Le Tennis Club de Boulogne Billancourt** (19 bd Anatole-France, 92100 Boulogne-Billancourt/01.46.03.84.49/ M° Boulogne-Jean Jaurès) has 28 hard courts. **Club Forest Hill** (4 rue Louis-Armand, 15th/01.40.60.10.00/ M° Balard/RER Boulevard Victor) has 12 branches in the Paris region. For **table tennis** fans, there are public tables on the quais at Stalingrad (you can expect an audience), and all the clubs in Paris where you can ping your pong are listed on www.tennisdetable.com.

Theatre

With thespian tights all in a bunch, you might think it's curtains for French theatre. *Au contraire* – there's international and home-grown talent to an absurd degree.

France holds the theatre in such high regard that recent government plans to reform the unemployment system – and dramatically reduce benefit to theatre, cinema and audio-visual artists – set many a codpiece a-throbbing with indignation. Festivals and events across France in summer 2003, including Avignon Festival, were cancelled as a result of strikes by *intermittents*. The new season's solidarity may prove to threaten more of the same, so it would be wise to look before you book.

But the show must go on. In Paris, the 2004 season is marked, surprisingly, by the paucity of French plays. Though ye olde regulars like Racine, Molière and Feydeau will be around, they have been pushed aside, allowing a flood of international productions and directors to come front and centre. Theatres such as the **Odéon, Théâtre d'Europe** attract diverse works, often performed in their own languages, and the **Théâtre International de Langue Française** represents all Francophones at **La Villette** (01.40.03.93.95/ www.tilf.fr). The international festivals, especially **Festival d'Automne** (September to December) and spring's **Festival de l'Imaginaire** (01.45.44.72.30/ www.mcm.asso.fr), bring top-class talent to France.

Here in town, nearly native Peter Brook at the **Bouffes du Nord** still reigns as the most influential director, although Ariane Mnouchkine at her **Théâtre du Soleil** shares the spotlight with Patrice Chéreau, who presided over the 2003 Cannes Film Festival. Paris continues to vogue with musicals; **Théâtre de Châtelet** (*see chapter,* **Music: Classical & Opera**) will resurrect Broadway revivals and St-Exupéry's *Le Petit Prince* will go onto a second season (without Daniel Lavoie). But not all of the action is in town. Some of the most uninhibited productions can be found outside the Péripherique; taking a jaunt out of town might be well worth the trip (*see chapter,* **Beyond the Périphérique**). Notables to visit include Peter Sellars at the **MC93** (01.41.60.72.72/www.mc93.com) in Bobigny or Nanterre's **Théâtre des Amandiers** (www.tem-nanterre.com).

English productions abound, despite the lack of an institutionalised Anglophone theatre company, but reliable troupes include **Dear Conjunction** and **OnStage Theatre Company**, who both perform at the Sudden Theatre (14bis rue Ste. Isaure, 18th/ 01.42.62.35.00). The cellar of the Théâtre de Nesle (8 rue de Nesle, 6th/01.46.34.61.04) is also a go-to if you're in need of the native tongue, and the **Théâtre de Verdure du Jardin Shakespeare** in the Bois de Boulogne (08.20.00.75.75) welcomes London's Tower Theatre to perform the Bard's works in June.

National theatres

Comédie Française

Salle Richelieu *pl Colette, 1st (01.44.58.15.15/ www.comedie-francaise.fr). M° Palais Royal.* **Box office** 11am-6pm daily. **Tickets** €11-€30; €10 under-27s (1hr before play). **Credit** AmEx, MC, V. **Map** p406 H5. **Théâtre du Vieux-Colombier** *21 rue du Vieux-Colombier, 6th (01.44.39.87.00/ www.comedie-francaise.fr). M° St-Sulpice.* **Box office** 1-6pm Mon, Sun; 11am-7pm Tue-Sat. **Tickets** €26; €19 over-60s; €13 under-27s. **Credit** MC, V. **Map** p405 G7. **Studio Théâtre** *Galerie du Carrousel (99 rue de Rivoli), 1st (01.44.58.98.58/ www.comedie-francaise.fr). M° Palais Royal.* **Box office** 5.30pm on day (Mon, Wed-Sun). **Tickets** €13; €7.50 under-27s. **Credit** MC, V. **Map** p405 H5.

The Comédie Française is the grandmother of Parisian venues. From 16 May, the historic Salle Richelieu will be buffing the marble and putting new springs in the chair where Molière popped his clogs during a performance of *Le Malade Imaginaire*, reopening on 15 October with the same play. The Left Bank Théâtre du Vieux-Colombier, founded 'to combat the cowardice of commercial theatre', anticipates Brigitte Jacques-Wajeman's interpretation of Racine's *Britannicus*. The 136-seat Studio Theatre, named after Stanislavsky and Moscow's First Studio-Theatre of Art, nourishes actors with contemporary plays and readings and hosts early evening short plays (6.30pm) and salons in the Carrousel du Louvre. *Wheelchair access (call ahead).*

Théâtre National de Chaillot

Palais de Chaillot, 1 pl du Trocadéro, 16th (01.53.65.30.00/www.theatre-chaillot.fr). M° Trocadéro. **Box office** 11am-7pm Mon-Fri; 1pm-5pm Sun; *telephone* 11am-7pm Mon-Sat. **Tickets** €18.50-€31; €16-€25.50 concessions; €10-€19 under-26s. **Credit** MC, V. **Map** p404 B5.

Popular, accessible plays (classic and modern), dance and musical theatre are programmed for Chaillot's mammoth 2,800-seat, 1930s theatre, while more experimental fare can be found in its smaller

Comédie Française

theatre space. Noteworthy British author Martin Crimp's *Face au Mur* is on the docket and if, Brecht's your bard, Irina Brook takes on *La Bonne Ame de St-Tchouan. Wheelchair access (call ahead).*

Odéon, Théâtre de L'Europe

Temporary address (until 2006): Aux Ateliers Berthier, 8 bd Berthier, 17th (01.44.41.36.36/ www.theatre-odeon.fr). M° Porte de Clichy. **Box office** *telephone* 11am-6.30pm Mon-Sat (or ticket office an hour and a half before the show). **Tickets** €7.50-€26. **Credit** MC, V. **Map** p401 E1.

Closed until 2006 for a total overhaul, the flagship European theatre has been relocated up north to an ex-warehouse converted into a 500-seat theatre. Georges Lavaudant directs *Matériau Platanov*, drafted material by young Chekhov discovered in a Moscow safe. *Wheelchair access (call ahead).*

Théâtre National de la Colline

15 rue Malte-Brun, 20th (01.44.62.52.52/ www.colline.fr). M° Gambetta. **Box office** 11am-6pm Mon-Tue; 11am-7pm Wed-Fri; 1pm-7pm Sat; 2-5pm Sun if play on. **Tickets** €26; €21 over-60s; €13 under-30s; €18 Tue. **Credit** MC, V. **Map** p403 Q5.

This is the place for the nurturing of contemporary talent. Playwrights such as Valère Novarina and directors such as Stanislas Norday (directing Feydeau's *La Puce à l'Oreille* in May and June) get the billing. It is also stages French versions of Pinter (long gaps are not hard to translate). *Wheelchair access (call ahead).*

Right Bank

Théâtre de la Ville/Les Abbesses

Théâtre de la Ville *2 pl du Châtelet, 4th (01.42.74.22.77/www.theatredelaville-paris.com). M° Châtelet.* **Box office** 11am-7pm Mon; 11am-8pm Tue-Sat; *telephone* 11am-7pm Mon-Sat. **Map** p406 J6.
Les Abbesses *31 rue des Abbesses, 18th. M° Abbesses.* **Box office** Tue-Sat 5-8pm. **Map** p402 H2. **Tickets** €15-€22; half-price on day under-27s. **Credit** MC, V.

This year's season boasts 84 programmes, 31 exhibitions and 399 performances ranging from cutting-edge, controversial theatre and dance to standards like Shakespeare's *Much Ado About Nothing* and *Richard II.* The Abbesses spinoff hosts Anita Picchiarini's version of *La Fin de Casanova.*

Théâtre du Rond Point

2bis rue Franklin D Roosevelt, 8th (01.44.95.98.21/ www.theatredurondpoint.fr). M° Franklin D Roosevelt. **Box office** noon-7pm Tue-Sat; noon-4pm Sun and day of show; *telephone* 11am-1pm, 2-7pm Mon-Fri; noon-7pm Sat (01.44.95.98.10). **Tickets** €19-26; €12-under-30s. **Credit** MC, V. **Map** p400 E4.

Director Jean-Michel Ribes, famed for his *Théâtre sans Animaux*, brings contemporary French authors to the stage. There are debates, a hipster restaurant, a slick book store, and a cabaret, all bringing life to the space off the Champs-Elysées.

La Bruyère

5 rue La Bruyère, 9th (01.48.74.76.99/ www.ddo.fr/labruyere). M° St-Georges. **Box office** 11am-7pm Mon-Sat. **Tickets** €13-€32. **Credit** MC, V. **Map** p401 H2.

This is where feelgood box-office smashes like *Popcorn* and *Visiting Mr Green* can make Francophones feel warm and fuzzy. Here Stephan Meldegg put *Stones in their Pockets* into French; you'll see it in 2004 if it manages to do just that.

Théâtre de l'Athénée-Louis Jouvet

7 rue Boudreau, sq de l'Opéra-Louis-Jouvet, 9th (01.53.05.19.19/www.athenee-theatre.com). M° Opéra. **Box office** *winter* 1-7pm Mon-Sat; 1 hour pre-show; *summer* 1-6pm Tue-Fri. **Tickets** €6-€28. **Credit** MC, V. **Map** p401 G4.

This long-established theatre puts on French and foreign classics in an Italianate pearl of a salle. The studio upstairs caters to smaller contemporary works. *Wheelchair access (call ahead).*

Les Bouffes du Nord

37bis bd de la Chapelle, 10th (01.46.07.34.50/ www.bouffesdunord.com). M° La Chapelle. **Box office** 11am-6pm Mon-Sat. **Tickets** €8-€24.50. **Credit** MC, V. **Map** p406 K2.

True theatre worshippers cannot come to Paris without paying tribute to legendary director Peter Brook, whose experimental company the CICT is based at the famously unrenovated venue. Stéphane Lissner's co-direction has added classical music and opera, and Carla Bruni too will be appearing in 2004.

The French Monty

Monty Python in French? Implausible as it sounds, our Gallic cousins have received a healthy injection of humour 'so British', kindly served in their own language. Over the past two years *Monty Python's Flying Circus*, followed by *Monty Python 2*, directed by Thomas Le Douarec, have scored a hit in Paris theatres, at the Edinburgh Fringe and in London. Now, nothing tickles the French more than a well-played jeu-de-mots, a cutting satire or boudoir farce and, at surface level, perhaps, the humour of Monty Python seems a far cry from their usual fun-filled evenings of raucous literary debate and beret beat poetry. In French comedy categorisation (and who but they would attempt to categorise laughs?) 'first degree' humour is a comedy of childish obscenity, slap-stick peepee/caca jokes that, no matter the context, guarantees a cheap laugh. 'Second degree', however, requires more provocation and takes the art to a more ironic, intellectual level. But Monty *is* philosophy. Monty *is* satire. Monty *is* sex. Monty is *French*, people.

The Beatles of comedy, Graham Chapman, John Cleese, Terry Jones, Michael Palin and Terry Gilliam, with their hoity-toity Oxbridge wit, are perhaps pompous enough to teach those French a thing or two about holistic pet shop policies. In the 1980s, when the first Monty Python stage show appeared live at the Hollywood Bowl, philosophers stroked beards and scratched pensive heads during a game of football while 'Kick the ball you silly nits!' is shouted from the stands. The French production, however, owes more to Beckett and the theatre of the absurd. For both, life boils down to the crude notion that 'it' is one big buffoonerie.

Oh those rude keepers of the grail have been at it for years. Satire and farce have shared a candlelit romance in the closets of French theatre since the days of Molière, whose constant mockery of bourgeois society neatly parallels those yacking Yorkshiremen with snifters comparing stories of destitute childhoods with snifters from the comfort of a Chesterfield. Granted, given the ultra-liberal atmosphere of Paris and given the show is not broadcast on late-60s matronly telly, it does lose a bit of shock-value. One French critic commented that High Court judges disrobing into pink lacys become just another man dressed in women's unmentionables. As if! And in a place where sex and nudity are part of acceptable culture, a bare-assed how's-your-father scenario might be, well, banal. Despite this, the addition of a female in the cast and lots of rear-end nudity do fulfil sexy quotas enough for those of a Gallic persuasion.

But it is Ionesco-like inertia that holds the production together, with subtitles that dutifuly follow for Anglophones trying to keep up. Le Douarec says he 'purposely chose sketches that are more visual, to appeal to a more universal audience'. His troupe, Charles Ardillon-Gauriat, Grégoire Bonnet, Yavan Garouer, Philippe Vieux and the first-ever Python-ette Marie Parouty do come close to winning the incontinent olympics. 'It was quite hard some of the time to work out which sketch was actually being done,' commented Michael Palin after seeing the performance in Edinburgh last summer. 'Sometimes they hit the mark exactly, sometimes they miss the mark, and sometimes they miss it so completely that it is quite extraordinary.' Look out for a reprise when the troupe returns from London this year.

Cartoucherie de Vincennes

Route du Champ de Manoeuvre, bois de Vincennes, 12th. M° Château de Vincennes, then shuttle bus or bus 112. **Théâtre du Soleil** *(01.43.74.24.08/ www.theatre-du-soleil.fr).* **Théâtre de l'Epée de Bois** *(01.48.08.39.74).* **Théâtre de la Tempête** *(01.43.28.36.36/www.la-tempete.fr).* **Théâtre de l'Aquarium** *(01.43.74.99.61/ www.theatredelaquarium.com).* **Théâtre du Chaudron** *(01.43.28.97.04).*

Five independent theatres are housed in ex-army munitions warehouses in the woods of Vincennes. Walk into Ariane Mnouchkine's **Théâtre du Soleil** and you may see actors powdering up or the *grande dame* herself behind the ticket booth. **Théâtre de l'Epée du Bois** and **Théâtre du Chaudron** are often overlooked despite their excellent, if smaller-scale programming. The **Théâtre de la Tempête** always features a top-class programme by its resident troupe, and **Théâtre de l'Aquarium** is an outlet for new repertoires and forms.

Left Bank

Théâtre de la Huchette

23 rue de la Huchette, 5th (01.43.26.38.99). M° St-Michel. **Box office** 5-9pm Mon-Sat. **Tickets** €16 one play, €25 both plays; €12.50 students under 25, €19 both plays. **Credit** MC, V. **Map** p406 J7.

Nicolas Bataille's original production of Ionesco's *La Cantatrice Chauve* has been playing here for more than 50 years, however young playwrights still come clutching freshly penned scripts in hopes of seeing their names on the bill. *Wheelchair access.*

Théâtre Lucernaire

53 rue Notre-Dame-des-Champs, 6th (01.45.44.57.34). M° Notre-Dame-des-Champs. **Box office** 2-9pm Mon-Sat. **Tickets** €10-€20. **Credit** AmEx, MC, V. **Map** p405 G9.

This ex-factory turned bustling arts centre is a favourite haunt for students, housing two 130-seat theatres, a cinema, a café and various exhibitions. The repertoire, directed by Laurent Tertzieff, occasionally features new work, but usually reverts to reliable commercial successes.

Guichet-Montparnasse

15 rue du Maine, 14th (01.43.27.88.61). M° Montparnasse-Bienvenüe. **Box office** *telephone* 2-7pm Mon-Sat. **Tickets** €17; €12 students, over-60s, Mon. **No credit cards. Map** p405 F9.

In a minute 50-seat auditorium, this lively fringe venue features everything from the grand classics to new writing, showcasing small companies and new directing and acting talent. Several short productions are shown each night.

Théâtre de la Cité Internationale

21 bd Jourdan, 14th (01.43.13.50.50/ www.theatredelacite.ciup.fr). RER Cité Universitaire. **Box office** 2-7pm Mon-Sat. **Tickets** €18; €12.50 over-60s; €9.50 students, under-26s, Mon. **Credit** MC, V.

As the name suggests, this outward-looking, modern theatre, led by Nicole Gautier, former cabinet official in the Ministry of Culture, is one of Paris' most chic subsidised spots and focuses on world contemporary 'intellectual' theatre and theatre forms, as well as dance and music. The cheap rate on Mondays is cool, as is the friendly snack bar.

Théâtre de l'Athénée-Louis Jouvet

Trips Out of Town

Features

Trips Out of Town

Surround yourself with beauty. Astaire did it. Liberace did it. Dame Barbara Cartland did it. The urban personification of all three – Paris – does it too.

Stately Châteaux

Versailles

For an old hunting lodge nicknamed 'little house of cards', Versailles is not doing too badly. Centuries of makeovers have made it one of the largest, most sumptuously clad châteaux in France – a veritable bouquet of bad taste and brilliance, and an absolute must-see. Architect Louis Le Vau first embellished the original building after Sun King Louis XIV took an ego-knocking during a visit to Vaux-le-Vicomte, the impressive residence of his finance minister, Nicolas Fouquet. Painter Charles Le Brun decorated the interior, and André Le Nôtre revamped the gardens, turning boggy marshland into terraces, pools and paths.

After Le Vau's death, Jules Hardouin-Mansart took over as principal architect in 1678, dedicating the last 30 years of his life to adding the two main wings, the Cour des Ministres and Chapelle Royale. In 1682 Louis moved in and thereafter rarely set foot in Paris. In the 1770s, Louis XV chose his favourite architect Jacques Ange Gabriel to add the sumptuous Opéra Royal, sometimes used for concerts by the Centre de Musique Baroque (01.39.20.78.10), and still fully equipped with the original spy holes from where Louis' bodyguards kept an eye on him. With the fall of the monarchy in 1792, most of the furniture was lost but the château was saved from demolition after the 1830 Revolution by Louis-Philippe.

Versailles is showy, but it is also a masterpiece. The architectural magnificence of the classical facades, the 73m-long Hall of Mirrors (where the treaty of Versailles was signed in 1919), the King's Bedroom, where Louis held his celebrated *levées* in the presence of around 100 male courtiers; the Apollo Salon, and the Queen's Bedroom, where queens gave birth in full view of the court, are more than impressive. The **Gardens** are also magnificent works of art. Stretching over 815 hectares, they include formal parterres, ponds, wooded parkland and sheep-filled pastures, as well as the recently restored Potager du Roi, the king's vegetable garden. Statues of the seasons, elements and continents, many commissioned by Colbert in 1674, are scattered throughout, and the spectacular series of fountains is served by an ingenious hydraulic system, pumping water from a 200km network of channels and aqueducts in the Versailles area. Each Sunday afternoon from April to October, the great fountains in the gardens are set in action, to music, in the Grandes Eaux Musicales; while seven times a year the extravagant Fêtes de Nuit capture the ancient finery of the Sun King's celebrations.

After so many extensions the palace lost whatever homely feel it may ever have had. In 1687 Louis had Hardouin-Mansart build the pink marble **Grand Trianon** in the north of the park away from the protocol of the court. Louis lodged there with Mme de Maintenon and Napoléon Bonaparte later also stayed there with his second Empress, Marie-Louise.

The Petit Trianon, built for Louis XV's mistress Mme de Pompadour, is a perfect example of Neo-Classicism. Marie-Antoinette, played out her visions of peasantry at the nearby Hameau de la Reine, a fairytale farm.

A recent addition to a day out at Versailles is a chance to see the newly restored Sun King's stables, home to a *haute école* equestrian school, **l'Académie du Spectacle Equestre**.

Château de Versailles

78000 Versailles (01.30.83.76.20/ www.chateauversailles.fr). **Open** *Apr-Oct* 9am-6pm Tue-Sun. *Nov-Mar* 9am-5pm Tue-Sun. **Admission** €7.50; €5.30 after 3.30pm; free under-18s. Jump the queues: Gate D takes you direct to the Grands Appartements and Appartements Privés: call ahead to reserve (01.30.83.77.88). All inclusive 'Passport' tickets are available for €20 (€14.50 Nov-Mar) from RER stations.

Grand Trianon/Petit Trianon

Open *Apr-Oct* noon-6pm daily; *Nov-Mar* noon-5pm daily. **Admission** €5; €3 after 3.30pm; free under-18s.

Gardens

Grand Parc Open dawn-dusk daily. **Admission** free (Grandes Eaux 01.30.83.78.88; €5 ; free under 10s). **Petit Parc Open** *Apr-Oct* 9am-6pm. **Admission** €3; free in winter, when most statues are protected by a tarpaulin. **Potager du Roi** (01.39.24.62.62). **Open** *Apr-Oct* 10am-6pm daily (guided tours only Sat, Sun). **Admission** €4.50; guided tours €6.50.

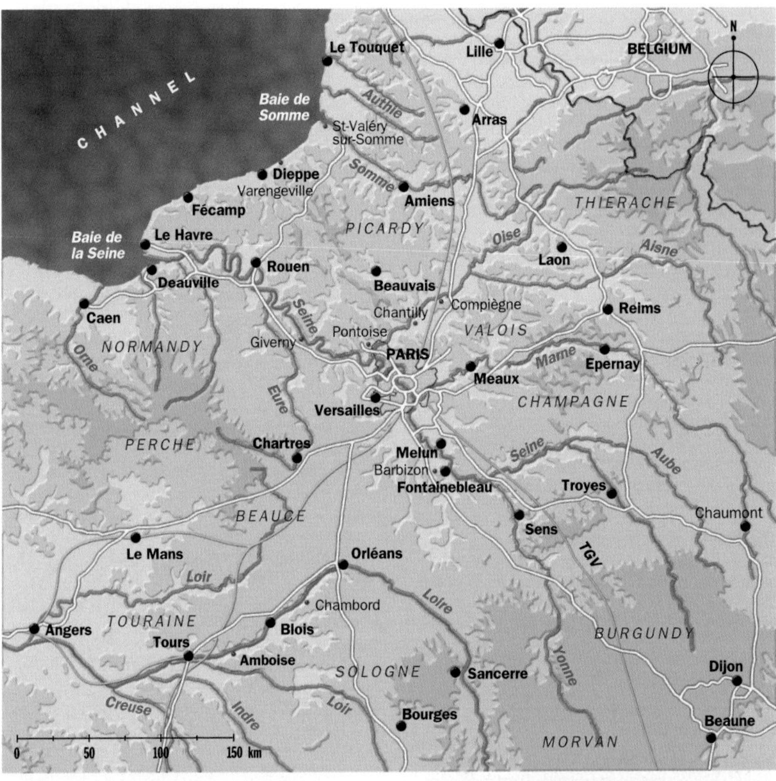

Académie du Spectacle Equestre

Grandes Ecuries, Château de Versailles (01.39.02.07.14). RER C Versailles-Rive Gauche. **Open** *Les Matinales des écuyers* (practice and visit) 9am-noon Tue-Fri; 11am-2pm Sat, Sun. *Reprise Musicale* (performance and visit) 2-3pm Sat, Sun. Closed Jan to mid Feb. **Tickets** *Les Matinales* €7; €3 5-18s; free under-5s. *Reprise Musicale* €15; €7 under-18s. **Credit** MC, V.

Where to eat

Le Chapeau Gris (7 rue Hoche/01.39.50.10.81) has a good €26 menu and €17 lunch menu. **Les Trois Marches** (Hôtel Trianon Palace, 1 bd Reine, 01.39.50.13.21), where the Treaty of Versailles was signed, is for a splurge.

Getting there

By car

20km from Paris by A13 or D10.

By RER

RER C Versailles-Rive Gauche.

Chantilly

Cream-coloured Chantilly looks like an exemplary French Renaissance château with its attractive domes and turrets standing high above the surrounding lake. In reality, much of the original palace was destroyed during the Revolution, leaving the main wing to be reconstructed in the 19th century by avid art collector, the Duc de Condé. Chantilly still houses the Duc's remarkable collections, with three paintings by Raphael, Filippo Lippi's *Esther and Assuarus* and the *Très Riches Heures du Duc de Berry* medieval book of hours (facsimile only usually on show).

Today the park, designed by royal gardener Le Nôtre, is rather run-down, but it is gradually being spruced up. The extensive canal system, an artificial 'hamlet' that in fact predated Marie-Antoinette's at Versailles, the recently restored Princes' Kitchen Garden, the 19th-century English garden and the daffodil flowerbeds are all well worth a gander.

The château's handsome Great Stables were ordered by Prince Louis-Henri de Bourbon (who believed that he would be reincarnated as a horse) and housed 240 horses, 500 dogs and almost 100 palfreys and hunting birds. Since 1982 it has contained the **Musée Vivant du Cheval** (*see chapter* **Children**). The town of Chantilly has a bustling equestrian centre, with many racing stables and a major racetrack which hosts the prestigious Prix de Diane Hermès in June.

South of the château spreads the **Forêt de Chantilly**. A pleasant walk of around 7km circles the four small lakes, the Etangs de Commelles, and passes the Château de la Reine Blanche, a mill converted in the 1820s into a pseudo-medieval hunting lodge.

Worthy of note is **Senlis**, 9km east of Chantilly. Bypassed since its glory days as birthplace of the French monarchy in the tenth century, its historical centre contains quaint, half-timbered streets, some handsome mansions, a Gothic cathedral and the remains of the Gallo-Roman amphitheatre and city wall.

Château de Chantilly

Musée Condé, 60500 Chantilly (03.44.62.62.62/ www.chateaudechantilly.com). **Open** *Mar-Oct* 10am-6pm Mon, Wed-Sun; *Nov-Feb* 10.30am-12.45pm, 2-5pm Mon, Wed-Sun. **Park Open** *Mar-Oct* 10am-6pm daily. *Nov-Feb* 10.30am-5pm Mon, Wed-Sun. **Admission** €7; €6 12-17s; €2.80 4-12s; park only €3; €2 4-11s; free under-4s. **Credit** MC, V.

Where to eat

La Carrousel du Musée Vivant du Cheval (03.44.57.19.77) has an excellent €10 set meal. The château restaurant **La Capitainerie** also offers good French food in the old castle kitchens (03.44.67.40.00), with three courses for around €25.

Getting there

By car

41km from Paris by A1, exit Chantilly or N16 direct.

By train

SNCF Chantilly from Gare du Nord (30 mins), then 30min walk or short taxi ride.

Compiègne & Pierrefonds

North of Paris, the hunting forest of Compiègne separates two very different, yet intriguing châteaux. The **Château de Compiègne**, on the edge of the old town, was designed by architect Jacques Ange Gabriel and is a monument to Louis XV's obsession with hunting. It was completed in 1788; however, with the onslaught of the Revolution in 1789, Louis never actually basked in its classical charms. In fact nobody benefited from the palace until Napoléon I took it over in 1807. He ruthlessly remodelled the interior for his second wife, Marie-Louise. The Imperial decor remains and is stuffed with eagles, bees, palms and busts of the great self-publicist. Napoléon III also left his mark at Compiègne, where he and Empress Eugénie hosted lavish house parties every autumn. His most popular legacy was the highly efficient heating system, which still works today and makes a visit to the château bearable even in the depths of winter. As well as the apartments, the château shelters two museums: the **Musée de la Voiture** is devoted to early transport, from Napoléon I's state coach to an 1899 Renault, and the **Musée du Second Empire et l'Impératrice** shows works by Boudin and Carpeaux, and the Bonaparte family history.

In the forest 4km from Compiègne by D973 is the **Clairière de l'Armistice**, a memorial to the site where the Germans surrendered to Maréchal Foch, ending World War I, on 11 November 1918 (it is also where in 1940 the French surrendered to the Germans but one tends to mention that less frequently at dinner parties). The clearing features the spot where the combatants' two railway lines met, a statue of Foch and a reconstruction of his railway-carriage office.

At the opposite edge of the forest lies the neo-medieval **Château de Pierrefonds**. At first sight, it looks like something straight out of a Hans Christian Andersen fairy story. Yet it deserves a detour. Napoléon I was charmed by the ruins of the original 14th-century castle, and bought them for 2,950 francs. In 1857, Napoléon III asked Viollet-le-Duc to restore one tower as a hunting lodge. But the project grew and the fervent medievalist ended up reconstructing the whole edifice, in part using the remaining foundations, in part borrowing elements from other castles, or simply inventing his own fantastical brand of medieval revival. Grand baronial halls harbour elaborately carved Gothic chimneypieces. The magnificent Salle des Preuses has a fireplace sculpted with nine women (one a likeness of Empress Eugénie).

Château de Compiègne

5 pl du Général-de-Gaulle, 60200 Compiègne (03.44.38.47.00). **Open** 10am-5pm Mon, Wed-Sun. **Admission** €5.50 château and museum; €4 château only; €3 18-25s; free under 18s. **No credit cards.**

Château de Pierrefonds

60350 Pierrefonds (03.44.42.72.72). **Open** *1 Sept-14 May* 9.30am-12.30pm, 2-6pm Mon-Sat; 9.30am-6pm Sun. *15 May-1 Sept* 9.30am-6pm daily. Closed public holidays. **Admission** €5.50; €3.50 17-25s; free under 17s. **No credit cards.**

Château de Chantilly. *See p349.*

Where to eat & stay

In Compiègne, **Rive Gauche** (13 cours Guynemer/ 03.44.40.29.99) does inventive cuisine (menus €30-€35). The **Hôtel Les Beaux-Arts** (33 cours Guynemer/03.44.92.26.26, double €72) is a cosy hotel.

Getting there

By car

Compiègne is 80km from Paris by A1. To reach Pierrefonds from Compiègne take the N31 towards Soissons, then follow signs.

By train

From Gare du Nord.

Fontainebleau

Fontainebleau is a congenial town, dominated by three major elements: the sumptuous royal palace which takes over the town centre, the hunting forest with its amazing rock formations, and the INSEAD business school (the 'European Harvard') on the edge of the forest, which adds a distinctly cosmopolitan touch.

The **Château de Fontainebleau** is bite-sized compared to the sprawling grandeur of places such as Versailles, and 300 years of mish-mashing styles has given it its distinctive charm. In 1528, François 1er brought in Italian artists and craftsmen to help architect Gilles le Breton transform what was a neglected royal lodge into the finest Italian Mannerist palace in France. This style, noted for its grotesqueries, contorted figures and crazy fireplaces, is still visible in the Ballroom and Long Gallery. Henri IV then added a tennis court, Louis XIII built a double-horseshoe entrance staircase, Louis XIV and XV added classical trimmings. Napoléon redecorated in Empire style before leaving France for exile from the front courtyard, known ever since as the Cour des Adieux.

With its ravines, rocky outcrops and mix of forest and sandy heath, the **Forest of Fontainebleau** where François 1er liked to hunt, is the wildest slice of nature near to Paris and now popular with Parisian weekenders for walking, cycling, riding and rock climbing. The GR1 is a popular hiking trail signposted straight from the station at Bois-le-Roi, 30 minutes from Gare de Lyon, and the Centre Equestre des Basses Masures is a favourite for horse riders (SNCF Fontainebleau/ 01.64.24.21.10).

Château de Fontainebleau

77300 Fontainebleau (01.60.71.50.60). **Open** *Oct-May* 9.30am-5pm Mon, Wed-Sun; *June-Sept*, 9.30am-6pm Mon, Wed-Sun. Closed 1 Jan, 1 May, 25 Dec. **Admission** €5; €4 18-25s; free under 18s. **Credit** V.

Versailles. *See p348.*

Where to eat & stay

Pedestrianised rue Montebello is lined with restaurants. **Jungle House** at No 5 (01.64.22.15.66) serves excellent, authentic African and Afro-Indian dishes. Lunches by chef William Lesaulnier at **Au Délice Impérial** (1 rue Grande/01.64.22.20.70, €7-€18) are inventive and stylish. Some rooms at the **Hôtel de Londres** (1 pl Général de Gaulle/ 01.64.22.20.21/www.hoteldelondres.com, double €90-€150) have balconies overlooking the château.

Getting there

By car

60km from Paris by A6, then N7.

By train

Gare de Lyon to Fontainebleau-Avon (35 mins), then bus marked Château.

Vaux-Le-Vicomte

Never try to outdo your boss. The cheesy grin will always be followed by the knife in the back. This is the rule Nicolas Fouquet (1615-1680), protégé of the ultra-powerful Cardinal Mazarin, should have stuck to when he bought the site for his sumptuous country château in 1641. In 1653 he was named Surintendant des Finances, and decided to build an abode that matched his position. He assembled three of France's most talented men for the job: painter Charles Lebrun, architect Louis Le Vau and landscape gardener André Le Nôtre.

Fouquet's fatal mistake came in 1661 when he invited the Sun King to a huge inaugural soirée. Guests were entertained by jewel-encrusted elephants and spectacular Chinese fireworks. Lully wrote music for the occasion; Molière did a comedy. The King, who was 23 and ruling for the first time, was outraged by his minister's show of grandeur. Shortly afterwards Louis had Fouquet arrested, and his embezzlement of state funds exposed in a show trial. All of his personal effects were taken by the crown and the court sentenced him to exile; Louis XIV commuted the sentence to solitary confinement. Fouquet is sometimes thought to have been the 'Man in the Iron Mask'.

As you round the moat, the relatively sober frontage gives way to the stunningly Baroque rear aspect. The most telling symbol of the fallen magnate is the unfinished, domed ceiling in the elliptical Grand Salon, where Lebrun only had time to paint the cloudy sky and one solitary eagle. Fouquet's *grand projet* did live on in one way, however: it inspired Louis XIV to build Versailles – using Fouquet's architect to do it. Every cloud, and all that.

The spectacular fountains spout from 3-6pm on the second and last Saturday of the month, Apr-Oct. The biggest draw, though, are the candlelit evenings, which transform the château into a palatial jack-o-lantern.

Vaux-Le-Vicomte

77950 Maincy (01.64.14.41.90). **Open** *29 Mar-11 Nov* 10am-6pm daily (château closed 1-2pm Mon-Fri). **Admission** €12; €9 6-16s, students, over-60s; free under-6s. **Candlelit visits** *3 May-11 Oct* 8pm-midnight Sat; *July, Aug* 8pm-midnight Fri. **Admission** €15; €13 6-16s, students, over-60s; free under-6s. **Credit** MC, V.

Getting there

By car

60km from Paris by A6 to Fontainebleau exit; follow signs to Melun, then N36 and D215.

By coach

Paris-Vision (01.42.60.30.01) runs half-day and day trips from Paris.

Châteaux of the Loire

Seat of power of the Valois kings, who preferred to rule from Amboise and Blois than Paris (more game, fewer strikes), the Loire valley became the wellspring of the French Renaissance. François 1er was the main instigator, bringing architects, artists and craftsmen from Italy to build his palaces, and musicians and poets to keep him amused. Royal courtiers followed suit with their own elaborate – but too elaborate – residences.

First up is the enormous **Château de Chambord** (02.54.50.40.00; 02.54.50.50.00 for events). François 1er's masterpiece, it took 1800 men to build it and was probably designed in part by Leonardo da Vinci. Built in the local white stone, it's a magnificent example of architecture from the French Renaissance, with details such as the playfully ingenious double staircase – it was possible to go up or down without crossing someone coming the other way – to the wealth of decoration and the 400 draughty rooms. Watch your feet though. In August 2003 one room caved in so some rooms may still be closed to the public.

In total contrast of scale is the charming **Château de Beauregard** (02.54.70.40.05) nearby at Cellettes. Its main treasure is the unusual panelled portrait gallery, depicting in naïve style 327 famous men and women. The park contains a modern colour-themed garden designed by Gilles Clément.

From here the road to Amboise follows an attractive riverside stretch, under the looming turrets of the **Château de Chaumont** (02.54.51.26.26) past roadside wine cellars dug into the tufa cliffs (with numerous opportunities to indulge). The grounds of Chaumont are used for an innovative garden festival from June to October (02.54.20.99.22).

The lively town of Amboise, not far from Tours, grew up at a strategic crossing point on the Loire. The **Château Royal d'Amboise** (02.47.57.00.98) was built within the walls of a medieval stronghold, although today only a (still considerable) fraction of Louis XI's and Charles VIII's complex remains. The château's interiors span several styles from vaulted Gothic to Empire. The exquisite Gothic chapel has a richly carved portal, vaulted interior and, supposedly, the tomb of Leonardo da Vinci.

It's a short walk up the hill, past several cave dwellings, to reach **Clos Lucé** (02.47.57.62.88), the Renaissance manor where Leonardo lived at the invitation of François 1er for the three years before his death in 1519. There's an enduring myth of a (so far undiscovered) tunnel linking it to the château. Currently celebrating 550 years since Leonardo's birth with a host of exhibitions and special events, the museum focuses on Leonardo as Renaissance Man: artist, engineer and inventor, with models of his inventions (sadly not functional). An oddity just outside town is the 18th century pagoda of Chanteloup, built when *chinoiserie* was all the rage.

South of Amboise, the **Château de Chenonceau** (02.47.23.90.07) occupies a unique site spanning the river Cher. Henri II gave the château to his beautiful mistress Diane de Poitiers, until she was forced to give it up to a jealous Catherine de Médicis (wise move), who commissioned Philibert Delorme to add the three-storey gallery that extends across the river. Chenonceau is usually packed with tourists in summer, but its watery views, original ceilings, fireplaces, tapestries and paintings (including *Diane de Poitiers* by Primaticcio) are well worth seeing.

Rising magically from an island in the river Indre west of Tours, **Azay-le-Rideau** (02.47.45.42.04) is the quintessential fairytale castle, especially when viewed during the nocturnal garden visits in summer. Built 1518-27 by the king's treasurer, it combines the turrets of a medieval fortress with the new Italian Renaissance style.

Villandry (02.47.50.02.09) is famous for its spectacular Renaissance knot gardens. Most unusual is the colourful and appetisingly aromatic *jardin potager*, where the patterns created with artichokes, cabbages and pumpkins compose the ultimate kitchen garden. It is also, of course, an inspiration to any allotment fan's sense of possibility.

If you don't have time to see them all, a trip to the **Parc des Minis Châteaux** (02.47.23.44.44) in Amboise is a good way to quench castle fever.

Where to stay

At the heart of the park in Chambord, the **Hôtel Restaurant du Grand St-Michel** (pl St-Louis/ 02.54.20.31.31, double €49-€69) faces the château. Amboise is a pleasant, centrally placed stopping-off point. In town, try the **Lion d'Or** (17 quai Charles Guinot/02.47.57.00.23, double €51-€74) which also has a restaurant. For a taste of château life, try the **Château de Pray** (02.47.57.23.67/ http://praycastel.online.fr, double €101-€165) at Chargé, 3km outside town. There are more hotels and restaurants in Tours.

Getting there

By car

Take the A10 to Blois (182km), or leave at Mer for Chambord. An attractive route follows the Loire from Blois to Amboise and Tours, along the D761.

By train

From Gare d'Austerlitz to Amboise (2hrs) and TGV from Gare Montparnasse to Tours (70 mins).

Great Minds

The splendour of Paris and its surrounding *départements* has long been a source of inspiration for brain boxes. Luckily, even for us less gifted mortals, much of the original beauty still remains today and can be found within an hour's journey from the French capital.

Villandry

Impressionist haunts

North of Paris, charming **Auvers-sur-Oise** has a whole canvas of painters to its name; Van Gogh, Daubigny, Corot, Daumier and Cézanne all stayed here towards the end of the 19th century. Modern **Auvers** can't escape their colourful influence, either. Illustrated panels around town let you compare paintings to their locations today. The tiny attic room at the **Auberge Ravoux** (01.30.36.60.60) that Vincent rented on 20 May 1890 for 3.50 francs is open to the public and gives and an evocative sense of the artist's stay. The **Atelier de Daubigny** (01.34.48.03.03), built by the successful Barbizon school artist in 1861, is still decorated with murals by Daubigny, his son and daughter and his friends Corot and Daumier. The 17th-century **Château d'Auvers** (01.34.48.48.50) offers an audiovisual display about the Impressionists, while the **Musée de l'Absinthe** (01.30.36.83.26) is devoted to their favourite drink. A new addition to the itinerary is the **Maison du Dr Gachet**, the home of Van Gogh's mentor (01.30.36.81.27). Auvers can be combined with a visit to **Montmorency**.

To the west of Paris, **Giverny** – made immortal by Monet's paintings of his flower garden – is another art institution. Though besieged by busloads of tourists, the natural charm of the pink-brick house (**Fondation Claude Monet** 02.32.51.28.21), where Monet moved with his mistress and eight children in 1883, and the glorious gardens, including the water garden with its weeping willows and bridge, survive intact. Up the road, the **Musée Americain Giverny** (02.32.51.94.65), devoted to the American artists who followed the Impressionists, also has a wide-ranging programme of temporary exhibitions.

From the 1830's onwards, the leafy rural hamlet of **Barbizon**, on the edge of the **Fôret de Fontainebleau** became another sanctuary for painters. Corot, Théodore Rousseau, Daubigny and Millet all settled, paving the way for Impressionism with their new concern for peasant life and landscape. Other artists soon followed and stayed at the **Auberge du Père Ganne** (01.60.66.22.27), painting on the walls in lieu of rent (try it, kids). The inn is an over-sanitised museum, but the artists' charming sketches and paintings can still be seen.
The **Office du Tourisme** (01.60.66.41.87) is in the former house of Théodore Rousseau. Prints by Millet and others can be seen in the **Maison-atelier Jean-François Millet** (01.60.66.21.55), where Millet moved in 1849 to escape cholera in Paris. Most of these sights are all on the Grande Rue. Plaques point out who lived where.

Useful information

Auvers-sur-Oise

Where to eat Vincent's old pad, the Auberge Ravoux (pl de la Mairie/01.30.36.60.60, *menu* €25-€32) does good, simple food (no rooms). **By car** 35km north of Paris by A15 exit 7, then N184 exit Méry-sur-Oise for Auvers. **By train** Gare du Nord or Gare St-Lazare direction Pontoise, change at Persan-Beaumont or Creil, or RER A Cergy-Préfecture, then bus (marked for Butry). **By coach** Paris-Vision (01.42.60.30.01) runs tours from Paris.

Giverny

Where to stay Chambres d'hôtes Le Bon Maréchal (1 rue du Colombier/02.32.51.39.70, double €46-€62) is a comfy bed and breakfast. **By car** 80km west of Paris by A13 to Bonnières and D201. **By train** Gare St-Lazare to Vernon (45 mins); then taxi or bus.

Barbizon

Where to eat & stay La Bohème (35 Grande Rue/01.60.66.48.65) has a good-value €28 menu. The Auberge Manoir du St Hérem (29 Grande Rue/01.60.66.42.42) has €22-€30 *menus* and double rooms for €46-€57. **By car** 57km from Paris by A6, then N7 and D64. **By train** Gare de Lyon to Melun, then taxi (12km).

Highbrow 'hoods

An hour southwest of Paris is picturesque **Montfort L'Amaury**, home to dandy composer Maurice Ravel and setting for Victor Hugo's poem *Ode aux ruines*. Hugo wrote the romantic verses after seeing the 16th-century rampart ruins. Ravel's house, Le Belvedere, is now an eerie museum (**Musée Maurice Ravel** 01.34.86.07.43), left exactly as it was when he died in 1937 and filled with the small toys and curiosities that fed the artist's mind during his lifetime. He composed two concertos for piano and orchestra here in 1931, including one left-handed piano piece for his friend who lost his right arm in the war. The rest of the town, with its back streets and 15th-century church, is also worth a look. The **Bureau de Tourisme** (01.34.86.87.96) in rue Amaury offers a useful *Randonnée Culturelle* (guided walk).

As with many satellite towns, **Montmorency**, 13km north of the capital, has not escaped Paris' urban engulfment. In the 18th century, however, it was a tranquil spot lined with oaks. Philosopher Jean-Jacques Rousseau came here in 1756 to escape the 'dirt and smoke' of Paris. His two-storey town house is now home to the **Musée Jean-Jacques Rousseau** (01.39.64.80.13). It was from here that Rousseau wrote his poignant pieces, *La Nouvelle Héloïse*, *Emile* and *Le Contrat Social.* The museum shows a reconstitution of how the house would have been when the great mind lived in it with his wife (once servant) Thérèse Levasseur. The garden was completely redesigned by Rousseau himself.

For a sleepy town, **La Ferté-Milon** with its breathtaking castle ruin at the end of the Canal de l'Ourcq that runs north-east of Paris, boasts associations with names such as Leonardo da Vinci, Jean Racine, Jean de la Fontaine and Gustave Eiffel. It was here that the young Leonardo was invited by François 1er to conceive the first ever plan to turn the Ourcq river into a canal heading into Paris. France's great dramatist Jean Racine was born here in 1639. His house is now the **Musée Jean Racine** (03.23.96.77.77). A few Corot paintings are also thrown in for good measure from when he visited in 1858. La Fontaine (famous for his fables) married Racine's cousin in the Notre Dame church in 1647, and Gustave Eiffel designed the metal footbridge over the river Ourcq. As if that wasn't enough, the 14th-century castle ruin is stunning and played a role in the Hundred Years' War.

Useful information

Montfort-L'Amaury

Where to eat L'Entre-mets (16 place Robert Brault/01.34.86.07.43) offers traditional French food in an excellent setting with a €10 lunch *menu*. **By car** 40km west of Paris by A13, then A12 and N12 at Dreux. **By train** Gare Montparnasse direction Houdan or Dreux to Monfort L'Amaury-Méré.

Montmorency

Where to eat La Maison Jaune (7 av Emile/ 01.39.64.69.38) does exceptional food at a reasonable price, with a €14 *menu*. **By car** 15km north of Paris by A1 (Porte de la Chapelle), exit Beauvais. **By train** Gare du Nord to Enghien-les-Bains via Pontoise, then bus 15A and 15M to Montmorency.

La Ferté-Millon

Where to eat Les Ruines (2 place du Vieux Château/03.23.96.71.56) is in an inspiring location with a range of *menus*, €11-€25. **By car** 70km northeast A4 or N2 to Meaux, then D405 and D936 to La Ferté-Millon. **By train** Gare de l'Est direction Reims to La Ferté-Millon.

Beside the Seaside

Dieppe & Varengeville

Dieppe became a popular seaside resort in the 19th century when the Duchesse de Berry persuaded her aristocratic buddies that bathing in the freezing waters of the English Channel was a fashionable way for Parisians to spend the summer. Since then, it has remained a veritable 'Paris-Plage', tempting many a city dweller to come for a chilly dip and a fish meal. The charming area around the harbour along quai Henri IV is prettier than ever now that ferries from Britain go to a new container port. At one end the Tour des Crabes is the last remnant of fortified wall (Dieppe has been an important port since the Middle Ages). The maze of old streets between the harbour and the newer quarters fronting the promenade contains numerous brick sailors' houses and the fine Gothic churches of St-Jacques, once a starting point for pilgrims to Compostella, and St-Rémi. The seafront offers plenty of activities for kids, with mini-golf, pony rides, a children's beach and lawns filled with kite flyers (the international kite festival is in September). The shingle beach is overlooked from the cliff top by the gloomy **Château de Dieppe** (02.35.84.19.76), now the municipal museum, which has carved ivories and paintings by Pissarro and Braque. On particularly aromatic days a southerly wind wafts a coffee smell up from the Nescafé factory that sits in the neighbouring river valley.

Leave town by the D75 for a twisting, breathtakingly scenic drive along the cliffs all the way to Etretat. This is the so-called Alabaster Coast, its many alleged 'moods' immortalised by Monet. Just outside Dieppe is **Varengeville-sur-Mer**, celebrated for its clifftop churchyard where Cubist painter Georges Braque (who also designed the stained-glass in the church) and composer Albert Roussel are buried. Here too is the **Parc du Bois des Moustiers** (02.35.85.10.02), an English garden planted by Lutyens and Gertrude Jekyll, famed for its spectacular rhododendrons and memorable views; the unusual 16th-century **Manoir d'Ango** (02.35.85.14.80) has a galleried courtyard and unusual dovecote.

8km south of Dieppe is the decorative early 17th-century **Château de Miromesnil** (02.35.85.02.80) where the writer Guy de Maupassant was born in 1850. (He left it at the age of one, possibly not of his own volition.) The building has a fascinating historic kitchen garden. Nearby, dominating a little hill at Arques la Bataille, are the ruins of a 10th-century feudal castle.

Where to eat & stay

In Dieppe, head towards the harbour, along quai Henri IV to find countless fish restaurants offering delicious local cider. Best money-comfort ratio has to be **Hôtel de l'Europe**, (63 bd de Verdun/ 02.32.90.19.19, from €60 for a double room), famed for its cocktails and next door to the Bellevue restaurant.

Auvers-sur-Oise. *See p355.*

Getting there

By car

Dieppe is 170km north-west from Paris. Take the A13 to Rouen and then the A151.

By train

From Gare St-Lazare (2½ hours).

Tourist information

Office du Tourisme de Dieppe

Pont Jehan Ango, 76204 Dieppe (02.32.14.40.60). **Open** *July, Aug* 9am-1pm, 2-8pm Mon-Sat; 10am-1pm, 3-6pm Sun. *Sept-June* 9am-1pm, 2-7pm Mon-Sat.

Baie de Somme

Although the Somme is synonymous with the carnage of World War I, its estuary is an area of extreme natural beauty. The estuary region boasts a rich variety of wildlife and has a gentle, ever-changing light that has attracted artists and writers. There are many picturesque villages and a beautiful coastline that varies from long beaches and rolling dunes to pebbles and cliffs. The bay has an astounding 2,000 hectares of nature reserves and France's first maritime reserve was created here in 1968, with some 200 bird species, notably winter migrants, recorded at the **Parc Naturel du Marquenterre** (St-Quentin-en-Tourmont/ 03.22.25.03.06). Nearby **La Maison de l'Oiseau** (Lanchères/03.22.26.93.93) is a nature reserve which looks after countless species of birds, many endangered.

A popular tourist steam train, the **Chemin de Fer de la Baie de Somme** (03.22.26.96.96) tours the bay in summer between Le Crotoy, Noyelles, St-Valéry-sur-Somme and Cayeux.

The panorama around the bay at the small fishing port of Le Crotoy inspired Jules Verne to write *20,000 Leagues Under the Sea* and drew Colette, Toulouse-Lautrec and Arthur Rimbaud. It boasts the only south-facing sandy beach in northern France and as such is a busy resort, with hotels, guest houses and campsites, plus restaurants serving excellent fresh fish; there are opportunities for watersports (03.22.27.04.39), hunting, fishing and tennis.

Across the bay, **St-Valéry-sur-Somme**'s well-preserved medieval upper town has a commanding position, and plenty of history. It was from here that William the Conqueror set sail in 1066, and Joan of Arc passed through as a prisoner in 1430. The upper town contains a Gothic church and château, part of the former abbey. A small chapel overlooking the bay houses the tomb of St-Valéry. In the lower town, the **Ecomusée Picarvie** recreates aspects of traditional village life. Strolling from the port to the bay, you can see some impressive late-19th-century villas. Consult tide times: at low tide the sea goes out nearly 14km; it comes back again in less than five hours.

At the tip of the bay, **Le Hourdel** consists of a few fishermen's houses and a dock where the fishing boats sell their daily catch. Here is your best chance to see seals from the largest colony in France. Lying below sea-level, **Cayeux**, three miles south, was a chic resort in the early 1900s. It has beautiful sand beaches at low tide, often almost completely deserted. The seafront is captivatingly dressed with wooden cabins and planks in a 2km promenade.

Ecomusée Picarvie

5 quai du Romeral, St-Valéry-sur-Somme (03.22.26.94.90). **Open** *Apr-Sept* 2-6pm. Closed Oct-Mar. **Admission** €4; €2.50 4-14s.

Parc Naturel du Marquenterre

03.22.25.03.26. **Open** *Apr-Sept* 9.30am-5pm daily; *Oct-Nov* 10am-4pm daily. **Admission** €9.50; €7 6-18s, students, disabled.

Where to eat & stay

In St-Valéry-sur-Somme, **Le Nicol's** (15 rue de la Ferté/03.22.26.82.96, *menu* €13-€29) does excellent fare. The **Relais Guillaume de Normandie** (46 quai Romerel/03.22.60.82.36, double €56) is a welcoming hotel.

Getting there & around

By car

Le Crotoy is 190km from Paris by N1 or A15 and N184, then A16 motorway (exit Abbeville Nord).

By train

The closest train station is Noyelles-sur-Mer, just after Abbeville, about 2hrs from Gare du Nord. Limited local buses serve villages on the bay. Bikes can be hired at St-Valéry-sur-Somme (03.22.26.96.80).

Tourist information

Office du Tourisme Le Crotoy

1 rue Carnot, 80550 Le Crotoy (03.22.27.05.25). **Open** *Sept-June* 10am-noon, 2-6pm Mon, Wed-Sun. *July, Aug* 10am-7pm daily.

Office du Tourisme St-Valéry

2 pl Guillaume le Conquérant, 80230 St-Valery-sur-Somme (03.22.60.93.50). **Open** *May-Sept* 9.30am-12.30pm, 2-6pm daily.

Cathedral Cities

Chartres

Described by Rodin as the 'French Acropolis,' **Chartres cathedral** bursts up out of the lonely Beauce plains with monumental glory. Seen from afar, its mismatched spires and breathtaking silhouette literally dominate the scenery. Up close, it's not bad either. The sublime stained glass and doorways bristling with sculpture embody a complete medieval world view, with earthly society and civic life reflecting the divine order. Chartres was a pilgrimage site long before the cathedral was built, ever since the Sacra Camisia (said to be the Virgin Mary's lying-in garment) was donated to the city in 876 by the king.

When the church caught fire in 1194, locals had a whip round to raise the necessary funds to reconstruct it, taking St-Denis as the model for the new west front, 'the royal portal' with its three richly sculpted doorways. The stylised, elongated figure columns above geometric patterns still form part of the door structure.

Inside the cathedral, another era of sculpture is represented in the lively 16th-century scenes of the life of Christ that surround the choir. Worthy of note is the circular labyrinth of black and white stones in the floor. Such mazes used to exist in most cathedrals, but most have been destroyed.

The cathedral is, above all, famed for its stained-glass windows depicting Biblical scenes, saints and medieval trades in brilliant 'Chartres blue', punctuated by rich reds. If you want to decipher the medieval messages that lie behind the windows and sculpture alike, take one of the educational, erudite and entertaining tours given in English by Malcolm Miller (02.37.28.15.58/€10, €5 students). The tower is worth the climb for its fantastic view.

The cathedral may seem to take over the town from a distance, but once inside the narrow medieval streets, with their overhanging gables, glimpses of it are only occasional. Wander past the iron-framed market hall, down to the river Eure, crossed by a string of attractive old bridges, past the partly Romanesque Eglise St-André (now an exhibition and concert centre) and down the rue des Tanneries, which runs along the bank.

Another fine church is the Gothic **Eglise St-Pierre**, which has magnificent stained glass and a Romanesque porch-belfry.

There's a good view from the Jardin de l'Evêché, located at the back of the cathedral and adjoining the **Musée des Beaux-Arts** (29 Cloître Nôtre-Dame/02.37.36.41.39). Housed in the former Bishop's palace, the collection includes some fine 18th-century French paintings by Boucher and Watteau, as well as some distinctly creepy medieval sculptures.

Another big-time Chartres tourist attraction is the fabulous **COMPA** (pont de Mainvilliers/ 02.37.36.11.30), a converted engine shed near the station that gives a lively presentation of the history of agriculture and food (great

Medieval madness

Ever wondered what happens to French medieval cities once their haymaking days are over? The answer lies in Provins, 80km east of Paris. This UNESCO classified city is one of the most intact medieval towns in France and it has a unique form of merrymaking that makes it well worth a detour from the flat Brie countryside surrounding it. Enter through the ramparts and you step into an obscure universe where modernity and medievalism coexist – so much so that residents spend most of the year dressed up as their middle-age predecessors. This archaic form of ancestor worship does seem a crayon short of a brass rubbing, but it puts Provins on the map. Streams of tourists arrive each year to witness the re-enactment of forgotten practises in a *bona fide* medieval setting.

The festivities usually start with Falconry by La Société de Vol Libre. Over 80 falcons, vultures and eagles soar with acrobatic fury overhead wolves, camels and men galloping on horseback (01.60.58.80.32, every day April to November). Chivalry is kept well and truly alive in the knights' jousting tournament. Wannabe Lancelots indulge their fantasies by charging at each other with long sticks to remove a ring on a mast in the centre of the arena (every Sunday between June and September). Seizing the ramparts is an equally popular pastime: every year artisan Renaud Beffeyte constructs war machines copied from genuine medieval texts and engravings, putting them into spectacular action between April and June.

The challenging feminine skills of baking corn dollies and *niflette* (Provins' gastronomic speciality, a tart covered in custard) are the forms of fun chosen by most Maid Marians during the festival. (Corn dollies by Annie Lebel, 5 rue de la Chapelle St-Jean, 01.64.00.10.73).

Spectacular they may be, but the celebrations are reassuringly not all there is to see in Provins and even when men aren't in tights, the city has a lot to offer. By the 12th century, it was a centre for European medieval trade fairs, had its own system of weights and measures, its own currency and its own cloth industry. Remnants of such a great past don't disappear that easily. In fact, despite a close shave during the Revolution, some of the best models of medieval architecture, town planning and hydraulic systems in the world are still found in Provins. La Tour César and the 5km of ramparts (01.64.60.26.26) are fine examples of medieval military architecture dating from the reign of Henri le Libéral in the 12th century. The Place du Châtel brings together a whole caboodle of medieval buildings with the St-Thibaut Church, the Hôtel de la Coquille mansion, the Croix des Changes monument in the centre of the square and the Wishing Well next to the cross. La Grange aux Dîmes (01.64.60.26.26) was a 12th-century storage building that now shelters an informative exhibition on the workings of medieval Provins trade fairs. And La Maison Romaine (01.64.01.40.19) is the earliest example of a Provins stone structure. Today it is a fascinating museum featuring a range of art from Renaissance paintings to Merovingian sarcophagi.

Useful information

Where to eat Try the Hostellerie de la Croix d'Or in the Ville Basse (1 rue des Capucins/01.64.00.01.96) or L'Auberge de la Grange in the Ville Haute (3 rue St-Jean/ 01.64.08.96.77) for good traditional French cuisine. **Tourist Office** 01.64.60.26.26.

location for a first date) from 50,000BC to the present day, with the emphasis on machinery, from vintage tractors to old fridges. Whatever fluffs your rice, eh?

Where to eat

La Vieille Maison (5 rue au Lait/02.37.34.10.67) has good classical cooking (*menu* €26). Facing the cathedral, the **Café Serpente** (2 Cloître Notre Dame/02.37.21.68.81) triples as café, tearoom and restaurant. **L'Estocade** (1 rue de la Porte Guillaume/ 02.37.34.27.17) has a riverside terrace where you can enjoy a four-course *menu* for €22.50.

Getting there

By car

88km from Paris by A10, then A11.

By train

From Gare Montparnasse.

Tourist information

Office du Tourisme

pl de la Cathédrale, 28000 Chartres (02.37.18.26.26). **Open** *Apr-Sept* 9am-7pm Mon-Sat; 9.30am-5.30pm Sun; *Oct-Mar* 10am-6pm Mon-Sat; 10am-1pm, 2.30-4.30pm Sun.

The best Religio-cities

Two other cathedral cities are definitely worth a visit:

Beauvais: 75km from Paris

The Cathédrale de Beauvais has the tallest Gothic vault in the world and a curious astrological clock from the 1860's. The **Musée Départemental de l'Oise** (03.44.11.43.83) traces the region's illustrious heritage, while **Manufacture Nationale de la Tapisserie** (24 rue Henri Brispot/ 03.44.05.14.28) shows how weavers recreate traditional Beauvais tapestry. **Office du Tourisme:** 1 rue Beauregard/03.44.15.30.30.

Amiens: 100km from Paris

The Cathédrale d'Amiens is one of the biggest cathedrals in Europe measuring 112.7m in height. The **Musée de Picardie** (48 rue de la République/03.22.97.14.00) houses three collections: archaeology, medieval and fine art. The **Zoo** (Esplanade de la Hotoie/03.22.69.61.00) cares for animals, including two new elephants.

Lille

Lille, European Capital of Culture 2004 (*see p363*), is on a crossroads between the Netherlands, France, Belgium, Germany and Britain. One of the great wool towns of medieval Flanders, it became part of France in 1667. A buzzing city filled with a lively mix of popular and high culture and the futuristic Eurolille showcase business complex, it continues to innovate and renovate with many architectural projects going on around town. Come for La Braderie on the first weekend in September: dating back to medieval times, the wonderfully anarchic 'clear-out' sees streets lined with jumble and antique stalls.

In Vieux Lille, some fine Renaissance houses have been renovated, including the 1652-53 Vieille Bourse on the Grand' Place at the historic heart of the city. The adjoining place du Théâtre has the 19th-century Nouvelle Bourse, a pretty opera house and the rang de Beauregard, a row of late 17th-century houses. The tourist office is in the Gothic Palais Rihour started in 1454 by Philippe Le Bel, Duc de Bourgogne. Nearby is Lille's finest church, the Gothic **Eglise St-Maurice**.

The **Musée de l'Hospice Comtesse** (32 rue de la Monnaie/03.20.49.50.90) contains some fantastic displays of Flemish art, furniture and ceramics. Nearby, on place de la Treille, is Lille's cathedral, begun 150 years ago and only completed in 1999. Do try to make time to visit the modest brick house where De Gaulle was born (9 rue Princesse/03.28.38.12.05).

You'll find one of France's very best art collections at the palatial **Musée des Beaux-Arts** (pl de la République, 03.20.06.78.00), including works by Rubens, Jordaens, El Greco, Goya, David, Delacroix and Courbet. The **Musée d'Art Moderne** (1 allée du Musée, Villeneuve d'Ascq, 03.20.19.68.68) houses works by Picasso, Braque, Derain and Modigliani amid a landscaped sculpture garden. In nearby Roubaix, the new **Musée d'Art et d'Histoire** (23 rue de l'Espérance, Roubaix, 03.20.69.23.60) occupies a stunning art deco swimming pool.

Where to eat & stay

Bistros line the rue de Gand. Try chic **L'Huîtrière** (3 rue des Chats-Bossus/03.20.55.43.41), or brasserie **Alcide** (5 rue des Debris-St-Etienne/03.20.12.06.95). Stop for tea at pâtisserie **Méert** (27 rue Esquermoise/ 03.20.57.07.44). For a leisurely stay, try the **Hôtel de la Treille** (7-9 pl Louise de Bettignies/ 03.20.55.45.46, double €69-€74), a pleasant modern hotel, the simple **Hôtel de la Paix** (46*bis* rue de Paris/03.20.54.63.93, double €73-€78) or the new Hermitage Gantois (224 rue de Paris/03.20.85.30.30, double €190-€240) in a 16th-century brick hospice.

Chartres. *See p358.*

Getting there

By car

220km from Paris by A1; 104km from Calais.

By train

TGV from Gare du Nord (1hr) or 1hr 35 min by Eurostar from London.

Tourist information

Office du Tourisme

pl Rihour, 59002 Lille (03.20.21.94.21). **Open** 9.30am-6.30pm Mon-Sat; 10am-noon, 2-5pm Sun.

Reims

Reims, with its **Cathédrale Notre-Dame** cherished by French Royalists as the coronation church of most French monarchs dating all the way back to Clovis in 496, has been an important city since Roman times. The present church was begun in 1211 and its rich Gothic decoration includes thousands of figures on the portals; the Kings of Judea high above the rose window show how sculptural style developed over the centuries. Copies have replaced many of the carvings since heavy shelling in World War I so go next door to the former archbishop's palace, Palais de Tau, where you can see some of the originals close up. It is possible that some of the masons from Chartres also worked on Reims, but the figures generally show more classical influence in their drapery and expression. Look out for the winsome 'smiling angel' sculpture and St Joseph on the west front, and the elaborate foliage on the capitals inside.

A few streets south of the cathedral, the **Musée des Beaux-Arts** (8 rue Chanzy/ 03.26.47.28.44) has some wonderful portraits of German princes by Cranach and 26 canvases by Corot. From the museum, head down rue Gambetta (though it's quite a trek) to the Basilique St-Rémi, which honours the saint who baptised Clovis. Built 1007-49, it is the embodiment of architectural progression from Romanesque style in the 11th century to the Gothic style of the 13th. Don't miss the ten remarkable 16th-century tapestries depicting the life of St-Rémi in the **Musée St-Remi** (53 rue Simon/03.26.85.23.36) next door.

Reims is, of course, at the heart of the Champagne region. Many leading producers of the famous bubbly are based in the town and offer cellar visits explaining the skilful process. The **Champagne Pommery** cellars (03.26.61.62.56/tours mid Mar-mid Nov daily) occupy Gallo-Roman chalk mines 30m below ground and are decorated with art nouveau bas-reliefs by Emile Gallé. **Taittinger** (03.26.85.84.33) doesn't look like much like a lorra lorra laffs until you head downstairs: on the first level are the vaulted Gothic cellars of a former monastery with a Roman crypto-portique; below are the eerily, strangely beautiful, Gallo-Roman chalk quarries.

Where to eat & stay

Haute-cuisine mecca is Gérard Boyer's **Château des Crayères** (64 bd Henri-Vanier/03.26.82.80.80) in a Second Empire château southeast of town. His former partner, chef Fabrice Maillot, runs the lively bistro **Au Petit Comptoir** (17 rue de Mars/ 03.26.40.58.58); another Boyer-trained chef is at the good-value **La Vigneraie** (14 rue de Thillois/ 03.26.88.67.27). Countless cafés and brasseries line lively place Drouet d'Erlon, as well as a number of hotels. If you want to stay the night the **Grand Hôtel du Nord** at No 75 (03.26.47.39.03, double €53.40) has bright, well-tended rooms and English-speaking staff. If you fancy staying at a working champagne domain give **Ariston Fils Champagne** a call. They don't have many rooms but spoil their guests (4-8 Grande Rue, Brouillet/03.26.97.43.46).

Getting there

By car

150km by A4.

By train

From Gare de l'Est about 90min.

Tourist information

Office du Tourisme

2 rue Guillaume-de-Machault, 51100 Reims (03.26.77.45.25). **Open** *mid-Apr to mid-Oct* 9am-7pm Mon-Sat; 10am-6pm Sun. *Mid-Oct to mid-Apr* 9am-6pm Mon-Sat; 10am-5pm Sun.

Rouen

The capital of Normandy features a historic centre with lots of half-timbered buildings and narrow streets, while the port areas by the Seine were almost totally destroyed by bombing during World War II and were reconstructed in the 1950s. Begun in the 12th century upon the site of a Romanesque church (the crypt of which remains intact), the **Cathédrale Notre-Dame** spans the Gothic period from the early north tower to the flamboyant late 15th-century Tour de Beurre. Nearby, the tourist office occupies a fine Renaissance house, while the Gros Horloge gateway, with its famous ornamental clock, spans the busy medieval rue du Gros-Horloge, leading to still more picturesque streets of half-timbered houses.

Two more Gothic churches are worth a visit, the **Abbatiale St-Ouen** and the **Eglise St-Maclou**, as well as the fanciful Flamboyant Gothic Palais de Justice. Near the Abbatiale St-Ouen, the **Musée de l'Education** (185 rue Eau-de-Robec/02.32.82.95.95) presents a lively view of French education since the 15th century over two floors of a half-timbered house. The striking, contemporary Eglise Ste-Jeanne d'Arc, adjoining a funky modern market hall on place du Vieux-Marché, is a boat-shaped structure with a swooping wooden roof and stained glass windows recovered from a bombed city church. **The Musée des Beaux Arts** (1 pl Restout/02.35.71.28.40) numbers masterpieces by Gérard David, Velázquez, Perugino and Caravaggio, some wonderful oil studies by Géricault (a native of Rouen) and several Monets and Sisleys.

Where to eat and stay

Best-known gourmet stop is **Restaurant Gill** (9 quai de la Bourse/02.35.71.16.14), home to fish specialist Gilles Tournadre (*menus* €38-€73), who also runs the less formal **37** (37 rue St-Etienne des Tonneliers/02.35.70.56.65). Among the many bistros on place du Vieux-Marché are local favourite **Les Maraîchers** (No 37, 02.35.71.57.73) and **La Couronne** (No 31, 02.35.71.40.90), which claims to be the oldest inn in France. **Hôtel de la Cathédrale** (12 rue St-Romain/02.35.71.57.95/www.hotel-de-la-cathedrale.com, double €54-€61) and **Hôtel du Vieux-Carré** (34 rue Ganterie/02.35.71.67.70, double €55) are two attractive, central hotels.

Getting there

By car

137km west of Paris by A13.

By train

From Gare St-Lazare. Check times: fast trains take about an hr; slow ones about 2½ hours.

Tourist information

Office du Tourisme

25 pl de la Cathédrale, 76000 Rouen (02.32.08.32.40). **Open** *May-Sept* 9am-7pm Mon-Sat; 9.30am-12.30pm, 2.30-6.30pm Sun. *Oct-Apr* 9am-6.30pm Mon-Sat; 10am-1pm Sun.

Troyes

Stroll along the timbered rue Champeaux and don't miss the ruelle des Chats, an atmospheric narrow lane which leads up to the **Eglise Ste-Madeleine**, the city's oldest church. Nearby, the **Basilique St-Urbain** represents an apogee of Gothic architecture.

Pass through café-lined place du Maréchal-Foch, with the handsome 17th-century Hôtel de Ville, and cross a canal into the oldest part of the city around the **Cathédrale St-Pierre St-Paul**. Part of the impressive facade is by Martin Chambiges, who also worked on the cathedrals at Sens and Beauvais. **Musée d'Art Moderne** (pl St-Pierre/03.25.76.26.80) is a must for lovers of early 20th-century art, especially Derain. The **Maison de l'Outil** (7 rue de la Trinité/03.25.73.28.26) has a fascinating array of tools. Next to the cathedral in the Abbaye St-Loup, the **Musée des Beaux-Arts et d'Archéologie** (4 rue Chrétien de Troyes/03.25.76.21.68) has fine Gallo-Roman bronzes.

Where to eat

At **Le Clos Juillet** (22 bd du 14 Juillet/03.25.73.31.32) chef Philippe Colin specialises in modernised regional dishes.

Getting there

By car

150km southeast of Paris by A6 and A5.

By train

From Gare de l'Est (75 mins).

Tourist information

Office du Tourisme

16 bd Carnot, 10000 Troyes (03.25.82.62.70). **Open** 9am-12.30pm, 2-6.30pm Mon-Sat.

Lille, European City of Culture 2004

It's Lille's turn to show what it's got in its cultural bowl. The Flanders town has been glitzed-up big time and, unlike with previous cities of culture, this year the programme extends to the whole region. Here's our pick.

Out in the streets

Arriving by train at **Gare Lille-Flandres** you'll be welcomed by a light installation by designer Patrick Jouin who has used coloured filters over the glazed vault. Outside, the revamped rue Faidherbe metamorphoses throughout the year. **Le Chemin des Etoiles** (until early Feb), a modern sci-fi walkway, will be succeeded by a cacophany of Shanghai neon (Mar), the mechanical beasties of the **Galerie de Monstres** (mid-July to mid-Aug) from Berlin collective Dead Chickens, and a 30-metre high bamboo jungle (Sept-Oct). Lucie Lom's topsy-turvy **La Forêt Suspendue** (end Apr-end June) sees trees hanging upside-down over the Grand' Place. All year long, artists' lighting projects and **Microfolies** crop up all over town, from a hall of mirrors in Eurolille business complex by minimalist composer Terry Riley, and Vincent Dupont-Rougier's treehouse love seats, to François Azambourg's travelling dinette.

Visual arts

Dig on down in **Flower Power** (until 22 Feb), the tripartite exhibition at the Palais des Beaux-Arts, Palais Rameau and Musée de l'Hospice Comtesse, featuring artists such as Andy Warhol and Gilbert & George. The Musée d'Art Moderne at Villeneuve d'Ascq stars Fluxus genius **Robert Filliou** (until 28 Mar). The magnificent Baroque church of Ste-Marie-Madeleine provides the setting for **Du Côté de Chez...** projects by Miwa Yanagi, Peter Greenaway, Chiharu Shiota and Erwin Redl. The future is the theme in the exuberant concept cars of **Voitures du Futur** and **Robots** (both until 7 Mar) at the former postal sorting office, the Tri Postal, next to the station. Spring kicks off with Flemish master **Rubens** (6 Mar-14 June). Many of his greatest works, including *La Descente de la Croix* are on show in the Palais des Beaux-Arts.

Performing arts

The magnificent Opéra de Lille reopens after renovation with a programme of opera that goes from **Puccini** (11-23 Mar) and **Handel** (3-9 Oct) to a creation by **Aperghis** (17-20 Nov), and cutting-edge dance from **Saburo Teshigawara** (28 May-9 June), **William Forsythe** (10, 11 May) and American hoofer **Bill T Jones** (26-28 Nov). Theatre guru Peter Brook raises the curtain on **Tierno Bokar** (Théâtre du Nord, 20 Sept-14 Oct).

Practical information

For the full programme and ticket reservations, check out the regularly updated website www.lille2004.com. Bookings can also be made up to three days in advance by phone on 08.90.39.20.04 (from outside France 00.33.359.579.400), or in person at the Office du Tourisme de Lille and the Tri Postal. In the three days before an event, remaining tickets are on sale at the venue.

Directory

Directory

Getting Around

Arriving & leaving

By air

Roissy-Charles-de-Gaulle airport

Most international flights arrive at Roissy-Charles-de-Gaulle airport, 30km north-east of Paris. Its two main terminals are some way apart, so it's important to check which is the right one for your flight if you are flying out. 24-hr information service in English: 01.48.62.22.80/www.adp.fr (under 'flight schedules'). The **RER B** is the quickest and most reliable way to central Paris (about 40 minutes to Gare du Nord; 45 minutes to Châtelet-Les Halles, €7.60 single). A new station gives direct access from Terminal 2 (including Air France flights); from Terminal 1 you take the free shuttle bus. RER trains run every 15 minutes, 5.24am-11.56pm daily. SNCF information: 80.91.36.20.20.
Air France buses (€10 single, €17 return) leave every 15 minutes, 5.45am-11pm daily, from both terminals, and stop at Porte Maillot and pl Charles-de-Gaulle (35-50 min trip). Air France buses also run to Gare Montparnasse and Gare de Lyon (€11.50 single, €19.55 return) every 30 minutes (45-60 minute trip), 7am-9.30pm daily. There is also a bus between Roissy and Orly (€15.50) every 20-30 minutes, 6am-11pm daily. Information: 08.92.35.08.20/ www.cars.airfrance.fr. The RATP **Roissybus** (€8.20) runs every 15 minutes, 5.45am-11pm daily, between the airport and the corner of rue Scribe/rue Auber (at least 45 minutes); tickets are sold on the bus. Information: 08.36.68.77.14.
Paris Airports Service is a door-to-door minibus service between the airports and hotels, running 24-hr daily. It works on a 'the more passengers the less you pay' system. Roissy prices from €23 for one person to €11.25 each for eight people sharing; Orly €21 for one to €8.50 each for eight sharing (reserve ahead on 08.21.80.08.01/www.parisairportservice.com).
Airport Connection (01.44.18.36.02/www.airport-connection.com; reservations 7am-8pm) runs a similar service, 5am-8pm, at €25 per person, €16 each for two or more. **Taxis** are the least reliable and most expensive means of transport. A taxi to central Paris can take 30-60 mins depending on traffic and your point of arrival. Expect to pay €30-€50, plus €1 per piece of luggage. **Km2** (01.45.16.28.56) runs **motorbike taxis** aimed largely at executives. Roissy-Charles de Gaulle to Versailles about €90; Orly to La Défense about €70.

Orly airport

French domestic and several international flights use Orly airport, 18km south of the city. It also has two terminals: Orly-Sud (mainly international flights) and Orly-Ouest (mainly domestic flights). English-speaking information service on 01.49.75.15.15, 6am-midnight daily. **Air France buses** (08.92.35.08.20/www.cars.airfrance.fr; €7.50 single, €12.75 return) leave both terminals every 15 minutes, 6am-11.30pm Mon-Fri, 7am-10.30pm Sat, Sun, and stop at Invalides and Montparnasse (30-45 minutes). The RATP **Orlybus** at Denfert-Rochereau leaves every 15 minutes, 5.35am-11.05pm daily (30-minute trip); tickets (€5.50) are available on the bus. Information: 08.92.68.77.14. The high-speed **Orlyval** shuttle train runs every seven minutes (6am-11pm daily) to RER B station Antony (Orlyval and RER together cost €8.80); getting to central Paris takes about 35 minutes. Alternatively, catch the **Orlyrail** (€5.35) to Pont de Rungis, where you can take the RER C into central Paris. Trains run every 15 minutes, 6am-11pm daily; 50-minute trip. A **taxi** into town takes 20-40 minutes and costs €16-€26, plus €1 per piece of luggage. The minibus and Km2 services listed above also run to and from Orly.

Paris Beauvais airport

Beauvais, 70km from Paris, is served by **Ryan Air** (03.44.11.41.41/www.ryanair.com) flights from Dublin and Glasgow, and **Mytravellite** (01.55.69.81.66/ www.mytravellite.com) from Birmingham. A bus service (€10) between the airport and Porte Maillot leaves 20min after each arrival and 2hr 45min before each departure. Tickets can be bought at the arrival lounge or from the Beauvais shop at 1 bd Pershing, 17th. Information: 08.92.68.20.64/ www.aeroportbeauvais.com.

Airline contacts

Aer Lingus 01.70.20.00.72/ www.aerlingus.com
Air France 08.20.82.08.20/ www.airfrance.fr
American Airlines 08.10.87.28.72/www.aa.com www.americanairlines.com
bmibaby +44 (0)890 710 081/ www.bmibaby.com
British Airways 08.25.82.54.00/ www.britishairways.fr
British Midland 01.41.91.87.04/ www.flybmi.com
Continental 01.42.99.09.09/ www.continental.com
Easyjet 08.25.08.25.08/ www.easyjet.com
KLM & NorthWest 08.90.71.07.10/www.klm.com
United 08.10.72.72.72/ www.united.com

By car

For travelling between France and the UK by car, options include tunnel **Le Shuttle** (Folkstone-Calais 35mins) (08.10.63.03.04/ www.eurotunnel.com); seacat **Hoverspeed** (Dover-Calais,

Newhaven-Dieppe) (03.21.46.14.00/ www.hoverspeed.com); ferries **Brittany Ferries** (08.25.82.88.28/www.brittany-ferries.com), **P&O Stena Line** (01.55.69.82.28/www.posl.com) and **SeaFrance** (08.25.04.40.45/ www.seafrance.com).

Shared journeys

Allô-Stop *1 rue Condorcet, 9th (01.53.20.42.42/ 08.25.80.36.66) www.allostop.net).* **Open** 10am-1pm, 2-6.30pm Mon-Fri; 10am-1pm, 2-5pm Sat. **Credit** MC, V. Call several days ahead to be put in touch with drivers. There's a fee (€4.50 under 200km; up to €10 over 500km), plus €0.50 per km to the driver. Routes most travelled: Cologne, Lyon, Marseille, Nantes, Rennes, Toulouse.

By coach

International coach services arrive at the Gare Routière Internationale Paris-Galliéni at Porte de Bagnolet, 20th (M° Galliéni). For reservations (in English) call **Eurolines** on 08.92.69.52.52) (€0.34 min), or in the UK 01582-404511/www.eurolines.fr.

By rail

The new, speedier **Eurostar** train between London and Paris now takes 2 hours 25minutes direct; slightly longer for trains that stop at Ashford and Lille (due to be reduced further in the next few years). You must check in at least 30 minutes before the train is due to leave. Passports must be carried on the Eurostar. Eurostar trains from London Waterloo (01233-617575/www.eurostar.com) arrive at Gare du Nord (08.92.35.35.39, €0.34/min; www.sncf.fr) with easy access to public transport and taxi ranks (the huge queues do move fairly quickly). **Bicycles** can be transported as hand luggage provided they are dismantled and carried in a bike bag. You can also check them in at the Eurodispatch depot at Waterloo (Esprit Parcel Service: 08705-850850) or the Sernam depot at Gare du Nord (08.25.84.58.45) up to 24 hours in advance. A Eurostar ticket must be shown and the service costs £20 or €45.75.

Travel agencies

Havas Voyages
26 av de l'Opéra, 1st (01.53.29.40.00/ www.havasvoyages.fr). M° Opéra. **Open** 10.30am-7pm Mon-Sat. **Credit** AmEx, V. General travel agent with more than 15 branches in Paris.

Nouvelles Frontières
13 av de l'Opéra, 1st (08.25.00.08.25/www.nouvelles-frontieres.fr). M° Pyramides. **Open** 9am-8pm Mon-Sat. **Credit** MC, V. Agent with 16 branches in Paris.

USIT *6 rue de Vaugirard, 6th (01.42.34.56.90/08.92.88.88.88/ www.usitconnections.fr). M° Odéon.* **Open** 10am-7pm Mon-Fri; 10am-6pm Sat. **Credit** MC, V. Provides coach, air and train tickets for under-26s and others.

Maps

Free maps of the Métro, bus and RER systems are available at airports and Métro stations. Other brochures from Métro stations are *Paris Visite – Le Guide*, with details of transport tickets and a small map, and the *Plan de Paris*, a fold-out map that also indicates *Noctambus* night bus lines. Useful maps sponsored by Galeries Lafayette and Printemps can be picked up at most hotel receptions. A Paris A-Z (called *Plan de Paris*) can be bought from newsagents or stationers (*papeteries*). The blue-covered *Paris Pratique* is particularly clear and compact.

Public transport

The public transport system (**RATP**) consists of bus routes, the Métro (underground), the **RER** suburban express railway (which interconnects with the Métro inside Paris) and two suburban tramways. Paris and its suburbs are divided into eight travel zones; zones 1 and 2 cover the city centre. Information 6am-9pm daily, 08.36.68.77.14/in English 08.36.68.41.14 (€0.34/ min); www.ratp.fr. **SNCF**, the state railway system, serves the French regions and international (*Grandes Lignes*) and the suburbs (*Banlieue*). Information: 08.36.35.35.35/www.sncf.com.

Fares & tickets

RATP **tickets** and passes are valid on the Métro, bus and RER. Tickets and *carnets* can be bought at Métro stations, tourist offices and *tabacs* (tobacconists); tickets can be bought on the bus. Keep your ticket in case of spot checks and to exit from RER stations. Individual tickets cost €1.30; it's more economical to buy a *carnet* of ten tickets for €10. *Carte Orange* travel passes (passport photo needed) offer unlimited travel in the relevant zones for a week or month. A *Coupon Mensuel* (valid from the first day of the month) zones 1-2 costs €48.60. A weekly *Coupon Hebdomadaire* (valid Mon-Sun inclusive) zones 1-2 costs €14.50 and is better value than *Paris Visite* passes – a three-day pass for zones 1-3 is €18.25; a five-day pass is €26.65, with discounts on some tourist attractions. A one-day Mobilis pass goes from €5.20 for zones 1-2 to €18.30 for zones 1-8 (not including airports).

Métro & RER

The Paris **Métro** is at most times the quickest and cheapest means of travelling around the city. Trains run daily 5.30am-12.40am. Individual lines are numbered, with each direction named after the last stop. Follow the orange *correspondance* signs to change lines. Some interchanges, notably Châtelet-Les Halles, Montparnasse-Bienvenüe and République, involve a long walk. The exit (*sortie*) is indicated in blue. The high-speed Line 14, Météor, links the new Bibliothèque Nationale to Madeleine and has just reached Gare St-Lazare. Pickpockets and bag-snatchers are rife on the Métro – pay special attention as the doors are closing. The five **RER** lines (A, B, C, D and the new Eole) run 5.30am-1am daily across Paris and into commuterland. Within Paris, the RER is useful for making faster journeys – for example, Châtelet-Les Halles to Charles de Gaulle-Etoile is only two stops on the RER compared with eight on Métro Line 1. The €1.30 Métro tickets are valid for RER journeys within zones 1-2.

Buses

Buses run from 6.30am until 8.30pm, with some routes continuing until 12.30am, Mon-Sat, with a more limited service on selected lines on Sundays and public holidays. You can use a Métro ticket, a ticket bought from the driver (€1.30) or a travel pass. Tickets should be punched in the machine next to the driver; passes should be shown to the driver. When you want to get off, press the red request button, and the *arrêt demandé* (stop requested) sign above the driver will light up.

Night buses

After the Métro and normal buses stop, the only public transport – apart from taxis – are the 18 **Noctambus** lines, between place du Châtelet and the suburbs (hourly 1.30am-5.35am Mon-Thur; half-hourly 1am-5.35am Fri, Sat). Routes A to H, P, T and V serve the Right Bank and northern suburbs; I to M, R and S serve the Left Bank and southern suburbs. Look out for the owl logo on bus stops. A ticket costs €2.40 and allows one change; travel passes are valid.

River transport

Batobus (www.batobus.com). River buses stop every 15-20 mins at: Eiffel Tower, Musée d'Orsay, St Germain-des-Prés (Quai Malaquais), Notre-Dame, Jardin des Plantes, Hôtel de Ville, Louvre, Champs-Elysées (Pont Alexandre III). They run June-Sept 10am-9pm; Apr-Oct 10am-7pm. A single ticket costs €2.50 for one stop, €2.50 for each stage thereafter; one-day pass €10, (€5.50 children, €8 students, €6.50 Carte Orange holders); two-day pass €12.50 (€6.50, €9, €9); season-ticket €45. Tickets can be bought at Batobus stops, RATP ticket offices and the Office de Tourisme.

Trams

Two modern tramlines operate in the suburbs, running from La Défense to Issy-Val de Seine and from Bobigny Pablo Picasso to St-Denis. They connect with the Métro and RER and fares are the same as for buses.

Rail services

Several attractions in the suburbs, notably Versailles and Disneyland Paris, are served by the RER. Most locations farther from the city are served by the SNCF state railway; there are few long-distance bus services. The TGV high-speed train has revolutionised journey times and is gradually being extended to all the main regions.

SNCF Reservations/Tickets SNCF national reservations and information: 08.92.35.35.35 (€0.34 per min) www.sncf.com. **Open** 7am-10pm daily.

SNCF information (no reservations) in the Ile de France: 08.91.36.20.20. **Open** 6am-10pm daily.

Tickets can be bought at any SNCF station (not just the one from which you'll be travelling), SNCF shops and travel agents. If you reserve online or by phone, you can pay and pick up your tickets from the station or have them sent to your home. SNCF automatic machines (*billeterie automatique*) only work with French credit/debit cards. Regular trains have both full-rate White (peak times) and cheaper Blue periods. You can save on TGV fares by purchasing special cards. Carte 12/25 gives under-26s a 25%-50% reduction; without it, under-26s are entitled to 25% off. Buy your ticket in advance to secure the cheaper fare. Pensioners over 60 benefit from similar terms with a Carte Senior. Before you board any train, validate your ticket in the orange *composteur* machines located by the platforms, or you might have to pay a hefty fine.

Paris mainline stations

Gare d'Austerlitz: Central and SW France and Spain.
Gare de l'Est: Alsace, Champagne and southern Germany.
Gare de Lyon: Burgundy, the Alps, Provence, Italy.
Gare Montparnasse: West France, Brittany, Bordeaux, the Southwest.
Gare du Nord: Northeast France, Channel ports, Eurostar, Belgium and the Netherlands.
Gare St-Lazare: Normandy.

Taxis

Paris taxi drivers are not known for their charm, nor for infallible knowledge of the Paris street plan – if there's a route you would prefer, say so. Taxis can also be few and far between, especially at rush hour or early in the morning. Your best bet is to find a taxi rank (*station de taxis*) – on major roads, crossroads and at stations – marked with a blue sign. The white light on a taxi's roof indicates the car is free. A glowing orange light means the cab is busy. Taxi charges are based on area and time: A (7am-7pm Mon-Sat, €0.60 per km); B (7pm-7am Mon-Sat, all day Sun; 7am-7pm Mon-Sat suburbs and airports, €1.00 per km); C (7pm-7am daily suburbs and airports, €1.20 per km). Most journeys in central Paris average €6-€12; there's a minimum charge of €5, plus €0.90 for each piece of luggage over 5kg or bulky objects, and a €0.70 surcharge from mainline stations. Most drivers will not take more than three people, although they should take a couple and two children. Don't feel obliged to tip, although rounding up by €0.30-€0.70 is polite. Taxis are not allowed to refuse rides because they are too short and can only refuse to take you in a particular direction during their last half-hour of service – however, in practice these rules are blatantly ignored. If you want a receipt, ask for *un reçu* or *la note* (compulsory for journeys of €15.25 or more). Complaints should be made in writing to the **Bureau de la réglementation publique de Paris**, 36 rue des Morillons, 75732 Paris Cedex 15.

Phone cabs

The following accept telephone bookings 24-hrs. However, you also pay for the time it takes your radioed taxi to get to where you are and there is no guarantee they will actually turn up. If you wish to pay by credit card, mention this when you order.

Credit cards over €15.24: **Alpha** 01.45.85.85.85. **Artaxi** 01.42.06.67.10/www.artaxi.fr; **G7** 01.47.39.47.39/01.41.27.66.99 (in English);

Km2 (motorbikes 01.45.16.28.56/www.k-m-2.com (Mon-Fri 7.30am-7pm); **Taxis Bleus** (01.49.36.10.10/ www.taxis-bleus.com).

Driving

If you bring your car to France, you will need to bring the registration and insurance documents – an insurance green card, available from insurance companies and the AA and RAC in the UK, is not compulsory but is advisable. As you come into Paris you will inevitably meet the Périphérique, the giant ring road that carries traffic in, out and around the city. Intersections, which lead onto other main roads, are called *portes* (gates). Driving on the Périphérique is not as hair-raising as it might look, even though it's often congested, especially during rush hour and at peak holiday times. The key word is confidence. If you've come to Paris by car, it can be a good idea to park at the edge of the city and use public transport which is generally a reliable way to navigate the city. A few hotels have parking spaces which can be paid for by the hour, day or by various types of season tickets. In peak holiday periods, the organisation Bison Futé hands out brochures at the motorway *péages* (toll stations), suggesting less-crowded routes. French roads are divided into *Autoroutes* (motorways, with an 'A' in front of the number), *Routes Nationales* (national 'N' roads), *Routes Départementales* (local, 'D' roads) and tiny, rural *Routes Communales* ('C' roads). *Autoroutes* are toll roads (*péages*), although some sections, including most of the area immediately around Paris, are free. Motorways have a speed limit of 130km/h (80mph), though this is not adhered to with any degree of zeal by many French motorists. The limit on most *Routes Nationale*s is 90km/h (56mph); within urban areas the limit is 50km/h (30mph), 30km/h (20mph) in selected residential zones.

Traffic information for the Ile-de-France: 08.26.02.02.22/www.bison-fute.equipement.gouv.fr.

Breakdown services

The AA or RAC do not have reciprocal arrangements with an equivalent organisation in France, so it is advisable to take out additional breakdown insurance cover, for example with *Europ Assistance* (01.41.85.85.41/ www.europassistance.co.uk). If you don't have insurance, you can use its service (01.41.85.85.85) but it will charge you the full cost. Other 24-hour breakdown services in Paris include: **Action Auto Assistance** (01.45.58.49.58); **Adan Dépann Auto** (01.42.66.67.58).

Driving tips

• At intersections where no signposts indicate the right of way, the car coming from the right has priority. Many roundabouts now give priority to those on the roundabout. If this is not indicated (by road markings or a sign with the message *Vous n'avez pas la priorité*), priority is for those coming from the right.
• Drivers and all passengers must wear seat belts.
• Children under ten are not allowed to travel in the front of a car, except in special babyseats facing backwards.
• You should not stop on an open road; pull off to the side.
• When drivers flash their lights at you, this means that they will not slow down and are warning you to move out of their path or keep out of the way.
• Friendly drivers also flash their lights to warn you when there are *gendarmes* lurking in the vicinity.
• Try to carry plenty of change, as it's quicker – and less stressful – to make for the exact-money line on *péages*; but, if you are caught short, cashiers do give change and *péages* accept credit cards.

Parking

There are still a few free on-street parking areas left in Paris, but they are, unsurprisingly, often full. If you park illegally, you risk getting your car clamped or towed away (*see below*). It is forbidden to park in zones marked for deliveries (*livraisons*) or taxis. Parking meters have now been replaced by *horodateurs*, pay-and-display machines, which take special cards, *carte de stationnement* (€15 or €30 available from *tabacs*). Parking is often free at weekends, after 7pm and in August. There are numerous underground car parks in central Paris. Most cost €2.30 per hour; €18.30 for 24 hours; some offer lower rates after 6pm and many offer various types of season ticket. Information: www.saemes.com

Clamps & car pounds

If you've had your car clamped, contact the local police station. There are eight car pounds (*préfourrières*) in Paris. You'll have to pay a €96.10 removal fee plus €4.60 storage charge per day, and a parking fine of €35 for parking in a no-parking zone. Bring your driving licence and insurance papers. But before you can pay, you need to find that treasured vehicle – not a small task given the labyrinth that represents the world of impounded cars in Paris and the affability of those who run it. Here goes. Once clamped, your car will first be sent to the *préfourrière* closest to where it was snatched. The six *préfourrières* correspond – roughly – to the following districts: **Les Halles** 1st, 2nd, 3rd, 4th (01.40.39.12.20); **Bercy** 5th, 12th, 13th, 14th (01.53.46.69.20); **Pantin** 10th, 11th, 19th, 20th (01.44.52.52.10); **Balard** 6th, 7th, 14th, 15th, 16th (01.45.58.70.30); **Foch** 8th, 16th, (01.53.64.11.80); **Poucet** 9th, 17th, 18th (01.53.06.67.68). After a 72-hr spell in the *préfourrière*, if no-one comes to claim it your car will be sent to one of the following two *fourrières* (pounds): **Paris Nord Macdonald** 1st-4th, 8th-10th, 16th-19th (01.40.37.79.20); **Paris Sud Bonneuil** 5th-7th, 11th-15th, 20th (01.45.13.61.40). But, if your car is deemed not necessarily worth retrieving, it will be sent to one of the following *fourrières*: **Paris Nord La Courneuve** 1st-4th, 8th-10th, 16th-19th (01.48.38.14.81); **Paris Sud Clichy** 5th-7th, 11th-15th, 20th (01.47.31.22.15). Information: www.prefecture-police-paris.interieur.gouv.fr.

Car hire

To hire a car you must normally be 25 or over and have held a licence for at least a year. Some agencies accept drivers aged 21-24, but a supplement of €20-€22 per day is usual. Take your licence and passport with you.

Hire companies

Ada 01.45.54.63.63/08.25.16.91.69/www.ada-location.fr.
Avis 08.20.05.05.05/www.avis.com.
Budget 08.25.00.35.64/www.budgetrentacar.com.
Calandres 04.93.76.03.50. Has a *flotte prestige* of luxury cars from cabriolets to Ferraris (for those who've held a licence for at least five years). **EasyRentacar** www.easyRentacar.com.
Europcar 01.30.43.82.82. **Hertz** 01.39.38.38.38/www.hertz.com.
Rent-a-Car 08.92.69.46.95/www.rentacar.fr.
Valem 01.43.14.79.79/www.valem.fr.

There are often good weekend offers (Fri evening to Mon morning). Week-long deals are better at the bigger hire companies – with Avis or Budget, for example, it's around €240 a week for a small car with insurance and 1,750km included. The more expensive hire companies allow the return of a car in other French cities and abroad. Bargain companies may have an extremely high charge for damage, so read the small print before signing on the dotted line.

Chauffeur-driven cars

First Limousine
(01.41.40.84.84/www.carey-first.com). **Open** 24-hr daily. **Prices** from €145 sedan airport transfer; €240 for four hours. **Credit** AmEx, DC, MC, V.

International Limousines
(01.41.66.32.00/www.inter-limousines.com). **Open** 24-hr daily. **Prices** from €48/hr + €16 meal allowance for a chauffeur-driven car (minimum 4 hours); half-day guided tours from €214. **Credit** AmEx, DC, MC, V.

Cycling

Since 1996, the Mairie de Paris has been promoting cycling in the city. There are now almost 200km of bike lanes and there are even plans for a bicycle 'Périphérique' circling Paris. Mayor Delanoë has continued with predecessor Jean Tiberi's enthusiasm, although his big summer 2002 splash, the 3km of the Right Bank closed for cyclists, rollerbladers and pedestrians beside Paris-Plage, was clearly aimed at leisure rather than commuter cyclists. The Itinéraires Paris-Piétons-Vélos-Rollers – scenic strips of the city that are closed to cars on Sundays and holidays – have been consistently multiplied; the city website (www.paris.fr) can provide you with an up-to-date list of routes and a downloadable map of cycle lanes. A free *Paris à Vélo* map can also be picked up at any Mairie or from bike shops. Cycle lanes (*pistes cyclables*) run mostly N-S and E-W. N-S routes include rue de Rennes, av d'Italie, bd Sébastopol and av Marceau. E-W routes take in the rue de Rivoli, bd St-Germain, bd St-Jacques and av Daumesnil. You could be fined (€22) if you don't use them, which is a bit rich considering the lanes are often blocked by delivery vans and the €137.20 fine for obstructing a cycle lane is barely enforced. Cyclists are also entitled to use certain bus lanes (especially the new ones, which are set off by a strip of pavement): look out for a traffic sign with a bike symbol. The Bois de Boulogne and Bois de Vincennes offer paths away from traffic although they are still criss-crossed by roads bearing menacing motor vehicles.
Don't let the Parisians' blasé attitute to helmets and lights convince you it's not worth using them. Be confident, make your intentions clear and keep moving are the best words of advice for cyclists – and beware of scooter-mounted bag-snatchers and (believe it or not) bum-pinchers.
If the thought of peddling around alone in a city known for the verve of its drivers fazes you, consider joining a guided bike tour (*see p75*, **Guided Tours**).

Cycles & scooters for hire

Note that bike insurance may not cover theft: be sure to check before you sign on the dotted line.

Atelier de la Compagnie *57 bd de Grenelle, 15th (01.45.79.77.24).* **Open** 9.30am-7pm Mon-Fri. Closed 3 weeks in Aug. **Credit** MC, V. A scooter for €30 per day or €130 per week. Deposit of €1,200, plus passport, required.

Maison Roue Libre *1 passage Mondétour, 1st (08.10.44.15.34). M° Châtelet. Plus (Mar-Oct) four RATP cyclobuses at Stalingrad, pl du Châtelet, porte d'Auteuil and parc Floral in the Bois de Vincennes (01.48.15.28.88/www.citefutee.com/sortir/roue_libre.php).* **Open** 9am-7pm daily. **Credit** MC, V (for weekend hire only). Bike hire costs €3 an hour; €12 a day. Helmets come free. Passport and €150 deposit required.

Paris-Vélo *2 rue du Fer-à-Moulin, 5th (01.43.37.59.22/www.paris-velo-rent-a-bike.fr). M° Censier-Daubenton. Also (15 Apr to 15 Oct) in the Bois de Boulogne (rond-pont du Jardin d'Acclimatation) and the Bois de Vincennes (av Daumesnil, by Lac Daumesnil).* **Open** 10am-7pm daily. **Credit** MC, V. Good selection of mountain bikes (*VTT*) and 21-speed models for hire. Five hours costs €12, a weekend €30, a month €116. Passport and €300 deposit required.

Walking

Exploring by foot is the very best way to discover Paris; just remember that to anything on wheels (and this includes cyclists and in-line roller skaters), pedestrians are the lowest form of life. Crossing Paris' multi-lane boulevards can be lethal to the uninitiated, as the 3,000 or so pedestrians who finish up in hospital – or worse – each year learn. Brits, of course, must realise that traffic will be coming in an opposite direction from the one to which they are accustomed – and that zebra crossings mean little. By law, drivers are only fully obliged to stop when there is a red light. Even then, a lot of drivers will take a calculated risk (your personal safety is not likely to be a high factor in that calculation). Where there is a crossing, whether or not it has a flashing amber light or a sign saying *Priorité aux Piétons*, most drivers will ignore pedestrians. Safety in numbers can help – or use the Métro underpass if there is one.

Resources A-Z

Addresses

Paris arrondissements are reflected in the last two digits of the postal code, eg. the 5th arrondissement 75005, the 12th 75012. The 16th arrondissement is subdivided into two sectors, 75016 and 75116. Some business addresses have a more detailed postcode, followed by a Cedex number which indicates the arrondissement. *Bis* or *ter* is the equivalent of 'b' or 'c' after a building number.

Age restrictions

You must be 18 or over to drive, and 18 in order to consume alcohol in a public place. There is no age limit for buying cigarettes. The age of consent for heterosexuals and homosexuals is 15.

Attitude & etiquette

Parisians take manners seriously and are generally more courteous than their reputation may lead you to believe. If someone brushes you accidentally on the Métro they will more often than not say '*pardon*'; you can do likewise, or reply '*C'est pas grave*' (don't worry). In shops it is normal to greet the assistant with a '*Bonjour madame*' or '*Bonjour monsieur*' when you enter and say '*au revoir*' when you leave. The question of '*vous*' and '*tu*' is a difficult one for English speakers. Strangers, people significantly older than you and professional contacts should be addressed with the more respectful '*vous*'; friends, relatives, children and dogs as '*tu*'. Among themselves young people often launch straight in with '*tu*'.

Business

The best first stop in Paris for initiating business is the CCIP (*see* **Useful Organisations**, *below*). Banks can refer you to lawyers, accountants and tax consultants. Other US and British banks provide expatriate services.

Conventions & conferences

The world's leading centre for international trade fairs, Paris hosts over 500 exhibitions a year.

CNIT *2 pl de la Défense, BP 321, 92053 Paris La Défense (01.43.95.37.00/www.parisexpo.fr). M°/RER Grande Arche de La Défense.* Mainly computer fairs.

Palais des Congrès *2 pl de la Porte-Maillot, 17th (01.40.68.22.22/www.palaisdescongres-paris.com). M° Porte-Maillot.*

Paris-Expo Porte de Versailles *15th (01.43.95.37.00/www.parisexpo.fr). M° Porte de Versailles.* Paris' biggest expo centre, from fashion to pharmaceuticals.

Parc des Expositions de Paris-Nord Villepinte *SEPENV 60004, 95970 Roissy-Charles de Gaulle (01.48.63.30.30/www.expoparisnord.com). RER B Parc des Expositions.* Trade fair centre near Roissy airport.

Courier services

Chronopost (*Customer service: 08.25.80.18.01/www.chronopost.com*). **Open** 9am-8pm Mon-Fri; 9am-1pm Sat. **Credit** MC, V. This overnight delivery offshoot of the state-run post office is the most widely used service for parcels of up to 30kg.

UPS *(0800.877.877/www.ups.com)* **Open** 8am-7pm Mon-Fri; 8am-1pm Sat. **Credit** AmEx, MC, V. International courier services.

ATV *(01.41.72.13.63/www.atoutevitesse.com).* **Open** 24-hr daily. **No credit cards.** 24-hr bike or van messengers. Higher rates after 8pm and at weekends.

Secretarial services

ADECCO International *14 pl de la Défense, 92974 Paris La Défense (01.49.01.45.06/www.adecco.fr). M° Grande Arche de La Défense.* **Open** 8.30am-12.30pm, 2-6.30pm Mon-Fri. Large international employment agency specialises in bilingual secretaries and office staff – permanent or temporary workers available.

Translators & interpreters

Certain documents, from birth certificates to loan applications, must be translated by certified legal translators, listed at the CCIP (*see below*) or embassies. For business translations there are dozens of reliable independents.

Association des Anciens Elèves de L'Esit *(01.44.05.41.46).* **Open** by phone only 9am-6pm Mon-Fri. A translation and interpreting cooperative whose 1,000 members are graduates of L'Ecole Supérieure d'Interprètes et de Traducteurs.

International Corporate Communication *3 rue des Batignolles, 17th (01.43.87.29.29). M° Place de Clichy.* **Open** 9am-1pm, 2-6pm Mon-Fri. Translators of financial and corporate documents plus simultaneous translation.

Useful organisations

American Chamber of Commerce *262 rue de Fbg-St-Honoré, 8th (01.53.89.11.00/www.faccparisfrance.com). M° Ternes. (Closed to the public, calls only.)*

British Embassy Commercial Library *35 rue du Fbg-St-Honoré, 8th (01.44.51.34.56/www.amb-grandebretagne.fr). M° Concorde.* **Open** 10am-1pm, 2.30-5pm Mon-Fri, by appointment. Stocks trade directories, and assists British companies that wish to develop or set up in France.

CCIP (Chambre de Commerce et d'Industrie de Paris) *27 av de Friedland, 8th (01.55.65.55.65/ www.ccip.fr). M° Charles de Gaulle.* **Open** 9am-7.30pm Mon-Fri. This huge organisation provides a variety of services for people doing business in France and is particularly useful for small businesses. Pick up the free booklet *Discovering the Chamber of Commerce* from the head office (above). **Branch:** *Bourse du Commerce, 2 rue de Viarmes, 1st (01.53.40.46.00). M° Louvre-Rivoli or Chatelet.* **Open** 9am-1pm, 2-5.30pm Mon-Fri. Contains a free library and bookshop. **Branch:** *2 rue Adolf Jullien, 1st. M° Louvre-*

Rivoli or Châtelet. **Open** 8.30am-12.30pm, 1.30-4.35pm. Support for businesspeople wishing to export their goods and services to France. **Legal advice line:** 08.92.70.51.00. **Open** 9am-5.30pm Mon-Thur; 9am-1pm Fri.

Chambre de Commerce et d'Industrie Franco-Britannique *31 rue Boissy d'Anglas, 8th (01.53.30.81.30/ fax 01.53.30.81.35/ www.francobritishchamber.com). M° Madeleine.* **Open** 2-5pm Mon-Fri. This organisation promotes contacts through conferences and social/cultural events. It publishes its own trade directory as well as *Cross-Channel*, a trade magazine.

INSEE (Institut National de la Statistique et des Etudes Economiques) Salle de consultation: *195 rue de Bercy, Tour Gamma A, 12th (01.41.17.66.11/08.25.88.94.52/ www.insee.fr). M° Bercy.* **Open** 9.30am-12:30pm, 2-5pm Mon-Thu, 9.30-12.30pm, 2-4pm Fri. The mother of seemingly every statistic that dissects French economy and society. Visit the reading room or search the website for free stats.

US Commercial Service *US Embassy, 2 av Gabriel, 8th (01.43.12.28.14/fax 01.43.12.21.72/ www.buyusa.gov/france). M° Concorde.* **Open** 9am-6pm Mon-Fri, by appointment. Aids US companies looking to export to France. Advice by fax and e-mail.

Customs

There are no customs on goods for personal use between EU countries, provided tax has been paid in the country of origin.

Quantities accepted as being for personal use are:

- 800 cigarettes, 400 small cigars, 200 cigars or 1kg loose tobacco.
- 10 litres of spirits (over 22% alcohol), 90 litres of wine (under 22% alcohol) or 110 litres of beer.

For goods from outside the EU:

- 200 cigarettes, 100 small cigars, 50 cigars or 250g loose tobacco.
- 1 litre of spirits (over 22% alcohol) or 2 litres of wine and beer
- 50g perfume
- 500g coffee

Visitors can carry up to €7,600 in currency (www.finances.gouv.fr).

Tax refunds

Non-EU residents can claim a refund (average 12%) on VAT if they spend over €175 in any one day and if they live outside the EU for more than six months per year. At the shop ask for a *bordereau de vente à l'exportation*, and when you leave France have it stamped by customs. Then send the stamped form back to the shop. *Détaxe* does not cover food, drink, antiques, services or works of art.

Climate

Month	Average monthly temperature:		Average monthly rainfall:	
	Celsuis	Fahrenheit	mm	inches
January	7.5º	45.5º	56	2.2
February	7.1º	44.8º	42	1.7
March	10.2º	50.4º	36	1.4
April	15.7º	60.3º	40	1.6
May	16.6º	61.9º	56	2.2
June	23.4º	74.1º	52	2.0
July	25.1º	77.2º	58	2.3
August	25.6º	78.1º	60	2.4
September	20.9º	69.6º	53	2.1
October	16.5º	61.7º	48	1.8
November	11.7º	53.1º	48	1.8
December	7.8º	46.0º	48	1.8

Disabled travellers

Time Out guides include wheelchair access in listings, but it's always wise to check beforehand. Other places are accessible to wheelchair users but do not have adapted toilets.

APAJH (Association pour Adultes et Jeunes Handicapés) *26 rue du Chemin Vert, 11th (01.48.07.25.88/www.apajh.org). M° Chemin Vert.* Advice for disabled people living in France.

Association des paralysés de France *22 rue du Père-Guérain, 13th (01.44.16.83.83). M° Place d'Italie.* **Open** 9am-12.30pm, 1.30-6pm Mon-Fri (closes 5pm Fri). Publishes *Guide 98 Musées, Cinémas* (€3.81) listing cinemas and museums accessible to those with limited mobility, and a guide to restaurants, monuments and other sights.

Platforme d'accueil et d'information des personnes handicapées de la Marie de Paris has a Freephone 08.00.03.37.48 which gives advice (in French) to disabled persons living in or visiting Paris. The Office de Tourisme's website **www.parisbienvenue.com** also givesuseful information for disabled visitors.

Getting around

Neither the Métro nor buses are wheelchair-accessible, except Métro line 14 (Méteor), bus lines 20, PC (Petite Ceinture) and some No 91s. Forward seats on buses are intended for people with poor mobility. RER lines A and B and some SNCF trains are wheelchair-accessible in parts. All Paris taxis are obliged by law to take passengers in wheelchairs. The following offer adapted transport for the disabled. You should book 72hrs in advance.

Aihrop *(01.41.29.01.29).* **Open** 9.30 am-noon, 12.30-7.30pm Mon-Fri. Closed Aug. Transport to and from the airports, book 48 hours in advance.

GiHP *24 av Henri Barbusse, 93000 Bobigny (01.41.83.15.50/www.gihpidf.asso.fr).* **Open** 6.30am-7pm Mon-Fri.

Drugs

French police have the power to stop and search anyone; it's always wise to keep any prescription drugs in their original containers, and, if possible, to carry copies of the original prescriptions. If you're caught in possession of illegal drugs you can expect a prison sentence and/or a fine. **Centre DIDRO** (*01.45.42.75.00/www.didro.net*) is an excellent source of advice for young people with drug problems. *See also* **Health**, **Helplines**.

Electricity & gas

Electricity in France runs on 220V. Visitors with British 240V appliances can change the plug or use an adapter (*adaptateur*). For US 110V appliances, you will need to use a transformer (*transformateur*) available at the Fnac and Darty chains or in the basement of BHV. Gas and electricity are supplied by the state-owned Electricité de France-Gaz de France. Contact EDF-GDF (01.45.44.64.64/www.edf.fr/ www.gazdefrance.com) about supply, bills, or in case of power failures or gas leaks.

Education

Language

Most of the large multinational language schools such as **Berlitz** (www.berlitz.com) have at least one branch in Paris. If you just want conversation practice **Konversando** (01.47.70.21.64/ www.konversando.fr) specialises in exchanges and conversation.

Alliance Française
101 bd Raspail, 6th (01.42.84.90.00/ww.alliancefr.org). M° St-Placide. Non-profit French-language school, with beginners and specialist courses starting every month, plus a *médiathèque*, film club and lectures.

British Institute
11 rue Constantine, 7th (01.44.11.73.83/ www.bip.lon.ac.uk). M° Invalides. Linked to the University of London, the 4,000-student Institute offers English courses for Parisians, and French courses (not beginner). Also offers a degree course and MAs.

Ecole Eiffel
3 rue Crocé-Spinelli, 14th. (01.43.20.37.41/www.ecole-eiffel.fr). M° Pernéty. Intensive classes, business French, and phonetics.

Eurocentres
13 passage Dauphine, 6th (01.40.46.72.00/ www.eurocentres.com). M° Odéon. Intensive classes with emphasis on communication. Has a *médiathèque*.

Institut Catholique de Paris
12 rue Cassette, 6th (01.44.39.52.68/www.icp.fr). M° St-Sulpice. Traditional courses in French language and culture. Students must be 18 or above, but don't have to be Catholic.

Institut Parisien
87 bd de Grenelle, 15th (01.40.56.09.53). M° La Motte Picquet-Grenelle. Dynamic private school offers courses in language and French civilisation, business French, plus evening courses if there's demand.

La Sorbonne – Cours de Langue et Civilisation
47 rue des Ecoles, 5th (01.40.46.22.11 ext 2664 through 75/www.fle.fr/sorbonne). M° Cluny-La Sorbonne/RER Luxembourg. Classes for foreigners ride on the name of this eminent institution. Teaching is grammar-based. Courses are open to anyone over 18 and fill up quickly.

Specialised

Many of the prestigious Ecoles Nationales Supérieures (including film schools La Fémis and ENS Louis Lumière) offer summer courses in addition to their full-time degree courses – ask for *formation continue*.

Adult education courses
Information: www.paris.fr) or from your local Mairie. A huge range of inexpensive adult education classes is run by the City of Paris, including French as a foreign language, computer skills and applied arts.

American University of Paris
31 av Bosquet, 7th (01.40.62.07.20/www.aup.edu). RER Pont de l'Alma. An international college awarding four-year American liberal arts degrees (BA/BSc). Contact the Division of Continuing Education (102 rue St-Dominique, 7th/01.40.62.05.84) for evening classes and summer school.

Christie's Education Paris
Hôtel Salomon de Rothschild, 11 rue Berryer, 8th (01.42.25.10.90/ www.christies.com/education). M° George V. The international auction house offers a one-year diploma, ten-week intensive courses and specialisations. A four-day course in English explores the 'art of living' at the court of Louis XIV.

CIDD Découverte du Vin
30 rue de la Sablière, 14th (01.45.45.44.20). M° Pernéty. Wine tasting and appreciation courses (some in English) at all levels.

Cordon Bleu
8 rue Léon-Delhomme, 15th (01.53.68.22.50). M° Vaugirard. Courses range from three-hour sessions on classical and regional cuisine to a nine-month diploma aimed at those embarking on a culinary career.

Ritz-Escoffier Ecole de Gastronomie Française
38 rue Cambon, 1st (01.43.16.30.50/ www.ritzparis.com). M° Opéra. Offers everything from afternoon demos in the Ritz kitchens to diplomas, but it doesn't come cheap. Courses are in French with English translation.

Travel info

For up-to-date information on travel to a specific country – including the latest news on safety and security, health issues, local laws and customs – contact your home country government's department of foreign affairs. Most have websites packed with useful advice for would-be travellers.

Australia
www.dfat.gov.au/travel
Canada
www.voyage.gc.ca
New Zealand
www.mft.govt.nz/travel
Republic of Ireland
www.irlgov.ie/iveagh
UK
www.fco.gov.uk/travel
USA
www.state.gov/travel

Ecole du Louvre
Porte Jaugard, Aile de Flore, Palais du Louvre. quai du Louvre, 1st (01.55.35.17.35/ www.ecoledulouvre.fr). M° Palais Royal-Musée du Louvre. Art history and archaeology courses. Foreign students not wanting to take a degree can attend lectures.

INSEAD
bd de Constance, 77305 Fontainebleau (01.60.72.40.00/ www.insead.edu). Highly regarded international business school offers a ten-month MBA in English. Not a bad place to name-drop on your CV (only if you've actually been here).

Parsons School of Design
14 rue Letellier, 15th (01.45.77.39.66/www.parsons-paris.pair.com). M° La Motte-Picquet-Grenelle. Subsidiary of New York art college offers BFA programme in fine art, fashion, photography, marketing and interior design.

Spéos – Paris Photographic Institute
7 rue Jules-Vallès, 11th (01.40.09.18.58/ www.photography-education.com). M° Charonne. Full-, part-time and summer programmes. Exchange programmes with four art schools, including the Rhode Island School of Design.

Student life

Cartes de séjour and housing benefit

Take a deep breath before you read this lot. Foreign students wishing to qualify for housing benefit or to work legally during their course in Paris must get a *Carte de Séjour* (*see p387*). You may then (note the 'may') be eligible for the ALS (*Allocation de Logement à Caractère Social*), which is handled by four CAFs (*caisses d'allocations familiales*), by *arrondissement*. The '*calculez votre aide au logement*' feature of their website (www.caf.fr) allows you to see how much you'll receive. www.droitsdesjeunes.gouv.fr gives information on your rights.

Centre de Réception des Etrangers
(EU and non-EU students) *Hôtel de Police, 114/116 av du Maine, 14th (01.53.71.51.68/ www.prefecture-police-paris. interieur.gouv.fr). M° Gaité or Montparnasse.* **Open** 9am-4pm Mon-Fri.

CAFs *19 rue Pot de Fer, 5th (08.20.25.75.10), M° Place Monge; 101 rue Nationale, 13th, M° Nationale; 18 rue Viala, 15th, M° Dupleix; 67 av Jean-Jaurès, 19th, M° Laumière.* **Open** 8.30am-4pm Mon-Fri.

Accommodation

The simplest budget accommodation for medium-to-long stays can be found at the **Cité Universitaire** or *foyers* (student hostels). Another option is a *chambre contre travail* – free board in exchange for childcare, housework or English lessons. Look out for ads at language schools and the American Church. For cheap hotels and youth hostels, *see chapter* **Where to Stay**. As students often cannot provide proof of income, a *porte-garant* (guarantor) is required who will guarantee payment of rent and bills.

Cité Universitaire
19 bd Jourdan, 14th (01.44.16.64.46/48/www.ciup.fr). RER Cité Universitaire. **Open** offices 8.30am-7pm Mon-Fri. Foreign students enrolled on a university course, or interns who are also studying, can apply for a place at this campus of halls of residence (but be forewarned: only about 10% of the students that apply get in). Rooms must be booked for the entire academic year. Rents are around €300-€400/month single, €200-€300 per person double. UK citizens must apply to the Collège Franco-Britannique, and Americans to the Fondation des Etats-Unis.

CROUS (Centre régional des oeuvres universitaires et scolaires) *39 av Georges-Bernanos, 5th (01.40.51.36.00/ www.crous-paris.fr). Service du Logement: (01.40.51.55.55). RER Port-Royal.* **Open** 9am-5pm Mon-Fri. Manages all University of Paris student residences, posts ads for rooms and has a list of hostels. Requests for rooms must be made by 1 April for the next academic year. CROUS also runs cheap canteens (listed on website) and is the clearing house for all *bourses* (grants) issued to foreign students. Call the Service des Bourses on 01.40.51.37.35.

UCRIF (Union des centres de rencontres internationales de France) *27 rue de Turbigo, 2nd (01.40.26.57.64/ www.ucrif.asso.fr). M° Etienne Marcel.* **Open** 9am-6pm Mon-Fri. Operates cheap, short-stay hostels from four help centres: 5th (01.43.29.34.80); 12th (01.44.75.60.06); 13th (01.43.36.00.63); 14th (01.43.13.17.00).

Student & youth discounts

To claim the *tarif étudiant* (around €1.52 off some cinema seats, up to 50% off museums and standby theatre tickets), you must have a French student card or an International Student Identity Card (ISIC), available from CROUS, student travel agents and the Cité Universitaire. ISIC cards are only valid in France if you are under 26. Under-26s can get up to 50% off rail travel on certain trains with the SNCF's Carte 12/25 and the same reduction on the RATP with the 'Imagine R' card.

Working

Foreign students can legally work up to 20hrs per week. Non-EU members studying in Paris must apply for an *autorisation provisoire de travail* from the DDTEFT. CROUS's job service (01.40.51.37.52 through 57) places students in part-time jobs.

DDTEFT (Direction Régionale du Travail, d'Emploi et du Formation Professionelle)
109 rue Montmartre, 75084 Paris Cedex 02 (01.44.76.69.30/ www.travail.gouv.fr).

Useful organisations

CIDJ (Centre d'information et de documentation jeunesse)
101 quai Branly, 15th (01.44.49.12.00/www.cidj.com). M° Bir-Hakeim/ RER Champ de Mars. **Open** 10am-6pm Mon, Wed, Fri; 10am-7pm Tue, Thur; 9.30am-1pm Sat. Library gives students advice on courses and careers; youth bureau of ANPE (Agence Nationale Pour l'Emploi/www.anpe.fr) helps with job applications.

Edu France
173 bd St-Germain, 6th (01.53.63.35.00/www.edufrance.com). M° St Germain des Près. **Open** Mon-Fri 9am-6pm (call as hours vary). **Fees** €200-€500. Government-run organisation promotes the French university system abroad and assists foreign students in France. The website has some useful free information.

Maison des Initiatives Etudiantes (MIE)
50 rue des Tournelles, 3rd (01.49.96.65.30/www.paris.fr). Offers Paris-based student associations resources such as meeting rooms, grants and on-line computers. Its future plans include creating a radio station for students (Radio Campus Paris).

Socrates-Erasmus Programme
Britain: *UK Socrates-Erasmus Council, RND Building, The University, Canterbury, Kent CT2 7PD (01227-762712).* **France:** *Agence Erasmus, 10 pl de la Bourse, 33080 Bordeaux Cedex (05.56.79.44.00/ www.socrates-france.org).* The Socrates-Erasmus scheme enables EU students with reasonable written and spoken French to spend a year of their degree in the French university system. Applications must be made through the Erasmus co-ordinator at your home university. Non-EU students should find out from their university whether it has an agreement with the French university system. US students can find out more from MICEFA (26 rue du Fbg-St-Jacques, 14th, 01.40.51.76.96/www.micefa.org).

Relais d'accueil (Foreign students helpdesk) *Cité Universitaire, 19 bd Jourdan, 14th. RER Cité Universitaire. CROUS de Paris, 39 av Georges-Bernanos, 5th. RER Port Royal. Information (01.43.13.66.46/www.eduparis.net). Sept-Nov.* By-appointment advice on housing, getting a bank account, a Carte de Séjour, social security and university registration is available to foreign students at the two addresses above.

Embassies & consulates

There's a full list of embassies and consulates in the *Pages Jaunes* (or www.pagesjaunes.fr) under '*Ambassades et Consulats*'. Consular services are for citizens of that country (passport matters, etc) while a separate visa service operates for foreign nationals applying for visas.

Australian Embassy
4 rue Jean-Rey, 15th (01.40.59.33.00/ www.austgov.fr). M° Bir-Hakeim. **Consular services** 9.15am-noon, 2-4.30pm Mon-Fri; **Visas** 10am-12am Mon-Fri.

British Embassy
35 rue du Fbg-St-Honoré, 8th (01.44.51.31.00/ www.amb-grandebretagne.fr). M° Concorde. **Consular services** *18bis rue d'Anjou, 8th.* **Open** 9.30am-1pm, 2.30-6pm Mon, Wed-Fri; 9.30am-4.30pm Tue. **Visas** *16 rue d'Anjou, 8th (01.44.51.33.01/ 01.44.51.33.04).* **Open** 9am-noon Mon-Fri; by phone 2.30-5pm Mon-Fri. British citizens wanting consular services (new passports etc) should note that the long queue extending along rue d'Anjou is for the visa department – for other nationalities wanting visas to visit Britain. Bypass this and walk straight in at No 18*bis*.

Canadian Embassy
35 av Montaigne, 8th (01.44.43.29.00/www.amb-canada.fr). M° Franklin D. Roosevelt. **Consular services** *(01.44.43.29.02).* **Open** 9am-noon, 2-4.30pm Mon-Fri. **Visas** *37 av Montaigne (01.44.43.29.16).* **Open** 8.30-11am Mon-Fri.

Irish Embassy
12 av Foch, 16th. **Consulate** *4 rue Rude, 16th (01.44.17.67.00). M° Charles de Gaulle-Etoile.* **Open** (consular/visas) 9.30am-noon Mon-Fri; by phone 9.30am-1pm, 2.30-5.30pm Mon-Fri.

New Zealand Embassy
7ter rue Léonard de Vinci, 16th (01.45.01.43.43/ www.nzembassy.com/france). M° Victor-Hugo. **Open** 9am-1pm, 2pm-5.30pm Mon-Fri (closes 4pm Fri). *July, Aug* 9am-1pm, 2-4.30pm Mon-Thur; 9am-2pm Fri.
Visas 9am-1pm Mon-Fri. Visas for travel to New Zealand can be applied for using the website www.immigration.govt.nz.

South African Embassy
59 quai d'Orsay, 7th (01.53.59.23.23/www.afriquesud.net). M° Invalides. **Open** by appointment; by phone 8.30am-5.15pm Mon-Fri. **Consulate and visas** 9am-noon.

US Embassy
2 av Gabriel, 8th (01.43.12.22.22/ www.amb-usa.fr). M° Concorde. **Consulate and visas** *2 rue St-Florentin, 1st (01.43.12.22.22). M° Concorde.* **Open** (consular services) 9am-12.30pm, 1-3pm Mon-Fri. **Visas** phone 08.99.70.37.00 or check website for non-immigration visas.

Emergencies

Most of the following services operate 24-hr a day. In a real medical emergency such as a road accident, call the Sapeurs-Pompiers, who have trained paramedics.

Police **17**
Fire (Sapeurs-Pompiers) **18**
Ambulance (SAMU) **15**
Emergency (from a mobile phone) **112**
GDF (gas leaks) 08.10.43.32.75
EDF (electricity) 08.10.33.39 + number of *arrondissement* (01-20)
Centre anti-poison 01.40.05.48.48
See also **Health: Accident & Emergency, Doctors; Helplines**.

Health

Nationals of non-EU countries should take out insurance before leaving home. EU nationals staying in France are entitled to use of the French Social Security system, which refunds up to 70% of medical expenses. British nationals should obtain form E111 from a post office before leaving the UK (or E112 for those already in treatment). If you are staying for longer than three months, or working in France but still paying NI contributions in Britain, you will need form E128 filled in by your employer and stamped by the NI contributions office in order to get a French medical number. Consultations and prescriptions have to be paid for in full at the time, and are reimbursed on receipt of a completed *fiche*. If you undergo treatment the doctor will give you a prescription and a *feuille de soins* (statement of treatment). Stick the little stickers from the medication onto the *feuille de soins*. Send this, the prescription and form E111, to the local **Caisse Primaire d'Assurance Maladie** to retrieve your reimbursement.
For those resident in France more and more doctors (especially in Paris) now accept the Carte Vitale, which allows them to establish a virtual *feuille de soins* and you to pay only the non-reimbursable part of the bill. Information on the health system can be found at www.ameli.fr. You can track your refunds with Allosecu (08.20.90.09.00/€0.12 per minute).

Accident & emergency

Note that many hospitals specialise in one type of medical emergency or illness. Consult the Assistance Publique's web site (www.ap-hop-paris.fr) for details. In a medical emergency call the Sapeurs-Pompiers or SAMU (*see p376* **Emergencies**). Following (in order of arrondissement) are Paris hospitals with 24-hr accident and emergency services:

Adults

Hôpital Hôtel Dieu
1 place du Parvis Notre-Dame, 4th (01.42.34.82.34).

Hôpital St-Louis *1 av Claude Vellefaux, 10th (01.42.49.49.49).*

Hôpital St-Antoine
184 rue du Fbg-St-Antoine, 12th (01.49.28.20.00).

Hôpital de la Pitié-Salpêtrière
47-83 bd de l'Hôpital, 13th (01.42.16.00.00).

Hôpital Cochin
27 rue du Fbg-St-Jacques, 14th (01.58.41.41.41).

Hôpital Européen Georges Pompidou
20 rue Leblanc, 15th (01.56.09.20.00).

Hôpital Bichat-Claude Bernard
46 rue Henri Huchard, 18th (01.40.25.80.80).

Hôpital Tenon
4 rue de la Chine, 20th (01.56.01.70.00).

Children

Hôpital Armand Trousseau
26 av du Dr Arnold Netter, 12th (01.44.73.74.75).

Hôpital St Vincent de Paul
82 av Denfert Rochereau, 14th (01.40.48.81.11).

Hôpital Necker
149 rue de Sèvres, 15th (01.44.49.40.00).

Hôpital Robert Debré
48 bd Sérurier, 19th (01.40.03.20.00).

Private Hospitals

American Hospital in Paris
63 bd Victor-Hugo, 92200 Neuilly (01.46.41.25.25/www.american-hospital.org). M° Porte Maillot, then bus 82. **Open** 24-hr. English-speaking hospital. French Social Security refunds only a small percentage of treatment costs.

Hertford British Hospital
(Hôpital Franco-Britannique) 3 rue Barbès, 92300 Levallois-Perret (01.46.39.22.22). M° Anatole-France. **Open** 24-hr. Most of the medical staff speak English.

Complementary medicine

Académie d'homéopathie et des médecines douces
2 rue d'Isly, 8th (01.43.87.60.33). M° St-Lazare. **Open** 10am-6pm Mon-Fri. Health services include acupuncture, aromatherapy and homeopathy.

Contraception & abortion

To obtain the pill (*la pilule*) or the coil (*stérilet*), you need a prescription, available on appointment from the first two places below or from a *médecin généraliste* (GP) or gynaecologist. Note that the morning-after pill (*la pilule du lendemain*) is available from pharmacies without prescription but is not reimbursed. Spermicides and condoms (*préservatifs*) are sold in pharmacies and supermarkets, and there are condom machines in most Métro stations, club lavatories and on some street corners. If you are considering an abortion (*IVG* or *interruption volontaire de grossesse*) but want to discuss options in detail you may get better information and counselling from the *orthogénie* (family planning) department of a hospital than from the two organisations below (see www.ap-hop-paris.fr for where IVG is offered). While abortion rights are strongly grounded in France, some doctors remain opposed. Ultrasound examinations to ascertain the exact stage of pregnancy are obligatory.

Centre de planification et d'éducation familiales *27 rue Curnonsky, 17th (01.48.88.07.28). M° Porte de Champerret.* **Open** 9am-5pm Mon-Fri. Free consultations on family planning and abortion. Abortion counselling on demand; otherwise phone for an appointment.

MFPF (Mouvement français pour le planning familial)
10 rue Vivienne, 2nd (free info: 08.00.80.38.03 or 01.42.60.93.20). M° Bourse. **Open** 9.30am-7.30pm Mon-Fri; 9.30am-12.30pm Sat. Phone for an appointment for contraception advice and prescriptions. For abortion advice, turn up at the centre at one of the designated time slots. The approach here, however, is brusque.
Branch: 94 bd Masséna, 13th (01.45.84.28.25/ open 10am-3.30pm Wed; 11am-4pm Fri).

Dentists

Dentists are found in the *Pages Jaunes* under *Dentistes*. For emergencies contact:

Urgences Dentaires de Paris
(01.42.61.12.00). **Open** 8am-10pm Sun, holidays.

SOS Dentaire *87 bd Port-Royal, 13th (01.43.37.51.00). M° Gobelins, RER Port-Royal.* **Open** Call for an appointment as hours vary. Phone service for emergency dental care.

Hôpital de la Pitié-Salpêtrière (*see above*, **Accident & Emergency**) offers 24hr emergency dental care.

Doctors

A complete list of GPs is in the *Pages Jaunes* under *Médecins: Médecine générale*. To get a Social Security refund, choose a doctor or dentist who is *'conventionné'* (state registered). Consultations cost €20 upwards, of which a proportion can be reimbursed. Seeing a specialist costs more.

Centre Médical Europe
44 rue d'Amsterdam, 9th (01.42.81.93.33/dentists 01.42.81.80.00). M° St-Lazare. **Open** 8am-7pm Mon-Fri; 8am-6pm Sat. Practitioners in all fields, charging minimal consultation fees.

House calls

SOS Infirmiers *(Nurses) (01.47.07.00.73).* **House calls** 8pm-midnight; daytime Sat-Sun; the cost is generally €22.87.

SOS Médecins *(01.43.37.77.77 or 08.20.33.24.24).* Home visits at least €60 if you don't have French social security; €30 if you do, before 7pm; from €50 after.

Urgences Médicales de Paris *(01.53.94.94.94)*. Doctors make house calls around the clock for €31-€55 per visit. Some speak English.

Eyes

Branches of Alain Afflelou (www.alainefflelou.com) and Lissac (www.lissac.com) stock hundreds of frames and can make prescription glasses within the hour. For an eye test you will need to go to an *ophtalmologiste* – ask the optician for a list. Contact lenses can be bought over the counter if you have your prescription details.

Hôpital des Quinze-Vingts
28 rue de Charenton, 12th (01.40.02.15.20). Specialist eye hospital offers on-the-spot consultations for eye problems.

SOS Optique *(01.48.07.22.00/ www.sosoptique.com)*. 24-hr repair service for glasses.

Pharmacies

Pharmacies sport a green neon cross. Paris has a rota system of *pharmacies de garde* at night and on Sunday. A closed pharmacy will have a sign indicating the nearest open pharmacy. Staff can provide basic medical services like disinfecting and bandaging wounds (for a small fee) and will indicate the nearest doctor on duty. *Parapharmacies* sell almost everything pharmacies do but cannot dispense prescription medication. Toiletries, sanitary products and cosmetics are often cheaper in supermarkets.

Night pharmacies

Pharma Presto *(01.42.42.42.50/ www.pharma-presto.com)*. **Open** 24-hr. Delivery charge €39 from 8am-6pm; €54 6pm-8am. Delivers prescription medication (non-prescription exceptions can be made). Will also chauffer your ailing pet to the vet.

Pharmacie des Halles
10 bd de Sébastopol, 4th (01.42.72.03.23). M° Châtelet. **Open** 9am-midnight Mon-Sat; 9am-10pm Sun.

Dérhy/Pharmacie des Champs
84 av des Champs-Elysées, 8th (01.45.62.02.41). M° George V. **Open** 24-hr.

Matignon *2 rue Jean-Mermoz, 8th (01.43.59.86.55). M° Franklin D. Roosevelt.* **Open** 8.30am-2am daily.

Pharmacie Européenne de la Place de Clichy
6 pl de Clichy, 9th (01.48.74.65.18). M° Place de Clichy. **Open** 24-hr.

Pharmacie de la Place de la Nation
13 pl de la Nation, 11th (01.43.73.24.03). M° Nation. **Open** 8am-midnight daily.

Pharmacie d'Italie
61 av d'Italie, 13th (01.44.24.19.72). M° Tolbiac. **Open** 8am-2am Mon-Sat; 9am-midnight Sun.

STDs, HIV & AIDS

Centre Medico-Sociale (Mairie de Paris)
2 rue Figuier, 4th (01.49.96.62.70). M° Pont-Marie. **Open** 9am-6.30pm Mon, Tue, Thur; 1.30-6.30pm Wed, Fri; 9.30-12.30pm Sat. Free, anonymous tests (*dépistages*) for HIV, Hep B and C and syphillis (wait one week for results). Excellent counselling.

Le Kiosque Info Sida
36 rue Geoffroy l'Asnier, 4th (01.44.78.00.00). M° St-Paul. **Open** 10am-7pm Mon-Fri; 2-7pm Sat. Youth association offering info on AIDS and health. Face-to-face counselling service.

FACTS *(01.44.93.16.69/www.facts-line.com)*. **Open** 7-9pm Mon, Wed. English-speaking crisis line gives info and support for those touched by HIV/AIDS and runs groups for friends and relatives.

SIDA Info Service
(08.00.84.08.00). **Open** 24-hr. Confidential AIDS information in French. English-speaking counsellors 2-7pm Mon, Wed, Fri.

Helplines

SOS Dépression
(01.40.47.95.95). **Open** 24-hr. People listen and/or give advice. Can send a counsellor or psychiatrist to your home in case of a crisis.

SOS Help *(01.46.21.46.46)*. **Open** 3-11pm daily. English-language helpline .

Alcoholics Anonymous in English
(01.46.34.59.65/www.aaparis.org). 24-hr recorded message gives details of AA meetings at the American Church or Cathedral (*see p384,* **Religion**).

Narcotics Anonymous
(01.43.62.12.72/01.48.58.50.61/ www.nafrance.org). Meetings in English three times a week.

The Counseling Center
(01.47.23.61.13). English-language counselling service, based at the American Cathedral.

113 Phone service for help with drug, alcohol and tobacco problems.

ID

French law demands that some form of identification is carried at all times. Be ready to produce a passport or *Carte de Séjour* in response to that old police refrain '*Papiers, s'il vous plaît*'.

Insurance

See p376, **Health**.

Internet

After a slow start, use has skyrocketed. It is now possible get cable access in most of Paris.

ISPs

Noosnet (08.25.34.54.74/ 08.00.114.114/www.noos.com).

America Online (08.26.02.60.00/www.aol.fr).

Club-Internet (08.26.02.70.28/ www.club-internet.fr).

CompuServe (03.21.13.49.49/ www.compuserve.fr).

Microsoft Network (08.25.82.78.29/www.fr.msn.com).

Wanadoo (France Télécom) (08.10.63.34.34/www.wanadoo.fr).

Free (www.free.fr).

Internet access

Access Academy *60-62 rue Saint-André des Arts, 6th (www.accessacademy.com) M˚ Odeon* **Open** 8am-2am daily.

Café Orbital *13 rue de Médicis, 6th (01.43.25.76.77). RER Luxembourg.* **Open** 10am-8pm Mon-Fri; 10am-8pm Sat, Sun.

Clickside *14 rue Domat, 5th (01.56.81.03.00). M° Maubert-Mutualité.* **Open** 10am-midnight Mon-Fri; 1pm-11pm Sat-Sun.

Cyber Cube *12 rue Daval, 11th (01.49.29.67.67/www.cybercube.fr). M° Bastille.* **Open** 10am-10pm daily. Many hotels offer Internet access, some from your own room.

Language

See p388, **Essential Vocabulary**, and *p184,* **Menu Lexicon**, for food terms.

Legal advice

Mairies can answer some legal enquiries. Phone for times of free *consultations juridiques*.

Direction départmentale de la concurrence, de la consommation, et de la répression des fraudes
8 rue Froissart, 3rd (01.40.27.16.00). M° St-Sébastien-Froissart. **Open** 9-11.30am, 2-5pm Mon-Fri. This subdivision of the Ministry of Finance deals with consumer complaints.

Palais de Justice Galerie de Harlay
Escalier S, 4 bd du Palais, 4th (01.44.32.48.48). M° Cité. **Open** 9.30am-noon Mon-Fri. Free legal consultation. Arrive early.

SOS Avocats *(08.25.39.33.00).* **Open** 7-11.30pm Mon-Fri. Closed July, Aug. Free legal advice by phone.

Libraries

All *arrondissements* have free public libraries. For a library card, you need ID and evidence of a fixed address in Paris.

American Library
10 rue du Général-Camou, 7th (01.53.59.12.60/ www.americanlibraryinparis.org). M° Ecole-Militaire/RER Pont de l'Alma. **Open** 10am-7pm Tue-Sat (shorter hours in Aug). **Admission** day pass €11; annual €96. The largest English-language lending library in continental Europe. Receives 400 periodicals, plus popular magazines and newspapers (mainly American).

Bibliothèque Historique de la Ville de Paris *Hôtel Lamoignon, 24 rue Pavée, 4th (01.44.59.29.40). M° St-Paul.* **Open** 9.30am-6pm Mon-Sat. Closed first two weeks in Aug. **Admission** free (bring ID and a passport photo). Reference books and documents on Paris history in a Marais mansion.

Bibliothèque Marguerite Durand
79 rue Nationale, 13th (01.45.70.80.30). M° Tolbiac or Place d'Italie. **Open** 2-6pm Tue-Sat. Closed 3 weeks in Sept. **Admission** free. 40,000 books and 120 periodicals on women's history and feminism. Collection includes letters of Colette and Louise Michel.

Bibliothèque Nationale de France François Mitterrand
quai François-Mauriac, 13th (01.53.79.59.59/ www.bnf.fr). M° Bibliothèque. **Open** 10am-8pm Tue-Sat; noon-7pm Sun. Closed 2 weeks in Sept. **Admission** day pass €3; annual €30. Books, papers and periodicals, plus titles in English. An audio-visual room lets you browse photo, film and sound archives. *Wheelchair access.*

Bibliothèque Publique d'Information (BPI) *Centre Pompidou, 4th (01.44.78.12.71/ www.bpi.fr). M° Hôtel de Ville/RER Châtelet-Les Halles.* **Open** 12am-10pm Mon, Wed-Fri; 11am-10pm Sat, Sun. **Admission** free. Now on three levels, the Centre Pompidou's vast library has a huge international press section, reference books and language-learning facilities. *Wheelchair access.*

BIFI (Bibliothèque du Film)
100 rue du Fbg-St-Antoine, 12th (01.53.02.22.30/www.bifi.fr). M° Ledru-Rollin. **Open** 10am-7pm Mon-Fri. Closed 2 weeks in Aug. **Admission** €3.50 day pass; €34 annual; €15 students annual. Film buffs' library offers books, magazines film stills and posters, as well as films on video and DVD.

Documentation Française
29 quai Voltaire, 7th (01.40.15.72.72/ www.ladocumentationfrancaise.fr). M° Rue du Bac. **Open** 10am-6pm Mon-Wed, Fri; 10am-1pm Thur. Closed Aug and first week Sept. The official government archive and central reference library has information on French politics and economy since 1945.

Locksmiths

Numerous 24-hr emergency repair services handle plumbing, locks, and sometimes car repairs. Most charge a minimum €18-€20 call-out (*déplacement*) and €30 per hour, plus parts. Charges are higher on Sunday and at night.

Allô Assistance Dépannage (08.00.00.00.18). No car repairs.

Websites

www.absolufeminin.com
The last word on fashion and shopping.
www.culture.fr
News on all aspects of art and culture in France
www.eduparis.net
A useful introduction for foreign students arriving in Paris.
www.fnac.com
Great for booking tickets to all sorts of events.
www.fusac.fr
Resources and contacts for anglophones in Paris.
www.leparisien.com
The capital's daily newspaper.
www.mappy.fr
Plan the best route through Paris and France.
www.meteo.fr/temps
Forecasts from the meteorological office.
www.pagesjaunes.fr
On-line phone directory with maps and photographs.
www.paris-anglo.com
Articles and directory from an expat angle.
www.paris-art.com
The latest contemporary arts events including a calender.
www.paris.org
The city from Métro maps to museum opening times and lots of links.
www.parissi.com
Good for clubbing and concert news.
www.paris-touristoffice.com
The organ of the official Paris Tourist Board (available in English).
www.timeout.com
A list of the month's current events, and an extensive guide to hotels, restaurants and the arts. Simply the best.

Numéro Un Dépannage (01.40.71.55.55). No car repairs.

SOS Dépannage (01.47.07.99.99). Double the price of most, but claims to be twice as reliable.

Lost property

Bureau des Objets Trouvés *36 rue des Morillons, 15th (08.21.00.25.25/ www.prefecture-police-paris.interieur.gouv.fr). M° Convention.* **Open** 8.30am-5pm Mon-Thur; 8.30am-4.30pm Fri. Visit in person to fill in a form specifying details of the loss. This may have been the first lost property office in the world, but it is far from the most efficient. Horrendous delays in processing claims mean that if your trip to Paris is short you may need to nominate a proxy to collect found objects after your return, although small items can be posted. If your passport was among the lost items you will need to go to your consulate to get a single-entry temporary passport in order to leave the country.

SNCF lost property Some mainline SNCF stations have their own lost property offices.

Media

Magazines

Arts & listings

Three pocket-sized publications compete for basic Wed-to-Tue listings information: **Pariscope** (€0.40), the Parisian cinema-goer's bible, which includes **Time Out Paris** in English; the thinner **Officiel des Spectacles** (€0.35); and trendy **Zurban** (€0.80). Linked to Radio Nova, monthly **Nova** gives rigorously multi-ethnic information on where to drink, dance or hang out. **Technikart** tries to mix clubbing with the arts. Highbrow TV guide **Télérama** has good arts and entertainment features and a Paris listings insert. *See also below* **Le Monde** *and* **Le Figaro**.
There are specialist arts magazines to meet every interest. Film titles include intellectual **Les Cahiers du Cinéma**, glossy **Studio** and younger, celebrity-geared **Première**.

Business

Capital, its sister magazine **Management** and the weightier **L'Expansion** are worthwhile monthlies. **Défis** has tips for the entrepreneur, **Initiatives** is for the self-employed.

English

On the local front, **Time Out Paris** is a six-page supplement inside weekly listings magazine **Pariscope**, available at all news stands, covering selected Paris events, exhibitions, films, concerts and restaurants. The quarterly **Time Out Paris Free Guide** is distributed in bars, hotels and tourist centres, and the **Time Out Paris Visitors' Guide** is on sale in newsagents across the city. **FUSAC** (France-USA Contacts) is a small-ads free-sheet with flat rentals, job ads and appliances for sale.

Gossip

The French appear to have an almost insatiable appetite for gossip. Launched in 2003 **Public** gives weekly celebrity updates. **Oh La!** (sister of Spain's *Hola!* and UK's *Hello!*) showcases celebs. **Voici** is the juiciest scandal sheet while **Gala** tells the same stories without the sleaze. **Paris Match** is a French institution founded in 1948, packed with society gossip and celebrity interviews, but still regularly scoops the rest with photo shoots of international affairs. **Point de Vue** specialises in royalty and disdains showbiz fluff. Monthly **Entrevue** aims to totillate and tends toward features on bizarre sexual practices.

News

Weekly news magazines are an important sector in France, taking the place of weighty Sunday tomes and offering news, cultural sections as well as in-depth reports. Titles range from solidly serious **L'Express** and **Le Point** to the traditionally left-wing **Le Nouvel Observateur** and sardonic, chaotically arranged **Marianne**. Weekly **Courrier International** publishes a fascinating selection of articles from newspapers all over the world, translated into French.

Women, men & fashion

Elle was a pioneer among women's mags and has editions across the globe. In France it is weekly and spot-on for interviews and fashion. Monthly **Marie-Claire** takes a more feminist, campaigning line. Both have design spin-offs (**Elle Décoration**, **Marie-Claire Maison**) and Elle has spawned foodie **Elle à Table**. **DS** aims at the intellectual reader, with lots to read and coverage of social issues. **Vogue**, read both for its fashion coverage and big-name guests, is rivalled when it comes to fashion week by **L'Officiel de la Mode**. The underground go for more radical publications **Purple** (six-monthly art, literature and fashion tome), **Crash**, and the new wave of fashion/lifestyle mags: **WAD** (We Are Different), **Citizen K**, **Jalouse** and **Numéro**. Men's mags include French versions of lad bibles **FHM**, **Maximal**, **Men's Health**, and the naughty **Echo des Savanes**.

Newspapers

The national dailies are characterised by high prices and relatively low circulation. Only 20% of the population reads a national paper; regional dailies hold sway outside Paris. Serious, centre-left **Le Monde** is essential reading for business people, politicians and intellectuals. Despite its highbrow reputation, subject matter is surprisingly eclectic, although international coverage is selective. It also publishes **Aden**, a Wednesday Paris-listings supplement.
Founded post-68 by a group that included Sartre and de Beauvoir, trendy **Libération** is now centre-left, but still the read of the *gauche caviar*, worth reading for wide-ranging news and arts coverage. The conservative upper and middle classes go for **Le Figaro**, a daily broadsheet with a devotion to politics, shopping, food and sport. Sales are boosted by lots of property and job ads and the Wednesday **Figaroscope** Paris listings. Saturday's edition contains three magazines which rockets the price from €1 to €4. For business and financial news,

the French dailies **La Tribune**, **Les Echos** and the weekly **Investir** are the tried and trusted sources. Tabloid in format, the easy-read **Le Parisien** is strong on consumer affairs, social issues, local news and events and vox pops, and has a Sunday edition. Downmarket **France Soir** has gone tabloid. **La Croix** is a Catholic, right-wing daily. The Communist Party **L'Humanité** struggles to exist, as does the Party itself. Sunday broadsheet **Le Journal du Dimanche** comes with **Fémina** mag and a Paris. section. **L'Equipe** is a big-selling sports daily with a bias towards football; **Paris-Turf** caters for horse-racing fans.

English papers

The Paris-based **International Herald Tribune** is on sale throughout the city; British dailies, Sundays and **USA Today** are widely available on the day of issue at larger kiosks in the centre, though often without their supplements.

Satirical papers

Wednesday-published institution **Le Canard Enchainé** is the Gallic *Private Eye* – in fact it was the inspiration for the *Eye*. It's a broadly left-wing satirical weekly broadsheet that's full of in-jokes and breaks political scandals. **Charlie Hebdo** is mainly bought for its cartoons.

Radio

A quota requiring a minimum of 40% French music has led to overplay of Gallic pop oldies and to the creation of dubious hybrids by local groups that mix some words in French with a refrain in English. Trash-talking phone-in shows also proliferate. Wavelengths are in MHz.

87.8 France Inter State-run, MOR music, international news and concerts by rock newcomers.

90.4 Nostalgie As it sounds.

90.9 Chante France 100% French *chanson*.

91.3 Chérie FM Lots of oldies.

91.7 France Musiques State classical music channel has brought in more *variété* and slush to its highbrow mix of concerts, contemporary bleeps and top jazz.

92.1 Le Mouv' New public station aimed at luring the young with pop and rock music.

93.1 Aligre From local Paris news to literary chat.

93.5/93.9 France Culture Verbose state culture station.

94.8 RCJ/Radio J/Judaïque FM/ Radio Shalom Shared wavelength for Jewish stations.

95.2 Ici et Maintenant/Neo New stations hoping to stir local public debate about current events.

96 Skyrock Pop station with loudmouth presenters. Lots of rap.

96.4 BFM Business and economics.

96.9 Voltage FM Dance music.

97.4 Rire et Chansons A non-stop diet of jokes – politically incorrect or just plain lousy – and pop oldies.

97.8 Ado Music for adolescents.

98.2 Radio FG Beloved of clubbers for its up-to-the-minute what's on announcements this popular station broke free from its gay status in 1999.

99 Radio Latina Great Latin and salsa music.

100.3 NRJ Energy: national leader with the under-30s.

101.1 Radio Classique More classical pops than France Musique.

101.5 Radio Nova Hip hop, trip hop, world, jazz.

101.9 Fun Radio Now embracing techno alongside Anglo pop hits.

102.3 Ouï FM Ouï rock you.

103.9 RFM Easy listening.

104.3 RTL The most popular French station nationwide mixes music and talk programmes.

104.7 Europe 1 News, press reviews, sports, business, entertainment. Much the best weekday breakfast news broadcast, with politicians interviewed live.

105.1 FIP Traffic and weather bulletins, what's on in Paris and a brilliantly eclectic mix of jazz, classical, world and pop.

105.5 France Info 24-hr news, weather, economic updates and sports bulletins. As reports get repeated every 15 minutes, it's guaranteed to drive you mad – good though if you're learning French.

106.7 Beur FM North African music and discussion.

For up-to-date info on TV and radio see www.csa.fr.

English

You can receive the **BBC World Service** (648 KHz AM) for its English-language international news, current events, pop and drama. Also on 198KHz LW, from midnight to 5.30am daily. At other times this frequency carries **BBC Radio 4** (198 KHz LW), for British news, talk and *The Archers* directed at the home audience. **RFI** (738 KHz AM) has an English-language programme of news and music from 7-8am, 2-3pm and 4.30-5pm daily; www.rfi.fr

Television

TF1 The country's biggest channel, and first to be privatised in 1987. Reality shows, dubbed soaps and football are staples.

France 2 State-owned station mixes game shows, chat, documentaries, and the usual cop series and films.

FR3 The more heavyweight of the two state channels offers regional, wildlife and sports coverage, debates and *Cinéma de Minuit*, late-night Sunday classic films in V.O. (original language).

Canal+ Subscription channel shows recent films, exclusive sport and late-night porn. A weeks worth of the satirical puppets show *Les Guignols* is broadcast unscrambled on Sunday at 1.40pm.

Arte/France 5 Intellectual Franco-German hybrid Arte shares its wavelength with educational channel France 5 (3am-7pm).

M6 Imports sci-fi series and made for TV movies. Homegrown programmes include *Culture Pub* (about advertising) and cheesy talent-seeker *Fame Academy*.

Cable TV & satellite

France offers a decent range of cable and satellite channels but content in English remains limited. CNN and BBC World offer round-the-clock news coverage. BBC Prime keeps you up to date on *Eastenders* (omnibus Sun 2pm), while Teva features original-language comedy *Sex and the City*.

Noostv (08.00.114.114/ www.noos.fr). The first cable provider to offer an interactive video service via Internet. Packages from €19 per month ('Noos Pass').

Money

The euro

On 1 January 2002 euro currency became the official currency in France. If you still have francs left over, only the Banque de France or the Trésor Public now offer free exchanges (coins until 17 Feb 2005, notes until 17 Feb 2012). Foreign debit and credit cards can automatically be used to withdraw and pay in euros, and currency withdrawn in France can be used all over the euro zone. Daylight robbery occurs, however, if you try to deposit a euro cheque from any country other than France in a French bank: they are currently charging around €15 for this service, and the European parliament has backed down on its original decision that cross-border payments should be in line with domestic ones across the euro zone. Good news for Brits though – if you transfer money from the UK to France in euros you'll pay the same charges as if Britain were within the euro zone (watch the exchange rate carefully though).

Useful websites

www.banque-france.fr

www.euro.gouv.fr Official website; information, updates and online franc-euro converter.

www.xe.com/ucc Universal live rate currency converter.

ATMs

Withdrawals in euros can be made from bank and post office automatic cash machines. The specific cards accepted are marked on each machine, and most give instructions in English. Credit card companies charge a fee for cash advances, but rates are often better than bank rates.

Banks

French banks usually open 9am-5pm Mon-Fri (some close at lunch); some banks also open on Sat. All are closed on public holidays, and from noon on the previous day. Note that not all banks have foreign exchange counters. Commission rates vary between banks. The state Banque de France usually offers good rates. Most banks accept travellers' cheques, but may be reluctant to accept personal cheques even with the Eurocheque guarantee card, which is not widely used in France.

Bank accounts

To open an account (*ouvrir un compte*), French banks require proof of identity, address and your income (if any). You'll probably be required to show your passport, *Carte de Séjour*, an electricity/gas or phone bill in your name and a payslip/letter from your employer. Students need a student card and may need a letter from their parents. Of the major banks (BNP, Crédit Lyonnais, Société Générale, Banque Populaire, Crédit Agricole), Société Générale tends to be most foreigner-friendly. Most banks don't hand out a *Carte Bleue/Visa* until several weeks after you've opened an account. A chequebook (*chéquier*) is usually issued in about a week. *Carte Bleue* is debited directly from your current account, but you can choose for purchases to be debited at the end of every month. French banks are tough on overdrafts, so try to anticipate any cash crisis in advance and work out a deal for an authorised overdraft (*découvert autorisé*) or you risk being blacklisted as '*interdit bancaire*' – forbidden from having a current account – for up to 10 years. Depositing foreign-currency cheques is slow, so use wire transfer or a bank draft in euros to receive funds from abroad.

Bureaux de change

If you arrive in Paris early or late, you can change money at the **American Express** bureaux de change in the terminals 1 (01.48.16.13.70), 2D (01.48.16.63.81) and 2F (01.48.16.48.40) at Roissy and at Orly Sud (01.49.75.77.37) airports, which are open 6.30am to 11 or 11.30pm daily. **Thomas Cook** has bureaux de change at the main train stations. Hours can vary.

Gare d'Austerlitz 01.53.61.92.40. **Open** 10am-6pm daily.

Gare Montparnasse 01.42.79.03.88. **Open** 8am-7pm daily.

Gare St-Lazare 01.43.87.72.51. **Open** 8am-7pm Mon-Sat; 10.45am-6pm Sun.

Gare du Nord 01.42.80.11.50. **Open** 7am-11.25pm daily.

Gare de l'Est 01.42.09.51.97. **Open** Mon-Sat 7am-10pm, 7am-7pm Sun.

Credit cards

Major international credit cards are widely used in France; Visa (in French *Carte Bleue*) is the most readily accepted. French-issued credit cards have a special security microchip (*puce*) in each card. The card is slotted into a card reader, and the holder keys in a PIN number to authorise the transaction. Non-French cards also work, but generate a credit slip to sign. In case of credit card loss or theft, call the following 24-hr services which have English-speaking staff: **American Express** 01.47.77.72.00; **Diners Club** 08.10.31.41.59; **MasterCard/Visa** 08.92.70.57.05.

Foreign affairs

American Express *11 rue Scribe, 9th (01.47.77.79.28/ www24.americanexpress.com/ France). M° Opéra.* **Open** 9am-4.30pm Mon-Fri. **Bureau de change** (01.47.77.77.58). **Open** 9am-6.30pm Mon-Fri; 9am-5.30pm Sat. Travel agency, bureau de change, poste restante (you can also leave messages here for other card holders Euro-travelling), card replacement, travellers' cheque refund service, international money transfers and a cash machine for AmEx cardholders.

Barclays *6 rond point des Champs-Elysées, 8th (01.44.95.13.80/www.barclays.fr). M° Franklin D Roosevelt.* **Open** 9.15am-4.30pm Mon-Fri. Barclays' international Expat Service handles direct debits, international transfer of funds, etc.

Global Change *150 av des Champs-Elysées, 8th (01.45.61.05.62) M° Charles de Gaulle-Etoile.* **Open** 24-hr. Other branches have variable hours. No commission.

Travelex *52 av des Champs-Elysées, 8th (01.42.89.80.32/www.travelex.fr). M° Franklin D. Roosevelt.* **Open** 9am-9.30pm daily. Hours of other branches (over 20 in Paris) vary. Issues travellers' cheques and travel insurance and deals with bank transfers.

Western Union Money Transfer 48 post offices provide Western Union services (call 08.25.00.98.98). Money transfers from abroad should arrive within 10-15 minutes. Charges paid by the sender. This branch of the CCF bank (and four other branches located in tourist neighbourhoods) also act as an agent for Western Union, offering the same. *CCF Change, 4 rue du Cloître-Notre-Dame, 4th (01.43.54.46.12)/ www. intl.westernunion.com). M° Cité.* **Open** 9am-5.10pm daily (till 6pm in summer).

Citibank *125 av des Champs-Elysées, 8th (01.53.23.33.60/ www.citibank.fr). M° Charles de Gaulle-Etoile.* **Open** 10am-6pm Mon-Fri. Existing clients get good rates for transferring money from country to country, preferential exchange rates and no commision on travellers cheques.

Opening hours

Standard opening hours for shops are 9am/10am-7pm/8pm Mon-Sat. Some shops close on Mon. Shops and businesses often close at lunch, usually 12.30-2pm. Many shops close in August. While Paris doesn't have the 24-hr consumer culture beloved of some capitals, some branches of Monoprix stay open until 10pm. Also most areas have a local grocer that stays open until around 9.30 or 10pm and will often open on Sundays and public holidays too – although you do pay for the convenience

24-hr florist Elyfleur *82 av de Wagram, 17th (01.47.66.87.19). M° Wagram.*

24-hr newsagents include: *33 av des Champs-Elysées, 8th. M° Franklin D. Roosevelt; 2 bd Montmartre, 9th. M° Grands Boulevards.*

24-hr garage Select Shell *6 bd Raspail, 7th (01.45.48.43.12). M° Rue du Bac.* This round-the-clock garage has a large if pricey array of supermarket standards from the Casino chain. No alcohol sold 10pm-6am.

Late-night tabacs La Brazza *86 bd du Montparnasse, 14th (01.43.35.42.65). M° Montparnasse-Bienvenüe.* **Open** 24-hr daily.

La Favorite *3 bd St-Michel, 5th (01.43.54.08.02). M° St-Michel.* **Open** 7am-2am Mon-Fri; 8am-2am Sat, Sun.

Photo labs

Photo developing is often more expensive than in the UK or USA. **Fnac Service**, **Photo Station** (www.photostation.fr) and **Photo Service** (www.photoservice.com) have numerous branches.

Police stations

The French 999/911 is 17 (18 for fire, 15 for ambulence) and 112 from a mobile, but don't expect a speedy response. Trying to bring the police closer to the public, the Préfécture de Police has established 94 different outposts in the city. If you are robbed or attacked, you should report the incident as soon as possible. You will need to make a statement (*procès verbal*) at the *point d'accueil* closest to the site of the crime. To find the nearest one, phone the Préfecture Centrale (08.91.01.22.22) day or night, or consult their website, www.prefecture-police.paris.interieur.gouv.fr. Stolen goods are unlikely to be recovered, but you will need the police statement for insurance purposes.

Postal services

Post offices (*bureaux de poste*) are open 8am-7pm Mon-Fri; 8am-noon Sat. All are listed in the phone book: under Administration des PTT in the *Pages Jaunes*; under Poste in the *Pages Blanches*. Most post offices have automatic machines (in French and English) that weigh your letter, print out a stamp and give change, saving you from wasting time in an enormous queue. You can also buy stamps and often envelopes at a tobacconist (*tabac*). For info see www.laposte.fr

Main Post Office *52 rue du Louvre, 1st (01.40.28.76.00). M° Les Halles or Louvre-Rivoli.* **Open** 24-hr for Poste Restante, telephones, stamps, fax, photocopying and some banking operations. This is the best place to get your mail sent if you haven't got a fixed address in Paris. Mail should be addressed to you in block capitals, followed by Poste Restante, then the post office's address. There is a charge of €0.50 for each letter received.

Recycling & rubbish

The city has a new system of colour-coded domestic recycling bins. A yellow-lidded bin can take paper, cardboard cartons, tins and small electrical items; a white-lidded bin takes glass. All other rubbish should go in the green-lidded bins except for batteries (all shops that sell batteries should accept them), medication (take it back to a pharmacy), toxic products (call 08.20.00.75.75 to have them picked up) or car batteries (take them to an official tip or return to garages exhibiting the '*relais verts auto*' sign). Green hive-shaped bottle banks can be found on street corners.

Allô Propreté *(08.20.00.75.75/ www.paris.fr).* **Open** 9-5pm Mon-Fri. Recycling information and collection of cumbersome objects.

Religion

Churches and religious centres are listed in the phone book (*Pages Jaunes*) under *Eglises* and *Culte*. Paris has several English-speaking churches. The *International Herald Tribune*'s Saturday edition lists Sunday church services in English.

American Cathedral
23 av George V, 8th (01.53.23.84.00/ www.us.net/amcathedral-paris). M° George V.

American Church in Paris
65 quai d'Orsay, 7th (01.40.62.05.00/ www.americanchurch.paris.org). M° Invalides.

Emmanuel Baptist Church of Paris
56 rue des Bons Raisins, 92500 Rueil-Malmaison (01.47.51.29.63/www.ebcparis.org).

Kehilat Geisher *10 rue de Pologne, 78100 St Germain-en-Laye (01.39.21.97.19).* The Liberal English-speaking Jewish community has rotating services in Paris and the western suburbs.

La Mosquée de Paris
2 pl du Puits de l'Ermite, 5th (01.45.35.97.33).

St George's Anglican Church *7 rue Auguste-Vacquerie, 16th (01.47.20.22.51/ www.stgeorgesparis.com). M° Charles de Gaulle-Etoile.*

St Joseph's Roman Catholic Church *50 av Hoche, 8th (01.42.27.28.56/www.stjoeparis. org). M° Charles de Gaulle-Etoile.*

St Michael's Church of England *5 rue d'Aguesseau, 8th (01.47.42.70.88/ www.saintmichaelsparis.org). M° Madeleine.*

Renting a flat

Northern, eastern and southeastern Paris are generally cheapest for flat rental. Expect to pay roughly €20 per month/m² (€700 per month for a 35m² flat, and so on). Studios and one-bedroom flats fetch the highest prices proportionally; lifts and cellars will also boost the rent.

Flat hunting

Given the shortage of accommodation in Paris, it is a landlord's world out there so you will need to search actively, or even frenetically, in order to find an apartment. The site www.logement.com is a reassuring place to start. In addition to giving reliable information about most aspects of the real estate world, it also provides links to at least 20 other sites that list rental ads. Click on, for example, www.explorimmo.fr, which lists rental ads from *Le Figaro* as well as specialised real estate magazines. Thursday morning's *De Particulier à Particulier* (www.pap.fr) is a standby for those that want to rent directly from the owner, but be forewarned, most apartments go within hours. Fortnightly *Se Loger* (www.seloger.com) is worth checking out also, though most ads are through agencies. Flats offered to foreigners are advertised in the *International Herald Tribune* and English-language fortnightly *FUSAC* (www.fusac.fr); rents tend to be higher than in the French press. There are also assorted free ad brochures that can be picked up from agencies. Private landlords often set a visiting time; prepare to meet hordes of other flat-seekers and have your documents and cheque book on hand. After the success of *Loft Story* and *Friends*, young French people who have traditionally rented a small studio of their own are eagerly getting into the idea of flat-sharing (*colocation*). Les Jeudis de la Colocation, is a monthly event organised by the flatshare website www.colocation.fr the first Thursday of every month. Would-be flatsharers pay €7 (including a drink) to meet possible flatmates/soulmates at a roving location, recently at Six-Seven, 65-67 rue Pierre Charron, 8th M° Franklin D. Roosevelt. Call to verify (08.92.23.15.15).

Rental laws

The minimum lease (*bail de location*) on an unfurnished apartment is three years (though the tenant can give notice and leave before this period is up); furnished flats are generally one year. During this period the landlord can only raise the rent by the official construction inflation index. At the end of the lease, the rent can be adjusted, but tenants can object before a rent board. Tenants can be evicted for non-payment, or if the landlord wishes to sell the property or use it as his own residence. It is illegal to throw people out in winter. Landlords will probably require you to present a dossier with pay slips (*fiches de paie/bulletins de salaire*) showing three to four times the amount of the monthly rent, and, for foreigners in particular, to provide a financial guarantor (someone who will sign a document promising to pay the rent if you scarper without paying). When taking out a lease, payments usually include the first month's rent, a deposit (*une caution*) equal to two month's rent, and an agency fee, if applicable. It is customary for an inspection of the premises (*état des lieux*) at the start and end of the rental, the cost of which (around €150) is shared by landlord and tenant. Landlords may try to rent their flats *non-declaré* – without a written lease – and get rent in cash. This can make it difficult for tenants to establish their rights – which is one reason landlords do it.

Bureau de l'information juridique des proprietaires et des occupants (BIPO) *6 rue Agrippa-d'Aubigné, 4th (01.42.76.31.31). M° Sully-Morland.* **Open** 9am-5pm Mon-Fri. Municipal service provides free advice (in French) about renting or buying a flat, housing benefit, rent legislation and tenants' rights.

Centre d'information et de défense des locataires *9 rue Severo, 14th (01.45.41.47.76). M° Pernety or Convention.* **Open** By appointment 10am-12.30pm, 2.30-3.30pm Mon-Fri. Will help you sort out problems with landlords, rent increases, etc.

Shipping services

Hedley's Humpers *6 bd de la Libération, 93284 St-Denis (01.48.13.01.02/ www.hedleyshumpers.com). M° Carrefour-Pleyel.* **Open** 9am-1pm, 2-6pm Mon-Fri. Closed 3 weeks in Aug. **Branch:** *102 rue des Rosiers, 93400 St-Ouen (01.40.10.94.00). M° Porte de Clignancourt.* **Open** 9am-1pm Mon, Fri; 9am-6pm Sat, Sun. Specialised in transporting furniture and antiques. **In UK:** *3 St Leonards Rd, London NW10 6SX, UK (0208 965 8733).* **In USA:** *21-41 45th Road, Long Island City, New York NY 11101, USA (1.718.433.4005).*

Smoking

Although smoking seems to represent a quintessential part of French life (and death), the French government and public health groups have recently been trying to wage war against the cigarette on several fronts. Smoking is now banned in most public spaces, such as theatres, cinemas and on public transport and increasingly strident anti-smoking campaigns include a TV ad from Nicorette with a girl kick-boxing a man-sized cigarette. Health warnings on cigarette packets are now huge and prices have skyrocketed. Restaurants are obliged to provide a non-smoking area (*espace non-fumeurs*), however, you'll often end up with the worst table in the house, and there's no guarantee other people seated in the section won't light up anyway. For more information about quitting smoking, contact the Tabac Info Service helpline (08.03.30.93.10/ www.tabac-info.net). If you are a dedicated smoker, you'll soon learn the hard way that most tabacs close at 8pm (*but see p383* **Opening Hours**). Some bars have cigarettes behind the bar, generally only on sale to customers who stay for a drink.

Telephones

Cellphones

The three companies that rule the cell phone market in France are:

Bouyges Telecom (08.10.63.01.00/ www.bouyguestelecom.fr).

France Telecom/Orange (08.25.00.57.00/www.orange.fr).

SFR (08.05.80.08.05/www.sfr.fr).

A subscription (*abonnement*) will normally get you a free phone if you sign up for a minimum of one year. Two hours' calling time a month costs about €35/month. International calls are normally charged extra – a lot extra.

Dialing & codes

All French phone numbers have ten digits. Paris and Ile de France numbers begin with 01; the rest of France is divided into four zones (02-05). Mobile phone numbers start with 06; 08 indicates a special rate (*see below*). If you are calling France from abroad leave off the 0 at the start of the ten-digit number. Country code: 33. To call abroad from France dial 00, then country code. Since 1998 other phone companies have been allowed to enter the market, but France Télécom still has the monopoly on basic service.

France Telecom English-Speaking Customer Service
08.00.36.47.75. **Open** 9am-5.30pm Mon-Fri. Freephone information line in English on phone services, bills, payment, Internet.

Public phones

Most public phones in Paris use (in the majority France Télécom) phonecards *télécartes*. Sold at post offices, tobacconists, airports and train and Métro stations, cards cost €7.40 for 50 units and €14.75 for 120 units. For cheap international calls you can also buy a card with a microchip *télécarte à puce* or *télécartes pré-payées* with a numerical code that you dial before making a call, these can be used on domestic phones too. Travelex's International Telephone Card can be used in more than 80 countries (from Travelex agencies *see p382*). Cafés have coin phones, while post offices usually have card phones. In a phone box, the digital display screen should read *Décrochez.* Pick up the phone. When *Introduisez votre carte* appears, insert your card into the slot. The screen should then read *Patientez SVP. Numérotez* is your signal to dial. *Crédit épuisé* means that you have no more units left. Finally, hang up (*Raccrochez*), and don't forget your card. Some public phones take credit cards. If you are using a credit card, insert the card, key in your PIN number and *Patientez SVP* should appear.

Operator services

Operator assistance, French directory enquiries (renseignements), dial 12. To make a reverse-charge call within France, ask to make a call en PCV.

International directory enquiries 32.12, then country code. €3 per call.

Telephone engineer dial 10.13.

International news (French recorded message, France Inter), dial 08.92.68.10.33 (€0.34 per min).

Telegram all languages, international 08.00.33.44.11; within France 36.55.

Time dial 36.99.

Traffic news dial 08.26.02.20.22

Weather dial 08.99.70.12.34 (€1.35 then €0.39 per min) for enquiries on weather in France and abroad, in French or English; dial 08.92.68.02.75 (€0.34 per min) for a recorded weather announcement for Paris and region.

Airparif (01.44.59.47.64). Mon-Fri 9am-12.30pm, 1.45-5.45pm. Information about pollution levels and air quality in Paris and Ile-de-France: invaluable for asthmatics.

Telephone directories

Phone books are found in all post offices and most cafés. The *Pages Blanches* (White Pages) list people and businesses alphabetically; *Pages Jaunes* (Yellow Pages) list businesses and services by category. Online versions can be found at www.pagesjaunes.fr.

Telephone charges

Local calls in Paris and Ile-de-France beginning with 01 cost €0.11 for three minutes, standard rate, €0.04 per minute thereafter and only apply to calls towards other land phones. Calls beyond a 100km radius (province) are charged at €0.11 for the first 39 seconds, then €0.24 per minute. International destinations are divided into 16 zones. Reduced-rate periods for calls within France and Europe: 7pm-8am during the week; all day Sat, Sun. Reduced-rate periods for the US and Canada: 7pm through to 1pm Mon-Fri; all day Sat, Sun.

Cheap providers

Getting wise to market demand, smaller telephone providers are becoming increasingly prolific and popular, as rates from giant France Télécom are not exactly bargain-basement. The following can offer alternative rates for calls (you will still need to rent your telephone line from France Télécom):

Onetel www.onetel.fr.

3U Télécom 08.05.10.16.45.

Le 7 www.le7.fr.

Télé 2 08.05.04.44.44.

9 Télécom 08.00.95.99.59/www.9online.fr.

Fast Télécom 01.46.98.20.00.

Téléconnect 08.05.10.25.05.

AT&T Direct Local access number: 0800-99-00-11.

Primus 01.53.43.94.01/www.primus.com.

Free www.free.fr. With the Freebox (Free's modem for ASDL connection) €29.99 per month gets you ten hours of free calls to fixed lines (additional calls: €0.01 per minute), €0.19 per minute to mobiles and €0.03 per minute for most international calls.

Special-rate numbers

0800 Numéro Vert Freephone.

0810 Numéro Azur €0.11 under 3 min, then €0.04 per min.

0820 Numéro Indigo I €0.118 per min.

0825 Numéro Indigo II €0.15 per min.

0836.64/0890.64/0890.70 €0.112 per min.

0891.71 €0.15 per min.

0891.67/0891.70 €0.225 per min.

0836/0892 €0.337 min. This rate applies mostly to ticket agencies, cinema and transport information lines.

10.14 France Télécom information: Free (except from mobile phones).

Minitel

France Telecom's Minitel, launched in the 1980s, is a videotext service available to any telephone subscriber, though the Internet has made it virtually redundant. If you come across one of these beige plastic boxes, dust it off then dial 3611 for Minitel directory in English, wait for the beep, press *Connexion*, type MGS, then *Envoi*. Then type *Minitel en anglais* for the English service.

Ticket agencies

The easiest way to reserve and buy tickets for concerts, plays and matches is from a **Fnac** store. You can also reserve on www.fnac.com or by phone (08.92.68.36.22; 9am to 8pm Mon-Sat) and pick them up at one of their *points de vente* (see site for complete list) or pay with your credit card and have them sent to your home. **Virgin** has teamed up with Ticketnet to create an online ticket office (www.virginmega.fr). Tickets can also be purchased by phone (08.25.02.30.24) and sent to your home for a €5.35 fee.

Fnac Forum des Halles
1st (01.40.41.40.00/www.fnac.com). M° Les Halles/RER Châtelet-Les Halles. **Open** 10am-7.30pm Mon-Sat. **Credit** AmEx, MC, V.

Virgin Megastore
52 av des Champs-Elysées, 8th (01.49.53.50.00). M° Franklin D. Roosevelt. **Open** 10am-midnight Mon-Sat. **Credit** AmEx, DC, MC, V.

Time & seasons

France is one hour ahead of Greenwich Mean Time (GMT). France uses the 24-hr system (eg. 20h for 8pm).

Tipping

A service charge of 10-15% is legally included in your bill at all restaurants, cafés and bars. However, it is polite to either round up the final amount for drinks, and to leave a cash tip of €1-€2 or more for a meal, depending on the restaurant and, of course, on the quality of service you receive.

Toilets

Automatic street toilets are not as terrifying as they look. You place your coin in the slot, and – open sesame – you're in a disinfected wonderland (each loo is completely washed down and disinfected after use, so don't try to avoid paying by sneaking in as someone is leaving: you'll end up covered in bleach). Once in, you'll have 15 minutes in which to do the bizzo. If a space-age-style lavatory experience doesn't appeal, you can always nip in to the loos of a café, although theoretically reserved for customers' use, a polite request and a smile should win sympathy with the waiter. Fast food chain toilets often have a code on their toilet doors which is made known to paying customers only.

Tourist information

Espace du Tourisme d'Ile de France *Carrousel du Louvre, 99 rue de Rivoli, 1st (08.26.16.66.66/ www.paris-ile-de-france.com). M° Palais Royal.* **Open** 10am-7pm daily. Information showcase for Paris and the Ile-de-France.

Maison de la France/French Travel Centre *178 Piccadilly, London W1J 9AL (0906-824 4123/ www.franceguide.com).* **Open** 10am-6pm Mon-Fri; 10am-5pm Sat. Information on visiting France. Can also reserve train tickets for France and other European countries.

Office de Tourisme et des Congrès de Paris
From May 2004: *25-27 rue des Pyramides, 9th, (08.92.68.30.30 €0.34/min recorded information in English and French/www.paris-touristoffice.com). M° Pyramides.*

Size charts

Women's Clothes

British	French	US
4	32	2
6	34	4
8	36	6
10	38	8
12	40	10
14	42	12
16	44	14
18	46	16
20	48	18

Women's Shoes

British	French	US
3	36	5
4	37	6
5	38	7
6	39	8
7	40	9
8	41	10
9	42	11

Men's Suits

British	French	US
34	44	34
36	46	36
38	48	38
40	50	40
42	52	42
44	54	44
46	56	46
48	58	48

Men's Shoes

British	French	US
6	39	7
7 1/2	40	7 1/2
8	41	8
8	42	8 1/2
9	43	9 1/2
10	44	10 1/2
11	45	11
12	46	11 1/2

Information on Paris and the suburbs, shop, *bureau de change*, hotel reservations, phonecards, museum cards, travel passes and tickets. Multilingal staff.

Before May 2004 (and beyond) branches can be found at the following addresses: *11 rue Scribe, 9th . M° Opera.* **Open** 9am-6.30pm Mon-Sat. Closed Sun, 1 Jan, 1 May, 25 Dec. *Gare de Lyon, 20 bd Diderot, 12th, M° Gare de Lyon.* **Open** 8am-6pm, Mon-Sat. Closed Sundays and public holidays. *Gare du Nord, 18 rue de Dunkerque, 10th, M° Gare du Nord* **Open** 12.30pm-8pm daily, closed 25 Dec, 1 May. Temporary branches in Montmartre's place du Tertre and in the Carrousel du Louvre may also be extended after May 2004.

Visas

European Union nationals do not need a visa to enter France, nor do US, Canadian, Australian or New Zealand citizens for stays of up to three months. Nationals of other countries should enquire at the nearest French Consulate before leaving home. If they are travelling to France from one of the countries included in the Schengen agreement (most of the EU, but not Britain, Ireland, Italy or Greece), the visa from that country should be sufficient. For stays of over three months, *see below,* **Cartes de Séjour**.

Weights & measures

France uses only the metric system; remember that all speed limits are in kilometres. One kilometre is equivalent to 0.62 mile (1 mile = 1.6km). Petrol, like other liquids, is measured in litres; one UK gallon = 4.54 litres; 1 US gallon = 3.79 litres).

Women's Paris

Paris is not especially threatening for women, although the precautions you would take in any major city apply: be careful at night in areas like Pigalle, the rue St-Denis, Stalingrad, La Chapelle, Château Rouge, Gare de l'Est, Gare du Nord, the Bois de Boulogne and Bois de Vincennes. If you receive unwanted attention a politely scathing *'N'insistez pas!'* ('Don't push it) makes your feelings clear. If things get too heavy, go into the nearest shop or café and ask for help.

CIDFF *7 rue du Jura, 13th* (01.42.17.12.34). M° Gobelins. **Open** 1.30-5.30pm Tue-Thur (Mon by phone 9am-12.30pm).The Centre d'Information et de Documentation des Femmes et des Familles offers health, legal and professional advice for women.

Violence conjugale: Femmes Info Service *(01.40.33.80.60).* **Open** 7.30am-11.30pm Mon-Sat. Telephone hotline for battered women, directing them towards medical aid or shelters.

Viols Femmes Informations *(08.00.05.95.95).* **Open** 10am-7pm Mon-Fri. Freephone in French gives help and advice to rape victims.

Working in Paris

All EU nationals can work legally in France, but should apply for a French social security number and *Carte de Séjour*. Some job ads can be found at branches of the **Agence nationale pour l'emploi (ANPE)/** www.anpe.fr, the French national employment bureau. This is also the place to go to sign up as a *demandeur d'emploi,* to be placed on file as available for work and possibly to qualify for French unemployment benefits. Britons can only claim French unemployment benefit if they were already signed on before leaving the UK. Non-EU nationals need a work permit and are not entitled to use the ANPE network without valid work papers.

CIEE *112ter rue Cardinet, 17th (01.58.57.20.50/ www.councilexchanges-fr.org). M° Malesherbes.* **Open** 9am-6pm Mon-Fri. The Council on International Educational Exchange provides three-month work permits for US citizens at or recently graduated from university ('Work in France' programme), has a job centre, mostly for sales and catering, and a housing placement service for those participating in the programme.

Espace emploi international (OMI et ANPE) *48 bd de la Bastille, 12th (01.53.02.25.50/ www.emploi-international.org). M° Bastille.* **Open** 9am-5pm Mon, Wed-Fri; Tue 9am-noon. Provides work permits of up to 18 months for Americans aged 18-35 and has a job placement service.

The Language Network *(01.44.64.82.23/01.43.08.35.19).* Helps to orient native English speakers who wish to teach.

Job ads

Help-wanted ads sometimes appear in the *International Herald Tribune*, in *FUSAC* and on noticeboards at language schools and the American Church. Bilingual secretarial/PA work is available for those with good written French. If you are looking for professional work, have your CV translated, including French equivalents for any qualifications. Most job applications require a photo and a handwritten letter (employers often use graphological analysis).

Cartes de Séjour

Officially, all foreigners, both EU citizens and non-Europeans, who are in France for more than three months must apply at the Préfecture de Police for a *Carte de Séjour,* valid for one year. Those who have had a *Carte de Séjour* for at least three years, have been paying French income tax, can show proof of income and/or are married to a French national can apply for a *Carte de Résident,* valid for ten years.

CIRA (Centre interministeriel de renseignements administratifs) *(0821.08.09.10 0.12€/min/www.service-public.fr).* **Open** 9am-12.30pm, 2-5.30pm Mon-Fri. Advice on French admin procedures.

Préfecture de Police de Paris Service Étrangers *7-9 bd du Palais, 4th (01.53.71.51.68/ www.prefecture-police-paris.interieur.gouv.fr). M° Cité.* **Open** 9am-4pm Mon-Fri. Information on residency and work permits for foreigners.

Essential Vocabulary

In French the second person singular (you) has two forms. Phrases here are given in the more polite *vous* form. The *tu* form is used with family, friends, young children and pets; you should be careful not to use it with people you do not know sufficiently well. You will also find that courtesies such as *monsieur, madame* and *mademoiselle* are used much more than their English equivalents.

General expressions

good morning/afternoon, hello *bonjour;* **good evening** *bonsoir;* **goodbye** *au revoir;* **hi** (familiar) *salut;* **OK** *d'accord;* **yes** *oui;* **no** *non;* **How are you?** *Comment allez vous?/vous allez bien?;* **How's it going?** *Comment ça va?/ça va?* (familiar); **Sir/Mr** *monsieur (Mr);* **Madam/Mrs** *madame (Mme);* **Miss** *mademoiselle (Mlle);* **please** *s'il vous plaît;* **thank you** *merci;* **thank you very much** *merci beaucoup;* **sorry** *pardon;* **excuse me** *excusez-moi;* **Do you speak English?** *Parlez-vous anglais?;* **I don't speak French** *Je ne parle pas français;* **I don't understand** *Je ne comprends pas;* **Speak more slowly, please** *Parlez plus lentement, s'il vous plaît ;* **Leave me alone** *Laissez-moi tranquille;* **How much?/how many?** *combien?;* **Have you got change?** *Avez-vous de la monnaie?* **I would like...** *Je voudrais...* **I am going** *Je vais;* **I am going to pay** *Je vais payer;* **it is** *c'est;* **it isn't** *ce n'est pas;* **good** *bon/bonne;* **bad** *mauvais/ mauvaise* **small** *petit/petite;* **big** *grand/grande;* **beautiful** *beau/belle;* **well** *bien;* **badly** *mal;* **expensive** *cher;* **cheap** *pas cher;* **a bit** *un peu;* **a lot** *beaucoup;* **very** *très;* **with** *avec;* **without** *sans;* **and** *et;* **or** *ou;* **because** *parce que* **who?** *qui?;* **when?** *quand?;* **what?** *quoi?;* **which?** *quel?;* **where?** *où?;* **why?** *pourquoi?;* **how?** *comment?;* **at what time/when?** *à quelle heure?;* **forbidden** *interdit/défendu;* **out of order** *hors service (hs)/en panne;* **daily** *tous les jours (tlj);*

On the phone

hello (telephone) *allô;* **Who's calling?** *C'est de la part de qui?/Qui est à l'appareil?;* **Hold the line** *Ne quittez pas*

Getting around

Where is the (nearest) Métro? *Où est le Métro (le plus proche)?;* **When is the next train for... ?** *C'est quand le prochain train pour... ?;* **ticket** *un billet;* **station** *la gare;* **platform** *le quai;* **entrance** *entrée;* **exit** *sortie;* **left** *gauche;* **right** *droite;* **straight on** *tout droit;* **far** *loin;* **near** *pas loin/près d'ici;* **street map** *le plan;* **road map** *la carte;* **bank** *la banque;* **is there a bank near here?** *est-ce qu'il y a une banque près d'ici?;* **post office** *La Poste;* **a stamp** *un timbre*

Sightseeing

museum *un musée;* **church** *une église;* **exhibition** *une exposition;* **ticket** (for museum) *un billet;* (for theatre, concert) *une place;* **open** *ouvert;* **closed** *fermé;* **free** *gratuit;* **reduced price** *un tarif réduit*

Accommodation

Do you have a room (for this evening/for two people)? *Avez-vous une chambre (pour ce soir/pour deux personnes)?;* **full** *complet;* **room** *une chambre;* **bed** *un lit;* **double bed** *un grand lit;* **(a room with) twin beds** *une chambre à deux lits;* **with bath(room)/shower** *avec (salle de) bain/douche;* **breakfast** *le petit déjeuner;* **included** *compris;* **lift** *un ascenseur*

At the café or restaurant

I'd like to book a table (for three/at 8pm) *Je voudrais réserver une table (pour trois personnes/à vingt heures);* **lunch** *le déjeuner;* **dinner** *le dîner;* **coffee** (espresso) *un café;* **white coffee** *un café au lait/café crème;* **tea** *le thé;* **wine** *le vin;* **beer** *la bière;* **mineral water** *eau minérale;* **fizzy** *gazeuse;* **still** *plate;* **tap water** *eau du robinet/une carafe d'eau;* **the bill, please** *l'addition, s'il vous plaît*

Behind the wheel

no parking *stationnement interdit/ gênant;* **toll** *péage;* **speed limit 40** *rappel 40;* **petrol** *essence;* **speed** *vitesse;* **traffic moving freely** *traffic fluide*

Shopping

may I try this on? *est-ce que je pourrais essayer cet article?;* **do you have a smaller/ larger size?** *auriez-vous la taille en-dessous/au dessus?;* **I'm a size 38** *je fais un 38;* **I'll take it** *je le prends;* **does my bum look big in this?** *cela me fait-il de grosses fesses?*

The come on

do you have a light? *vous avez du feu?;* **what's your name?** *comment vous vous appellez?;* **would you like a drink?** *vous voulez boire un verre?;* **your place or mine?** *chez toi ou chez moi?* (nb: you need a certain style to carry the last one off without appearing tragically geeky).

The brush-off

leave me alone *laissez-moi tranquille;* **fuck off** *va te faire foutre.*

Staying alive

be cool *restez calme;* **I don't want any trouble** *je ne veux pas d'ennuis;* **I only do safe sex;** *je ne pratique que le safe sex.*

Numbers

0 *zéro;* **1** *un, une;* **2** *deux;* **3** *trois;* **4** *quatre;* **5** *cinq;* **6** *six;* **7** *sept;* **8** *huit;* **9** *neuf;* **10** *dix;* **11** *onze;* **12** *douze;* **13** *treize;* **14** *quatorze;* **15** *quinze;* **16** *seize;* **17** *dix-sept;* **18** *dix-huit;* **19** *dix-neuf;* **20** *vingt;* **21** *vingt-et-un;* **22** *vingt-deux;* **30** *trente;* **40** *quarante;* **50** *cinquante;* **60** *soixante;* **70** *soixante-dix;* **80** *quatre-vingts;* **90** *quatre-vingt-dix;* **100** *cent*

Days & months

Mon *lundi;* **Tue** *mardi;* **Wed** *mercredi;* **Thur** *jeudi;* **Fri** *vendredi;* **Sat** *samedi;* **Sun** *dimanche;* **Jan** *janvier;* **Feb** *février;* **Mar** *mars;* **Apr** *avril;* **May** *mai;* **June** *juin;* **July** *juillet;* **Aug** *août;* **Sept** *septembre;* **Oct** *octobre;* **Nov** *novembre;* **Dec** *décembre*

Further Reference

Books

Non-fiction

Alan Sokal *Fashionable Nonsense: Postmodern Intellectuals' Abuse of Science.* So they really didn't know what they were talking about.
Margaret MacMillan *Paris 1919: Six Months That Changed the World* A hearty read, it details the division of Europe.
Petrus Abaelardus & Heloïse *Letters* The full details of Paris' first great romantic drama.
Antony Beevor & Artemis Cooper *Paris after the Liberation* Rationing, liberation and existentialism.
Rupert Christiansen *Tales of the New Babylon* Blood and sleaze in Napoléon III's Paris.
Vincent Cronin *Napoleon* A fine biography of the great megalomaniac.
Noel Riley Fitch *Literary Cafés of Paris* Who drank where.
Alastair Horne *The Fall of Paris* Detailed chronicle of the Siege and Commune 1870-71.
Ian Littlewood *Paris: Architecture, History, Art* Paris' history and its treasures.
Patrick Marnham *Crime & the Académie Française* Quirks and scandals of Mitterrand-era Paris.
François Maspero *A Journey Through the Paris Suburbs* Our society discussed on the train.
Nancy Mitford *The Sun King; Madame de Pompadour* Great gossipy accounts of the courts of the *ancien régime*.
Douglas Johnson & Madeleine Johnson *Age of Illusion: Art & Politics in France 1918-1940* French culture in a Paris at the forefront of modernity.
Renzo Salvadori *Architect's Guide to Paris* Plans, illustrations and a guide to Paris' growth.
Simon Schama *Citizens* Giant but wonderfully readable account of the Revolution.
Alice B Toklas *The Alice B Toklas Cookbook* How to cook fish for Picasso, by the companion (and cook) of Gertrude Stein.
Theodore Zeldin *The French* Idiosyncratic and entertaining survey of modern France.

Fiction & poetry

Louis Aragon *Paris Peasant* A great Surrealist view of the city.
Honoré de Balzac *Illusions perdues; La Peau de chagrin; Le Père Goriot; Splendeurs et misères des courtisanes* Some of the most evocative novels in the 'Human Comedy' cycle, all set in Paris.
Baudelaire *LeSpleen de Paris* Baudelaire's prose poems with Paris settings.
Simone de Beauvoir *The Mandarins* Paris intellectuals and idealists just after the Liberation.
Louis-Ferdinand Céline *Mort à crédit* Vivid account of an impoverished Paris childhood.
Michel Houellebecq *Platform* Naughty boy of French literature tackles sexual tourism.
Victor Hugo *Notre Dame de Paris* Quasimodo and the romantic vision of medieval Paris.
Guy de Maupassant *Bel-Ami* Gambling and dissipation.
Catherine Millet *The Sexual Life of Catherine M* Bonkography par excellence.
Patrick Modiano *Honeymoon* Evocative story of two lives that cross in Paris.
Georges Perec *Life, A User's Manual* Intellectual puzzle in a Haussmannian apartment building.
Raymond Queneau *Zazie in the Metro* Paris in the 1950s: bright and very *nouvelle vague*.
Nicolas Restif de la Bretonne *Les Nuits de Paris* The sexual underworld of Louis XV's Paris, by one of France's most famous defrocked priests.
Jean-Paul Sartre *Roads to Freedom* Existential angst as the German army takes over Paris.
Georges Simenon The *Maigret* series. Many of Simenon's novels featuring his laconic detective provide a vivid picture of Paris and its underworld.
Emile Zola *Nana, L'Assommoir, Le Ventre de Paris* Vivid accounts of the underside of the Second Empire.

The ex-pat angle

Ernest Hemingway *A Moveable Feast* Big Ern drinks his way around 1920s writers' Paris. Give that butch, bibulous beast a macho award, eh?
Henry Miller *Tropic of Cancer, Tropic of Capricorn* Low-life and lust in Montparnasse.
Anaïs Nin *Henry & June* More lust in Montparnasse with Henry Miller and his wife.
Adam Gopnik*From Paris to the Moon* A 'New Yorker' in Paris raises a family in this alien city.
Gertrude Stein *The Autobiography of Alice B Toklas* Ex-pat Paris, from start to finish.

Film

Les Bronzés (1978) Classic comedy about cheeky cod pieces taking over Club Med.
Etre et Avoir (2002) Touching Crowned school days documentary
Carry On Don't Lose Your Head (1966) Brit-pack *Carry On* team's take on the ins and outs of the revolution.
The Rebel (1960) Tony Hancock satire on ex-pat artistes who come to Paris for the sake of their art. Our hero founds the *Infantile* school of painting.

Sounds

Sympathique, *Pink Martini* 'Je ne veux pas travailler' and other dinner party starters by some French singing Americans.
L'Histoire de Melody Nelson, *Serge Gainsbourg* On the cover, she covers her bun in the oven with a teddy bear. Super sexy.
Frank Sinatra and Sextet live in Paris 1962 He came, he swung, he conquered, they dug.
I Love Paris The compilation that will put you in the mood for all those special moments.
Moon Safari, *Air* Relaxing, ambient beeps and sonics from that *rara avis,* a credible French pop group.
Song for Europe, *Roxy Music* Bryan Ferry croons like a *chansonnier* in immaculate heart-broken Geordie style.
The Paris Concert, *Thelonius Monk* A blend of the experimental and the romantically gentle.

Index

Index

WHERE TO STAY

BARS & CAFÉS

RESTAURANTS

Note: numbers in italics indicate a photograph; numbers in **bold** *indicate major entries*

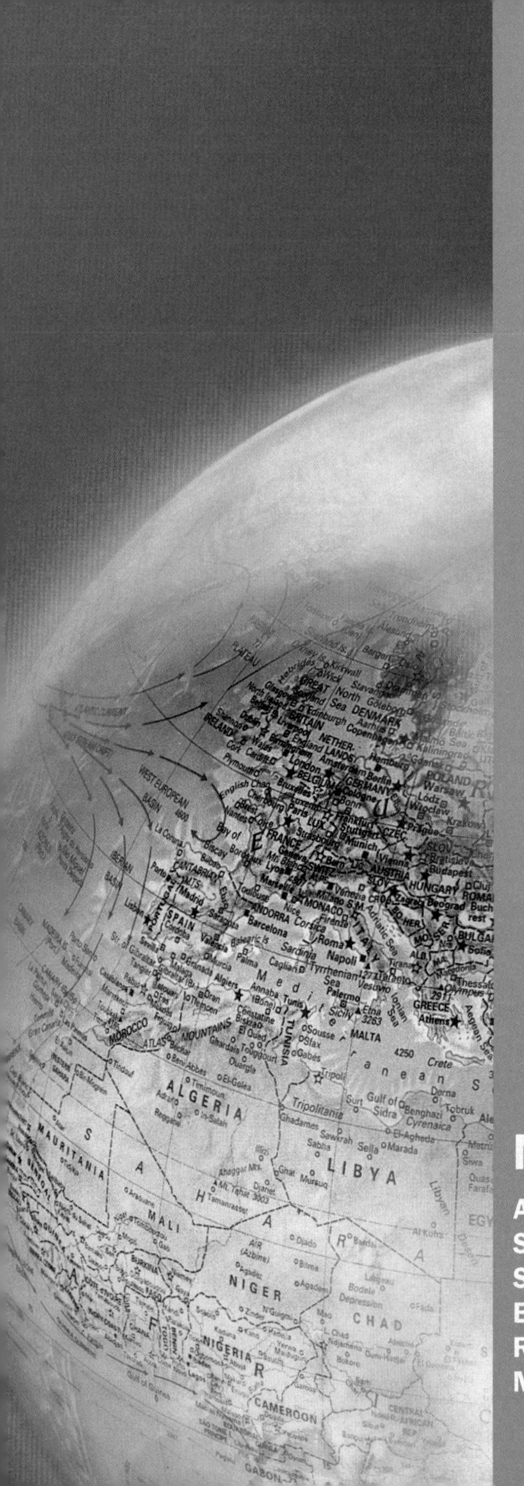
ALGERIA
LIBYA
NIGER
CHAD
MALI
MAURITANIA
NIGERIA
CAMEROON
MOROCCO
TUNISIA
SPAIN
FRANCE
GREECE
MALTA
HUNGARY
AUSTRIA
POLAND
DENMARK
IRELAND
Crete
Sicily
Sardinia
Corsica

Maps

Paris Arrondissements

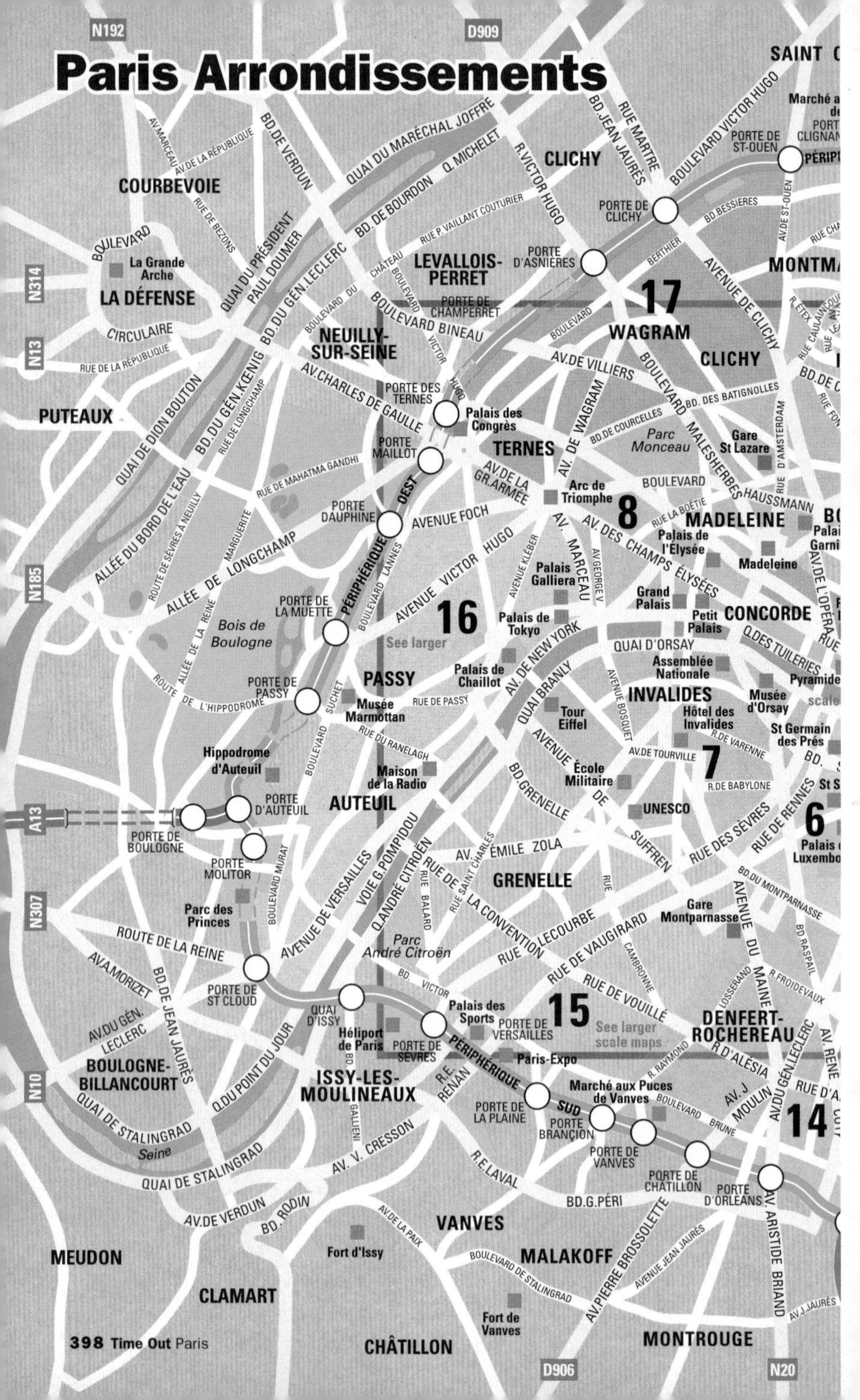

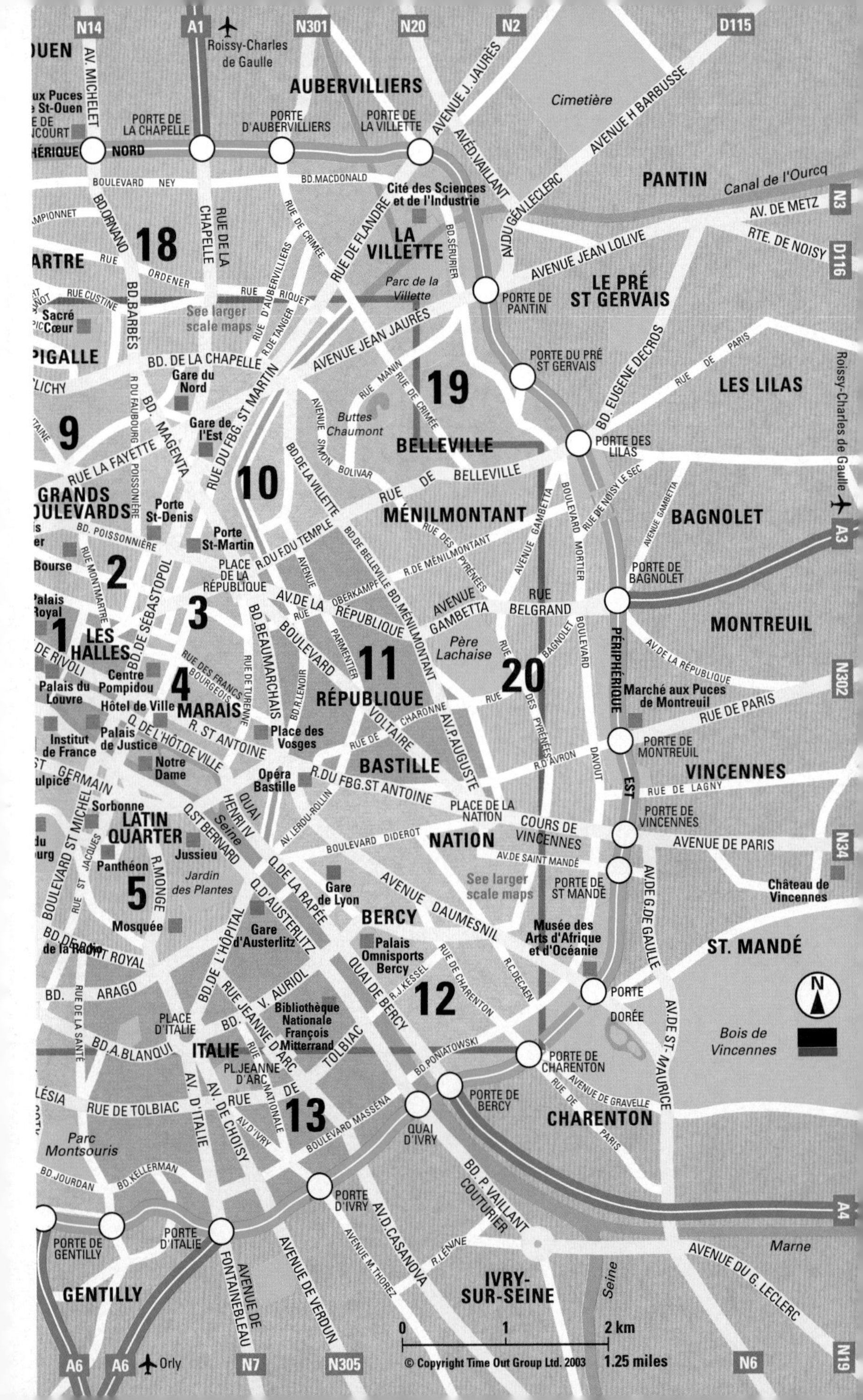
N14
A1
Roissy-Charles de Gaulle
N301
N20
N2
D115
AUBERVILLIERS
Cimetière
PANTIN
Canal de l'Ourcq
N3
D116
AV. DE METZ
RTE. DE NOISY
AVENUE H BARBUSSE
AVENUE J. JAURÈS
AV.ÉD.VAILLANT
AV.DU GÉN.LECLERC
AVENUE JEAN LOLIVE
LE PRÉ ST GERVAIS
PORTE DE PANTIN
PORTE DU PRÉ ST GERVAIS
BD. EUGENE DECROS
RUE DE PARIS
LES LILAS
PORTE DES LILAS
Roissy-Charles de Gaulle
A3
BAGNOLET
AVENUE GAMBETTA
RUE DE NOISY LE SEC
PORTE DE BAGNOLET
MONTREUIL
AV.DE LA RÉPUBLIQUE
N302
Marché aux Puces de Montreuil
RUE DE PARIS
PORTE DE MONTREUIL
VINCENNES
RUE DE LAGNY
PORTE DE VINCENNES
AVENUE DE PARIS
N34
Château de Vincennes
AV.DE G.DE GAULLE
ST. MANDÉ
PORTE DORÉE
Bois de Vincennes
AV.DE ST. MAURICE
CHARENTON
AVENUE DE GRAVELLE
RUE DE PARIS
A4
Marne
AVENUE DU G. LECLERC
N19
N6
Seine
IVRY-SUR-SEINE
AVENUE DE VERDUN
N305
AVENUE DE FONTAINEBLEAU
N7
A6
A6
Orly
GENTILLY
PORTE DE GENTILLY
PORTE D'ITALIE
PORTE D'IVRY
AV.D.CASANOVA
AVENUE M.THOREZ
R.LÉNINE
BD. P. VAILLANT COUTURIER
QUAI D'IVRY
PORTE DE BERCY
PORTE DE CHARENTON
BD.POINTATOWSKI
BOULEVARD MASSÉNA
13
RUE DE TOLBIAC
Parc Montsouris
BD.JOURDAN
BD.KELLERMAN
AV. D'ITALIE
AV. DE CHOISY
AV.D'IVRY
RUE NATIONALE
PL.JEANNE D'ARC
ITALIE
PLACE D'ITALIE
BD.A.BLANQUI
RUE DE LA SANTÉ
BD. ARAGO
BD.DE PORT ROYAL
RUE JEANNE D'ARC
BD.V. AURIOL
Bibliothèque Nationale François Mitterrand
TOLBIAC
QUAI DE BERCY
R.J.KESSEL
12
RUE DE CHARENTON
R.C.DECAEN
Musée des Arts d'Afrique et d'Océanie
AVENUE DAUMESNIL
BERCY
Palais Omnisports Bercy
Gare de Lyon
Q.DE LA RAPÉE
Q.D'AUSTERLITZ
Gare d'Austerlitz
BD.DE L'HÔPITAL
Jardin des Plantes
Mosquée
5
R.MONGE
Panthéon
Jussieu
LATIN QUARTER
Sorbonne
BOULEVARD ST MICHEL
RUE ST JACQUES
Q.ST BERNARD
QUAI HENRI IV
Seine
BD. LERDU-ROLLIN
BOULEVARD DIDEROT
NATION
PLACE DE LA NATION
COURS DE VINCENNES
AV.DE SAINT MANDÉ
PORTE DE ST MANDÉ
See larger scale maps
BASTILLE
Opéra Bastille
R.DU FBG.ST ANTOINE
R.D'AVRON
DAVOUT
EST
PÉRIPHÉRIQUE
20
RUE DES PYRÉNÉES
Père Lachaise
RUE BAGNOLET
BOULEVARD
RUE BELGRAND
AVENUE GAMBETTA
BOULEVARD MORTIER
MÉNILMONTANT
R.DE MÉNILMONTANT
RUE DES PYRÉNÉES
11
RÉPUBLIQUE
VOLTAIRE
RUE DE CHARONNE
AV.P.AUGUSTE
BD.MÉNILMONTANT
BD.DE BELLEVILLE
AVENUE PARMENTIER
OBERKAMPF
BD.R.LENOIR
BD.BEAUMARCHAIS
BOULEVARD
AV.DE LA RÉPUBLIQUE
Place des Vosges
MARAIS
4
R. ST ANTOINE
RUE DE TURENNE
RUE DES FRANCS BOURGEOIS
Hôtel de Ville
Q. DE L'HÔTEL DE VILLE
Notre Dame
Palais de Justice
Institut de France
ST GERMAIN
Centre Pompidou
Palais du Louvre
RUE DE RIVOLI
LES HALLES
1
Palais Royal
RUE MONTMARTRE
Bourse
2
BD.DE SÉBASTOPOL
3
PLACE DE LA RÉPUBLIQUE
R.DU F.DU TEMPLE
Porte St-Martin
Porte St-Denis
BD. POISSONNIÈRE
GRANDS BOULEVARDS
RUE LA FAYETTE
9
10
BD. MAGENTA
R.DU FAUBOURG POISSONNIÈRE
Gare de l'Est
Gare du Nord
RUE DU FBG. ST MARTIN
BD.DE LA VILLETTE
BD. DE LA CHAPELLE
PIGALLE
Sacré Cœur
RUE CUSTINE
BD.BARBÈS
RUE ORDENER
18
BD.ORNANO
RUE DE LA CHAPELLE
BOULEVARD NEY
PÉRIPHÉRIQUE NORD
PORTE DE LA CHAPELLE
PORTE D'AUBERVILLIERS
PORTE DE LA VILLETTE
BD.MACDONALD
Cité des Sciences et de l'Industrie
LA VILLETTE
Parc de la Villette
RUE DE FLANDRE
RUE DE CRIMÉE
RUE D'AUBERVILLIERS
RUE RIQUET
R.DE TANGER
See larger scale maps
AVENUE JEAN JAURÈS
BD.SÉRURIER
19
RUE MANIN
Buttes Chaumont
AVENUE SIMON BOLIVAR
BELLEVILLE
RUE DE BELLEVILLE
AV. MICHELET
Marché aux Puces de St-Ouen
N
0
1
2 km
1.25 miles
© Copyright Time Out Group Ltd. 2003

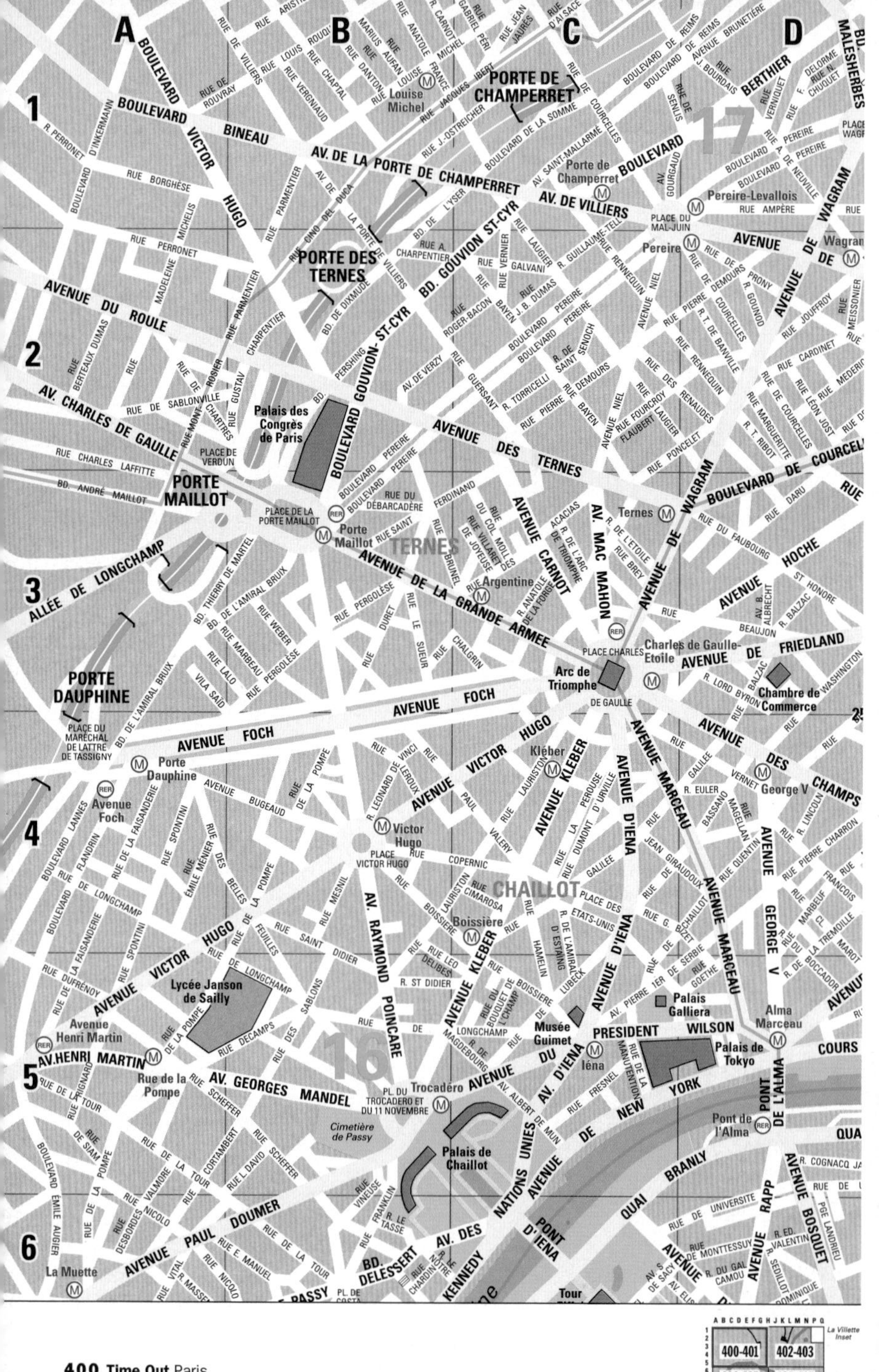

A
B
C
D
1
2
3
4
5
6
17
16
PORTE DE CHAMPERRET
Louise Michel
BOULEVARD VICTOR HUGO
BOULEVARD BINEAU
AV. DE LA PORTE DE CHAMPERRET
AV. DE VILLIERS
Porte de Champerret
Pereire-Levallois
PLACE DU MAL-JUIN
Pereire
AVENUE DE WAGRAM
Wagram
BD. MALESHERBES
BOULEVARD BERTHIER
BOULEVARD PEREIRE
BOULEVARD DE REIMS
BOULEVARD DE LA SOMME
RUE DE COURCELLES
PORTE DES TERNES
BD. GOUVION ST-CYR
BOULEVARD GOUVION-ST-CYR
AVENUE DU ROULE
AV. CHARLES DE GAULLE
Palais des Congrès de Paris
AVENUE DES TERNES
PORTE MAILLOT
PLACE DE VERDUN
PLACE DE LA PORTE MAILLOT
Porte Maillot
RUE CHARLES LAFFITTE
BD. ANDRÉ MAILLOT
TERNES
Ternes
BOULEVARD DE COURCELLES
AVENUE DE LA GRANDE ARMEE
AVENUE CARNOT
AV. MAC MAHON
ALLÉE DE LONGCHAMP
Argentine
AVENUE HOCHE
AVENUE DE FRIEDLAND
PLACE CHARLES DE GAULLE
Charles de Gaulle-Etoile
Arc de Triomphe
Chambre de Commerce
PORTE DAUPHINE
PLACE DU MARÉCHAL DE LATTRE DE TASSIGNY
AVENUE FOCH
Porte Dauphine
Avenue Foch
AVENUE VICTOR HUGO
Kléber
AVENUE KLEBER
AVENUE D'IENA
AVENUE MARCEAU
AVENUE DES CHAMPS
George V
AVENUE GEORGE V
Victor Hugo
PLACE VICTOR HUGO
RUE COPERNIC
CHAILLOT
PLACE DES ETATS-UNIS
Boissière
AV. RAYMOND POINCARE
Lycée Janson de Sailly
Palais Galliera
Musée Guimet
Avenue Henri Martin
AV. HENRI MARTIN
Rue de la Pompe
AV. GEORGES MANDEL
AVENUE PRESIDENT WILSON
Iéna
Palais de Tokyo
Alma Marceau
COURS
Trocadéro
PL. DU TROCADERO ET DU 11 NOVEMBRE
Cimetière de Passy
Palais de Chaillot
AVENUE DE NEW YORK
PONT DE L'ALMA
Pont de l'Alma
AV. DES NATIONS UNIES
PONT D'IENA
QUAI BRANLY
AVENUE RAPP
AVENUE BOSQUET
AVENUE PAUL DOUMER
BD. DELESSERT
AV. DES KENNEDY
La Muette
BOULEVARD ÉMILE AUGIER
Tour
400-401
402-403
404-405
406-407
La Villette Inset

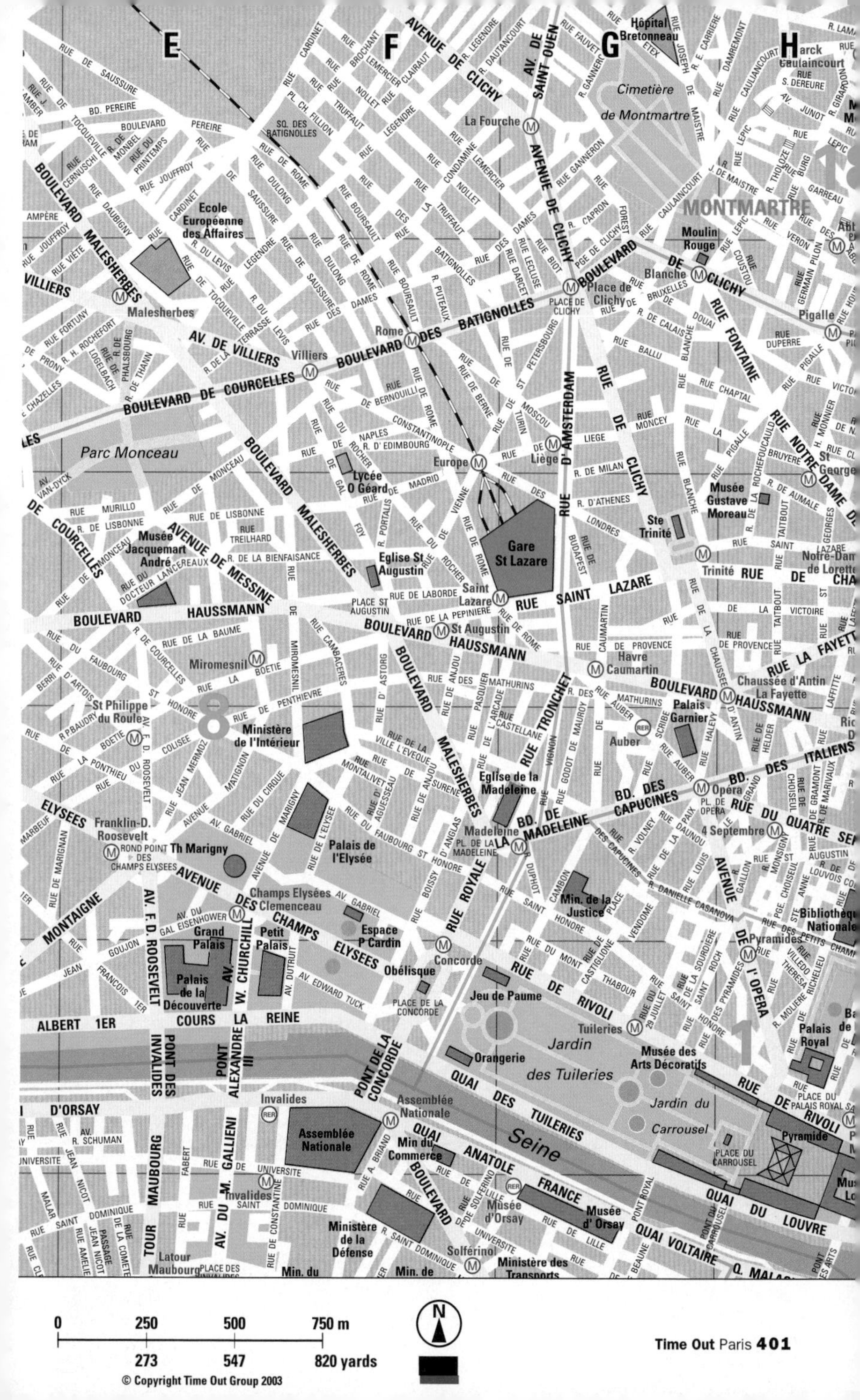
E
F
G
H
Hôpital Bretonneau
Cimetière de Montmartre
MONTMARTRE
Moulin Rouge
Blanche
Pigalle
La Fourche
Place de Clichy
Ecole Européenne des Affaires
SQ. DES BATIGNOLLES
Malesherbes
Villiers
Rome
Parc Monceau
Europe
Liège
Lycée C Géard
Gare St Lazare
Saint Lazare
Eglise St Augustin
St Augustin
Musée Jacquemart André
Musée Gustave Moreau
Ste Trinité
Trinité
Notre-Dame de Lorette
St Georges
Miromesnil
St Philippe du Roule
Ministère de l'Intérieur
Havre Caumartin
Chaussée d'Antin La Fayette
Palais Garnier
Auber
Opéra
4 Septembre
Eglise de la Madeleine
Madeleine
Palais de l'Elysée
Franklin-D. Roosevelt
Th Marigny
Champs Elysées Clemenceau
Espace P Cardin
Grand Palais
Petit Palais
Palais de la Découverte
Obélisque
Concorde
Jeu de Paume
Min. de la Justice
Pyramides
Bibliothèque Nationale
Tuileries
Jardin des Tuileries
Orangerie
Musée des Arts Décoratifs
Jardin du Carrousel
Palais Royal
Pyramide
Seine
Invalides
Assemblée Nationale
Min du Commerce
Musée d'Orsay
Ministère de la Défense
Solférino
Ministère des Transports
Latour Maubourg
8
1
BOULEVARD DE COURCELLES
BOULEVARD DES BATIGNOLLES
BOULEVARD DE CLICHY
BOULEVARD MALESHERBES
BOULEVARD HAUSSMANN
AVENUE DE CLICHY
AV. DE SAINT OUEN
RUE D'AMSTERDAM
RUE DE CLICHY
RUE SAINT LAZARE
RUE TRONCHET
RUE ROYALE
BD. DES CAPUCINES
BD. DES ITALIENS
AVENUE DES CHAMPS ELYSEES
AVENUE MONTAIGNE
RUE DE RIVOLI
QUAI DES TUILERIES
QUAI ANATOLE FRANCE
QUAI VOLTAIRE
QUAI DU LOUVRE
COURS LA REINE
PONT DE LA CONCORDE
PONT ALEXANDRE III
PONT DES INVALIDES
AVENUE DE L'OPERA
0
250
500
750 m
273
547
820 yards
N
© Copyright Time Out Group 2003

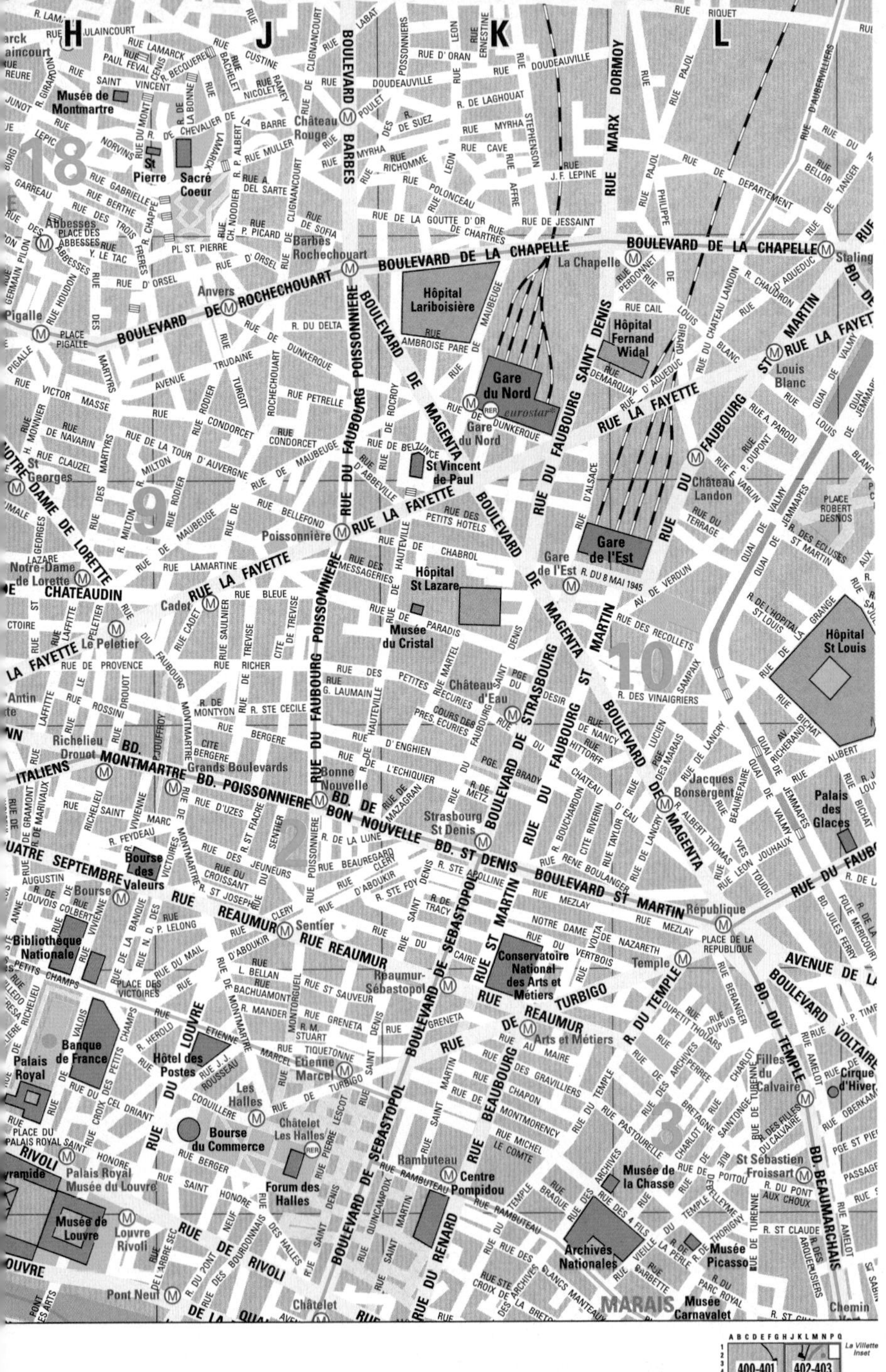
H
J
K
L
18
9
10
2
3
Musée de Montmartre
St Pierre
Sacré Coeur
Château Rouge
Barbès Rochechouart
Abbesses
Place des Abbesses
Pigalle
Place Pigalle
Anvers
Boulevard de Rochechouart
Boulevard de la Chapelle
La Chapelle
Hôpital Lariboisière
Gare du Nord
eurostar
Hôpital Fernand Widal
Louis Blanc
Rue La Fayette
Boulevard de Magenta
Rue du Faubourg Poissonnière
Rue du Faubourg Saint Denis
Boulevard Barbès
Rue Marx Dormoy
St Vincent de Paul
St Georges
Poissonnière
Château Landon
Place Robert Desnos
Gare de l'Est
Notre-Dame de Lorette
Chateaudun
Cadet
Hôpital St Lazare
Musée du Cristal
Hôpital St Louis
Le Peletier
Château d'Eau
Richelieu Drouot
Grands Boulevards
Bd. Montmartre
Bd. Poissonnière
Bonne Nouvelle
Bd. de Bon Nouvelle
Bd. St Denis
Strasbourg St Denis
Boulevard de Strasbourg
Rue du Faubourg St Martin
Jacques Bonsergent
Palais des Glaces
Bourse des Valeurs
Bourse
Boulevard St Martin
République
Place de la République
Rue Reaumur
Sentier
Bibliothèque Nationale
Place des Victoires
Conservatoire National des Arts et Métiers
Temple
Réaumur-Sébastopol
Rue Turbigo
Arts et Métiers
Avenue de la République
Boulevard Voltaire
Banque de France
Palais Royal
Hôtel des Postes
Etienne Marcel
Les Halles
Filles du Calvaire
Cirque d'Hiver
Bourse du Commerce
Châtelet Les Halles
Rambuteau
Centre Pompidou
Musée de la Chasse
St Sebastien Froissart
Palais Royal Musée du Louvre
Forum des Halles
Musée de Louvre
Louvre Rivoli
Rue de Rivoli
Boulevard de Sebastopol
Rue du Renard
Archives Nationales
Musée Picasso
Bd. Beaumarchais
Bd. du Temple
Pont Neuf
Châtelet
Marais
Musée Carnavalet
A B C D E F G H J K L M N P Q
La Villette Inset
400-401
402-403
404-405
406-407

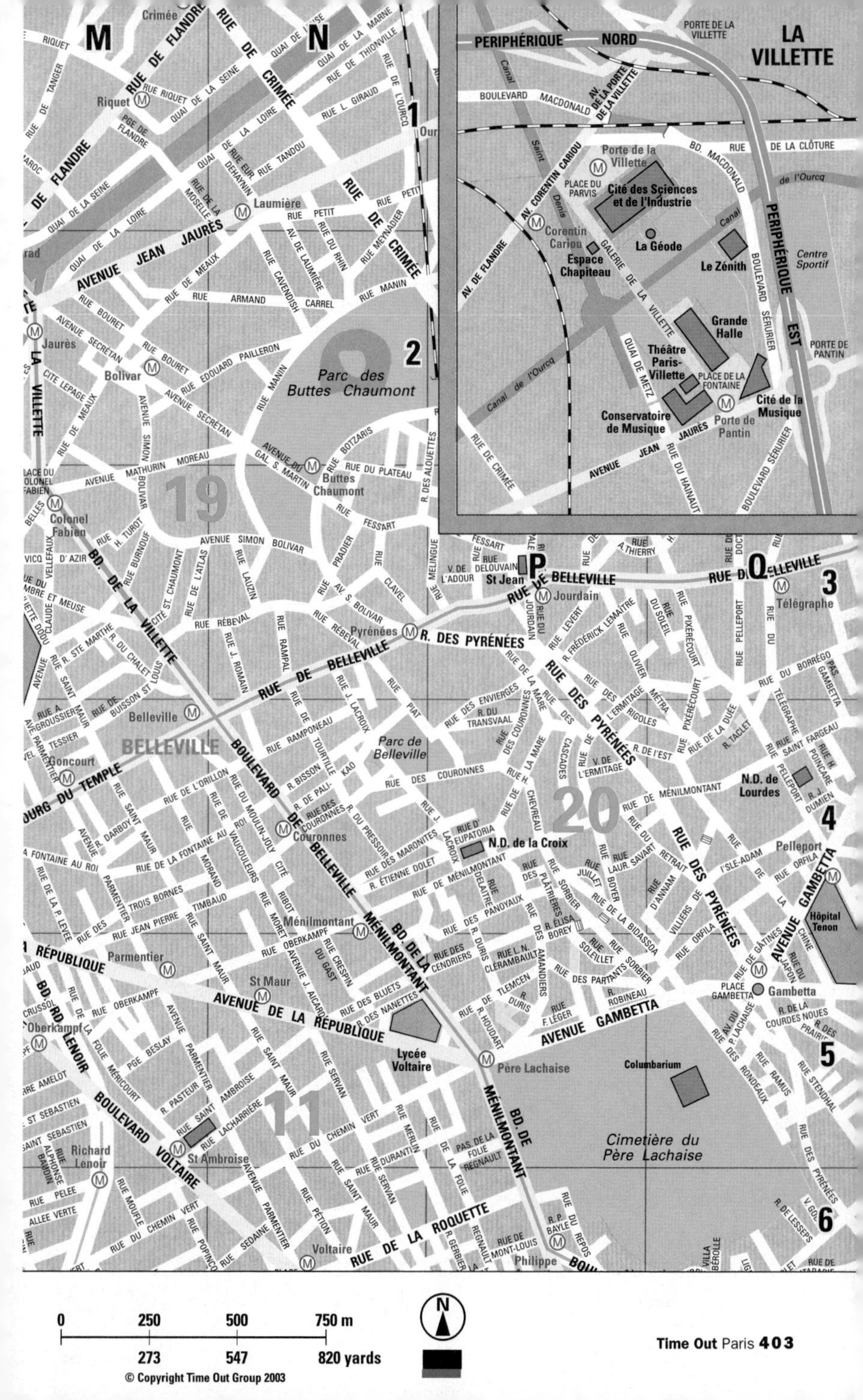

M
N
P
Q
1
2
3
4
5
6
19
20
11
LA VILLETTE
PERIPHÉRIQUE NORD
PERIPHÉRIQUE EST
PORTE DE LA VILLETTE
BOULEVARD MACDONALD
AV. DE LA PORTE DE LA VILLETTE
BD. MACDONALD
RUE DE LA CLÔTURE
Canal Saint Denis
Canal de l'Ourcq
AV. CORENTIN CARIOU
AV. DE FLANDRE
Porte de la Villette
PLACE DU PARVIS
Cité des Sciences et de l'Industrie
La Géode
Corentin Cariou
Espace Chapiteau
GALERIE DE LA VILLETTE
Le Zénith
Centre Sportif
BOULEVARD SÉRURIER
Grande Halle
Théâtre Paris-Villette
PLACE DE LA FONTAINE
PORTE DE PANTIN
Cité de la Musique
Conservatoire de Musique
Porte de Pantin
QUAI DE METZ
AVENUE JEAN JAURÈS
RUE DU HAINAUT
RUE DE CRIMÉE
BOULEVARD SÉRURIER
Crimée
RIQUET
RUE DE FLANDRE
RUE DE TANGER
RUE RIQUET
Riquet
QUAI DE LA SEINE
QUAI DE LA LOIRE
QUAI DE LA MARNE
QUAI DE THIONVILLE
QUAI DE L'OURCQ
RUE L. GIRAUD
RUE TANDOU
RUE EUR. DEHAYNIN
RUE DE LA MOSELLE
PGE DE FLANDRE
Laumière
RUE PETIT
AV. DE LAUMIÈRE
RUE DU RHIN
RUE MEYNADIER
AVENUE JEAN JAURÈS
RUE DE MEAUX
RUE ARMAND CARREL
RUE CAVENDISH
RUE MANIN
RUE BOURET
AVENUE SECRÉTAN
Jaurès
Bolivar
RUE EDOUARD PAILLERON
CITÉ LEPAGE
BD. DE LA VILLETTE
Parc des Buttes Chaumont
AVENUE SIMON BOLIVAR
AVENUE DU GAL S. MARTIN
Buttes Chaumont
RUE BOTZARIS
RUE DU PLATEAU
R. DES ALOUETTES
AVENUE MATHURIN MOREAU
PLACE DU COLONEL FABIEN
Colonel Fabien
RUE H. TUROT
RUE BURNOUF
CITÉ ST. CHAUMONT
RUE DE L'ATLAS
RUE LAUZIN
RUE FESSART
RUE PRADIER
RUE CLAVEL
RUE MELINGUE
RUE DELOUVAIN
V. DE L'ADOUR
St Jean
RUE DE BELLEVILLE
Jourdain
RUE DU JOURDAIN
Télégraphe
RUE PELLEPORT
Pyrénées
R. DES PYRÉNÉES
RUE RÉBEVAL
RUE J. ROMAIN
RUE RAMPAL
RUE DE BELLEVILLE
RUE J. LACROIX
RUE PIAT
RUE LEVERT
RUE FRÉDÉRICK LEMAÎTRE
RUE OLIVIER MÉTRA
RUE PIXÉRÉCOURT
RUE DU BORRÉGO
PAS. GAMBETTA
RUE DU TÉLÉGRAPHE
RUE SAINT FARGEAU
RUE DES PYRÉNÉES
RUE DE LA MARE
RUE DES ENVIERGES
R. DU TRANSVAAL
RUE DES COURONNES
RUE DES CASCADES
V. DE L'ERMITAGE
RUE DES RIGOLES
R. DE L'EST
RUE DE LA DUÉE
R. TACLET
N.D. de Lourdes
R. J. DUMIEN
RUE H. POINCARÉ
Belleville
BELLEVILLE
BOULEVARD DE BELLEVILLE
Goncourt
FAUBOURG DU TEMPLE
RUE SAINT MAUR
Parc de Belleville
RUE RAMPONEAU
RUE DE TOURTILLE
R. BISSON
R. DE PALI-KAO
RUE DE L'ORILLON
RUE DU MOULIN-JOLY
RUE DE LA FONTAINE AU ROI
RUE DES COURONNES
Couronnes
R. DU PRESSOIR
RUE DES MARONITES
R. ÉTIENNE DOLET
RUE D'EUPATORIA
N.D. de la Croix
RUE DE MÉNILMONTANT
RUE DES PLATRIÈRES
RUE SORBIER
RUE BOYER
RUE DE LA BIDASSOA
RUE D'ANNAM
VILLIERS DE L'ISLE-ADAM
Pelleport
RUE ORFILA
AVENUE GAMBETTA
Hôpital Tenon
RUE DE LA CHINE
RUE DU JAPON
RUE DE GÂTINES
PLACE GAMBETTA
Gambetta
R. DE LA COURDES NOUES
RUE TROIS BORNES
RUE JEAN PIERRE TIMBAUD
RUE OBERKAMPF
Ménilmontant
BD. DE LA MÉNILMONTANT
RUE DES CENDRIERS
RUE L. N. CLÉRAMBAULT
RUE DES AMANDIERS
RUE DES PARTANTS
R. ROBINEAU
AVENUE GAMBETTA
RUE DE TLEMCEN
R. DURIS
RUE F. LÉGER
RUE R. HOUDART
RÉPUBLIQUE
Parmentier
St Maur
AVENUE DE LA RÉPUBLIQUE
Lycée Voltaire
Père Lachaise
Columbarium
Cimetière du Père Lachaise
RUE DES RONDEAUX
AV. DU P. LACHAISE
RUE STENDHAL
RUE RAMUS
RUE DES PYRÉNÉES
R. DE LESSEPS
BD. RD LENOIR
Oberkampf
RUE DE CRUSSOL
RUE DE LA FOLIE MÉRICOURT
PGE BESLAY
AVENUE PARMENTIER
R. PASTEUR
RUE SAINT AMBROISE
RUE LACHARRIÈRE
RUE SAINT MAUR
RUE SERVAN
RUE DU CHEMIN VERT
RUE MERLIN
RUE DURANTI
PAS. DE LA FOLIE REGNAULT
BD. DE MÉNILMONTANT
RUE AMELOT
ST SEBASTIEN
Richard Lenoir
BOULEVARD VOLTAIRE
St Ambroise
RUE ALPHONSE BAUDIN
RUE PELEE
ALLEE VERTE
RUE MOUFLE
RUE POPINCOURT
RUE SEDAINE
RUE PÉTION
Voltaire
RUE DE LA ROQUETTE
RUE GERBIER
RUE DE MONT-LOUIS
R. P. BAYLE
RUE DU REPOS
Philippe
VILLA BÉROLLE
0
250
500
750 m
273
547
820 yards
N

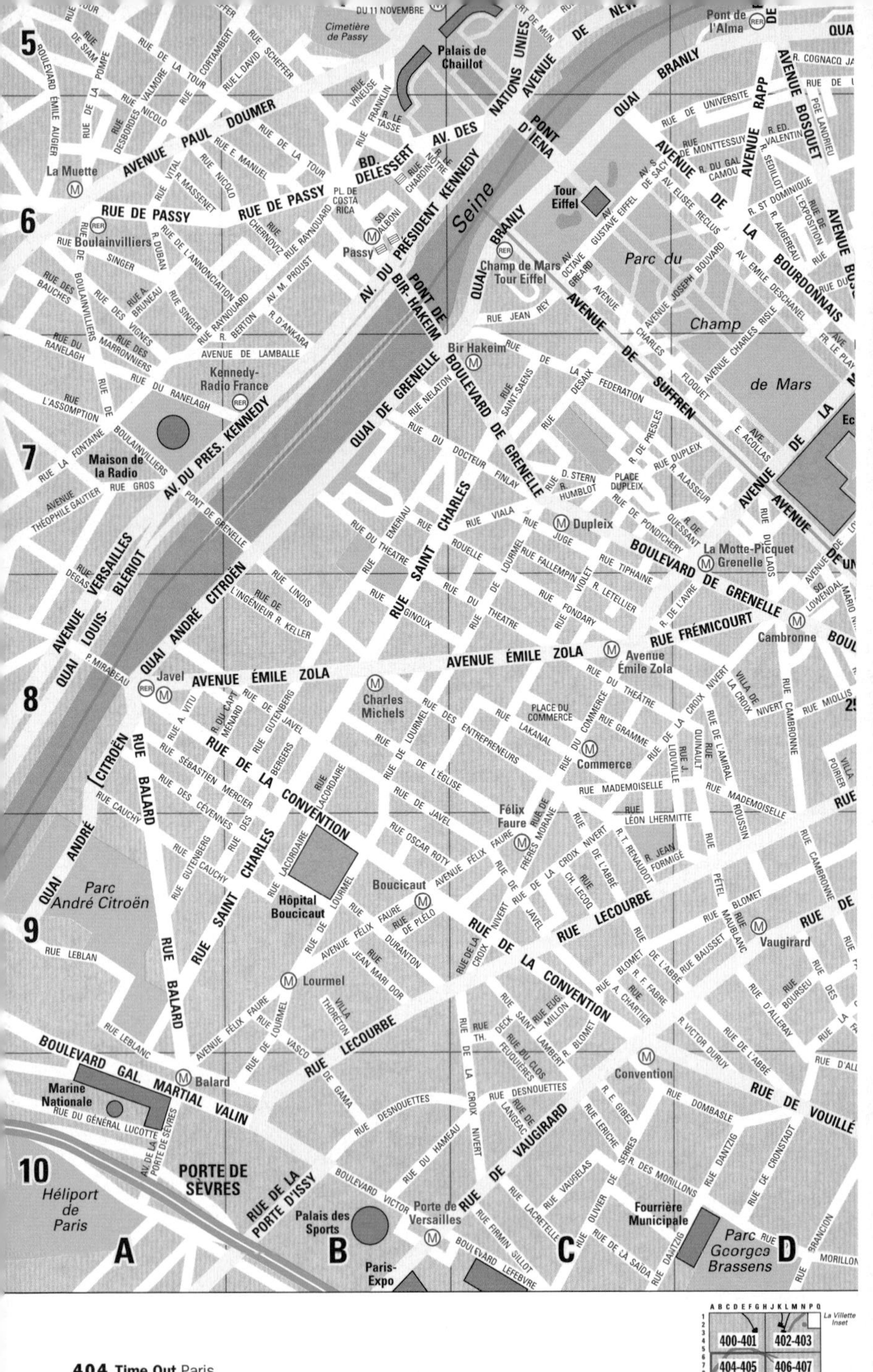
Cimetière de Passy
Palais de Chaillot
Pont de l'Alma
Avenue Paul Doumer
Rue de Passy
La Muette
Boulevard Émile Augier
Rue de la Pompe
Rue Boulainvilliers
Avenue des Nations Unies
Avenue de New
Quai Branly
Avenue Rapp
Avenue Bosquet
Pont d'Iéna
Bd. Delessert
Pl. de Costa Rica
Passy
Av. du Président Kennedy
Seine
Tour Eiffel
Champ de Mars Tour Eiffel
Parc du Champ de Mars
Avenue de la Bourdonnais
Avenue de Suffren
Pont de Bir-Hakeim
Bir Hakeim
Avenue de Lamballe
Kennedy-Radio France
Rue du Ranelagh
Maison de la Radio
Av. du Pres. Kennedy
Quai de Grenelle
Boulevard de Grenelle
Rue Saint Charles
Dupleix
Place Dupleix
La Motte-Picquet Grenelle
Pont de Grenelle
Avenue Versailles
Quai Louis-Blériot
Quai André Citroën
Rue Linois
Avenue Émile Zola
Rue Frémicourt
Cambronne
Javel
Charles Michels
Avenue Émile Zola
Place du Commerce
Commerce
Rue de la Convention
Rue Balard
Félix Faure
Hôpital Boucicaut
Boucicaut
Parc André Citroën
Rue Lecourbe
Vaugirard
Lourmel
Rue Leblanc
Boulevard Gal. Martial Valin
Balard
Marine Nationale
Convention
Rue de Vouillé
Rue de Vaugirard
Porte de Sèvres
Héliport de Paris
Rue de la Porte d'Issy
Palais des Sports
Porte de Versailles
Paris-Expo
Boulevard Victor
Boulevard Lefebvre
Fourrière Municipale
Parc Georges Brassens
Rue Dantzig
5
6
7
8
9
10
A
B
C
D
400-401
402-403
404-405
406-407
La Villette Inset

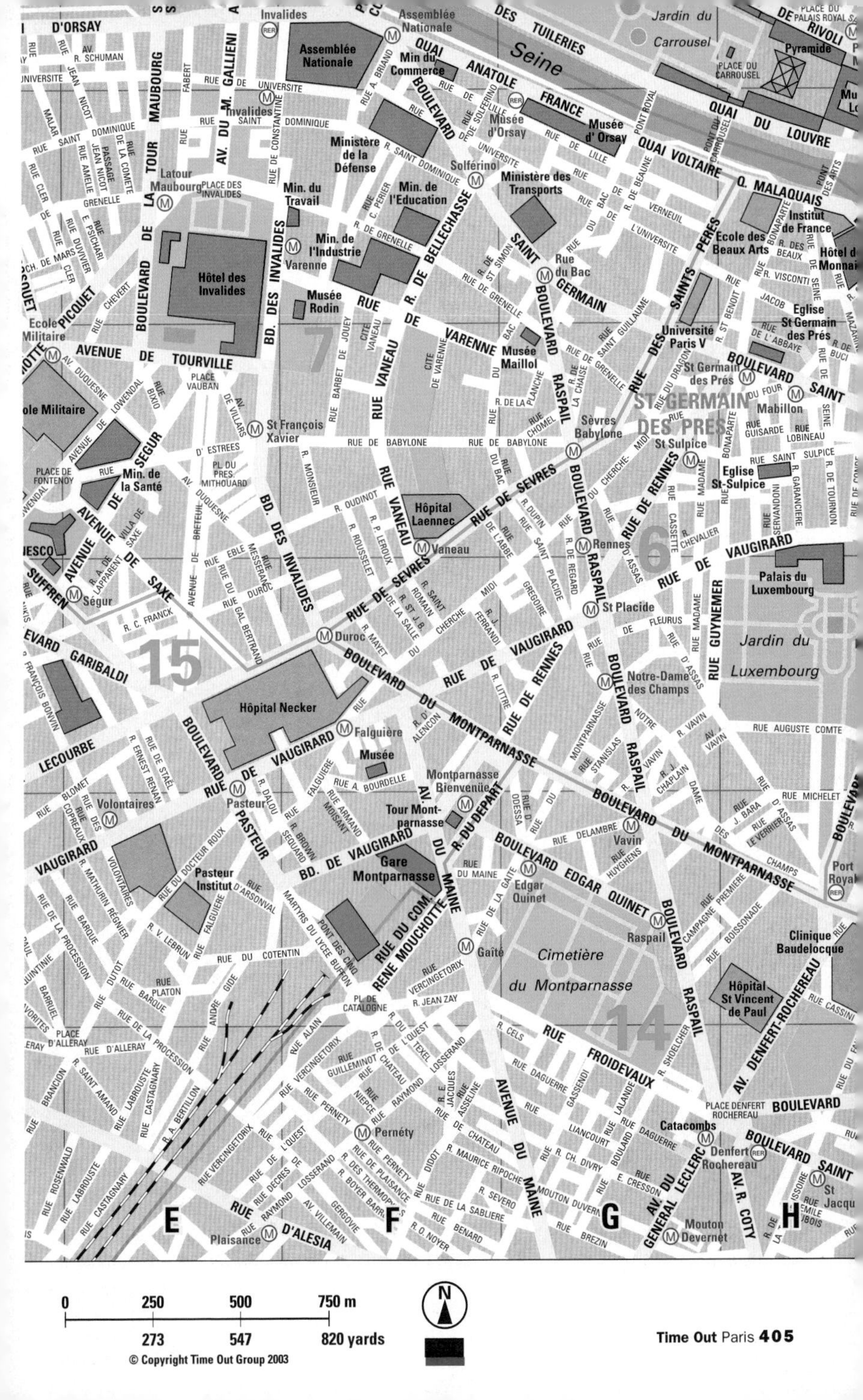
Invalides
Assemblée Nationale
Jardin du Carrousel
Place du Palais Royal
Rivoli
Pyramide
Place du Carrousel
Seine
Quai des Tuileries
Quai Anatole France
Quai du Louvre
Quai Voltaire
Q. Malaquais
Musée d'Orsay
Min du Commerce
Ministère de la Défense
Solférino
Ministère des Transports
Institut de France
Ecole des Beaux Arts
Hôtel de la Monnaie
Latour Maubourg
Place des Invalides
Min. du Travail
Min. de l'Education
Min. de l'Industrie
Varenne
Hôtel des Invalides
Musée Rodin
Rue du Bac
Boulevard Saint Germain
Université Paris V
Eglise St Germain des Prés
St Germain des Prés
Mabillon
Musée Maillol
Ecole Militaire
Avenue de Tourville
Place Vauban
St François Xavier
Rue de Babylone
Sèvres Babylone
St Sulpice
Eglise St-Sulpice
Ecole Militaire
Place de Fontenoy
Min. de la Santé
Unesco
Avenue de Ségur
Avenue de Saxe
Ségur
Hôpital Laennec
Vaneau
Rue de Sèvres
Rennes
Rue de Rennes
Rue de Vaugirard
Palais du Luxembourg
Jardin du Luxembourg
St Placide
Duroc
Notre-Dame des Champs
Boulevard Garibaldi
Hôpital Necker
Falguière
Boulevard du Montparnasse
Musée
Montparnasse Bienvenüe
Tour Montparnasse
Gare Montparnasse
Volontaires
Pasteur
Pasteur Institut
Vavin
Boulevard Edgar Quinet
Edgar Quinet
Raspail
Boulevard Raspail
Port Royal
Clinique Baudelocque
Cimetière du Montparnasse
Gaîté
Hôpital St Vincent de Paul
Pl. de Catalogne
Rue Froidevaux
Av. Denfert-Rochereau
Place Denfert Rochereau
Catacombs
Denfert Rochereau
Pernéty
Avenue du Maine
Plaisance
Rue d'Alésia
Mouton Duvernet
Av. du Général Leclerc
Av. R. Coty
St Jacques
7
6
15
14
E
F
G
H
0
250
500
750 m
273
547
820 yards
N

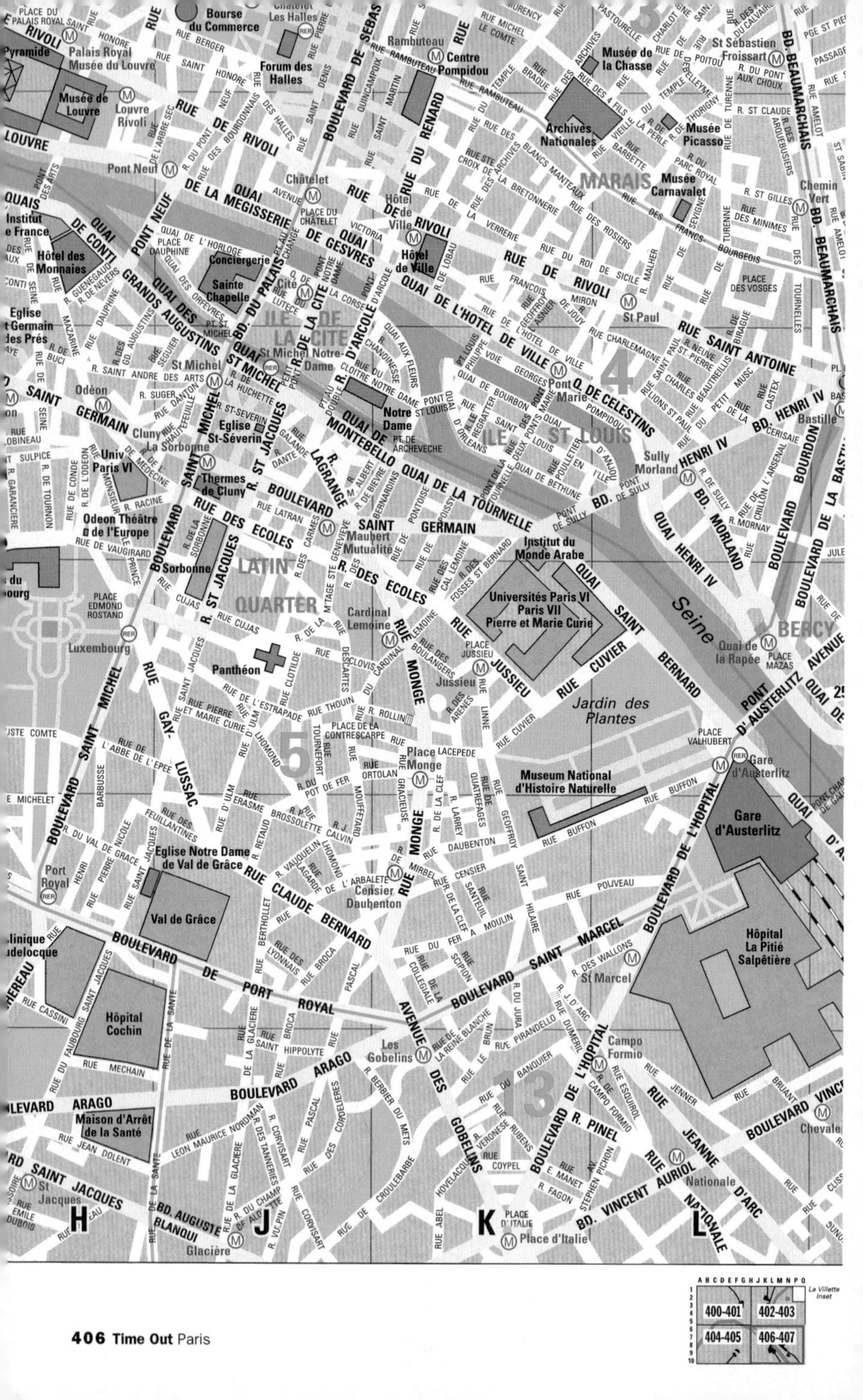
Bourse du Commerce
Châtelet Les Halles
Forum des Halles
Rambuteau
Centre Pompidou
Musée de la Chasse
St Sébastien Froissart
Palais Royal Musée du Louvre
Pyramide
Musée de Louvre
Louvre Rivoli
Archives Nationales
Musée Picasso
Pont Neuf
Châtelet
MARAIS
Musée Carnavalet
Chemin Vert
Hôtel de Ville
Institut de France
Hôtel des Monnaies
Conciergerie
Sainte Chapelle
Cité
ILE DE LA CITE
St Michel Notre-Dame
St Paul
Eglise St Germain des Prés
St Michel
Odéon
Notre Dame
Pont Marie
ILE ST LOUIS
Bastille
Cluny La Sorbonne
Eglise St-Séverin
Univ Paris VI
Thermes de Cluny
Sully Morland
Odeon Théâtre de l'Europe
Maubert Mutualité
Institut du Monde Arabe
Sorbonne
LATIN QUARTER
Cardinal Lemoine
Universités Paris VI Paris VII Pierre et Marie Curie
Seine
BERCY
Luxembourg
Panthéon
Jussieu
Quai de la Rapée
Jardin des Plantes
Place Monge
Museum National d'Histoire Naturelle
Gare d'Austerlitz
Port Royal
Eglise Notre Dame de Val de Grâce
Censier Daubenton
Val de Grâce
Hôpital La Pitié Salpêtière
St Marcel
Hôpital Cochin
Campo Formio
Les Gobelins
Maison d'Arrêt de la Santé
Chevaleret
Nationale
St Jacques
Glacière
Place d'Italie
BOULEVARD SAINT GERMAIN
RUE DE RIVOLI
BOULEVARD SAINT MICHEL
RUE MONGE
BOULEVARD DE PORT ROYAL
BOULEVARD ARAGO
BOULEVARD SAINT MARCEL
BOULEVARD DE L'HOPITAL
AVENUE DES GOBELINS
BD. VINCENT AURIOL
BD. BEAUMARCHAIS
RUE SAINT ANTOINE
QUAI SAINT BERNARD
RUE CLAUDE BERNARD
3
4
5
13
H
J
K
L

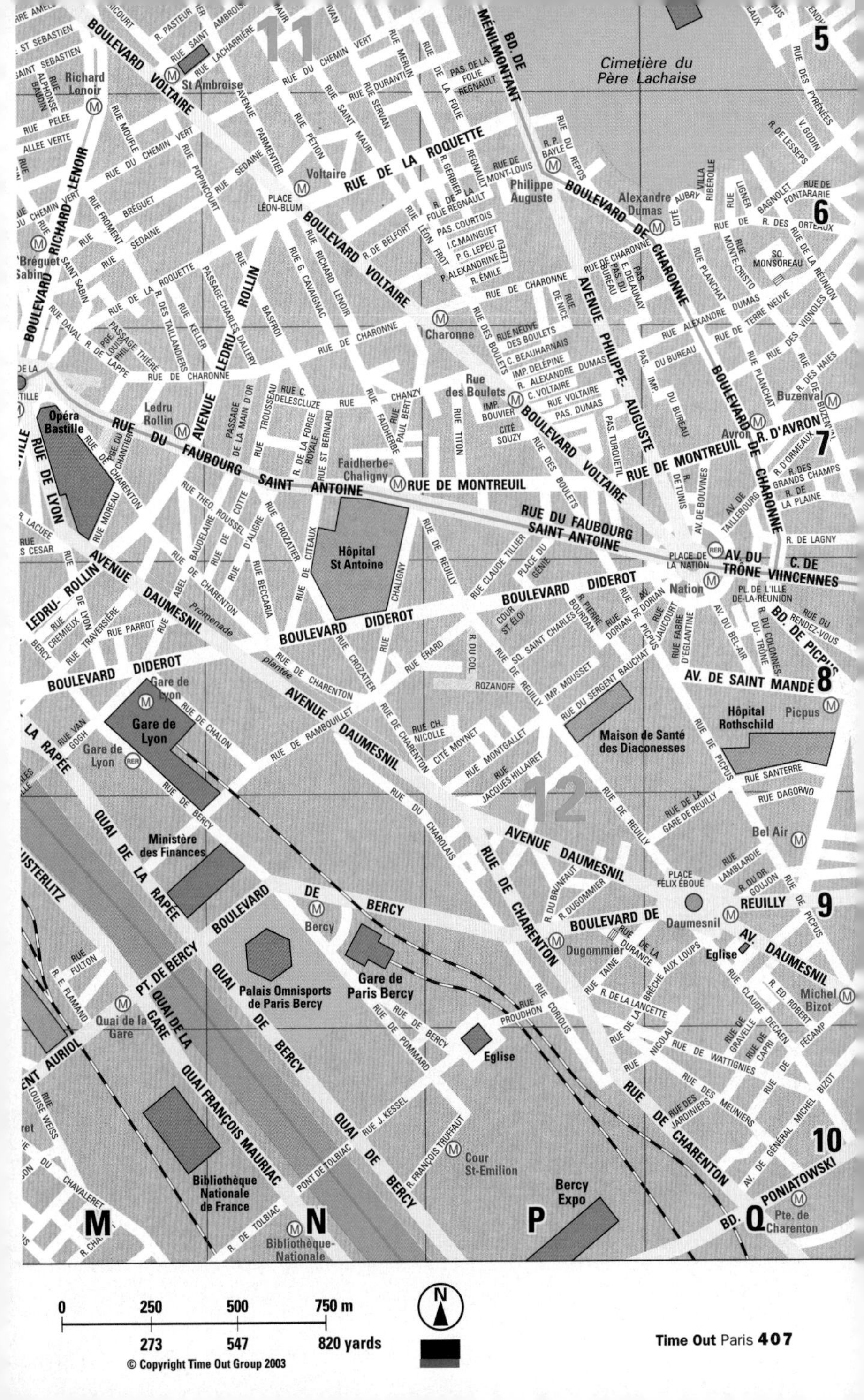
11
12
5
6
7
8
9
10
M
N
P
Q
Cimetière du Père Lachaise
BOULEVARD VOLTAIRE
BOULEVARD RICHARD LENOIR
BD. DE MÉNILMONTANT
RUE DE LA ROQUETTE
RUE DE CHARONNE
BOULEVARD DE CHARONNE
AVENUE PHILIPPE-AUGUSTE
AVENUE LEDRU-ROLLIN
RUE DU FAUBOURG SAINT ANTOINE
RUE DE MONTREUIL
R. D'AVRON
AV. DU TRÔNE
C. DE VINCENNES
PLACE DE LA NATION
BOULEVARD DIDEROT
AVENUE DAUMESNIL
RUE DE LYON
RUE DE CHARENTON
RUE DE REUILLY
RUE DE PICPUS
BD. DE PICPUS
AV. DE SAINT MANDÉ
BOULEVARD DE REUILLY
BOULEVARD DE BERCY
QUAI DE LA RAPÉE
QUAI DE BERCY
QUAI DE LA GARE
QUAI FRANÇOIS MAURIAC
PT. DE BERCY
PONT DE TOLBIAC
RUE DE TOLBIAC
BD. PONIATOWSKI
AV. DE GÉNÉRAL MICHEL BIZOT
RUE DE TAILLANDIERS
RUE DU CHEMIN VERT
AVENUE PARMENTIER
RUE SAINT MAUR
RUE DES BOULETS
RUE DE RAMBOUILLET
RUE CROZATIER
RUE DE CITEAUX
RUE DE WATTIGNIES
RUE DES MEUNIERS
RUE DE POMMARD
RUE DU CHAROLAIS
Promenade plantée
Richard Lenoir
St Ambroise
Voltaire
Place Léon-Blum
Philippe Auguste
Alexandre Dumas
Charonne
Rue des Boulets
Buzenval
Avron
Ledru Rollin
Opéra Bastille
Faidherbe-Chaligny
Hôpital St Antoine
Nation
PL. DE L'ILLE DE-LA-RÉUNION
Hôpital Rothschild
Picpus
Maison de Santé des Diaconesses
Gare de Lyon
Ministère des Finances
Bercy
Palais Omnisports de Paris Bercy
Gare de Paris Bercy
Eglise
Dugommier
Daumesnil
Place Félix Éboué
Bel Air
Michel Bizot
Quai de la Gare
Cour St-Emilion
Bercy Expo
Bibliothèque Nationale de France
Bibliothèque-Nationale
Pte. de Charenton
0
250
500
750 m
273
547
820 yards
N

Street Index

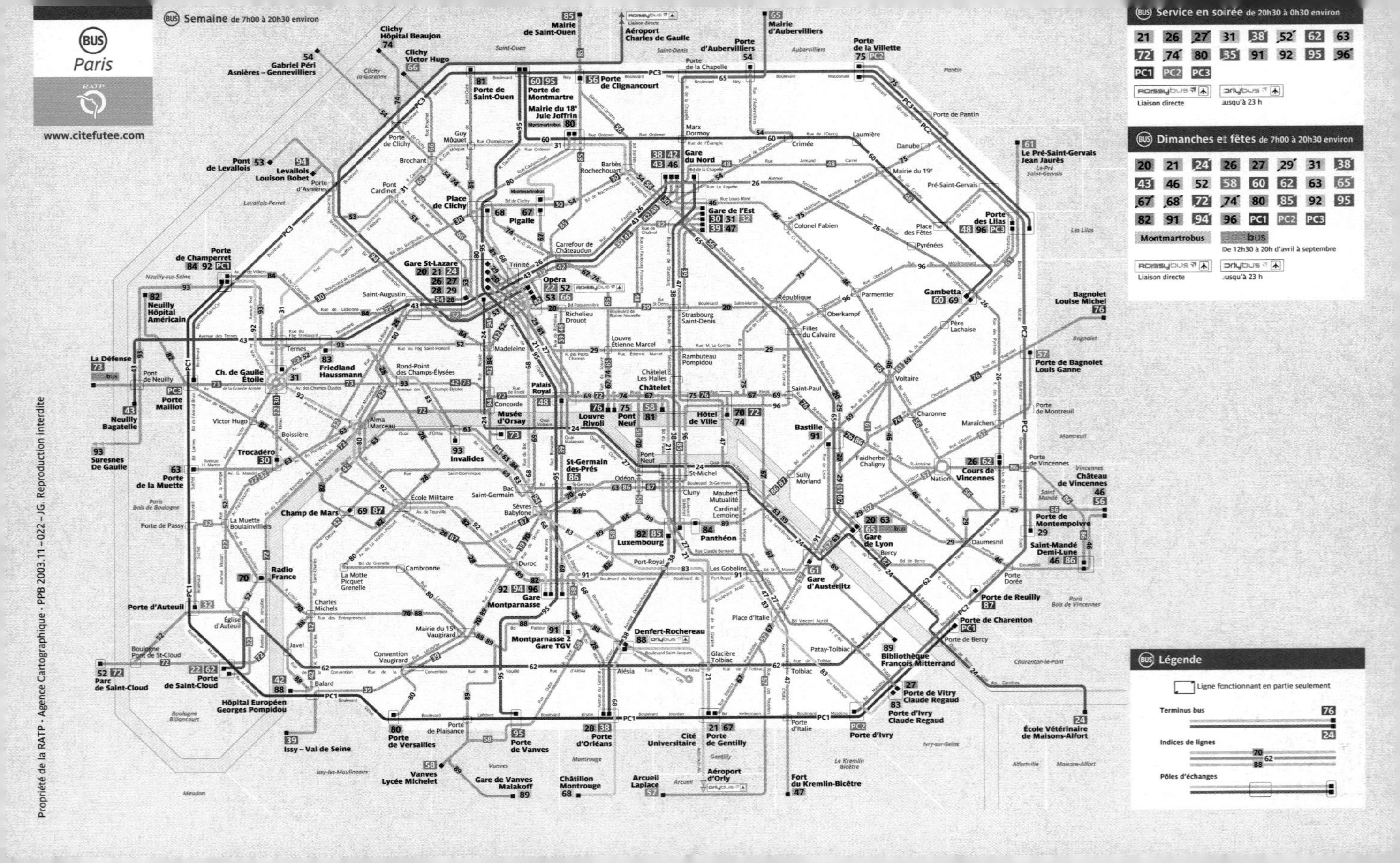

BUS Paris
RATP
www.citefutee.com
Semaine de 7h00 à 20h30 environ
Service en soirée de 20h30 à 0h30 environ
21 26 27 31 38 52 62 63
72 74 80 35 91 92 95 96
PC1 PC2 PC3
ROISSYBUS Liaison directe
ORLYBUS jusqu'à 23 h
Dimanches et fêtes de 7h00 à 20h30 environ
20 21 24 26 27 29 31 38
43 46 52 58 60 62 63 65
67 68 72 74 80 85 92 95
82 91 94 96 PC1 PC2 PC3
Montmartrobus
De 12h30 à 20h d'avril à septembre
ROISSYBUS Liaison directe
ORLYBUS jusqu'à 23 h
Légende
Ligne fonctionnant en partie seulement
Terminus bus
Indices de lignes
Pôles d'échanges
Propriété de la RATP - Agence Cartographique - PPB 2003.11 – 022 – JG. Reproduction interdite
Mairie de Saint-Ouen
Aéroport Charles de Gaulle
Mairie d'Aubervilliers
Porte d'Aubervilliers
Porte de la Villette
Clichy Hôpital Beaujon
Clichy Victor Hugo
Gabriel Péri Asnières – Gennevilliers
Porte de Saint-Ouen
Porte de Montmartre
Mairie du 18e Jule Joffrin
Porte de Clignancourt
Porte de la Chapelle
Porte de Pantin
Pont de Levallois
Levallois Louison Bobet
Porte d'Asnières
Porte de Clichy
Guy Môquet
Brochant
Pont Cardinet
Marx Dormoy
Crimée
Laumière
Danube
Mairie du 19e
Le Pré-Saint-Gervais Jean Jaurès
Gare du Nord
Barbès Rochechouart
Place de Clichy
Pigalle
Gare de l'Est
Colonel Fabien
Place des Fêtes
Pré-Saint-Gervais
Porte des Lilas
Pyrénées
Porte de Champerret
Neuilly Hôpital Américain
Gare St-Lazare
Trinité
Carrefour de Châteaudun
Opéra
Saint-Augustin
République
Oberkampf
Parmentier
Gambetta
Bagnolet Louise Michel
La Défense
Pont de Neuilly
Ternes
Friedland Haussmann
Ch. de Gaulle Étoile
Madeleine
Richelieu Drouot
Strasbourg Saint-Denis
Filles du Calvaire
Père Lachaise
Louvre Étienne Marcel
Rambuteau Pompidou
Rond-Point des Champs-Élysées
Porte Maillot
Neuilly Bagatelle
Concorde
Palais Royal
Châtelet Les Halles
Châtelet
Saint-Paul
Voltaire
Porte de Bagnolet Louis Ganne
Victor Hugo
Alma Marceau
Musée d'Orsay
Louvre Rivoli
Pont Neuf
Hôtel de Ville
Bastille
Charonne
Porte de Montreuil
Maraîchers
Suresnes De Gaulle
Boissière
Trocadéro
Invalides
St-Germain des-Prés
Odéon
St-Michel
Sully Morland
Faidherbe Chaligny
Cours de Vincennes
Nation
Porte de Vincennes
Château de Vincennes
Porte de la Muette
École Militaire
Bac Saint-Germain
Sèvres Babylone
Cluny
Maubert Mutualité
Cardinal Lemoine
Champ de Mars
Luxembourg
Panthéon
Gare de Lyon
Bercy
Porte de Montempoivre
Saint-Mandé Demi-Lune
Porte de Passy
La Muette Boulainvilliers
La Motte Picquet Grenelle
Cambronne
Duroc
Port-Royal
Les Gobelins
Gare d'Austerlitz
Daumesnil
Porte Dorée
Radio France
Gare Montparnasse
Charles Michels
Porte d'Auteuil
Église d'Auteuil
Mairie du 15e Vaugirard
Montparnasse 2 Gare TGV
Denfert-Rochereau
Place d'Italie
Patay-Tolbiac
Porte de Reuilly
Porte de Charenton
Porte de Bercy
Bibliothèque François Mitterrand
Boulogne Pont de St-Cloud
Javel
Convention Vaugirard
Alésia
Glacière Tolbiac
Tolbiac
Parc de Saint-Cloud
Porte de Saint-Cloud
Balard
Hôpital Européen Georges Pompidou
Porte de Vitry Claude Regaud
Porte d'Ivry Claude Regaud
Porte de Plaisance
Porte de Versailles
Porte de Vanves
Porte d'Orléans
Cité Universitaire
Porte de Gentilly
Porte d'Italie
Porte d'Ivry
École Vétérinaire de Maisons-Alfort
Issy – Val de Seine
Vanves Lycée Michelet
Gare de Vanves Malakoff
Châtillon Montrouge
Arcueil Laplace
Aéroport d'Orly
Fort du Kremlin-Bicêtre

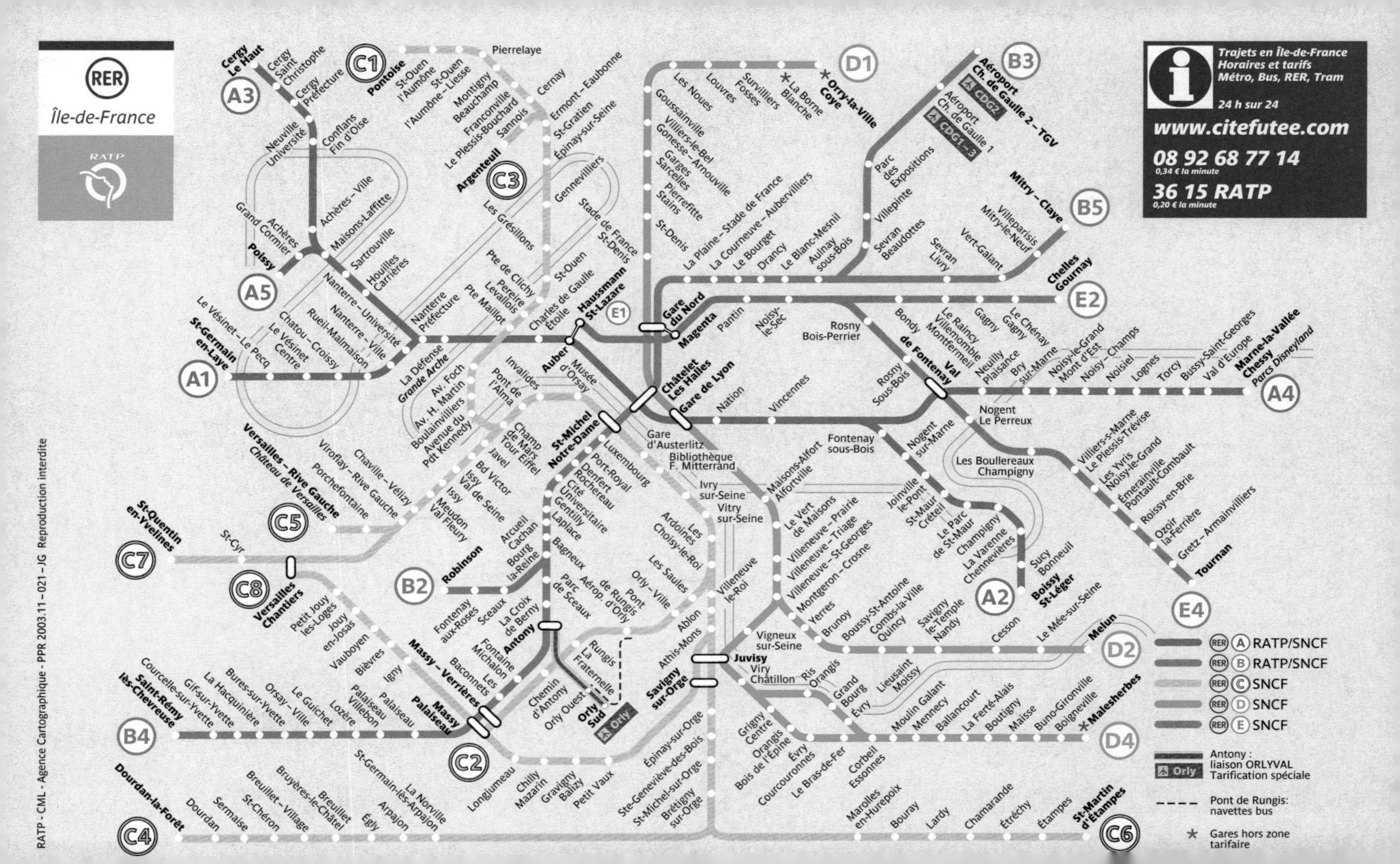

RATP - CML - Agence Cartographique - PPR 2003.11 – 021 – JG Reproduction interdite
RER
île-de-France
RATP
Trajets en Île-de-France
Horaires et tarifs
Métro, Bus, RER, Tram
24 h sur 24
www.citefutee.com
08 92 68 77 14
0,34 € la minute
36 15 RATP
0,20 € la minute
A1 St-Germain-en-Laye
Le Vésinet – Le Pecq
Le Vésinet Centre
Chatou – Croissy
Rueil-Malmaison
Nanterre – Ville
Nanterre – Université
Nanterre Préfecture
La Défense Grande Arche
Charles de Gaulle Étoile
Auber
Châtelet Les Halles
Gare de Lyon
Nation
Vincennes
A2 Boissy St-Léger
Sucy Bonneuil
La Varenne Chennevières
Le Parc de St-Maur
Champigny
St-Maur Créteil
Joinville-le-Pont
Nogent-sur-Marne
Fontenay-sous-Bois
A3 Cergy Le Haut
Cergy St-Christophe
Cergy Préfecture
Neuville Université
Conflans Fin d'Oise
Achères – Ville
Maisons-Laffitte
Sartrouville
Houilles Carrières
A4 Marne-la-Vallée Chessy Parcs Disneyland
Val d'Europe
Bussy-Saint-Georges
Torcy
Lognes
Noisiel
Noisy – Champs
Noisy-le-Grand Mont d'Est
Bry-sur-Marne
Neuilly Plaisance
Nogent Le Perreux
Val de Fontenay
Rosny Sous-Bois
A5 Poissy
Achères Grand Cormier
B2 Robinson
Fontenay-aux-Roses
Sceaux
Bourg-la-Reine
B3 Aéroport Ch. de Gaulle 2 – TGV
Aéroport Ch. de Gaulle 1
CDG2
CDG1 – 3
Parc des Expositions
Villepinte
Sevran Beaudottes
Aulnay-sous-Bois
Le Blanc-Mesnil
Drancy
Le Bourget
La Courneuve – Aubervilliers
La Plaine – Stade de France
Gare du Nord
St-Michel Notre-Dame
Luxembourg
Port-Royal
Denfert Rochereau
Cité Universitaire
Gentilly
Laplace
Arcueil Cachan
Bagneux
La Croix de Berny
Antony
Fontaine Michalon
Les Baconnets
Massy – Verrières
Massy Palaiseau
Palaiseau
Palaiseau Villebon
Lozère
Le Guichet
Orsay – Ville
Bures-sur-Yvette
La Hacquinière
Gif-sur-Yvette
Courcelle-sur-Yvette
B4 St-Rémy-lès-Chevreuse
B5 Mitry – Claye
Villeparisis Mitry-le-Neuf
Vert-Galant
Sevran Livry
Orly Ouest
Orly Sud
Orly
Parc de Sceaux
Aérop. d'Orly
Pont de Rungis Aérop. d'Orly
Rungis La Fraternelle
Chemin d'Antony
C1 Pontoise
St-Ouen l'Aumône
St-Ouen l'Aumône – Liesse
Pierrelaye
Montigny Beauchamp
Franconville Le Plessis-Bouchard
Cernay
Ermont – Eaubonne
St-Gratien
Épinay-sur-Seine
Gennevilliers
C3 Argenteuil
Les Grésillons
St-Ouen
Pte de Clichy
Pereire Levallois
Pte Maillot
Neuilly Porte Maillot
Av. Foch
Av. H. Martin
Boulainvilliers
Avenue du Pdt Kennedy
Javel
Champ de Mars Tour Eiffel
Pont de l'Alma
Invalides
Musée d'Orsay
Gare d'Austerlitz
Bibliothèque F. Mitterrand
Ivry-sur-Seine
Vitry-sur-Seine
Les Ardoines
Choisy-le-Roi
Villeneuve-le-Roi
Ablon
Athis-Mons
Juvisy
Savigny-sur-Orge
Épinay-sur-Orge
Ste-Geneviève-des-Bois
St-Michel-sur-Orge
Brétigny-sur-Orge
Marolles-en-Hurepoix
Bouray
Lardy
Chamarande
Étréchy
Étampes
C6 St-Martin d'Étampes
C4 Dourdan-la-Forêt
Dourdan
Sermaise
St-Chéron
Breuillet – Village
Breuillet Bruyères-le-Châtel
Égly
Arpajon
St-Germain-lès-Arpajon
La Norville
C2 Massy Palaiseau
Longjumeau
Chilly Mazarin
Gravigny Balizy
Petit Vaux
Orly – Ville
Les Saules
Pont de Rungis
C5 Versailles – Rive Gauche Château de Versailles
Porchefontaine
Viroflay – Rive Gauche
Chaville – Vélizy
Meudon Val Fleury
Issy
Issy Val de Seine
Bd Victor
C7 St-Quentin-en-Yvelines
St-Cyr
C8 Versailles Chantiers
Jouy-en-Josas
Petit Jouy les-Loges
Vauboyen
Bièvres
Igny
D1 Orry-la-Ville Coye
La Borne Blanche
Survilliers Fosses
Louvres
Les Noues
Goussainville
Villiers-le-Bel Gonesse-Arnouville
Garges Sarcelles
Pierrefitte Stains
St-Denis
E1 Haussmann St-Lazare
Magenta
Pantin
Noisy-le-Sec
Bondy
Le Raincy Villemomble Montfermeil
Gagny
Le Chénay Gagny
E2 Chelles Gournay
Rosny Bois-Perrier
E4 Tournan
Gretz – Armainvilliers
Ozoir la-Ferrière
Roissy-en-Brie
Émerainville Pontault-Combault
Les Yvris Noisy-le-Grand
Villiers-s-Marne Le Plessis-Trévise
Les Boullereaux Champigny
D2 Melun
Le Mée-sur-Seine
Cesson
Savigny le-Temple Nandy
Lieusaint Moissy
Combs-la-Ville Quincy
Boussy-St-Antoine
Brunoy
Yerres
Montgeron – Crosne
Villeneuve – St-Georges
Villeneuve – Triage
Villeneuve – Prairie
Le Vert de Maisons
Maisons-Alfort Alfortville
Vigneux-sur-Seine
Viry Châtillon
Ris Orangis
Grand Bourg
Évry
Grigny Centre
Orangis Bois de l'Épine
Évry Courcouronnes
Le Bras-de-Fer
Corbeil Essonnes
D4 Malesherbes
Moulin Galant
Mennecy
Ballancourt
La Ferté-Alais
Boutigny
Maisse
Buno-Gironville
Boigneville
RER A RATP/SNCF
RER B RATP/SNCF
RER C SNCF
RER D SNCF
RER E SNCF
Orly Antony : liaison ORLYVAL Tarification spéciale
Pont de Rungis: navettes bus
* Gares hors zone tarifaire

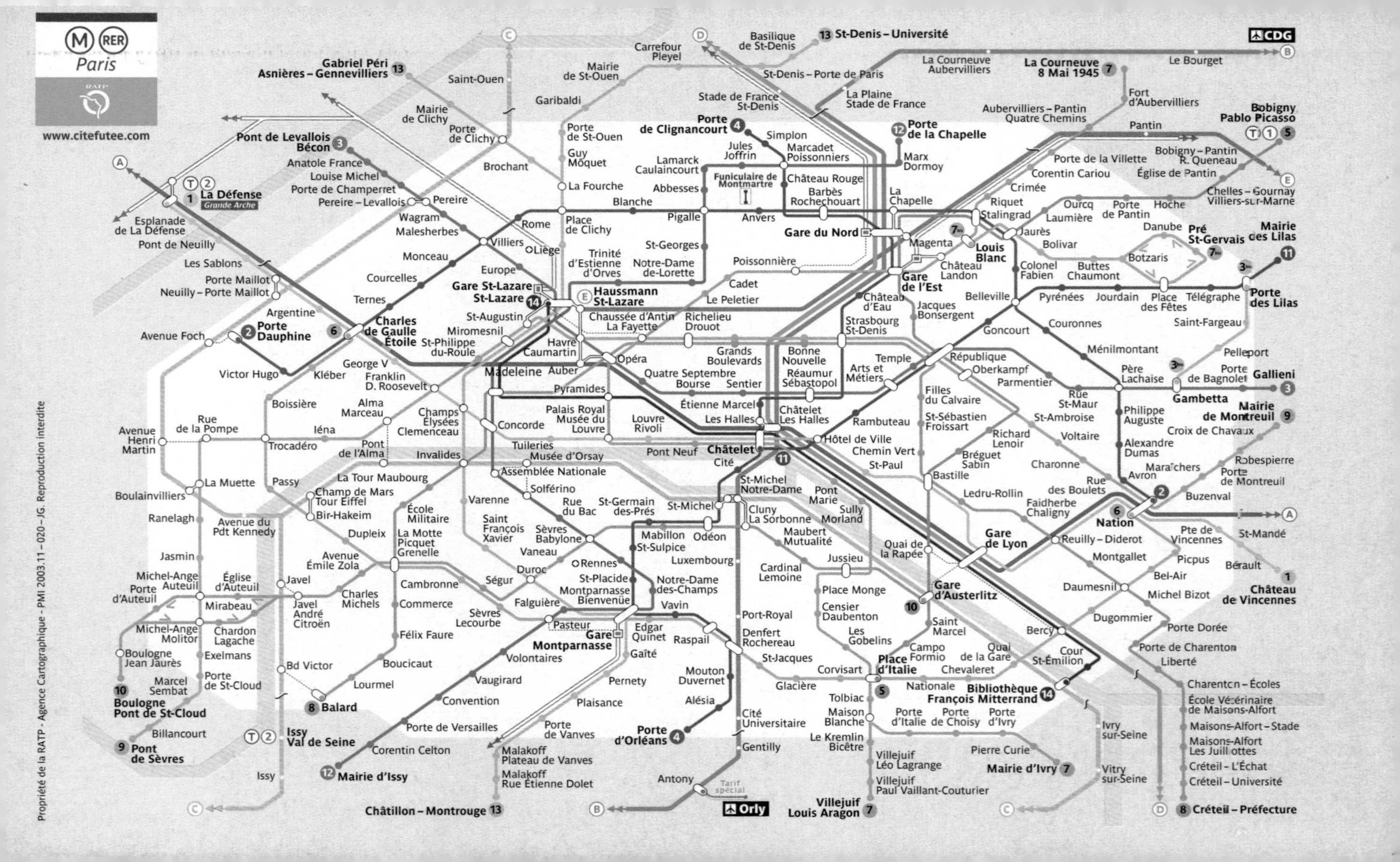
M RER
Paris
RATP
www.citefutee.com
Propriété de la RATP - Agence Cartographique - PMI 2003.11 – 020 – JG. Reproduction interdite
Gabriel Péri
Asnières – Gennevilliers 13
Saint-Ouen
Mairie de Clichy
Porte de Clichy
Garibaldi
Mairie de St-Ouen
Carrefour Pleyel
Basilique de St-Denis
13 St-Denis – Université
CDG
St-Denis – Porte de Paris
Stade de France St-Denis
La Plaine Stade de France
La Courneuve Aubervilliers
La Courneuve 8 Mai 1945 7
Le Bourget
Fort d'Aubervilliers
Aubervilliers – Pantin Quatre Chemins
Bobigny Pablo Picasso
T 1 5
Pantin
Bobigny – Pantin R. Queneau
Église de Pantin
Porte de la Villette
Corentin Cariou
Crimée
Chelles – Gournay
Villiers-sur-Marne
Pont de Levallois Bécon 3
Anatole France
Louise Michel
Porte de Champerret
Pereire – Levallois
Pereire
Brochant
Porte de St-Ouen
Guy Môquet
La Fourche
Porte de Clignancourt 4
Simplon
Jules Joffrin
Marcadet Poissonniers
Lamarck Caulaincourt
Funiculaire de Montmartre
Château Rouge
Abbesses
Barbès Rochechouart
12 Porte de la Chapelle
Marx Dormoy
La Chapelle
T 2
La Défense
1 Grande Arche
Esplanade de La Défense
Pont de Neuilly
Les Sablons
Porte Maillot
Neuilly – Porte Maillot
Wagram
Malesherbes
Monceau
Courcelles
Ternes
Villiers
Rome
Liège
Place de Clichy
Blanche
Pigalle
Anvers
Gare du Nord
Magenta
Riquet
Stalingrad
Jaurès
Ourcq
Laumière
Porte de Pantin
Hoche
Danube
Pré St-Gervais
Mairie des Lilas
7bis
Bolivar
Botzaris
Louis Blanc
Château Landon
Colonel Fabien
Buttes Chaumont
11
3bis
Porte des Lilas
Trinité d'Estienne d'Orves
St-Georges
Notre-Dame de-Lorette
Poissonnière
Cadet
Le Peletier
Europe
Gare St-Lazare
St-Lazare 14
E
Haussmann St-Lazare
Gare de l'Est
Château d'Eau
Jacques Bonsergent
Belleville
Pyrénées
Jourdain
Place des Fêtes
Télégraphe
Saint-Fargeau
Argentine
Charles de Gaulle Étoile
6
Avenue Foch
2 Porte Dauphine
St-Augustin
Miromesnil
St-Philippe du-Roule
Chaussée d'Antin La Fayette
Richelieu Drouot
Strasbourg St-Denis
Goncourt
Couronnes
Ménilmontant
Pelleport
Victor Hugo
Kléber
George V
Franklin D. Roosevelt
Havre Caumartin
Opéra
Grands Boulevards
Bonne Nouvelle
Temple
République
Oberkampf
Parmentier
Père Lachaise
Porte de Bagnolet
Gallieni 3
Gambetta
Madeleine
Auber
Quatre Septembre
Bourse
Sentier
Réaumur Sébastopol
Arts et Métiers
Rue St-Maur
Philippe Auguste
Mairie de Montreuil 9
Croix de Chavaux
Boissière
Alma Marceau
Champs Élysées Clemenceau
Pyramides
Palais Royal Musée du Louvre
Étienne Marcel
Les Halles
Châtelet Les Halles
Rambuteau
Filles du Calvaire
St-Sébastien Froissart
St-Ambroise
Voltaire
Alexandre Dumas
Robespierre
Avenue Henri Martin
Rue de la Pompe
Iéna
Trocadéro
Concorde
Louvre Rivoli
Hôtel de Ville
Richard Lenoir
Bréguet Sabin
Avron
Maraîchers
Porte de Montreuil
Pont de l'Alma
Invalides
Tuileries
Musée d'Orsay
Pont Neuf
Châtelet
Cité
Chemin Vert
St-Paul
Bastille
Charonne
Rue des Boulets
2
Buzenval
A
La Muette
Passy
La Tour Maubourg
Assemblée Nationale
St-Michel Notre-Dame
Pont Marie
Ledru-Rollin
Faidherbe Chaligny
6 Nation
Pte de Vincennes
St-Mandé
Boulainvilliers
Champ de Mars Tour Eiffel
Bir-Hakeim
École Militaire
Varenne
Solférino
Rue du Bac
St-Germain des-Prés
St-Michel
Cluny La Sorbonne
Sully Morland
Maubert Mutualité
Quai de la Rapée
Gare de Lyon
Reuilly – Diderot
Montgallet
Picpus
Bérault
1 Château de Vincennes
Ranelagh
Avenue du Pdt Kennedy
Dupleix
La Motte Picquet Grenelle
Saint François Xavier
Sèvres Babylone
Vaneau
Mabillon
Odéon
Luxembourg
Jussieu
Cardinal Lemoine
Bel-Air
Daumesnil
Michel Bizot
Jasmin
Avenue Émile Zola
Duroc
Rennes
St-Sulpice
St-Placide
Notre-Dame des-Champs
Montparnasse Bienvenüe
Place Monge
Censier Daubenton
Gare d'Austerlitz
10
Michel-Ange Auteuil
Porte d'Auteuil
Église d'Auteuil
Javel
Javel André Citroën
Charles Michels
Cambronne
Ségur
Commerce
Falguière
Vavin
Port-Royal
Les Gobelins
Saint Marcel
Dugommier
Porte Dorée
Mirabeau
Michel-Ange Molitor
Chardon Lagache
Félix Faure
Sèvres Lecourbe
Pasteur
Gare Montparnasse
Edgar Quinet
Raspail
Denfert Rochereau
St-Jacques
Campo Formio
Quai de la Gare
Chevaleret
Bercy
Cour St-Émilion
Porte de Charenton
Liberté
Boulogne Jean Jaurès
Exelmans
Bd Victor
Boucicaut
Volontaires
Gaîté
Mouton Duvernet
Corvisart
Place d'Italie
Glacière
Nationale
Bibliothèque François Mitterrand 14
Charenton – Écoles
École Vétérinaire de Maisons-Alfort
Maisons-Alfort – Stade
Maisons-Alfort Les Juilliottes
Créteil – L'Échat
Créteil – Université
8 Créteil – Préfecture
Marcel Sembat
Porte de St-Cloud
10 Boulogne Pont de St-Cloud
Lourmel
Vaugirard
Convention
Pernety
Plaisance
Alésia
Tolbiac
Maison Blanche
Porte d'Italie
Porte de Choisy
Porte d'Ivry
Ivry sur-Seine
Vitry sur-Seine
Billancourt
9 Pont de Sèvres
8 Balard
Porte de Versailles
Porte de Vanves
Porte d'Orléans 4
Cité Universitaire
Le Kremlin Bicêtre
Pierre Curie
Mairie d'Ivry 7
T 2
Issy Val de Seine
Issy
Corentin Celton
12 Mairie d'Issy
Malakoff Plateau de Vanves
Malakoff Rue Étienne Dolet
Châtillon – Montrouge 13
Gentilly
Antony
Tarif spécial
Orly
Villejuif Léo Lagrange
Villejuif Paul Vaillant-Couturier
Villejuif Louis Aragon 7
C
D
B